WEST FRONT OF THE STAR CHAMBER, FROM PALACE YARD.
From Smith's 'Antiquities of Westminster.'

Les Reportes del Cases
in
Camera Stellata

1593 TO 1609

FROM THE ORIGINAL MS. OF

JOHN HAWARDE

OF THE INNER TEMPLE, ESQUIRE, BARRISTER-AT-LAW

EDITED BY

WILLIAM PALEY BAILDON, F.S.A.

OF LINCOLN'S INN, ESQUIRE, BARRISTER-AT-LAW

With a New Introduction and Notes by
Thomas Garden Barnes

Professor of History & Law Emeritus
Co-Director, Canadian Studies Program
University of California, Berkeley

THE LAWBOOK EXCHANGE, LTD.
Clark, New Jersey
2008

ISBN-13: 978-1-58477-900-1
ISBN-10: 1-58477-900-4

The quality of this reprint is equivalent to the quality of the original work.

The Lawbook Exchange, Ltd.
33 Terminal Avenue
Clark, New Jersey 07066-1321

Please see our website for a selection of our other publications and fine facsimile reprints of classic works of legal history:
www.lawbookexchange.com

Library of Congress Cataloging-in-Publication Data

England and Wales. Court of Star Chamber.
Les reportes del cases in Camera stellata, 1593 to 1609 : from the original ms. of John Hawarde / edited by William Paley Baildon ; with a new introduction and notes by Thomas Garden Barnes.
p. cm.
Originally published: London : Priv. print [by Spottiswoode & Co.], 1894.
Includes bibliographical references and index.
ISBN-13: 978-1-58477-900-1 (cloth : alk. paper)
ISBN-10: 1-58477-900-4 (cloth : alk. paper)
1. Law reports, digests, etc.--Great Britain. I. Hawarde, John, 1571?-1630. II. Baildon, W. Paley (William Paley), 1859-1924 III. Title.
KD7865.2.S7E54 2008
349.420264--dc22

2008023378

Printed in the United States of America on acid-free paper

INTRODUCTION

Hawarde's *Les Reportes* fits Thomas Gray's poetic conceit, "Many a flower is born to blush unseen, And waste its sweetness on the desert air." It remained in manuscript from its compilation, apparently uncirculated and certainly not copied, until the industrious William Paley Baildon transcribed, edited, and introduced it, and the owner of the manuscript, Alfred Morrison, "Privately Printed" it in 1894 in a print-run of 250 copies. It has never had a chance of being a best-seller, even in the limited understanding of that term in legal historical publications. Which is a pity, because there is no comparable single source for Star Chamber cases in print for that crucial period, from 1596 to the end of the first decade of the next century, when Lord Keeper Thomas Egerton framed its widest jurisdiction, reformed its procedures, and spurred the expansion of the criminal law of misdemeanors by its case-law. Moreover, it remains the most complete printed report of cases in Star Chamber for any period. It seldom finds its way onto the market and commands a high price when it does. Its republication is long overdue.

A word about the editor and his text is in order. William Paley Baildon (1859-1924), son of a Southport, Lancashire, iron merchant, was a barrister with chambers at 5 Stone Buildings, Lincoln's Inn, who enjoyed a comfortable real property practice at the Chancery bar. He has been variously described as an antiquarian or historian: the former term does not do him justice and the latter diminishes his contributions to English legal history retrieved from the archives. Baildon was a prominent figure in that cohort of British autodidactic mediaevalists that arose in the last quarter of the nineteenth century, many of whom did not hold academic appointments but worked tirelessly in transcribing, translating, and editing records of the courts and private muniments. His chambers were a five-minute walk down Chancery Lane to the

Public Record Office, and he made good use of it. A founding member of the Selden Society, he was the editor of its third volume, *Select Civil Pleas* (1890) and produced two more volumes, one with the illustrious Frederic William Maitland, and the last on *Select Cases in Chancery, 1364-1471* (1896). He also compiled the two volume *Admissions to Lincoln's Inn from 1420* (1893) and undertook the daunting task of publishing the *Black Books of Lincoln's Inn*, the principal record of the Inn, completing four volumes (1897-1904) before he died. His antiquarian bent was concentrated on Yorkshire, particularly the ancient village of Baildon near Bradford in the West Riding, and the family which dominated it for half a millennium; he wrote a fifteen-part history of *Baildon and the Baildons* (1913-1926). Between 1895 and 1918 he edited six volumes of early records for the Yorkshire Archaeological Society. Other family histories (including *The Hawardes of Tandridge, County Surrey* in 1894, for which he had gathered the material that provided his biographical sketch of the reporter), a number of articles, and many contributions to the antiquarian journal *Notes & Queries* marked a fecund scholar of the remote past.[1]

Such a scholarly pedigree lends great credibility to Baildon's fifty-nine page introduction and the extensive scholarly apparatus, including informative appendices, that graces the text. It also assures us that his transcription and translation of Hawarde's manuscript attains the high standard that his cohort achieved in their editing of original documents. It does. Alfred Morrison's manuscript was acquired by the Carl H. Pforzheimer Library in New York.[2] Many years ago I spent a long day there comparing Baildon's text to the manuscript, and afterwards fine-toothed it from microfilm. Baildon's transcription was meticulous, and errors—mostly in the headnote of the case showing the presence, title, date, etc.—very few indeed. His translation of Law French was skillful. And his use of précis to abridge some material was restrained and careful, though one case (Calvin's Case in Exchequer Chamber, 12 May 1608, pages 349-366, touching Scotsmen's rights under English law since the union of the crowns in 1603) was much too abbreviated, considering how important it was legally and politically.

Baildon's introduction, pages xl to lxiii, provides a useful, balanced—and as far as his reliance on printed sources on Star Chamber, particularly William Hudson's treatise,[3] permitted—searching summation of the site, constitution, composition, jurisdiction, and procedure of the Star Chamber in Hawarde's day. His skepticism concerning the whiggish canard that Star Chamber "used" torture braved the conventional wisdom of nineteenth-century historians, and proved to be correct.[4] He was, in fact, remarkably free of the priggish condemnation of the court and the willful ignorance of the contributions it made to the modern law of misdemeanor current among his contemporaries. The additional material provided in the table of attendance by the Councillors and judges and the twenty-six appendices containing matter relevant to some of the more important cases reported by Hawarde is extremely valuable in understanding the early Stuart Star Chamber.

About John Hawarde (c.1571-1631) we know a great deal, thanks to Baildon's assiduous research carefully opened in his introduction. Hawarde was the son of a London fishmonger and his second wife, the daughter of a London merchant. The father, a successful businessman, purchased extensive properties in and around Tandridge, Surrey. John in his middle-teens sojourned at one of the Inns of Chancery—thereby acquiring some familiarity with legal instruments—and from Clifford's Inn entered the Inner Temple in 1588. It took him ten years to complete the exercises for the bar, possibly less because of indolence than because in common with his generation of aspiring barristers he was an inveterate court-watcher. Attendance at the courts was a large part of the Inns' educational experience. It was also good entertainment, especially if the court was the Star Chamber with its eminence and grandeur, *causes célèbres*, exciting creativity in making a new law of misdemeanor, and the chance to listen to the advocacy of the most golden-throated leaders of the bar. Where else could one witness the following exchange between the two legal titans of the age, in Atty Gen v. Sir Robert Dudley, 1 May 1605, over admissability of evidence taken before the case was filed?

> The Lo. Chauncellor [Thomas Egerton, Lord Ellesmere] seemed to be in some sorte of the same opinion [with the defense's submission], whereat Mr. Atturnie [Sir Edward Coke] was very much mooued, & Conceaved it a wronge offered to him, . . .The Lo. Chauncellor seemed to be of another opinion; then ye Attornie desired to be hearde, for it Concerned ye kinge & ye Common weale, & he would appeale to ye Che. Justice [KB, Sir John Popham] whoe had serued in his place [Attorney General] longe, & sayde yf it mighte not be allowed him he woulde speake no more in the cause, & layde awaye his bookes, & pressed to be hearde in his appealle. The Lor. Chauncellor made aunsweare he showlde be hearde, & he [the Chancellor] woulde speake to[o], & be hearde in that place, for he woulde not be out braued; he knewe what he sayde & he hearde & learned it before euer Mr. Atturnie had: . . . [Hawarde, p. 203]

The first quarter of his reports were done before Hawarde was called, comprising 142 of the 224 Star Chamber cases in the work. The discrepancy between the number of pages and the number of cases is in great part explicable by the fact that his early effort was more sparing and economical and included more interlocutory matter than the later cases, appropriate to the student. After his call he became more prolix, almost as if he was luxuriating in the spectacle of the cases. There is no indication in the reports that Hawarde was ever of counsel in Star Chamber litigation. His masterful quashing of a witness's testimony on interrogatories was in Chancery [Hawarde, pp.116-117]. His appearance as counsel in a case of riot and forcible entry was at a special sessions pursuant to statute at Godstone, Surrey, two miles from his seat at Tandridge [Hawarde, pp. 139-143]. In fact, while there is no record of an appearance at trial, he did sign pleadings in three Star Chamber cases between 1610 and 1619, two of which were from Surrey.[5] In this, he was in a good company. For the period 1603-1625, there were about 1550 barristers who might have practiced in Star Chamber. The proceedings for the court for that period indicate 1250 counsel signed pleadings (bills, answers, special pleadings, replication, rejoinder, etc.). Of these, 5 per cent signed 40 per cent of the pleadings. Of the rest, many signed only once, and few signed more than three or four instruments.[6] Hawarde fit solidly into the latter category. He had a practice that was based on his own county, doing business including trial work in a number of jurisdictions, of which Star Chamber was probably the least prominent. He was a justice of the peace (of the quorum) of Surrey, served as coroner for the county, and was a Member of Parliament for the nearby borough of Bletchingley in 1621 and 1624. He did not cut a figure in debate and perhaps the most memorable aspect of his political career was the dispute over his election in 1624. Such offices attracted what was a modest professional clientele, including such neighboring gentry as Sir Nicholas Carew and Sir Thomas Gresham. Having inherited the Tandridge estates on the death of his father in 1610, Hawarde's connection with the metropolis became increasingly tenuous. It was no accident that the last case he reported was in February 1609. Made a bencher of the Inner Temple in 1613, he did his professional and domestic duty by being Lent Reader in 1615 on an unknown subject. His most direct connection with Star Chamber came in November 1613, when he was named defendant with twenty-one others in a bill brought by Jacob Torado against a London merchant, Robert Bossoch, Hawarde, and an ecclesiastical court official, charging perjury, vexatious litigation, champerty, and conspiracy. The case had no legs: Hawarde was named as a barrister of the Middle Temple, the defense countered that Torado was a bigamist, Hawarde's answer was a clean traverse, and the action went no further.[7]

How good a reporter was John Hawarde? One point must be made at the outset. "Reporting" was a relatively new phenomenon which by the end of the sixteenth century was clearly distinguishable from the cases recounted in the Year Books of the high middle-ages. Edmund Plowden (c.1518-1585) is credited with being the first "modern reporter," producing a volume for the reigns of Edward VI to Elizabeth I that banished the anecdotal Year Book genre in favor of concise factual statement and legal conclusion in the case. He was the first to publish his reports in his own lifetime. His contemporary, James Dyer (1510-1582), was even more highly concentrated on the law of a case, and his *Reports*, published shortly after his death, had immediate success and wide circulation. Plowden and Dyer probably featured "more often than any other printed books in legal commonplaces of the late Elizabethan and Jacobean period."[8] Hawarde, in common with his fellow students at the Inns in the 1590s, would have been thoroughly familiar with those early reports, and they would have served as his model. It shows. Hawarde was meticulous in developing the factual background to a case—indeed, this was testified to by his predilection to luxuriate in the great events in Star Chamber. He sought and achieved great clarity and directness in setting down the legal arguments and judicial determinations in cases. In accord with the new canons of "reporting," Hawarde sought doctrine in the cases, substantive law rather than adjective law. That makes his reports seem familiar to us, capable of being grasped, understood, relevant, useful. If nothing else, that makes their republication compelling.

Hawarde's 224 Star Chamber cases reflect the range of the court's jurisdiction in the first decade of the seventeenth century. The crimes charged are clear, and because the reports concentrate on trial and sentence more than on interlocutory motions and orders the extent of Star Chamber's contributions to the new misdemeanors is abundantly clear. By the nature of the English bill by which Star Chamber proceeded, every action involved more than one crime charged. A charge of conspiracy/combination was usually thrown into an already over-long bill primarily to snare the principal defendant's witnesses into the action and so impeach their testimony. For that reason conspiracy is largely excluded from this reckoning. But of the 379 specific charges in these cases, the largest proportion was the crimes of violence which had always been the staple of the court's business: 114, of which 67 were riot/rout, 18 involved destruction of property, 27 were assault, and 2 involved hunting. The second largest category was crimes against justice:

perjury 22, subornation of officials 20, contempt of court and abuse of legal process 19, maintenance/champerty/embracery 18, vexatious litigation 6, and conspiracy to indict for felony 1. To this category can be added many of the 27 charges against officials, especially JPs, for malfeasance and the 8 charges of malfeasance by lawyers. Crimes of covin constituted 80 of the offences: forgery 40, fraud 25, extortion 11, counterfeit instruments and impersonation 3, and embezzlement 1. Crimes in denigration of status included 27 defamation and 1 abduction of a girl underage to make prey of her estate. One very small category received at least passing attention: inchoate crime. In four cases, conspiracy was charged as a substantive crime rather than as merely a procedural device. Moreover, there is one case in which the charge came to no more than an attempt, and was punished. Though Star Chamber's willingness to reprehend simple inchoate crime was about a decade away, the essence of the offense is clear in 1595 in Earl of Salisbury v. Talbot [Hawarde, pp. 16-19].

Given the always considerable weight of private prosecutions in Star Chamber by litigants seeking advantage in suits elsewhere, usually involving real property or chattels real, the large number of prosecutions by the Attorney General for the King, either by information or upon confession *ore tenus*, for crimes against the state, in denigration of religion, violation of royal proclamations, and injury to the commonweal is worth noting: sedition 6, subversion 3, denigration of religion 9, violation of proclamations 7, and engrossing etc. 6. These 31 charges included, of course, the *causes-célèbres* of great matters of state. The Attorney General, especially Sir Edward Coke, was energetic in such matters, and there was clear policy in punishing those who forestalled or engrossed markets in food which made a succession of bad crop-years worse, those who enclosed arable, and those who were building ramshackle tenements rapidly filling up the mile between the western end of London and the palace of Westminster.[9] There were to be many more such prosecutions to the ends of state pressed with even greater vigor after 1620. By 1630 the Attorney General's causes *pro Rege* began to chase away the private litigant, whose matter even when it was put down on the cause-list would drop off it when the Attorney General rose to move his cases.[10]

There is no reason to believe that Hawarde cherry-picked his cases. Of course, he would not have resisted the temptation to attend when great cases came to trial. Over all, however, the scope of the trials set down in his reports is comparable to the range revealed in the records of the pleadings and proofs in the Star Chamber preserved in the Public Record Office at Kew.[11] He provides the conclusion to a great many cases for the period which cannot be retrieved from any other source. The printed reports—those in the English Reports series—provide just under 200 cases for Star Chamber from the late-sixteenth century to its abolition in 1641, of which the largest single group (41 cases) is in Moore's Reports. There exist in manuscript in archives, muniments, and libraries around the English-speaking world reports of a further 1500 cases in Star Chamber, all but a very few from the mid-1590s onwards. Hawarde's *Les Reportes* is emblematic of the genre but far superior to the run of the reports. And for Star Chamber cases in print, it is simply peerless. Hawarde covers a period for which few reported cases in Star Chamber exist at all, and even fewer of cases afforded such extensive treatment.

That he saw fit to report the charges given by the Lord Chancellor to the judges of the central courts before they set off on their assize circuits at the end of Hilary Term (Lent assizes) and the end of Trinity Term (Summer assizes) was a bonus. There are ten of them, from Summer 1595 to Lent 1609, only one of which is available elsewhere,[12] out of seventeen charges extant between Summer 1595 to Lent 1614. The importance of this political theatre cannot be overstressed. It occurred on the first day post-term when the Star Chamber disposed of motions before retiring for dinner in the early afternoon to consider pleas for mitigation of sentence. The presence of Privy Councillors was always large and the three chief and nine puisne justices of the King's Bench, Common Pleas, and Exchequer were in attendance, along with as many justices of the peace as were still around Westminster before going home to their counties after the term concluded. The Lord Chancellor's charge was always delivered with great solemnity, he spoke with the authority and at the behest of the King himself and with the concurrence of the Privy Council. The charge laid out in direct and mandatory terms what particular matters of regal policy and law and order the judges were to implement with forthrightness and vigor. It was the bulliest pulpit the King could command save at the opening of Parliament.[13] After 1610, he parliamentary pulpit became less frequent and considerably more perilous for the monarch's interests and his ministers' morale.

Perhaps the greatest contribution of Hawarde's *Les Reportes* is what they reveal about the early evolution of the agenda of Sir Thomas Egerton, Lord Keeper of the Great Seal and afterwards Baron Ellesmere and Lord Chancellor from May 1596 until his death in March 1617, for the Star Chamber over which he presided. Egerton was the only lawyer who could rival Coke in learning, constrain him politically, and humble him in court. Hawarde supplies plenty of evidence to that effect. Egerton was bent on doing substantial justice in Star Chamber, and was willing and able to develop new law by continuous elaboration and sophistication. Great malefactors he hit hard. His object all sublime was not to fit the punishment to the crime, but to the criminal: *Dignitas delinquentis auget culpam*—the dignity of the criminal increases his guilt—was his favorite aphorism and often dressed his sentence in causes touching magnates [Hawarde, pp.162, 229, 235, 288]. Outraged by defamation, Egerton encouraged its punishment in Star Chamber. He believed the private litigant should benefit from trial success by receiving damages. As a procedural reformer, he fought against the viscous deceleration caused by an entrenched clerical bureaucracy, the dilatoriness of lawyers, and the shifts of litigants that threatened to slow Star Chamber to a standstill. That accounted for his frequent attacks on the incompetence of advocates and vexatious activities of solicitors and common law attorneys in stirring suits. He enjoyed considerable success in implementing his agenda. He was able to cope with the increasing load of litigation in Star Chamber. He enjoyed less success in Chancery, where he did not have the same power to control the ornate clerical apparatus there which he had wielded as Master of the Rolls from 1594, held in conjunction with the Keepership from 1596 until he surrendered the Rolls in 1603. Perforce, he came into conflict with Coke, most openly in Star Chamber because Coke was at virtually every sitting as Attorney General, 1596 to 1606, and afterwards as Chief Justice of the Common Pleas and member of the Court. The tension was not originally so much over ideological differences or even because of any rivalry between common law and equity, but for personal and temperamental reasons. Egerton's affection for Sir Francis Bacon guaranteed Coke's hostility. After Calvin's Case (1608), which revealed real fissures between Ellesmere and Coke in point of law over the King's prerogative powers, the division between them grew steadily.[14] Hawarde, though, no longer attended Star Chamber to witness the chasm widen.

We must be grateful for John Hawarde's painful labor in seeing so much and writing down so much about what he saw in Star Chamber. *Les Reportes* remains, for want of better, the best place to begin to determine what went on in that extraordinary tribunal.

Thomas G. Barnes
May 2008

NOTES

1. Baildon's correspondence, historical and genealogical notes, deeds, extracts, pedigrees, drawings—particularly of the megalithic site on Baildon Moor—are in the Yorkshire Archaeological Society and the West Yorkshire Archive Service.
2. Pforzheimer Library: MS. 36. Alfred Morrison (1821-1897) was an art, autograph, and gem collector of great wealth seated in Wiltshire. Carl H. Pforzheimer Sr. and Jr., bankers both, were manic bibliophils, in the cut of Morrison. In 1986, thanks in part to H. Ross Perot, the University of Texas Austin acquired the bulk of the collection, including Hawarde's MS. which is now in the Harry Ransom Humanities Center Library.
3. *Treatise of the Court of Star Chamber,* written in 1621, printed by Francis Hargrave, 2 Collectanea Juridica (1792).
4. Thomas G. Barnes, "Star Chamber Mythology," 5 American Journal of Legal History (1961) pp. 1-11.
5. For the plaintiff: Public Record Office: STAC8/249/24, abduction of a Surrey gentlewoman's daughter to make a prey of her estate, bill Nov. 1619. For the defendant: STAC8/199/7, London merchants falling out, charges of defamation, maintenance, and vexatious suits, bill May 1615; STAC8/99/25, signed jointly and as junior with Randulph Crewe, answer of a Surrey JP to charges of his malfeasance in not acting against rescuers of oxen taken in distraint for arrears of rent, bill June 1610.
6. Thomas G. Barnes, "Star Chamber Litigants and Their Counsel, 1596-1641," *Legal Records and the Historian*, J. H. Baker ed. (London, 1978) pp. 25-27.
7. PRO: STAC8/282/28. The mistake in his professional ascription was telling: the plaintiff was engaged in a try-on, intended more for vexation than victory. The defendants were represented by two future judges—John Walter and Robert Heath—and the pre-eminent leader at the Star Chamber bar, William Hudson. For further biographical information on Hawarde, including his considerable estate, see Thomas G. Barnes's entry for Hawarde in the *Oxford Dictionary of National Biography* (Oxford, 2004).
8. J. H. Baker's profile of Dyer in the *Oxford Dictionary of National Biography* (Oxford, 2004). See Baker's editions of *Reports from the Lost Notebooks of Sir James Dyer,* 109 & 110 Selden Society (1993-1994).

9. Thomas G. Barnes, "The Prerogative and Environmental Control of London Building in the Early Seventeenth Century: The Lost Opportunity," 58 California Law Review (1970) 1332-1363.
10. Thomas G. Barnes, "Due Process and Slow Process in the Late Elizabethan-Early Stuart Star Chamber," 6 American Journal of Legal History (1962) pp. 221-249 and 315-346.
11. The class, STAC8, consists of 8228 files of proceedings—pleadings and proofs—in 314 boxes, consisting of parchment engrossments of the pleadings and interrogatories and depositions taken by commission, and paperbooks of depositions taken in the Star Chamber clerk's office by the registrar, *List and Index to the Proceedings in Star Chamber for the Reign of James I (1603-1625) in the Public Record Office, London, Class STAC8,* 3 vols., Thomas G. Barnes ed., American Bar Foundation (Chicago, 1975). The order and decree books vanished in the seventeenth century. For the nature of the records, see Thomas G. Barnes, "The Archives and Archival Problems of the Elizabethan and Early Stuart Star Chamber," *Prisca Munimenta: Studies in Archival & Administrative History Presented to Dr. A.E.J. Hollaender,* Felicity Ranger ed., University of London Press (1973) 130-149.
12. Before Lent assizes 1605, Hawarde, p. 186, reported in Moore's Reports 755 and also available in MS. sources for Moore, British Library: Additional MS. 48061 and Folger Library: MS. V. a. 133.
13. See *Somerset Assize Orders, 1629-1640,* Thomas G. Barnes ed., 65 Somerset Record Society (Frome, 1959) and Thomas G. Barnes, "A Charge to the Judges of Assize, 1627/8," 24 Huntington Library Quarterly (1961) 251-256.
14. Both Sir John Baker on Egerton and Alllen Boyer on Coke provide balanced assessments of the Ellesmere-Coke antagonism in their respective profiles of the titans in the *Oxford Dictionary of National Biography* (Oxford, 2004).

Les Reportes del Cases

in

Camera Stellata

1593 TO 1609

FROM THE ORIGINAL MS. OF

JOHN HAWARDE

OF THE INNER TEMPLE, ESQUIRE, BARRISTER-AT-LAW

EDITED BY

WILLIAM PALEY BAILDON, F.S.A.

OF LINCOLN'S INN, ESQUIRE, BARRISTER-AT-LAW

Privately Printed

1894

250 Copies privately printed for ALFRED MORRISON, *Esquire*

INTRODUCTION

I. *The Manuscript*

The manuscript from which this volume has been printed is one of the well-known collection of Alfred Morrison, Esq., of Fonthill House, Tisbury, Wiltshire, and 16 Carlton House Terrace, London.[1] It is a folio volume of 364 pages, 11¾ by 7¾ inches, and, with the exception of being slightly injured at the top by damp, is in very good condition. This damage is mostly confined to the first few leaves, and is chiefly to be regretted because the author's signature has all disappeared except the lower part of the flourish. On one fly leaf is written "10*s*. 0*d*.," which probably represents the price which the writer paid for his blank book, and below, in a very minute hand, is the following:

Scipionis Epitaphium.

Deuicto Hanibale, capta Carthagine atque aucto
Imperio, hos Cineres marmore tectus habes,
Cui non Europa, non obstitit Africa, quondam;
Respice res hominum quam brevis vrna premit.

At p. 146 are fifteen blank leaves: these, as explained in the text, were evidently left with the intention of writing thereon certain proclamations, speeches, etc., which are

[1] An account of Mr. Morrison's MSS. will be found in the 9th Report of the Historical MSS. Commission, p. xvii; and Appendix II. p. 406.

referred to in the writer's account of the death of Queen Elizabeth and the accession of King James I. This intention was, however, not carried out. There are also two blank pages at pp. 203, 204, and one at p. 300, as to which see n. 3, p. 328 of this volume.

The MS. is written partly in English and partly in a curious mixture of Law French, Latin, and English, of which a few specimens are printed. The former portions are printed *verbatim*, and are marked by inverted commas. The portions not in English have been translated, but it has not been deemed advisable to make a free translation into modern English. This would have been in many parts very difficult, and in some parts well-nigh impossible, and, moreover, the advantage of so doing seems very doubtful; the original therefore has been followed as closely as possible. The difficulty of translating (and this applies also to the transcribing of the English portions) is much increased by the want of punctuation in the MS. There are a few commas and colons here and there, and an occasional period and dash, but practically the MS. is almost unpunctuated.

Most of the abbreviations could be represented by ordinary type; the few that could not have been extended: these are ꝓ for 'pro,' p̃ for 'pre' or 'pri,' ꝑ for 'per' or 'par,' õ for 'om' or 'on,' and a few others.

It is curious to note the writer's almost invariable use of a capital C at the beginning of words.

The name on the fly leaf, as has already been stated, has been destroyed by damp, but fortunately on p. 72 of the MS. (p. 111 of this volume) the writer had occasion to mention his own name. He himself, it seems, had become an object of suspicion to the Privy Council, and was summoned to appear before that body at Greenwich. He says, '*Jeo, John Hawarde del Inner temple, va al Courte al Greeneswiche oue vn messenger del Chamber del roigne, nosme*

Mr. George Cobham, mise pur moy par le commaundemente del roigne et son counselle.'

I have referred to the volume of Acts and Ordinances preserved at the Privy Council Office in Whitehall, but the record there does not throw any additional light on the proceedings. The entry is as follows:

17th of May, 1600 This present daie John Hayward of the Inner Temple, gent., beinge by their Ll^s [Lordships'] Warrant sent for, entered his apparaunce, and was hereby enioyned in theire Ll^s names to giue his attendaunce vpon their Ll^s in theire syttinges to answere that wch might be abutted against him.

Saturday, 17 May, 1600. In the Afternoon.

Present:	L. Keeper	Mr Secretary Cecill
	L. Treaso^r	L. Cheefe Justyce
	L. Admirall	
	L. Northe.	

But for this fortunate circumstance, there would have been nothing to show by whom the MS. was written.

A word must be said about the numerous references in the MS. to cases and authorities. Hawarde, as he himself tells us (p. 357), wrote up his volume from rough notes taken in Court, but, with some exceptions, he does not appear to have verified his references at all. This is the more unfortunate because many of them must have been taken from MS. authorities which cannot now be identified. The printed volumes in his time were few; the Year Books and a few volumes of Reports and Commentaries were all. In the majority of cases, therefore, there is no means of checking him, but in Calvin's case (p. 349) we are able to test his accuracy. This case was reported at considerable length by Coke (*Reports*, vii. fol. 1), and Lord Ellesmere's judgment was printed as a pamphlet.[1] Judged

[1] See *post*, p. 349, n. 1.

by these two authorities, Hawarde must be pronounced inaccurate and careless, though of course this in no way detracts from the general correctness of these reports. I have looked in the most obvious places in order to verify his references, but in many cases I have failed to do so and can only assume that there is some mistake. In these instances (and they are many) I have been reluctantly obliged to give up the search, after much wasted time, and I can only console myself with the remark made by Coke (p. 296), *ubi non possum discernere, non teneor divinare.*

It is only fair to Hawarde to mention that the earlier part of the book shows signs of careful editing. References are corrected and added, headings are put to the cases, and copious marginal notes. Hawarde succeeded to the family property on his father's death in March 1611, and it is quite likely that this may have occasioned a discontinuance of his legal labours.

The only liberties I have taken with the text have been to add the titles of cases in the margin, and a few marginal notes, where omitted by Hawarde.

Calvin's case has been abridged for the reasons stated on p. 349. The names of the Privy Councillors and Judges sitting each day have in most cases been omitted in order to save space; they will be found in a Table at the end of this Introduction, and the names of those in attendance on any particular day can easily be picked out.

The volume includes a few cases at Sessions (mostly those in which Hawarde was himself concerned as Counsel), in the King's Bench, in Chancery, in the Court of Wards, one (Calvin's case) in the Exchequer Chamber, and the trial of the Gunpowder Plot traitors before a Special Commission. But as by far the greater part of the book is concerned with the Star Chamber, it has been thought best to preserve Hawarde's own title to his MS.

In addition to reports of cases, Hawarde gives an interesting account of Queen Elizabeth's death, and the accession of James I. He also gives at considerable length the Lord Chancellor's annual charges to the Judges of Assize and Justices of the Peace; these are referred to in Part III. of this Introduction.

II. *The Author*

We have seen that the writer of the MS. was one John Hawarde of the Inner Temple. Thanks to the clue afforded by this piece of information, I have been enabled to gather the following particulars about him and his family.

John Hawarde [1] or Hayward was the third, but eldest surviving son of Henry Hawarde, Citizen and Fishmonger of London, by his wife Agnes, daughter and heir of Thomas Castell or Castle of London, merchant. John entered his pedigree at the Visitation of Surrey in 1623,[2] from which we learn that Henry Hawarde, his father, was the son of Thomas, who was the son of Richard, who was the son of Michael Hawarde of Hayward Castle in Wales. In Add. MS. 12478, fo. 52, this place is called 'Ramond Castle in Wallia.'

Mr. W. S. Ellis, in an article in *The Herald and Genealogist* (vi. 372), makes some very severe remarks upon the 'unreliableness' of certain pedigrees in the Heralds' Visitations, and he selects the pedigree of Hawarde from the Visitation of 1623 as an illustration; asserting that, as tested by deeds, it is manifestly wrong in the earlier generations. Speaking of John Hawarde, who entered the pedigree in question, he asserts that the errors in the pedigree arise 'from information evidently furnished by the head of the family then living.' 'This person' (he goes on) 'does not

[1] The name is spelt in various ways, but John and his son, Sir William, always use the spelling Hawarde in their signatures. In the Visitation pedigree the name is spelt Hayward.

[2] Harleian MSS., 1433, fo. 102; 1561, fo. 162; etc.

seem to have known the name of his own grandfather.' Mr. Ellis refuses to accept the alleged Welsh origin of the family, and therein he may possibly be right. 'Hayward Castle' has a suspicious sound about it, and we know that the heralds of the period cannot always be relied upon. Mr. Ellis then states that in his opinion the Hawardes of Tandridge, and the other families of the name in the neighbourhood, were probably all descended from one Richard Hayward (who died Dec. 9, 1529) and Anne his wife, whose brass is (or was) existing in Westerham church.[1] The brass is not perfect, as the effigies of the wife and four sons are missing, those of Richard himself and six daughters yet remain. This is all likely enough, and the date of death would fit in very well for John Hawarde's great-grandfather, whose name is given in the Visitation pedigree as Richard. Mr. Ellis then quotes from Manning and Bray's *History of Surrey* (ii. 387), to the effect that the manor of Oxted *alias* Bursted was conveyed by Richard Hayward to his son Henry, Sept. 2, 32 Elizabeth, 1590. This is the only evidence that Mr. Ellis produces to support the statement that John Hawarde did not know his grandfather's name. Turning to Manning and Bray (*loc. cit.*), I find that the authority there given is 'Donation MS. Brit. Mus. 4705.' This turns out to be Additional MS. 4705, and the extraordinary mode of referring to it seems to be due to the fact that on the back of the volume is recorded 'Ex Dono S. Lethieullier, Arm.' The volume is an Index to the licenses to alienate lands held *in capite*. Unfortunately for the critic it is not stated in that MS., nor in the original license in the Record Office,[2] that Henry Hawarde was Richard's son. It is clear that Mr. Ellis could not find the 'Donation MS.,' and relied too implicitly on Manning and Bray. But what becomes of all his

[1] Thorpe, *Registrum Roffense*, 1029.

[2] Exchequer of Account, Alienation Office, vol. 4, fol. 375; see *post*

sarcasm? There is not the slightest reason to doubt the accuracy of the pedigree on this point.

To resume, HENRY HAWARDE, John's father, apparently began to purchase property in Tandridge and the neighbourhood about 1560. In Michaelmas Term of that year he was plaintiff in a Fine in which Richard Bostock and Catherine his wife were deforciants, concerning two messuages and lands in Tandridge.[1]

His name is found frequently in the Feet of Fines after this, generally as plaintiff, relating to property in Tandridge, Tatsfield, Farleigh, Croydon, Oxted, and elsewhere. In 1572, he acquired from John Rede and Bartholomew Rede, esquires, the manor of Gaston, *alias* Gasson, *alias* Garston, and lands in Blechingley, Godstone, Warlingham, Chelsham, Caterham, Saunderstead, Waldingham and Tandridge.[2]

In 1577, another Fine was levied relating to the same property in which John Rede and Elizabeth his wife were the deforciants.[3]

This John Rede was the son of another John Rede who had been the principal grantee of the land belonging to Tandridge Priory at the dissolution of the Monasteries.[4] John Rede the son in 1576 conveyed by Fine to Richard Bostock,[5] gentleman, the Manor of Tanrygge *alias* Tanrydge *alias* Northall *alias* le Pryorye, the Manor of Oxsted *alias* Berstead *alias* Bursted in Oxsted, the site of the late Monastery of Tanrydge, and 20 messuages, and lands, and £3 rent in Tandridge and elsewhere, also the Rectories of Tandridge and Crowherst, with their great and small tithes, and half the Rectory of Wolcomsted *alias* God-

[1] Feet of Fines, Surrey, Mich. 2 & 3 Eliz.

[2] Feet of Fines, Surrey, Mich. 14 & 15 Eliz. License to alienate dated Sep. 13; Patent Roll, 14 Eliz., part 2.

[3] Feet of Fines, Surrey, Hil. 19 Eliz. License to alienate dated Sep. 12; Patent Roll.

[4] Brayley, *Hist. of Surrey*, iv. *pass.* See *The History of Tandridge Priory*, by Major Alfred Heales, F.S.A., F.R.S.L.

[5] See *post*, p. 258.

stone, with its great and small tithes, and the advowson of the Vicarage.[1] A considerable part of this property was subsequently purchased by the Hawardes. The Manor of Burstead in 1577 was sold by Bostock to one Edward Johnson,[2] who, in 1582, conveyed it by Fine to Richard Hawarde of Oxted,[3] together with the tithes of Tandridge, and five messuages and lands and 26*s.* 8*d.* rent in Tandridge and Oxted. Brayley, following Manning and Bray, says that this Richard Hawarde was Henry's father;[4] I have already examined the accuracy of this statement. I believe that this Richard was Henry's brother. But however this may be, in 1590 Richard conveyed the property to Henry; it had possibly been conveyed to Richard as Henry's trustee.

In 1587 Richard Hawarde had a license to alienate to Henry Hawarde and his heirs certain lands called Abbeys and other land in the parish of Tandridge. Dated Sept. 2, 29 Eliz.[5]

In the same year a pardon was granted to Henry 'Heywarde,' Citizen and Fishmonger of London, for acquiring to himself and his heirs from John Rede or Reade, esquire, by an Indenture dated Feb. 18, 23 Eliz., 1580–1, two messuages, etc., in Oxted and Tandridge, without license. Dated Nov. 13, 29 Eliz.[6]

In 1590 a license was granted to Richard Hawarde to alienate the Manor of Biersted *alias* Bursted in Oxsted and lands in Oxsted to Henry 'Haywarde,' Citizen and Fishmonger of London, and his heirs, 2 Sept. 32 Eliz.[7]

A Fine was levied of the same Manor together with a messuage, lands, and 40*s.* rent in Oxted and Tandridge, in

[1] Feet of Fines, Surrey, Mich. 18 & 19 Eliz. License to alienate dated Oct. 1, 18 Eliz.

[2] Brayley, iv. 172. See *post*, p. xxxiii.

[3] Feet of Fines, Surrey, Trin. 24 Eliz. License to alienate dated May 2, 24 Eliz.

[4] iv. 172.

[5] Exchequer of Account, Alienation Office, vol. 4, fol. 180.

[6] *Ibid.*

[7] *Ibid.*, fol. 375.

1599, in which Fine Henry was plaintiff and Richard deforciant.[1]

The Tandridge Hall property was part of that conveyed to Richard Hawarde by Edward Johnson in 1582, and when it was acquired by Henry does not appear. Brayley[2] simply states that it was sold to one of the family of Hawarde. All I can say with certainty is that it was after 1582, in which year, as we have seen, it was sold by Johnson to Richard Hawarde, and before 1598, which is the date on the panelling still existing at the Hall. It was most probably included in the license to alienate of Sept. 2, 1587, set out above. This date is strongly confirmed by the pleadings in a Chancery suit in that year, relating to a messuage having the sign of the Galley, in Thames St.[3] In his answer, Henry states that shortly before he had 'diuerse greate somes of monye then to paye;' this payment had no doubt something to do with the purchase of Tandridge Hall. Again on March 23, 1587–8, he borrowed £640 from George Gardiner of Lincoln's Inn, gent., on the security of a farm called 'Skidhill' in the parishes of Cudham, Kent, and Chelsham, Surrey, a farm called 'Logiers' and another called 'Merchauntes' in Chelsham; the money was further secured by a bond for 1000 marks.[4] In August following he sold to Joan, widow of Edward Palmer of Chelsham, yeoman, a farm called 'Jennens' or 'Washmerstreate' at Cudham, for £105.[5] The purchase money was paid to Catherine Bassock, of London, widow (who afterwards became Henry's third wife), and the sale is said to have been 'at the speciall instaunce and requeste of Will'm Bowlle, yeoman ussher to our saide soueraigne ladye the

[1] Feet of Fines, Surrey, Mich. 41 & 42 Eliz.

[2] iv. 182. Its identity appears clear from the particulars of Sir William Hawarde's estate, *post*, p. xxxiii, where mention is made of a charge of 23*l*. a year granted by Edward Johnson before the purchase by Sir William's [grand-] father.

[3] See Appendix XXIV., where the pleadings are printed at some length.

[4] Close Roll, 30 Eliz., parts 15 and 25.

[5] *Ibid.*, part 17.

Quene's Maiestie, and John Philip th'elder of Cuddam in the Countie of Kent yeoman.' In 1589, Dec. 1, he gave a bond to Michael Gardiner of Grindford magna, clerk, for 500 marks, as security for the performance of the covenants of a deed dated Nov. 22 in the same year.[1] This was probably another mortgage. The Fine levied on this occasion shows that Henry's second wife, Agnes, died before 1590. In Hilary Term of that year a Fine was levied between William Seyliard, esquire, plaintiff, and Henry Haywarde and Catherine his wife, George Gardiner, gentleman, and Michael Gardiner, clerk, and Margaret his wife, deforciants, of a messuage and lands in Cudham, co. Kent, and of land in Chelsham, co. Surrey.[2]

The name of Henry Hawarde occurs in several Fines after this date and before 1611 (the year of his death), but some of these documents (and perhaps all of them) may refer to Henry the son.

In 1592, Henry obtained a grant of arms; Sable, two bars argent, in chief a talbot passant of the first: crest, a talbot's head couped, argent, collared sable, ringed argent, In the Visitation pedigree,[3] this coat is quartered with Argent, three castles gules, the arms of Agnes Castell, Henry's second wife. It is there stated that 'The first coate & creste [were] given by William Dethick, Garter, to Hen. Hayward of Tandridge, in Com. Surrey, 10 Aprill, 34 Q. Elizabeth, 1592.' It may be noted that in her will Catherine, Henry's widow, speaks of her cousin George Dethick, so she may have been related to Garter.

Henry had three wives. The first, Elizabeth, is mentioned in a Fine in 1563 relating to her property in Bermondsey.[4] This marriage is not recorded in the Visitation pedigree; it may be presumed that she had no issue. The second wife was Agnes, daughter and heir of Thomas

[1] Close Roll, 32 Eliz., part 35.

[2] Feet of Fines, Divers Counties, Hil. 32 Eliz.

[3] *Loc. cit.*

[4] Feet of Fines, Surrey, East. 5 Eliz.

Castell of London, merchant. She was the mother of a numerous family. The two eldest sons, Richard and Henry, died in their father's lifetime without issue;[1] John, the third son, was thus heir to his father. He was the writer of the MS. printed in this volume. There were five other sons, Rowland, a Bachelor of Divinity; William; Thomas (described in the pedigree as of Aberffeld, probably Arborfield, co. Berks), married and had issue a daughter married to William Thorold of Lincolnshire; Edmond, married in Ireland and had issue several sons; Michael, died without issue.[2] Thomas, Edmond and Michael are mentioned in their father's will in 1610,[3] the others were probably dead. There were also two daughters, Agnes or Anne, married 1. John Gardiner of Jenningsbury, co. Hertford, and 2. Francis Bowyer; Joan, married one Bacon and had a daughter Elizabeth.

Henry's third wife was Catherine Bassock, widow; she was married to him before 1590, and survived him. As will be seen from her will (*post*), she was the mother of John Hawarde's first wife Agnes Wilkinson, and must therefore have been the widow of William Wilkinson. She also mentions her only son, Robert Bassock. She made her will on April 6, 1614, being then of Stepney; she desired to be buried in the choir of S. Mary at Hill, Billingsgate, near her parents and kindred; she appointed her 'loving and only sonne' Robert Bassocke her executor, and bequeathed to him £100 due to her by her son-in-law, John Hawarde, of the Inner Temple, esquire, by agreement with Henry Hawarde, her late husband, 'out of the goodes which fell vnto his parte in my Righte vppon the decease of my vncle Younge'; 'I do allso earnestlie desire my sayed sonne in Lawe to be kynde and carefull of his children

[1] Heralds' College MS., Benefactors, ii. 74.

[2] Inquisition *post mortem*. Richard was entered at the Inner Temple, Nov. 16, 1577; he is described as late of Clifford's Inn.

[3] See *post*.

which god hath sent hym by my daughter Agnes Wilkenson, theire deceased mother;' she bequeathed 20*s*. to her brother-in-law Thomas Jones of Ratcliffe, 20*s*. to her cousin George Dethicke, 20*s*. to Elizabeth wife of William Bostocke, 40*s*. to Anne Elliott her maid. By a nuncupative codicil, without date, she bequeathed 'To her daughter Agnes Hayward, her three children, to eache of them a peece of gould of twentie twoe shillinges; To her daughter Catherine certeyne of her childebed lynnen, which she did call for to be brought vnto her, and caused yt to be tyed vp in a Bundell by yt self for her.' Proved June 8, 1614.[1]

Henry Hawarde died at Tandridge, March 24th, 1610, seised of considerable property in and around Tandridge. The Inquisition taken after his death is unfortunately in bad condition, the right margin being quite illegible. It is dated at Lambeth, July 30th, 1612. From it we learn that he was seised of the capital messuage known as Tandridge Hall, of other property in Tandridge, of the manors of Gasson *alias* Garston, Oxsted *alias* Birsted *alias* Bursted in Oxsted, of the manor or capital messuage and farm of Westhall [in Oxted], and of 11 messuages, 200 acres of land, 40 acres of meadow, and 200 acres of furze and heath, in the towns and parishes of Blechingley, Godstone. . . . Warlingham, Catterham, Chelsham, Farley, Titsey and Sanderstead, in the county of Surrey. In 1572, he settled certain property on himself and Agnes his then wife for their lives, with remainder to Richard, his eldest son, in tail male, remainder to Henry, his second son, in tail male, remainder to John his third son in tail male, remainder to John's right heirs. The two eldest sons, Richard and Henry, died in their father's lifetime without issue. In 1594, Henry Hawarde, the father, settled the manor of Garstone on himself and Katherine, his then wife, for their lives, with remainder to his son John and Agnes, his then

[1] P.C.C., Reg. Lawe, fol. 65.

wife, and the heirs of the body of John, with various remainders over. In 1606, he settled the manor of Oxted *alias* Birstead on John and his heirs male, with various remainders over. In 1606–7 he settled the residue of his property on himself for life, with remainder to his son John and his heirs male, with various remainders over. John was his son and heir, aged 40.[1]

Henry's will is dated Sept. 26, 1610, and was proved April 18, 1611. He desires to be buried 'as neere to the Corps of my deceassed wief as convenientlie maye be'; he bequeaths 10*s*. for the repair of the west end of Waldingham Church; 'And whereas I latelie at myne onely charge erected twoe Pillers of stone at the west ende of the Parrishe Churche of Tanridge, and amended alsoe the decayed foundations of the Thirde Pillar before standinge to the sayde ende, and did alsoe levell and pave there the Floore of the churche porche, and sett vp a Sonne Dyall in Stone & Bricke vppon the South syde of the same churche,'[2] his executor is to maintain the same during his life; To 20 poor and God-fearing householders in Blechingley, 20*s*.; the like in Godstone and Oxted; To 12 poor men of Tandridge, each a coat, containing 1½ yards of broad cloth of London measure, price 6*s*. 8*d*. the yard; To 13 poor wives or widows of Tandridge, each a gown containing 2¾ yards of broad cloth of the same price; These poor men and women are to attend his funeral and after the ceremony are to have dinner and 1*s*. apiece; To Elizabeth, daughter of his daughter Joan Bacon, £20; To his wife, Catherine, a legacy of £100, and an annuity of £50 in lieu of dower or jointure, with power of distress. He requests his son and

[1] Inquisition *post mortem*, Chancery, 10 James I., part 2, no 131.

[2] Tandridge Church has a nave and two aisles; on the south side are two pillars forming the nave arcade, but on the north side there is only one pillar, the place of the other being taken by a massive square pier of rather curious construction. There are thus three pillars in the nave. I think these must be the three pillars referred to above. The 'Sonne Dyall in Stone & Bricke' has disappeared.

heir [John] to allow his wife [Catherine] to live in his house at Tandridge, during her widowhood, 'and soe muche the rather for that I have for the better satisfaccion of them bothe lately bestowed greate charges vppon th'inlargement thereof;' To each of his sons, Thomas, Edmund and Michael, an annuity of £10, with power of distress; To his son Michael and his heirs his freehold land in Titsey, 'for the better enlargemen^{t} of my coppyhold there descendinge vnto him by the custome of the saide Manno^{r};' He mentioned a mortgage from Richard Hawarde of Woldingham; He appointed his son John executor and residuary legatee. One Henry Haward was a witness.[1]

John Hawarde, the writer of the MS., was, as we have seen, 40 years old at his father's death in 1611; he was therefore born about 1571. I cannot ascertain that he went to either University. He was entered at Clifford's Inn, as the custom then was, before becoming a student of an Inn of Court. He was admitted a student of the Inner Temple in 1588; the entry in the Admission Register is as follows:

Johannes Haywarde *de Tandryge in Com. Surr. et nuper de Cliffordes Inn, Generosus, admissus est in Societate istius Comitive in Cons' xx^{s} premanibus solut', xxiij die Novembr' anno r. R^{ne} Eliz. xxxj^{o}* [1588].

Plegii, George Rawe,
Ro. Heath.

The *y* of Haywarde has been struck through.

He was called to the Bar, Nov. 3, 1598, and was made a Bencher, Nov. 28, 1613; he was Reader in 1625.

In the Inner Temple Hall is a shield bearing these arms: Argent, on a pile sable, three crescents of the first; and underneath it is written, JOHANNES HAYWARD AR: LECTOR QVADR: A.D. 1614. This must, I think, refer to

[1] P.C.C., Reg. Wood, fol. 37.

John Hawarde of Tandridge, but the arms belong to another family.

He practised in the Courts of Chancery and Star Chamber, and also at the local Assizes and Sessions; his name appears in Foss's list of Counsel for the reign of James I. In 1597, he filed a Bill of Complaint in the Star Chamber, which will be found in App. XXV.

His name appears as a Justice of the Peace and Quorum for Surrey, in a list dated May 20, 1608.

John Hawarde was apparently married before 1586, although he could not have been more than 15 years old. In Hilary Term of that year a Fine was levied between Richard Hayward, demandant, and John Hayward and Agnes his wife, deforciants, of a barn and lands in Mitcham.[1] As the deforciants warranted against the heirs of Agnes, it would seem that the property dealt with belonged to her.

In 1609-10 he is described as 'senior' in a Fine levied between himself and William Valentine, plaintiffs, and Richard Haywarde, deforciant, of a messuage and lands in Woldingham, Chelsham and Oxted; to hold to John and William and the heirs of John.[2]

His name also occurs in other Fines at this period.

In 1613, John settled the Manor of Burstead on his second wife, Elizabeth, for life, with remainder to his own heirs male.[3] By a new settlement in 1630, his sons John and William were the remainder-men to the exclusion of the eldest son Humfrey.[4] This is partially explained by John's will (*post*), where we learn that Humfrey was undutiful and unthrifty. How much of John's other property was included in this last settlement I cannot say; but it would seem from John's will, and from the Fine of 1650 (*post*), that the whole of his property was settled so as to exclude his eldest son. Manning and Bray state (ii. 305) that John

[1] Feet of Fines, Surrey, Hil. 28 Eliz.
[2] *Ibid.*, Hil. 7 James I.
[3] Brayley, *Surrey*, iv. 172.
[4] *Ibid.*

settled the reversion of the Manor of Garston and certain lands, after the deaths of himself and Elizabeth his wife, on William, and the reversion of the Manors of Bursted and Westhall on John, with remainder to William; an estate at Tandridge was limited to Thomas, son of John and Elizabeth, and mention was made that John the son had a good estate of his own. The date of the deed is given as Sept. 10, 1630. Brayley[1] says the Manor of Garston 'descended' to Sir William Hawarde, who was the eldest son of the second marriage, and this is borne out by the Royalist Composition Papers (*post*), but the Tandridge property undoubtedly went to John, the second son of the first marriage.

In 1620, Hawarde was elected Member of Parliament for the Borough of Blechingly, co. Surrey, and again in 1624. On this second occasion a petition was presented against his return, and the facts of the case will be found set out in a collection of 'Certain Cases of Election of Burgesses to the Parliament, collected by Mr Serjeant Glanvile.'[2] The case begins thus:

'A Petition was exhibited by Henry Lovell gent. supposing, that, Whereas Sir Miles Fleetwood knight, and the said Mr Lovell were duly chosen Burgesses for the Borough, yet John Heyward esquire was unjustly returned, instead of the said Mr Lovell, and prayed relief and reformation in the premises: where in few days after, another petition was exhibited by the Borough-holders of the said Borough, justifying the said return and election of Mr Heyward, and charging the said Mr Lovell and one Mr Harris, Parson of Belchingley aforesaid, with several misdemeanours; in attempting to disturb the due election and return of Mr Heyward; procuring a colour of election for the said Mr Lovell, and a return of him thereupon; and for a

[1] iv. 109.
[2] State Papers, Domestic, Addenda, James I., vol. 43, no. 62.

practice and endeavour from thenceforth to innovate and alter the true and ancient custom of election, time out of mind used within the said Borough; praying that some punishment might be inflicted upon the said Mr Lovell and Mr Harris.' The case is set out at considerable length; the election took place on February 22nd, 21 James I., 1624. The matter was eventually decided in favour of Hawarde, who was declared to be duly elected; Lovell was considered to have 'committed an offence against the liberties and priveledges of the commons in Parliament,' for which it was ordered that he 'be committed prisoner to the Tower, there to remain during the pleasure of the house, and not to be enlarged till he had made his submission, and acknowledged his fault upon his knees at the bar of the house.' Harris was found to have committed several offences against the liberties and privileges of the house, 'deserving the more punishment in regard he had abused the pulpit to his own private and malicious ends. And for such his offences he should be brought as a Delinquent to the bar of the said house, to be there sharply reproved and admonished for such his faults, and to confess the same there, upon his knees, and humbly desire the pardon of the house, and upon the Sunday sevennight shewing in the Pulpit of his parish Church, in the entrance to his Sermon, again to witness the same fault, desiring the love of his neighbours and promising a reformation.'

John Hawarde was twice married. His first wife was Agnes, daughter and heir of William Wilkinson of London, merchant, to whom he was married before 1586 [*ante*]; by her he had issue Humphrey, aged 25 in 1623, John, and Agnes,[1] who is said in Harleian MS. 1561, fo. 162, to have been executed, July 4th, 1634. Agnes the wife was presumably living in 1598, when her initials were placed on the panelling at Tandridge Hall. See *post*. His second

[1] She is called Anne in the Inq. *post mortem* of her father; *post*.

wife was Elizabeth, daughter of William Angell of London, Fishmonger to James I., and Serjeant of the Acatery[1] to James I. and Charles I.; she was the widow of William Watts, 2nd son of Sir John Watts, knt., Lord Mayor of London; by her he had issue William, Thomas, Catherine, Susan (married 1. Robert Greenway, gent., 2. Arthur Spenser, gent.), Frances (married Edward Downer of Southampton, merchant), Thomazin (died unmarried), Jane (married William Fletcher of Mitcham, co. Surrey, gent.; they were married at Streatham, Feb. 3, 1651),[2] Dorothy (died unmarried), Mary and 'Margett.' The two last probably died young; the other daughters were living in 1646.[3] Thomas the son was dead in that year.

Hawarde's will was dated July 1, 1630, and proved Feb. 11 following. He recites that he has 'settled and estated all my landes, goodes and Chattalls by seueral deedes, drawne and engrossed wth mynowne hande, for the provision of my wife and all my children.' He excludes his 'vndutifull and vnthriftie sonne, Humfrie Haward, from all colour of ever challengeing any parte of my reall or personall estate.' He appoints his wife, Elizabeth, executrix.[4]

He died in January, 1630–1.

The Inquisition taken after his death sets out these settlements at some length.

Inquisition taken at Southwark, Nov. 4, 8 Charles I., 1632, after the death of John Haward, esq.; long before

[1] Acatery, a sort of check between the clerks of the King's kitchen and the purveyors. Crabb, *Tech. Dict.*

A Bill of Complaint, dated Nov. 17, 1617, by William Angell, esquire, 'his ma^tie's^ Fyshemonger,' against Sir William Foster, late of Crowhurst, knight, and William Foster, esq., his son and heir apparent, relating to property in Crowhurst, Lingfield, Oxted, Tandridge and Limpsfield, which the Fosters had sold to John Halsey or Haulsey, citizen and Merchant Taylor of London, for 3,450*l.*, and which had afterwards been purchased from him by William Angell 'for a greate somme of money.' This bill was drawn by John Hawarde and is signed by him at the foot.

Chancery B. & A., James I, A. 4, no. 2.

[2] *Col. Top. et Gen.*, iii. 312.

[3] See *post*, p. xxxiii.

[4] P.C.C., Reg. St John, fol. 13.

his death he was seised of a capital messuage called Tanridge Hall, and of divers lands, etc., thereto belonging, and also of 100 acres of land, 60 acres of meadow, 200 acres of pasture and 120 acres of wood in the parish of Tanridge; also of the Manors of Gasson or Garston and Oxsted or Birsted or Bursted in Oxsted; also of the Manor, capital messuage and farm of Westhall; also of 10 messuages, 200 acres of land, 40 acres of meadow, 400 acres of pasture, 200 acres of wood and 200 acres of furze and heath in the towns and parishes of Bletchingley, Godstone or Walkhamsted, Tanridge, Oxsted, Warlingham, Caterham, Chelsham, Farley and Saundersted. By an Indenture dated Feb. 26, 1613, made between Haward of the one part and William Angell, esq., Martin Freeman, esq., and John Angell, gent., son and heir apparent of William (being a settlement made in contemplation of a marriage between Haward and Elizabeth Watts, widow of William Watts, esq., and eldest daughter of William Angell), Haward settled the Manors of Garston, Bursted and Westhall, and certain property in Tandridge, to the use of himself for life, remainder to the use of the said Elizabeth for life as her jointure, remainder to the heirs male of the body of John, remainder to John's right heirs; and as to Tandridge Hall and all his other property, to the use of John and the heirs male of his body, with remainder to his right heirs. A Fine was levied, Hil. 4 Car. I. [1628–9], between William and John Angell, plaintiffs, and John Hawarde, deforciant, of all the above property, in confirmation of the said settlement. Hawarde was also seised of a messuage in Tandridge which he lately purchased. By an Indenture dated Sept. 10, 1630, made between himself of the first part, John Hawarde junior his 2nd son described as of the Inner Temple gent., of the 2nd part, and John Angell of Crowhurst, co. Surrey, Esq., and James Angell, Citizen and Fishmonger of London, of the 3rd part, reciting the former settlement, and that a recovery had been suffered in Hilary Term, 15 James I. [1617–8], of all the said Manors and lands, in order to enable John the father to limit and secure the same from Humphrey Hawarde his eldest son and his great and many debts, and to provide for John's other children; and reciting a Fine levied Hil. 4 Charles I., to effect the same object; and reciting an Indenture dated Feb. 16, 1629–30, made between the same parties, by which John Hawarde the father revoked the estate tail created by the marriage settlement of 1613, and gave himself an estate in fee simple in reversion after the death of his wife, Elizabeth; It was witnessed that Hawarde the father resettled all his property as follows:— to himself for life, remainder to Elizabeth for life, remainder as to the Manor of Garston to William, eldest son of John and Elizabeth, and his heirs, and as to the Manors of Bursted and Westhall, with remainder to John Hawarde the son and his heirs male; as to Tandridge Hall and all Hawarde's other property, including a garden plot in Trinity and Huggin Lane, London, to John Hawarde the father for life, remainder to John the son and the heirs male of his body, remainder to the said William Hawarde and the heirs male of his body, remainder to Thomas the 2nd son of John the father and Elizabeth and the heirs male of his body, with remainder to the right heirs of the said Thomas for ever. John Hawarde the son is to pay to Anne Hawarde eldest daughter of John H. the father, £40 a year for her maintenance for life; to Catherine, Susan, Frances, Thomasin, Jane and Dorothy Hawarde, the daughters of John the father, £500 each, and shall in the meantime allow them £8 per cent on their respective amounts for their maintenance; William and Thomas Hawarde, the sons of John the father and Elizabeth, are each to have £500 and interest at £8 per cent during their minority for their maintenance. 'And whereas the said Humfry Haward is by birth the eldest sonne of the said

John Haward the father and by the Course of the Common lawe his heire, yet in regard he hath alwaies beene an vndutifull and disobedient Child and liued a vaine Course of life to vex and greeve his aged father, and standes greatly indebted and much endangered by many, whereby if any thinge might descend vnto him or should be estated vpon him others would haue it from him and neyther he nor any other Child of the said John Haward the father be any way the better for it, Therefore the full intent and meaninge of the said John Haward the father and of these presentes is, That the said Humfry Haward shall haue noe part of the reall or personall estate of the said John Haward the father.' Nevertheless John the son is to pay Humphrey £20 a year for life. Part of the lands are charged with an annuity of £23 granted by Edward Johnson, gentleman, deceased, and other part with an annuity of £10 devised by Henry Haward, deceased, to his son Thomas for life; and all the lands are charged with £8 3*s.* 7*d.* a year payable to the King, and 7*s.* 4*d.* every 5th term for respite of homage. If John the son attempts to sell any of the property, or fails to pay any of the legacies or charges on the estate, then the whole to go to William on the like conditions.

John Hawarde senior died March 1, 6 Car. I., 1630–1;[1] Humphrey is son and next heir, and was aged 25 at the death of his father.[2]

Tandridge Hall and certain lands in Tandridge are held of Edward Bostock Fuller, esq., as of his Manor of Tandridge and Northall, in free and common socage by a rent of 10*s.*, and they are worth 20*s.* a year. The other lands in Tandridge and the Manors of Garston, Bursted and Westhall, and the 10 messuages and lands in Blechingley, Godstone, Tandridge, Oxted, Warlingham, Caterham, Chelsham, Farley and Saundersted, are held of the King

[1] This is a mistake; his will was proved Feb. 11, 1630-1.
[2] This is also wrong.

in chief by knight's service; the first mentioned property is worth 10*s*. yearly, the three Manors are worth the same.[1]

Elizabeth Hawarde, John's widow, was living in 1650, (see *post*). She held her Court at Bursted Oct. 5, 1641.[2]

John Hawarde's Signature from the Inner Temple Admission Register.

Humphrey Hawarde, John's eldest son, was baptised at the Church of S. Dunstan in the West, April 15, 1598.[3]

He was admitted to the Inner Temple, October 28, 1613, being described as of Tandridge and late of Clifford's Inn, gentleman.

He was disinherited by his father, as we have seen, and very little appears to be known about him. The following from the State Papers is the only item I have been able to discover.

1631, June 17.—Henry Edlin of Addington, Surrey, yeoman, petitioned the Privy Council, stating that long since he became bound as surety for one Humphrey Hayward, esq., for divers sums, which cost him 100*l*. at least; having bonds to secure himself, he 'arreasted the said Hayward twice, whoe both times was rescued, & about half a yeare past in a ryotous manner was taken away from the Bayliffes by one Sr Fraunci Leigh of Addington, knight, & by his freinds & seruants at his appointement, who came violentlie wth swordes, pitchforks, staues, & throwing of stones, & tooke the saide Hayward from the Bayliffes'; 'being not able to contend in lawe wth the saide Sr Fraunci (hee being a man of greate wealth & power), [the petitioner] is therefore like to loose all his said money, the said Hayward now living priuatelie in Milford laine, where

[1] Inq. *post mortem*, Chancery, 11 Car. I., part 3, no. 170.
[2] Manning & Bray, ii. 387. [3] *Col. Top. et Gen.* v. 367.

he cannot be arreasted.' The case was referred to the Judges of Assize for relief.[1]

1631, November 28.—Sir George Vernon and Sir James Weston, Barons of the Exchequer, reported that Edlin had several times made default at the times appointed by them to hear his complaint, and that they had therefore been unable to proceed in the matter.[2]

Sir Francis Leigh of Addington was the eldest son of Sir Oliph Leigh; he was admitted to the Inner Temple, October 10, 1610, when John Hawarde (the writer of the MS.) was one of his pledges; he was knighted at Newmarket, December 11, 1618.

Humphrey Hawarde died without issue.[3]

JOHN HAWARDE, second son of John, was admitted a student of the Inner Temple, November 26, 1615.

By an Indenture dated December 15, 1631, John Hawarde of London, gent., mortgaged to Arthur Mowsse the elder, Citizen and Fishmonger of London, and Arthur Mowsse the younger, his son, for the sum of 324*l.*, a messuage, etc., called the White Horse in Sydon Lane *alias* Seethinge Lane in the parish of All Saints Barking near the Tower of London, and two messuages in Thames Street 'at Belynsgate,' which Robert Bassock, deceased, devised to Hawarde by his will. An annuity of 26*l.* was payable out of part of the premises to Frances Manninge, widow, late the wife of the said Robert Bassock.[4]

John sold all his paternal estate to his half-brother, Sir William Hawarde, probably before 1642. Manning and Bray[5] give 1649 as the date of this transaction, and mention a deed dated February 7, 1649[50]. This, however,

[1] State Papers, Domestic, Charles I., vol. 194, no. 23.

[2] *Ibid.*, vol. 203, no. 86.

[3] Heralds' College MS., Benefactors, ii. 74.

[4] Close Roll, 7 Charles I., part 32. Robert Bassock was the only son of Catherine Wilkinson, 3rd wife of Henry Hawarde; see *ante*.

[5] ii. 379.

appears to have been a deed by which Sir William resettled the property, and the actual purchase may very well have taken place some years before. The Civil War was no doubt responsible for the delay.

The Fine levied on this occasion is as follows:

Hilary Term 1649–50, Fine between Henry Bysshopp, Esq., and Edward Thurland, Esq., plaintiffs, and Elizabeth Haward, widow, William Haward, Knight, and Martha his wife, and John Haward, Esq., deforciants of the Manors of Garston, Beirsted and Westhall, and of 20 messuages, 3 cottages, 23 barns, 20 stables, a water-mill, a pigeon-cote, 23 gardens, 23 orchards, 400 acres of land, 50 acres of meadow, 390 acres of pasture, 200 acres of wood, 100 acres of furze and heath, and common of pasture for all cattle, in Tandridge, Godstone, Bletchingley, Oxted, Caterham, Warlingham, Saunderstead and Crowhurst.[1]

It is not quite clear how much of this property had belonged to John. According to the settlement of 1630 (*ante*) the Manor of Garston belonged to William and the Manors of Bursted and Westhall and the Tandridge property belonged to John. But the particular of Sir William's estate (*post*) refers to the various estates as if they all belonged to Sir William, and ignores John altogether. It is clear, then, that at the date of the particular, John had already conveyed his share of the property to William. It will be noticed that in a list of Sir William's debts owing in 1642, he is said to owe John 660*l.*; this no doubt represents part of the purchase money. It was still unpaid in 1651 (*post*).

John is stated in the settlement of 1630 to have had a good estate of his own; we have seen that he had property in the City of London which was left to him by Robert Bassock (who was half-brother of John's mother), and the next document shows that he had also property in Essex.

By an Indenture dated February 1, 23 Charles I., 1647–8,

[1] Feet of Fines, Surrey, Hil. 1649–50.

John Hawarde of the Inner Temple, gentleman, leased to Richard Elcox of Fobbing, co. Essex, gentleman, in consideration of 200*l.*, diet and other necessaries, the capital messuage called Sprevers Hall, and all his lands in Fobbing, for a term of 99 years, at a rent of 20*l.* during Haward's life, and after his death at a peppercorn rent.[1]

John Hawarde died without issue,[2] but when I cannot say.

Sir William Hawarde, the eldest son of John's second marriage, was knighted by Charles I. at Sudeley Castle, September 9, 1643.

He purchased most of the family property from his half-brother John, probably in 1642,[3] that is to say Tandridge Hall, and the Manors of Bursted and Westhall. He sold these Manors, as well as that of Garstone in 1681 to John Borrough, esquire.[4]

He was admitted a student of the Inner Temple, November 10, 1635.

He was a Gentleman of the Honourable Privy Chamber in Ordinary to Charles I., Charles II.,[5] James II. and William III.[6]

Sir William married at Christ Church, Oxford, September 4, 1643,[7] Martha, youngest daughter of John Acton of London, Goldsmith to Charles I., second son of Thomas Acton of Elmley Lovett, co. Worcester, and brother and heir of Charles Acton. She was living in 1681, when she was a party to a Fine (set out *post*), and probably died in 1689. By her Sir William had 4 sons and 6 daughters.

1. John, died an infant. 2. William, of whom *post.*
3. John, aged about fifteen in 1672. 4. Marma-

[1] Close Roll, 1650, part 10, no. 5.
[2] Heralds' College MS., Benefactors, ii. 74.
[3] Brayley, *Surrey*, iv. 172, 182. See *ante*.
[4] *Ibid.* See *post*.
[5] Heralds' College MS., Benefactors, ii. 74.
[6] Chester's *Westminster Abbey Registers*, 223. Carlisle's *Gentlemen of the Privy Chamber*.
[7] Chester's *Westminster Abbey Registers*, 223.

duke, aged 10 in 1672. 1. Northamptonia, Northamptona, or Northampton, married to Sir John Henden of Biddenden, co. Kent, knt., at Streatham, August 28, 1660.[1] The marriage allegation in the Register of the Vicar-General of the Archbishop of Canterbury is dated August 20, 1660; Sir John is described as a bachelor, about twenty-eight years of age, the lady is described as a spinster, about fifteen years of age; the license was for the churches of Streatham, Tandridge, or S. Gregory, London. 2. Elizabeth. 3. Thomazin. 4. Martha. 5. Catherine, died an infant. 6. Jane.

The above particulars as to Sir William's family have mostly been obtained from a MS. in the Heralds' College, for which I am indebted to the kindness of H. F. Burke, Esq., F.S.A., Somerset Herald. The volume is known as 'Benefactors, vol. 2,' and is entitled 'The Armes and Descents of several Noble-Persons and others who have Contributed Moneys towards rebuilding ye College of Armes; at the Request and by the Solicitation of Francis Sandford, Esqr, now Lancaster Herald, at that time Rougedragon Pursivant of Arms; with a Catalogue of the Benefactors and the Summes of Money by them Paid.' The Hawarde pedigree begins with Henry, Sir William's grandfather, and includes Sir William's children; it is dated May 9, 1672.

At the top is a shield with the following arms:—Quarterly of six. 1. Sable, two bars argent, in chief a talbot passant of the last; *Hawarde*. 2. Azure, on a bend argent between two leopards' faces or, three martlets gules. 3. Argent, a chevron between three talbots passant sable. 4. Ermine, on a chief azure three lions rampant argent. 5. Argent, three towers triple lowered gules; *Castle*. 6. Gules, a fess vair, in chief an unicorn passant between two

[1] *Col. Top. et Gen.* iii. 312.

mullets or, within a bordure engrailed of the last; *Wilkinson.* Opposite to the last quartering is this note: 'the last coat ought not to be quartered by Sr Will: Haward.'

Sir William espoused the cause of Charles I in the Civil War. Some interesting details about him and his property are recorded in the Royalist Composition Papers.

'His delinquency that he diserted his owne dwellinge and went to Oxford and liued there whiles it was a Garrison held for the Kinge against the Parliam^te^, and remayned there for some tyme.' [1]

He appears to have been a somewhat lukewarm Royalist. He states in his petition that he 'was neuer in Armes ag^t^ the Parlym^t^,' [2] and that as early as December, 1645, he had the intention to submit himself. An affidavit of William Evans and Christopher Hudson, two of Sir William's servants, states, that they, 'attending vpon their Master Sr William about Michaelmas last [1645] att Oxford, heard the sayd Sr William frequently expresse his resolutions of comming from thence, and submitting himselfe to the Parliam^te^, and that he would sende to his mother in Surrey to procure him a passe from the Parliam^t^ for his safe comming, by the meanes of her Freind Mr Darley, one of the members of the Honor^ble^ house of Commons: and that they are very confidently persuaded, if such a passe had then bin procured, and sente to the sayd Sr William, he would not haue fayled to haue come away; the sayd Sr William often expressing to boeth of them that the wante of a passe was the onely cause of the delaying his comming away.' [3] The pass was procured, and Richard Hunt, 'seruante to Mrs Elizabeth Haward of Tandridge, widd.,' was despatched with it. He says, 'about Michaelmas last past [1645], the sayd Richard Hunt was commanded by his Mistresse, the sayd Elizabeth Haward, to try if he could gett to Oxford, and

[1] State Papers, Domestic, Interregnum, G. 196, no. 733.
[2] *Ibid.*, no. 736.
[3] *Ibid.*, no. 744.

carry a passe to her sonne, Sr William Haward, for his safe comming away to the Parliam^{t}, which passe, as he conceaues by his Mistresses expressions, was signed by the Speaker of the Honor^{ble} house of Commons, and procured by the meanes of Mr Darley. And that he wente as farre as Henley on his way, but durst not carry the passe any farther by reason of the frequent passings up and downe of Souldiers on boeth sides.' [1]

The particular of Sir William's estate is as follows:

'He is seized of an estate to him & his heires in reuersion after the decease of Elizabeth his mother of & in the manno^{r} of Garston wth the rightes, members & app^{r}tenn^{ces} scituate in Bleachingleigh & Godstone in the County of Surrey, of the yerely value before these troubles of 80^{li}.

'That by Indenture dated 10° Sept. 1630 made betweene John Haward, the Compounder's father, on the first parte, John Haward the sonne, on the second parte, and certayne trustees on the third part, for the consideracions therein expressed, the said John Haward the father did soe settle the landes hereafter mencioned as that the Compounder standeth seized of an estate to him & his heires in revercion after his mother's decease of & in the manno^{rs} of Biersted & Westhall & the Hillish land wth their appertenn^{ces} in the County of Surrey, wch weare of the yerely value before these troubles of 105^{li} 0^{s} 0^{d}.

'And of an estate in possession to him & the heires males of his body of and in a Capitall messuage and certaine other Farmes, landes & ten^{tes} in Tandridge & other neighbouring parishes, & of a garden plott scituate in Trinity Lane & Huggyn Lane, London, of the yerely value of 209^{li} 08^{s} 00^{d}.

'Upon Condicion that the Compounder shall pay

'To Katheryne Haward, eldest daughter of John Haward & Eliz.—500^{li}.

[1] *Ibid.*, no. 730.

'To Suzan Haward their second daughter—500^{li}.

'To Fraunces their third daughter—500^{li}.

'To Thomazyne Haward their Fourth daughter—500^{li}.

'To Jane Haward their fifth daughter—500^{li}.

'To Dorathy Haward their sixth daughter—500^{li}.

'To Thomas Haward now deceased their second sonne, which is lefte by his will to Joane Haward his widdowe—500^{li}.

'Togeather wth Interest after the rate of 8^{li} per centum, w^{ch}, from the death of John the father who dyed in January, 1630 [1631], till their seuerall ages of 21 yeres or dayes of mariage, amountes yearly to 280^{li}, which the Compounder conceives is more then the land charged wth the same cann satisfy.

'And wth the paym^{t} of 23^{li} per annum for euer, graunted, before the Compounder's [grand]father purchased the same, by Edward Johnson to be issueing out of the said landes, and of the annual charge of 8^{li} 3^{s} 4^{d} for a tenth to the king, *prout* the same Indenture, whereof he craues allowance.

'He is interessed or hath right to 1250^{li} bequeathed vnto Martha, the Compounder's wiefe, by the will of her father, wch is payable, as he Conceiues, out of the estate of Sr Henry Skipwith, Kn^{t} & Barronett, of Leicestershire, a delinquent, wch he feares is almost desperate, The fyne for wch he desires he may haue tyme to pay into this hono^{ble} Committee [the Committee for Compounding], when he receives the same.'[1]

The six sisters were all living at Tandridge in September, 1646; all the portions mentioned above were then unpaid.[2]

His fine was fixed in January, 1646–7, at one sixth, which amounted to 437*l.* 14*s.* 0*d.*[3]

On July 8, 1652, Dame Martha, his wife, refused to take

[1] *Ibid.*, no. 747. [2] *Ibid.*, no. 749. [3] *Ibid.*, p. 734.

the oath of abjuration, and two thirds of her jointure was ordered to be sequestered accordingly.[1]

On June 19, 1651, an information was lodged against him by Captain Cassibilan Burton:—'That the said Sr William Haward gave in vpon his particuler when hee compounded That there was due vnto him the summe of Fifteene hundred poundes or thereaboutes in right of his wife, out of Sr Henry Skipwith his estate, which was desperate, and desired when hee had recovered it, hee might bee admitted to compound for it, which was accordingly graunted, Since which time the said debt of 1500^{li} hath bin receaued above fifteene monthes agoe by the said Sr William, and not yet offered to bee compounded for; Besides, when the said Sr William gave in this as a desperate debt, hee was in actuall possession of 400^{li} per annum of Sr Henry Skipwith's estate in the Countie of Leicester, wch was morgaged for the said debt, and did att the same time & afterwardes receave the profittes towardes $paym^t$ thereof vntill the said landes were sould to pay the aforesaid debt.'[2]

'I, Henry Proby, Common Seriant at lawe of the Citty of London, doe certifie that about the eight day of November, 1647, Sr William Haward, knight, informed mee that he had bin aboue three yeares marryed vnto Martha, one of the daughters and late orphan of John Acton, late Citizen & Goldsmith of London deceased, & desired mee to let him know his wife's portion and where the same was remayning,& therevpon I did certifie him that her portion was 1250^{li} 12^s $8^d\frac{1}{2}$, & that the same togeather with the like portion for Jane and Edward two other of the children & orphans of the said John Acton was secured by Sr Henry Skipwith, knight & barronett, by a lease bearing date on or about the 27th day of June Anno d^{ni} 1640, made vnto Mr Alderman Pennington, & other Aldermen

[1] *Ibid.*, G. 30, fo. 442. [2] *Ibid.*, A. 118, no. 1.

of the Citty of London, of the Mannor of Prestwold and other lands in ye County of Lecester for the terme of 99 yeares; And that afterwardes vpon Complaint made vnto the Court of Lord Maior & Aldermen that the said portions were not payed, It was thought fitt & directions given accordingly that the said Lease should be sold for payment of the s^d^ portions. . . . And that afterwards the said Trustees by order & direction of the said Court on or about the 12th day of february, 1649, [did] assigne the said Lease vnto Mr Alderman Pack, wherevpon the seuerall porcions afores^d^ were paid and discharged, wch portions were to euery of them 1250^li^ 12^s^ 8^d^½ apeece principall money, and interest for the forbearance of the same, but how much I cannot remember. Dated the 7th day of this instant July, 1651.'[1]

A list of debts owing by Sir William before May, 1642, and still unpaid in October, 1651, amounting in all to 860*l*. Among them a debt of 660*l*. due to John Haward of London, gentleman.[2]

Probably in 1642 or earlier, Sir William purchased from his half-brother John all John's share of the family property in Surrey. The 660*l*. due from Sir William to John in 1651 probably represents part of the purchase money. By a deed dated February 7, 1649–50, Sir William's estates, including the Tandridge property and the Manors of Bursted and Westhall purchased from John, and the Manors of Oxted and Garston, were resettled; Elizabeth Hawarde (widow of John H. the father, and mother of Sir William), and John H. the son were parties. Elizabeth's jointure was confirmed during the joint lives of herself and Sir William, but if he died first, then those estates (the Manors of Garston, Bursted, and Westhall) were to be the jointure of Sir William's widow, and Elizabeth was to have Tandridge Hall and other property in lieu thereof; and, subject to the

[1] *Ibid.*, no. 3. [2] *Ibid.*, no. 7.

said jointures, all the property was settled on Sir William and his heirs male, with remainder to him in fee.[1] The Fine levied on this occasion has already been set out.

In 1661 Sir William was elected M.P. for Bletchingley,[2] the constituency which his father represented in 1620 and 1624.

In 1681, according to the county histories, Sir William, Dame Martha, his wife, and William, his son and heir apparent, sold all their Surrey property to John Borrough, esq. The only evidence I can find of this transaction is a Fine in Michaelmas Term of that year between Borrough, plaintiff, and Sir William and his wife, deforciants of the Manors of Beirsted and Garston, and 12 messuages, 3 cottages, 10 barns, 10 stables, a water-mill, a dove-cote, 12 gardens, 10 orchards, 300 acres of land, 90 acres of meadow, 140 acres of pasture, 240 acres of wood, 200 acres of furze and heath, and 28*s*. rent, in Tandridge, Godstone, Bletchingley, Oxted, Caterham, Warlingham, Saunderstead and Crowhurst.[3] This supports the statement as to the sale to a certain extent, but on the other hand I find Sir William continued to be described as of Tandridge for more than 20 years afterwards.

In an Indenture dated July 14, 3 James II. [1687], Sir William Hawarde is described as of Tandridge, and is stated to be one of the surviving Trustees for the sale of the King's Fee Farm Rents.[4]

His name occurs with the same description in various other Indentures up to May 11, 1 Anne [1702].[5]

It seems strange that Sir William should continue to describe himself of Tandridge twenty years after he had sold the property, though of course he might have reserved a life interest in it.

[1] Manning and Bray, ii. 379, 387.
[2] *Ibid.*, ii. 294.
[3] Feet of Fines, Surrey, Mich. 33 Car. II.
[4] Close Roll, 3 James II., part 6, no. 3.
[5] *Ibid.* 1 Anne, part 10, no. 14.

On March 24, 1688-9, Lady Martha *Haywood* was buried in the West Cloister at Westminster Abbey. Mr. Chester suggests, with great plausibility, that she was the wife of Sir William *Hayward* or Hawarde.[1] The mis-spelling of the surname is probably due to the carelessness of the clerk who made the entry, and it was not at all unusual at that period for a knight's wife to be referred to as 'Lady' with her Christian name.

The deed of May 11, 1702, is the last record I have found of Sir William; and I can find no evidence of his death or burial, nor of any will or letters of administration.

Sir William Hawarde's signature, from the Royalist Composition Papers.

WILLIAM HAWARDE, son and heir of Sir William, was aged about 24 in 1672;[2] he was admitted a student of the Inner Temple, February 7, 1663–4.

I have not been able to trace him or his family any further.

TANDRIDGE HALL, as has already been stated, was sold to John Borrough in 1681. After various transfers, it was purchased by Lady Clayton, wife of Sir Kenrick Clayton, together with the Manor of Garston, and in 1808 it belonged to Sir William Clayton, Bart. From him it was purchased by Joseph Wilks, esquire, who converted the old farm-house

[1] *Westminster Abbey Registers*, J. L. Chester, 223.

[2] Heralds' College MS., Benefactors, ii. 74.

into a residence for himself.[1] It is now the property of the Earl of Cottenham, and is occupied by W. H. Charlesworth, Esquire, who very kindly allowed me to see the house. The exterior has been stuccoed and lime-washed, so that it is impossible to say how much of Henry Hawarde's work is still standing. Brayley says :[2]—' Many of the rooms are ancient and appear to be nearly in their pristine state. One apartment is wainscotted throughout ; over its carved mantel piece is the date 1598, and on each side are the initials of the Haward family. It is probable that this mantel piece, which is of a handsome character, formerly ornamented the dining-room, as that apartment is said to have been wainscotted previously to the time when Mr Wilks effected his alterations (after 1808). Fragments of carving, similar to that of the mantel piece, are found in other parts of the house.' ' Over the vestry fireplace [Tandridge church] is an oak carving from Tandridge Hall in the same style as the mantel piece already referred to. It is in three compartments ; flowers, scrolls, etc., occupying the north and the centre ; and the south, what appears to be the head of a jester. Its age is probably that of the mantel piece, 1598 ' [p. 185].

At the present day the only room showing any signs of antiquity is the wainscotted room referred to by Brayley. It is a low room on the first floor, and is now used as a chapel. The wainscotting is plain, with a carved frieze of simple design, and is in capital preservation. The mantelpiece is a nice specimen of the carved woodwork of the period ; it has been cleaned and restored at some comparatively recent time. At the sides above the mantelpiece are two small panels, 6 in. × 7½ in., with inlaid patterns of boxwood and ebony, and in the centre is a smaller design in a similar style, with the date 1598. These are figured below. The initials are those of Henry Hawarde and

[1] Brayley's *Hist. of Surrey*, new ed. by Edward Walford, no date, iii. 381.
[2] iv. 182.

Catherine his wife, on the left, and of John Hawarde and Agnes his wife, on the right. The woodwork in this room shows no sign of having been removed, and I believe it is in its original position.

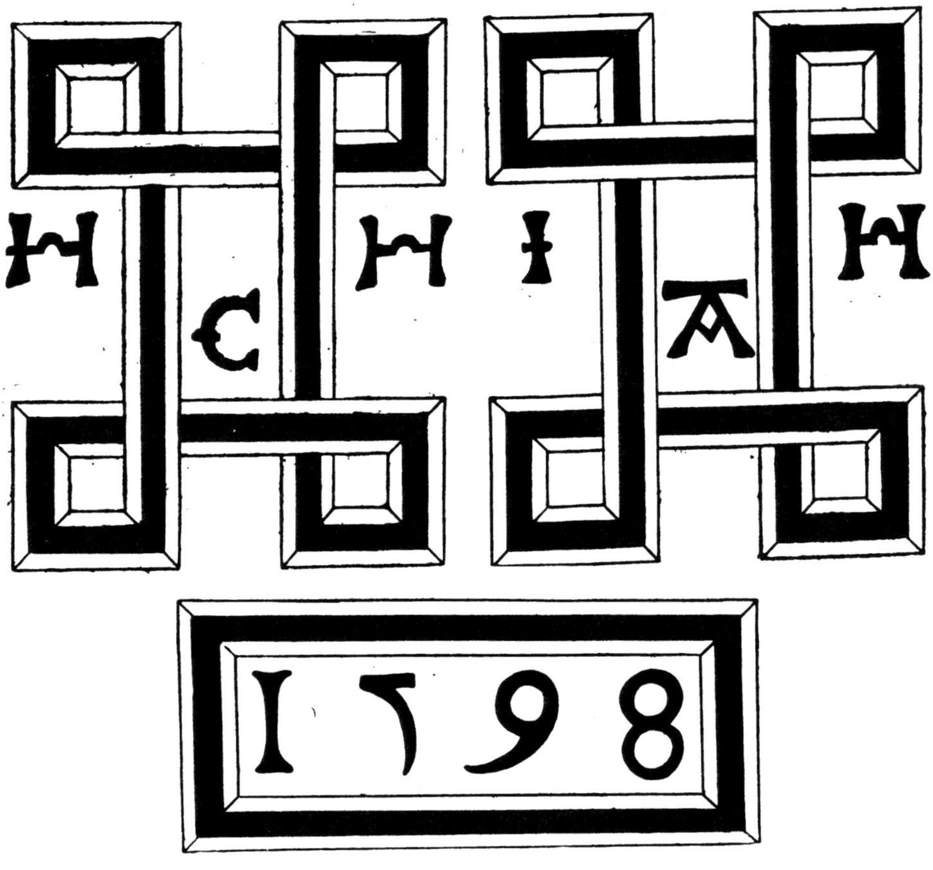

The carving mentioned by Brayley as being in Tandridge Church is not now to be found, nor are the fragments of carving which he says existed in other parts of the house. The Hall seems to have fallen into decay during the last century, and has since suffered much from alterations. In 1674 Sir William Hawarde paid Hearth Tax on 19 hearths, which shows that the house was then of considerable size.[1] Sir Marmaduke Gresham had 22 hearths in his house at Titsey at the same date.

III. *The Court of Star Chamber.*[2]

A. *History.*

The origin of the Court of Star Chamber, though not exactly lost in the mists of antiquity, must certainly be sought for at an earlier period than that of any of the superior courts of justice in this country, excepting only the House of Lords and the Privy Council.

At a very early period of our legal history, soon after the Conquest in fact, we find that there was but one superior, or King's Court in existence, namely, the Court held before the King himself and his Council. They were the law-makers and law-interpreters too; the Court was at once the executive, the law court, and the legislature; the King was at once the ruler and the judge.[3]

The system was based upon the theory that the King was the principal fount of justice in his kingdom, and was bound to look into and to right the wrongs of his subjects. This Court of the King and his Council was called the King's Hall or Court (*Aula Regis*, or *Curia Regis*), and naturally had to sit wherever the King happened to be for the time being. From it arose from time to time the Courts of King's Bench, Common Pleas, Exchequer, and Chancery. The details of these various divisions are well known, and it is unnecessary to go into them here.[4]

By the establishment of these various courts the Council

[1] Exchequer, L. T. R., Lay Subsidies, 188–496.

[2] For this part of my Introduction I am largely indebted to a very able paper on the Star Chamber by John Bruce, F.S.A. (*Archæologia*, vol. xxv. 1834), Hudson's Treatise on the Star Chamber (*Collectanea Juridica*, vol. ii.), Dicey's *Privy Council*, etc.

[3] Dicey.

[4] The separation of the first three of these Courts was in all probability accomplished not later than 1164–1174. Dicey.

got rid of the greater part of their judicial functions, but they still retained a certain residuum which was exercised from time to time. Occasional points of law were reserved for their opinion,[1] and pleas were frequently heard before them.[2] The Council also exercised to a certain extent the functions which the Council of Judges performs nowadays, in regulating the procedure of the other Courts; they devised new writs when necessary, and so on. The cases heard by the Council were chiefly those in which the inelastic forms of the common law could give no remedy, and it is from this branch of the Council's jurisdiction that the Court of Chancery may be said to have arisen. Other cases heard by the Council were those which in their nature were cognizable at common law, but which from individual circumstances were of great importance or of an extraordinary character. 'Wherever, in fact, either from defect of legal authority to give judgment, or from want of the might necessary to carry their decision into effect, the law courts were likely to prove inefficient, then the Council stepped in, by summoning before it defendants and accusers.' [3] It is this part of the Council's functions which subsequently came to be called the Court of Star Chamber. Such cases were where 'it were a "heinous trespass" for which it was necessary to provide speedy remedy; if the one party was so rich and the other so poor, that right was not likely to be done in the Courts below' [Bruce], or the like. In such cases, on complaint being made by petition, the Council used either to send for the parties, and determine the case before them, or to issue a commission of *oyer* and *terminer* to inquire into the matter. In all such cases, petition was made nominally to the King for his special interference, and this form continued in the Star

[1] *Bracton's Note Book*, F. W. Maitland, iii. 234, 467, 499, etc.; *Abbreviatio Placitorum*, 320; Selden Soc., *Select Civil Pleas*, W. P. Baildon, i. 190.

[2] *Bracton's Note Book*, and *Abbreviatio Placitorum*, *passim*.

[3] Dicey.

Chamber until its abolition. The petition was addressed to the King, praying that he would send for the defendant to appear before himself and his Council. After the institution of Parliament by Edward I. the House of Commons, jealous of the power of the Council, petitioned against it at various times. Probably for this reason the appointment of special commissions ceased during the reign of Edward III., and all cases were heard before the Council itself.

BIRD'S-EYE VIEW OF WESTMINSTER, 1578.
(From Ralph Aggas's Map.)

It was in this reign that the name of the court first arose, as to which a little digression will be necessary.

King Edward III. made large additions to the Palace of Westminster, including S. Stephen's Chapel, and many other buildings; and it was in 1347, towards the middle of his reign, that a new council chamber was built. This Chamber, the Star Chamber, was part of a range of buildings situated on the east side of Palace Yard, most of

EAST FRONT OF THE STAR CHAMBER, FROM THE THAMES.
From Smith's 'Antiquities of Westminster.'

which were apportioned to the office of the Exchequer. The last remaining part of these buildings was taken down as recently as 1836.[1] The original room seems to have been repaired or rebuilt at the end of Elizabeth's reign; the initials 'E. R.' and the date 1602, were carved over one of the doors.[2] An illustration of this stone is given in Smith's *Antiquities of Westminster* (1807), and is here reproduced on a larger scale. A view of the interior of the Star Chamber is given by Brayley and Britton [*op. cit.*], and two views of the exterior of the building are given by Smith [*op. cit.*]; these three plates are here reproduced. Smith also has a plate of the very fine ceiling of the Star Chamber,

CARVING OVER THE ENTRANCE TO THE STAR CHAMBER.
(*Enlarged from Smith's 'Antiquities of Westminster.'*)

and details of parts of the stone and woodwork will be found in *A Guide for drawing the Acanthus*, by I. Page, London, 1843. Some of these are reproduced on the next page.

Page says:—'Immense paneled and ornamented doorways, large handsome fireplaces,—an illustration of which I have given in the annexed plate, and which was added, to complete the room (bought by the Hon. Lieut.-Colonel Cust), of the internal fittings at the Star Chamber, or King's Palace, which he had fitted up at his own mansion, as it stood in Old Palace Yard, Westminster. The ceiling of that was most elaborate,—it was purely Gothic; and, at

[1] *History of the Ancient Palace and late Houses of Parliament at Westminster*, Brayley and Britton, p. 231.

[2] *Ibid.*, p. 442. Smith, *op. cit.* See *post*, p. 463.

each extremity, terminated with the white and red rose of York and Lancaster, the port-cullis, and the pomegranate, which, with the fleur-de-lis, was a very favourite ornament of that time' [p. 196]. This passage is so delightfully vague that it has been quoted *verbatim*. A small plan is given of the elaborate ceiling, but the illustration of the fireplace is difficult to identify; moreover it is not at all clear from the passage quoted whether the fireplace in

question was actually part of the Star Chamber, or was added by Colonel Cust from some other room.

We can fix the date of the erection of the original building within a few months. In 1344 we learn from the Parliament Roll that the Council of our Lord the King, and the Justices and other sages of the law, were assembled *en la*

THE INTERIOR OF THE STAR CHAMBER.

From Britton and Brayley's 'History of Westminster Palace.'

Chambre du Conseil pres de l'Escheqier.[1] This was the old Council Chamber. The new chamber was apparently built on the same site. It was commenced in 1347, and finished in the following year. I have extracted the accounts of the building from various sources; they will be found in Appendix XXVI.

The earliest record I have found of the name of the Star Chamber is in or about 1348, where it is referred to as the 'Sterred Chambre.'[2] The next is dated 1355, and is to the effect that on March 7th in that year William de la Pole senior, knight, came *in Camera Stellata in palacio Westm' prope pontem regium coram venerabilibus Patribus Johanne Archiepiscopo Ebor., Cancellario, et Willelmo Wynton' Episcopo, Thesaurario, et Bartholomeo de Burgherssh, Camerario ipsius domini Regis, et Thoma de Brembre, Custode privati sigilli Regis, Johanne de Bello campo et aliis de consilio eiusdem Regis,* and there delivered up certain deeds and letters patent of the King to be cancelled, and also brought a deed to be enrolled by which he released to the King all his right in certain property. At the same time his sons Sir Thomas de la Pole and Edmund de la Pole came *coram dicto consilio iu eadem Camera* on the like business.[3]

In 1366, we find a variation in the name, as appears from the following:

Fait arememberere que Isabella qui feu la femme Monsr Wauter Fauconberge vient le meskirdy proschein apres la feste de touz Seintz l'an du regne nostre s^r^ le Roi quarantisme a Westmonst' en la Chaumbre du conseil esteillee pres de la resceite de l'escheqier.[4]

This was a matter relating to Isabel's dower and may well have been the judgment in a suit actually heard before the Council; it is mentioned that the Chancellor, the Treasurer, *et autres du Conseil* were present.

[1] *Rot. Parl.*, ii. 154.

[2] See *post*, p. 462.

[3] Close Roll, 29 Edw. III. m. 26 *d.* I am indebted to the late Miss Emily Holt, 'Hermentrude,' for this reference.

[4] Close Roll, 40 Edw. III. m. 3 *d.*

In the following year, 1367, a further variation is recorded.

Processus inter Jacobum Daudeleye & Elizabeth' uxorem Nicholai Daudeleye coram consilio habitus [margin]. *Et sur ceo nostre s^r le Roi fist venir le dit Monsr James deuant son counseil, c'est assauoir, Chaunceller, Tresorer, Justices, & auters sages assemblez en la Chaumbre des esteilles pres de la receite a Westm' lendymain de l'ascension.*[1]

In the first case the addition of the words *prope pontem regium* and in the two other cases *pres de la resceite* identifies the room with the site mentioned in 1344, and also with the new buildings built by Edward III.

An early English variation of the name was 'Sterne Chamere.' Soon after the death of Henry V., the then Chancellor, Thomas Langley, Bishop of Durham, delivered up the Great Seal to Henry VI. at Windsor. Henry handed it over to Simon Gaunstede, Keeper of the Rolls of the Chancery. As Keeper thereof, Simon took it with him to London, and on the morrow of Michaelmas, *in quadam camera vocata le Sterne chamere infra palacium domini Regis Westm'*, sealed certain letters patent with it in the presence of the said Bishop of Durham and other Lords.[2] The earliest English form is 'Sterred' chamber.[3]

Various explanations have been given of the name, some fanciful, some ridiculous. There is no doubt whatever that the Star Chamber was so called because it was decorated with stars. The very form of the name ought to be sufficient to show this, in Latin *Camera Stellata*, or *Camera stellarum*, in French, *Chaumbre estoillee* or *Chaumbre des esteilles*, in English 'Starred,' 'Sterne,' or 'Star' Chamber. I suppose it is because this meaning is too simple and obvious that so much ingenuity has been displayed in find-

[1] Close Roll, 41 Edw. III. m. 13.

[2] Close Roll, 1 Hen. VI. m. 21 *d.* I am indebted to the late Miss Holt for this reference. Starn, Sterne, a star. Halliwell.

[3] *Post*, p. 462, and see Close Roll, 32 Hen. VI.

ing others. Hudson's remarks on this point are very quaint. He says:[1]

'Some think it is so called of *Crimen stellionatus* because it handleth such things and cases as are strange and unusual: some of *stallen.* And so I doubt not but *Camera stellata* (for so I find it called in our antient Year-books) is most aptly named; not because the Star-Chamber, where the Court is kept, is so adorned with stars gilded, as some would have it; for surely the chamber is so adorned, because it is the seat of that Court, *et denominatio* being *a præstantiori magis dignum trahit ad se minus;* and it was so fitly called, because the stars have no light but what is cast upon them from the sun by reflection, being his representative body; and as his majesty himself was pleased to say, when he sat there in his royal person, representation must needs cease when the person is present. So in the presence of his great majesty, the which is the sun of honour and glory, the shining of those stars is put out, they not having any power to pronounce any sentence in this court, for the judgment is the king's only; but by way of advice they deliver their opinions, which his wisdom alloweth or disalloweth, encreaseth or moderateth, at his royal pleasure: which was performed by his most excellent majesty with more than Solomon's wisdom in that great cause of the *Countess of Exeter* against *Sir Thomas Lake*; where his majesty, during the dignity of that court, sat five continual days in a chair of state elevated above the table about which his lords sat; and after that long and patient hearing, and the opinions particularly given of his great council, he pronounced a sentence more accurately eloquent, judiciously grave, and honourably just, to the satisfaction of all the hearers, and of all the lovers of justice, than all the records extant in this kingdom can declare to have been, at any former time, done by any of his royal progenitors.

[1] *Op. cit.*, p. 8.

To conclude then, I suppose the name to be given according to the nature of the judges thereof, which I hope agreeth with the name of the chancery and other courts of this kingdom.' The derivation from *Crimen stellionatus* will be found set out in the text.[1]

A more plausible theory is Blackstone's.[2] He suggests that the Star Chamber was so called because it was used as a depository for certain Jewish contracts or bonds, which were called *starra,* from the Rabbinical or Chaldaic *Shetar* or *Setar*; that in the course of time the meaning of the Jewish 'stars' was forgotten, and then the words Star-chamber were naturally rendered in Latin *Camera stellata*; etc. There are several difficulties in this derivation. First, the short space of time between the banishment of the Jews in 1290 and the mention of the 'Sterred Chambre' in 1348, only 58 years; it seems hardly possible that the real meaning of the name could have been so soon forgotten by the officials of the Palace. 2. The theory involves an involuntary pun or confusion of meanings which is only possible in English, and as the language of the Court would be French and that of its records either French or Latin, probably the latter, it is difficult to see how such confusion could arise. 3. The earliest English form of the name seems to have been not 'star,' but 'sterne,' or 'starred,' chamber, which was still used as late as the reign of Henry VIII. The word starred is the exact equivalent of *stellata* or *estoillée*, and is synonymous with starry; an epithet which could be appropriately applied to a room whose ceiling was decorated with stars, but which could not well be used of a room which was a depository for '*starra*.' 4. It seems quite clear that the name 'Starred Chamber' was applied to a new room. If Blackstone's theory were correct, we should expect to find some mention of it by that, or some kindred name, during the time that the

[1] P. 123; see also p. 15. [2] *Commentaries*, iv. 266.

room was used (as alleged) as a depository for *starra*, or, at any rate, shortly afterwards. But no, there is no trace of any 'Star Chamber' until Edward III. built his new Council Chamber, and christened it after the most prominent feature of its decoration.

In commenting on Blackstone's suggestion, the late Mr. John Caley, F.S.A., says: 'At first view this etymology seems plausible; but it will not bear the test of examination.' . . . 'There appears, therefore, in the present instance, no reason to depart from the usual derivation; which is that the roof of the Star Chamber was anciently ornamented with gilded stars; and though no actual proof can be at this time produced of that fact, it is supported by the testimony of two such able authorities as Sir Edward Coke, in his *Institutes* [4th Instit. 66], and Sir Thomas Smith, *De Republica Anglorum* [lib. ii. cap. 4].'[1]

The House of Commons, as I have said, was very jealous of the power and authority of the Council, and frequently petitioned against it.[2] During the reign of Richard II. these petitions seem to have had no result. 'The politic Henry IV. evaded the petitions or qualified his consent so as to render it unavailing. The attempts of the Commons were equally unsuccessful during the reign of Henry V.; but in the next reign the authority, which had been so long contested, seems to have been in some degree settled and confirmed by parliamentary sanction.'[3] In the eighth year of that reign (1429–30) it was laid down that, of those causes determinable at common law, the only ones to

[1] 'On the Origin of the Jews in England'; *Archæologia*, vii. 389. It is only fair to mention that Blackstone's theory has found favour in the sight of Prof. F. W. Maitland. 'Star Chamber; so called, says popular etymology, because the roof must have been adorned with stars; so called, thinks erudition, because in this part of the old Exchequer the Jews, not yet expelled from England, had to deposit their *starra*, or as we might say, register their bills of sale, since *starrum* is excellent Anglo-Hebræo-Latin for a written bond or covenant.' *English Illustrated Magazine*, 1883, p. 11. Prof. Dicey on the other hand supports the starry ceiling theory.

[2] *Rot. Parl.* iii. 267.

[3] Bruce. *Rot. Parl.* iv. 201, 343; v. 407.

be tried before the Council, that is, in the Star Chamber, were those 'in which the complaint was against a man of great influence, or the suitor was too poor to prosecute his cause in the inferior courts, or in which the Council saw other reasonable cause.'[1] In theory this was excellent; to protect the lowly against the great, the poor against the rich, was an endeavour which all were likely to praise. But the Council were the sole judges of what constituted 'other reasonable cause,' and they put a very elastic interpretation on that rather ambiguous phrase. It was in this way that the unscrupulous ministers of despotic princes were enabled to use this Court as a tremendous weapon against their political opponents.

In the reign of Henry VII. an Act of Parliament was passed which defined certain offences which were to be tried before the Council. These offences were: 1. Maintenance. 2. Giving of liveries. 3. Having retainers. 4. Imbracery. 5. The receipt of money by jurors. 6. Certain misdemeanours in Sheriffs. 7. Routs and riots. Many writers have thought that this Statute (3 Hen. VII. cap. 7) created the Court of Star Chamber. That this is an error I think is apparent from what I have already said. 'That the powers given by the Act of 3 Henry VII. were exceeded, is stated in 16 Charles I., cap. 10,[2] but in fact Henry's statute seems neither for good nor for bad to have exerted influence over the growth of the Star Chamber. The judges in that Court were the whole of the Council. The crimes punished by it consisted of many others than those enumerated in the Act. The penalties inflicted were not those assigned by the statute.'[3]

The following early instances of the Star Chamber as a Court of Justice are quoted from Hudson [p. 15 *et seq.*].

'Temp. *H.* 6; One Danvers was there purged of the

[1] Bruce. [2] The Act abolishing the Star Chamber.
[3] Dicey.

razure of a record by these words, *in camera stellata consilii regis*, and he which did raze it sentenced for the same. And *Ralph Lord Cromwell* was attempted to be slain by one *Talboys*, and a multitude of others, sitting in council in the Star Chamber at Westminster; and in 31 *H.* 6 the same *Ralph Lord Cromwell* was there acquitted for accusation of suspicion of treason made against him by one *Colson* a priest.

'And after *H.* 6's successor, being *E.* 4, being assisted with his council, heard the cause of *Master and poor brethren of the hospital of S. Leonard's in York* against *Sir Hugh Hastings, Wormerdel, and others,* for a thrave of corn of every ploughland in Yorkshire, Cumberland, Westmoreland, and Lancashire; for the which they, being very poor, were not able to sue at the common law; or rather for that the suits would have been infinite. And another like was heard before the king and his council for the *Abbot of Bury St. Edmund's* against one *Tristram* and others of that town, for turbulent election of the aldermen, where they had no corporation nor head but the abbot: and it appeareth by the report of *Hussey, Ch. Just.* 1 *H.* 7 that *E.* 4 sat in the Star Chamber in conference with his lord's, and took their oaths for execution of divers laws, which, as he saith, he saw when he was attorney to king *E.* 4.

'And although *R.* 3. reigned but a short time, yet it appeareth in our Year-books that he sat twice in person in the Star Chamber; the one time to hear the cause of the Spanish merchant; and the other, to be resolved by the judges of three questions which he there propounded unto them.[1] But the English Solomon *H.* 7 as well before the stat. 3 *H.* 7. 1. as long after, kept it as an established court of settled justice, and there in person himself deliberated of great matters; as of the intercourse of Burgundy, the marriage of prince Arthur, and the like: and many causes

[1] See p. 301.

concerning titles of land were there determined, possession orderly established upon shewing their evidence, and security always taken for keeping the peace: and about the tenth, eleventh, and twelfth years of that king these cases were more often heard before the president of the council than before the chancellor, treasurer, or privy seal; whereby it is most manifest, by the subsequent as by the precedent practice, that the Court then sat not by virtue of that statute, the president of that council not being mentioned therein, but sat as they antiently had done, and by as antient, if not more antient, authority than any court in Westminster Hall.'

I may mention incidentally that 'the Court of Star Chamber' was the only popular title of the Court; the official title was always 'The Lords of the Council sitting in the Star Chamber.'

In the reigns of Henry VIII. and Elizabeth, the private business of the Court seems to have increased enormously. Part of the calendar of causes in the former reign has been printed in the Appendix to the 49th Report of the Deputy Keeper of the Public Records, and the rest is in MS.; for the reign of Elizabeth a MS. calendar exists in four arge folio volumes. It is much to be regretted that the calendar stops here, in consequence of which the pleadings and depositions for the two succeeding reigns are practically inaccessible. I know of no class of Public Records which give a more vivid and picturesque view of the social and domestic life of the period than the Star Chamber documents; it is therefore to be hoped that the continuation of the calendar for the reigns of James I. and Charles I. will shortly be put in hand.

No records of the Court, other than the pleadings and depositions, are known to exist. The Decree and Order Books are missing. In a Report of a Committee of the House of Lords in 1719 it is stated that 'the last notice of them that could be got was that they were in a house in St. Bartholomew's Close, London.'

In the reign of James I. the Court does not seem to have been much abused by the ministers of the Crown, but under Charles I. it was used as an instrument for oppression of the worst kind; and it was in this period that the Court acquired that unenviable reputation which has rendered it a by-word in English history, and which finally led to its overthrow. The cases of Hampden, Lilburne, and Prynne are typical examples.

One of the first acts of the Long Parliament was to appoint a committee to inquire into the jurisdiction of the Star Chamber and in the mean time to stay all proceedings there. This was in December 1640. In March 1641 a bill for regulating the powers of the Court was read a first time. As this was not deemed sufficiently drastic, another bill was introduced a few days later entitled 'An Act for Regulating of the Privy Council and for taking away the Court commonly called the Star-Chamber;' 16 Car. I., cap. 10. This bill finally passed the Commons on July 3, 1641, and shortly afterwards became law. The preamble recites part of Magna Charta and various other statutes which the Star Chamber was supposed to infringe; section 2 gives four reasons for passing the Act, viz.:—that all causes heard in the Star Chamber can be dealt with just as well at common law; that the reasons for the 'erection and continuance' of the Court have now ceased; that 'the Proceedings, Censures and Decrees of that Court, have by Experience been found to be an intolerable Burthen to the Subjects, and the Means to introduce an arbitrary Power and Government;' that the 'Council-Table' has of late assumed the power of intermeddling in civil causes, 'and hath adventured to determine of the Estates and Liberties of the Subject, contrary to the Law of the Land and the Rights and Privileges of the Subject.' Section 4 abolished the Courts of the

Council of the Marches of Wales, the Council in the Northern Parts, the Council of the Duchy of Lancaster, and the Exchequer of the County Palatine of Chester. The two former, namely, the Court of the Council of the Northern Parts, and the Court of the Council of the Marches of Wales, were branches, as it were, of the Star Chamber. They will be found mentioned several times in this volume. In their practice and procedure they were similar to the parent Court, and they were abolished, as we have seen, by the same statute.

B. *Constitution and Procedure.*

Originally the whole of the Council sat as judges, or at any rate had the right to do so. In the reigns of Henry VII. and VIII. the number attending is said to have been nearly forty. At a later date, which cannot be exactly determined, only peers and Privy Councillors sat. Those peers who were not Privy Councillors discontinued attending in the time of Elizabeth.[1] The largest number mentioned in this volume is 19, the smallest 5. Upon some important occasions in the reign of Charles I. the attendance amounted to 24 or 26.[2] The Lord Chancellor or Lord Keeper was the President.[3] The Lords Treasurer, Privy Seal, High Admiral, and the other Privy Councillors generally sat; also the Archbishop of Canterbury and such other Bishops as were of the Privy Council; the Lords Chief Justices of the King's Bench and the Common Pleas, and the Lord Chief Baron. In addition, the Council could and did require the presence of certain other judges when it was deemed necessary, a practice which seems to have been first authorised by the statute of 3 Hen. VII. The sentence of the majority was the sentence of the Court, and the Lord Chancellor had a casting vote.

[1] Bruce.

[2] Rushworth, ii. 475.

[3] Bruce states (*loc. cit.*) that the Lord Chancellor alone had the power of assessing damages and awarding costs. That this is an error appears abundantly in the text.

The procedure was threefold. 1. The Attorney-General could lay a written information, as was done in the Court of King's Bench. 2. The Attorney-General could complain *ore tenus* without a written information, but this could only be done when the defendant confessed the offences laid against him. Theoretically the King or Queen was present at the sittings of the Court; it was *coram domino Rege in Camera Stellata coram Consilio ibidem.*[1] Richard III. is said to have sat there judicially,[1] also Henry VII. and James I., the two 'British Solomons,' and several other monarchs as mentioned by Hudson above.

In 1602, John Manningham writes as follows:—'In the Star Chamber the benche on that part of the roome where the Queene's armes are placed is alwayes vacant; noe man may sitt on it, as I take it, because it is reserved as a seate for the Prince, and therefore before the same are layed the purse and the mace, as notes of autority.'[2]

'The *ore tenus* proceedings before the Council originated either in "soden reporte," which is the phrase used in the regulations of the time of Henry VI., and which I understand to mean private, and probably secret, information, given to the Council; or "by the curious eye of the State and King's Council prying into the inconveniences and mischiefs which abound in the Commonwealth."[3] The person accused or suspected was immediately apprehended and privately examined. If he confessed any offence, or if the cunning of his examiners drew from him, or his own simplicity let fall, any expressions which suited their purpose, he was at once brought to the bar, his confession or examination was read, he was convicted *ex ore suo*, and judgment was immediately pronounced against him.'[4]

3. The procedure between private individuals was much the same as in the Court of Chancery. The plaintiff filed

[1] See p. 302.
[2] *Manningham's Diary*, Camden Soc., p. 53.
[3] Hudson.
[4] Bruce.

a bill of complaint, then the defendant put in an answer, to which he was sworn. If he refused to swear to his answer, or refused to answer at all, it was considered a confession of the bill, and judgment was given accordingly. The evidence was taken by interrogatories and depositions.

When a question of fact arose that could be more conveniently tried at common law, the Court directed an issue to be drawn up, tried in one of the common law courts before a jury, and the verdict certified into the Star Chamber.

'When the defendant had put in his answer, the plaintiff proceeded to examine him upon written interrogatories—a practice most scandalously abused, being employed, as Hudson admits, "like a Spanish Inquisition, to rack men's consciences, nay to perplex them by intricate questions, thereby to make contrarieties, which may easily happen to simple men;" etc. To restrain this abuse Lord Keeper Bacon limited the examination to 15 articles, each containing two questions. [Lord Ellesmere further amended the practice in this respect.] If the defendant refused to answer the interrogatories, he was committed until he consented to do so. Hudson states that he knew some who continued in this confinement during their lives, and mentions as an instance one Thomas Ellis, who would not disclose the names of some persons set on by him to commit an outrage.'[1] After the examination of the defendant the parties proceeded to examine witnesses upon interrogatories.

Seven offences were usually punished in the Star Chamber: 1. Perjury, 2. Forgery, 3. Riot, 4. Maintenance, 5. Fraud, 6. Libels, 7. Conspiracy.[2] Building houses in London contrary to the various proclamations was punished here [pp. 318, 328]. The houses were generally ordered to be pulled down, which is, says Hudson, 'surely very necessary, if any thing would deter men from that horrible

[1] Bruce. [2] Hudson, p. 71.

mischief of encreasing that head which is swoln to a great hugeness already.' [1]

In addition to cases of these classes, the Star Chamber claimed, or at any rate exercised, considerable jurisdiction in cases of disputed customs of Manors, and other cases where there was a great number either of plaintiffs or defendants.[2] Also in controversies between merchant strangers and Englishmen, or between foreigners on both sides, restitution of ships and goods unlawfully seized, or deceits of merchants; [3] cases between corporations, abbats and convents, mayors and commonalties, bailiffs and burgesses, 'or betwixt great and mighty men, where intrest drew malice and partaking, which was dangerous to the peace.'[4] The King's Almoner always sued here for the goods of *felones de se*, or for deodands.

In addition to all these, Hudson mentions the following:—Attempts to commit certain offences, such as coining, burglary, murder, poisoning, etc.; black mailing; gifts from drunken men; partiality in executing writs; improper conduct in Justices of the Peace as such; gaming houses; duelling; 'inveigling of young gentlemen, and entangling of them in contracts of marriage to their utter ruin, to which no statute extendeth.'[5] As a curious example of the extraordinary jurisdiction claimed by the Court, Hudson mentions that one Brent was complained of for wasting his estate in lewdness, so that 'his wife and children had not wherewithal to maintain themselves; the Court directed the Master of the Rolls and the Under Treasurer to settle him in a course certain, and the Court ordered him to obey it.' [6]

A good deal of miscellaneous business was transacted by the Council in the Star Chamber besides its judicial functions. Amongst other things I may mention the Pro-

[1] Hudson, p. 108. [2] *Ibid.*, p. 53. [3] *Ibid.*, p. 55.
[4] *Ibid.*, p. 56. [5] *Ibid.*, p. 108. [6] *Ibid.*, p. 108.

clamation of Orders in Council, the holding of the Mint Assay, and the Lord Chancellor's annual charge or address to the Judges and Justices of the Peace. The last two are illustrated in this volume; an account of the Mint Assay will be found on page 38; the Chancellor's charges occur frequently, and some of them are given at considerable length, notably those in 1595 [p. 19], 1596 [p. 56], 1598 [p. 101], 1605 [p. 186], 1607 [p. 326], and 1608 [p. 367]. Great stress was laid upon the necessity for country gentlemen to reside at their country seats [pp. 20, 56, 106, etc.]. In 1596, the Queen commands 'all sortes of gentlemen of what sorte or qualitye soeuer. . . . presentely to repayre to there country dwellings, and there to make there continuall aboade' [p. 56]. In 1599, the Attorney-General is ordered to inform against all [country] gentlemen dwelling in London or Westminster [p. 106]. In 1608, the Lord Mayor is to 'make accounte what they are that lurke aboute the towne, and the Judges [are to] retorne the names of them that abyde not in there cuntrye dwelllinges & keepe hospitalitye' [p. 368]. Vagrants are especially disliked. All inns are to be searched, 'that none lodge but one night w^th^oute speciall cause' [p. 21]; 'there marke is idlenes and wastefull spending, for *egestas et inertia* are 2 cankers in the common wealthe' [p. 57]. In 1607, the Justices are admonished to 'looke carefullye to all seminaries[1] and there Followers, & to there conuenticles; to all vagrauntes, stronge to labor, yet idle, & like gentlemen in apparelle & diete, yet w^th^out meanes, lybellers & deuysers of plottes' [p. 326]. Benefit of clergy was not to be allowed more than once [p. 21]. The scarcity of corn was a constant source of anxiety. The attempts of the corn-dealers, or corn-masters, as they are often called, to 'ingross' that commodity, that is to hold up their stock in the hope of getting an enhanced price, had to be circum-

[1] Seminary priests.

vented somehow. Whether the dealers ever succeeded in getting an actual 'corner' in grain does not appear, but apparently they were always striving after that end. In 1595 the Justices of the Peace are ordered to attend the weekly markets to 'perswade the bringing of corne to furnishe the markets.' They were also to collect money for the purchase of corn, and to sell the same at every market without profit [p. 20]. In 1608, all exportation of corn was forbidden, the customs on importation were remitted, and the Lord Mayor was ordered to 'make prouisions from forren partes' [p. 367]. Some very curious speculations are there given as to the cause of the scarcity.

Some of the directions to the Justices of the Peace are very curious: they are to look after 'th'excesse of apparrell' among ladies of various degrees, which is called 'a pestilent canker in the Common wealthe,' causing 'the confusyon of all degrees' [p. 57]. What the ladies said to this, or what was the effect of the Justices' interference, we are not told. In 1605, a close time is urged, for 'yonge thinges of all kindes, beinge preserued & spared, the plentie thereof is more abundante all the yeare after' [p. 187]. The interests and welfare of the poor were well looked after, in theory at any rate. In 1598, the Assessors of the Subsidies are warned not for any cause to charge the meaner sort and disburden the better sort [p. 102]. In 1601, the Justices are charged to see 'that the sommes collected for the poore be ymployed accordinglye' [p. 368]; in 1607, they are 'to looke carefullye to sherifes and vndersheriffes & there officers, whoe buye and selle the people' [p. 327]; and generally they are to 'exercise Justice wth a Herculean courage' [p. 21]. Referring to monopolies and the rights of pre-emption claimed by the crown, we are told that the King 'can not holde his Crowne yf he showlde loose his prerogatiue, but he woulde haue it vsed tenderlye, & to the greateste ease to his people that mighte be' [p. 300].

The relation of the Judges to the Counsel practising before them in the Star Chamber seems very strange to our modern notions. A Barrister who had signed a Bill imputing perjury to certain ecclesiastical dignitaries, which was not proved, was ordered to be disbarred for seven years [p. 32]. In another somewhat similar case, the Solicitor-General was ordered to inquire whether the Counsel's name to the Bill was a forgery; if not, the Counsel was to be disbarred for ever [p. 55]. A trivial Bill was dismissed with costs, and the Counsel who signed it was fined £10, and debarred from all practice in the Star Chamber [p. 82]. A Barrister who had drawn certain insufficient answers was disbarred, and another, who had previously been disbarred for evil counsel, was restored to practice on his confession, penitence, and submission [p. 91]. On one occasion Lord Keeper Egerton addressed a Counsel in these terms: "You muste goe to schoole to learne more wytte; you are not well aduysed; you forgette yor place; &, to be plaine, it is a lye" [p. 43]. 'Scenes in Court' were not uncommon, and the 'plaintiff in person' was as great a nuisance then as now. In the case of Lady John Russell against the Earl of Nottingham, the plaintiff seems to have stated her case with great vigour, and the scene recalls very forcibly some famous female litigants of modern times [p. 275].

Generally speaking, the Court was not particularly chivalrous in its treatment of the fair sex. In 1596, the Lord Keeper ordered that a room adjoining the Court should be reserved for men of good account in the country, and for gentlemen 'towardes the lawe,' and should not be plagued with 'base fellowes' and women, or other suitors, as it had been [p. 39]. In 1602, it was ordered that no woman should be a suitor in any court in her own person [p. 161]. In that case the woman, who was 'clamorous and impudent,' was ordered to be whipped. The lords on one occasion held that it was 'incredible and not to be believed' that a man would accuse himself to a woman [p. 30]. 'If an action were brought against a wife for battery, and damages given, the husband shall pay it, for two reasons; the one that it was his folly to take such an unruly wife, the other for that it is the husband's duty to correct her ill manners.'[1]

On the whole I have no hesitation in saying that, as far as the present volume goes, substantial justice was done in the Court of Star Chamber. The number of bills dismissed shows that the Court did not hesitate to brand a groundless complaint as such, and in these cases the plaintiff was invariably fined and sometimes imprisoned. It was laid down by the Chancellor, Archbishop, and Treasurer as a maxim of the Court, that 'it were better to acquite 20 that are guyltie, than condempne one innocent' [p. 320], and I believe that the majority of the Judges tried to act up to this excellent precept.

On this point, I again quote Hudson, though I must admit he is not an altogether impartial witness. Complaining of the delays in the Court in his own time, he says:—'For I dare say, if the Lords should sit every day, as they did in *H.* 7 and *H.* 8's times, and handle causes of that nature they then did, no court of this kingdom would be so replenished with causes; so confident the people are of equality and justice there.'[2] Sir Thomas Smith in his *Commonwealth* (iii. 7) calls the Star Chamber 'the poor man's Court, in which he might have right without paying any money.'

A word may be said here about the magnitude of the fines imposed in the Star Chamber. Bruce says: 'in early instances there was a moderation in fines; but latterly they were inflicted in excess, not according to the estate of the delinquent, but in proportion to the supposed character of the offence;'[3] Hudson says that the ransom of a beggar

[1] Hudson, *loc. cit.* p. 140. [2] Page 28. [3] *Loc. cit.* p. 20.

and a gentleman was all one;[1] and many other writers have written in the same strain. It would seem, however, that the fines imposed by the Court were subject to 'taxation.' In Appendix VII. p. 411, will be found a very remarkable document which throws a great deal of light on the practice of the Court. It is a list of fines and the sums at which they were ultimately taxed. The difference in some cases is astonishing. £1,000 is reduced to £100, £500 to £30, £200 to £10, £50 to £5. We can only assume that the delinquent had satisfied the officers of the Court of his inability to pay the larger sum, and that he was consequently let off with the payment of the smaller. The list is the only document of the kind that I have seen, and contains but a small number of cases, but I see no reason to doubt that the taxation of fines applied to all cases in this Court. If that be so, the apparent excess of some of the fines imposed is at once explained, and the strictures based on these fall to the ground. Some of the fines, of course, really were enormous: for example, that of £30,000 imposed on the Earl of Northumberland [p. 292 *et seq.*]. Still, in that particular case, most people would hesitate to say that the sentence was too heavy, assuming that the Earl was really guilty of complicity in the Gunpowder Plot. And even there the balance was pardoned after £11,000 had been paid.

It is repeatedly stated, but on what authority I do not know, that the Star Chamber applied torture to its prisoners in order to extort a confession. Prof. Dicey mentions one case, that of Guy Fawkes, apparently forgetting that the Powder Conspirators were not tried in the Star Chamber at all, but before a Special Commission.

It should be borne in mind that the cruelty of the Star Chamber (apart from its political oppression) was the cruelty of the times rather than of the Court, and was

[1] Page 224.

largely due to statute law. For instance, the statute of 5 Eliz., cap. 14, punished the forgery of deeds by double damages to the party grieved, imprisonment for life, pillory, cutting off both ears, slitting the nostrils, and the forfeiture of all goods and the profits of lands for life. The punishment for brawling in churches, enacted by the statute of 5 Edward VI., cap 4, was equally barbarous. [See pp. 337, 371.] There also part of the punishment consisted in cutting off one or both ears, but the statute prudently provided an alternative in case the offender had no ears.

In conclusion, I cannot do better than quote from Mr. G. W. Prothero's interesting and able article on the Star Chamber in the *Encyclopædia Britannica.*

'Its procedure was not according to the common law; it dispensed with the encumbrance of a jury; it could proceed on mere rumour or examine witnesses; it could apply torture; it could inflict any penalty short of death. It was thus admirably calculated to be the support of order against anarchy, or of despotism against individual and national liberty. During the Tudor period it appeared in the former light, under the Stuarts in the latter.'

W. PALEY BAILDON.

5 Stone Buildings,
Lincoln's Inn.

Sept. vj., 1894.

ILLUSTRATIONS

TABLE OF PRIVY COUNCILLORS AND JUDGES SITTING IN THE STAR CHAMBER.[1]

ABBOT, GEORGE; *Bishop of London*, 1610.

He is mentioned on page 357 of the MS., as being present Oct. 12, 1608. It is, however, an error, as he was not appointed Bishop of London until 1610.

ADMIRAL, LORD; *see* Charles Howard.

ALTHAM, SIR JAMES; *Baron of the Exchequer*, Feb. 1, 1607; d. Feb. 21, 1617.

1608: May 31 [Exchequer Chamber].

ANDERSON, SIR EDMUND; b. *cir.* 1530; *Chief Justice of the Common Pleas*, May 2, 1582; d. Aug. 1, 1605.

1593: Nov. 16. **1594**: Feb. 6, 8; May 16. **1595**: Jan. 29; June 3. **1596**: Jan. 28, 30; Feb. 4, 11, 13; April 29; May 12, 19, 21, 25; June 18, 23, 25; July 1; Oct. 13; Nov. 24. **1597**: Feb. 4, 9, 11; April 22; Oct 14, 19, 21; Nov. 9, 11, 17. **1598**: May 24; June 30; July 6; Oct. 11. **1599**: May 16, 18; June 13, 22, 28. **1600**: Feb. 6; April 18; May 28; June 4; July 6; Oct. 10, 15. **1601**: June 17. **1602**: April 28; May 5, 7, 12; June 9, 11, 16, 18; Oct. 13, 15, 20, 22; Nov. 30. **1603**: May 13, 18, 20, 27; June 1, 3. **1605**: Feb. 13.

BANCROFT, RICHARD; *Bishop of London*, 1597; *Archbishop of Canterbury*, 1604; d. Nov. 2, 1610.

1600: Feb. 6; Oct. 10, 15. **1601**: June 17. **1602**: April 28; May 5, 7, 12; June 9, 16, 18; Oct. 13, 15, 20, 22; Nov. 30. **1604**: Oct. 10, 12, 17, 19. **1605**: Feb. 13; April 19, 24; May 1, 3, 5, 10, 14; Oct. 11, 16, 23; Nov. 8, 13, 15, 20, 22. **1606**: Jan. 31; Feb. 5, 13; May 9, 14, 16, 30; June 3, 27; Nov. 7, 19, 21, 26, 29. **1607**: Jan. 28; April 24, 29; May 1, 6; June 10; Oct. 23, 28; Nov. 4, 6, 13, 18, 20, 27. **1608**: Oct. 12; page 372; Nov. 9. **1609**: Feb. 14.

BLOUNT, SIR CHARLES, K.G.; 8th *Baron Mountjoy*; created *Earl of Devonshire*, July 21, 1603; d. April 3, 1606.

1604: Oct. 10, 12, 17, 19. **1605**: Feb. 13; May 1, 3, 5, 10, 14. **1606**: Jan. 27.

---

[1] In this table the year is treated as beginning on January 1.

BROOKE, SIR WILLIAM, K.G.; 10th *Baron Cobham*; succeeded 1558; d. March 6, 1597.

1596: April 29.

BRUCE, EDWARD; b. *cir.* 1548; *Master of the Rolls*, May 18, 1603; created *Baron Bruce of Kinloss*, July 8, 1604; d. Jan. 14, 1611.

1605: Feb. 13; May 14; June 16. **1609**: Feb. 14.

BUCKHURST, LORD; *see* Thomas Sackville.

BURGHLEY, LORD; *see*
Thomas Cecil,
William Cecil.

CÆSAR, SIR JULIUS; b. 1557; *Chancellor of the Exchequer*, April 11, 1606; *Master of the Rolls*, 1614; d. April 18, 1636.

1607: Oct. 14, 16, 21, 23, 28, 30; Nov. 4, 6, 13, 18, 20, 27. **1608**: Jan. 27; Oct. 12; page 372; Nov. 9. **1609**: Feb. 14.

CANTERBURY, ARCHBISHOP OF; *see*
Richard Bancroft,
John Whitgift.

CAREY, SIR GEORGE, K.G.; 2nd *Baron Hunsdon*; succeeded July 23, 1596; *Lord Chamberlain of the Household*; d. Sept. 9, 1603.

1598: July 6. **1599**: May 16.

CAREY, SIR HENRY, K.G.; created *Baron Hunsdon*, Jan. 13, 1559; *Lord Chamberlain of the Household*; d. 1596.

1593: May 16. **1594**: Feb. 8. **1595**: June 3. **1596**: May 21; June 23; July 1.

CECIL, SIR ROBERT; *Secretary of State* and *Chancellor of the Duchy of Lancaster; Master of the Wards*; created *Baron Cecil of Essendon*, May 13, 1603; created *Viscount Cranborne*, Aug. 20, 1604; created *Earl of Salisbury*, May 4, 1605; *Lord Treasurer*, 1608 [p. 331]; d. May 24, 1612.

1594: Jan. 30; Feb. 6. **1595**: July 4. **1596**: Feb. 6, 11. **1597**: Oct. 14. **1598**: June 30. **1600**: May 28. **1601**: June 17. **1603**: May 18; June 3. **1604**: Oct. 10, 12, 17, 19. **1605**: Feb. 13; May 1, 3, 5, 10, 14. **1606**: Jan. 27; June 3, 27. **1607**: Nov. 12 [Wards]. **1608**: May 31 [Exchequer Chamber].

CECIL, SIR THOMAS, K.G.; 2nd *Baron of Burghley*; succeeded 1598; created *Earl of Exeter*, May 4, 1605; *Lord President of the Council of the North*, 1599–1603; d. Feb. 8, 1623.

1603: May 13, 18, 20. **1604**: June 22; Oct. 17, 19. **1605**: Feb. 13; Oct. 16, 23, 25, 30; Nov. 8, 15, 20, 22. **1606**: Feb. 7; May 16, 23, 28, 30; June 3, 27; Oct. 31; Nov. 7. **1607**: Jan. 28; May 1, 6; Nov. 6, 13, 13, 20, 27.

CECIL, SIR WILLIAM, K.G.; *Chief Secretary*; created *Baron of Burghley*, Feb. 25, 1571; *Lord Treasurer*, 1572; d. Aug. 4, 1598.

1593: May 16. **1595**: June 3; July 2, 4. **1596**: Jan. 28, 30; Feb. 6, 11; April 29; May 12; June 18, 23, 25; Oct. 13, 15. **1597**: April 15, 20, 22; Oct. 26; Nov. 9, 11.

CHAMBERLAIN, LORD; *see*
George Carey,
Henry Carey,
Thomas Howard.

CHANCELLOR, LORD; *see* Thomas Egerton.

CLARKE, SIR ROBERT; *Baron of the Exchequer*, June 22, 1587; d. Jan. 1, 1607.

1598: July 6. **1599**: June 28. **1605**: Feb. 13.

CLENCHE, JOHN; *Justice of the Queen's Bench*, May 29, 1584; resigned 1602; d. Aug. 19, 1607.

1595: June 3. **1596**: July 1. **1598**: July 6. **1599**: June 28.

CLIFFORD, GEORGE; 3rd *Earl of Cumberland*; succeeded 1569; d. Oct. 30, 1605.

1605: May 3, 5, 10, 14.

COBHAM, LORD; *see* William Brooke.

COKE, SIR EDWARD; born Feb. 1, 1552; *Chief Justice of the Common Pleas*, June 30, 1606; *Chief Justice of the King's Bench*, Oct. 25, 1613; removed Nov., 1616; d. Sept. 3, 1633.

1606: July 10; Oct. 31; Nov. 5 [?], 7, 19, 21, 26, 29. **1607**: Jan. 28; April 24, 29; May 1, 6; June 10; Oct. 14, 16, 21, 23, 28, 30; Nov. 4, 6, 12 [Wards], 13, 18, 20, 27. **1608**: Jan. 27; May 31; June 4; Oct. 12; page 372; Nov. 9, 11.

COMMON PLEAS, CHIEF JUSTICE OF; *see*
Edmund Anderson,
Edward Coke,
Francis Gawdy.

COMMON PLEAS, JUSTICE OF; *see*
William Daniel,
Thomas Foster,
John Glanville,
George Kingsmill,
Thomas Owen,
Thomas Walmesley,
Peter Warburton.

CRANBORNE, VISCOUNT; *see* Robert Cecil.

CROKE, SIR JOHN; born 1553; *Justice of the King's Bench*, June 25, 1607; d. Jan. 23, 1620.

1603: May 31 [Exchequer Chamber].

CUMBERLAND, EARL OF; *see* George Clifford.

DANIEL, WILLIAM; *Justice of the Common Pleas*, Feb. 3, 1604; d. 1610.

1605: Feb. 13. **1608**: May 31; June 16.

DERBY, EARL OF; *see* Henry Stanley.

DEVEREUX, ROBERT, 2nd *Earl of Essex*; succeeded 1576; d. Feb. 25, 1601.

1594: Jan. 30; Feb. 6, 8. **1595**: Jan. 29; July 4. **1596**: Jan. 28, 30; Feb. 4, 11; Oct. 13. **1597**: Feb. 4, 9, 11; April 20. **1598**: May 24.

DEVONSHIRE, EARL OF; *see* Charles Blount.

DORSET, EARL OF; *see* Thomas Sackville.

EGERTON, SIR THOMAS; *Lord Keeper*, May 6, 1596; created *Baron Ellesmere*, July 21, 1603; *Lord Chancellor*, July 24, 1603; created *Viscount Brackley*, Nov. 7, 1616; d. March 15, 1617.

1595: June 3. **1596**: Feb. 13; May 12, 19, 21, 25; June 18, 23, 25; July 1; Oct. 13, 15; Nov. 24. **1597**: Feb. 4, 9, 11; April 15, 20, 22; Oct. 14, 19, 21, 26; Nov. 4, 9, 11, 17. **1598**: May 24, 26; June 28, 30; July 6; Oct. 11. **1599**: May 16, 18; June 13, 22, 28. **1600**: Feb. 6; April 18; May 28; June 4; July 6; Oct. 10, 15. **1601**: June 17. **1602**: April 28; May 5, 7, 12; June 9, 11, 16, 18; Oct. 13, 15, 20, 22; Nov. 30. **1603**: May 13, 18, 20, 27; June 1, 3. **1604**: June 22; Oct. 10, 12, 17, 19. **1605**: Feb. 13; April 19, 24; May 1, 3, 5, 10, 14; Oct. 11, 16, 23, 25, 30; Nov. 8, 13, 15, 20, 22. **1606**: Jan. 31; Feb. 5, 7, 13; May 9, 14, 16, 21, 23, 28, 30; June 3, 27; July 10; Oct. 31; Nov. 5 [?], 7, 19, 21, 26, 29. **1607**: Jan. 28; April 24, 29; May 1, 6; June 10; Oct. 14, 16, 21, 23, 28, 30; Nov. 4, 6, 13, 18, 20, 27. **1608**: Jan. 27; May 31; June 7, 16; Oct. 12; page 372; Nov. 9, 11. **1609**: Feb. 14.

ELLESMERE, LORD; *see* Thomas Egerton.

ESSEX, EARL OF; *see* Robert Devereux.

EXCHEQUER, CHANCELLOR OF; *see*
Julius Cæsar,
John Fortescue.

EXCHEQUER, CHIEF BARON OF; *see*
Thomas Fleming,
William Peryam,
Laurence Tanfield.

GLANVILLE, JOHN; *Justice of the Common Pleas*, June 30, 1598; d. July 27, 1600.
1598: July 6. **1599**: June 28.

HENNEAGE, SIR THOMAS; *Vice-Chamberlain.*
1593: Nov. 16. **1594**: Jan. 25, 30; May 16. **1595**: Jan. 29.

HERBERT, SIR JOHN; *Second Secretary of State*, May, 1600; d. July, 1618.
1601: June 17. **1602**: April 28; May 5; June 11, 16, 18. **1604**: Oct. 10, 12, 17, 19. **1605**: May 3, 5, 10; Oct. 11, 16, 23; Nov. 8, 15, 20, 22. **1606**: May 14, 21, 23, 30; June 3, 27; Oct. 31; Nov. 5 [?], 26. **1607**: June 10; Nov. 4, 6, 13, 18, 20. **1609**: Feb. 14.

HERON, SIR EDWARD; *Baron of the Exchequer*, Nov. 25, 1607.
1608: May 31 [Exchequer Chamber].

HOWARD, SIR CHARLES; 2nd *Lord Howard of Effingham*; *Lord Admiral*, 1585; created *Earl of Nottingham*, Oct. 22, 1596; d. Dec. 14, 1624.
1594: Jan. 30. **1595**: June 3; July 4. **1596**: Feb. 11; Oct. 15. **1597**: Feb. 4; Nov. 4. **1598**: June 30. **1599**: May 16; June 13. **1600**: May 28. **1601**: June 17. **1602**: April 28; Nov. 30. **1604**: Oct. 10, 12, 17, 19. **1605**: Feb. 13; Oct. 11. **1606**: Jan. 27; June 3, 27.

HOWARD, LORD; probably Lord Henry Howard, afterwards Earl of Northampton, *q.v.*
1595: July 4.

HOWARD, SIR HENRY, K.G.; created *Earl of Northampton*, March 13, 1604; *Lord Privy Seal*; d. 1614.
1603: May 27; June 1, 3. **1604**: June 22; Oct. 10, 12, 17, 19. **1605**: Feb. 13; April 19; May 1, 3, 5, 10, 14; Oct. 11, 16, 23, 25, 30; Nov. 22. **1606**: Jan. 27, 31; Feb. 5, 7, 13; May 9, 14, 16, 28, 30; June 3, 27; Oct. 31; Nov. 5 [?], 7, 19, 21, 26. **1607**: Jan. 28; April 29; May 1, 6; June 10; Oct. 14, 16, 21, 23, 28, 30; Nov. 4, 6, 13, 18, 20, 27. **1608**: Jan. 27; May 31; June 16; Oct. 12; page 372; Nov. 9, 11.

HOWARD, SIR THOMAS, K.G.; *Lord Chamberlain*; created *Earl of Suffolk*, July 21, 1603; *Lord Treasurer*, 1614; d. May 28, 1626.
1605: May 1, 8. **1606**: Jan. 27; June 3, 27.

HUNSDON, LORD; *see*
George Carey,
Henry Carey.

KEEPER, LORD; *see*
Thomas Egerton,
John Puckering.

KING'S BENCH, CHIEF JUSTICE OF; *see*
Edward Coke,
Thomas Fleming,
John Popham.

KING'S *or* QUEEN'S BENCH, JUSTICE OF; *see*
John Clench,
John Croke,
Edward Fenner,
Francis Gawdy,
Lawrence Tanfield,
David Williams,
Christopher Yelverton.

KINGSMILL, SIR GEORGE; *Justice of the Common Pleas*, Feb. 8, 1559; d. April, 1606.
1599: June 28. **1605**: Feb. 13.

KINLOSS, LORD; *see* Edward Bruce.

KNOLLYS, SIR WILLIAM, K.G.; *Comptroller of the Household*; created *Baron Knollys of Greys*, May 13, 1603; created *Viscount Wallingford*, Nov. 7, 1616; created *Earl of Banbury*, Aug. 18, 1626; d. May 25, 1632.
1597: Feb. 4, 9, 11; April 15, 20; Oct. 14, 26. **1598**: May 24, 26; June 28, 30; July 6. **1599**: June 28. **1600**: April 18; May 28; June 4; July 6; Oct. 15. **1601**: June 17. **1602**: April 28; May 7, 12; June 9; Oct. 15, 20, 22. **1603**: May 27; June 1. **1604**: June 22. **1605**: Feb. 13; April 19, 24; May 1, 3, 5, 10, 14; Oct. 11, 16, 23, 25; Nov. 13, 15, 20, 22. **1606**: Jan. 31; Feb, 5, 7; May 14, 16, 21, 28; June 3, 27. **1607**: April 24, 29; May 6; Nov. 4. **1608**: May 31; Nov. 11.

LONDON, BISHOP OF: *see*
George Abbot,
Richard Bancroft,
Richard Fletcher,
Thomas Ravis,
Richard Vaughan.

NORTH, ROGER, 2nd *Baron North*; succeeded 1564; *Treasurer of the Household*; d. 1600.
1596: Nov. 24. **1597**: Feb. 4, 9, 11; April 20, 22; Oct. 14, 26; Nov. 9, 11, 17. **1598**: May 24; June 28, 30; July 6. **1599**: May 16, 18; June 13, 22.

NORTHAMPTON, EARL OF; *see* Henry Howard.

NORTHUMBERLAND, EARL OF; *see* Henry Percy.

NOTTINGHAM, EARL OF; *see* Charles Howard.

Owen, Thomas; *Justice of the Common Pleas*, Jan. 21, 1594; d. Dec. 21, 1598.

1593: July 6.

Parry, Sir Thomas; *Chancellor of the Duchy of Lancaster.*

1608: Oct. 12; Nov. 11.

Pepper, Sir Cuthbert; *Attorney of the Court of Wards and Liveries*; July 9, 1607; d. Aug. 1608.

1607: Nov. 12 [Wards].

Percy, Sir Henry, K.G.; 9th *Earl of Northumberland*; succeeded 1585; d. 1632.

1603: May 18. **1604**: June 22; Oct. 10, 12, 17, 19. **1605**: Feb. 13; May 1, 3, 5, 10, 19.

Peryam, Sir William; b. 1534; *Chief Baron of the Exchequer*, Feb. 1593; d. Oct. 9, 1604.

1594: Jan. 25, 30; May 16. **1596**: Feb. 6, 13; April 29; June 18; Oct. 15. **1597**: Feb. 4; April 15, 20; Oct. 14, 26; Nov. 4. **1598**: June 28, 30; July 6. **1599**: June 28. **1600**: April 18. **1602**: April 28. **1603**: May 18; June 3.

Popham, Sir John; b. *cir.* 1531; *Chief Justice of the Queen's Bench*, June 2, 1592; d. June 10, 1607 or 1608.

1593: Nov. 16. **1594**: Jan. 25, 30; Feb. 6, 8; May 16. **1595**: Jan. 29; June 3; July 4. **1596**: Jan. 28, 30; Feb. 4, 6, 11, 13; April 29; May 12, 19, 21, 25; June 18, 23, 25; July 1; Oct. 13, 15; Nov. 24. **1597**: Feb. 4, 9, 11; April 15, 20, 22; Oct. 14, 19, 21, 26; Nov. 4, 9, 11, 17. **1598**: May 24, 26; June 28, 30; July 6; Oct. 11. **1599**: May 16, 18; June 13, 22, 28. **1600**: Feb. 6; April 18; May 28; June 4; July 6; Oct. 10, 15. **1601**: June 17. **1602**: April 28; May 5, 7, 12; June 9, 11, 16, 18; Oct. 13, 15, 20, 22; Nov. 30. **1603**: May 13, 18, 20, 27; June 1, 3. **1604**: June 22; Oct. 10, 12, 17, 19. **1605**: Feb. 13; April 19, 24; May 1, 3, 5, 10, 14; Oct. 11, 16, 23, 25, 30; Nov. 13, 15, 20, 22. **1606**: Jan. 27, 31; Feb. 5, 7, 13; May 9, 14, 16, 21, 28, 30; June 3, 27; July 10; Oct. 31; Nov. 5 [?], 7, 19, 21, 26, 29. **1607**: Jan. 28; April 24, 29; May 1, 6.

Privy Seal, Lord; *see* Henry Howard.

Puckering, Sir John; b. *cir.* 1544; appointed *Lord Keeper*, May 28, 1592; d. April 30, 1596.

1593: Nov. 16. **1594**: Jan. 25, 30; Feb. 6, 8; May 16. **1595**: Jan. 29; June 3; July 4. **1596**: Jan. 28, 30; Feb. 4, 6, 11, 13.

Queen's Bench; *see* King's Bench.

Ravis, Thomas; *Bishop of London*, 1607; d. Dec. 14, 1609.

1607: June 10; Oct. 14, 16, 21, 23, 28, 30; Nov. 4, 6, 13, 18, 20, 27. **1608**: Jan. 27; June 16; Oct. 12; page 372; Nov. 9, 11.

ROLLS, MASTER OF THE; *see*
Edward Bruce,
Julius Cæsar.

SACKVILLE, SIR THOMAS; created *Lord Buckhurst*, June 8, 1567; created *Earl of Dorset*, March 13, 1604; *Lord Treasurer*, 1599; d. April 19, 1608.

1593: Nov. 16. **1594**: Jan. 25, 30; Feb. 6; May 16. **1595**: Jan. 29; June 3. **1596**: Jan. 28, 30; Feb. 4, 6, 11, 13; April 29; May 12, 19, 21, 25; July 1; Oct. 13, 15; Nov. 24. **1597**: Feb. 4, 9, 11; April 15, 20, 22; Oct. 14, 19, 21, 26; Nov. 4, 9, 11, 17. **1598**: May 24, 26; June 28, 30; July 6; Oct. 11. **1599**: May 16, 18; June 13, 22, 28. **1600**: May 28; June 4; July 6; Oct. 10, 15. **1601**: June 17. **1602**: April 28; May 5, 7, 12; June 9, 11, 16, 18; Oct. 15; Nov. 30. **1603**: May 13, 18, 20, 27; June 1. **1604**: June 22; Oct. 10, 12, 17, 19. **1605**: Feb. 13; April 19; May 1, 3, 5, 10, 14; Oct. 11, 16, 23, 25, 30; Nov. 8, 13, 15, 20, 22. **1606**: Jan. 31; Feb. 5, 7, 13; May 9, 14, 16, 21, 23, 28, 30; June 3, 27; July 10; Oct. 31; Nov. 5 [?], 7, 19, 21, 26, 29. **1607**: Jan. 28; April 29; May 1, 6; Oct. 14, 16, 21, 23; Nov. 4, 6, 13, 18, 20, 27. **1608**: Jan. 27. **1609**: Feb. 14.

SALISBURY, EARL OF; *see* Robert Cecil.

SAVILE, SIR JOHN; *Baron of the Exchequer*, July 1, 1598; d. Feb. 2, 1607.

1598: July 6. **1599**: June 28. **1604**: Oct. 10, 12, 17, 19. **1605**: Feb. 13; May 14. **1606**: Jan. 27; Nov. 29.

SHREWSBURY, EARL OF; *see* Gilbert Talbot.

SNIGGE, SIR GEORGE; b. *cir.* 1545; *Baron of the Exchequer*, Oct. 14, 1604; d. Nov. 11, 1617.

1605: Feb. 13. **1608**: May 31; June 16.

SOMERSET, SIR EDWARD, K.G.; 4th *Earl of Worcester*; succeeded 1589; d. 1628.

1602: May 7, 12. **1604**: June 22. **1605**: Feb. 13; May 3, 14. **1606**: Jan. 27; June 3, 27. **1608**: May 31.

SOTHERTON, JOHN; *Baron of the Exchequer*, June 16, 1579; d. Oct. 26, 1605.

1598: July 6. **1599**: June 28.

STAFFORD, EDWARD, LORD; 3rd Baron; succeeded 1566; d. Oct. 18, 1603.

1594: Jan. 25.

STANHOPE, SIR JOHN; *Vice-Chamberlain*; created *Baron Stanhope of Harrington*, May 4, 1605; d. 1620.

1602: May 7. **1606**: June 27.

STANLEY, SIR HENRY, K.G.; 4th *Earl of Derby*; succeeded 1572; d. Sept. 25, 1593.

1593: May 16.

SUFFOLK, EARL OF; *see* Thomas Howard.

TALBOT, SIR GILBERT, K.G.; 7th *Earl of Shrewsbury*; succeeded 1590; d. 1626.

1602: April 28; May 5, 7, 12; June 9, 11, 16. **1603**: May 27. **1604**: June 22. **1606**: Feb. 13; May 21; June 3, 27.

TANFIELD, LAWRENCE; *Justice of the King's Bench*, Jan. 13, 1606; *Chief Baron of the Exchequer*, June 25, 1607; d. April 30, 1625.

1607: Nov. 12 [Wards]. **1608**: May 31.

TREASURER, LORD; *see*
Robert Cecil,
William Cecil,
Thomas Sackville.

VAUGHAN, RICHARD; *Bishop of London*, 1604; d. March 30, 1607.

1605: Feb. 13; April 19, 24; May 1, 5, 10, 14; Oct. 11, 16, 23, 25, 30; Nov. 8, 20, 22. **1606**: Jan. 31; Feb. 5, 7, 13; May 21, 23, 30; June 3, 27; Oct. 31; Nov. 7, 19, 21, 26, 29. **1607**: Jan. 28.

WALMESLEY, SIR THOMAS; *Justice of the Common Pleas*, May 10, 1589; d. Nov. 26, 1612.

1595: June 3. **1596**: Feb. 13; May 25; July 1. **1598**: July 6. **1599**: June 28. **1600**: Feb. 6; July 6. **1605**: Feb. 13. **1608**: May 31; June 16.

WARBURTON, SIR PETER; *Justice of the Common Pleas*, Nov. 24, 1600; d. Sept. 7, 1621.

1604: Oct. 10, 12, 17, 19. **1605**: Feb. 13; May 1, 3, 5, 10. **1608**: May 31; June 16.

WHARTON, PHILIP; 3rd *Baron Wharton*; succeeded 1572; d. 1625.

1605: May 8.

WHITGIFT, JOHN; *Archbishop of Canterbury*, 1583; d. Feb. 29, 1603–4.

1594: Jan. 25, 30; Feb. 6, 8; May 16. **1595**: Jan. 29; June 3; July 4. **1596**: Jan. 28, 30; Feb. 6, 11, 13; April 29; May 12, 19, 21, 25; June 18, 23, 25; July 1; Oct. 15; Nov. 24. **1597**: Feb. 4, 9, 11; April 15, 20, 22; Oct. 14, 19, 21, 26; Nov. 4, 9, 11, 17. **1598**: May 24, 26; June 28, 30; July 6; Oct. 11. **1599**: May 16, 18; June 13, 22, 28. **1600**: April 18; May 28; June 4; July 6; Oct. 10. **1601**: June 17. **1602**: April 28; May 5, 7, 12; June 9, 11, 16, 18; Oct. 13, 15, 20; Nov. 30. **1603**: May 13, 18, 20, 27; June 1, 3.

Les Reportes del Cases in Camera Stellata

In Camera Stellata, die Veneris, 25 Januarij, 1593, Elizab. 36, adonque presente, Sur Keeper, Archeuesque del Canterberye, Ch. Just. de Banco, Ch. Baron d'exchequer, L. Stafford, L. Bukherst, Sr Thomas Hennage vice-chamberlein, Sr John Fortescue, chaunceller d'exchequer. 1593-4 Jan. 25

The Attorneys in the Star Chamber are four, whose names are :— Names of the Attorneys

Mr Writington.

Mr Healle ; *afterwards Mr Lowman ; afterwards Mr Beston ; afterwards Beere.*[1]

Mr Johnes.

Mr Milles ; *afterwards Hudson.*[1]

Clerk, Mr Milles.

It was asked of Mr Writington by Mr Phillips, a Counsellor at the Bar, whether, if a bill in this Court be referred and certified as insufficient, it ought to be dismissed the Court as a matter of course [*de common course*], without motion. It was answered that it ought to be dismissed with costs as a matter of course, without motion. Bill dismissed as of course, or not

It was moved between Lane, plaintiff, and Gardiner and others, defendants. The case was for perjury, for this that Gardiner, in the Court of Wards upon proof there LANE v. GARDINER — Perjury

[1] These subsequent names in italics have been written at different times.

1593–4
Jan. 25

that he had sealed, subscribed and delivered a 'generall relleasse' to one Ryder, now dead, had deposed that it was not his deed; and so in this Court, being heard at St Albon's, it was ordered for the default of the plaintiff that he could not come to his books[1] which were in a house in London in which seven persons had died of the plague between October last and January,[2] and this was now moved to stay the hearing, but it could not prevail; and so, on the default of the plaintiff for want of the books,[1] they proceeded to hear the cause. Serjeant Yelverton and Serjeant Healle with the plaintiff. It was ordered by the whole Court that Gardiner, the defendant, be dismissed by the great favour of the court.

The same day Edgerton, the Queen's Attorney, moved for the committal of one now at large, but who had been before committed; and afterwards, when one of the plaintiff's men came to serve a writ on the defendant, the defendant wounded and maimed him. It was ordered by the Lord Keeper that he should be committed as before; and there should be an order for the future that no one who was a party [to any case], and no men or allies of either plaintiff or defendant, should have any warrant to serve the process of this Court, but that the men of the Warden of the Fleet alone [should serve process]. To this it was objected by the officers in Court that it was impossible for the Warden of the Fleet to have sufficient men to serve all the processes out of this Court, and that in some cases no one dare serve process but some of the plaintiff's men. So Milles[3] was ordered to find precedents in such cases, and to report them to the Court the next day.

Who shall serve process

[1] The word in the text is *liuers*; it seems to be used throughout the MS. in the sense of 'depositions,' and I have so translated it. The Star Chamber depositions extant at the Public Record Office are mostly stitched up in book form.

[2] See Calendar of State Papers, Domestic, 1591–94, for many references to the plague at this time. 'The plague is very hot in London and other places of the realm, so that a great mortality is expected this summer' (*ib.* p. 353). See also Cal. State Papers, Dom., Addenda, 1580–1625, p. 356.

[3] The Clerk of the Court; see p. 1.

In Camera Stellata, termino Hillarij, 30 Januar., Elizab. 36, coram le Lo. Keeper, l'archeuesque de Canterberye, l'erle de Essex, L. Admirall, Lo. Buckhurst, S[r] Tho. Hennage, S[r] John Fortescue, S[r] Robert Cicill, Ch. Just. de banco, et Chiefe Baron. 1593-4 Jan. 30

The hearing of the case was continued between Thomas Deighton and Elin Deighton, plaintiffs, and Robert Thorpe, Sir John Munsen, deceased, and others, defendants. The matters of the bill were, 1. the forgery of a will; 2. the publishing of two forged leases and procuring them to be antedated; 3. the forging of two assignments and a release, and other matters; 4. the suborning and maintenance of a juror by Sir [John] Munsen. DEIGHTON and DEIGHTON v. MOUNSON — Forgery

1. It was apparent that it was not a forged will; the plaintiff could not prove, as he endeavoured [to do], that his father's will was of no profit in his lifetime and [that] no executors were named [in it], For in the will produced to the Court, with a codicil to it, the Earl of Lincoln, Sir John Munsen, and others, were named executors; and the testator owed much more than he possessed,[1] and therefore there was no cause to forge a will. It was held that in law a will is good notwithstanding no executor be named in it; and to speak of 'hearesaye,' and to swear, are two [different] things. [p. 2] Will without executor

2. The leases were good notwithstanding the antedating, for a man may antedate a deed if it be not to any man's prejudice or to defeat any man's right: it was not proved to the Court that they were published with the knowledge of their being forged; for if any man publish a forged deed, not knowing it to be forged, it is not punishable. It was held by the Lord Keeper that notwithstanding it did not appear who forged the deed, still this Court could proceed to punish those who knowingly published such forged deeds. Antedating a deed; where good — Publication, without knowledge, not forgery

3 and 4. Nothing at all was proved at the last hearing proving soliciting in her own cause by Dame Munsen, and no other maintenance or subornation.

[1] *Fuit mult pluis en dette que auoyt.*

1593-4 Jan. 30

And because it appeared to the Court that the plaintiff Deighton was guilty of many heinous offences, as detected of perjury in this Court, of the subornation of his own witnesses, of procuring one named William Heighton to be perjured in the Queen's Bench, and another of his witnesses to be executed for murder, upon which an appeal was brought before in the Bench, being a Counsellor of 'Graies Inne,' and he demurred on the appeal, and thereupon was executed, and he proceeding in malice, vouched his dead father for forging a deed, and joined his mother as plaintiff in the bill with him, when it appeared by a certificate in Court that she did not know of this, but was greatly offended with it, and so the suit was 'malicious, vnnatural & wicked,' not only against father and mother, brother and sister, uncle and friends, and to their slander.

Defendants dismissed with costs

For all these causes it was agreed by the Court, by Sir John Fortescue, the Chief Justice of the Bench, Lord Buckherst, the Archbishop and the Lord Keeper, that the defendants, as to all the causes mentioned in the bill, ought to be and should be in the fullest manner dismissed the Court, with their costs, according to the former precedents of Sir [1] Yonge, Sir John Dauers, and others, and the plaintiff should pay a fine of £200, and be committed: against this were the Chief Baron, Sir Thomas Hennage and the Lord Admiral, alleging that the plaintiff was a gentleman, and had expended great sums in this suit, and not knowing his ability [to pay the fine] nor what his estate is, and being dubious of the precedent of the Court for fining or imprisoning in such a case. But the Lord Keeper proceeded with the sentence and gave this. For the Earl of Essexe and Sir Robert Cecill said nothing as they came late.

Fine 200l.

And it was the first hour of the day, so Blunt, Merrike and I went to dinner at Bilbye's, the Sub-Chancellor of the Exchequer. By Blunt: it is apparent that the Lord Keeper can give sentence by himself, notwithstanding it be

Lord Keeper gives sentence alone

[1] Blank in MS. Should be John; see p. 9.

against the whole Court, for the Lord Keeper, the Lord Treasurer and the Lord Privy Seal are the sole judges in this Court, and the other barons and lords are but assistants to them. Which is not the law, as I believe, for it proceeds by the majority of voices, not by experience. Blunte [said that] to 'forswear' is to do so in common talk, but 'perjury' is to be perjured in a Court of Record. And it was asked by a Counsellor at the Bar if the ancient order that the bill or answer should not exceed eighteen sheets and that in that case [the party] should pay the costs, [was in force,] and by another [Counsellor] if a frivolous bill of no value as of a 'cap-case doblet'[1] should be preferred in this Court, if it is allowable or not. Answer: The first in some [p. 3] cases is observed, in others not. As to the last question of a bill containing frivolous things, slanderous or malicious, or things of no value, in all these cases the Court should dismiss them with costs.

In Camera Stellata, Die Mercurij 6 Februarij, 1593, Elizab. 36, [1593–4,] termino Hillarij.[2]

1593-4 Feb. 6

PARSONS v. HERNE

Perjury

One Parsons, a 'hosteler,' plaintiff, against Herne,[3] defendant, a Bencher of 'Lincolne's Inne,' for perjury and misdemeanour, argued by the Counsel for the plaintiff, but not answered by the defendant's Counsel, but adjourned to the next day. It was moved by the Lords how these words should be understood when a man testifies in his deposition[4] that such a man swore or had said 'these wordes or the like in effecte.' By the Lord Keeper: no bill could be judged on such uncertain words, as in this case, because the words were 'that he did depose thus or the like in effect.'

Of what words they can judge

On the Friday next following, the bill being declared and [about] to be heard, the Court deferred the hearing

[1] Query. Halliwell gives as the meaning of cap-case, 'a small travelling case, or band-box.' What the expression means I cannot say.

[2] The names of the Councillors present, ten in number, are here set out in the MS. as on p. 1. It has not been thought necessary to repeat them every time, as they are all included in the Table at the end of the Introduction.

[3] Edward Heron.

[4] *Tesmoigne sur son liuer.*

1593–4 Feb. 6

because of the uncertainty of the words. And Serjeant Healle, of Counsel with the defendant, had agreed that the bill should be amended, which could not be done by the order of the Court without the agreement of the parties; and afterwards both parties agreed that a new bill should be preferred and those words amended, which the Court would not and could not do without the consent of both parties; and, to avoid precedents in such cases, it was ordered, on the motion of the Lord Keeper, that no man of base condition, such as an apprentice, horsekeeper, or suchlike, should be a plaintiff in this Court before he had [found] sufficient surety to perform the order of the Court. And from the proceedings in this case it would appear that this Court does not give judgment without apparent, pregnant and sufficient proof. But as to the former query regarding the uncertainty of the depositions of one witness, the whole Court held against the Lord Keeper, saying that when a man deposes that 'he said these wordes or the like,' it shall be taken [to mean] 'these wordes or wordes of the like sounde;' but when he says 'these wordes or the like in effecte' shall be understood 'the same wordes in sense and meaninge,' because no one would swear certainly or precisely to words. To this Bishop Flecher [1] said that perjury is a lie with an oath.[2]

Amendment without agreement, or not

No base man shall be plaintiff in this Court without good sureties

No judgment without good proof

Perjury, what

Suit in the Marches shall not be commenced here

On seeing letters from the President of Wales,[3] it was ordered that no suit, commenced or pending in the Marches, should be admitted or received into this Court; because it appears in this case that Morris was to appear before the President of the Marches, and for his contempt [in not appearing], a commission of rebellion was issued against him, and notwithstanding this, he has, this term, preferred a bill in this Court and has served a subpœna on the defendant.

[1] He is described in the list of judges present this day, ten in number, as *Do. Flecher donque euesque de worceter et amner al Roigne, et ore euesque de Londres.* He was not appointed Bishop of London until December 25, 1594, so that this part of the manuscript is evidently written up from notes.

[2] *Periuria est mendacium cum iuramento.*

[3] The President of the Court of the Marches of Wales.

In Camera Stellata, 8° Februar., die Veneris, Elizab. 36, termino Hillarij, [1593–4].[1]

[p. 4] 1593–4 Feb. 8

Parsons, pl. Herne, deft.

The former cause between Parsons and Herne[2] and Sleyford, who is now dead and so no cause to proceed against him. But the cause was sentenced as follows.

Perjury and other misdemeanours

First, the charges were perjury, in giving evidence to a jury in the Queen's Bench [*in banco Regis*] and of this [there were] two or three parts, as usurious taking of interest, &c., another misdemeanour when he was attached by process in the Bench, refusing contemptuously to appear, and on attachment against him, he procured interrogatories from the officer of the court, and, having had a conference with the defendant Sleyford, he wrote his answer and gave it to Sleyford, &c. This cause was three days in hearing, and at the end the Court thought that nothing was proved against Herne as to the perjury, although Weymarke (who was the man who had maintained Parsons' suit against Herne) had complained in Parsons' name so that he himself might be a witness, and has deposed directly against Herne, and Herne against him, but it was not read, but by the clear opinion of all the Court, he being the defendant and [there being] no deceit, it could be read and good credit given to it. Exceptions were moved against Weymarke, because if he recovered in this action he would again be interested in his land which he had sold to Sleyford. On which contract arose one part of the perjury, whether the sale was conditional or absolute, it being proved to be conditional, they forced an oath from Herne that it was an absolute bargain. As to the misdemeanour, the Chief Justices of both Benches held it clear that any man may, either by order of Court or by consent of the parties, procure interrogatories out of Court, and write his own answer. And so it was proved *viva voce* by one Felle, an officer of the Bench, that Weymarke's man had consented to the interrogatories being delivered to Herne; and Sleyford en-

[1] Ten Councillors were present, including the Earl of Essex and the Lord Chamberlain, who left before sentence was given.

[2] See p. 5.

1593–4 Feb. 8

If Interrogatories are delivered to a witness by consent, it is good

treated Herne, who was ill and doubtful if he would be alive the next term, to give him his answers in writing, which Herne did, praying Sleyford not to suffer them to be read by anyone but to deliver them again to him, but if he, Herne, died, then Sleyford was to use them for his own good. Which was allowed by the whole Court, and some of them had done the like. And also a deed was shown to the Court which was penned by Serjeant Harris and his hand [set] to it, and perused by Herne of counsel with Sleyford, in which the lands now demanded were granted by Sleyford to Weymarke, and in the same deed other lands previously sold were recited: and then follows 'he enfeffes, grauntes, &c., all his righte, intereste, &c., in the sayd premisses,' where it ought to be 'in the same premisses.' *Valde* good shift, and some oversight of Herne's. In the same deed bearing date of 9 May, 35 Elizab. '92, follows a proviso that Weymarke should pay on a certain day certain money and so have back his land, which [deed] was first dated ''92' but afterwards '8' was put in, and so it was made ''82,' a day past before the date, so that Weymarke should have his land back and give nothing for it, a shiftinge device and without any good intent.

'Cumming date'

[p. 5] Three days in hearing

But on the whole matter the cause continued three entire days and was argued at length with divers crossing of the Counsel at law, which was checked by the Court; the Court went to sentence as follows.

Rash deposing condemned, but defendant acquitted

John Fortescue, knight; checked Herne for his rash deposing and speaking regarding his oath, but this notwithstanding acquitted him as to the perjury and every part of it; and also as to the misdemeanour. And so did John Woolly, knight, but he blamed Herne for giving counsel to a usurer. These two did not give any charges.

Herne clearly acquitted

Lord Anderson, Chief Justice of the Common Bench, acquitted Herne of everything and would restore his good fame in the best sort that could be, and delivered some words in dislike of what John Woolye had uttered regarding usury.

The Chief Justice of the Bench also acquitted Herne of everything, and he to have restitution of his good name.

He would have this done by the plaintiff's confession in Lincoln's Inn or in this Court; and the said Parsons to be examined who were the maintainers of this suit and if they be of ability to pay costs to Herne.

What witnesses requisite to sentence perjury

Lord Buckherst said that perjury being the greatest offence, and that as the simplest man living ought to esteem [his good name] [1] rather than his goods or his life, we ought not to proceed to sentence this without proofs *luce clariores*, and witnesses *omni exceptione maiores*. And thus he agreed in all points with the Chief Justice of the Bench.

The Bishop of Worcester agreed with them, and argued some *diuinitas*, but the whole cause was opened by the Chief Justice of the Queen's Bench [*de banco Regis*].

Sir John Yonge and Sir John Dauers' case cited

Costs awarded to defendant

Confession

The Archbishop agreed with them, and so did the Lord Keeper. And he ordered that, according to the precedents of Sir John Yonge's and Sir John Dauers' and an Attorney's cases at St. Albans [2] term, the plaintiff, if his ability be such, shall pay costs to the defendant, and shall make confession in this Court of his slanderous complaint against Herne, and he shall be specially examined who were his procurers, aiders or assisters in this suit.

Commendation of this Court

Motion by the Queen's Counsel for costs for the Queen.

After sentence was given by the whole Court, the Queen's Attorney and Solicitor being present, the Attorney moved that, because this Court being the most honourable, worthy and grave Court that ever he had read or heard of in all Europe, and the Judges of this Court being Councillors of the Queen, peers of the realm, and for the deciding of causes here the Queen is content for them to depart from her side, therefore it will not be convenient that this Court should be abused before all others for men to wreck their malice and to spew their poison in slandering and defaming Her Majesty's subjects; for in other Courts an action on the case will lie for slanderous words. Thus in this case the Court being detained these three days, and nothing proved against the defendant who was acquitted *per totam curiam*, the precedents are that [the plaintiff] shall pay a fine to the Queen.

[1] Something of the sort seems necessary to make sense.

[2] When the Court sat at St. Albans; see p. 2.

[p. 6] 1593–4 Feb. 8

So the Lord Keeper moved for a new sentence, to which Fortescue said nothing, but Woollye and the Chief Justice of the Bench gave a fine to the Queen, the Chief Justice of the Common Bench having gone, and so Lord Buckhurst agreed on a £40 fine, also the Bishop of Worcester, the Archbishop of Canterbury and the Lord Keeper; if it should appear that the plaintiff is of ability, or any who are procurers, maintainers or actors in this suit, then to be fined a greater fine to the Queen than £40; and imprisonment if the precedent of the Court will warrant it, as it will *ut dicitur*.

LORD DUDLEY'S case

On the same day Lord Dudley moved against a former order for him to pay £4 costs because his commissioners did not assemble on the day appointed, although they were on that day at Quarter Sessions. But the Lord Keeper would not admit this [to be any excuse], because [Lord Dudley] could have appointed some other day, knowing before of the day of the Sessions. And so he would not alter the former order, for by this the courses here would be infinitely delayed.

1593 Nov. 16

In Camera Stellata, 16 Nouembris, An° Do^{ni} 1593.[1]

FANSHAWE, the MAYOR OF LONDON, and others *v.* WROTHE and others

The first motion was by Phillips on behalf of Fanstowe[2] of the Exchequer and the Mayor of London and others, plaintiffs, against Wrothe and others of Ware, defendants; Healle for them. The case was for the continuance of the River of Lee, leading from the town of Ware to London, without disturbance by such kind of riots as has been used these twenty years last past. And because divers of the defendants have answered but will not be sworn to their answers, [it was moved] that they be compelled to be sworn. And it was ordered by the Lord Keeper that they be sworn to their answers, and attachment will lie against them to

[1] Five Councillors were present. This sitting is of earlier date than the previous ones. I have kept it here in preference to moving it into its proper place, as showing that the MS. was probably written up from rough notes. The next five sittings are also out of their proper order.

[2] Thomas Fanshawe.

compel them to answer. And these matters were referred to both the Chief Justices.[1] And because the bills and answers were so long, and especially the interrogatories, which were four yards of parchment, the Judges themselves moved for a remedy for this. And the Lord Keeper ordained as a rule of Court that if any bill contains more than sixteen sheets of paper, then the plaintiff shall pay for the copying of all beyond the sixteen sheets for the use of the defendant; and so if the answer contain more than sixteen sheets of paper, then the defendant shall pay for the copying of all beyond the sixteen sheets for the use of the plaintiff. And so of interrogatories. And if in any of those sixteen sheets the Judges report any unnecessary matter which might be comprehended in fewer lines, then the party so in default shall pay costs.[2]

Serjeant Yelverton moved that whereas he for the plaintiff had named eight commissioners and the defendant had named six, of which six the plaintiff had elected two, and out of the said eight the defendant would not elect any, but took exception to all, that the Court would award an order to remedy this. Healle, one of the attorneys of the Court, to avoid this said that before this time the defendant and the plaintiff had agreed about their commissioners, and now the plaintiff prayed to have them remain their commissioners which the plaintiff [*sic* ? defendant] would not allow. And therefore no order to do the contrary, but it was ordered by the Court that its order shall be observed, and it is this, that in all cases both parties are bound by the usage of the Court to name six commissioners, and each party may take exception to four of them, and to allow the two of the six or otherwise to proceed with the commission alone. And so it was ordered in this case.

[1] The Report of the Lords Chief Justices is preserved among the State Papers. It is a very interesting document, but too long to quote here. See *post*, Appendix I.

[2] This sentence is an excellent example of the extraordinary mixture of Latin, French and English in which the MS. is written: *Si in ascun de eux* 16 *sheetes les Judges report ascun vnnecessary chose quel potuit esse comprehend in fewer lines*, &c.

[p. 7] 1594 Jan. 29

In Camera Stellata, die Martis, Januarij 29, termino Paschae [*sic*], Elizab. 37, 1594.[1]

Askew v. Earl of Lincoln — Maintenance, &c.

Ascoe, plaintiff, and the Earl of Lincoln, defendant, for maintenance, and for buying a statute merchant and prosecuting an extent thereon, for 'rasinge' a certificate out of Chancery and suborning one to do this, &c.; also when a jury was proceeding on the extent and execution thereof, being present and compelling the jury to appraise them again and below the value, and for waste in 'scindinge' and felling 1500 timber trees at Michaelmas to the destruction of the bark. The Earl's counsel moved that the bill was insufficient for these words, 'contrary to the lawes & statutes in that case provyded within two yeres laste paste did buye,' &c., and there are divers statutes against maintenance, and the action is not maintainable unless prosecuted within one year after the offence is committed. The Court ruled that the bill was good, because it is for the Queen, for whom two years is to be allowed. Phillips says that it is not for the Queen, because of this difference, when it is for the Queen, the words are 'informethe to yor ma^tie^,' but when it is for the party, the words are, 'complaynethe to yor ma^tie^.' But the Court was against him.

Another exception to the bill, that if it be in the disjunctive, it is bad, [was taken] by Yelverton, Serjeant, as, 'you committe perjurye in the 16th Interrogatory, and haue prosecuted th'extente, and contracted for the statute or caused some other,' &c. By the Chief Justices: It is good, and there is sufficient matter in the bill besides to maintain maintenance.

The third exception—the extent was taken with the privity of the Earl—is not a good exception: by the Court. But the time of the subornation must be declared, and also of the procurement of maintenance, and it was so agreed by the Court, and on the sight of the bill it appeared plainly. And thus the Counsel for Ascoe proved their matters against the Earl, and so ended the first day. But the cause was not answered on any other day in Court, but

[1] Nine Councillors were present.

was determined by the Lords in private, for the good credit of the Earl; for if the Earl had suffered the case to proceed, grave charges [*grande choses*] would have appeared against him. I was not informed what manner of fine was made.

In Camera Stellata, coram consilio ibidem 2 Julij anno Elizab. Reginae 37, termino Trinitatis.[1] 1595 Jul. 2

'Edward Talbot, plaintiff, and Woode, defendante. TALBOT *v.* WOODE — Slander

'The bill contaynethe the sclaunder of Woode the defend^te^ wherewith he hathe charged the plaintiff that he showld secretely intende the poyseninge of the Erle of Shrewseberye, his brother, by this defend^te^, which the defend^te^ did of late reueale to the Erle of Shrewsebery & his wyfe & to some of the priuye counsell (which was since a challenge of the Erle to the plaintiff by 2 sundry letters), and after 2 yeres and a halfe conceallinge of the same. For the sayd Wood hathe suggested that more then three yeres sythence this plaintiff wroughte secretely under hande with this defendante to poyson the sayd Erle by gloves, and concealed the same till June, 36 Elizab.; and Wood also pretendethe a forged deede of a 100^li^ anuitye *per annum*, graunted to him by the plaintiff to effecte the same; and that the plaintiff seemed to Woode, 17 Novembr. laste, to desire rather the ministringe of some pocion to the Earle, whereas the forged deede of anuity bearethe date the 28 of *Novembris* laste, which daye the gloues were boughte by Woode.

'The plaintiff's Councell did first enforce the impeachemente of Wood's credite by sundry deceitefull practyses in phisike, (he practisinge phisike being neyther lycensed nor graduate in any Vniuersitye), of oyle of stagges' bloode ministred to the Countesse of Shrewseberye for the gowte, of drinkinge 12 gallons of wine pretendinge to drawe the spirite of wyne, the ministringe of dyvers sophisticate oyles, receiptes, and other compositions, as oyle of waxe, butter, antimonie, licor[2] of pearle, the quintessence of creme, and

[1] The names of the Judges are not given.
[2] Liquor.

1595 Jul. 2 other distillations, the iest of the house and the counter, &c.

[p. 8] 'His trecherye wth the Erle and his Ladye in concealinge this practise 2 yeares & a halfe, & reuealinge to the plaintiff how the Erle had intelligence of all thinges spoken in the plaintiff's bedde chamber. His conceaued sorrowe for his vnfortunate happe in not reuealinge to the plaintiff the Erle's proces against the plaintiff before they were serued vpon him; for there were certeine controuersies for title of lande betwene th'erle & the plaintiff his brother, & the defendante gaue intelligence to the plaintiff at all times of all proceedinges vsed by the Earle in that Cawse.

'The forginge of the deede of the anuitye, prooved by the secrete seallinge of it, by the rasure of "Henry," and interposinge "Edward," in 2 places at the beginning, by lymitinge no estate but "duringe the naturall of the defendante," without "lyfe," & the deede neuer delyuered, the subscrybinge of 2 letters, viz: "E. T.," beinge neuer vsed to be so subscrybed by the plaintiff in any of his former grauntes.'

The Queen's Serjeant, Serjeant Healle, Serjeant Flemminge, Serjeant Lewkener, Jackson, Healle junior, of counsell with the plaintiff, and at the bar all day. Serjeant Yelverton, Serjeant Herne, Heskins, Phillips, Fuller, Crue, with the defendant, and at the bar all day.

'M[r] Attornie mooued that one beinge acquaynted with a practise of poyseninge, or the lyke, and dothe surcease his time in not reueallinge the same within a time conueniente, he is not to be receaued as a fitte wytnesse, and so alleaged the authoritie of Bracton. *Accusator post interuallum temporis non est audiendus*; & therefore in actes of parliamente of treason & felonie a certeine time is limited, in some a quarter, in others halfe, and in some a hole yeere, to be conuicted of the offence by them. And so agreed *per Dominum Thesaurarium totius Angliae.*

'Heskins first aunsweares for the defend[te] for his credite for thinges done in his youth, which, if they showlde be examyned, gentlemen of Innes of Courte & others haue done many worse practyses; & for his sophisticated drugges, manye Apothecaryes in the towne are in the like faulte; & endeauoured to disgrace some of the wytnesses produced one the plaintiff's behalfe; & he woulde have produced Bostoke and others *viua voce* for the defend[te's] credite, but the Courte woulde not allowe it but *ex assensu partium*, who woulde not agree. Then Sergeant Yeluerton woulde haue aunsweared the forgerye of the deede, but the Lordes forced him to aunsweare firste the substance, which was the practise of poyseninge, and then the color, viz.—the forginge of the deede of the anuitie, or els to leave the cawse to the censure [1] of the Cowrte. But Yeluerton preste the dependauncye and presente hearinge of one other bill, wherein the Erle was plaintiff and Edward Talbot defendante, conteyninge the practise of poyseninge; and ordered by this Courte that bothe causes showlde be hearde th'one after th'other successiuely, and not censured [2] before they were bothe hearde; but the Lordes vrged as before; & for that the time was spente they referred the sequel to the nexte hearinge; & the defend[te] was bounde for his apparaunce. And it was sayd *par Sur Thesorer* (for that the defendante made some doubte his cause would not be censured this terme, for that this terme was very shorte), that this Courte was a Courte of state, & tyed to no time, and therefore hathe a starre fixed, and called starre chamber, of the state thereof; & so the councell here, being the Quene's councell,[3] might sit & heare waighty causes 3 or 4 dayes after the terme. Likewise he spake for lawe, that if any man will practise phisike not lycensed, if he minister to any that dye after it, he is to be indicted of felony, and suffer deathe as a felon.

'But Serg. Yeluerton assaied to ouerthrowe the bill, and that the Courte could not geue any sentence vpon it for contayninge the forging of a deede that doth not declare any estate, &c., nor euer was delyuered.'

Concluded by the whole Court that in criminal cases

[1] Judgment. [2] Judged.
[3] That is, the Privy Council.

1595 Jul. 2

'one wytnesse suffysethe not,' but *testes luce clariores et omni exceptione maiores* may bring proof.

1595 Jul. 4

'The nexte daye,[1] being Friday, 4 Jul. 95, present Lo. Keeper, Sir Jo. Puck[ering], Lo. Tresorer, Sr Wm Cecill, Erle of Essexe, Deuereux, Lo. Admirall, Lo. Howarde, Sr Robert Cecill, Sr John Wollye, Sr Joh. Fortescue, Lo. Ch. Justice Popham, L'archeuesque de Canterb. Whitgift.

'Then Serg. Yeluerton and Heskins assaied to aunsweare the rest of the plaintiff's bill, and therein did vse all arte and science that the witte of man could; & so was replyde more learnedly by the Queene's Attornie. In so muche that, vpon the hearing of the learned councell one bothe sides, the Lordes sayd themselues they were in greate suspence to which side they showld incline, at the first holding Wood the defendante altogether in faulte, and upon the aunsweare making question of Talbot the plaintiff's innocency, and yet vpon the present reply condemning Wood for a most palpable machiuilian, his Councell pressing the courte with [p. 9] Circumstances of Wood's deuysing, & presumptions of speeche & letters, being all censured at the last both by the Lordes and plaintiff's counsell to be the damnable practises of Wood, in the traiterous Cariage of himselfe to his Lord and Lady and to this plaintiff. And so in shortenes[2] they ended that Cawse, but referred the sentencing & censuring thereof to be ioyned with the nexte cause that followed, as before.

EARL OF SHREWSBURY *v.* TALBOT

'Then Phillipes proceeded to the bill wherein the Erle of Shrew[sbury] was plaintiff and Edward Talbot, his brother, defend^te^ & one Whitington. The matter the bill conteyned was the purpose of Edward Talbot, by the practise of Wood, the defend^te^ in the former bille, to haue poysened the Erle, firste by gloues, & after by pocion or plaister; which th'erle did assaye to proue by no dyrecte wytnesses but Wood, who was not allowed, but taken as infamous, and by circumstances, at the firste seeming some-

[1] The next Court day. [2] Shortness.

what probable, but plainely aunsweared by the defendante. First, that Talbot showld insinuate into Wood's acquaintance by sending for him to Uckfeilde in Sussexe, where he dwelte, and sending diuers messages vnto him, by vsing his secrete aduise in many thinges, by often secrete conferences, by commending his skill and science in poysons, to poyson by smelles *paulatim*, and by presente dispache, a moste daungerous science, by hauing conference of the state of the Erle's bodye, by moouing the procurement of an anuitie for Wood to lyue amongste them, & by gyuing him 4 spurre ryalles [1] in a purse, etc. All these & more of the like nature were very learnedlye & forceably mooued by th'earle's councell, but all by probability, coniectures and presumptions; all wch were aunsweared wth greate learning, greater aduise & delyberacion, and with the greateste probability & presumptions that mighte be, and so conceaued & censured *per totam curiam.* The particuler aunsweares to these and all other the objections mooued by th'erles Counsell, I woulde, withoute presumption, particularise and abbreuiate in wrytinge, thoughe not with the like learninge in any degree as they were forceably and effectuallye opened to the Courte; but I thinke in so doinge I should loose my selfe, the grownde is to large to write throughe; for the openinge, aunswearinge & censuring of this one Cawse, forced the Lordes to sitte from 9 a clocke in the morninge vnto 6 a clocke at nighte, & neuer mooued. Th'erle's counsell endeauoured likewyse to discredite the defendante for his religion, his haughtines of minde, his prodigalitye, &c.; to prooue which they mooued that the defend^te^ showld spende 10,000 marks since the deathe of his Father, being not aboue three yeres sythence; [2] his religion, for defendinge one John Baldwin (a witnes produced one Wood's behalfe) who questioned whether there were a god; if there were, howe he showld be knowne; if by his worde, who wrote the same; if the prophetes & the Apostles, they were but men, *et humanum est errare*; & such like most damnable doubtes, & not suffered to be reade in the hearinge of this Courte;

[1] A gold coin, worth about fifteen shillings. [2] Since.

1595 Jul. 4 his haughtines of minde, that he showld saye to Wood, it was braue to be an Earle, & no estate sure but an Earle's, & that he could furnishe that place well, & when he trayuayled into France & Italye he was toulde he was borne to be an Earle[1] & such like; but not any one woorde hereof was proued, but wysely aunsweared by the defendante's Councell; & so conceaued *per curiam*. Then th'erle opened that the defend[te] showld practise & agree with Sir Edwarde Stapleton for the effecting of this poyseninge, & that he showld [p. 10] suborne a man of his, one of his name, to buye the gloues, & that Sir Edward Stapleton showld be a meete man so to do, for that he had in former time suborned wytnesses in this Courte; & this pointe the Courte seemed dubious a longe time, for that Wood had procured the Erle to produce wytnesses to proue this to be the man that had boughte the gloues: insomuche that the Cowrte was forced to sende for the millener[2] and his man that soulde the gloues, who denied vpon the sight of the sayd Stapleton that he cowld be the man. All which Woode hearinge, sayd that in his Conscience he thoughte he was not the man. So the palpable asse Woode was herein condemned (after long doubtinge,) for a verye villein & of Sathan's broode, being called *Diabolos* for that he is an accuser; for it could not be imagyned that Woode, concealing this practise onely to be assured of good proofe, as he himselfe confessed vpon his oathe, but that he would haue knowne his name that boughte the gloues with him, & some wytnesse to the seallinge of the deede of th'anuitie; of the which he did neyther; but it was god's worke he showld be espyed in time. So the Councell one bothe sydes proceeded very learnedlye, & to the greate admiration of all men, & beyond all expectation. But the Queene's Attornie craued his silence mighte not prejudice the defend[te]'s cawse, for whom he spake before, being plaintiff in the former bill, for now he could not speake for him, for that Edward Talbot was defendaunt, and for whome he would

[1] The prophecy was verified in 1616, when Edward Talbot succeeded his brother Gilbert, the plaintiff in this case, as eleventh earl of Shrewsbury.

[2] The old sense of milliner was a haberdasher, or seller of small wares. Skeat.

speake but for his oathe[1]; and he proued Woode to be no schollar for that he wrote false ortography, for "proces," "prossus," whereas every scholler knowethe "proces" to come of *procedendo*. *Issint Woode fuit Censure per totam curiam* (th'erle of Essexe & th'archebishope onely excepted, for which they were checkte by Her Matie afterwards), that he showlde ride from the Fleete to Westminster with his face to the horse taile, & there stand upon the pillorye, & so ride to the Fleete againe; & another daye from thence to Chepeside, to the pillorye there; fined to the Queene 500^{li}; imprisonmente at Her pleasure; and it was mooued by the Lo. Tresorer that if Woode woulde confesse his faulte & submitte himselfe to Mr Talbot at the assises where Mr Talbot dwelte, then the 500^{li} to be relleassed; which then he would not doe; but after some longe imprisonmente he confessed that he himselfe was the onely deuiser, procurer, acter, & plotter in all this action, for the which he loste bothe his eares upon the pillorye, was slitte in the nose, sealled in the foreheade, & censured to perpetual imprisonmente. Euery one of the Priuye Counsell at the hearinge beforesayd spake liberallye, learnedlye and exceeding wysely, to the hole cawse and euery perticuler thereof, but to sette downe euery speciall sentence or specialty mooued, I maye not take vpon me to doe, neyther will I trouble my selfe so muche, being an infinite labor. *Ideo sic finem facio*, 10 *Julii*, *An*° *Do*^{ni} 1595. Elizab. 37.' Sentence

In Camera Stellata, coram Consilio ibidem, le prochein jour apres le fine del Easter Terme, Elizab. 37, mense Junii 3°, die Martis, An° Do^{ni} 1595.[2] [p. 11] 1595 June 3

At the first sitting of the Court, those Justices of the Peace who lived in and near London were ordered to appear, &c., by special order, and then the Lord Keeper, being Sir John Puckring, delivered an oration given in charge to him by the Queen herself, and devised by her [*par sa devise* Proclamation

[1] This being a criminal prosecution, in which the Queen was theoretically interested as plaintiff, the Queen's Attorney could not appear for the defendant.

[2] For list of Councillors present, fifteen in number, see Table in Introduction.

1595
June 3

demesne] without any direction from her Council; and it was to this intent. And it commenced with the custom of making an oration to the Justices of each county at the end of Easter or Trinity term,[1] ' w[ch] vsage hathe of late yeeres bene discontinued, but now, considering the presente scarsitye, her Ma[tie] of her own speciall Care and regarde to her louinge subiectes hathe gyuen in charge, to vs (viz. Lords Keeper and tresorer) to delyuer in this place her owne speciall direction for the redresse hereof, in the audience of such Justices as are in Towne & of other of her Judges of Circuites of Assise whome we have requyred to be here.[2] Firste, for redresse of the presente wante of graine, it is thoughte good that diligence shall be vsed in the ouerlookinge of Certificates in former time made, accordinge to some former orders in that Case prouided, & the offences of Corne maisters & mongers to be punished wth greate seuerity, & the Justices of euery County to meete at euery of there markets weekelye to perswade the bringing of Corne to furnishe the markets, & if neede be to vse there authoritie therein; & allso in charitable manner they themselues to make a somme of monie, beinge thereto assisted by all those of the better sorte w[th]in the shire, and therew[th] to buye some quantitie of Corne, & to Cawse the same to be soulde in euery market w[th]oute any manner of gaine. & for more speedier redresse of the presente scarsity, Her Ma[tie's] pleasure is that all Justices of peace and all others whatsoeuer shall presentely resorte vnto there Cuntrye dwellinges, there to maintaine hospitality, vpon Her Ma[tie's] displeasure, all excuses layde aparte, except suche as are imployed in affaires concerning Her Ma[tie's] owne person, or in any office w[ch] concernethe Her selfe in speciall sorte. And for that the number of Justices of the peace are growne allmoste infinite, to the hinderaunce of Justice, th'one trustinge so much vnto another that there are more Justicers then Justice, & as th'old saying is many times[3] *multitudo*

[1] The writer here continues in nglish, probably giving the exact words of the Queen's charge.

[2] '*Fenner, Wamslowe, Gaudye et Clenche, Judges, par speciall commaundment adonque presente.*'

[3] Something apparently omitted here.

imperatorum destruit excercitum [*sic*], & of these many insufficiente, vnlearned, negligente and vndiscreete. Her Matie therefore, like a good huswyfe looking vnto all her houshold stuffe, tooke the booke in her owne handes, & in the sighte of vs, the Lo. Keeper and Tresorer, wente throughe & noted those Justices she would have Continue in Commission, & whome shee thoughte not meete, & willed vs to Consyder of the reste, & that this audience showld knowe this, that she would not haue any to be in Commission of the peace to serue her that showlde retaine to any other man, & *ideo* th'old statute of 3 H. 7 shee woulde showld be narrowly looke vnto.[1] Nor any that doe not lyue wth in the County, or that are not of sufficiente lyuing and Countenaunce, thereby to be a discredite to the reste. Or that are [p. 12] vnlearned & negligente in there places, & y^t the Justices of Assise showld looke narrowly vnto this, & they to remooue those that in discrecyon they thoughte not meete for the place: & the statute of retayners to be looked vnto, & bailes for Felons not baileable by lawe, there waches for the punishing of Rouges & idle persons, the searche of Innes & alehouses, that none lodge but one nighte wth oute speciall Cause, & euery one to looke wysely to the gouernemente of his Family, for that he is to aunsweare for euery seruaunte; the excesse in apparrell to be punished, & for the Chastisinge of all suche offences, the Justices of peace, being now but fewe, are to excercise Justice wth a Herculean Courage; & both they & the Judges of Assise to geue those thinges in speciall Charge at there seuerall meetinges wth in all Counties; & not to allowe the Clergye but once, or where it is not alloweable by lawe, for it is no pietye but wicked pitye.'[2]

In Camera Stellata, 16 Maij, Elizab. 35.[3]

1593 May 16

CROUCHE *v.* HUNGERFORD and others

Forgery

Walter Crouche, plaintiff, Sir Walter Hungerford and others, defendants. The case was for forging a deed, and

[1] This refers apparently to cap. 13, 'The King's Officers or Tenants shall not be retained by Liveries with others.' It was repealed 3 Car. I. cap. 4.

[2] Clergy, of course, means benefit of clergy.

[3] Eleven Councillors were present. This is the earliest sitting reported in this volume. See note 1, p. 10.

1593 May 16 — the point was the erasure of a word contained in the deed, to wit, [in the sentence] '*habendum sibi et assignatis suis*,' he erased '*assignatis*' and wrote '*heredibus*.' But at the end of the hearing, (for the case was two days in hearing.) Sir Walter Hungerford was acquitted for want of proof; for Crouche could not prove that the forgery was done by Hungerford himself; and so Sir Walter Hungerford was dismissed to the common law. The Lord Keeper cited that [the words] 'to hold to him and his assigns to his own proper use and to the use of his heirs and assigns' were adjudged in Boston's case to be an estate for life, and a fee simple in use.

Bill dismissed

[p. 13]

1595 Oct. 10

In Camera Stellata, coram consilio ibidem, termino Michaelis, Elizab. 37 & 38, Octobris 10, An° Do^ni^ 1595.[1]

GRESHAM *v.* BOOTHE and MARKHAM — Forgery

Kuke,[2] the Queen's Attorney, moved first for Dame Gresham against Boothe and Markham for forgery of deeds of 500 or 600 [*sic*] per an. in the lands of Thomas Gresham, knight, deceased, to be deeds of 21 years past; and he moved to have Boothe committed for not delivering up to the Court the deed supposed to be forged, as the Court formerly ordered, and to have the witnesses suppressed who were examined after publication; and to re-examine the witnesses as to the forged deed now in Court and unknown before. All which was granted by the Court. The infant Markham, being 19 years of age, elected Thomas Morgan, knight, as his guardian; and Morgan, having delivered up the deed to the Court, petitioned that he might be allowed to assist Markham in this suit as his guardian. The Court allowed this, but as [next] friend, and not as guardian, since Markham was not his pupil, but was of [*i.e.* over] the age of 14 years. A day for judgment is given in this term.[3]

[1] No names given.

[2] Sir Edward Coke.

[3] There are several references to this suit in the State Papers. See Appendix II. See also *post*, pp. 26, 29, 64.

ATT.-GEN. v. HUNTLY, PURNELL, and others

The Attorney informs against one Christopher Huntly of Boxeley in the county of Gloucester, Justice of the Peace, now restrained because an attaint is pending against him as Juror, and against three others named Purnell, 'clothes men,' who were robbed of £390 on the 1st of February last by one Bridges and one Guildford. The hue and cry was raised, and Huntly sent his servants and horses to pursue the felons. At two o'clock the same night the said felons came to Huntly's house, and he said to Guildford, "Why come you so late. There is a robbery done. I suspecte you." Then Guildford went away, and [Huntly] took Bridge and detained him. And three or four hours afterwards, Guildford was taken and brought to him. The Purnells having come, the felons confessed the fact, and delivered part of the money to Huntly, who kept the money and the felons in his own house for five or six days, and laboured with the Purnells for a composition on his giving up of the part of their money, and also for the residue. And the felons being brought by Huntly and the Parnells [*sic*] to two Justices, to wit, Dauers and Hayes, to be bailed, Huntly concealed their confession, and said that they were suspected; and the Parnells said that they were like those [who robbed them] and had such horses and cloaks. Whereupon the felons were bailed on bonds of £50 each, and have now escaped. And for this matter the two Justices of the Peace were fined £1000 each by Perriam, Chief Baron, at the Assizes in the country [*in pais*], the felons being then indicted by the said Huntly. But because this case greatly concerns the peace of the common weal, the Lords have resolved to sentence it in this Court, the parties being examined by Popham, Chief Justice, and Perriam, Chief Baron; and so they were sentenced upon [p. 14] their examinations only. And the two Justices of the Peace, not having been yet examined, are, by the order of the Court, to be examined by the Chief Justice and the Chief Baron, and they must not depart without receiving their sentence in this Court. In this matter it was agreed by all [the judges] to be the law, that if any one pursue a felon

1595 Oct. 10

and take back his money before the outlawry [of the felon], he shall be accessory to the felony, and he shall not have his money before the outlawry be stayed by the Queen's Attorney. Every subject is bound to pursue felons on a hue and cry, and to bring them to a Justice of the Peace by the constables. No one may make his house into a gaol to detain people there, but only for examination; the procuring of the money again ought not to delay the course of Justice, for [the felony] is even then punishable; but the promise and procuring of favour is good and lawful, the course of law not being delayed. By Anderson, C. J.: If there be grave suspicion, or the party be taken by a hue and cry, or with any of the goods [upon him], the Justices of the Peace should not allow bail.

Sentence

John Fortescue, knight.[1] The fault of Huntly was (1) keeping the felons five or six days in his own house without being examined, not being a Justice of the Peace, and they being felons by their own confession; (2) allowing them to hold conference with others; (3) the aiding and procuring of a composition; and (4) concealing the facts of the confession and the restoration of the money when before the two Justices. And for all these things, he was sentenced by him [Fortescue] to be imprisoned '*de course*' and to pay a fine of £500. The three Parnells were acquitted by him.

Perriam, Chief Baron, as a precedent for a case of such moment, and being better acquainted with the facts at the Assizes in the country, would have imposed a larger fine, but he agreed to £500, and imprisonment, and public confession at the Assizes in the country, and for each of the Parnells a £40 fine, imprisonment and public confession at the Assizes.

Both the Chief Justices agreed with him, and would have given a larger fine; but Lord Buckhurst, the Earl of Essex and the Lord Treasurer wished to diminish the fine (if it was not in disagreement with the former sen-

[1] The Judges in the Star Chamber gave their judgments in succession, beginning with the lowest in rank. The sentence of the majority was the sentence of the Court. See Introduction.

tence), and so did the Archbishop, since the root of the matter was not malice, corruption, subornation nor the desire of gain, and moreover they confessed the truth in everything; for the branches do favour life and honest friendship, but the blossoms the not punishing of malefactors; for a magistrate ought to punish a good man offending. But since they did not wish to disagree with the former sentence, they and the Lord Keeper agreed that Huntly should have imprisonment *de course,* a fine of £500, and should make public confession at the next Assizes, and the Parnells to be imprisoned, to pay fine of £40 each, and to make public confession at the Assizes. The Archbishop: *Ignorantia juris non excusat a toto sed a tanto.*

In a motion that one who was now discharged should be newly committed on another affidavit, the Court ordered that he should not be newly committed in the same matter, on a new affidavit, whether of the same person or of another. Motion

On a motion of the poor men of Denby in Wales, appearing here by process for riots, it was ordered that they should be dismissed, although it was certified by Baron Ewins[1] that the matter was meet to be heard in this Court; for the Council of the Marches in Wales has power to hear and determine the riots there; and this was agreed to by the whole Court. The case of the men of DENBIGH — Riot

And in the former case [Huntly's] it was laid down by Anderson, C. J., that before the time of Henry VII., felons could not be bailed. And the Lord Treasurer[2] reported a case, in the time of Edward VI., where the then Master of the Rolls, being an evil man, and having a quean or whore who robbed him, complained to the Chief Justice, then Mountague;[3] and the concubine carried the money back and placed it behind a door, and a man-servant of the HUNTLY'S case. [p. 15]

[1] Mathew Ewens, appointed one of the Barons of the Exchequer February 1, 1594. Foss.

[2] Sir William Cecil, appointed July 1572.

[3] Edward Montagu, Chief Justice of the Common Pleas.

1595 Oct. 10 Master of the Rolls took it, and the concubine besought the Master of the Rolls to be content, and so he certified to Justice Mountague that he had his money back, and Mountague was satisfied. But afterwards, Mountague, in the hearing of the said William Cecil, Lord Treasurer, besought Edward VI. for his pardon for the concubine and the servant, who had escaped.

In Camera Stellata, 28 Januarij, an° Elizab. Reginae 38, coram consilio ibidem, termino Hillarij. An° Do^{ni} 1595.[1]

1595-6 Jan. 28

POOLE *v.* KNEVET — Riot

Serjeant Drewe, the Queen's Serjeant, moved first in a case of Poole *v.* Sir Robert Knevet, where the hearing of two bills for divers riots had been stayed for the determination of a matter in law touching the title to the land, and that matter having now been tried, he moved to have a hearing for both bills, which depended on each other ; he was referred to the two Chief Justices.

ATT.-GEN. *v.* THROGMORTON and others

Kuke,[2] the Queen's Attorney, informed against one Throgmorton, esquire, Justice of the Peace for Gloucestershire, and three clerks, for deceit in presenting to an advowson of the Queen's. And he preferred articles against Throgmorton for him to be examined upon, and this was granted by the Court. One of the clerks went to the Bishop of Gloucester, and advised him to admit no one, for within fourteen days he would procure the warrant of the Lord Keeper for his own admittance, and in the meantime he appealed in the [Court of] Arches, to the prejudice of the Queen's title. The Attorney moved for a stay of the suit in the [Court of] Arches, and for a trial of the deceit, which was granted by the Court. But the Archbishop doubted if this Court could stay proceedings in the [Court of] Arches.

GRESHAM *v.* MARKHAM and BOOTHE

The Attorney moved again in the case of Dame Gresham *v.* Markham, junior, and Boothe,[3] both of whom

[1] Eight Councillors were present. [2] Sir Edward Coke.
[3] See p. 22, 29, 64.

were sentenced in this Court last term, and five forged deeds were condemned, one of which deeds is now in the hands of the said Markham. He [the Attorney] moved for the delivery of this deed, and for the examination of Markham and Boothe on interrogatories touching a letter penned [*sic*] by Boothe and written by Markham to the Attorney-General. For the closing of this matter Boothe had offered the Attorney 1000 'angelles' within certain days now last passed.

[p. 16]

LITTLETON and PARKER *v.* LORD DUDLEY and others

Riot, &c.

Phillips opened cause of hearing between Littleton and Parker, plaintiffs, and Lord Dudley and 68 others [defendants] for three riots and one misdemeanor; the first riot was in taking the beasts of the plaintiffs, with force and weapons, 'gunnes, bowes, & javelins;' the second and third riots in chasing them from one county to another by night with a multitude of armed men; and the misdemeanor in rescuing the said beasts from the bailiffs of the Sheriff when they came to replevy the beasts, &c.

Heskins for the defendants opened the cause as above, but alleged pardon for the riot, if riot it be, by the general pardon of 25 Elizabeth,[1] for the supposed riots were made in the 28 Elizabeth, on the 17th, 18th, and 19th days of October, and in the said pardon is only one exception material to this point, [namely,] "Excepted oute of this generall pardon all offences, contempts, disorders, couens, frauds, deceits and misdemeanors whatsoeuer heretofore committed by any person or persons, & whereof & for the wch any suite by bil, plaint or informacyon at any time wthin 4 yeres next before the last day of this present session of parliament is or shalbe commenced or exhibited in the Court of Starre Chamber at Westminster, & shalbe there the same laste daye of this session of parliamente dependinge." The Parliament commenced the 19th of February, A^{o} R. Elizabeth 35 [1593], and was dissolved on the 10th of April following. The riot was made 34 Elizabeth,[2] and a bill

[1] *Sic*, but appears to be a mistake for '35.' See pp. 34, 41.

[2] There seems to be some uncertainty about the date.

1595–6
Jan. 28

was preferred in December before the session of Parliament, and process issued in Hilary Term, before the Parliament, but returnable in Easter Term, after the dissolution of the Parliament. The question was if this bill was pending or not. By Popham, Chief Justice: If process was returned and so prosecuted with effect, it would have relation to the beginning. Anderson, [C. J.,] thought otherwise. The matter was referred to them.

Report by the Judges that it is pending *a principio*

Att.-Gen. *v.* Harward

Forgery

The Attorney-General, Serjeant Yelverton, and Fuller opened a cause for hearing between the Queen's Attorney, plaintiff, and Thomas Harward of Alborough in Norfolk, gentleman, for forgery in this manner. One Clement Harward, being seised of certain manors in Norfolk, devised them by writing to his wife for life, remainder to Robert Harward his nephew and the heirs male of his body, remainder to his niece and the heirs male of her body, and other remainders over, with divers legacies; and he gave nothing to Thomas Harward, who was not akin to him. Thomas Harward, seeing this testament, forged one in writing, limiting the land to the wife of Clement Harward for life, and an annuity of £20 to himself for life [*pur touts jours*],[1] with remainder of the lands to himself, and remainders over, &c. And so it was forgery in him. The defendant had an adjournment until the next day for his answer, and then forfeited his recognisance, with two sureties, by not appearing. The Attorney moved, and it was resolved by the whole Court, that if a man, in his illness, shall declare his will verbally touching his goods, and it is written out after his death, it is valid as to goods but not as to land. (Also if he write his intentions on the wall with a coal [query: *s'il escrie . . . . sur le walle oue un colle*]. The addition of two letters, 'C. H.,' to a testament after the death of the testator is forgery.)[2] The Attorney was of opinion that if anyone after the death of a man intestate should write a

[1] '*Pur an pur terme del vie del feme,*' erased. [2] In the margin

will dealing with his land, and should publish it, affirming it to be the intent of the intestate, that this would be forgery. But Phillips denied this, and it was doubted by others. End of this day.

[p. 17]

1595-6 Jan. 30

In Camera Stellata, 30 Januarij 38 Elizabeth [1595-6], coram consilio predicto, excepto Johanne Fortescue. B. de Londres fuit present ore.

GRESHAM v. MARKHAM and BOOTHE

Kuke, Attorney-General, moved in the case of Dame Gresham against Boothe and Markham junior,[1] touching a deed which the Court had ordered to be delivered up and cancelled, and which deed Markham had not yet delivered up, and for the non-delivery, and touching a letter penned by Boothe and written and sent by Markham to the said Attorney; and for this they were both committed [to be kept] close prisoners. "For," [said] the Lord Treasurer, "prisons are ordained for two reasons, the one for safe custody, and the other for correction." And the Court agreed that a forged deed can be cancelled by the order of this Court, even if the forger be not known, as in Sir Gilbert Gerard's case.

EARL OF PEMBROKE v. BARTLETT and others

It was moved by the Earl of Pembroke *v.* Sir Henry Bartlet, that whereas it was ordered by the Court that Sir H. Bartlet and divers others should pay the costs, when the Earl came to levy the costs he was resisted by force by Sir H. Bartlet and others. It was ordered that Sir H. Bartlet should make answer to this Court in person; for it was agreed that every one ought to have notice of the orders of this Court, and if any be grieved thereby, he should seek a remedy in the Court, and not resist the order, for this is a contempt.

ATT.-GEN. v. HARWARD

The former cause on the information of the Queen's Attorney against Thomas Harwood[2] was answered by

[1] See pp. 22, 26, 64. See also Appendix II.
[2] *Sic*; 'Harward' before. See p. 28.

1595-6 Jan. 30

Phillips and Serjeant Healle. And they endeavoured to disprove the evidence of Winter by divers circumstances, one as to accusing himself to a woman, which was incredible to the Lords that any man should accuse himself to a woman, and which was impossible to be believed. And finally they laboured to upset [*destroyer*] the bill as it lies, because the forgery is not applied to any estate certain, and the name of the lands is not certainly mentioned and [relying] on Diar, 12 Elizabeth, which was denied to be law.[1] Moreover the forgery was read as forgery at Common Law, which was before any Statute; and it was found that the lands were certainly named in the bill; and so they proceeded to sentence, which was agreed upon by all the Lords with one consent. Anderson first: It is a forgery in Harward, and therefore he is to be fined £500, and to be imprisoned during the Queen's pleasure, and to lose his two ears on the pillory. And they insist principally on this that as the said forged will follows in every respect the true will to the end, it proves that he had seen and read the true will before he published the forged one. Therefore it is well for every one to have good advice and very good witnesses if he wish to write or interpose any article in a will after the death of the testator; for it ought to be annexed as a codicil and not written in the will itself; and Ordinaries ought to have special care to receive special proof in the probate of wills. The Earl of Essex agreed with the sentence of the Court, and the rather, because a wise man, many hundred years before he sat in this place, complained of the injuriousness of the times (*quedam homines magis anulis quam animis*) that men, through their ill-governance of themselves, give more credence and faith to men's writings than to their words, and so it is to this day. Therefore the intentions of an evil man should be here examined, and he should be judged accordingly, and all magistrates ought to examine the intentions of men in their offences, and the ignorance of fact and the feebleness of the party, and so to punish evil intentions.

Sentence

[p. 18]

[1] Sir John Marvin's case, Dyer's Reports, fo. 288 a.

In Camera Stellata, 4° Februarij, 38 Elizabeth, [1595–6], coram consilio ibidem.[1] 1595–6 Feb. 4

The first motion was by the Queen's Attorney and Serjeant Yelverton, which was referred again to Lord Anderson, since the suggestion was false that he had not leisure to hear the cause, for he had heard [it] these three days. Motion

It was moved by the Lord Keeper on a letter sent to him by the Archbishop of York about a bill preferred in this Court for a perjury committed before them[2] at York; the question was if they could determine this at York; and it was agreed by the Judges that this Court could determine all perjuries in the whole of England, and Wales had an act of parliament to try perjuries, but it was doubted if they of York could. Therefore it was referred to the Judges; but it was agreed by the whole Court that the Star Chamber has jurisdiction for perjury committed before them of York. Motion

PETTIE v. JAMES and others — Perjury

It was moved by Phillips in the case of Dr. James. One Pettie had preferred a bill for perjury and subornation against Dr. James, Chancellor of Dorsette, the Archdeacon,[3] two ministers, the constables and churchwardens, for presenting that he held company with an ill woman, and for this he was twice convicted and punished; and the Chancellor bound him in £20 not to enter her house without honest company, and that this was contrary to the law, and that they, by virtue of their offices, had extorted more than three subsidies, &c. The honesty of the defendants was certified by divers grave and wise men, of great authority and known to the Court. And as to this slanderous bill, the Court, upon motion without demurrer (because this Court has no jurisdiction over those things not determinable here), sentenced the plaintiff to a fine of £200. But upon some

[1] Seven Councillors were present.
[2] This refers to the Court at York held before the Council of the North.
[3] There is no Chancellor of Dorset; Chancellor of Bristol and Archdeacon of Dorset are probably meant.

1595-6
Feb. 4

They reported a bad bill, and imposed a fine of 500*l.*, and pillory and public confession at the Assizes

doubts, the bill was referred to be considered by the Judges, and to seek for precedents for this, and if it was ruled as before in Sir Christopher Hatton's days,[1] when one Darrell, counseller at law, was committed to the Fleet, then one Mullinaxe in this case was to be disbarred for seven years and debarred from all practice, for putting his name to this bill. And it was ordered that no one but a Reader of an Inn of Court should put his hand to any bill in this Court. The Queen's Attorney moved that one Phillips should be allowed, who was a very great practiser in Chancery and here, and in good favour, but it was not to be admitted, although he was elected Reader at the Middle Temple in Lent following.

ATT.-GEN. *v.* GRESHAM and others

The Queen's Attorney informed against William Gresham of Norfolk, Justice of the Peace, and divers others, for that they, in 36 Elizabeth [1593–4], when men were being mustered there, did take money to discharge certain men when they were pressed for service, and to appoint others in their places; but the Court stayed the proceedings against Gresham for this day. And the others have Counsel at the bar who speak 'coldely,' for that the Lord Keeper would not allow what they wished, which was to avoid the information under the statutes of 2 Edward VI.,[2] and 4 Philip and Mary,[3] because [the defendants] are not captains, petty captains, nor lieutenants, nor have they charge of the men. [p. 19] But the Attorney informed at Common Law, on the 27th Book of Assizes the last article of the charge of Justices in Eyre at Kingeston[4] and on this he proceeded. The depositions[5] of the witnesses were written and made at the charge of the Attorney, but he said that afterwards the Queen would make allowance for this. And he read a sage speech of the princely care of the Queen for the peace of her realm and respecting the

[1] He died 1591.
[2] 2 and 3 Edw. VI. cap. 2: An Act for the Reformation of Captains and Soldiers serving in the Wars.
[3] 4 and 5 P. and M., cap. 3: An Act for the Taking of Musters.
[4] Folio 139, edition 1580.
[5] *Liuers.*

danger of such offences, which weakened the forces of the kingdom and made the people mutinous, &c. Lord Buckhurst greatly commended the Attorney for his fealty and trouble in finding these offenders in his native country,[1] where he [Lord Buckhurst] had great alliances and friends, and he encouraged him [Coke] by humble petition to continue on such a course, which was very good service to the Queen and her realm; and the Lord Keeper likewise. But the Earl of Essex inveighed with great force against such offences, which to him are more odious in the petty-officers and servants [*sic*; ? serjeants] than in magistrates and masters; and in commendation of the vigilance and policy in the governance of Her Majesty, [he said] this Island is more defensive by itself and has more uses of all warlike instruments than any Christian nation; moreover we do not hire foreign soldiers, but we are a defence in ourselves. Therefore the offence is the more grievous in this, that the liege and free people of this realm are sold like cattle in a market, to the great grief of Her Majesty, who regards more the love of her subjects and their good estate [? *bone safe*] than her own honour and revenues; and so it is true, as the Athenians said, *inuicti erimus quia insularii*, &c. Therefore he wished to impose a greater fine when prosecuted [?]; and if any of those that he himself had preferred (since he had preferred many 'captaines, liutenants, muster-makers and others that have charge of men') have offended in this manner, he wished, if the law allowed, to prosecute [*pursue*] them to death. The Bishop of London agreed with the Court, but he said that this [was] as the battle of the lion going before to the spoil, and the foxes, tigers, and wolves following after. The fine was imposed first by Sir John Fortescue, and allowed by the whole Court. Sentence

Funtstone, attorney at law, and Hammon, constable, fine 200 marks. [£133 13*s*. 4*d*.]

Botly, fine £100.

Browne, fine £100.

[1] *I.e.* county. Coke was born at Mileham, co. Norfolk, February 1, 1551–2. Foss.

1595–6 Feb. 4

Newarke, fine £40.
Clere, fine £100.
Sego [or Sege], fine £40.
Henarde, fine £20.
Freeman, fine £20.

And all were adjudged imprisonment during the Queen's pleasure, restitution of all parcels which they had taken, at the public assizes at Norfolk next ensuing, and public confession of their faults there, the deposing of the constables from their office, and confession and restitution [to be made] in the public place where the county elects such officers.

[p. 20] 1595–6 Feb. 6

In Camera Stellata, vj° Februarij, An° Elizab. R^nae^ 38, coram consilio ibidem.[1]

LITTLETON and PARKER v. EARL OF DUDLEY

The previous bill of Litleton and Parker, plaintiffs, and Lord Dudley, defendant,[2] was certified by the Judges to be sufficient, and therefore sentence was now [given]. The charges were two riots and a misdemeanour, in this manner, Lord Dudley assembled 300 men, of whom 69 have answered, and they drove 320 sheep and divers other cattle, belonging to the said Litleton, to the castle of Dudley, which is in Staffordshire, the town of Dudley is in another county,[3] and kept them there; Litleton afterwards replevied them, and Lord Dudley rescued them and assembled 400 men with 'pikes, bowes, staues, wth jauelins and other weapons, and at 4 a clocke in the nighte in October,' drove the said beasts 9 miles to a market; and because they could not sell them, they drove them back again with 600 men in all, and Lord Dudley himself with them. Lord Dudley made answer that a patent was made to the Earl of Northumberland in 1 Henry VI that he should have all outlaws' goods within his Castle of Dudley, and he seized Litleton's goods because he was outlawed, and in truth they were not Litleton's goods, save as executor of another. The Queen's Attorney said that

[1] Eight Councillors were present.
[2] See pp. 27, 41.
[3] Worcestershire.

the said patent was re-assumed in 22 Henry VI. The Lord Treasurer said that the answer could not be held good, for Lord Paget's case was similar and was adjudged bad.[1] Therefore, it was of no consequence, and he, with much vehemence, held him to the matter in question and contained within the depositions.[2] The other defendants answered that Lord Dudley commanded them, being his tenants and allies, to assist him to apprehend hunters in his chase, and they did not know otherwise, and no assault or affray was made. But Lord Dudley and all the others were fined for both riots and the misdemeanour, by Sir John Fortescue and the Chief Justice and the Chief Baron a larger sum, and by the Lord Treasurer and his son,[3] a lesser sum, because they knew his estate, and a broken Latin word intrudes in an estate *saluo sibi contenemento suo.*

But the Lord Chief Baron on the contrary, "If he has not the means let him pay with his body," and, "The greater the man the greater the punishment as an example to others;" and the riot was such as has not been heard of in the Queen's time, and the most part of the rioters were 'naylors,' to wit, '*minors de Coles,*' who live all their days in drink [*en boyer*], and if they were assaulted we know not what would follow, and *ignorantia juris non excusat a toto sed a tanto,* and they did wrong in obeying their lord and doing this unlawful act; and it is a rout if they assemble with weapons, and a riot if they do an unlawful act. Therefore let the servant beware how he perform his master's wish in unlawful acts, for the servant himself shall be punished.

So the Court disagreed as to the fine, the Lord Chief Justice and the others being for the greater fine, and the Lord Treasurer and his son for the lesser; but Lord Buckhurst, the Archbishop and the Lord Keeper agreed on a sum between the two, and this was the sentence of the Court:— Sentence
Lord Dudley for the first riot [to pay a fine of] 500 marks,

[1] The text is obscure, but this seems to be the meaning. See Dyer's Reports, folios 142 a, 308 a.

[2] *Liuers.*

[3] Sir William Cecil, Lord Burghley, and Sir Robert Cecil, afterwards Earl of Salisbury.

1595-6 Feb. 6 and all the others £20, and for the misdemeanour, each £5, and for the last [riot, Lord Dudley] £500, and each of the others £20. The Lord Treasurer would have imposed fines of £300 only on Lord Dudley for everything and £5 on each of the others, and the [Lord Chief Justice and the] others would have imposed 1000 marks on Lord Dudley and £40 on the others for the first riot, and £500 [on him] and £20 on the others for the other [riot].

[p. 21]

1595-6 Feb. 11

In Camera Stellata, Feb. 11, 38 Elizabeth [1595–6], coram consilio ibidem.[1]

Att.-Gen. *v.* Nixen and others

An information was laid by the Queen's Attorney against Nixen, Pepper, Ellis, Johnson and Anglesey for counterfeiting warrants under the hands of the Lord Keeper, the Lord Treasurer, the Earl of Essex, the Lord Admiral and Sir John Wollye, for the apprehending of papists, seminaries,[2] *agnes dei* and crucifixes etc., and for conveying 'ordinaunce,'[3] and for receiving money, and thus having collected divers sums and deceived the Queen's people. Nixen and Pepper have lost their ears for such offences by a former sentence of this Court. The three first have counterfeited divers warrants and affixed the hands of the Privy Councillors, and counterfeited the seal of the Lord Admiral; and they did separately [*un aper se*] inform the Lord Admirall that they could do good service to the realm and would detect one another; and the Lord Admiral suffered them to practise together, and promised them each a reward for detecting and apprehending the other, and so suffered them to go at large, which was not lawful in him, for he should have arrested them, and then procured one to detect and apprehend the other, and not suffered them to practise. Johnson was detected that he and Anglesey (by the coercion of Johnson), counterfeited the Privy Councillors' hands, and caused himself to be [made] captain, and forged a warrant for the lodging and main-

[1] Eleven Councillors were present.
[2] Seminary priests.
[3] That is, 'ordnance.'

tenance of divers men ; and because the Mayor of Lancaster refused to lodge them, he boxed his ears [*il done luy blowe del eare*]. The other three, wearing on their breasts a box with the Queen's arms as poursuivant [*purseuaunt*] within Lancashire, did threaten a priest that he had burnt a child in an oven, and for this he agreed with them and gave them £5. No evidence was produced of these matters, but all were confessed by the accused on their examination before the Attorney and the Solicitor. And so they went to sentence :—

It is agreed by the whole Court that this is a great and 'heynous' offence, and worthy to be punished with death ; and thus in the last parliament a bill was passed in the Upper House to make this felony, but the parliament being at an end, [the bill] was not made absolute. For this [offence] is the most dangerous mischief that can be, and the party cannot be satisfied for the offence against him and cannot have knowledge of it ; as the Lord Treasurer said, If my house be robbed, that is my fault, and if my horse be stolen, that is the fault of my horse-keeper, but of the counterfeiting of my hand and seal, I cannot have knowledge, and by this he may deprive me of my life. As [it happened] in the time of Edward VI., one [1] wrote divers blanks in recommendation of his secretary to the King of France, and subscribed them, and in one the secretary accused his master of treason to the King, and for this he would have died if he had not found his secretary, who confessed. And as to the counterfeiting of the hands of the Lord Treasurer, one has borrowed £100 from a merchant in Italy, and he [2] and the Lord Admiral have paid £20 to a merchant in Antwerpe for money borrowed from him on the counterfeit signatures. And so they were condemned by the whole Court. They were taken by Topcliffe, the public prosecutor of recusants and seminaries. The sentence was that Nixen, Pepper and [p. 22] Ellis should stand on the pillory and lose their ears if they Sentence have any, and be branded on the forehead with the letter

[1] Blank in MS. [2] The Lord Treasurer is still speaking.

1595–6 Feb. 11

F, and be condemned perpetually to the galleys; Johnson the same; but Anglesey (inasmuch as he wrote the names of the councillors through fear of a stab from Johnson), pillory and imprisonment for one year only. The Lord Treasurer moved that, inasmuch as such burnings in the ears and hands die out in a short time, they should be scarified on the balls of the cheeks with the letter F by a surgeon, and that some powder be put there to colour it, so that it would never vanish. But the others made no reply to this.

1595–6 Feb. 13

In Camera Stellata, Feb. 13, 1595 [1595–6], coram consilio ibidem.[1]

Motions

This was the day for motions, one peremptory and the other of the Serjeants, according to their precedence [*en antiquitye*]; but before the commencement of the Court in the Inner Chamber, Sir Richard Martin and a jury of goldsmiths brought their 'picktes'[2] to show the coins made two years before. And the Lords allowed the 'pictures,'[3] and the moneys, and also the trials of the metals, and there they stayed[4] till after dinner. It was then ordered that for every motion made on the last day of term, each motioner—that is, each Counsellor who makes a motion—shall pay 12*d.*, to be collected by the usher for the poor prisoners in the Fleete; and this was granted on the motion of Lord Buckhurst and Sir John Fortescue. And it was ordered that every one who is committed by this court shall not be suffered to go at large, and for this purpose Mr. Milles, the Clerk of the Court, was enjoined to go to the Fleete, and to view the prisoners committed there by this Court. It was ordered also on the motion of the whole Court that interrogatories shall be annexed to each commission that is issued, for the non-doing of this is the cause of great and frequent perjury; but when the commission is merely to have and take an answer, there shall

Trial of the Pix

Collection for poor prisoners

Interrogatories

[1] Nine Councillors were present.

[2] *I.e.* pix. Sir Richard Martin was Warden of the Mint.

[3] *Sic.*

[4] Query, *murront* for *demurront.*

be no interrogatories annexed, for they cannot be made before answer is given.

Order as to empty room

It was also ordered by the Lord Keeper that the empty room at the East side of the Court, 'of late inclosed wth a doore,' shall be reserved for men of good account in the country and for gentlemen 'towardes the lawe,' and shall not be plagued [*pester*] with 'base fellowes' and women or other suitors, as it has been.

PAULET *v.* PORTMAN

A long motion was made between the Lady Paullet and Sir Hughe Portman (who was made a knight when the Queen was at the Lord Keeper's house at Cewe [1]) for the publishing of two testimonies [*tesmoignes*], but for certain reasons the Court decreed that they should not be published.

1596 April 29

In Camera Stellata, 29 April, 1596, 38 Elizabeth, coram consilio ibidem.[2]

ATT.-GEN. *v.* SMITHE

Slanderous news

Kuke, the Queen's Attorney, moved against three for slanderous words against the Lord Admiral and the Earl of Essexe, but he proceeded only against one Smithe, on his confession, 'for spreadinge sclaunderous newes.' He laid his information under the statutes of 3 Edward I and Philip and Mary,[3] and [said] that without law [4] the Councillors could punish these offences in this Court at their discretion. Smithe had confessed that he, being a [p. 23] pressed soldier at Dover, and the news being there that the Spaniards were on the sea (which was false, for they were Hollanders and friends of the Queen), they were 'shipte,' bu as it turned out to be 'Grave Morris' [5] they were dismissed; and he came to London, and reported that the news was throughout the soldiers that the Lord Admiral's 'shippe

[1] Sir John Puckering, the Lord Keeper, entertained Queen Elizabeth at his house at Kew, December 13, 1595. (Foss.)

[2] Nine Councillors were present.

[3] Stat. 3 Edw. I. cap. 34: 'None shall report slanderous News whereby Discord may arise.' Stat. 1 and 2 Philip and Mary, cap. 3.

[4] Statute-law apparently is meant.

[5] Prince Maurice, Governor of the United Provinces.

1596 April 29

beinge searchte by th'erle of Essexe & openinge divers barrelles, wherein he supposed to haue bene gunpowder, he fownde ashes, duste & sande, & therevpon he Called him Traitor, and so theye Came bothe to the Cowrte, & there th'erle of Essexe & th'erle of Cumberlande before the Queene tooke the Lord Admiralle by the Berde & sayde "ah thou Traytor"; & this Smithe, traueylinge by Windsor, Called at the howse of a Justice of peace thereby for drinke, and reportinge the like there, was by the gentleman himselfe apprehended, for wch he was greately Commended; & Smithe was

Sentence

sentenced *per totam Curiam* to loose one of his eares vpon the pillorie at Westminster, the other at Windsor, to be whipped, & to haue a paper one his heade Contayning the wordes, & imprisoned duringe pleasure, & fined 20^li^, wch showlde haue bene farre greater but for his baseness, beinge a peasante & a boye. The Lo. Keeper, then Sr Joh. Puckringe, Cowld not be presente lyinge daungerousely sicke of a deade palsye.'[1]

AMISLOE'S case

The same day, four were sentenced to fines of £5 each and imprisonment for a riot made against one Amisloe, plaintiff, *per totam curiam*.

RIDGLY'S case

Ridgly, plaintiff, against others, for perjury in these words: 'He procured 4 to depose that there was suche a lease paroll agreede vpon at midsommer to beginne at Mich. followinge, in deposinge whereof &c., they haue committed periurye.' 1. It was moved by Phillipps that these words were not sufficient to charge him, because he had not said 'they did depose'; and so it seemed to the Judges. 2. Another thing that they have deposed that the said lease was sealed at Michaelmas, and so it is doubtful if it should be called 'lease' at the first agreement or not; it was agreed that it should be, for as the minister vouches and says in 'le Common praier booke' that 'I take thee &c. for my wyfe from this daye forwarde &c.' and neverthe-

[1] He died April 30, 1596. He was succeeded in the office of Lord Keeper by Sir Thomas Egerton, the Master of the Rolls.

less that day is a day of matrimony joined. But this was referred to Lord Anderson.

In Camera Stellata, Wednesday, May 12, Easter Term, 38 Elizabeth, 1596, coram consilio ibidem.[1] 1596 May 12

It was moved on a new matter in Lord Dudlye's case, before sentenced, that the offences were pardoned, but inasmuch as this was moved at the [former] hearing, and it was then resolved that they were not pardoned, it prevailed nothing.[2] LORD DUDLEY'S case

Cause of hearing between Susan Tilman, widow, plaintiff, and Edmond Tilman and Richarde Glover, defendants. The case was for the forgery of a deed by Robert Tilman, and maintenance by Richard Glover by presenting a cause in Chancery on a letter received from his friend. There was no proof of the forgery, but probabilities, presumptions, absurdities and inducements; which were opened and answered briefly; but because they were not large [?], it was ordered that the trial should be at common law as to the deed, and then this Court would proceed to sentence. Agreed to *per totam curiam.* TILMAN *v.* TILMAN and GLOVER — Forgery [p. 24]

Pardon for offences should be pleaded and shown in Court.

The Queen's Attorney informed against Robert Fisher for unnatural usage of his father, and for heretical and execrable words ('that Christe was no sauioure & the gospell a fable'), for forging an order in the Chancery to gain possession and rent to himself, and interposing defendants for plaintiffs, and [forging] the Register's hand to this, '& for wearing of dagges,[3] & comminge to Sergeaunte Healle & Mr. Crewe (being of counsell againste him) with dagges charged. For the forginge of th' order he was sentenced *per totam curiam,* imprisonmente,' till he ATT.-GEN. *v.* FISHER — Sentence

[1] Eight Councillors were present.
[2] See pp. 27, 34.
[3] A kind of pistol.

1596 May 12

find good sureties for his good behaviour, and £100 fine, 'to stande vpon the pillorye wth a paper, his eares not nailled; & for wearing of dagges, a fine of xx^{li}; For wearing of them *in terrorem populi dominae Reginae* is punished by the lawes, excepte it be the Quene's ministers.' For the insolence to his father he was pardoned, otherwise it is punishable here; but for his blasphemous heresy (since this Court has no jurisdiction in this matter), it was referred to the Archbishop to punish severely. And although there was not much testimony, yet by his outrage and impudence he was condemned. And, as the Lord Treasurer said, He who is once evil in the highest degree is always presumed to be evil, and [this man's] previous acts and subsequent life declare his impiety. [*Qui semel est malus in summo gradu semper presumitur esse malus, et ante acta et subsequens vita declare son impiousenes.*]

1596 May 19

In Camera Stellata, 19 May, Wednesday, Eliz. 38, Easter Term [1596].[1]

MARBERY v. CLARKE and others — Riot, &c.

There was a case of riot and maintenance, 'crossebilles,' Marbery against Clarke, Fishe, Jolde and others, of 'Barkeshire.' Phillippes and others for Marbery, Serjeant Healle and Hitchecocke for Clarke and the others. The manner of the riot was in a 'warrenne' of 'Cunnies,'[2] belonging to Marbery, which he held of the Queen. Clarke and others of the town pretended there was a custom to kill conies there, and this they did. Marbery coming to them, they delivered to him the Sheriff's warrant by one of his men, and he [Marbery] tore this, (which was greatly disliked by the Court,) although they told him that it was a warrant for his arrest; and afterwards they delivered another warrant to him, and so arrested him. In departing from them, he was struck and beaten and wounded with 'long pike, staffe, bowe and arrowes, sworde and tarket, &c.' Whereupon a cry was raised by the women, as Marbery was being carried to his house wounded, and his men coming

[1] Six Councillors were present.

[2] Conies.

up, he said "Kill them, kill them;" which speech the Court considered proceeded from 'choller & paine.' And so *per curiam* Clarke and Fishe were each fined £20 with imprisonment. The Lord Keeper [1] differed from the whole Court in his sentence, in aggravating the punishment, though this did not alter the sentence, as he said. He condemned the riot the more for the arrest, because they made the Queen's writ a colour for the execution of their malicious force; and the Sheriff was greatly blamed because he gave notice to Marbery of the writ against him, and then took his promise for his appearance, and did not arrest him, contrary to his oath. Hitchecocke [2] was sharply rebuked all day by the Lord Keeper, with such words as these—"you must goe to schoole to learne more wytte, you are not well advysed, you forgette yor place, & to be plaine, it is a lye;" and this because he enforced certain things contrary to, or not agreeing with, the depositions,[3] and very often he enforced matter which he conceived to make for him, but which was considered by the Court to be contrary to, and against, him. And it was adjudged that it was not maintenance for one person to prosecute a cause in the name of a town. Sentence

[p. 25]

Case of SPILMAN, SIMPSON, and others

Perjury

Another cause was moved as to a perjury against Spilman, 'iueller,'[4] Simpson, 'goldesmithe,' and others. Counsel supposed Spilman to be perjured as to the value of a silver fountain delivered to him. But as the estimation of this was dubious and diverse in each man's intelligence, and, as the Lord Keeper said, "A countryman would esteem and have more use for a whetstone than a diamond," and so [the plaintiff] was dismissed to have a trial at common law; and if an action on the statute would not lie at common law, then to receive trial here. Bill dismissed

[1] At this time Sir Thomas Egerton.

[2] One of the counsel for the defendants.

[3] *Liuers.*

[4] Probably John Spilman, the Queen's Goldsmith. In 1587 he was commissioned to provide all sorts of gold, jewels, diamonds, pearls, rubies, and other precious stones, and to take up diamond cutters, ruby cutters, agate cutters and other workmen, at her Majesty's prices. State Papers, Domestic, Eliz., vol. ccii. No. 43. In 1588 he had a paper-mill, where he employed German labour. *Ibid.* vol. ccxvii. No. 70.

1596
May 21

In Camera Stellata, Friday, 21 May, Easter Term, Elizabeth 38, [1596], coram consilio ibidem.[1]

ATT.-GEN. *v.* KINGE

Slander of the Lord Admiral

The Queen's Attorney, then Koke of the Inner Temple, informed against one Robert Kinge for words confessed by him against the Lord Admiral, to wit, that he had heard two persons say 'in Fleetestreete dialougewise that my Lo: Admirall was come to the Courte & prooued himselfe a traitor, and his barrelles of gunpowder were mixte wth sande'; which two supposed men were defendants in this Court, and the said Robert Kinge was solicitor in the cause against them in a bill touching a deed supposed to forged; and moreover he had procured articles or interrogatories to be written by Fuller, a Counsellor of 'Graies inne,' his man, and perused by him and subscribed with his hand, one of which articles was, if any 'did knowe my Lorde Admiralle to be a traitor, yea or no; a thinge never hearde of before, that a man of so great commaunde vnder her Ma[tie], so honorablye discended,[2] so trulye noble & of so worthye deserte, showld be lefte of recorde for euer that it was examyned in this Cowrte whether he were a true subiecte or no; a Course never hearde of before, & *ideo* worthy of the greater punishemente.' And for these offences the said Kinge was sentenced *per totam curiam* 'to loose both his eares vpon the pillorie, to be whipped, & imprisoned till he Could finde good suertye for his good behauioure, & fined 500 markes if he be of abilitye to paye it.' By the Attorney, No man is to report such news without good proof, and to no one save such as have authority to examine them and to punish, and every one who reports such news without his author and proof of it, shall be imprisoned and punished at the discretion of this Court. The article interposed and perused by Fuller was *per totam curiam* greatly disliked, and Fuller was 'notoriouselye rebuked' by all, and of this the Lord Chamberlain would acquaint the Queen, and the Lord Admiral may have his action against him; and Fuller

Sentence

[1] Eight Councillors were present.

[2] Sir Charles Howard, second Baron Howard of Effingham, was Lord Admiral at this time.

was ordered to attend at the 'counsell table' after dinner to know their pleasure. By the Lord Keeper, '"Fuller of all lawyers was the worste,"' and in this he showed no discretion, to write his hand to articles that he had not perused, which was his excuse, contrary to the oath of the party. *Sed quid sequitur nescio.* All the Court agreed that the punishment of Kinge would be juster if it had been much greater, and by the Lord Keeper, "The laws of Edgar and Ethelbert, kings of this land before the Conquest, were that a slanderer should lose his tongue, which would have been a just judgment for this person. And among the Lidians there was a law that the slanderer should be put to great torture and then put to death. And in this Court one was pilloried and fined for a slander on Sir John Fitzjames, Chief Justice of England,[1] a place [office] much inferior to that of the Admiral of England. And another was pilloried for slandering Sir Roger Chalmeley, Recorder of London;[2] and another for slandering a Bishop's Chancellor." Ruled *per curiam* that there cannot be a bill in this Court for the perjury of witnesses in a cause depending in this Court, before the cause be heard and sentenced; And a bill so preferred was dismissed with costs. Rule of Court

There was another case of perjury heard, but the parties were acquitted; and the Master of the Hospital at 'Knightes bridge'[3] (who was the plaintiff) was deposed from his place and fined for costs. For, it was laid down by the Judges, that this Court, in its discretion, may in such cases assess costs, as the Court may by statute in the cases of those who are non-suited in actions at common law. The Lord Keeper made delivery of his conceit for solicitors, and he said that he had not learned 'any lawe to allowe or to warrante them,' and that they are 'caterpillers *del common weale*,' [p. 26] MASTER OF KNIGHTS-BRIDGE HOSPITAL pl. Perjury

[1] He was appointed Chief Justice of the King's Bench in 1526, and retired in 1539. Foss.

[2] Sir Roger Cholmley was elected Recorder in 1535, and held the office for ten years. Foss.

[3] An ancient lazar-house or hospital. Among the records belonging to the Dean and Chapter of Westminster, is a state of the Lazar-house at Knightsbridge, as drawn up in the year 1595 by John Glassington, who was governor of the house. Mon. Aug., VI., 766. This John Glassington is probably the Master referred to in the text.

1596 May 21 and maintenance would lie against them; for at all times the laws and acts of Parliament give authority in cases necessary to make attornies, and therefore solicitors are not warrantable by any law, and therefore they should be punished and a remedy should be provided against them; and he promised that he would advise as to punishment against them and to abolish and extirpate all solicitors. He gave notice to the Counsellors that he would hear causes in this Court after dinner. And so he appointed two hours for motions only.

1596 May 25 **In Camera Stellata,** 25 Maij, Elizab. 38, termino paschae, 1596, le prochein ioure apres le terme, coram consilio ibidem.[1]

Motions

This was the day for motions only, for the referring of causes, dismissions and contempts. First the Attorney-General moved, then the Serjeants, and afterwards the bar, and a favourite at any time.

Rule of Court

It was ruled by the Court to be the usage of the Court, that if one committed to close prison will not answer the Clerk of the Court when he goes to take his answer, it shall be held to be a confession, and he ought not to be examined; for the former [point], the sentence in Boothe and Markham's case,[2] and on the last point, Ascoe's and the Earl of Lincoln's case.[3] And the Counsellors who are practisers should be well advised as to what manner of bills, demurrers, answers, etc. they put their hands; for the words "I hope I shall be able to proove," ought not to be contained in any bill or such record of the Court; for the Court is to judge according to what is alleged and proved; and in demurrer, the defendant should confess the things in the bill and demur if there should be no sufficient answer, and not speak of other things of his own knowledge.

I[4] put a case. I showed a lease to one, and he took it from me, and refuses to deliver it again. The question was

[1] Eight Councillors were present.
[2] See pp. 22, 26, 29.
[3] See p. 12.
[4] John Hawarde, the writer of the MS.

if this could be examined in this Court or not. By the Lord Keeper, It cannot.

Order of Court

Because the whole day was wasted in motions for dismissions, the Lord Keeper moved an ancient order of the Court, that he would write certain orders which should be perused by the Lords Chief Justices and the Attorney-General, and then be delivered to the Clerk of the Court for his observance: that the Clerk shall, in each term, deliver the names of those causes which have not been pursued for the three terms last before, and then the party to have notice that if he [? do not] appear in Court the fourth term he shall be dismissed without motion: and for the tediousness of suits, he would have the depositions[1] of the Court abridged and the fees 'accustomably payde;' but he gave precise and strict advertisement to Counsellors at law, saying that their profession is honorable, but 'if god be not at the getting, god will not be at the spendinge;' and to Justices of the Peace, and in particular to one Sir Harry Knevet for bailing one who was not bailable according to law.

[p. 27]
1596 June 1

In Camera Stellata, die Veneris, 18 Junij, An^{o} Do^{ni} 1596, termino trinitatis, Elizab. 38, coram consilio ibidem.[2]

Att.-Gen. v. Howe and East — Cosinage

The first case was an information by the Queen's Attorney against one Howe, a broker, and Easte, a solicitor, for 'coseninge diuers yonge gentlemen,' and procuring them to enter into bonds, statutes, recognizances and confessions of action by attorney (which bound them although under age, and which could not be avoided when they came to full age), and so of the confession of some such real action within age. They procured one Richard Cage, the only son of one John Cage of London, salter, and another [3] to swear in the Chancery, that they were of full age, in this manner: the said Howe and Easte drew a bill and an answer to it, and wrote two 'councellers' names to these, without

[1] *Les bookes.* [2] Six Councillors were present. [3] Blank in MS.

1596 June 18

their knowledge, and procured Doctor Hone to write his name to the said answer; thus they condemned the gentlemen body and soul; and these 'cosiners' procured money from the 'erle Lincolne' for the said gentlemen, and a condition with promise of defeasance, and a confession of the action on this and other bargains, for a 'perle looking glasse' of £100 and 'borders' of £120, and other merchandise to the value of £600, and other 'cosinages' as appears in their confession only. For which matters they were sentenced by the whole Court to have imprisonment for a year, and to be on the pillory at Westminster, at the Temple Gate, and in Cheape side, with papers on their heads, to be whipped all through the city [1] in the four terms of the year, and fined each £20. The Lord Treasurer 'would haue those y^t^ make the playes to make a Comedie hereof, & to acte it wth these names, & gaue good Counsell to there Fathers, y^t^ when they sende there sonnes to th'innes of Cowrte to haue one or too superintendentes ouer them that maye looke ouer them, & certify there Freindes of there manner of lyuinge, as by experience he hathe knowne to be commonly vsed.' By the Lord Keeper: The sentence is just; for this is a great and common offence; great, because it concerns all the pillars of the land and commonwealth, noble and ignoble; common, because one Williamson has a 'bedrolle' [2] of all young gentlemen in the town. And so it was adjudged by all to be a 'greevous offence' and worthy of death, who robbed them body and soul.

Sentence

Ceo est Justice ut poena paucis metus omnibus perueniat

ATT.-GEN. *v.* ENSTER and EGLES — Forgery

The Attorney also informed against one Enster, a minister, and Egles, the Clerk of a Justice of the Peace, for the forging of passports:—against Enster for forging six passports, and Egles 73; which was confessed by them. They were sentenced to be pilloried at the next Assizes, to be 'whopte' in Wilteshire, and fined each £5, and imprisonment. And this order shall not affect the ecclesiastical jurisdiction over the minister, but he shall be 'disgraded' and shall lose his benefice, as was moved by the Archbishop.

Sentence

[1] *Sur toute le citye.*

[2] A beadroll or list.

The cause of hearing between the Lady Russell, plaintiff, and Lovelace and others, defendants, for riot, in this wise; the said Lady had imprisoned two men of Lovelace's in her lodge, called the Porter's Lodge, adjoining her monastery of [1], and the said Lovelace came with nine or ten men, with unusual weapons and did 'breake the doore of the porter's lodge, & wth an axe breake the stockes and take awaye the prisoners,' when the said Lady was at dinner. The cause came to hearing by confession, and the said Lovelace, being a Justice of the Peace, was present at the said riot; and for this he was fined *per curiam* £40, and imprisonment. By the Lord Keeper: If any one be imprisoned without right and tortiously, no Justice of the Peace may retake him by force on his own account[2] and without bail (if he be bailable); and for such cases there is a writ *de Homine replegiando* and *Habeas Corpus*, to remove him to some Court. And in his [the Lord Keeper's] opinion, he was not a fit or meet man to be a Justice of the Peace. By the Lord Treasurer: This Lovelace is an ungrateful man, for he and his father are greatly indebted to the said Lady and Sir Edwarde Hobbye, the chief founders of him and his ancestors. When a man comes with a good intention (for Lovelace had answered 'that he came hoping to mooue the Ladye to releasse them & consente to the breaking of the stockes wth an axe and the freeing of the prisoners') and does or consents *male agere*, this is punishable, and is an offence in him.

RUSSELL *v.* LOVELACE and others — Riot

Sentence

[p. 28]

In Camera Stellata, 23 Junii, die Mercurii, termino trinitatis, Elizab. 38, coram consilio ibidem [1596].[3]

1596 June 23

The cause of hearing between Lady Davers,[4] plaintiff, and Sir Walter Longe, Mr. Edmond Longe, procurers and comforters of a riot, and Seallman, Bosse, Hawarden, Sewell and others, defendants, for a riot, and against one Stumpe, Counsellor at Law, of the Inner Temple, for advising them,

DANVERS *v.* LONGE and others — Riot, &c.

[1] Blank in MS.

[2] *De son teste demesne.*

[3] Seven Councillors were present.

[4] See *post*, p. 61 and Appendix III. Lady Davers or Danvers was the widow of Sir John Danvers.

1596 June 23

and against one Mathewes, Coroner, for extortion and misdemeanour in his office.

The offences against Mathewes were, that he, being the Coroner, and a man being killed and 'buryed 6 or 7 weekes,' directed his precept to another Hundred and not to the Hundred where the party was wounded, nor to the Hundred where he died; and before the appearance of the Jury, he [Mathewes] went to Sir Walter Longe and had conference with him and his friends, the Coroner being his servant, and the man who was killed being his servant also, and he did not take the body 'oute of the earthe,' (which by law he ought to have done), but he examined witnesses, and returned the office *super visum corporis se defendendo*; and because the body was infectious, through 'lyinge 7 weekes in th'earthe,' he examined witnesses and caused the inquest [to be adjourned] to the Assizes, to be better advised by the Judges there, which they did.[1] But the Court [of Star Chamber], because the day was wasted, and this matter having no affinity with the riot and therefore ought to be contained in another bill, awarded that another day should be determined if, on the understanding of the said cause, the Lord Keeper should think this [cause] apt to be sentenced here, for otherwise they would acquit them.

The occasion and manner of this outrageous and great riot (now detested and abhorred and grievously punished, together with all manner of misdemeanours) was in this wise. The said Sir John Davers (otherwise called Danvers)[2], now dead, was seised of a manor in Wiltshire ; and the tenants of his manor, having a waste or common (voidable, unprofitable and overgrown with brambles and briars, and not worth twelve [? pence] each acre), and containing 100 or 120 acres, besought the said Sir John Davers to enclose this, and to grant them common in other lands. The which was accorded them, and thereupon the said Sir John, 17 years now passed, granted to the said tenants common

[1] This is not very grammatical, but seems to mean that the Coroner asked the Judges for their advice, which they gave him.

[2] He has not been mentioned before.

in other lands and the profits of a certain wood, and enclosed the said voidable common with ditches, pales and 'quicksette hedges,' and grubbed and enriched it, so that now it is worth 13s. each acre; and he continued in quiet possession of the said common for 17 years now passed without any interruption.

But the said Sir John dying, the tenants conspired together to regain this enclosed common as before, and to effect this they collected a common purse, and went to Sir Walter Longe, who advised them to go to one Stumpe, dwelling within five miles of the said common, who advised them, as they informed [the Court], to go two only together and to destroy the pales, ditches and 'quicksettes,' which they did accordingly, and two only at a time went together and laboured to destroy the hedges, &c., and then another two, [and so on] to the number of 28, with bills and spades, and no weapons, and at no time but two together, and peaceably, without any force: therefore no riot. And Sir Walter Longe, three days before, at the Assizes, said, '"You shall see the hedges, ditches & pales be pluckte downe as faste as euer they were set vp;"' and at the time when [the tenants] were doing this, he rode there (there being no high way), and said '"Well done, Masters! This is the waye. If you doe not preuayle, I will gyue you as muche lande oute of my parke;" and "Holde together, for there was neuer multitude helde together & failled of there purpose." Edmond Longe to the like effecte.' And then the tenants complained by petition to the Lords of the Privy Council, who wrote to the Justices of the Peace there to examine and certify this, which they did accordingly; and certified to the Lords a great and outrageous riot. Whereupon the Lords wrote to 'Koke, attornie generall,' to prefer a bill in this Court with care and effect, which was done accordingly. And then the tenants delivered a petition to the Queen, containing very many falsehoods and suggestions, which petition she delivered to the present Lord Keeper, and it was this day read in Court. Upon the whole matter, it appeared that there was a great riot, and

p. 29]

1596 June 23

Sir Walter Longe was the author of it: but Edmond Longe was acquitted, because he was a witness against him. Sir Walter Longe was condemned because his words were mutinous, and would give occasion to rebellion; and for this he was sentenced by the whole Court.

Sentence

Sir Walter Longe, imprisonment and £100 fine.[1] Sealmann, Bosse, Hawarden, Sewell, each £100 fine and imprisonment.

All the other tenants were fined 100 marks and imprisonment.

The Lord Keeper wished to have some exemplary punishment on those who preferred the said suggested and false petition to the Queen: 'For it is a sinne againste allmighty god to instille any vntrothe into her Matie's sacred eares, who delightes onely in truthe, & her hole care is that truthe, equitye & iustice showld be wth equalle hand ministred vnto all her subiectes, & therefore it is o^r partes to punishe these offences, & to kepe all Cawses from her sacred Matie that maye harbor disquiete thoughtes in her diuine breste.'

[p. 30] 1596 June 25

In Camera Stellata, coram consilio ibidem, 25 Junii, termino trinitatis, Elizab. 38, An° Do^ni 1596, die Veneris.[2]

There were divers causes heard, and many were not ready, such dispatch being unexpected, and such causes in which the plaintiffs were not ready were dismissed, because they had procured a day of hearing.

WHEELER v. DEAN OF WORCESTER and others

There was a slanderous bill, in which Wheeler was the plaintiff (and not now ready) against the Dean of Worcester and others, who had sentenced him for incontinency; and this bill contained 74 offences in the Dean, and others in the High Commissioners and others in authority. The Lords wished to see the depositions,[3] and the next day sentenced the cause, a fine to the Queen, and costs and a fine to the defendants.

Sentence

[1] '£200' was written first. [2] Five Councillors were present.
[3] *Liuers.*

Another cause of abuse and misdemeanour in this wise: Two lewd and evil men came to Justice Clenche,[1] in good and decent apparel, to stand bail, and named themselves (being rogues and 'raskalles') by the names of proved and grave men, as by the name of the party now plaintiff, and thus bailed a man for a debt of £40; and the present plaintiff was arrested for this, and imprisoned in the 'gatehowse,' and paid the debt. Of which matter he complaineth here. It was adjudged by the whole Court, that the defendant should pay a fine to the Court of £100, and the costs, and the money recovered against the plaintiff, and should be imprisoned until he found sufficient bail for the discharge of this. By the Lords Keeper and Treasurer: It is a common course, and therefore odious. For it has happened on one occasion that a man has come with a 'curtizan' or 'drabbe' to the Common Pleas, and said that she was his wife, and so acknowledged a fine with her as with his own wife, whereas in truth she was a drab and courtesan.[2] And for the danger and 'communitie' of this, the greater punishment is necessary. Sentence

It was moved by the Lord Keeper, that inasmuch as the statutes were made, in causes of riots, in order to reduce and to punish violence, by giving the Justices of the Peace in the counties authority to give possession to him who has been removed by force, and [the Justices] at the present day do, for the most part, abuse the statutes, and make this a 'color & cloke' to remove possession from him who lawfully and peaceably has it, and to give it to their friends: but if I[3] have knowledge of them, for my part I will depose them from the Commission of the Peace without return, unless the Queen command that they be placed on the Commission [again].

In Camera Stellata, 1 Julii, le jour apres le terme de trinitye, Elizab. 38, An° Do^{ni} 1526, die jovis coram con- 1596 July 1

[1] One of the Judges of the Court of Queen's Bench, appointed 1584.
[2] The bearing of this on the case is rather obscure.
[3] The Lord Keeper.

1596 July 1

silio ibidem, Lo. Keeper, l'archevesque de Cant., Lo. Hunsdon, Lo. Buckherst, ambideux Lo. Ch. Justices, Justice Clenche, Justice Gawdy et Justice Wamslowe, per proclamacion in Chauncery le jour devant.

[p 31]

WHEELER v. DEAN OF WORCESTER and others

The former cause [1] was opened by Phillips, in which Wheeler is plaintiff and Dr. Willis, Dean of Worster, Dr. Puritie, Chancellor, and the Register,[2] and others, defendants. The hearing was tedious, and a slanderous libel, rehearsing all their lives, the interrogatories on the one side being 155, and on the other 125, and 77 witnesses were examined, interrogating things of doctrine and religion, over which this Court has no jurisdiction, and of which the Counsellor ought to be well advised, and of such tedious depositions.[3] And so the Court gave sentence, and vouched D. James' case for slander of him, where the party was imprisoned, pilloried and fined 100 marks.[4]

Justice Wameslowe, with great learning, reprehended the tediousness of tbe depositions [3] of this honourable Court aud of such state, inasmuch as a subject could pay four subsidies, or find 20 horses furnished for the defence of the realm, rather than [pay] the charge of these depositions[3]; and in the Common [Pleas ?] the processes are called *brevia*, 'briefes,' for that 'they showlde be shorte, and if they conteine false, vnnecessarye or superfluous matter, he shall be amerced:' also we have *De falso clamore*, 'for deceite allwayes hathe manye Collors & seekes shadowes, & therefore conteines much frivolous matter; but truthe is allwayes short & plane. His speache was graue, wyse & learned, politike and sauoringe of state, exceedingely wèll applyed to the time, & to his no smalle Commendacion.' For

Sentence

the fine, he, Gawdy and Clenche agree at 500 marks only to the Queen, imprisonment, and pillory 'sans naillinge,' and the depositions [3] to be withdrawn from the Court. But both the Chief Justices agreed on fines of 500 marks to the Queen, £100 to the Dean, 100 marks to the Chancellor, 500 marks to the Register, imprisonment, and to be nailed to the pillory

[1] See p. 52. [2] *I.e.* Registrar. [3] *Liuers.* [4] See p. 31.

in the place where the Council of Wales should be resident, and in Worster at the general Assizes; they vouched Sir John Yonge's case, and Smithe's, fined £300. But Lord Buckhurst, being informed of the substance and good ability of Wheeler, would increase the fines to 1000 marks to the Queen, and to the parties as before; for on his conscience he deserved ransom rather than fine, for he was not worthy to live; he concluded 'erudite & effectuallye,' with admiration. Lord Hunsden agreed in everything with him. The Archbishop spoke entirely of his own knowledge of the plaintiff and of the defendants especially in their commendation. And he agreed with all the punishment of 1000 marks [fine], imprisonment during the Queen's pleasure, nailing to the pillory in two places, and 'ingenious confession' of their offences, and 'to aske forgyveness' of the parties; and the depositions[1] to be withdrawn from the Court; and the 'ecclesiasticall proceedinges' against the plaintiff not to be stayed on account of the sentence of this Court, but to proceed with effect. The Lord Keeper disliked greatly the hugeness of the depositions[1] of the slanderous bill, and condemned the plaintiff for a notorious villain; and his offence is the greater in this, that he made this Court (of such authority and state that I[2] have not read nor heard of the like in the world) an instrument to publish of record his blasphemies, and to have the nobles of the land 'from her Matie's syde, vpon whose sacred person they showld attende,' to hear his slanders and libels, and thus a great shame to her Majesty and to this Court. And for this he agreed to fines of 1000 marks to the Queen, £100 to the Dean, 100 marks to the Chancellor, 50 marks to the Register, 'imprisonmente duringe pleasure, naillinge' at the pillory in two places, the depositions[1] to be withdrawn from the record; and he added that, for the shame done to this Court at Westminster, he should be pilloried there, or 'whipped from le Fleete: and for the Councellor whose name was to the bill, one Doynee, of Lincolne's inne, a man of the leste[3] learninge of all lawyers, Mr Sollicitor [general] to examine

Sentence

[p. 32]

[1] *Liuers.* [2] The Lord Keeper. [3] *I.e.* least.

1596 July 1

it whether his hande was forged, then the forgerer [*sic*] to be punished; if he himselfe did put it to, then to be disbarred for euer. For this faulte of sclaunderinge worde, *seditio regni*, was felonie, *et* in Kinge Canutus *et* Edgar dayes, Kinges of this realme before the Conqueste, he showlde loose his tonge; a very iuste lawe, & I doe wishe it might be executed in these dayes.'

By the Lord Chief Justice: The order of this Court as to interrogatories is, that the Counsellor's hand must be [set] to them.

Proclamation

The previous day proclamation was made in the Chancery that every Justice of the Peace and gentleman of 'sorte' and quality, in or near the City, should attend here to hear the Queen's commandment delivered 'grauely, eloquentely & very learnedlye, by the Lo. Keeper as followethe:

'Protestinge that it was not for fashion or custome, but her sacred Matie, of her godly & princely Care, dothe greately tender the religious & peaceable state of her people, & for that Cawse hathe delyuered in speciall Charge vnto me,[1] in the hearing of her Lordes here presente, to gyue her hole realme notice thereof in this peace; & to that ende, &c.

'Firste. her Matie speciallye requyrethe & Commaundeth, not onely all Justices of peace, but all sortes of gentlemen of what sorte or qualitye soeuer, wch haue lefte or forsaken there Country dwellinges & habitations to liue in Cityes or towne Corporates, presentely to repayre to there Country dwellings,[2] & there to make there Continuall aboade, as they will aunsweare to the Contrarye vpon there perill & her Ma$^{tie's}$ highe displeasure; for her Matie greately dislyketh the same, & expressely Commaundes all sortes presentely to retorne to there Countryes in regarde of eminente daungers, & yet the fainteste harte neede not to feare: but to be circumspecte & carefull, especiallye in the maritime partes, for *negligentia semper habet comitem*

[1] The Lord Keeper. [2] Compare this with the Proclamation, p. 19.

infortunium: & Edwarde the thirde, for neglecting this charge, did sease there landes & banished them; so a Justice of peace oughte to regarde his name, & so to doe iustely & for the peace of the lande, respecte his dutye & his oathe.

'2. For vagrande & idle persons, especiallye those wch flocke together, to punishe seuerely; there marke is idlenes & wastefull spending; for *egestas et inertia* are 2 Cankers in the Common wealthe: & amongste the Egiptians there was a lawe that Idle persons muste die *tamquam predo*.

'3. To haue circumspecte note of sclaunderers, who haue loose tonges, & to punishe them *non oscitanter*; for there are suche as will not feare to saye, *Non habemus partem in Dauid nec in filio eius*.

'4. For th'excesse of Apparrell in marchauntes' wyues & there daughters, lawyers' wyues & there daughters, gentlemen's wyues & there daughters, & in all degrees, to beginne wth some speciall instance; for hereby we prodigallye waste o^r^ patrimonie, & is a pestilent Canker in a Common wealthe, the Confusyon of all degrees; & therefore the lawes selected by proclamacion for this purpose must be reuyued.

'5. The presente dearthe (for I hope it is not scarcitye) to be prouyded for; & the Justices of peace, in there wisedomes, to aduise of some good Course to mitigate the prices.

'To looke to th'execucyon of the stat. of winchester [p. 33] for the due keepinge of there waches; to looke to Innes & alehouses, whome they lodge not aboue 2 nightes; & Justices of peace are bound to looke w^th^in there vice frank pledge, & to be a patterne for them not to entertaine titles, nor maintaine vniuste Cawses, nor to medle rashely wth forces, nor takinge or giuinge possessions, countenauncinge Cawses at the triall, or in discouraginge or incouraginge & instructinge Jurors: the Justices of Assise to looke very strictely to all these articles, & to be instructed who hathe bene forwarde in the reforminge hereof, & by particular

1596 July 1 instance what & how it is done, and not finde *omnia bene*, but to incourage where it is done, & to punishe where it is not done, & hereof to make accompte vnto her Matie, as she will seuerelye expecte it vpon her highe displeasure.

'My Lo. Chamberlin, he remembred one article giuen in charge by her Matie (but forgotten by my Lo. Keeper) for the Composition for her Ma$^{tie's}$ prouision for her housholde; for there are some wch as yet haue not Compounded, her Ma$^{tie's}$ pleasure is that if they Compounde not wth speede, (wch the Justices of peace muste procure to be done,) then her purueyours & takers to prouide for the housholde as in former times they haue vsed; & for that it is thoughte that the gentlemen are in most faulte that suche Composition is not made, it is therefore thoughte meeter that her Ma$^{tie's}$ prouision shalbe first purueyed & taken of the gentlemen & the better sorte wch doe refuse to compounde: & for Riots, it was ordered, *per totam curiam*, if any suche were Complayned of in this Cowrte as eyther mighte be ended by the Justices of the peace in the Country or not worthye of this Cowrte, then, allthoughe the Cowrte doe sentence it a ryot, the plaintife shall not haue any one penie Costes.'

re GARTER KING OF ARMS, BROOKE, and CLARENCIEUX.

Serjeant Harris moved for Garter, principal King of Arms,[1] against Brooke and Clarentius,[2] for reference of witnesses to Baron Ewens:[3] ruled by the Lord Keeper that both sides should be referred to him to examine what persons concern the matter and the point now in question, and what persons are material to it, and they to have continuance on each side, but otherwise not.

1596 Oct. 13

In Camera Stellata, coram consilio ibidem, 13 Octobris die Mercurii termino Michaelis, Elizabethae 38 & 39, Anno domini 1596.[4]

[1] Sir William Dethick.
[2] Robert Cooke.
[3] Matthew Ewens, Baron of the Exchequer.
[4] Seven Councillors were present.

The Attorney first moved on behalf of Edward Standen against Bullokes; he had purchased two manors for £4500, which were entailed on the Bullokes with proviso that if any heir committed, or entered into, any action of treason, felony, or praemunire, then the next [heir] should enter; and so a fine, and then a bargain and sale, and a lease were published, and possession was taken by Bulloke *pendente lite* 'since the bille & aunsweare;' which [? possession] was restored by order of the Court according to the course of this Court. STANDEN v. BULLOKE

[Marginal note.] The Lord Keeper wished him to be punished who advised this. By the Lord Treasurer: It is more evil advice than the Chief Baron's.[1]

The Attorney then informed, *ore tenus*, for the Queen, first against one Moulseworth, a merchant of London, for cosinage in this manner: he took bonds, statutes and recognizances from the son of one Harlacherden of Kent to the value of £3150, and a lease of all his land to commence from the death of his father, and all this for commodities of no value; but since this did not appear to the Court judicially, he was not sentenced for it. And the said Moulseworth, intending to have a statute for £300 from Zachee Harlackerden, the younger brother, who was within age, Lord Anderson, Chief Justice of the Common Pleas, refused to take any statute from him, finding him on examination to be within age; thereupon they went (knowing the said younger brother to be within age) to Doctor Hone, a Master of the Chancery, who took a recognizance from him. Moulesworth's offence was double: 1. Fraude or cosinage at common law (as [the A.G.] now informed), the taking of a statute or recognizance from an infant, knowing him to be within age, which is a great offence at common law, and so it was agreed by the whole Court: 2. Abusing a Judge, first the Chief Justice of the Common Pleas, who refused, and then Doctor Hone, the Master of the Chancery, which is a judicial place also. ATT.-GEN. v. MOULSWORTH — Cosinage [p. 34]

[1] I do not know to what this alludes.

1596
Oct. 13
Sentence

And for this Moulseworth was sentenced by the Court to be imprisoned, to pay a fine of £100, and to be pilloried. But the Lord Chief Justice of the Bench and the Earl of Essex did not agree to the pillory. And Sir John Fortescue was of opinion that he could only be sentenced on bill and answer, but this was negatived by the whole Court. And so the sentence of the Court was £100 fine, pillory, and imprisonment. The Lord Treasurer said that this corporation of cosiners was now discovered, but the estates of such adolescents did not deserve pity; and he wished to have Dr. Hone removed from his place in the Chancery, because he had at other times taken recognizances from other infants; and he said to the Lord Keeper, '"Haue you any neede of him?" and the Lord Keeper answered, "We haue many we neede not, and we neede many we haue not, for since I came to the place I could neuer learne how manye M^rs^ of the Chauncery there are, or by what authoritye they were made."' The Lord Treasurer answered, '"Then, my Lo., you had neede appointe some daye to muster them."' So the gravity, wisdom, and sincerity of Anderson were commended, and the indiscretion and folly of Dr. Hone were condemned, by all. It was agreed to be law by all, that if an infant acknowledge a fine, statute or recognizance while within age, and do not remedy this before he come to full age, he can never avoid those things which are matters of record. Therefore the fraud and the abuse of the Judge [1] are so much greater.

Att.-Gen. v. Robinson

Forgery

The Attorney informed also, *ore tenus*, against one Robinson (on the confession of himself and Hancocke the scrivener) for the forgery of two bonds in this wise: Robinson came to one Hancocke, a scrivener, saying that he had lost two bonds, and Hancocke said, '"I will helpe you for that;" & so he drawes 2 bondes in Henry Talbot's name, & sealles & delyuers them, & subscrybes "H. Talbot," after his deathe. So the scryuener drewe them & sealed, subscrybed & delyuered them by the direction of Robinson,

[1] The two offences mentioned above.

but told Mr Atturnie thereof when he had drawne them, & before he did sealle them, as Mr Atturnie himselfe did then alleage, to whome my Lo. Treso. sayd, "Then you were priuye to the forgerye."' Robinson was sentenced *per totam curiam*, to imprisonment, fine of £100, and pillory. And the Lord Treasurer said, '"It had neede be a Cli of woolle"; for the fellowe was poore.' Sentence

Bacon[1] of 'Grayes Inne' moved to dismiss for uncertainty a bill for a riot supposed to be made '"in 35 of her Matie's raigne or thereaboutes" where Parliament was that year,'[2] and also for the small value of the cause. It was referred to the Justices of that circuit where the riot was made, to examine into the certainty or sufficiency of the bill, and the weight [*momente*] of the cause. Motion

A cause was heard and sentenced between the Lady Davers, plaintiff, and Mathewes, attorney at law and now Coroner in Wiltshire, and Sir Walter Longe and Mr Edmonde Longe, defendants.[3] The cause was a misdemeanour in returning an inquest of office upon view of the body of [a man] killed by a servant of Sir Walter Longe's, when the body had not been viewed and the office was taken five weeks after the body was buried, and also for directing a warrant for the Queen's service generally (making no mention of the man who was killed, but of one who hanged himself), and for summoning twenty-five [men] of other Hundreds where Sir Walter Longe commands and is a Justice of the Peace, and no juror of the Hundred where the murder was done, nor [of the Hundred] where the body lay, the said Mathewes, the Coroner, being Solicitor and Steward of the Courts to the said Sir Walter Longe, and knowing the Hundreds, for he was an attorney at 'Davies Inne'[4] for twelve years, Undersheriff often, and Collector of Subsidies and Fifteenths in the same Hundred; and the [p. 35] DANVERS v. LONGE and others — Misdemeanour

[1] Francis Bacon.

[2] Doubtful. These are probably the uncertain words objected to.

[3] See p. 49, and Appendix III.

[4] The same as Thaive's or Thavies Inn in Holborn. See Herbert, *Inns of Court and Chancery*, p. 309.

1596 Oct. 13

inquisition also was returned *se defendendo*, 'the blowe [being] behinde the eare, most absurde.' Agreed for law by the Court that a Coroner by his oath ought to have his return *super visum corporis*, and when it is not *super visum corporis*, he acts wrongly and corruptly, '& oughte by the lawe [to] retourne those nexte adioyninge w^th^in the hundred where the murder was or the bodye lyes; for the Coroner's office [1] is in some kinde a conuiction, & no other Coroner can dealle wth it after office retorned,' but at the Assize or Quarter Sessions by indictment or otherwise, as was done [in this case]; and the jury inquired of Lord Anderson what manner of verdict they ought [to give], and he said "Follow your evidence," for which he was greatly commended. But Serjeant Harris and Glanvill advised the jury to find it *se defendendo*, which was grievously condemned; for they should not have advised them, not being a matter of law but of fact, and the jury ought not to take advice in such matters. So as to the sentence of the Court,

Sentence

Sir Walter Longe and Mr Edmonde Longe were dismissed but not acquitted by the sentence; but Mathewes was condemned *per totam curiam* for his subtle carriage, and so he was sentenced by all to be imprisoned, to pay a fine of £500, to lose his post of Coroner (which is in the Lord Keeper to do), to be removed from the 'under-sherifesship,' and never to be in office there, to be disbarred by Lord Anderson from his 'attorneshipe,' and by the Lord Keeper to be expelled from 'Davies Inne,' and to have a paper, and to go through Westminster Hall, and to be 'impilloride' there, and to be 'impilloride' with the paper on his head at the Assizes in the County where this was done; which was the sentence of the Court, as I conceive.

Motion

Hide, Counsellor at the bar, moved for a dismissal; to which the Lord Keeper answered that the clerk had orders that dismissals should go before him without motion; which is a good order to save clients very much money, as declared before in this book.[2]

[1] The inquisition or inquest.

[2] See p. 1.

In Camera Stellata, coram consilio ibidem, 15 Octobris, termino Michaelis, Elizab. 38, die veneris, An° Do^{ni}, 1596.[1] [p. 36] 1596 Oct. 15

Motions

Divers motions and orders on them before the hearing of causes, and three causes were sentenced this day, one of riot not apt for the Court.

SNELLE and HARGRAVE *v.* BODIE and others — Perjury

Snelle and Hargrave, plaintiffs, against Bodie, an informer in the Exchequer, and others, for perjury and subornation, and misdemeanour in Body as informer; Smithes, two of the defendants, were acquitted of perjury and subornation of perjury, and therefore dismissed; but Body and the other defendant were referred to common law, to have trial at the Assizes; and Bodie, the informer, was condemned by all, and his misdemeanour as informer and abuser of the laws was judged a good and apt matter to be sentenced in this Court. But for default of good proof and orderly proceedings by the Counsellors (who were gravely reprehended for their negligence), the last two were referred to common law.

Order of the Court

In this cause it was delivered as an order of the Court (by Milles, the Clerk) that if there are divers defendants and for several offences, if *subpoena ad audiendum judicium* be served on any of them, and on one of them only, it is sufficient, although there are three or four defendants or more, and their offences are several and diverse. To which the Lord Keeper answered that if it was the order of the Court, it ought to be observed, but if it was not, he would not admit or make any such order, because of the mischief and inconvenience that would ensue thereon.

SUTE'S case — Forgery and Perjury

Another cause of forgery and perjury against one Sute, esquire (late special attendant to the now Lord Treasurer), and it was in this wise. He obtains a copy of a Court-roll which had these words, *habere sibi secundum consuetudinem manerii*, and he writes it anew, and adds these words,

[1] Eight Councillors were present.

1596 Oct. 15 *habere sibi et heredibus secundum consuetudinem manerii,* and hangs this deed in the smoke, and 'smoke dryes it,' which was proved by three witnesses *omni exceptione maiores.* Then the perjury was in this way: he denied on his oath here that he had made this copy. The first bill was preferred for forgery only, and in his answer to this he was perjured. Then a new bill was preferred for perjury, and the Queen's Attorney informed in a third bill for forgery and perjury; but the forgery was pardoned by 31 Eliz., and as to this the sentence acquitted him *de poena* sed *non de culpa,* for the forgery was clearly proved. For the perjury he was sentenced to have imprisonment, a fine of 100 marks, and pillory with a paper. The Lord Treasurer desired to be spared from [giving] sentence, because it might be imagined that he spoke from spleen, for he had other matters in the Chancery against the said Sute, and so he did forbear.

Sentence

Corn

It was delivered by a resolution of the Judges that a man may give corn in exchange for corn, within the statute, and may sell it again, but may not give money for corn and sell it again.

1596 Nov. 24

In Camera Stellata, coram consilio ibidem, 24 Novembris, Eliz. 39, die Mercurii, An° Do^ni^ 1596.[1]

Att.-Gen. v. Boothes, Markham and others [p. 37]

The cause of hearing on an information by the Attorney wherein Dame Gresham is plaintiff and Roger Boothe, Cuthbert Boothe, John Markham junior, Josias Kerton and Edward Langden, defendants;[2] and now, Dame Gresham being dead, it was moved if this should be heard notwithstanding. And it was agreed *per totam curiam,* that by the custom of the Court and by special order, the Attorney could proceed if he wished, or otherwise the parties at their election, and so it was sentenced; and a precedent was cited to warrant this in the case of Sir Gilberte Garrette. The matters in the bill were a slan-

[1] Seven Councillors were present. [2] See pp. 21, 26, 28, and Appendix II.

dering of the sentence of this Court, given before this time, against Roger Boothe, Markham, and others, in which divers deeds of annuities and rent-charges were condemned as forgeries; and the now defendants have slandered the said sentence by saying that the said sentenced forged deeds were 'true & good deedes and they hope will prooue so.' The Attorney proved this by three or four unexceptional witnesses, by letters and petitions indited by Roger Boothe and Kerton and delivered by Markham and Kerton, and also by the gift of money to the witnesses to [make them] retract and to suborn them. And so by the whole Court their offences were deemed great and odious and worthy of death, and Roger Boothe the principal actor and contriver of all. And so he was sentenced by all 'to walke through Westminster Halle wth a paper one his heade, & to haue his eares naylled to the pillorye, to paye a thousande markes for fine, & to be imprisoned during his lyfe.[1] Kerton to be nailled to the pillorye wth a paper one his heade, to paye 500 markes for a fine & imprisoned during his life.' Langdon (who could not be found) pillory, £100 fine, and imprisonment. 'Cuthberte Boothe to stande one the pillory, 200^li.^ fine and imprisonmente. John Markham to stande one the pillory wth a paper, 100^li.^ fine & imprisonmente.' Sentence

By the Lord Keeper: This is a grievous offence and worthy of death, and by the duty of his place he ought to say something. Common custom holds this no offence, and it is now at such a pass that we ought to make laws according to men's offences. This Court, the most worthy, high and honourable Court in all Europe in this kind, replete with Judges come from the sacred side of her Majesty,

[1] Among the State Papers of 1595 is a grant of a pardon to Roger Booth, public notary, for all misdemeanours of which he and others are accused in the Star Chamber by Lady Anne Gresham, touching the forgery of several deeds of rent-charges out of the lands of the late Sir Thomas Gresham, and of release from a bond of £1000 for payment of £500, and from the sentence against him of standing in the pillory, having both his ears cut, and other grievous pains both corporal and pecuniary; granted because he has been many years a scrivener, and lived in honest reputation and credit. State Papers, Domestic, Elizabeth, vol. ccliv., No. 76. It would appear from the date of the trial that this document really belongs to 1596.

1596 Nov. 24

whose care is perpetually to administer judgment and justice to her subjects, without which they would not be governed, but [would be] apt for rebellion, insurrection, and all disorder, and this she gives in charge each day to her Privy Councillors, and to the Judges, and if I should conceal this, I should do shame to her Majesty, for she is the most careful, vigilant and 'respective' prince of her subjects that could be in the world, or ever was; wherefore the slander of this Court is the more offensive. Before the Conquest it was punished by Edgar and Canute by the loss of the tongue, and by the Lydians a slanderer was put to the torture and executed. Thought is free, but the tongue should be governed by knowledge. For to say "I thinke you are a traitor," an action on the case will lie, for on common voice and rumour a man may be imprisoned; and if one say "I thinke you are a theefe," an action will lie.

[p. 38]

1596–7 Feb. 4

In Camera Stellata, coram consilio ibidem, die veneris, 4° Februarij, 1596, Elizab. 39, termino Hillarij.[1]

EARL OF KENT and others *v.* ROTHERHAM and others

There was great expectation for the cause between the Earl of Kent,[2] Clarencieux,[3] and Brookesmouthe,[4] a herald, plaintiffs, against Rotheram and Garter, now named Dethike, defendants. The offences were supposed, 'the wearinge & partinge of the Erle of Kent his cote of his baronies of Ruthin, Hastinges & Wastinges, by Rotheram, giuen by Garter falsely, corruptely, contrarye to his owne bookes, & to his owne knowledge, & after giuinge the same Cote vnder his hande & sealle to th'erle of Kente, & yet lastelye making a testimonialle under the sealle of the office to countenaunce & warrante Rotheram's Coate; wherebye the Erle of Kente showlde loose all his lyuinge, his three baronies, & the Queene her Castle of Ruthin & a

[1] Twelve Councillors were present, including the Earl Marshall.

[2] Sir Henry Grey ,9th Baron Grey de Ruthyn and 6th Earl of Kent.

[3] Richard Lee, created 1594.

[4] Ralph Brookesmouth, or Brooke, York Herald.

1000li. lande *per annum* boughte of the late Erle of Kente. The title was thus opened. Edmonde, erle of Kente in 4 E. 4 [1] had issue Anthonye *par un venter* & George *par auter venter.'* Anthony died without issue; George entailed the land and the honours in special tail, and thus the now Earl of Kent had conveyed to him the land and the honours as heir in special tail. Rotheram and Garter say that true it is that Edmond had issue Anthonie, but Anthony had issue Katherine, who intermarried with our ancestor, Sir Thomas Rotheram; and Edmond, the father of Anthony, entailed the land and the baronies, but not the Earldom, to his heirs in special tail, and so Rotheram is heir in special tail. The issue [in the case] is, did Anthony die without issue or not. Of the whole matter there are three parts: 1, of the title to the arms or coats; 2, of the right to the baronies, which have continued in the Earls of Kent from 4 Edward IV. without question; 3, if Anthony had issue Katherine or not. As to the proof of the falsehood and corruption of Garter, a great offence in him, the Lord Keeper and the Lords Chief Justices doubted if it could properly be tried in this Court, and they judged that it could not. As to the title to arms, it should properly be decided by the Lord Marshall and the Lord Constable of England, and titles of honour and dignity, such as baronies and the like, are to be decided by the Queen herself, who is the head and fountain and disposer of all royalties, honours and dignities; and so it was decided between the Earl of Arundell and the Earl of Devonshire, 37 Henry VI.

Statute of 13 Richard II.

Lord Scroope and Gravener [*sic*], appeal to the King.

And it was so sentenced by the [majority of the] voices, but the Court was divided; and it was ruled by the Judges, to whom the Lords agreed [to refer], that it should not be dismissed; as to the issue, did Anthony have issue Katherine or not, it was referred to the common law, being a matter triable by the country; and after the trial of this, the

[1] Edmund, 4th Lord Grey de Ruthyn, created Earl of Kent by Edward IV.

1596-7 Feb. 4 falsehood, corruption, and malicious offence of Garter will be tried in this Court; for by many the offence was [deemed] great and heinous, and more worthy than many [p. 39] others to be sentenced in this Court. By the Earl of Essex: There cannot be a greater offence; for as God has reserved to Himself the authority to give virtue, so He has given to His vicar on earth, our Queen, the reward and remuneration of virtue, which are honours, baronies, and titles of dignity; and therefore to deceive her as to these rewards is a grievous offence and worthy of great punishment.

1596-7 Feb. 9 **In Camera Stellata,** coram Consilio ibidem, Mercurij, 9° Februar. An° Do^ni 1596, Elizab. 39, termino Hillarij.[1]

Causes dismissed for non-prosecution

Divers causes of perjury and forgery, appointed to be heard, were dismissed for non-prosecution, as well on the part of plaintiffs as of defendants, with costs, and fines to the Queen by the sentence of the Court.

1596-7 Feb. 11 **In Camera Stellata,** coram consilio ibidem, die Veneris, 11° Februar. Elizab. 39, ter^no Hillarij.[2]

GRIFFITHE and others, defendants

Riot and misdemeanour

One Griffithe and his servants were defendants for a riot, in this manner: the servants of the said Griffith, who was a Justice of the Peace, did grievously beat a man, and of this they acquainted their master and mistress, who assented to it. By the Judges: This case is not triable in this Court, but by an action at common law. But as to the misdemeanour of Griffithe, in allowing a battery on the part of his servants, he being a Justice of the Peace, and in offering a *supersedeas* or bond to another Justice of the Peace for their discharge, and in soliciting him for the non-certifying of their recognizance, for these misdemeanours in him as a Justice of the Peace he was sentenced, (Sentence) by the whole Court, to be deposed from the Commission of

[1] Nine Councillors were present. [2] Nine Councillors were present.

the Peace. The procurement of, and assent to, the battery were not proved in him, otherwise the Court would have fined him for it.

Rowlande Hille, plaintiff, against [1] Corbette for riot in this manner: by commanding his servants to challenge Hille and terrify him in his house, being [Corbette's] tenant; and it had no effect; but for this he [Corbette] was fined £40, and his servants £100 each. *Quicquid est extra causam est in persona,* and so *iudicium est suspiciosum et temerarium.*

HILL v. CORBETTE — Riot

Sentence

In the Chancery, on the last day of term, one was committed to the Fleet for buying a statute and a bond and suing thereon in the name of another, the which he confessed.

In the Chancery

And a fine and recovery were stayed *quia l'enfante en ventre sa mere.* Willoughbye and Willoughbye.

In Camera Stellata, coram consilio ibidem, Die veneris 15° Aprilis, An° Do^{ni} 1597, Elizab. 39, termino pasche.[2]

[p. 40] 1597 April 15

In the first cause of hearing the Attorney was plaintiff, and because process was not served but five days before, it was ordered that it should come in course the next day as the Queen's Attorney was a party, otherwise not.

ATT.-GEN., pl.

Aldworthe, plaintiff, Smallman and others, defendants, for riot and practice of conveying[3] an idiot. One was found an idiot in the Court of Wards on the surmise of Smallman, and was committed to his ward, and then he traversed the office and was found very simple and foolish but not an idiot from his birth, and it was so decreed in the Court of Wards; and he [the un-named idiot] was removed from Smallman, his stepfather, to Aldworthe, his uncle, and Smallman was ordered to account for £700 arrears, which

ALDWORTH v. SMALLMAN and others, — Riot, &c.

[1] Blank in MS.

[2] Seven Councillors were present.

[3] Carrying off or stealing. 'Convey, the wise it call: steale? foh: a fico for the phrase.' *Merry Wives of Windsor,* act i. sc. 3.

1597 April 15

he has not done. The supposed idiot, in the wardship of Aldrige [*sic*], lived in the country, and for the recovery from his infirmities, had a surgeon and his man there, with whom Smallman confederated, for £40 to the one and £10 to the other, to convey the idiot. They came with four others, with 'swordes, rapyers, & daggers, & 3 pistolles,' and seized the idiot forcibly. And for this riot and practice Smallman was fined £140, and each of the other four £40, and imprisonment according to the course of this Court.

Insidiatores viarum

Sentence

ALDRIGE and GOOGE *v.* WOOLRIGE and others

Aldrige and Googe, plaintiffs, Woolrige, Wheatecrofte and Partrige, defendants. Woolrige, by warrant of attorney, sued on a bond against Aldrige, who was bound for the debt but [was] not the principal [debtor], and by a supposed warrant of attorney, he [Woolrige] retained one Wheatecrofte, an attorney of the Common Bench, and paid both their fees for the plaintiff and the defendant also; which [Wheatecrofte] commenced a suit in the King's Bench, and took bail, and entered a *non sum informatus* in the name of one Partrige, who is ignorant of this and denies that he was ever privy to it. And he [Wheatecrofte] had judgment and execution in one term against Aldrige, without any notice or process served on him, whereas the course in the Bench is that a man shall be arrested on a *latitat* and shall have bail or shall prefer a bill in Middlesex. For this offence Woolrige was fined £100, and Wheatecrofte £300, and to be 'hurle over the barre at Westminster,' and never to be an attorney, nor to have any office in the law, to be expelled from 'Furnifolles Inne' for ever, and both of them to wear papers at Westminster and at the Assizes where they dwell.

Sentence

Order of the Court

Ruled that it is the custom of this Court that if there are two defendants for one offence, and the one is served with a subpoena *ad audiendum iudicium*, it is good for the other.

A warrant of attorney is an authority *et moritur cum persona*.

In Camera Stellata, coram consilio ibidem, Die Mercurij, 20 Aprilis, An° Do^{ni} 1597, Elizab. 39, termino paschae.[1] 1597 April 20

The Queen's Attorney informed first against one Panter for engrossing corn in Wiltshire in manner as follows: he procured a licence to buy and sell or badger corn; the words of the licence import that it was made in open Sessions by four Justices of the Peace where one was of the Quorum; but by the confession of the party, it was made after the Sessions, which was contrary to the Statute and a great offence in the Justices. The licence was made in Somersetshire to badger corn in Wiltshire with the consent of the Justices there; and he badgered there without their consent; and sold the corn in market at the instant the bell had rung, whereas by the orders of the Council it should not be sold within two hours after the bell has rung. For which offence, Thirne, a Justice of the Peace there (for which he was greatly commended and for his careful provision for the poor this dear year) caused the Constable to sell his corn to the poor 8^{d} under the price he had paid for it. Whereupon the said 'badger' of corn, Panter, arrested the Constable and recovered £8 against him, and imprisoned him for seven weeks. The Lord Chief Justice, with the Queen's 'Councelle' examined this, and on [Panter's] confession, proceeded here. *Prima facie* it seemed to the Lord Treasurer that this cause should be punished by the Justices of the Peace, but afterwards it was sentenced here by the whole Court; and for the example of this time principally, he was adjudged by all to be imprisoned, 'to stande vpon the pillory wth an empty sacke in his hande, a paper one his head, to paye 5$^{li.}$ to the Queene, 10$^{li.}$ to the party Constable & all his Costes.' And because he had been in the livery of one Harman, he and his master have forfeited £5 for each month. And the Lords would have a bill preferred against the said Harman for retaining.

ATT.-GEN. *v.* PANTER

[p. 41]

Sentence

[1] Ten Councillors were present.

1597
April 20

Att.-Gen.
v.
Wades and
others

Forgery, &c.

The Attorney, plaintiff, 'Michaell' Wades, Johnes, and Bedelles, defendants: Wades had arrested a gentlewoman named Oliffe Kebleworth on three several actions of the value of £1500, and had her in prison, and forged a warrant under the hand of the Archbishop of Canterbury and others of the High Commissioners, and procured one Justice Yonge to command that the woman should not be bailed; and then the said Wades agreed with her, and procured a discharge from Justice Yonge, and for £15 released the gentlewoman and all actions. He pleaded "Not guilty," and on interrogatories he made answer, "I can say nothing." Whereupon it was ruled by the Court that, by the course of the Court, it is held as a confession, and the cause may be judged immediately without other examinations. The defendant's counsel moved that the Court could not judge on the bill, but it was ruled by all that if a complaint be made generally, 'contrary to the lawes & statutes in that case prouyded,' it is in the election of the Court to judge this according to the statute or according to common law; but if the bill be upon any special statute, this should be followed and the matter proved to be an offence within the statute, otherwise the Court will not judge it. And if a bill complain of an offence done after a pardon, it is not material as to the date or day of the act or deed, although the bill and the deed differ in date; thus it may be proved that this is a forged deed; as at common law, if a man pleads "*nul tiel recorde*," and it appears to be the same record in substance without difference, even if the date or day differ, it has to be adjudged good.

Bedelles and Johnes, the one in the house with Wades, and Johnes his servant, on whom no process had been served, beat and barbarously and inhumanly used a man, wounding him 'wth a Codgell vpon the legges, treading of him in the durte,' when he came to execute an order of the Chancery to take possession of the land of the said Wades, who stands 'in his doore & sees all this.'

Senten

For the first offence Wades was fined 100 marks, and 'to stande vpon the pillorye wthoute nayllinge, a paper one his heade, & imprisonmente'; and for the other offence, 'Bedelles 100 markes fine and Wades 100 markes, and bothe to stande vpon the pillorye wth papers, & imprisonmente till they put in good suerties for there good abearinge.'

In Camera Stellata, coram consilio ibidem, Die Veneris, 22 Aprilis, Eliza. 39, An° Do[ni] 1597, termino pasche.[1] 1597 April 22

ATT.-GEN. v. JOHNES and THOMAS

Forgery of Hall marks, &c.

The Queen's Attorney informed against Johnes and Thomas, goldsmiths in London, for that it was ordained in the time of Edward III. 'that all plate showlde be thus alayd [2] sterling of the standarde, the wardens of the Company showlde veiwe weekely what plate is made, & there is a saer [3] sworne to take sae [4] & set one the Companie's marke, w[ch] is the Alphabeticall letter, the libbarde's [5] heade appointed by E. 3, they lyon appointed by H. 8, and euery Goldsmithe's marke w[ch] remayneth in there halle: & all these are Commaunded to be vpon all plate w[ch] is solde: but Johnes & Thomas had made diuers peeces of plate, & allayed them w[th] Copper allay, 12[d] in euery ounce, & had Counterfeyted the alphabeticall letter, the libbarde's heade, [p. 42] the lyon, the marke of the Companye, & set them all too, & solde them w[th]oute assaye; & euery freeman of this Company is sworne to the Contrary, so (*par ascuns*) they might be proceeded w[th]all for periury: but for these deceites & falsehoodes they were sentenced by the hole Courte to weare papers heere vpon the pillorye, & to loose eyther of them an eare one the pillorye at Cheapesyde, & to goe w[th] papers where they dwelle, to paye eyther 100[li.], & imprisonmente; for this was condemned for a greater faulte then robbery, for by this we knowe not how many nor whoe are robbed; & to Coyne monie is treason, *Ideo* this is a greate offence.'

Sentence

[1] Seven Councillors were present.
[2] Alloyed.
[3] Assayer.
[4] Assay.
[5] Leopard's.

1597
April 22

Moodye, Sheriff of Wiltshire, def.

Moodye, Sheriff, defendant, and others: execution for £7 in Wiltshire, and Bridges advised to chase cattle from Somerset into Wiltshire, saying that this was but trespass [?]; and this was done, and £7 10^s 0^d was received by the execution. This was in 31 Elizabeth, and Moodie, the Sheriff, not being acquainted with this, directed a new execution and took five cows, and sold them to his tenants for £7, and received the money, and retains it to this day. This was adjudged to be extortion in him, and not excepted [1] in the pardon of 35 Elizabeth, neither as to the offence nor the fine; and was sentenced by the Court, the Sheriff to pay £100 fine and be imprisoned, to restore all charges to the party according to the true value, the other parties each to pay £40 fine and be imprisoned, and Bridges to be disabled from practising the law.

Perjury and maintenance

Another cause for perjury and maintenance, in such a plea [2] 'that the plaintiff's Father was *non compos mentis* at suche a time,' which this Court would not determine; and so for default of good matter and proofs, [the bill] was dismissed. And as to the maintenance [the plaintiff?] did not prove the submission of the party [? the defendant], and so let him be whipped in the public market where he dwells.[3]

More, pl.

Riot

More, plaintiff, against husband and wife for riot. The husband is now dead, and there is no proof against the wife except the accusation of the husband, which, by the sentence of the Court, will not condemn the wife.

If a man plead in his answer Not Guilty, and will not answer the articles,[4] it shall be held as a confession.

1597
April 23

S. George's Day, Whitehalle, 23 Aprilis, die Sabbati, Elizab. 39.

The Royal Court being at Whitehall, great solemnity for the Order of the Garter was observed, being S. George's day. 'Firste morning Sarvice in the Chappell wth solemne

[1] 'Included' seems to be meant.
[2] Query, *plite* for *pleit*.
[3] This case is very obscure.
[4] *I.e.* the interrogatories.

musike & voyces, Doc. Boolle[1] then playing, the Lordes of the order then presente; then Comming & retyring they make 3 congies to the seate Royalle & so departe; & some howre after they come againe before her Matie wth all the officers of Armes, & then Commeth the Queene, three Ladyes Caryinge her trayne, wch then were the Countes of warwike, the Countes of Northumberlande & the Countes of Shrewseberrye, th'erle of Bedforde carryinge the sworde before her, 6 pencyeners Carying a riche Canopye ouer her heade; & then after there seuerall Congees, there is shorte seruice, the Clergie all in there riche Copes, wth the princely musike of voyces, organes, Cornettes & sackebuttes; & in like order her Matie goes one precession & so returnes, & shee & the reste of the order offer at the highe altar, & so seruice endes, & shee departes: then goes many princely seruices, at the firstes soundes many trumpettes, after playes 2 drommes & the fyfe. The names of the Lordes nowe of the order were these.

'Lo. Treserer	L'erle d'essexe
'Lo. Admirall	Erle of Northumberlande
'Lo. Buckherst	Erle of Shrewsebery
'Lo. Sheffeilde	Erle of Worster
'Lo. Boroughe	Erle of Comberlande

'The erles of pembroke & Ormond were absente.

'new
'made
'were } [2]

In Camera Stell.ta, coram consilio ibidem, 14 Octob. 1597, Elizab. 39, Veneris, termino Michaelis.[3] [p. 43] 1597 Oct. 14

Kooke of the Inner Temple, Attorney-general to the Queen, informed, *ore tenus*, on the confession of the parties ATT.-GEN. pl. — Ingrossing corn, &c.

[1] Dr. John Bull; for an account of him see *Dictionary of National Biography*.

[2] Blank in MS. Five Knights were elected; for their names, see *Memorials of the Order of the Garter*, by G. F. Beltz, 1841, p. clxxxiii.

[3] Ten Councillors were present.

1597 Oct. 14

themselves, for ingrossing corn, and for buying and selling the same out of market, contrary to the proclamations made in the years 1586 and 1594, and to a printed book made by the Queen in the 37th year of her reign and continued now, and also contrary to the letters of the Council delivered in charge to the Justices of Assize and of the Peace.

He also informed for ingrossing of land and converting houses[1] of husbandry and tillage to cottages (by taking and occupying the land without them), contrary to the statutes of 4 Henry VII. cap. 19, 27 Henry VIII. cap. 22, 7 Henry VIII. cap. 1, 5 Elizabeth, cap. 2.

ATT.-GEN. v. FRAMINGHAM and others — Ingrossing corn, &c.

Edward Framingham of Norfolk, for converting thirteen houses into cottages and tenements, and reserving the land for his own occupation, and for ingrossing corn, and buying and selling the same out of market, imprisonment, fine of £500, confession of his fault in Cheapside and in Norfolk, and £40 to the poor people, and to restore the houses with the land to husbandry again, and disabled from being Constable (for he was now High Constable).

Daniel Shanke and a 'malstere,' for ingrossing, imprisonment, and £20 fine, and confession of their fault.

Mathie Sotherton, the same fault and punishment.

Richard Whale, gentleman, the same.

William Pette, gentleman, the same.

Robarte Cupite, Thomas Birad, Thomas Bowde, Richard Westgauge, and the parson of a church, Thomas Taverner,
[p. 44] Roberte Buller [?], and others, each to have imprisonment, a fine of £40, and to restore the land to the houses.

ATT.-GEN. v. TIRRETTE and SHELTEN

He informed also against one John Tirrette and William Shelten, 'saltpeter men,' who, under colour of a commission granted by the Queen to George Evelin, John Evelin and Richard Hille[2] to make gunpowder for the provision and

[1] *Huises.*

[2] I cannot find the date of their appointment as gunpowder makers to the Queen, but it was before December 3, 1588, when certain quantities of saltpetre were ordered to be delivered to Evelyn and Hill, the gunpowder makers, to perform

defence of the realm, and to their deputies, these two persons, supposed to be deputies of the deputies of the patentees, made warrants to charge divers Hundreds in Suffolke with the carriage of wood and liquor [1] and other necessaries, at inconvenient times, or to agree with them for a sum of money; which [money] they received for 260 loads, whereas they carried but 80 loads. And they directed their warrant to a High Constable, who made his warrant accordingly. For these offences they were sentenced to have imprisonment, fine of £20 each, the pillory (and by the better opinion to be nailed), and confession. The Constable was fined £20, imprisonment, and confession, with expulsion from his office. Sentence

Egestas et ignauia pestis reipublicae. Lord Keeper on ingrossing

Maior fames ex rapacitate quam ex siccitate. By the Lord Keeper: These ingrossers are great offenders, and, by the law in the time of Edward I., they should be banished 31 Edw. I. from the town where they dwell; they are the 'decaiers' and ruiners of the commonwealth, for *omnis respublica est bene disposita*, first, for the life of the subjects, 2, to live in the fear of God, 3, to live in peace and plenty: but this ingrossing and converting of houses of tillage into cottages is the cause of idleness and felony: and the negligence of some Justices of the Peace ought to be certified to remove them, and the work of others also certified for their commendation and encouragement. [*Margin.*] He observed that government [*politica*] is strict and severe to execute letters and orders of councils.

In Camera Stellata, coram Consilio ibidem, Mercurij, 19 Octobris, Elizab. 39, An^o^ Do^ni^ 1597, ter^no^ Michaelis.[2] 1597 Oct. 19

their bargain. State Papers, Domestic, Elizabeth, vol. ccxix. No. 7. In August 1599, John Evelyn and others had a licence, for ten years, for the sole making of saltpetre and gunpowder. State Papers, Docquet.

[1] *Ligne et licor.*

[2] Six Councillors were present.

1597
Oct. 19

Att.-Gen. v. Parker and others

Ingrossing corn, &c.

Kooke, the Attorney-General, informed *ore tenus*, on the confession of the parties themselves, against Frauncis Parker, Nicolas Osborne, and others, 'malsters' of Kent, for ingrossing, and buying and selling corn out of market, contrary to the statutes of 5 Edw. VI. cap. 14, 13 Eliz. cap. 22, and 5 Eliz. cap. 12, and contrary to the orders [p. 45] now in force by virtue of proclamations (upon which alone they proceed now and give sentence, and not on any statute), for the Queen by her royal prerogative has power to provide remedies for the punishment or otherwise of exorbitant offences as the case and times require, without parliament; and forestalling was [an offence] at common law.

43 Ass. Pl. 38[1] Fits[herbert] Ass. 354, cited by the Lord Keeper, where one Lombarde, for forestalling lands, was fined and ransomed by the King's Council; and a ransome is all that he hath, goods and land, and all that he hath in the world.

These ingrossers were examined by Bacon, Counsel at Large to the Queen, who made a long oration of the parts of the statutes against ingrossers and forestallers, and to no purpose,[2] and also of the divine and princely regard of the Queen, Her sacred Majesty, with whose intent towards him he was so blessed as to be privy, and all not to the purpose: for the Lord Keeper and others of the Queen's Council, and the Judges also, being so instructed, intend redress for such offences and many others in the common wealth[3] by the Queen's prerogative only, and by proclamation, councils, orders, and letters; and thus their decrees and councils, proclamations and orders, shall be a firm and forcible law, and of the like force as the common law or an Act of Parliament. And this is the intent of the Privy Councillors in our day and time, to attribute to their councils and orders the vigour, force and power of a firm law, and of higher virtue and force, jurisdiction and 'preheminence,' than any positive law, whether it be the

[1] "Le Liver des Assises & plees del Corone," &c., 1580; the case cited in the text is on fol. 276.

[2] This apparently refers to the statutes.

[3] *in le weale publique.*

common law or statute law. And thus in a short time the Privy Councillors of this realm would be the most honourable, noble and commanding lords in all the world, and [have] the majesty of prince and ruler of the greatest reverence in all the world. And this appears to me[1] to be their intent for two other reasons now moved by the Lord Keeper, that they do proceed also against the builders of cottages (as follows) on the proclamation and not on the statute, and that in a short time he thought to punish the remissness and negligence of some Justices of the Peace and others in authority, who are content to grace themselves with this, in executing the letters of the Privy Council [p. 46] as to the orders concerning corn, and for other proclamations against cottages, and other statutes and things; and in my knowledge, these letters touching corn were sent by the Lords of the Privy Council to the Judges at the Assizes, and by them to the chief Justices of the Peace in each county [only], and so divers Justices of the Peace never knew the substance of them, nor of the Council's orders concerning grain. But *ignorantia legis non excusat.*

Francis Parker had been an ingrosser for sixteen years, and had every year carried corn to London in a boat, without a licence; and for this he was fined £500 to the Queen, imprisonment, £20 to the poor, to go to Westminster Hall with papers, and to confess his fault. Sentence

Nicolas Osborne and the others were fined for ingrossing, each £40, and imprisonment.

Att.-Gen. *v.* Negoose and others

* Proclamation 7 July, 22 Eliz., 1580

The Attorney-General also informed against Negoose and others for building cottages iu London "contrary to the proclamation," * and not "contrary to the statute 35 Eliz. cap. 6." For this they were fined, one £100, another £40, and another £20, the houses to be destroyed for their base condition, and the timber to be sold for the benefit of the poor. If there be any 'brothelle howses,' to burn them standing, if it can be done without peril, otherwise to burn them in the fields; and those which

[1] The writer of the MS., John Hawardes.

1597 Oct. 19

are beautiful and spacious edifices, to convert them into garners and storehouses for grain and other merchandise.

SMITHE *v.* IRENMAN

Misdemeanour

There was a cause of hearing between Smithe and Irenman,[1] an attorney, on a bill and answer, by order, because he confessed to this in his answer. There was a misdemeanour in Irenman,[1] being an attorney in the Common Pleas, in returning a *venire facias* in this way: he had a *venire facias* returned by the Sheriff under his hand and seal, and he lost this, and procured a new one from the Clerk of the Writs, and he himself subscribed the name of the Sheriff, and put the Sheriff's seal to it; and he justified the doing of this as the common use of many other attorneys of the Common Bench, and that in debt and trespass it is an ordinary thing that the attorney returns this without the Sheriff. By Anderson, [p 47] Chief Justice of the Common Bench: But this is erroneous and worthy of great punishment, and he would examine and reform this, and it would be a virtue in Ingram [*sic*] to accuse them; and "*multitudo peccatorum non tollit sensum peccati nec poenam, sed minuit pudorem peccatorum.*"[2]

Another misdemeanour in Irenman[1] was in altering a panel in this way: he had the panel, and finding at the commencement of it three or four names of favourites of the defendant, he wrote other three or four in their place, and transposed them to the lowest part of the panel.

Sentence

And for these misdemeanours he was fined £200, imprisonment, to have papers in Westminster Hall, confession in the Common Bench, and to be debarred from all practice as an attorney, and it was referred also to my Lord Anderson to expel him from the Common Bench for ever. And the Lord Keeper said that this is a great offence and worthy of very great punishment, for it confounds many laws; for the Sheriff is sworn to make good returns, and the Under-Sheriff is also sworn now-a-days, and cannot execute the office but once in three years, and he is to have a fee for each return; and by this false return subjects are grieved

[1] First written Ingram. [2] This word is doubtful.

and annoyed, the sheriff and under-sheriff are deceived, and the laws of no force; "For in my opinion (he said), in debt when there is a return on the original of *nichil*, and on *Alias* and *Capias* of *nihil*, or *non est inventus*, [made] by the Attorney of the party, without the sheriff, and then the defendant is sued to the exigent and outlawed, he would have an action on the case against the party who made the false return, when the defendant is [a man] of substance and easily to be found." And to this the Chief Justices said nothing, but seemed to agree as to the law. Lord Anderson, Chief Justice of the Common Bench, said that every attorney of the Common Bench took an oath to reveal every falsity and misdemeanour in the returning of writs, and other things, of all attorneys of the Court, if they knew of any; otherwise they were perjured if they did not do this.

FARINGTON'S case

Another cause of hearing on a bill and answer, William Farington, plaintiff, and ,[1] defendant. A bond was sealed by one William Farington, [the plaintiff's] third son, with additions [2] in all respects as if he was the father; [p. 48] and the father was arrested and paid the debt. And for this he sued the obligee in this Court. And when the matter appeared, William Farington the father prayed to be dismissed without costs; and this was allowed by the Court, if he would swear that he knew when he preferred his bill that his son William Farington was bound to the same obligee, with all the additions [2] of his father.

Bill dismissed without costs

MAYE *v.* EBDEN

Riot, &c.

Slanderous bill dismissed with costs, and withdrawn from the file for want of proof

Another cause of hearing between Maye, plaintiff, and Ebden, defendant, a man of good fame and credit in Sussex, and having £200 in lands. The bill was scandalous and slanderous, and a defamation of the defendant, and concerned supposed riots, and charged him in manner with felony and other misdemeanours. Divers witnesses were examined and proved nothing at all. And therefore the cause was dismissed, the bill withdrawn from the file and cancelled, and the plaintiff was fined £40 with imprisonment.

[1] Blank in MS.

[2] This word is used in the sense of descriptions.

1597 Oct. 19 — Motion — Costs for attachment on insufficient affidavit

Sergeant Healle moved for costs of appearance on attachment for contempt for non-appearance on process supposed to be served, because the attachment was procured on an affidavit insufficient to warrant it. The parties made an affidavit that they did not know of the process, and that it was never served on them. Wherefore it was ordered that the clerk who made the warrant of attachment on this insufficient affidavit should pay the costs of the parties who were never served with the process; and therefore there is no contempt in them, and they shall have their costs.

1597 Oct. 21

In Camera Stellata, coram Consilio ibidem, die Veneris, 21° Octobris, 1597, Elizab. 39, termino Michaelis.[1]

KERKAM *v.* SMITHE and others — Misdemeanour — Bill dismissed

Kerkam, plaintiff, Smithe and others, defendants, for misdemeanours, for this that he[2] took upon himself to deliver one hundred loads of hay ('of heye, good, sweete & marchantable, suche as Plumsted marshe dothe yeelde'). This was admitted to be the whole of the matter, and therefore the cause was dismissed with costs; and the Counsellor, Cleighton of the Inner Temple, who put his hand to the bill, was fined £10, and debarred by the Lord Keeper from all practice in this Court.

Perjury

Another cause of hearing for perjury, in effect as follows: in a trial at common law, relating to common *pur cause del vicinage,* fourteen were sworn to prove it, and in Chancery fourteen others were sworn to prove it. And on a bill to prove them perjured, fourteen were examined in this Court, and the Court was moved if it be fit to sentence this or not, for if this Court convict any one of them of perjury, the other twenty-seven are also convicted thereof. And thereupon the Court dismissed the cause, and suspended the costs until the trial should be had at common law which is now pending; and this trial shall be pursued

[1] Six Councillors and Judges were present.
[2] It is not quite clear who is referred to: probably the defendant Smithe.

with effect, and when it is ended, the costs shall be taxed according as the trial goes to either side.

[p. 49]
BEVERLEY v. PITTES and others

Perjury, riot, and fraud

Another cause of hearing between a poor man, Beverley, plaintiff, and another poor man, Robert Pittes, and others, defendants, for perjury, riot and fraud. The perjury in Robert Pittes was in this form: at a trial in Somersetshire, he deposed that one William [1] the father, in 2 Elizabeth, gave a lease (which he had) by parol to his daughter, 'Jhone' [1] in marriage, whereas it was proved that the said William, the father, in 4 Elizabeth, by his will gave the lease to his eldest son ,[1] with remainder to his younger son, and gave other legacies to his daughters. And the witnesses to this demise are supposed to be the witnesses to the said parol lease, who are now dead, and were also the witnesses to divers leases made by the said eldest son; and the eldest son and his issue enjoyed the said lease, by force of the said demise, all their lives, to this day without interruption. And the daughter, 'Johne' ,[1] never claimed this in her life-time, but since her death, her daughter took a husband, and they procured this Pittes to swear thus, whereas the father, William ,[1] disliked the marriage, and never agreed to it. And while [Pittes] swore that [the father] made this parol lease at the time of the marriage, it was proved that he was not at the marriage. And Robert Pittes himself confessed his perjury, saying, 'For that you haue shorne me of woolles tenemente you promysed me for helpinge you to this lande, I will goe to London & make knowne all yor knauerye.' As to the riot, it was in cutting and carrying the corn of this land, with force and weapons, before it was ripe. The fraud was in another, one ,[1] who sold the land by composition to this plaintiff for £50, and warranted it against all former sales, whereas he had sold it before to divers persons and by several diverse conveyances.

Sentence

Pittes was condemned of perjury, fined £40, being a

[1] Blank in MS.

1597 Oct. 21

poor man, 'to stande one the pillorye at Westminster wth one eare nailled, & at th'assizes in Sommersetshire wth another eare nailled, & imprisonmente.'

The others, for the riot, were suspended until their answer should be found in the Court, which was now missing.

Another for the fraud and riot was fined £100, and imprisonment, and the repayment of the money that the plaintiff had paid him, and the possession of the land to the plaintiff.

By the Lord Keeper: A parol lease is a perjured lease if there was not communication before and perfect contract since, by good witnesses and for good considerations.

[p. 50]

Phillips was assigned by the Court *in forma pauperis* to be of the plaintiff's counsel, Sergeant Healle with the defendant *in forma pauperis*. The cause was tedious and intricate, the depositions [1] great and very many, and because they have drawn exquisite pleas [2] in this case, the Lord Keeper greatly commended them, and encouraged others by their virtuous example.

1597 Oct. 23

In Curia Regali, Solis, 23 Octobris, Elizab. 37, An^{o} Do^{ni} 1597. In the morning, Charles Howard, Baron of Effingham, Lord Admiral of England, was created Earl of Nottingham to him and his heirs male, by Patent, and he was also made Lord High Steward of England. Camden, the Antiquary and Schoolmaster of Westminster, was made Clarencieux King of Arms.

PARLIAMENTE. 39 Elizab. 1597. Ceremony del ceo

The commencement of the High Court of Parliament, Monday, the 24th of October, 39 Elizabeth, A.D. 1597. Between the hours of 9 and 12 o'clock, the Knight Marshall, Sir Thomas Garrette, cleared the way, and then came the Masters of the Chancery, Dr. Hone, Dr. Stanhop, Dr. Carewe, Dr. Amye, and others, the Queen's Counsel, Flemminge the Solicitor, Kooke the Attorney, Drewe the Queen's Sergeant, the Masters of the

[1] *Liuers.* [2] Query. *Ils ont trands pluis exquisite.*

Requests, Cæsar and Herberte, the Judges of the Law, the Barons of the land, the Bishops, the Earls, the officers of the Household, the Lord Keeper, the Earl of Cumberlande carrying the sword, the Marques of Winchester carrying the cap, the Earl of Worster leading the 'emptye horse,' then comes the Queen, drawn in an open chariot[1] by two white horses with red manes, then an 'empty' horse and an 'emptye riche coache,' and then the ladies in their degree, upon good horses. By good report, there were 8 or 10 killed in the press. The Lord Chief Justice of England was unhorsed and in great danger. It was one o'clock before the Queen came. She heard a sermon in Westminster Church; Watson, Bishop of Chichester, preached. The Earl of Sussexe was instituted High Marshall for this day, but afterwards the Earl of Essexe was created Earl Marshall of England.

In Camera Stellata, coram consilio ibidem, Mercurij, 26 Octobris, 1597, ter^no^ Mich^is^, Elizab. 39.[2] [p. 51] 1597 Oct 26

The first cause of hearing was between Edward Everarde, plaintiff, Greene and others, defendants, for riot; and because the plaintiff would not make affidavit of his own knowledge, but only on report, that the process was served on the defendants 14 days before the day of hearing, and because the order for hearing did not limit any certain day, [the case] was delayed by the Court and a new day of hearing had to be procured, for the course [practice] of this Court, on the hearing of any cause, is first to read an affidavit, or to have it sworn *viva voce* in Court, that process was served 14 days before the day of hearing.

EVERARDE *v.* GREENE and others — Riot

Cause de hearing deferre per defalt d'affidavit de proces servie

Doient este 14 jours meane ente le proces servie et le joure de hearinge

Devant chescun hearing affidavit doit este fait que proces est servie sur son science demesne

Another cause of hearing was between James Rider of Yorkshire, and his 4 [*sic*] sons (thus opened by counsel), plaintiffs, against Hue Hare of the Inner Temple, and Sir John Sauvelle of Yorkeshire, and others, defendants, for falsifying a verdict, riot, and other misdemeanours. Phillips,

RIDER and others *v.* HARE, SAVILLE, and others — Falsifying a verdict,

[1] *Charrette.*

[2] Nine Councillors and Judges were present.

1597
Oct. 26

riots, and other misdemeanours, oppressions, &c.

Parolls incertein in bille referre deste consyder per Ch. Just. et Ch. Bar.

Matter de pais et matter de recorde diversity in bille in Camera Stellata

"Or to the like effect": good matter about this

Counsel for the defendants, moved divers uncertain points in the bill, one that he did counterfeit divers things, or to the like effect, another for the procurement by Hue Hare, and [not] showing what he procured nor the time of this. And for these and other uncertainties the bill was referred to the Chief Justice and the Chief Baron, and on their report, if the bill be good, to be heard here on the 11th of November next.

By the Attorney: If a bill rehearse matter *in pais*, which is not of record, to such or such a purpose, 'or the like in effecte,' it is not good, thus of perjury, or action on the case for slanderous or defamous words; but where it rehearses matter of record, it is good.

[p. 52]

HORE
v.
JOHNES and others

Riot, and disobeying and rescue[1] of warrants of Justices of Assize and Justices of the Peace

Three riots and a misdemeanour by the parson of a church on the Sabbath day

Defendants proclaimed rebels

Rescue in a riotous manner of a warrant for good abearing made by a Justice of Assize, and also by a Justice of the Peace

The three causes of hearing between Thomas Hore, plaintiff, and Laurence Johnes, parson of a church, and Alice his wife, and others, defendants, for three several riots and a misdemeanour; the said Laurence Johnes and his wife only have answered, and now the Court and Counsel proceed with them only, the others being attached upon proclamations of rebellion. A warrant for good behaviour[2] [had been] granted by Lord Anderson, then Justice of Assize there, against the [defendant; plaintiff in MS.] Laurence Johnes; he disobeyed this with force and arms on the Sabbath day before divine service, and wounded divers persons; and the same the next day; and also on another day, he in like manner disobeyed a warrant for his good "abearing" issued by a Justice of the Peace; and at another time, he arrested the plaintiff without a warrant, and brought him within Salsebery jurisdiction, and feigned[3] and devised divers actions for great sums against him. To all this [the defendant] pleaded "not guilty," but all the matters were substantially proved against him and his wife. And for these offences, Sir John Fortescue and the Archbishop would fine him £100, with imprisonment and restoration to the party of his damages. But by all the

[1] Seems to be used in the sense of resistance to.
[2] *Per le bone abearinge.* [3] *Feige* in MS.

others of the Court, he was fined 500 marks, imprisonment without return in haste or enlargement, referred to the Archbishop to depose him from his degree and his ministry, and then to have exemplary punishment by the pillory with confession at the next Assizes; and his wife £40 and imprisonment. The other defendants, who are sought for on proclamations of rebellion, to be indicted before the Justice of Assize and punished by him. Also the Lord Keeper moved that it is a great abuse, and worthy of grave punishment, to devise feigned actions on the case, or of felony, or treason, or such, and then to take the body of the party in execution, or to vex him with actions of great value.

Fine 500 marks, imprisonment without enlargement, deposition from his ministry, pillory and confession

The wife: Fine £40, and imprisonment

Abuse in feigning of great actions after arrest on action on the case or the like

Ruled by the Court: If anyone arrest men by a ticket of paper to appear in this Court, and no process is had out of this Court for their appearance (which may appear by the certificate of Cotton, the officer of the Court), on the affidavit of anyone so served, the party offending shall be committed to the Fleet and punished at the discretion of the Court.

Paper tickets without original process

[p. 53]

Be it noted as well that this Court observes strictly [the rule] of having the service of process appear by affidavit, otherwise they will not give credence to it. So in all causes of hearing, "Counsellers" at the bar ought to open the bill and answer truthfully as they are, without addition or detraction, and show what is proved in the depositions [*liuers*], and rely on this only, and not on any other collateral things, even where these are not only necessary, substantial, probable, and true [1] but [also] things material and effectual; they should move these later,[2] and refer the consideration of them to the wisdom of the Court, and never press the Court with them.

Affidavit as to service of process *et bon matter del ceo*

Observation as to causes of hearing

What evidence is material on hearing, what not

In Camera Stellata, coram Consilio ibidem, Veneris, 28 Octobr. '97, Elizab. 39, ter^{no} Mich^{is}.[3]

1597 Oct. 28

[1] *voyer.*

[2] *Leinter.*

[3] No names are given.

1597 Oct. 28

EGERTON v. STARKY and others — Riot

£300 fine for three several riots

Egerton, plaintiff, Starky and others, defendants. The cause between Egerton and Starky was heard, concerning three riots by Starky and others; [Starky] was fined £300 for the three several riots, and each other defendant, £20; and if they have not the ability [to pay], then Starky to pay all. I [1] was not then in Court, but [this is] by the report of another then present.

1597 Nov. 4

In Camera Stellata, coram Consilio ibidem, Veneris, 4 Novembris, '97, Elizab. 39, ter^no^ Mich^is^.[2]

Perjury. The principal acquitted, the accessory is discharged; [also] by the death of the principal perjuror

Divers causes of hearing: one of perjury against one defendant, and of subornation and procuring of the same in the other defendant. Since the publication of the depositions, the defendant against whom the perjury was charged has died; and by the sentence of all the Court, the suborner or procurer of the perjury is discharged by the death of the perjuror.

[p. 54]

LA MOTE'S case — Forgery, riot, and 'practise'

No forgery

What riot; what not

The other cause was the supposed forgery of the will of a woman, with riot and 'practise' in one La Mote, a French preacher, and others, good merchants in Southampton. The forgery was in this manner: The preacher and the other merchants came to the woman, who was in a grievous malady and 'senceles,' and they devised a will and published it. The riot, that they, as executors, having the house, and a stranger claiming a chest and certain money in it, they ejected him by force, but without weapon or blow. The 'practise,' that the preacher and the others by colour of a will of the plaintiff's elder brother, made twenty years ago, sued an action of detinue in the Court of 'Pypowders' [3] in Southampton, and recovered £300. And for the forgery and riot all the defendants were held

[1] John Hawarde, the writer of the MS.

Seven Councillors and Judges were present.

[3] The Court of Pie-powder (*pied puldreaux*, a pedlar) was a Court held in fairs and markets, to administer justice to buyers and sellers, and for redress of disorders committed there. See Jacob's *Law Dict.*

acquitted, and the bill was withdrawn from the file, and the party who sued this by letter of attorney [*i.e.* the plaintiff] to confess this in the congregation at Southampton and to pay a fine of £20 to the Queen. And the 'practise' is referred to the Bishop of Winchester and Flemminge, the King's [*sic*] Solicitor.[1] The preacher was greatly commended, and certified by several of great credit to be a pious, erudite, honest and virtuous man, and (by the Lord Admiral) of a noble house in France. And as to the forgery they did not prove that it would benefit themselves; therefore *Cuy bonum.* And as to the riot, if a stranger come to my house and will not depart, but remain in it against my good pleasure, it is lawful for me to expel him by force.

Defendants acquitted; plaintiff fined £20, imprisonment, confession in the congregation

Riot, and good matter of this

Another cause, [2] plaintiff, Smithe, attorney of the 'Guilde Halle en Londres,' defendant, for erasing a record. Debt upon an obligation [bond] was sued; and judgment given [on the bond], and entered by the clerk of the Town Clerk in the Sheriff's Court, and it was agreed by Wilbram, attorney for the defendant, and Smithe, attorney for the plaintiff, that, if he should show the obligation before such a day, then the judgment should be void; and Smithe, on the 'veiwe' of the obligation, erased the judgment and altered all the substance of it by agreement with the clerk of the Court and with Wilbram, the attorney for the other party. It was adjudged by the Court to be no offence in Smithe, since it was not corruption, deceit, trickery, nor fraud; but it is not a good thing to be allowed, since the Records are sacred things, and cannot be altered without the Judge in Court.

SMITHE's case — Erasing a record

[p. 55].

Defendant acquitted

Ruled by the Lord Keeper that when a plaintiff in this Court prosecutes his case by letter of attorney and disburses money for the plaintiff or defendant, he shall pay costs if the case be sentenced against him.

Case prosecuted by letter of attorney, and the costs for this

[1] Thomas Fleming, Solicitor-General.

[2] Blank in MS.

1597 Nov. 4

REDE *v.* BOOTHES

If a man will not answer interrogatories, it shall be held as a confession

The processes of this Court

In a motion by Cooke, the Queen's Attorney, between Rede and Boothes, the order of the Court is that if the defendant will not answer, *tenetur pro confesso*; thus, if a man prefers a bill and [the defendant] will not answer it, it is not held as a confession; but on this answer the plaintiff shall serve interrogatories, and if the defendant will not answer these, *tenetur pro confesso*. The processes of this Court are subpoena, attachment, proclamation of rebellion and commission of rebellion, and a pursuivant of arms [to be] one of the commissioners.

1597 Nov. 9

In Camera Stellata, coram Consilio ibidem, 9 Novembris, 1597, Elizab. 39, ter^no^ Mich^is^.[1]

Plaintiffs *in forma pauperis* sentenced to have exemplary punishment. A man, pillory and papers. A woman to be whipped in Bridewelle

Divers causes of hearing in which the plaintiffs were *in forma pauperis*, and because they did not prove the assertions in their bill [*sic*], and had no ability to pay the fine to the Court nor the costs to the party, it was adjudged by the Court that they should have corporal punishment, the one imprisonment, pillory and papers, the other, a woman, to be whipped in Bridewelle.

Hearing referred to show cause. *Habeas corpus* awarded of a prisoner in Court

Another cause of hearing was referred 'to shewe cawse' on the next day, and *habeas corpus* was awarded to have the party in Court on the next day, he being now in prison on an execution.

BLOMER'S case

'Counsellor,' of the Middle Temple, of no learning, nor honesty, committed [p. 56]

One Blomer, 'Counseller del middell temple,' was reported by the Lord Keeper to be a man generally reputed of no learning and of no honesty, but having a volubility of speech, a great audacity and 'impudencye'; on affidavit made that he suborned witnesses, he was committed to the Fleet; for it is the custom of this Court, on affidavit of disobeying process of the Court, or other proceedings, 'practise,' or misdemeanour, to commit [the offender] to prison.

[1] Eight Councillors and Judges were present.

In Camera Stellata, coram Consilio ibidem, Veneris, 11 Novembris, 1597, Elizab. 39, ter^no^ Mich^is^.[1] 1591 Nov. 11

The Attorney first moved against the engrossers of corn, against whom he proceeded by bill; and ten [of the defendants] have answered imperfectly, which [answers] were [referred] to the two Chief Justices, who certified them to be insufficient; [the defendants were ordered] to give £10 to the poor. The Lord Keeper moved that the Counsellors [*i.e.* Counsel] who devised these answers should be disbarred, especially as the Queen was a party; and thereupon the Lord Keeper moved also that Coomes of the Middle Temple, Counsellor, who had been disbarred from practise half a year ago for evil counsel in devising that the Queen should have no benefit of traitors or felons, or any lord [?], should now on his confession and penitency and submission be restored to practise again.

ATT.-GEN. *v.* Engrossers of corn

Engrossers fined £10 to the poor, for bad answers certified by the Chief Justices

Counsel fined for bad answers

Coomes restored to practise on submission and confession

The cause referred the last day in which James Parrye of Hereforde, esquire, was plaintiff against Roger Bodenham and other eight, defendants, for perjury and subornation and other misdemeanours, was now heard. The bill was '9 foote longe,' measured by the Lord Treasurer, and contained five skins of parchment, with the hand [signature] of Lancaster, 'Counsellor of Graies Inne,' to it. But the Attorney and Phillips, for the plaintiff, certified the Court that the bill was insufficient; but because the plaintiff said confidently that they confessed the perjury, it was referred to the Attorney and Phillips, and on their certificate to be sentenced accordingly, and not before.

PARRYE *v.* BODENHAM, and others

Perjury and subornation

Lancaster, Counsellor for a tedious bill

Another cause of hearing in which Lawrence Hyde, Counsellor of the Middle Temple, and Henry Hide, his brother, were plaintiffs, George Corrielle, clerk, John Baillie and Robert Bailie and others, defendants, for maintenance, champerty and riot. The Earl of Pembroke,

HIDE *v.* CORRIELLE, BAILIE, and others

Maintenance, champerty and riot

[1] Eight Councillors and Judges were present.

1597 Nov. 11

patron of a church 'presentative,' and the Ordinary, in 3 E[dward] VI, enfeoffed the plaintiff's ancestor in fee of the said parsonage, as of a parsonage impropriate; and the plaintiffs, and those whose estate they have, enjoyed the same accordingly up to the 36th [year] of Elizabeth now Queen. The defendants, with malice, and on pretence of a lease made for the trial of the title, maintained suits against the plaintiffs, etc., and disbursed money. But the riot was not proved. And it was certified by Justice Wamsloe [1] that the Court could proceed on the bill either under the statute [2] or at common law. But because on the whole matter some points of law arose, and the matter was not apparently proved, the Court was divided as to the sentence. The Chief Justices declared this to be maintenance, and [decreed] a forfeiture of the whole value of the land, and two of the defendants to be fined each £100. Sir John Fortescue, Lord Buckherst, Lord Northe, the Lord Treasurer, the Archbishop and the Lord Keeper, on the contrary, referred this to the common law, since it was not proved directly; but they greatly condemned maintenance; and the Lord Keeper agreed with the two Chief Justices as to the fine of £200 against two of the defendants.

[p. 57]. Parsonage presentative and impropriate; diversity

Stat. 32 Hen. VIII. cap. 9

Court divided in judgment

Sentence

Maintenance condemned

And upon this case were moved divers good matters: By all—That they do not favour impropriations, and that these cannot be made now-a-days but by Parliament, and they were always created by Parliament, by 31 and 32 Hen. VIII. [3] "of dissolutions," and before by other statutes, and by these have now become lay things. Their commencement was before the Conquest by the corruption of Abbats and other men of religion, when noblemen gave land to a small abbey, or founded an abbey or other house of religion, and they had small lands or possessions, the Abbats devised that they could give parsonages before

Impropriations not favoured, and cannot be made but by Parliament

Their origin and commencement

[1] Thomas Walmsley, Judge of the Common Pleas.

[2] The Bill of Bracery and buying of Titles, 32 Hen. VIII. cap. 9.

[3] 31 Hen. VIII. cap. 13; 32 Hen. VIII. cap. 20.

presentative, and they took the profits of them, and in this way made them impropriate. But at this day the parson, patron and Ordinary cannot grant the tithes of a parsonage presentative, nor make it impropriate, but they may grant the glebe or charge it *imperpetuum*.

Parson, patron, and Ordinary cannot make impropriation

And on the statute of maintenance,[1] the Judges resolved that it is not material if the title be good or bad, if he has not had possession for one entire year before, or of the reversion or remainder of it, or has [not] taken the rents and profits of it for one entire year before.

Maintenance on good or bad title; no difference

In Camera Stellata, coram Consilio ibidem, Mercurij, 17 Novembris, 1597, Elizab. 40, ter^{no} Mich^{is}.[2]

[p. 58] 1597 Nov. 17

A cause of hearing in which a woman was plaintiff *in forma pauperis*; and because the bill was slanderous, and not proved, she was sentenced to be drawn with papers to the 'Brydewelle' and there whipped, for 'iustice is euen as well to the poore as the ryche, & it is her Ma$^{tie's}$ daylye Commaundemente to doe iustice to all sortes, & if her selfe be a partye.'

Woman sentenced for slanderous bill

Another cause of hearing *in forma pauperis*, Helis, plaintiff, Henry Farrar, defendant, for riot, forcible entry, and other misdemeanours. Phillips was assigned his Counsel a year past, and the plaintiff gave notice to him of it this term, and not before; and he [Phillips], being then of Counsel with the defendant, refused. Whereupon the plaintiff preferred a petition to the Lord Keeper, reciting that [Phillips] had contemptuously refused, and was of Counsel with the defendant, having perused his writings and depositions [*liuers*], which was false. And for this slander the plaintiff was sentenced to have imprisonment, to have papers in Westminster Hall, and the pillory there, and to be whipped at Cheapside, and the pillory there. And Phillips was fully acquitted with great credit by all

HELIS *v.* FARRAR

Riot, &c.

Forma pauperis grievously punished for slander of Phillips, Counsellor at law, by petition to the Lord Keeper

Sentence

[1] 32 Hen. VIII. cap. 9.
[2] Seven Councillors and Judges were present.

1597 Nov. 17 the Court, and especially favoured by the Lord Keeper, and very many arguments of this.

LUTTRELLE v. BAKER and others — Riot, &c. Great fine for riot in hunting deer

Another cause of hearing, George Luttrelle of Somerset, plaintiff, George Baker, James Fugars, defendants, for riot, and other misdemeanours in killing a 'deare' in Luttrelle's park. Upon confession, they were fined each £100, three years imprisonment or seven,[1] and to be bound with sureties for their good 'abearinge' for seven years, and not to hunt there again, and [to pay] damages to the party.

1598 May 24

In Camera Stellata, coram Consilio ibidem, Mercurij, 24 May, 1598, Elizab. 40, ter^{no} Paschae.[2]

SIR WALTER RAWLEYE, Lord of the Stanneryes. Warrant after judgment and execution

Motion against Sir Walter Rawleighe, Lord of the Stanneryes, because he had directed a warrant to imprison two men who had sued divers Tinners of the Stanneryes and had [obtained] judgment and execution against them, and after this he granted his warrant. Which was disallowed and disliked by the Court, and a day was given [him] to answer it.

[p. 59]

ATT. GEN. v. MARKHAM and BOOTHE — Delivery of a forged deed, or otherwise close prisoners

The Attorney moved against Markham and Boothe to deliver a deed supposed to be forged. It is ordered that if they do not deliver the deed to the Court by the next day then they shall be close prisoners, with fetters, and as strict diet as can be used for any prisoner.[3]

BEESTON v. MILLE — Extortion

Phillips moved in the case of Beeston against Mille, clerk of this Court, to have the interrogatories of both parties referred to Commissioners appointed by the Court, and attachments against those who would not be examined by the Commissioners, and to view Mille's books to have proofs from them; which was opposed by Sergeant Healle

[1] Perhaps the longer term was in default of paying the fine, or in default of finding sureties.

[2] Nine Councillors and Judges were present.

[3] See pp. 22, 26, 29, 64, and Appendix II.

of Counsel with Mille, who would thus become his own accuser; and the forfeiture of his office was also sought. But it was ruled by the Lord Keeper that the books are appurtenant to the Queen and not to Mille, and therefore the parties might command them, with Mille's clerk to see that they are not falsified; for the subjects have been abused and "polled" these fourteen years past by Mille, as by the books (which are the Queen's Records and appertain to each subject) it may appear and be proved.

RICHARD CALLARD *v.* JOHN PADDON, JOHN CORNISHE, and others

Perjury

Cause of hearing, Richard Callarde, plaintiff, John Paddon, John Cornishe, defendants; [they] were committed for perjury, fined 100 marks each, pillory and imprisonment. And the perjury was in this manner, at the Assizes in Devon. [Two other] defendants, Eustace Callarde and his wife, and others, came to Serjeant Glanvill for his advice, saying that the father of Eustace Callarde had assured lands in such a form: "Stande forthe, Eustace, & I will giue thee, reseruinge to mee & my wyfe an estate for oure too liues, suche landes, to thee & thy heires"; and thus they would swear, and not otherwise. Whereupon Glanvill said that it would not avail, but that if they would swear these words: "Stande forthe, Eustace, heere I doe gyve thee suche lande to thee & thy heires, reseruinge to mee and my wyfe an estate for oure 2 liues," [it would be sufficient]. And then at another Assizes they swore those words, and on their evidence it was found [in their favour] and judgment accordingly; but afterwards it was reversed in the Exchequer Chamber.

"Stande forthe, Eustace!"

[p. 60]

Procuring of perjury

Eustace Callarde and Sydwell his wife were convicted of procuring these witnesses to swear these words, and others to countenance the same. And for this they were adjudged to have the pillory, a fine of £40 and imprisonment. And it was moved by the Lord Keeper, that every Counsellor at Law ought to be discreet and of good government, for he is called 'Counsellor, not onelye to giue Councelle, but allsoe to keepe Counselle.' Also Serjeant Glanville had done well to direct that the evidence was not

Sentence

1598 May 24 good, if he had stayed there, and had not directed what would serve their purpose; for this caused the perjury. As in the case [of] Lane of Staffordshire, a deed was forged with words sufficient to defeat the Queen of a wardship, which the true deed did not. And also the great men in the counties ought to intermeddle with their own causes and not with other men's businesses, and not to write letters countenancing a cause, or for a juror to appear generally.

Riot

Eustace Callarde, John Callarde, Richard Corey, Edmond Bulle, Emotte Bulle, Johan Langbridge, were sentenced, each £20 and imprisonment, for a riot in entering into the house of Richard Callarde, the plaintiff, with force, and taking evidences and other things, which he [Eustace Callarde] re-delivered now by the sentence of the Court.

1598 May 26

In Camera Stellata, coram Consilio ibidem, Veneris, 26 May, 1598, Elizab. Rne 40. Termino Pasche.[1]

Sir Walter Rawlye; and good matter touching the Stanneryes

The former motion[2] which concerned Sir Walter Rawlye, Lord of the Stanneries, was moved again, and referred to the Judges, and the consideration of the Vice-Warden of the Stanneryes and the Steward of the same to make warrants after judgment and execution at common law, which is contrary to the Great Charter (*quod nullus liber homo imprisonetur*), and the common law is the surest and best inheritance that any subject hath, *et perde ceo et perde tout.*

[p. 61]

Searchers of London committed for contempt, and misdemeanours in their offices

The Attorney moved against the four Searchers of London for misdemeanours in their places, being now made an office, who ought to seal and measure all cloths, and do not do this, but take money from the 'clothyars,' since the close of the last parliament, £1500; and for contempt

[1] Seven Councillors and Judges were present.
[2] See *ante*, p. 94.

of the process of this Court served on them, they were committed.

RAWLEIGHE'S case — Outlawed man plaintiff shall not be answered

In the last case touching Sir Walter Rawleighe, a bill was preferred, and the defendant answered that the plaintiff was five several times outlawed, and showed the records, [and craved] judgment if he [the plaintiff] should be answered. By the Court: No. And the Attorney cannot proceed on this bill on behalf of the Queen, but must prefer a new bill in his own name.

FINCHE *v.* ANNATE and others — Conspiracy for misprision of treason

Cause of hearing, Finche, merchant and Controller of the Customs of London, plaintiff, Annate, Poell and Berrye, defendants, for conspiracy. Annate devised a letter in Finche's name, containing matter touching misprision of treason in 'coyninge doble pistolets,' and wrote this in Finche's name, being sealed; and he opened it and read it and took copies and published them; but the letter itself could not be viewed. The cause of this and the 'originalle' was malice, for Finche, being Controller of the Customs, would not suffer Annate's beer to pass 'transemare,' and therefore [Annate] devised this letter. And then when he had opened it and read it and published copies of the same, he took it to Sir Edward Hobby, a Justice of the Peace in Kent. It was 'vnhoneste' for him to open the letter, for if he doubted that it contained suspicion of treason, he ought to have carried it to the Justice of the Peace and delivered it to him. And this conspiracy was adjudged a great fault, and was sentenced by the whole Court: First, Annate, fine £200, to be nailed to the pillory, to have papers and imprisonment. For the coining of 'doble pistolets' is misprision of treason only, because it is a coin not allowed or stamped within this realm; otherwise if it were treason, he should lose his ears, and have perpetual imprisonment and should forfeit all his lands and goods for ever.

Sentence Fine, £200 pillory, papers and imprisonment

[p. 62] Poell, £100 fine, pillory and imprisonment

Poell was adjudged accessory and procurer of this, and was sentenced to a fine of £100, pillory and imprisonment. Berrye was acquitted.

1598 May 26 Controller should not be a merchant

It was said by the Court that the Controller ought not to be a merchant, but that this is punishable in another course [? Court].

Jurisdiction of the Star Chamber, which is great

Ruled by the Court, that if any Judge, Justice, officer or subject of the realm shall go beyond his bounds and limits, and misdemean himself in any manner, this Court has power and authority to examine and punish this; and this is clear law without any doubt or question.

1598 June 28

In Camera Stellata, coram Consilio ibidem, Mercurij, 28 Junij, termino Trinitatis, Elizab. 40, An° Do^{ni} 1598.[1]

Perjury referred to common law by reason of verdicts

Perjury confessed and not sentenced

All the four causes appointed to be heard this day did not come to sentence. One for perjury against five with whom two verdicts have past, and therefore it was referred for trial at common law by indictment or action on the statute. And because one had confessed the perjury, he was to be sentenced, but the Court respited him until the trial at common law, the other cross bill depending on this.

Cause dismissed for insufficient bill

Another was compounded; and the last for insufficiency and uncertainty of the bill for forgery, in which no certain time was limited, [was dismissed].

Dedimus potestatem will not be granted before contempt purged

Ruled by the Lord Keeper, that when contempt is committed, no *dedimus potestatem* shall be granted before the contempt be purged and answered.

LITLETON *v.* LITLETON

In what case defendants may be used as witnesses

Also ruled in the case of Gilberte Litleton, the father, plaintiff, and John Litleton, his son, defendant, that if a plaintiff complain against several defendants for divers particular and several offences, and not [against] any two of them for one and the same offence, [one] defendant may use the [other] defendants as witnesses in all matters

[1] Eight Councillors and Judges were present.

with which they are not charged by the plaintiff in his bill; and this is the rule of the Court.

Koke, the Queen's Attorney, was absent by reason of the death of his wife, Monday, 26 June, 1598;[1] and last term Justice Beamonde[2] and Serjeant Drewe[3] died. Wife of the Queen's Attorney died Justice Beamond and Serjeant Drewe died

In Camera Stellata, coram Consilio ibidem, Veneris, 30 Junij, termino Trinitatis, Elizab. 40, An° Do^ni^ 1598.[4] [p. 63] 1598 June 30

QUEEN'S SERJEANT *v.* BULLE and others

Slander

Information by the Queen's Serjeant and Solicitor against Benjamin Bulle, servant to Lady Paget, now wife to one Sr Edwarde Carewe, on confession by the party of slanderous words against the Lord Chief Justice of the Bench [Sir John Popham]. One Deere was apprehended by one Barnes, a Justice of the Peace in Middlesex, on suspicion of a robbery and murder, and was examined by him, and conducted to Newgate, and at the trial there, before both the Chief Justices, the Recorder and divers others, he was indicted, arraigned, and condemned; and a woman named Marye Graye, having given evidence against the prisoner, the said Bulle many days after the trial approached her in Kent Street, and said to her, "Nowe, Graye, hathe god put into thy minde yet to saye the truthe concerninge Deere; I durste sweare vpon all the bookes in the worlde that he coulde not be guyltye of the murder & Robberye; if he were, he were woorthye of ten thousande deathes; the matter shall be hearde againe before the Councelle w^th^in 4 dayes, & then you shall be all hearde; god put into thy harte to saye the truthe;" and many other words sounding to retract the evidence after the trial,

[1] Bridget, daughter and heir of John Paston, esq., of Huntingfield, co. Suffolk. Foss, vol. vi. p. 109. On p. 111, it is stated that she died on June 27; the text here says June 26.

[2] Francis Beaumont, Judge of the Common Pleas, died April 22, 1598.

[3] Edward Drew, of the Inner Temple, appointed Queen's Serjeant, 1596.

[4] Eleven Councillors and Judges were present.

1598 June 30 and to re-examine the matter before the Council. Which was adjudged by the whole Court to be a heinous offence against the Queen and her dignity, against the common justice of the land, and a slander of the same, and a great defamation of the Lord Chief Justice of England; and he [the Lord Chief Justice] was acquitted of this, and discharged, and delivered with very much and very great fame, commendation, credit, reputation and honour, and by all adjudged to be the most grave, wise and just judge that ever before had possessed his place; and as to the trial itself, Lord Anderson, the Recorder of London, Barnes and Crompton,[1] reported in the hearing of the Court, that it was the most just that could be; inasmuch as the prisoner had a copy of the indictment (which he could not have without the warrant of the Queen's Counsel) and of the examinations of the witnesses on both sides, as well to acquit him as to accuse him, and he was reprieved also for [p. 64] many days. And Sr Edwarde Carewe confessed (being present at the said trial), that if he himself had been of the Jury, he would, on the same evidence, have condemned him, which aggravates and increases the offence now in question. And it was said by the Lord Keeper that if the Chief Justice had been found guilty of this offence, in the first place, he would draw the vengeance of God on all the land for innocent blood, he had abused the Queen and her justice, for she is the body and we are the parts of the body, and it is her continual charge "Serue not mee in knowledge, wisedome or eloquence, but serue mee in the Feare of god, & doe Justice equallye to all my subiectes in the feare of god." And this would have been his punishment, as the precedent is 24 Edward III.: Sir William Thorpe, Chief Justice of England, was accused of taking bribes; whereupon the King directed a grave Commission of the most honourable lords of the land, who examined the matter, and found him guilty of taking of one £10, of

[1] Probably two barristers who had been present at the trial. Crompton's name is given by Foss in a list of Counsel during Queen Elizabeth's reign. Barnes is not mentioned.

another £20, and in all not £60, and condemned him to death, and to forfeit all his goods and land for ever; and the cause of his judgment was 'for that he had falselye, iniustlye, & trayterouslye, & rebelliouselye, as muche as in him laye, offended the kinge's ma^stie^, his lawes, his Crowne & dygnitye.'[1] And the Lord Keeper extolled greatly the Chief Justice of his own knowledge, but said, to avoid flattery, *cum sapiens laudatur in facie, flagellatur in corde*. And by the whole Court, Bulle was sentenced to have imprisonment, £200 fine, to be nailed with papers to the pillory at Westminster, again at Newgate, and again in Cheapside, and each term that he should remain in prison, to carry papers on the pillory at Westminster. Sentence

In Camera Stellata, coram Consilio ibidem, Jovis, 6 Julij, Elizabeth. 40, An^o^ Do^ni^ [1598], le prochein joure apres Trinitye terme.[2] 1598 July 6

This was a day for motions only, as is always the custom, and after the Queen's Counsel had moved, the Lord Keeper delivered an exhortation[3] to the Judges and Justices by the commandment of the Queen, strictly delivered to him on the last Sabbath day at the Court. In the first place the Queen had an especial care and regard that all this Long Vacation the peace of her Church and of her land should be in all manner of ways maintained and preserved; and she charged the Judges here (who are trained in the knowledge of the laws, and touching whom [p. 65] the Queen has conceived a good opinion as to their justice and honesty, and therefore has advanced them to great dignity in justice, and which [Judges] are now to traverse all the realm in their several circuits for the common Justice of the realm), to have especial care and regard to preserve this according to the ancient laws of the realm, as they would render a strict and severe account thereof to

Motion day

Exhortation to Judges and Justice

[1] See Foss's *Judges*, vol. iii. p. 527.

[2] Seven Councillors are named, *et touts les Justices d'ambideux bankes et les barons del exchequer et diuers Justices del Peace.*

[3] Compare this with the other proclamations, pp. 19, 56, and *post*, p. 106, etc.

1598 July 6 her Majesty; and especially to regard the negligence of some Justices of the Peace, and the forwardness of others, and to punish the one and to recompense the other, and to make report of this to her Majesty; and since the peace of the Church, (thanks be to God,) is well preserved, but the disturbers of the peace of the land are 'sturdye Rouges & idle vagrant baggers,' these ought to have their punishment with great severity according to the purpose of the new statute.[1]

Also, the Justices of the Peace are to depart out of London to their rural habitations, and there to observe hospitality and to guard the Justice and good governance of the land, as they would answer the contrary in great contempt of her Majesty, her crown and royal dignity, and receive severe punishment for their former contempts in the like manner, contrary to divers worthy proclamations, commandments and exhortations; and to avoid the name of 'baskette' Justices of the Peace,[2] or the receipt of greater things.

And as to the subsidies lately given by Parliament[3] and now to be assessed, the Queen said nothing, or sparingly, but he [the Lord Keeper], of his own authority, charged the 'cessors' [assessors] to have especial care and regard to the just 'cessinge' of this, and not for any cause to charge the meaner sort of the people and discharge or disburden the better sort of the people, and with intent to gain freeholders in the county; for it is great deceit and a great sin to violate a promise to a friend, but to violate a promise and fidelity to the Queen herself and to God is more odious and detestable, for now indeed it is a certain debt due to her Majesty.

1598 Oct. 11 **In Camera Stellata,** coram consilio ibidem, Mercurij, 11 Octobris, Elizabethae 40, An^{o} Do^{ni} 1598.[4]

[1] 39 Eliz. cap. 4; An Act for punishment of Rogues, Vagabonds, and sturdy beggars.

[2] The basket Justices were so called because they allowed themselves to be bought over by presents of game. Wynter, *Curiosities of Civilization*, p. 493.

[3] 35 Eliz. cap. 12, 13.

[4] Six Councillors and Judges were present.

The first cause for hearing, Frier, plaintiff, and others, defendants ; and when the cause was appointed to be heard, the parties, by petition delivered to the Lord Keeper, procured a reference of the matter to the 'Attornie generalle,' to certify if it be fit for this Court; and the parties then agreed; and for this the plaintiff was sentenced to pay a fine to the Queen. FRIER'S case / Fine for compromising a case

Another cause for hearing, Scrogs, plaintiff, and [1] defendant, and divers others, for riot and maintenance; but the bill contained forgery and perjury [also], which were not proved; and for this the plaintiff was fined £10 for a false claim. And the Court was divided if it was riot or not, because there were no weapons nor blows, but only carrying hay with 'piclepronges,'[2] and no blows. But the Lord Keeper and others ruled this to be a riot, because they resisted a distress and 'piche le partye ouer the hedge,' and threatened him. And for this [they were] fined £20, notwithstanding that it was a small riot and not worthy of this Court; but because the country would not find it,[3] they sentenced it, and also because he would not replevy the beasts, which is the best trial, for all the title would appear by the pleading in the avowry. [p. 66] SCROGS, pl. / Riot, maintenance, etc. / Plaintiff fined / Sentence.

In Camera Stellata, coram Consilio ibidem, Mercurij, 16 Maij, Elizab. 41, An° Do[ni] 1599; adonque presente, Lo. Keeper, et Lo. Buckhurst adonque install Lo. Tresorer in le Chauncery et in l'eschequer, Lorde Admyralle adonque Erle de Nottingham, Lo. Chamberlin, Lo. Northe, L'archeuesque de Canterberye, ambideux Ch. Justices, et S[r] John Fortescue. 1599 May 16.

Edmund Kidermaister,[4] plaintiff, Maurice Hale, Richard Baum and divers others, women, defendants, 'for riots, routes & unlawefull assemblyes & other misdemeanours.' For the KIDERMAISTER v. HALE and others / Riot

[1] Blank in MS.

[2] Pikel a pitchfork, a hay fork. *North.* Halliwell.

[3] Had a Grand Jury thrown out a bill relating to it?

[4] Perhaps Ridermaister.

1599 May 16

first riot, each £10 and imprisonment; for the second riot, each £20 and imprisonment; for the third riot, each £30 and imprisonment; and the women to be punished with the 'kuckinge stoole,' and the men to stand on the pillory 'bareheaded & in woman's apparrelle.'

1599 May 18

In Camera Stellata, coram Consilio ibidem, Veneris, 18 Maij, Elizab. 41, An° Do^ni^ 1599; adonque presente Lo. Keeper, Lo. Tresorer, L'archeuesque de Canterberye, Lo. Northe, ambideux Ch. Justices, un esteant priuye Counseller,[1] et Sr John Fortescue.

BAILIFF OF SOUTHWARKE and others fined for extortion

The Bailiff of Southwarke and two of his men were (for extortion and other misdemeanours) fined, the Bailiff £100, his two men each £40, to stand on the pillory in three several places, and to have papers, and the two men to be whipped.

1599 June 13

In Camera Stellata, coram consilio ibidem, Mercurij, 13° Junij, tr^no^ Trinitatis, Elizab. 41, An° Do^ni^ 1599.[2]

ATT.-GEN. v. MISON

Contempt of authority and seditious words

[p. 67]

Cause of hearing, by information of the Attorney, against one [3] Mison, for seditious words in contempt of Justices of the Peace and their authority on the orders as to Corn and the poorer people in the time of the great dearth, and for seditious words against the Council and the Queen (viz. :—"they are knaues, I will keepe none of there bastardes, my goodes are my nowne,[4] they, nor the queene, nor the Councelle haue to doe wi^th^ my goodes, I will doe what I liste wth them," etc.). He was fined £100, imprisonment, to wear papers, to confess his fault, and to be bound for his good abearing.

£100 fine, imprisonment, for good abearing, papers and confession

ATT.-GEN. v. LUDLOWE

'depopulacions'

Another cause of hearing by information of the Attorney against Ludlowe of Wiltshire, a gentleman of good account

[1] From this it appears that the Judges who sat from time to time in the Star Chamber were not necessarily Privy Councillors.

[2] Eight Councillors and Judges were present.

[3] Blank in MS.

[4] *I.e.* mine own.

and great substance, for converting arable land to pasture, for the destruction of houses of husbandry and building cottages, to the 'depopulacion,' contrary to the late statute of 39 Elizabeth.[1] He was acquitted by the sentence, because [his] offences were committed before 39 Elizabeth, and so were pardoned by the statute; and the building and erecting of cottages is not to be punished in this [Court],[2] but by the Justices of Assize. Acquitted

In Camera Stellata, coram Consilio ibidem, Veneris, 22 Junij, Elizab. 41, An° Do^{ni} 1599, termino Trinitat.[3] 1599 June 22

Cause of hearing between Rochester and Rochester for forgery of a will; in these words "I giue all my landes wheresoeuer &c.," he forged "whereso for euer"; it was lengthily debated for two entire days, and at last was adjourned to Michaelmas term because they wanted probation to prove forged deeds which were pretended by the bill to be forged. ROCHESTER v. ROCHESTER — Forgery

Cause of hearing between Fleetewoode, a grave preacher, and Bankes of 'Lankashire,' in time past a Citizen of London; he was fined 500 marks, two of his servants for 'greeuous batterye' £40 apiece, and the others 40 marks, all [to suffer] imprisonment, and Bankes to be bound for his good behaviour, and to pay his servants' fines and £40 for the wounds to one of the plaintiff's servants. FLEETEWOODE v. BANKES — Riot. Fines, 500 marks, £40, 40 marks, £40, imprisonment, good abearing; master to pay for the servant

Another cause of hearing between Williams and others, plaintiffs, and Lhoyde, defendant, for extortions, and many other misdemeanours and grievous offences. He was fined 1000 marks, to stand on the pillory in three several places in Wales, imprisonment, and good abearing during his life. He sued divers processes in other names, and took money, and divers offences of a like nature. WILLIAMS and others v. LHOYDE — Extortions and other misdemeanours. Imprisonment, pillory in three places, fine 1000 marks, good abearing during life

[1] Chapter 2. [2] 'Course' in MS.
[3] Seven Councillors and Judges were present.

[p. 68] 1599 June 28

In Camera Stellata, coram consilio ibidem, Jovis, 28 Junij, le prochein jour puis Trinity terme, Elizab. 41, An° Do^ni 1599; adonque presente l'archeuesque, Lo. Keeper, Lo. Tresorer, Sr Wm Knowles, ambideux Ch. Justices et Sr John Fortescue et touts les Judges d'angliterre.

Charge in Trinity term

The Lord Keeper delivered a speech given to him in charge by the sacred majesty of the Queen,[1] 'whoe in her princelye regarde of the peace & good of all her people, & in her royall Care of the generall Justice of all her lande, hathe now, as many other times, giuen specialle Charge for all gentlemen that now lodge in London or Westminster to repayre to there Cuntrye dwellinges, *et* to maintayne hospitalitye, *et* to people the realme, *et* to set the poore to worke: & for Justices of peace to remember there names, they are Conseruators *et* Justices, & there oathe: not to domineere & Countenaunce Cawses, *et* contemne those wch doe good & call them busybodyes & depraue them: some doe nothing or euell, being grand reteyners, boulster causes, & in one shire of late at Easter Cessions, being orderlye sommoned & many Justices in the shire, not one there but the *Custos Rotulorum* onelye;' the Judges to advise for punishment of this, and the Judges to examine the service of each Justice and to give account for this, what 'felons, vagrand persons, alehowses,' &c., and to remove from the bench those that are drones and not bees, with disgrace and punishment; and the diligent and industrious to notify to the Queen to encourage them.

And the Attorney-general shall make a certificate of all gentlemen who now dwell in London or Westminster, and shall inform against them.

As to the taxing of the subsidy granted for the preservation of the realm, the Queen abhors all unjust taxations, and requires just and equal proportions from rich and poor.

[1] See pp. 19, 56, 101, and *post*.

In Camera Stellata, coram Consilio ibidem, Mercurij, 6 Febr., 1599,[1] Elizab. 42. 1599-1600 Feb. 6

JEFFERYES v. MOUNTAGUE

Riot, etc.

Jefferyes of Sussexe (brother of Baron Jeffryes,[2] now deceased), plaintiff, Mountague, defendant, for riot and other misdemeanours. Mountague, 20 July, entered on the land called "Grove lands" peaceably with five men usually attendant on him, with their usual weapons, and not otherwise, and then he built cabins and with two men without weapons kept this possession, and on the 6th of August, in the night, with 20 persons with sickles (and not otherwise), reaped the corn there growing, and peaceably carried it; and Mountague commanded that there should be no resistance and no violence if there should be any interruption; and he offered sequestration of the profits until the trial should be had of this case in the [p. 69] Bench. Query 41 Elizabeth, 15.[3] This was adjudged by the Court to be no riot, and also because no re-entry was ever actually made by Jefferyes; but for the misdemeanour in reaping the corn in a 'rayning' night, and for the mischief and example of this, and the inconvenience that would ensue, they fined all the defendants each five marks, but without imprisonment, which ought to be particularly excepted by the Court, otherwise it is due as of course. So there is a judgment in [this] Court for waste of a ditch [held] in common, by night; for the deeds of night are odious even if they be lawful; for a lawful thing may be unlawfully performed. And there is a case in our books if a parker or forester suffer hunting, he shall forfeit his office, but if there be hunting in the night, he shall not forfeit it; for [he] is not bound to guard his game in the night, for the night is ordained for all men and beasts to have rest, unless ravenous and 'devouringe beastes.' But

No riot, misdemeanour punished for reaping and carrying corn in the night

Sentence

Night deeds odious

[1] 1600 in modern reckoning. Six Councillors and Judges were present.

[2] John Jeffrey, appointed Chief Baron of the Exchequer, Oct. 12, 1577, died before Nov. 17, 1578. His daughter and heir married Edward Montague of Boughton. Foss. Edward Montague was perhaps the defendant in the present case. He was created Baron Montagu of Boughton 1621.

[3] *Sic.*

1599-1600 Feb. 6

this small offence should have punishment in the country, by indictment or otherwise, where it can be proved.

Perjury on indictment shall not be punished here, but by indictment

Barrator, who; and good abearing against him.

By Koke, Attorney-general, a man giving evidence on an indictment by the Queen, shall not be sued here for perjury, but shall be tried by indictment again; so of 'barrettye'; and a barrator, (by the Lord Keeper,) is such an one who moves 'debate, contentions, quarrelles & suites' for some little thing, and of no value or moment; and of such he would grant the good behaviour as soon as of a 'wandring roague.'

1600 April 18

In Camera Stellata, coram consilio ibidem, Veneris, 18 Aprilis, An° Do^{ni} 1600, An°que Elizab. R^{ne} 42.[1]

Surrey.

BRISTOWE v. LECHEFORDE and others

Henry Bristowe, plaintiff, against Richard Lecheforde, Justice of the Peace, three of his sons and divers of his servants, defendants.

Three riots and misdemeanour

The matters were three riots, and a misdemeanour in making warrants against the plaintiff to vex him in the title to land, *colore officii.* They were all proved. And one man was mortally wounded, and expended in surgery £5; and corn in a barn was destroyed to the value of £7. The defendant Lecheforde was fined by the whole Court 1000 [p. 70] marks, three of his sons and two of his servants were fined £1000, each £200 by himself, five (or six)[2] others of his servants were fined £500, each £100 by himself; the

Fined £2200

total sum of all their fines £2200; and if any of them shall not be of sufficient ability to pay their fines, then Lecheford, the defendant, by the sentence of the Court, is to pay all; and each is to have imprisonment; and the defendant Lecheforde at the next Assizes in Surrey is to make confession on a stool, and to remain there while the decree be

Richard Bostoke discharged from Commission of Peace

read; and Richard Bostoke, by the sentence of the Lord Keeper, both Chief Justices and the Chief Baron, was discharged and dismissed from the Commission of the Peace, because he agreed that Lecheford might set his hand to

[1] Seven Councillors and Judges were present. [2] Interlined.

any warrant made by him, which he had now done, and Bostoke on his examination confessed this; which (by the Lord Keeper) is contempt of the Queen and his Commission of the Peace and of his oath; and because he is content to be a 'pockette' Justice,[1] he is unworthy of the Commission of the Peace. It was decreed also by the Court that he who was wounded and paid £5 for the healing of his wounds,[2] should have his costs if the 'presydente'[3] of the Court would warrant it; also he that had his corn destroyed to have his damages if there be any 'presydente' in Court that will warrant this; because neither of the two was party to the bill. And Bostoke was not in the bill, but since he was in the proofs, the Lord Keeper seized upon this, and would have his sentence parcel of the decree. The Counsel on the part of the defendant endeavoured to quash the bill, First, because there was no certain limit of time when the riots were made, but it was allowed [by the Court] that there was a certain time; 2. otherwise because he was not charged particularly with offences as Justice of the Peace, and it was allowed also for this and 'in particularitye'; 3. otherwise that they could not be sentenced as procurers of the riot since they were not so charged; but it was good notwithstanding, because in the words, rioters and other misdemeaners, all rioters and procurers of riots are contained.

The Order of the Garter.

[p. 71]
1600
April 20
'Sur Chattois, Gouernor de Deepe,' at S. George's Feast, for the French King

Die Solis, 20 Aprilis, An° Do^ni 1600, An°que Elizab. R^n e 42. 'S^ur Chattois, Lord gouernor de Deepe,'[4] came to Godstone, accompanied by Ersefeilde, the High Sheriff of Surry and Sussexe, Sr Walter Couert, and divers other gentlemen of Surrey and Sussex, and came to Croydon to dinner with Sr Thomas Garrette,[5] Knight Marshall, and

[1] Perhaps the same as a 'basket Justice;' see note on p. 102.

[2] We were previously told that the wounds were mortal!

[3] *I.e.* precedent.

[4] "This last ambassador from France, the Governor of Dieppe, has brought great protestations of sincerity," etc. Cal. State Papers, Domestic, April 13th (?), 1600. [p. 428.]

[5] Sir Thomas Gerard, appointed May 23, 1597.

1600 April 20

Sir Fraucis Carewe accompanied him, and he was attended by one hundred men and servants [*garsons*] of France, all of whom had horses prepared by commandment of the Queen. The said Lord lay the night before at Grinsted, and the night before at Lewse, and came to England to solemnize the Order of S. George in the name and stead of the French King, his master, who was chosen a Knight of the Order of S. George two or three years before, and the Garter was sent to him by the Earl of Shrewseberrye ; but the said Sieur Chattois came now to be installed for him, and to solemnize this in his name and for his person.

At S. George's Feast at Greenwich, 23 April, 1600, the said Governor of Deepe then present, and these Knights of the Garter then present :—

The Earl of Notingham,[1]

Lord Buckhurst, Lord Treasurer and Lord President of the Garter,[2]

The Earl of Shrewseberrye,[3]

The Earl of Cumberlande,[4]

The Earl of Northumberland,[5]

The Earl of Worster,[6]

Lord Sheffeilde,[7]

Lord Howard of Walden,[8]

Lord Hunsden,[9]

Sir Henry Lee,[10]

The Earl of Sussexe,[11]

Lord Cobham,[12]

Lord Scrope,[13]

Absent :

The Earl of Pembroke,[14]

The Earl of Ormond,[15]

[1] Charles Howard, 1st Earl.

[2] Thomas Sackville, 1st Baron ; afterwards Earl of Dorset.

[3] Gilbert Talbot, 7th Earl.

[4] George Clifford, 3rd Earl.

[5] Henry Percy, 9th Earl.

[6] Edward Somerset, 4th Earl.

[7] Edward Sheffield, 3rd Baron.

[8] Thomas Howard, 1st Baron.

[9] George Carey, 2nd Baron.

[10] Of Quarendon, Bucks, Master of the Ordnance and Ranger of Woodstock. See *Dict. of Nat. Biog.*

[11] Robert Ratcliffe, 5th Earl.

[12] Henry Brooke, 6th Baron.

[13] Thomas Scrope, 10th Baron Scrope of Bolton.

[14] Henry Herbert, 2nd Earl.

[15] Thomas Butler, 10th Earl.

The Earl of Essexe [1] and
Lord Mountioye.[2]

'Lo. [Howard] of Effingham [3] caryed the swerde, Th'erle of Darbye [4] & the Erle of Rutlande [5] supported Her Matie, the Lad. Marques [6] & the Lad. Oxforde [7] carryed Her Ma$^{tie's}$ trayne & the Lo. Herberte [8] supported the trayne; Th'erle of Hertford,[9] Lo. Gray,[10] Sr Robert Carey,[11] Sr Edward Stafford,[12] Sr Wm Russell,[13] Sr Edward Norris,[14] Sr Thom. Gerrard & others to accompanye the Ambassador.'

Before the Council at Greenewiche. [p. 72] 1600 May 16

'Veneris; 16 die Maij, in Whitson weeke, An^{o} Do^{ni} 1600, An^{o} Elizab. R^{nae} 42,' I, John Hawarde of the Inner Temple,[15] went to the Court at Greenewiche with a messenger from the Queen's Chamber, named Mr George Cobham, [who was] sent for me by commandment of the Queen and Her Council, and by their warrant, which here follows in these words:—

'Theise shalbe to wille & requyre you to make yor p^{r}sente & undelaide repaire vnto ye Inner Temple in London or to any other place where you shall heare of the aboade of one Heywarde of the Inner Temple, & by vertue hereof to Commaunde him, all delayes & excuses sette aparte, to Come forthwth & in yor Companye to the Cowrte to aunsweare suche matters as maye be obiected againste

1 Robert Devereux, 2nd Earl.

2 Charles Blount, 8th Baron, afterwards 1st Earl of Devon.

3 William Howard, eldest son of the Earl of Nottingham; he was summoned to Parliament as Lord Howard of Effingham during his father's lifetime.

4 William Stanley, 6th Earl.

5 Roger Manners, 5th Earl.

6 Perhaps the Marchioness of Winchester, wife of William Paulet, 4th Marquis. She was a daughter of Sir Thomas Cecil, afterwards Earl of Exeter.

7 Elizabeth, daughter of Thomas Trentham, Esq., wife of Edward de Vere, 17th Earl of Oxford and Great Chamberlain.

8 William, Lord Herbert of Cardiff, eldest son of Henry, 2nd Earl of Pembroke.

9 Edward Seymour, 1st Earl.

10 Thomas, Lord Grey of Wilton, 16th Baron.

11 Fourth son of Henry, 1st Lord Hunsdon.

12 Afterwards 4th Baron Stafford.

13 Fourth son of Francis, 2nd Earl of Bedford.

14 Governor of Ostend, 3rd son of Henry, 1st Baron Noris.

15 This seems to be the only place where the writer of the MS. mentions his own name. See Introduction.

1600 May 16

him. And hereof you & he maye not faylle. From the Cowrte at Greenewiche the 12th of May 1600.

'Jo. Cant. Tho. Egerton T. Buckhurst
'Notingham. Ro. North
'Will. Knollys Jo. Popham

'To George Cobham, one
'of ye messengers of Her Matie's
'Chamber.'

And on this warrant I was examined the next day at the 'Counsell table,' on my knees, touching the delivery of the copy of a letter from Lady Riche to the Queen concerning the Earl of Essexe[1]; and on producing my authority for this, I was discharged with good 'credite & commendacyon'; paying fees to Mr Wade, Clerk of the Council, 1r [2] for recording my appearance, 6*s* 8*d* for entrance in a bond for 100 marks to appear on notice given at my chamber, and 6*s* 8*d* for this bond, and to the messenger 4 nobles,[3] where his fee is vjs. 8d. each day and 4d. each mile.

[p. 73]

1600 May 28

In Camera Stellata, coram consilio ibidem, Mercurij, 28 Maij, Ano Doni 1600, Anoque Elizab. Rnae 43.[4]

Lincolnshire

CLAUGHTON *v.* GUSTARDE and others

Forging of a warrant by an attorney of the Common Bench

Cause of hearing. Thomas Claughton, g[entleman], plaintiff, Thomas Gustarde, an attorney of the Common Pleas, defendant, 'for forginge a warrante, as an vnder sheryfe wrytinge for a *Capias* but had none, & so wthoute any originall made a warrant wth a blanke for the name.' For which he was fined £40, sequestered for life [*a touts jours*] from being an attorney, and imprisonment. Gregorye Ward and Richard Boothe, other defendants, for misdemeanour in executing this warrant on 'Palme Sondaye,' in the church while the parson was reading a homily and

Arrest in a church in time of divine service

[1] See Appendix IV.

[2] Probably one royal, a gold piece worth 15*s*.

[3] A noble is 6*s*. 8*d*.

[4] Nine Councillors and Judges were present.

preparing them for the Communion, but the defendants arrested him in the church, and taking from him an obligation [a bond], and saying to him that he must receive the Communion another day. And this was adjudged by the whole Court to be a great offence, and for this they were fined £200, imprisonment, and confession in a penitent manner on their knees in the church in time of divine service. Sentence

And it was cited by the Lord Keeper that Sir John Ratclyffe, a Sheriff, made a warrant on a *Capias*, with a blank for the name, and was fined for this.

Wiltshire.

BELLAMY *v.* LIDCOTT, and others

Riot; distraining beasts and selling them in another county

Thomas Bellamy, plaintiff, John Lidcott and others, defendants, for riot and other misdemeanours. The defendant, for claim of a rent, distrained beasts '*dammage feasant*,' and drove them into Surrye, another county, and there sold them: and for this he was fined ,[1] with imprisonment; and he had no Counsel, nor made any manner of defence, but his answer was read. Sentence

Nullus de cetero faciat ducere districtiones quas fecerit, extra comitatum in quo captae fuerint. Marlbrige, fo. 16, cap. 6

In Camera Stellata, coram Consilio ibidem, Mercurij, 4 Junij, An° Doni 1600, An°que Elizab. Rnae 42.[2]

[p. 74] 1600 June 4

PLAYER'S case

Fine for saving a man from the gallows

One Player of Glostershire was fined £100, and to be bound for his good behaviour, confession of the fault and imprisonment, for practising with the Sheriff and others to save a prisoner 'from the gallowes'; and the plaintiff slandered all the Justices in Glostershire and Snegge, 'Counsellor' at Law; and for this it was ordered that inasmuch as the bill could not be withdrawn from the Court, (because the sentence is founded on it), the 'acquytalle & cleere dismissing' of Snegge and the others should be ingrossed on the back of the bill, and thus should remain of record.

[1] Blank in MS. [2] Seven Councillors and Judges were present.

1600 June 4

ASCEWE v. EARL OF LINCOLN

Ascewe and the Earl of Lincolne.[1] Ruled in this case that the Earl is not bound to take notice of the judgment of this Court on the showing of an order of this Court by the party only, but [he is bound] on the showing of this by the Clerk and the Officer of the Court, or on *subpoena* out of the Court to execute the judgment of the Court, which is the most proper course.

1600 July 6

In Camera Stellata, coram Consilio ibidem, Veneris, 6° Julij, An° Do^ni^ 1600 An°que Elizab. R^næ^ 42.[2]

ATT.-GEN. *ex parte* MAYOR, etc. of LONDON v. BAYNAM and others

Riot and misdemeanour

Koke, the Queen's Attorney, informed by a bill on behalf of the Mayor,[3] Aldermen and City of London against Sir Edmonde Baynam, knight,[4] and Badger, Grauntam and Dutton, gentlemen, and Williamson, 'vintener in Breadestreete,' for riots and other misdemeanours in this manner: Sir Edmonde Baynam, Badger, Grauntam and Dutton went to supper in Breadestreete at the 'Marmaide,' where Williamson dwells and is a taverner, and there they supped and there they stayed until two 'a clocke,' in disorder and excess of drink; and then they departed, with 'Rapyers drawne,' and menaced, wounded and beat 'le Wache in Fridaye streete et en Paule's Churcheyarde,' and did utter seditious words. But they confessed their faults, and submitted themselves to the Court, and proved that all was done 'in drinke & heate.' And for these misdemeanours each of them was fined £200 and imprisonment, but Williamson was acquitted by the sentence, yet the Chief Justice, the Lord Treasurer and the Lord Keeper [would have] fined him £40 because he was *Causa sine qua non*. But because he was known [to be] an honest man and of good government and would not suffer music and illegal games in his house, and sent for the Constable for [to keep] good order, he was acquitted by the sentence. And it was there delivered that no taverner or 'alekeeper' ought to suffer or receive company after 9 o'clock, and

[p. 75]

Sentence

[1] See *ante*, p. 12.

[2] Eight Councillors and Judges were present.

[3] Sir Nicholas Mosley.

[4] See another case of his, *post*, p. 165.

because drunkenness is now so common, and general, and odious, (as to drink 'by bushell measure, dozen, & yarde'), it was delivered as law that a common drunkard may be bound for his good behaviour, as well as an 'Ingrosser, Regrator, or forstaller'; for the one ingrosses to sell again for lucre, and the other destroys himself and the store, which is the cause of the 'causeles dearthe' now: and it seems that this sentence was 'gracyouse & favourable' by reason of their confession, submission and drunkenness.

Another cause of hearing was lengthily debated against Sir Thomas Jones for collecting great sums for musters, armour and other munitions, and not [so] employing it; which was adjourned to Michaelmas Term.[1] SIR THOMAS JONES'S case [p. 76]

In Camera Stellata, coram Consilio ibidem, Veneris, 10 Octobris. Termino Michaelis, 42 Elizab. An° Do^ni 1600.[2] 1600 Oct. 10

The great case of Sir Thomas Jhones, one of the 'Deputye Leiuetenauntes' in Wales of the Earl of Pembroke, 'Lo. Presydente' there. The Attorney-general informed against him for the extortion of great sums by colour of his office, and taxing and levying [the same] to find soldiers when there was a 'Countermaunde' of this, and for taxing great sums, 'ouerpryzinge artyllerye,' gaining by the 'saille' of this, [obtaining] too great allowance for each 'souldyar,' for not restoring 'muskats' until the bill[3] was preferred, and for collecting £600 after the 'Countermaunde,' and for combining with the other Deputy Lieutenant to use his hand [signature], (and to this purpose Lecheforde and Bostoke's case was vouched,[4]) for refusing to restore [the £600] to them on complaint to the Judges of Assize, and for committing some for complaint made to the Lord President. Moore and Brocke with the Attorney. ATT.-GEN. *v.* JOHNES — Extortion as Deputy Lieutenant

[1] See below.
[2] Seven Councillors and Judges were present.
[3] The bill in this cause.
[4] See *ante*, p. 108.

1600 Oct. 10

Exception to the bill for uncertainty over-ruled

Owen Wood's case vouched

Sergeant Healle, Phillips and Walter with Sir Thomas Jones. They endeavoured to destroy the bill for uncertainty in charging with the offences 'done by them,' named, '3 or 4 or some of them,' and for this purpose they vouched Owen Wood's case, in which the defendant in his examination confessed himself to be guilty, which made the former uncertainty more certain, as it was in both cases; and notwithstanding this the Judges and the Court ruled [the present bill] good and certain, taking a difference [distinguishing] where it is between party and party and where the Queen is a party, for then on confession the Queen may proceed *viva voce*. And it was delivered by the Lord Keeper that there ought to be in each County two Deputy Lieutenants at least, and anything done by one only is void; and the Lieutenant of a County does not make them, but they are named to the Queen and she herself makes them. By the Attorney: *Leges silent arma.*

Two Deputy Lieutenants in each county, and the act of one only void

Election of Deputy Lieutenants; at all times made by the Queen herself.

The defence was adjourned to another day, but the Attorney proceeded with his proof against the other defendants, captains, mustermasters, constables and others, for extorting fees for the discharge of pressed men, and other offences; the defence to which was adjourned to another day.[1]

[p. 77]

1600 Oct. 11

In Cancellaria, Sabbati, 11 Octobr., ter^no^ Mich., 42 [Elizabethae].

A good note to be observed in examination of witnesses by commission.

Note of a commission to examine witnesses, and the quashing of it

The Lord Keeper, who now is Sir Thomas Egerton, being a commissioner, an article was interrogated [i.e. a question was asked] if such an one died seised of certain wastes. The plain people and ignorant deposed readily that he was seised and died seised. Whereupon I[2] demanded and said, namely, '"Heare you mee, Father, doe you knowe what it is to be seised or to dye seised?";

[1] See *post*, p. 117. [2] John Hawarde, the writer of the MS.

"Sir," saythe hee, "I knowe what I saye, I care not for yor Choppinge for Logique"; wherevpon I Caused the Clerke to wryte this his aunsweare allso as parte of his examynacyon; & then sayde his Commissioner, "Father, you meane he was possessed & tooke the profittes to the time of his deathe"; he aunsweared, "I, Sir, I,[1] god's blessing of yor harte." All which I Cawsed the Clarke to enter, & herevpon the Cawse never proceeded Farther.'

In Camera Stellata, coram consilio ibidem, Mercurij, 15 Octobris, 42 [Elizabethae], Mich.[2] 1600 Oct. 15.

Sir Thomas Jhones' ease was again adjourned.[3] JONES'S case

BLAGE v. ALLEN

Forgery by erasure in a bond

Cause of forgery was heard, between Blage, plaintiff, and Allen, a Londoner, defendant. The said Allen took one Blage, the plaintiff's son, for his apprenticeship and communication, and an agreement was made that the said Blage, the father, should be bound in an obligation of £100 for his good service, and thus it was drawn on paper, entered in the scrivener's book and thus sealed and delivered, an obligation bound in £100; and then the defendant Allen erased this and made it *in centum marcis*, instead of *in centum libris*; and then [on] his hard usage of the apprentice, and complaint made of this, he refused to show the bond; and on the award of the Aldermen, (to whom complaint was made), he was committed to prison until he showed the bond, and on showing it he was delivered; and the Aldermen and their Recorder declared that the bond was void on account of the erasure in it [and the insertion of] these words, *in centum marcis* ([there being] no indorsement before the sealing of it), for *in centum libris*. Afterwards, on trial of this, verdict was found that the obligation was erased, and this is the forgery intended by the bill, which is founded generally and not on the statute, and particularly to decipher the offence and

Centum libris erased, and *centum marcis* [written]

Obligation void for erasure without indorsement before sealing

[p. 78]

Verdict found, erasure, and for this the bond void

Bill for forgery, general

[1] Equivalent to "Aye, Aye, Sir."

[2] Six Councillors and Judges were present.

[3] See *ante*, p. 115.

1600 Oct. 15

misdemeanour. And to prove this forgery, one Peter Blage, utter barrister of the Inner Temple, and the scrivener, and others, were examined. And for this the defendant in the bill for forgery [Allen] preferred a cross bill for perjury against them for their evidence and depositions in the bill for forgery.

Cross bill for perjury; crossing of justice. Peter Blage accused falsely of perjury

The defendant in the first bill [Allen] urged that it was not forgery but a misdemeanour, and so pardoned by [the general pardons of] 31 and 35 Elizabeth; for the obligation was made in 26 Elizabeth and the bill was in Court in 38 Elizabeth and thus not within the pardon of 39 Elizabeth. The Lord Keeper and Anderson ruled that if a man wish to aver a general pardon and the benefit of it, he must take it in pleading and in his answer, or otherwise he will lose it; for it is a picking of clients' purses 'to spynne it oute in lengthe,' and then to destroy the bill on a pardon.

Misdemeanours, but not forgery, pardoned by 31, 35 and 39 Eliz.

Rule that the benefit of a general pardon must be claimed in pleading, or it will never be had in this Court

Also, by some pardons the offences are pardoned, but some persons are not capable of this, as some offences are excepted, but the parties and their persons are not excepted, and therefore of necessity they ought to show this in pleading.

Offences pardoned, but not the persons guilty

Offences excepted in general pardon, but not persons

And by both the Judges[1] and the Lord Keeper: It is not forgery if it be not to the prejudice and hurt of another; and if it be solely to the prejudice of the party himself, and no other can be grieved by it, it is not forgery by the statute nor at common law.

Forgery, what

It is not forgery if it be not to the prejudice of a third person, or another has cause of grief than the party himself

Lord Anderson, Sir William Knowlles, the Bishop of London and the Lord Treasurer by their sentence, acquitted the defendant and cleared him as well of the forgery as of the misdemeanour; but Popham, Chief Justice of the Bench, and the Lord Keeper [would have] convicted the plaintiff [*sic*; Allen] of the misdemeanour and fined him £20, and acquitted him of forgery, for there was no certain time of the forgery and no certain person for the forger. But the most voices are the sentence and judgement of the Court.

'Most voyces make the iudgemente'

Allen acquitted of forgery and misdemeanour

Majority give sentence

[p. 79]

As to the cross bill for perjury, in as much as there was

[1] The two Chief Justices.

no proof, the Attorney-general moved for a fine to the Queen and a fine and costs to the defendants, *pro falso clamore*, and the withdrawal of the bill from the file.

Cross bill for perjury

And the Court sentenced the plaintiff Allen[1] for his false claim and 'sclaunderous bille,' £40 fine to the Queen, £5 to each defendant and his costs, and the bill to be withdrawn from the file of this Court.

Allen fined for false claim, £40 to the Queen, £5 to each defendant and his costs

Bill withdrawn from the file

In Camera Stellata, coram Consilio ibidem, Termino Trinitatis, Elizab. 43, An° Do^{ni} 1601, Veneris, 17 Junij.[2]

1601 June 17

Att.-Gen. *v.* Daniell

Coke, Attorney-general, informed, *ore tenus*, against one John Daniell, gentleman, for 'Cosyninge' the Countess of Essexe in manner as follows:—The Earl of Essexe being in trouble and a prisoner at the Lord Keeper's house, and the Countess of Essexe, being then in child-bed at Walsingham House, she delivered a 'riche Caskette' of letters to one of her women, a 'duche' woman named Reoua,[3] (in whom the Earl and the Lady of Essexe reposed great confidence and trust, and which woman was four or five years before married to the said John Danyelle), to the intent that the said woman would keep it secret and safe, containing very many letters of love and passion and kindness, which had been between the Earl and his wife as well before the marriage between them as after, and [containing] no other thing; and then the said John Daniell one morning looking for his slippers, tossed and tumbled the bed in his house at Charinge crosse, and under the 'boulster' found this rich casket, and the same presently opened and took twenty or thirty of the letters, and reading them, carried them to Peter Bales, a notary in the Old Baillye, and carried also to him paper of the same largeness, and practised with Peter Bales 'to Copye

Information *ore tenus* by the Attorney-general against John Daniell for cosening the Countess of Essexe

Daniell a gentleman of blood and of an ancient house

The Countess esteemed these letters the best contentment and comfort that she had in the time of affliction of her husband

This opened and closed again, but in what fashion did not appear to the Court

Bales a rare and excellent scribe for all hands

[1] Plaintiff in the cross bill, and defendant in the other.

[2] Eleven Councillors and Judges were present.

[3] Her christian name was Jane. She says that she is the daughter of Ryhova, Governor of Ghent. See Appendix V.

1601 June 17

Counterfeiting the Earl of Essex's letters

them, Counterfeytinge the Erle's hande, wth the same characters, the lyke distance of lynes, the beginninge & endinge of euerye lyne wth the same wordes & letters, & this alleaginge that the Countesse of Essexe wylled him so to doe for her; & afterwardes the sayde John Danyelle, Comminge to Peter Bales to see if he had wrytten the letters, found him Copyinge of them, & for the more speedye Copyinge of them, the sayde Danyelle reade the letters to the sayde Bales as he Copyed them; & the sayde Bales, castinge his eye to the sayd Danyelle, espyed a paper in his hande of 4 or 5 lynes of Danyell's owne hande wrytinge, & then Bales sayde, "Mr Danyelle, if I thoughte there were any thinge Contayned in any of theise letters that mighte be daungerouse to my Lo. of Essexe, or hurtefull to the state, I woulde haue a Constable & apprehende you for it;" & therevpon Danyelle snachte awaye the letters & wente his waye: for this Danyelle had for 4 or fiue yeeres paste serued my Lo. of Essexe, & hauinge suite againste a College in Oxforde, vsed my Lorde of Essexe so that he obtayned his letters in his behalfe, & therebye prevayled againste the College; but not longe after, my Lo vnderstandinge how Danyelle had abused him, & how grosselye he had playde the knaue wth the College & Vniuersitye, he thruste him oute of seruice, & wrote his letters againste him; & euen after the same manner did he vse my Lo. Tresorer, & the Lo. Tresor^r so vsed him as before the Lo. of Essexe did, in wrytinge againste him, beinge better informed; wherevpon Danyell faylled in his suites, & the College preuayled againste him: Herevpon Danyelle, in the mallyce of his harte, intended & soughte to be reuenged of my Lo., & as it is moste probable had a meaninge eyther to inserte these lynes of his owne hande wrytinge into my Lord's letters, thereby to drawe my Lorde into daunger, or else to haue Copyes thereof by him, to haue made a Contynuall praye of my Ladye, as after it maye appeare: The Ladye of Essexe, hearinge that some of theise letters were dyuulged, was muche disquyeted therew^th, & therevpon sent for Reoua,

[p. 80]

Practise of Danyell, to endanger the Earl of Essex, as is probable

The original cause of Danyell's malice against the Earl of Essexe

Danyelle's wyfe, & demaunded her Caskette, whoe fetched her the same, & shee presentelye myssinge 20 or 30 of the letters, was muche troubled therewth, & sente for Danyelle, whoe at the firste denyed them, but afterwardes Came to the Ladye againe, & tolde her that he was muche distressed & felte manye wantes, was muche indebted & his lande morgaged & his estate greatelye decayed, her Lorde & shee bothe had made him many greate promysses, if shee woulde be now therefore Contente to giue him a peece of monye, he woulde helpe her to the letters; & he sayde the matter in them contayned was suche that the Lorde Cobham & Sr Walter Rawlye woulde giue 3000$^{li.}$ to gette them, & so insysted longe vpon the somme of 3000$^{li.}$. The good Ladye, muche mooued wth the wante of them, & moste desyrouse to gaine them againe, lefte him not, but importuned & perswaded him by all the wayes & meanes shee Coulde, not Caringe to gyue all that euer shee were woorthe or coulde make rather then shee woulde goe wthoute them; & to that purpose vsed the ayde of Sir Edwarde Dyar to drawe him to some Composition; wherevpon in the ende it was agreede he showlde haue 1720$^{li.}$, & so at one entyre payemente the good Countesse, by the salle of her Jewelles & other her beste thinges of woorthe, payde him 1720$^{li.}$, & he delyuered her the letters, but they were but the Counterfeyte copyes of them neyther, for the letters themselves he kepte by him. & not Contente herewth, he broughte a generall Relleasse, & woulde haue had bothe the Erle & the good Ladye to haue sealled; but the Ladye, moste vnwyllinge that the Erle showlde in any kinde haue any manner of knowledge that theise priuate letters of Complementes of loue & affectyon betwene them were discouered to the worlde, entreated that her Lorde might not be vsed, but was Contente for her owne parte to sealle the relleasse; & so did, wch was shewed in Cowrte, whereas more properlye he showlde haue sealled a Relleasse to the Ladye vpon the Receipte of the monye. And the Lo. of Essexe himselfe, hearinge of this Counterfeytinge of his letters, sayde, when the Lordes Came to him to his

'Daniell practisethe' to cosen the Countess out of money

[p. 81]

Danyell demands £3000

Lord Cobham and Sir Walter Rawly abused, for they being in Court did protest that they never knew Danyell, and also Danyelle did protest that he never spoke with them

Madame of Essexe, in her entire love to her husband, does not wish to have cause for a breach of love

The Countess gives Danielle for the letters £1720 by the sale of her jewels

Counterfeit copies delivered

The Countess seals a general release to Danyell

On this counterfeiting of the Earl's hand, he suspects a practise in some one of state

1601 June 17

howse the morninge that he rose, amongste other things, that his lyfe was soughte & that his hande was Counterfeyte, & the lyke speeches he vsed at his arraignemente, therebye layinge an imputation of a blemyshe vpon the state; wch her Matie hearinge of, (her greateste Care beinge to doe iustice to all, & her owne woordes are that *shee wyll haue her wyndinge sheete vnspotted*,[1] & that it is her contynuall charge to her Officers aboute her that all her people maye be iustelye & righteouselye dealte wthall,) woulde in any case haue her Atturnye generall to proceede to haue this punished wth all seueritye, accordinge to his demeryte of his odyous & vilde [*sic*] trecheryes *in addinge afflyctyon to afflyction.*[1]

Delivered by the Lord Keeper

The Queen hath great care of justice and judgment

The words of Secretary Cecill

[p. 82]

'The sayde Danyelle, beinge examyned by the Lo. Cheife Justice & the Attornye, Confessed all the matters bothe in substaunce & circumstaunce, & alleadged this onelye in excuse of himselfe, that perusinge the letters, & not beinge able to reade them, he Caryed them to Bales to Coppye them, to make him therebye the better able to reade them; whereas he had Confessed in his examynation that he, lykinge the methode of them, Caryed them to Bales to Coppye them; & Bales in his examinacyon saythe that he reade them to him when he was wrytinge of them: for the monye he receaued, he sayde it was for his maryage portyon, wch he neuer had any before; & to that purpose, the daye before the hearinge, he wroughte a vilde [*sic*], audacyous & impudente letter to the good Countesse, alleaginge therein that he maruayled shee woulde so seuerelye proceede againste him in that fashyon, (whereas in truthe it was the Queene's suite & her owne dyrectyon to her Atturnye), protestinge that his wyfe was neuer pryuye to his hauinge the Caskette or letters; & whereas the somme of 1720$^{li.}$ p^{d} him was in Consyderation of his marryage, as Sir Edwarde Dier coulde telle, & therefore prayde accordinge to the psalmiste, "From lyinge lyppes & a deceytefulle tounge, the Lorde delyuer mee"; a phrase of wrytinge muche Condemned by all the Lordes, & his trecherouse Caryage towards his M^{r} bitterlye spoken

'Daniell's feeble excuse'

There was never any communication before as to any marriage portion

Which letter the said Countess sent this morning to the Attorney, and it was read.

Erova [*sic*] cleared of any privity of the cozenage of her husband

[1] Underlined in MS.

againste, & muche enuyed & hated of all men, & of all kinde & sortes of people.

'In the ende, after longe debatinge, he, accordinge to a Former letter & petition of his delyuered to my Lo. Keeper, demanded Counselle, but it was resolued by the Judges that he coulde not haue Counselle, because it was matter of facte onelye & Confessed by him, as in the case of the Erle of Arundelle & the Erle of Herteforde, that coulde haue no Counselle. But hauinge greate lybertye of speache gyuen him, and gyuinge no reasonable aunsweare to anye thinge, it was sentenced by all the Courte to be *Crimen falsi, doli, et mali,*[1] & no punishmente to greate for him, it was *Culpa stellionata.* As *a learned Antiquarye sayde*[1] in the parliamente howse, that he doubted whether this Courte were so called of the starre that was in it, or for that *crimina stellionata* are here iudged & punished. He was adiudged to be naylled to the pillory wth papers, to perpetuall imprysonmente, & 3000^li.^ Fyne, the somme that he did firste demaunde: *lex tallyonis*: & all the Lordes woulde be humble suitors to her Matie that shee woulde be pleased oute of her graciouse bountye to bestowe some good porcyon of it vpon the good Countesse, to whom they did all attrybute many greate & woorthye Commendacyons, extollinge & muche Commendinge her rare vertues, her greate loue & kinde faithe to her Lorde, her true, vertuous patyence, her modeste, sober & temperate Carryage, her forwarde zeal & perseueringe in suite for my Lorde to his laste trouble, & in conclusyon adiudge that nothinge wanted in her of moste rare & perfecte vertue & dutye.'[2]

Counsel not allowed; as in [the cases] of the Earl of Arundelle and the Earl of Herteforde

Daniell wished to have Serjeant Healle and Tanfeilde as Counsel

Secretary Herberte used these words

Vouched by Secretary Cecill

[p. 83]

Pillory with papers, perpetual imprisonment, and £3000 fine

Lex tallionis

The Countess to have a portion of this fine

Secretary Cecill named £2000 as the allowance by the Queen to the Countess

The good Countess greatly commended, as [is] well deserved

Very many virtues commended in the Countess

Stellionatus crimen a Jurisconsultis dicitur, quando quis alterum callida quadam impostura defraudat: ut si quis rem alii obligatam, dissimulata obligatione, per calliditatem alii vendiderit, aut si quis merces corruperit, aut imposturam fecerit, cuius nulla ordinaria poena est, sed extraordinarie plectitur, et ad presidem spectat cognitio. Dictus stellionatus

[1] Underlined in MS.

[2] Frances, Countess of Essex, was daughter and heir to Sir Francis Walsingham, and widow of Sir Philip Sydney.

1601
June 17

a stellionis natura, quo nullum animal homini fraudulentius inuidet. *Plin., lib.* 30, *cap.* 10. *Cutem enim quam quotannis ponit, protinus deuorat, ut praeripiat homini praesentissimum comitialis morbi remedium. Inde est* (*inquit Plinius*) *quod stellionum nomen in maledictum est translatum. Calepin.*[1] *fol.* 1444.

ATT.-GEN. *v.* TYFFANYE

Assault in Fleetestrete, in the daytime

Information *ore tenus* for gagging Mrs. Whittingham

Whittingham the son practises against his mother

'The same daye were too others that were bretheren, called John Tyffanye & Thomas Tyffanye, proceded againste by Mr Atturnye, *ore tenus*, & vpon there owne Confessyon, for a greate outrage & assaulte made as followethe, viz.: That they tooe, by the deuyse & practyse of one Nicolas Whittingham, did in the daye time Come into a howse in Fleetestreete where Mrs Whittingham dwellethe, mother to the sayde Nicolas Whittingham, & there one of them tooke the mayde & gagged her & bounde her armes, th'other goes vp & pretendes to viewe the same to take a lodginge for a westerne gentn, & assayles her by the throate, & woulde haue forced her wth his dagger in her mouthe to haue gagged her, but shee stryuinge & makinge greate noyse, he tooke a rugge from the bedde, & wrapped her in it, & all moste smothered her wth lyinge & syttinge vpon her; and then th'other broughte vp the mayde & layde her in the Chamber by her; & by reason of the greate noyse they made, the neighbors came & knocked at the Doore, & then they vngagged the mayde, & prayed them to be good vnto them, & to let them oute at a backe doore; but before they coulde gette awaye the Companye Came in & tooke them; & beinge examyned, they Confessed as before: & so bothe these cawses were sentenced together; they were sentenced to haue imprisonmente duringe the Queene's pleasure, to be Fyned 500li., to be retorned to Newgate from whence they came, a pillorye to be sette vp in Fleetestreete ouer againste the howse where they vsed this violence, & there firste to be whipped, then to be sette vpon the pillorye, & to be gagged wth the same gagges, each wth his owne gagge, that they vsed to the sayde Mrs Whitting-

[p. 84]

Two causes sentenced *simul et semel.* Imprisonment, fine £500, pillory in Fletestrete, to be whipped, to lose their ears and to be gagged. *Lex tallionis*

[1] Ambrosius Calepinus, *Dictionarium Latinae Linguae.*

ham & her mayde, & then to loose there eares; & so this iudgemente was executed accordingelye vpon Fridaye nexte followinge.'

Execution of the judgment

Talio equalis retributio, idque in malam partem ut si cui quis oculum eruerit, idem ille patiatur. Calepine, fol. 1508.

In Camera Stellata, coram Consilio ibidem, Mercurij, 28 April, An° Do^ni 1602, An°que Elizab. R^nae 44, Ter^no Pasche.[1]

1602 April 28

Coke, the Queen's Attorney, informed on the relation of [2] Chamberlain, Under-Sheriff of ,[2] against Pierce and Twine, and others, for riot and a fraudulent deed, in manner as follows: Pierce, being indebted to Twine and others, made secretly and sealed and delivered a general deed of gift of all his goods to Twine, with intent to defraud the other creditors, and this deed was antedated, and was a deed poll. Pierce kept this deed, used the goods, sold the goods, marked the sheep, in the subsidy seised himself of these goods, and this deed did not appear before the Under-Sheriff came with the Queen's writ for execution for another debt; and then divers [men], by the appointment of Pierce and Twine, resisted the execution and the Sheriff by force, wounding, beating and maiming him, and this continued three or four several days. And there assembled at one time one hundred persons, and they continued their resistance in the names of Pierce and Twine by colour of the said gift of goods made to Twine, and saying that Twine wished to keep them safely and without damage; the four principal actors were named Clarke, and when others came the usual word was, "Whoe willte thou stande for?" the answer, "For Twine," and, "Whosoeuer will take goods heere, I will haue the Puddinges oute of his bellye," etc. The Sheriff committed divers [persons] for the force and riot; Twine brought [actions for] false imprisonment. Audelie, a friend of Twine's, was bound to

ATT.-GEN. *ex parte* CHAMBERLAIN *v.* PEARCE and others

Riot and Fraud
General gift of all goods by deed poll antedated; donor kept this, used the goods, sold part of them, etc.
The Sheriff resisted by force and beaten and maimed
Riot and rescue continued four several days
[p. 85]
One hundred persons assembled against the sheriff, by procurement of the defendants
Tumultuous and rebellious words
The sheriff committed the rioters, who brought 'false imprisonment.'
The sheriff also craved aid from a Justice of the Peace

[1] Twelve Councillors and Judges were present.

[2] Blank in MS. The case is reported by Coke, *Twyne's Case*, part iii., fo. 84*b*. See also, Smith's *Leading Cases*.

1602
April 28

Judgment confirmed on [writ of] error in the Exchequer

Cross bill in this Court against the Sheriff.

Twine maintains all costs of each suit

Proof of fraud and secrecy

the Sheriff by his goods, the Sheriff by his return charged himself with the goods; Twine brought a writ of error in the Exchequer, where the judgment was confirmed; Twine preferred a cross bill against the Sheriff in this Court; the depositions [*liuers*] in this Court [reach] to letter K; divers suits between the Sheriff and Audelye for the debt recovered on the execution, and divers defendants in this Court; Twine maintained the charge[s] of all [the defendants]: and the Scrivener, who made the [deed of] gift, deposed that it was made with intent to defraud other creditors, and secretly made, and so it was resolved to keep it; Twine confessed as much in effect: and yet in truth Peirce was indebted *bona fide* to Twine in £1100, and had made two earlier gifts of his goods for payment of his debt to Twine, but not general [gifts], and therefore they are of no value to satisfy the debt; and therefore Peirce, *bona fide* for the payment and satisfaction of all his debt to Twine, made this general gift of all his goods: which was a thing greatly disliked by the Court, namely, that Twine had taken two former gifts of goods.

Peirce *bona fide* in debt to Twine, and for payment of this made a general gift

Practise in Twine condemned by the Court

Recorder of London, counsel with the defendant

Crooke, Recorder of London,[1] was of Counsel with Twine; he did not defende the riots, but excused Twine, because he was not present at the riots, nor at the sealing and delivery of the gift, nor procured it, nor had cognizance of it; and he had been a man of good estate, but being a simple, weak man, and over-reached by these 'suertishippes & shiftes,' he is minus [*sanse*] £1100, and without means to have this; and he will be undone for ever, if this Court has not commiseration for him, and does not give him 'gratiouse relleife'; he submitted himself in all humility to the gracious censure of this honourable Court. He [Crooke] was commended for his discretion, judgment, learning and good and reverent regard to this Court in the delivery of this speech.

[p. 86]
Fashion of a good and discreet excuse and submission

But Serjeant Heale, Hutton and Toppam, of Counsel also with Twyne, did not make any defence for the riot, nor for the rioters, but excused Twine because he did not

[1] John Croke, afterwards a Judge of the King's Bench.

procure this, nor comfort them [the rioters], nor have cognizance of it. And as to the fraud, they endeavoured to acquit him in law, and for this moved a point on a proviso in the Statute of 13 Eliz. cap. 5, made against fraudulent gifts, deeds, grants, alienations, etc. This cause was heard on the last day, when this point was moved by Serjeant Heale, but when he ought to have opened it [this day ?], he discreetly departed from the bar [of the Court], and it was referred to the consideration of the judges this day; and now Toppam moved audaciously and 'peremptorie' on clear law, and cited judgments for this. First in Diar, 5 Mary, fol. 160, plea 44.[1] A man bound with two sureties in £40 to be paid at two days, for their assurance by Indenture sells to them beasts [? as if] for £40 paid, proviso, if he discharge and save them harmless, etc., the sale to be void, and it is agreed that he may occupy [retain possession]: he fails in the first payment, and afterwards is *felo de se*. Award in the Star Chamber that the Almoner shall have the beasts and discharge the sureties. Diar[2] against all, because the property is in the vendees, on breach of condition. Query if the wife who continues her quarentine,[3] may defend the possession with force. By the Lord Keeper: It was the best alms[4]: and in Diar are reports as he heard them [and also] opinions and doubtes, and thus are strange things printed, which detract greatly from the authority of Diar's book: but he said that he was a literate and reverend man.

Matter in law to discharge the fraud under statute of 13 Eliz. cap. 5

Commended by the Lord Keeper for his silent departure

5 Mary, Diar, fol. 160, plea 44

Another case of Bankrupts in the Attorney's book, part 2, fol. 25, Trin. 31 Eliz.[5]

Statute of Bankrupts 13 Eliz. cap. 7

This case is stronger against him than for him, and on the true reason of the said case, all fraud is condemned and equality commended, and all are in equal right. Cato says *Ipse etenim leges cupiunt ut iure regantur*. And equal

[1] Blank in MS. See Dyer's Reports, ed. 1794, vol. ii., fol. 160*b*.

[2] James Dyer, a Judge of the Court of Common Pleas, 1557; Chief Justice C.P. 1559.

[3] The forty days during which a widow was allowed to occupy the house before the entry of the heir.

[4] The goods of a *felo de se* were forfeited to the crown, and distributed by the Royal Almoner.

[5] Smith *v.* Mills, Coke's Reports, ed. 1826, vol. i. p. 481.

1602
April 28

distribution should be made according to the quantity of their debts.[1]

Query the report in the Queen's Bench

Another case cited in the Queen's Bench, Sydnam's case.

[p. 87]
Toppam, 'Counsellor,' disgraced and touched with impudency and audacity
Submission and reverence to the Court required and commended

All these cases were answered by the Attorney, and with offence he opposed Toppam, who, by default of intelligence, impudently vouched these cases, while the Recorder, a more reverend and judicial man, used other kind of submission and reverence to the authority of this Court.

Resolution by the Judges as to fraud
The proviso in the Statute of 13 [Eliz.] is flattering and deceitful
Fine for the fraud and riot, two persons £400
Confession at the Assizes, pillory and £40 fine
Woman rioter fined £10
The Sheriff commended; small number of sheriffs without corruption
The Sheriff allowed £200 on the precedent of Banke's case
All fines to be levied of one only if the others are not of ability

And so it was resolved by all the Judges that the deed was clearly fraudulent, and, by Popham, the proviso in the Statute of 13 [Eliz.] is a flattering proviso and does not seem to aid if it be well understood. And for the riot and fraud together, Peirce and Twine were fined each £200, the other defendants each £40, imprisonment, and the Clarkes, being the principals, confession at the next Assizes, and the pillory, and [bonds for their] good behaviour; a woman fined £10; all imprisonment as of course. The Sheriff, to incourage the others, (there being a small number without corruption,) and inasmuch as he had, for the execution of the Queen's writ, proceeded without corruption to adventure his life and to lose his blood, and he had complained of this in this Court, to have £200, to be paid by Peirce and Twine and any other defendant who is able; and in the same way, all the fines shall be levied of him who is most able.

Linwood vouched.
Seven badges of fraud
[p. 88]

By the Judges and the Lord Keeper: The deed has all the badges of fraude: First, (as Linwoodde notes), it is general of all the goods, '*the shirte from the backe & breade from the mouthe*'[2]; 2. The intent to defraud other creditors; 3. It is antedated; 4. It is a deed poll; 5. The donor keeps it; 6. The donor himself uses and sells the goods; 7. The gift is secretly kept, and not known before the execution. And thereupon the Lord Keeper and the Chief Justice advised 'Counsellors & practisers' to be laborious to have intelligence and knowledge of their

Advice to counsellors and practisers of the law

[1] This paragraph is the writer's comment. [2] Underlined in MS.

clients' causes, and with good discretion and judgment, honestly to provide and devise for them, and to have very good regard to the reverend personages and Judges of this Court, and not audaciously and impudently to defend or deliver any thing, and not [to speak] confidently and immodestly, to the scandal and detraction of the reverent respect to this Court and to the counsel thereof. For the cases put by Toppam may well beseem a moot, but not this place, for they are not well understood. And as to the cases in Diar and in the Attorney's book, they are both directly against him, and in Diar's case, this Court was of opinion that the Almoner should have the goods, and in good and 'principalle almes' should satisfy the sureties.

Reverence is to be given to the Court, and to the counsel of it

Answer to the cases put by Toppam, with *caveat*

And as to the Sheriff, he was much commended and encouraged, and others by his example; and when he summoned a jury to try whose the beasts were, it was needless and not usual, for he could take the beasts without a jury; and also when he procured a Justice of the Peace to assist him, he might have had a *posse comitatus*; and if he killed any one who resisted him, he could justify it by the law. By the Chief Justice: It is a resurrection[1] and a rebellious riot; and if the Sheriff on this resistance had made proclamation and, after proclamation made, they continued in resistance, they could be, and ought to be, proceeded against in another kind; for they resist the Queen and her royal authority, and therefore it differs from cases between party and party.

In levying execution it is not necessary to have a jury

Sheriff may have the *posse comitatus*, and may kill those who resist

Resurrection and rebellious riot

After proclamation resistance is felony

Resistance to the sheriff, in execution of a writ, is resistance to the Queen and her royal authority

In Camera Stellata, coram Consilio ibidem, Mercurij, 5 Maij, 1602, An°que Elizab. R^nae 44.[2]

[p. 89]

1602 May 5

Coke, Queen's Attorney, informed on the relation of Christofer Merrike of the Inner Temple, utter barrister, against Robert Pye,[3] defendant, of the Inner Temple, also utter barrister, for practice as to the life, lands and goods of the said Cristofer Merrike, for perjury touching the

QUEEN'S ATTORNEY *ex parte* MERRIKE *v.* PIE, a counsellor

Murder, robbery, perjury, and other misdemeanours

[1] Apparently used in the sense of insurrection, a rising.

[2] Nine Councillors and Judges were present.

[3] See Appendix VI.

1602 May 5

execution of this, and for other misdemeanours, as follows, namely :—

Money lent

Merrike, Febr. 1601, at the request of Pie, delivered to him £3 for a week; Pie did not repay this within three months, after Merrike had often demanded and sent for it, and at last threatened the arrest of Pie.

Acquittance demanded on repayment

Whereupon Pie, on July, carried 56*s.* to Merrike's chamber in the Inner Temple, and offered payment of this; Merrike said that he had lent £3, and without acquittance, and therefore he would not deliver any acquittance. Pie

Money abated on account of a wager

Case as to the age of an infant

replied that 4*s.* was to be abated for a wager, touching a case, that Merrike had lost to Pie, because Pie averred that when an infant enters upon the twenty first year he is of full age, Merrike on the contrary [said] that not before he had accomplished the twenty one years fully, days and hours.

Violence offered in taking money and an ink-horn [?]

Indictment for taking the same [p. 90]

Whereupon Pie refused to pay the 56*s.*, and Merrike with violence took the money and Pie's ink-horn [? ; *galiere*],[1] and beat him. Whereupon Pie indicted Merrike at Newgate, and gave instructions to one Grove, the clerk there, to fashion the indictment as follows :—[2]

The Clerk framed the indictment on the instruction of Pie. He was examined and deposed this. Grove an honest and sufficient clerk in the opinion of Shrewsbery and the [Lord] Keeper

Pie gives evidence to the Grand Inquest on the indictment

Pie himself was sworn to the indictment and gave evidence at the Grand Inquest [i.e. to the Grand Jury] that it was on the Queen's high way and that he [? Merrike] took to flight; whereupon a true bill was found.

Three of the Jury deposed what was Pie's answer on particular demand

The Recorder commended for his good discretion and grave judgment. Not robbery nor felony

Merrike arraigned and acquitted

The Recorder, John Crooke, seeing the indictment and knowing the parties, demanded of the Grand Inquest who gave evidence, and what evidence he gave; they answered as above. Whereupon the Recorder conferred at the bar with Pie, and said that this could not be either robbery or felony, and therefore advised him to be careful how he proceeded. The next day Pie was enjoined to proceed to the indictment; Merrike, then present, was arraigned. Pie, confidently and impudently, gave the same evidence,

[1] This word is spelled *galire* in the text and *galiere* in the margin. Cotgrave's Dictionary, 1673, gives *gallere*, an ink-horn.

[2] Here is a blank space.

whereupon he was committed to the Sheriff and bound to appear in this Court the next term. The same night after the indictment, Pie went to the court at Grenewige, and there acquainted Ferdinando, servant and musician in the Privy chamber, that one of good estate had committed felony and had forfeited his goods and lands, and demanded his letter to divers of the bench to have a gracious hearing by the Queen; whereupon [Ferdinando] wrote a letter to Sir Robert Wrothe and others, and so [the case] went to trial; and on the arraignment, Merrike was acquitted by the same jury as indicted him on the Grand Inquest. Then the Benchers of the Inner Temple examined this, and put Pie out of Commons, and referred him to the next Parliament[1]; and they suspended Merrike in Commons for a time of forbearance, but in a short time restored him. But at the next Parliament they examined the matter at large, and put Pie out of the House [i.e. the Inner Temple], and degraded him from the Bar and from all practice: and in the same vacation the Queen's Attorney and the Recorder took Pie's examination in writing, when he confessed all, and subscribed his hand: and thereupon the Attorney in Michaelmas Term next following informed *ore tenus* on this confession against Pie, when Pie denied it to be his hand, and said that it was not rightly [*dumente*] taken, and prayed to have the benefit of the law, [25] Edw. III. cap. [4] *quod nullus liber homo imprisonetur sans iudgmente*, and that he should not be condemned before bill and answer: Whereupon it was ordered by the Court that the Attorney should inform at once, because now Parliament is sitting [*continue*] and a pardon is expected, but if this cause be not heard before the pardon, the Lord Keeper would have care that this [case] should be excepted from the pardon if the bill was pending before the pardon: Phillips was assigned as Counsel with Pie, but when he saw Pie's answer, he moved for and obtained an order for his discharge: Pie was committed to the Fleete, and there remained until the

Pie committed, and bound to appear in the Starre Chamber

Ferdinando moved to beggar Merrike's lands and goods

Pie labours for an indifferent trial by the Queen

Acquittal by the same jury as found him guilty

[p. 91]

Pie put out by the Bench

Merrike suspended by the Bench

Pie put out of the House by the Parliament, to lose his chamber, to be disbarred, and [debarred] from all practice

The Attorney and the Recorder took Pie's confession, and in form *ore tenus*

Pie denied his hand and confession and prayed the benefit of the law

The Lord Keeper provides that Pie shall not have the benefit of the pardon.

Phillips, the Counsel assigned to Pie, is discharged by order on his dislike of the answer. Pie continues a prisoner in the Fleet until the time of sentence

[1] The meetings of the Benchers are so called.

1602 May 5 [p. 92]

Pie confesses, but without submission

sentence of the cause was heard. Pie did not submit himself, but in substance confessed all in his answer, and did not excuse himself in a reasonable or sensible word, but audaciously and impudently scandalized with imputations not only the Attorney, the Recorder and Merrike, but all the Judges and Justices, without any colour of cause. And he examined no witnesses, but Merrike examined Grove and three of the Grand Jurors and those witnesses which Pie said he had for himself and for the Queen, and they all deposed plainly and directly against Pie. To which he answered nothing, but only [said], "God knows the truth of all, and they may as well depose any thing [else] against me as this; for may I be hanged, and my neck cut off [*sic*] if this be true." And at last he craved the benefit of the Statute of 20 Edward I., *De defensione juris*, that no one should be admitted to sue before he has found surety to answer the issues and damages, etc. And thus he would take away the jurisdiction of this Court (as in the former Statute that he vouched), the authority of the Queen, which is present here, of her Council, of all original writs, and of all Justice. Then he craved the consideration of the Court inasmuch as the bill and the offences in it were not particular, and he was not charged with committing them contrary to the statutes and laws of this realm. But this notwithstanding [the bill] was held good by the Court and these exceptions [were considered] frivolous, Pie having superficial knowledge or taste of this, but not intellect.

Pie's own witnesses depose against him

The opinions of the Lord Keeper, the Chief Justices and the Attorney

[p. 93]

Merrike commended as a good student and of good behaviour

Malice and envy of Pie much noted by the Lord Keeper

Serjeant Woodde was examined in Court *viva voce*

Merrike was commended by the Attorney as a good student and of as good conversation as any in the Temple: But Pie falsely scandalized him for coveting and beggaring his brothers, taking forfeitures, suing men without cause, and otherwise cruel and extorting 'courses' in general without cause or colour: And [Pie] also imputed falsely that the Recorder had taken £10 from Merrike for a fee before the commencement of this suit, and as to this he vouched Serjeant Woodde, who cleared the Recorder of this imputation, and said of Merrike that he had intermeddled with Pie honestly, pitifully and conscionably.

Pie's offence was condemned by the whole Court to be horrible and odious, and the offence of robbery, murder and perjury against God; for, by the Bishops,[1] the breach of all the law is comprehended in this: *Diliges Deum toto corde, et proximum tuum sicut teipsum*. And by the ancient law *Voluntas reputabatur pro facto*. By the law of God and the Civil Law, *oculus pro oculo, dens pro dente, manus pro manu*, etc., and also *per legem talionis*: And Pie had intended murder and robbery in his heart, which is an offence before God: And the offence is more odious and detestable in this, that he has made Justice a murderer and robber.

Pie's offence contains murder, robbery, and perjury

The intent of murder, robbery, or perjury, is an offence before God

Lex talionis before followed

By the Lord Treasurer, and then by the Lord Keeper

[p. 94]

Sentence on Pie

Pie was sentenced to a fine of 1000 marks, pillory at Westminster and there to lose one ear, papers, from [Westminster] Hall to ride with his face to the horse's tail to 'Temple gate,' and there to be pilloried and to lose the other ear, and perpetual imprisonment.[2] As for Merrike, he was acquitted with great favour and grace, and delivered from all imputation of 'intemperancye' or 'heate.' And since they were both professors of the law, [the Court] exhorted them that have authority to admit to the bar, to have care to name those that were literate, honest and religious, and in the admittance of such to the House [Inn], for if they had had [such care], they would never have admitted Pie to the House, but he would have pursued his father's trade, who was a butcher; and [they should] not have calls by the dozens or scores, as now is the use: For the good and literate professors of the law are as good members of the Commonwealth as any others, but the ignorant and bad professors of the law are as 'daungerouse vermin' to the Commonwealth as 'Caterpillers,' etc. [*sic*].

Pie fined 1,000 marks, nailed to the pillory, ears, horse, perpetual imprisonment

Merrike acquitted with grace

Lord Keeper and the Chief Justices

Caveat as to calls to the bar and admittances at the Inns of Court

Good professors of the law are good members, and on the contrary. By the Lord Keeper

[1] The Archbishop of Canterbury and the Bishop of London.

[2] 'Pie, another barrister of the Inner Temple, stood on the pillory before the Temple Gate, and lost his ears, for plotting the death of a fellow lawyer, by way of justice.' State Papers, Dom., Eliz., 284, No. 14. John Chamberlain to Dudley Carleton.

1602
May 7

In Camera Stellata, coram Consilio ibidem, Veneris, 7° Maij, 1602, An°que Elizab. R^{nae} 44. Tr^{no} Pasche.[1]

WINSTON
v.
THROCKMORTON

Extortion and other several offences Answer, not guilty

[p. 95]

Murder and accessory to it

Sir Thomas Throckmorton assumed to acquit the accessory to the murder for 800*l*.

Honourable personages scandalised without cause

Good apology by the Counsellor in giving evidence. The Lord Keeper said that this aggravated the offence

Fountains and rivers of Justice

A Statute taken for 1600*l*. to acquit [him] of felony. This is extortion [even] if the money be not paid

Sir Henry Winston informed against Sir Thomas Throckmorton for 'diverse heynouse offences,' in number now only nine, to all of which Sir Thomas pleaded Not Guilty. The first was for great extortion,[2] namely :—

One Lewis in the County of Monmouth was barbarously murdered by his 'Cosin Germain,' also named Lewse [*sic*], who was indicted, arraigned and executed for it; and another Lewis, brother to him who was murdered, being accessory to the murder, and the wife intending to proceed against him, he repaired to the said Sir Thomas Throckmorton, who assumed to acquit him and discharge him; and to this [end] advised and conferred with the said Lewis that money and large sums would have to be expended to procure this, and some great personages would have to be used to effect it. And therefore he imposed imputation on the Earl of Pembroke and his Lady, the Lord Admiral and the Chief Justice, without cause or probability of any colour. And therefore at the commencement [*a l'entraunce*] of the evidence, Phillips, of Counsel with the plaintiff, made apology that, notwithstanding the Earl of Pembroke and his Lady were by the said Sir Thomas injuriously scandalized, yet it would plainly appear that they were clear, and so proved by the Earl himself, by the depositions of others, and by the confession of Sir Thomas himself. The Attorney said, as to the others, that it was a great slander, for 'no harte in Englaunde did ever Conceaue or had anye thoughte of Corruption in them; & if theise Fountaines be thus scandalized wth Corruption, what shall wee poore brookes look for.' Sir Thomas Throckmorton, being a Justice of the Peace and one of the Council of the Marches, April 35 Elizabeth, took a statute for £1600 from the said Lewis without defeasance, but the intent and agreement was that the said Sir Thomas should

[1] Eleven Councillors and Judges were present.

[2] For the others see *post*, p. 137, *et seq.*

have £800 for freeing the said Lewes, which sum was paid to the said Sir Thomas; and to prove this he produced Sir Thomas's letters, and the depositions of Lewes and others.

Coventrie, Crue, Hutton, Toppam, and others, of [p. 96] Counsel with the defendant, did not defend the offence nor extenuate it, but they confessed that it was an offence in Sir Thomas, who submitted himself in all humility to the Court; and they all affirmed that in the first place it was not an offence of such a nature and quality as to receive sentence here, for it was not extortion, and so it was pardoned by the Statute of 39 Elizabeth, if it be outside or after the pardon of 35 Elizabeth; and Sir Thomas craved the benefit of Her Majesty's gracious pardon. And that it is not extortion is thus proved: Firstly, the said Sir Thomas is not a Justice of the Peace, nor ever was, in the County of Monmouthe, nor in any other County but in the County of Gloster only; and when one is of the Council of the Marches, their authority is only when they are appealed to and have instructions, and not otherwise; and Sir Thomas was never sworn, and so was not a Judge, Justice, or other officer in the County of Monmouthe, and therefore no extortion. And also the said Sir Thomas took and received the money, not to his own use, but to give and pay it to others; and thus he disbursed it to the use of Lewis, and therefore no corruption or extortion in him. Also the said Lewis intended *bona fide* to intermarry with the daughter of the said Sir Thomas, and he was never indicted or arraigned for the felony, but Sir Thomas thought in his conscience that he was innocent, and not guilty of [the crime]; and also the wife of the murderer had the indictment against her husband removed into the Queen's Bench, where it was quashed for insufficiency; therefore the accessory cannot be indicted; for by law, where the principal is not *legitimo modo attinctus et convictus*, the accessory cannot be [put] in jeopardy of his life.

Extortion and *quomodo* pardoned. The pardons of 39 and 35 Elizabeth

Authority of the Council of the Welsh Marches

Principal not sufficiently convicted, accessory is acquitted

And firstly, as to whether it was extortion or not, the Court seemed to be of opinion that it was, and also that it was

1602 May 7

excepted from the pardon of 39 Elizabeth; but the consideration of this was reserved that the Judges might deliver their opinions on the next day.[1] And upon this was now much good matter delivered touching extortion and its nature to devour him who uses it, and the difference between extortion and bribery in a Judge or Officer, the grievousness [p. 97] of the offence, as to the punishment of Sir William Thorpe, Chief Justice of England, for adjourning the trial of a felon to the next Assizes following, for which offence he was indicted, arraigned, and executed for high treason; and this was confirmed by Act of Parliament, so heinous, grievous and odious is the offence of corruption and extortion in a Judge.[2]

Chief Justice attainted of high treason for adjourning a trial

Council of Wales

Much good matter was delivered by the Lord Keeper and others touching the authority of the Council of Wales, under the Statutes of 26 Henry VIII., cap. 4 & 6, and 34 Hen. VIII., cap. 26, [by which] the President and Council were created. And therefore if a man be made a Judge by patent and be not sworn, still he is a Judge, and shall be punished for extortion or corruption as a Judge: and that he is not sworn is his own fault, and he shall be punished for this. So is the case of the Council of Wales, who are made by patent, and, within all the Marches of Wales, each has good and equal authority; but if they are not named to the Council and [? do not] receive instructions from the Queen, they cannot sit nor have an allowance for their 'dyete' at the Queen's charge. This point also was referred to the Judges to consider.

Judge by patent and not sworn is a Judge

[1] Their opinion is given *post*, p. 137.

[2] This worthy was appointed Chief Justice of the King s Bench in 1346. In 1350 he was charged with having taken bribes, and was found guilty by the special Commissioners appointed by King Edward III. to investigate the matter. It was not, however, for adjourning trials, but for staying writs of exigent, that Thorpe received the bribes. He was committed to the Tower, and all his lands and goods were ordered to be seized into the King's hands, until the royal will and pleasure should be known. The King, by a writ dated Nov. 19, 1350, declared that the proper punishment was that Thorpe should be degraded and hanged, and directed the Commissioners to pass sentence accordingly, which they did. However, his life was spared, and Coke says that he eventually received a full pardon. The record and process were afterwards laid before the Parliament, which confirmed the judgment. Foss. This appears to be the Act of Parliament referred to in the text.

By the Lord Keeper: If a defendant in this Court be charged with several offences and is a delinquent in his defence, then all manner of proof is to be extended, with any kind of favourable and gracious interpretation, to charge and condemn him; and this is the use and rule of this Court.

Delinquent defendant shall have no favour

Also a use or rule observed in this Court [is], if the plaintiff has examined witnesses on interrogatories which are published, the defendant shall not re-examine them or other witnesses on new interrogatories, but on those first ones only.

No re-examination on new interrogatories

In Camera Stellata, coram Consilio ibidem, Mercurij, 12 Maij, 1602. Elizab. 44. Trno Pasche.[1]

[p. 98]

1602 May 12

The same cause between Sir Henry Winston and Sir Thomas Throckmorton.[2] It was opened now that in Michaelmas Term, 43 and 44 Eliz., Sir Henry Winston was plaintiff against Sir Thomas Throckmorton, who was sentenced and fined 1000 marks for a fraudulent deed, pronounced by two verdicts to be fraudulent; and after those verdicts, the said Sir Thomas bargained for this deed secretly and subtilely that he had not notice of this and that he purchased this and to whom the assignment was made. And in Hilary Term, 44 Eliz., Sir Thomas Throckmorton was plaintiff against the said Sir Henry, who was fined £1000 for 'intemperancye *et* batteryes' as Justice of the Peace, in resisting warrants, and principally for procuring an indictment for felony and burglary to be made and found petty larceny.

WINSTON *v.* THROCKMORTON

The plaintiff and defendant formerly sentenced in this court

Fine of 1000 marks against Sir Thomas for fraud

Fine of 1000*l.* against Winston, Knight, for altering an indictment

The Judges resolved that the offence of the said Sir Thomas was extortion and not excepted in the pardons of 35 or 39 [Elizabeth], and that he was a justice of oyer and terminer in this county.[3]

Resolution of the judges as to extortion

The second offence with which they charged the said Sir Thomas was that he by his bailiff seized the sheep of one

Defendant discharged of this offence

[1] Ten Councillors and Judges were present.

[2] See *ante*, p. 134.

[3] These points had been referred to them; see *ante*, p. 136.

1602 May 12

Mason on suspicion that he was guilty of the death of one who [had been] eight months buried. After [which time, Sir Thomas] procured the Coroner to raise him, and by a jury of his tenants to inquire concerning his death; and he spoke to the Coroner and the Jurors for the favour that they would not acquit so evil a man, so that as lord of the Manor, he should have chattels of felons. And he bound [Mason] over at three Assizes, when he was discharged by proclamation; and then he was pressed, through the information of the said Sir Thomas, and sent after the Captain to Bathe for service in Ireland. And he returned without his Captain's warrant, and was then committed by the said Sir Thomas: but the time of this offence was uncertain, and so was pardoned by 35 Elizabeth.

p. 99]

Time of the offence uncertain, and therefore pardoned

Whereupon good matter was resolved by all the Judges, the Attorney and the Lord Keeper, that if a man take money as 'presse-monie,' and be in charge of his Captain, and then depart without warrant, it is felony by the statute of 3 Henry VII., which is not repealed but continues in force. (And therefore the Attorney advises students of the law to read the Statutes at large, and not to trust to the Abridgements.) And it is good discretion in any Justice of the Peace to commit such a person, and for the like offence divers [persons] were executed at Mildende, and now it is necessary to publish this.

Felony if he depart when he has taken press-money

A good thing to read the Statutes at large and not the Abridgments

Departure when pressed is punishable with imprisonment and death

The third offence. One [1] Neste, was seised of land in tail, having issue two sons; both the sons were accused of murder; the said Sir Thomas took a bond from the younger son of £200 for the payment of £100 after his father's death, to condemn his elder brother of the said murder, and another bond of £200 for the payment of £100 after his father's death, to discharge himself of robbery and felony.

Time of this uncertain, and therefore pardoned also

The fourth offence. In taking money to discharge pressed soldiers; but this was against Garlike and other two servants of the said Sir Thomas, and not against Sir Thomas himself.

Taking money to discharge pressed soldiers, a great offence.

[1] Blank in MS.

And so on the whole matter, the said Sir Thomas was, for the first offence only, the extortion, fined 2000 marks, with imprisonment and public confession at the next Assizes.

Throckmorton fined 2,000 marks, imprisonment, and confession at the Assizes

Garlike, for taking money to discharge pressed soldiers, was fined £40, with imprisonment and restitution to the parties: and the others were fined £20, with imprisonment and restitution.

[p. 100]

Garlike fined 40*l*., the others 20*l*., imprisonment, and satisfaction

Special Sessions at Godstone,[1] Jovis 27 Maij, 1602. Elizab. 44, before Richard Bostoke, William Forster, William Gainseforde and John Turner, Justices of the Peace and Judges there.

1602 May 27

Between William Gardiner and George Etheridge, for riots and forcible entries. Edward Coomes of the Middle Temple of Counsel with Gardiner, and myself[2] with Etheridge.

ETHERIDGE *v.* GARDINER and others

Riot and forcible entry

William Gardiner seised of a messuage and lands named Legham, on the last day of May, 39 Elizabeth, made a lease to Edward Branden for 21 years, of all messuages, lands, tenements, woods, underwoods, and other profits, commodities, and hereditaments, with the appurtenances, etc., (except all timber trees, with free egress and regress to carry them, etc.,) paying £110 yearly at the two feasts or within 20 days after any of the feasts, and if it should happen that the said rent should be in arrear for the space of ten days after the said 20 days, the same being lawfully demanded within the hours of two and five of the same said day [the tenth day] at the 'Cobbarde en Graies Inne Halle in Midd.,' that then, etc.; And on January 12, 40 Elizabeth, the said Edward Brandon, for £220, assigned his lease and term to the said George Etheridge, who entered, and was, and is, possessed of the same accordingly. And the said William Gardiner demanded the rent accord-

[1] In the county of Surrey.

[2] John Hawarde of the Inner Temple, the writer of the MS The Hawardes lived at Tandridge, which is close to Godstone.

1602 May 27 ing to the condition of the lease, and for non payment thereof, entered on the land, made a lease, and brought *eiectione firme*; and the said George Etheridge brought a bill in Chancery; and now at this Session, George Etheridge preferred three several bills of indictment for forcible and riotous entry.

The first was that William Gardener, William Bromloe, Mathew Hatton, John Dodde, John Crumlin, Alan Beste, and William Harlinge, May 8, 44 Elizabeth, with force and arms, *manu forti*, 'riotose *et* routouse,' in disturbance of the peace, with weapons offensive and defensive, entered into [p. 101] the gate-house of Legham, and assaulted and beat the servants and cattle of the said George Etheridge and expelled them, contrary to the laws and statutes in that case made and provided.

The second was that John Dodde, William Kinge, and James Walter, May 12, 44 Elizabeth, entered on the land with force, 'riotose & routose,' and burnt five wooden carts, and diverted [*sic*, ? overturned] a load of coals.

The third was that William Kinge, Mathewe Hatton, Richard Ratcliffe, Alan Beste, Thomas Dennis and Robert Wrighte, May 14, 44 [Elizabeth], entered on the land again, with force as before, and chased and beat the beasts; and this continued until May 18 aforesaid, and they diverted a 'wane' of coals.

Lambert, fo. 149 Bro. Forcib. ent. 29 Crompt. fo. 63 Stat. 8 Hen. VI., cap. 9 Fitzherbert Nat. Bre. 249 4 Mar. Diar. 141 Lambert, fo. 187 Crompt. fo. 61 3 Hen. VII. 1° et 10 21 Hen. VII. 39, Fineux Crompt. fo. 62

The evidence to prove this was direct; and the first position was, that all manner of force is condemned by law; but where one has been in quiet possession for three whole years, without interruption, such a person may guard his possession by force. And that would be said [to be] quiet possession without interruption, if [you] and all yours be not actually driven out, and removed out. And if he, or those whose estate he hath, have been in possession for three years, he may defend his possession with such force and company as he hath in his house, but he may not bring armour, nor company, nor 'shotte' to guard it. For, it is said, a man may justify battery of another in defence of the possession of his goods, by 21 Edw. III., 34, *a multo fortiori* for the defence of his house, which is his hold and castle. 20 Hen. VI., 11

And also, if one has rent or other thing for which he may distrain, he may not distrain by force, for then it is punishable by 8 Henry VI., cap. 9, and 15 Richard II., cap. 2. 43 Ass. pl. 6 22 Hen. VI., 23 49 Ass. 7 2 Hen. VII. 16

Also that in an indictment for forcible entry, the title is not material, for if he use force, on good or bad title, it is all one. And therefore, if A disseise B, and B oust A by force; A shall be restored to possession of the land, and yet he is a disseisor. But in an action or indictment of trespass, the force depends on the validity of the title; and indictment for force is only by the Queen. [p. 102] 22 Hen. VI., 18 Lambert, fo. 158 Lambert, fo. 144 7 Hen. VI., 13 & 40

And so, firstly I proved the three years' possession and no actual ouster, and the entry by force and with weapons; and upon the whole matter our three indictments were found.

GARDINER *v.* ETHERIDGE and others — Riots, &c.

At the same time also, the said Mr Gardiner preferred five several indictments against George Etheridge and his servants for five several riots and forcible detainers of the said messuage and land of Legham, and gave in evidence the lease, and used the testimony of the parties formerly indicted. Whereupon I moved firstly, that in no case is the title itself to be examined; moreover, the matter in law is with us, and the tender was according to the condition; and the said Gardiner has brought an ejectment since his re-entry, and they could not now judge the title: and so [I] pressed them to prove a lawful entry and an actual ouster, both of which could not be proved; for on enforcement that they were for the Queen, they had favourable hearing, and their evidence was heard at large, notwithstanding I challenged the witnesses, being first charged for the former riot and force, and thus they swore for the clearing of themselves. And therefore I moved that the jury might first find our three indictments, and then to give the other evidence. Query these two last points. And all this notwithstanding, the jury found all "*Ignoramus*"; and after this verdict, Counsel moved to have the appearance of

1602 May 27 two [of the defendants] recorded; for Mr Bostoke, hearing and having knowledge of the riot and force, went to the land, and there finding two of Mr Gardiner's men, bound them to appear at this Session, and after the taking of their appearance, and recording it, he delivered *cerciorare* to remove all indicted with William Gardener and William Bromlie.

[p. 103] Also I moved that the charges of divers of the Justices and Jury should be borne by the said Gardiner, because this Session was not on the complaint of any one, but the Justices themselves having knowledge of [the affair] appointed it of themselves, being the neighbouring Justices 'inhabitant penall' by 13 Henry IV., cap. 7; for, by 8 Henry VI. cap. 9, if a session be held on a complaint of force, the party who complains shall bear the charge, but if Query. it be on account of a riot, the Queen shall bear the charge.

In our case we had not brought the indictment under 8 Henry VI. cap. 9, but generally, "against the laws and statutes and riotously and routously, *manu forti*, they did enter"; and they brought indictments of riot only, the one of which bore date before any of ours, and the indictment is the complaint that the Statute intends. Therefore we are to be discharged from the costs and charges, and the Queen or the said Gardiner must pay them. But Gardener refused to pay a penny, and the charges in all amount to £5; but at last the Justices persuaded [Gardiner] that he should pay five nobles, and Etheridge [should pay] the residue,[1] which was hard. Query.

At last after much persuasion by the Justices, and at the great and instant desire of the inhabitants of Godstone, Gardiner and Etheridge were content and agreed to refer all matters to the arbitrament of the said four Justices,[2] and with their consent a motion should be made to the Lord Keeper for a commission to those four to examine and determine all causes between them, all pending actions to be stayed, and all wood to remain without being removed,

[1] Five nobles amounts to 1*l*. 13*s*. 4*d*.
[2] Those holding the Special Session; see *ante*, p. 139.

so that the Justices could view the wood at Midsummer following.

In Camera Stellata, coram Consilio ibidem, Mercurij, 9 Junij, Elizab. 44, An°que Do^{mi} 1602. Tr^{no} Trinitat.[1] [p. 104] 1602 June 9

Before the hearing of causes, the Attorney moved for the reference of a demurrer on an information sent in by him against a libeller, for an 'infamouse libelle':[2] Phillips defended the plea and said that [it was] not a demurrer, for a former bill was preferred in this Court for the same offence and taken again out of the Court, by the order of the Court and with the assent of the parties, and so he craved the judgment of the Court: But the Queen's Attorney, notwithstanding this, if he find cause to gain a fine for the Queen, may proceed by information: And so it was ruled by the Court. And he said that he did not wish to compound a libel, for it is a growing vice, and there are more infamous libels [now] within a few days than ever there were in the ages last past.

Motion

Difference between demurrer and former judgment of the Court

Bill taken out by order, still the Queen's Attorney may proceed by information

Libels condemned

The Lord Keeper upon this and the motion following, did greatly reprehend demurrers, being frivolous, and always for delay; thus it is a common motion, "I praye referre a Demurrer," being a thing of course that when it is found insufficient, the party shall pay small costs: but it is necessary that for any insufficient demurrer the party shall pay very many and great costs, according to the quality of the damage of him who is thus delayed. To this the Chief Justice agreed, and, by way of advice, did exhort Counsellors at Law not to permit their clients to demur without good and sufficient cause, and this with judgment and discretion, otherwise the Court would tax them with weakness, and defect of knowledge, discretion and judgment.

Lord Keeper on demurrers

Good costs for each frivolous demurrer

Good counsel for the practicers of the law

[1] Nine Councillors and Judges were present.

[2] Probably the case against Michael Cawley and others; see *post*, pp. 146, 147, and Appendix VII.

1602
June 9

[p. 105]

PLYMOUTH WATER-WORKS case

Sir Francis Drake conveys the river to Plimmouth

Serjeant Healle, now Queen's Serjeant,[1] moved that whereas by 27 Elizabeth, cap. 20, the river of Mewe [Meavy] is to be brought by the Maior & 'Cominaltye' of Plimmouth to the town of Plimmouthe, which was done by the industry and charge of Sir Fraunicis Drake,[2] to the great commodity of the town, the country, the Queen's Navy in the harbour there, and for the public good otherwise in the making of tinne, and by the benefit of the fresh water, and whereas a bill was preferred two years ago against [3] Grenefeilde and others for the riotous stopping of the course thereof, and for throwing down the banks and fosses; and a demurrer was entered thereupon, and certified [to be] insufficient; and now since Easter Term, the fosses and banks are thrown down and stopped, to the prejudice not of the town only, but of the public good; and thereupon he moved that, according to the course of the Court, it should be ordered that the River should be continued in the same course as it was at the time of the bill preferred. And the Lord Keeper ordered this accordingly, saying, that it was not material, even if it be not the course of the Court, for in such great cases, in which there was great mischief, and it was so necessary for the public good, a precedent was not necessary to direct them, but they could make an order according to the necessity and nature of the thing itself.[4]

Course of the Court

Precedent not required where the case is great and necessary, and for the public good

[1] 'Sergeant Heale was made the Quenes sergeant this sommer, and rode circuit with Judge Gawdie in Sussex, Surrey, Kent, Essex, and Hartfordshire, wherein he plaide such pranckes, and so demeaned himselfe, that he is become both odious and rediculous.' *Chamberlain's Letters*, Camden Soc., p. 152.

[2] 1589. 'Also this yere the composytyon was made betwene the town and Sir Fraunces Drake for the bringinge of the river of Meve to the towne, for which the towne haue paid hym ii C li., and more C li., for which he is to compounde with the lordes of the lande over wich it commeth.'

1590. 'This yere on the daye of December Sir Fraunces Drake kneight, beganne to bringe the ryuer of Meve to the towne of Plymouthe which, beinge in lenght about 25 myles, he with great care and diligence effected, and brought the river into the towne the xxiiijth day of Aprill then next after.' MSS. of the Corporation of Plymouth. *Hist. MSS. Comm.*, 9th Rep. App. pt. i. p. 278.

[3] Blank in MS.

[4] See Appendix VIII.

A cause was heard between Plowden and Blundell, plaintiffs, against Braughton, Counsellor of the Inner Temple, Powelle, Hues, and others, for riot and other misdemeanours.

PLOWDEN and BLUNDELL v. BRAUGHTON and others

Riot and other misdemeanours

The father of Plowden, being a grave lawyer,[1] a man of great judgment and honesty, having a lease from the Queen of the Rectory of Bishop's Castle in Shropshire, at the rent of £19 13*s.* 4*d.* *per annum*, and two decrees for this in the Exchequer, the defendant Braughton, having a lease of the Rectory of Lidberrye-northe, adjoining the Rectory of Bishop's Castle, intended [i.e. pretended] that this passed also by his lease, and by colour of this intended a year before to take the tithes, and would 'shuffle' for them, and procured labourers twenty miles distant by means of Hues, a Justice of the Peace, who sent them, and with them Braughton sent his servants, with carts and weapons, to carry the tithes, and they maimed and wounded the servants of Plowden; and Braughton, with other gentlemen, saw this, and did not countermand it.

[p. 106]

Riot in taking tithes

Misdemeanour in procuring labourers

The misdemeanour was that Braughton, being a Judge in three Counties in Wales,[2] procured before himself as Judge an informer content to have his name used, while Braughton would maintain the suit at his own cost. But this was not proved by any one but one only, who had been sentenced to suffer at the pillory for perjury and other offences, which the Court would not suffer to be read, as he was sentenced before the suit commenced. For a Judge, in his just and honest courses, will be protected by this Court with grace and favour, and the proof to accuse him must be plain and apparent, and such evidence is only *ad informandam conscientiam*; but if he do evil and offend, this Court will punish him with great and heavy

Acquittal of the misdemeanour because no proof

Judge favoured in well-doing, and on the contrary

Proof to accuse a judge must be clear and without exception

[1] Edmund Plowden, of the Middle Temple, son of Humphrey Plowden of Plowden, in the parish of Lydbury North, Shropshire. Plowden Hall, which is still in the possession of the family, is a half-timbered building of the Elizabethan and Jacobean periods. It contains a private chapel and two hiding-places; which are probably accounted for by the fact that Edmund Plowden the lawyer was a staunch Roman Catholic. There is a full-length recumbent monument to his memory in the Temple Church.

[2] A Justice of the Peace.

1602 June 9

Braughton fined 200*l.* and imprisonment, and 'disjusticed'

[p. 107]

A Councillor of the Marches can only be removed by the Queen

punishment. Braughton, being an erudite man, and in a place of justice and dignity for his virtue and erudition, *et quanto maior est dignitas tanto magis fuerit plus reum* [*sic*], was fined £200, and removed from [his office as] Justice of the Peace, but being of the Council of the Marches, he is made by the Queen, and she gives him instructions, and he cannot be removed but by her. Two other defendants, gentlemen, each [fined] £100, the other defendants £20 each, and imprisonment. Braughton to pay the fines of the others who are not of ability. The Lord Keeper moved that the parties maimed should have their expenses and some recompence; *ad quod nihil fuit responsum.*[1]

PIKE'S case

Order to have those whipped who prefer petitions for trial at common law, after the cause is sentenced

The Lord Keeper moved that a man named Pike, after this court had sentenced [pronounced] a deed to be forged and [ordered] it to be cancelled, had moved by petition to him to have a trial at Common Law, and his wife, in time before, had preferred such a petition to the Queen and to him [the Lord Keeper]; And it was ordered by the Court that if she did this again, she should be lashed; and as to the right the husband had, the Court answered nothing.

ASCEWE *v.* EARL OF LINCOLN

The Earl of Lincolne conforms himself after contempts and imprisonment

The Queen's Attorney moved between the Earl of Lincolne and Ascewe.[2] Now the Earl, after many contempts and disobeyings of orders and decrees of the Court, after conference with the said Attorney, submitted himself to the order of the Court, and craved a reference to two Judges to assess the damages; which was ordered accordingly.

Infamous libel against Privy Councillors

The Attorney may use the

[p. 108]

messenger

He moved also that he, having preferred information against three for an infamous libel against some of state for conveying £3,000,000 out of the realm,[3] etc., had seized the principal of them after attachment by a messenger, and he prayed to have several of the others committed; and if he did not answer the interrogatories within a brief time, to be held *pro confesso.* And all was ordered accordingly.

[1] See *post*, p. 147.

[2] See *ante*, pp. 12, 114.

[3] Probably the case against Michael Cawley and others, see *ante*, p. 143, and below.

In Camera Stellata, coram consilio ibidem, Veneris, 11 Junij, 1602, Elizab. 44, Tr^no^ Trinitat.[1] 1602 June 11

ATT.-GEN. v. CAWLEY and others — Libel

The Attorney moved, in the great case of Caullye for libel, to have a short day to examine them.[2]

BRAUGHTON v. PLOWDEN and others — Riot

Idle and frivolous bill

The cross bill was heard, Braughton and others, plaintiffs, against Plowden, Blundell and others, defendants, for riots.[3] It was a great bill, containing 66 sheets of paper, and much idle and frivolous matter against himself, as, after folio 40, "they assemble riotouselie & goe together in most freindelye & louing mann^r^," etc., that no resistance was offered, and such ridiculous matter as moved very much laughter. But the Lord Keeper said, "Althoughe it be good to be merrye some time, & this be St Barnabas daye, the longeste daye in the yeere, yet let vs not spende the hole daye in this place wth wordes to no purpose." *Facetiae*

Riot in taking tithes. A man may do a just thing, but not justly; a right thing, but not rightly

The riot was supposed to be made in taking the tithes of the Rectories of Bishop's Castle and Lidberrie Northe by colour of a lease in Braughton supposing them to be one entire thing, as on the day before, and the other lease to be void, being on a 'concealde title' and *a die datus*; and it was in like manner as before, namely:—

Braughton uses a discreet course

Braughton, on the day before the supposed riot, went to Plowden's house, and offered him that there might be a trial as to the tithes in question, or that Judge Owen,[4]

[1] Eight Councillors and Judges were present.

[2] The defendants were William Elston, Gilbert Wilkinson, Anthony Atkinson and Michael Cawley. They had published divers libels on the Privy Council, the Lord Treasurer, and others. State Papers. Dom., Eliz., vol. 283, No. 7.

'The last day of the terme, at the Starre Chamber, Atkinson, Wilkinson, Elson, and Cawley, the accusers of the Lord Treasurer, were, after a longe and tedious hearing, condemned in a fine, to be whipt, to stand on the pillorie and lose theire eares, and to the gallies, or perpetuall imprisonment. The first and the third found some litle favour, and were dispensed withall for whipping and their eares, in consideration the one was very penitent, and had revealed the whole plot and drift; the other for that he was a souldier, and so more subject to discontentment.' *Chamberlain's Letters*, Camden Soc., p. 144.

'On Wensday last Atkinson and his fellowes had theire payment in Cheapside according to the sentence in the Star Chamber.' *Ibid.*, p. 145. See *ante*, pp. 143, 146, and Appendix VII.

[3] See *ante*, p. 145.

[4] Thomas Owen, one of the Judges of the Common Pleas.

1602 June 11

being in the country, might determine the matter. Plowden required until the next day to answer this, and [p. 109] seemed to allow of it in good fashion. The next day, which is the day on which the riot is supposed to have been made, Braughton heard that Plowden had assembled 60 people and taken the tithes. Whereupon Braughton, and some of his servants with a cart, went to the place and inquired for Plowden, who was not there. Braughton sent for Plowden where he was at the Commission. Whereupon Plowden coming on horseback and a man with him on horseback, with a bow and arrows, and others of his men followed him with 'Welshe hookes, rapiers & daggers, pistolls, bowes & arrowes, &c.' And Braughton then offered Plowden that he should take a lease, and then Braughton would bring an action for the trial of the title, or on the contrary. Plowden refused, saying that he would take the tithes by force in despite of all, and so he was advised; and he said to Braughton, "Let him take a sheaffe if he dare."

Unlawful weapons are punishable, even if it be to defend lawful possession

Braughton makes a good and discreet offer

Plowden badly advised, a just thing should be justly [done], and a right thing, rightly

On the whole matter and the long bill, this one sole offence was proved, and was heard and sentenced; for the Court would not suffer the Counsel of the now plaintiff to produce or to read any thing concerning or touching the former riot which was sentenced the day before, in which the servants were maimed. Still it was vouched that in the case of ,[1] a riot was sentenced in the defendant and plaintiff also; and so it might be by the rule of this Court.

A matter sentenced ought not to be impugned by reading the proof condemning others in a cross bill for the same offence. Case vouched against this. Query

Ployden [*sic*], solely for the unlawful weapons and force of his servants, was fined £100 and imprisonment, but the others of his servants were not proved by special names, and therefore were acquitted and dismissed with costs.

Plowden fined 100*l.* and imprisonment; the others dismissed with costs

Blundell's counsel was much disliked by the Court, as to the taking of the tithes by force; and Braughton's offer was much commended for the 'speedie & indifferente tryalle' as to the tithes.

Blundell gave evil counsel; done in his anger [or madness, *furie*]

[1] Blank in MS.

Another cause of hearing was between Sparke, plaintiff, and Sparke and Tyler, defendants, for forgery and erasure in a will. If a man write the name of the testator, after his death, to his will [*testamente*], in the presence of those who are witnesses to his will [*volunte*], it is good. Agreed by the Lord Keeper [that it is] the same as to altering anything in the will, such as blotting or bluring; and thus it was done in this case. And the party himself who did it had no benefit by it. The erasure was not proved. Therefore on the whole matter the plaintiff was fined £20 to the Queen and £20 to the two defendants *pro falso clamore*.

SPARKE *v.* SPARKE and TYLER

Forgery and erasure

[p. 110]

A will may be altered after the death of the testator

Plaintiff fined 20*l.*, and the defendants have costs, 20*l.*

Phillips moved the opinion of the Court in Hele and Prestwoodde's case, heard last term, when I was not present, but as I heard by report, this is the case: Prestwoodde, a gentleman of good condition, prescribed to have a way and passage in the yard and close by the house of a tenant of Healle's (and it seems in truth that this is an ancient way and *via regia*), to carry timber from his land, and had not any other passable way; the servants of Prestwoodde came with the team in a peaceable manner, and broke the hedge and diverted the ditch in attempting to pass, but the tenant came [with] a 'forreste bille' and other weapons, and resisted them, and beat the oxen. Prestwoodde himself came after his servants with his usual man who attended on him, in a peaceable manner without weapons, and persuaded them to permit the cart to pass, which they did, the others saying that they would be better prepared for their return, etc.

HELE *v.* PREST-WOODDE

Riot

Riot for using a highway

On the whole matter the Court gave sentence, there being ten [Judges] in Court. Five [of them] condemned Prescotte [*sic*] as guilty of a riot, and his servants [also]. Five others acquitted the servants of all and Prescotte [*sic*] of the riot but not of the misdemeanour, but of this they found Prescotte [*sic*] himself guilty. Now the question is if he be acquitted or condemned, and if the voices being equal, the sentence should not be taken to condemn the

If the Court give equal voices, which is the sentence? There is none as it seems, for the Clerk enters nothing

Good question. Query

[p. 111]

1602 June 11

party, because it is to the Queen's benefit. The Court wished to consider this. By the Attorney: it seems that the precedent of the Court in such a case is that the sentence for the Queen's benefit should be taken. Others to the contrary. Query.

Equal voices in felony or treason, the party is acquitted

If it be in a case of felony or treason, as in Lord Dacre's case in the time of Henry VIII.,[1] if the voices are equal, the party is acquitted, for it is *in favore vitae*, which is a thing that the law favours ('*life, libertie and dower*').

Man acquitted of riot by equal voices

But if a man be charged in this Court with riot and other misdemeanour, and five condemn him [for the riot], and five condemn him for the misdemeanour but not for the riot, then he is acquitted of the riot: by the Lord Keeper.

Course when a forged deed is confessed

The Queen's Attorney informed [in a case] of forgery; the deed was confessed, and ought to be brought into Court and there remain until the cause be heard in [due] course of the Court; but the Attorney moved that, inasmuch as it now appeared that the '*counterpane*' [*sic*] of [the deed] was cancelled, that this also might be brought into Court. The Lord Keeper said, "First examine upon this deed, which is confessed and not cancelled, and if there appear any cause, then the other deed, which is cancelled, should also be brought into Court."

If the counterpart of a forged deed should be brought into Court

Yelverton, Judge, and Lord Burleighe, as to the place of Vice-President

In the Council Chamber, the day before, after dinner, the matter between Judge Yelverton and the Lord Burleighe was heard, for that the said Yelverton took the place of the Vice-President of the Council of Yorke.[2] But what sentence was given thereupon, I have never heard.

[p. 112]

Judge Yelverton sitting to hear *Nisi Prius*, and Lord Burleighe being in the Commission with him and the

[1] William, Lord Dacre, was acquitted of high treason, 26 Henry VII.

[2] The Council of the Northern Parts, which met at York.

"Mr Touse told that in the last cirquit into Yorkeshire the Vice President of Yorke would have had the upper hand of Justice Yelverton, but he would not yeld." 1602, May 3 *Manningham's Diary*, Camden Soc p. 40.

See Appendix IX.

President there, and placed in the Commission before him, came to him and sat by him on the bench. And [Yelverton] called for the Abridgment of the Statutes, and turned to Statute ,[1] which says that no one shall sit by the Justice of *Nisi Prius* when he is on the Bench hearing [causes]; and he caused the said Statute to be read, and prayed the Lord Burleighe to hear this and to observe it. Which was read accordingly; and the Lord Burleighe took this in great disgrace and departed. And thereupon the said Judge Yelverton was summoned to the Council Chamber at Westminster after the said Star Chamber day; and there Secretary Cecille[2] reprehended the Judge that he had, out of the pride of his heart, done this to disgrace the said Lord Burleighe. The Judge replied that he had shamed him. The Lord Admiral was bitter against the Judge, and said that he thought that the professors of the law would press their honours, titles and dignities from them. The Lord Keeper and both the Chief Justices for the Judge. The Secretary said that the Council of State could alter or order the placing of persons of honour or office: but the Chief Justice answered that the Council of State could not alter the course of the Common Law, 'he woulde be sorrye yt coulde.' It was then ruled that Lord Burleighe had been shamed, and that the Judge should give him place. And it was also moved there that the Judge should make confession at Yorke and there submit himself, but on this the Court then varied. But on the Sabbath day next following, at the Council table at the Court at Grenewige (the Chief Justice then absent), it was ordered and decreed that the Judge should make his confession at the Assizes at Yorke next following, and there should make his submission. But the Queen of her grace, and on his humble petition, dispensed with this, and thereupon he changed his circuit.

[1] Blank in MS.

[2] Sir Robert Cecil, who was Secretary and Chancellor of the Duchy of Lancaster.

1602 June 16

In Camera Stellata, coram Consilio ibidem, Mercurij, 16 Junij, Elizab. 44, 1602, Ter^no^ trinitat.[1]

Att.-Gen. *ex parte* Boothe [p. 113] *v.* Agar — Forgery

Cause of hearing. The Attorney informed on behalf of a '*pouer wydowe*' named Boothe, plaintiff, against Agar, grocer and Deputy Receiver to the Queen, defendant, for forging three acquittances, and procuring her lease of the '*Swanne oue deux neckes*' house, in S. Laurence Lane, to be forfeited, in procuring the acquittances, bearing date before the day of the forfeiture, and he made new acquittances bearing date after the day of the forfeiture, and entered through the forfeiture, and procured a new lease in his own name, and promised the plaintiff this, and took money of her, and then refused to lease or assign it to her without a great sum of money, and also swore that the acquittances did not bear date before the day of forfeiture but after the day of forfeiture, and it was proved that they bore date before the day of forfeiture. But the matter not being clear, but in every way dubious, the Counsel for the defendant offered to give the plaintiff £80, the sum that the lease cost, or to assign the term, which was accepted by the Court; and so dismissed and not sentenced.

Dismissed and not sentenced

Roper *v.* Martin — Libel

Another cause; the Attorney informed on the relation of one [2] Roper, goldsmith, against [2] Martin, stationer, for an infamous libel. They both being rivals for a lady, Martin framed an infamous libel against [Roper] in fashion of a letter, and sent it to Roper, and put to it the name of "Tom tell trothe," and in this disgraced him with purpose to defeat him with the lady, who had a large portion, and to whom Roper is now married. This libelling was much disliked by the community, and [is] a danger to it; otherwise this was ridiculous and foolish. But for the example of this, [Martin] was fined £100, pillory in Cheapeside, and confession there. The Lord Keeper cited the precedents of Bashe and others.

Sentence

[1] Ten Councillors and Judges were present.
[2] Blank in MS.

In Camera Stellata, coram Consilio ibidem, veneris, 18 Junij, 1602.[1] [p. 114] 1602 June 18

It was moved by the Queen's Attorney [in the case] of Halle against Fitscheuerelle. The said F. was brought by the Sergeant at Arms for contempt of an order of the Court, and now he has obeyed it, and Halle arrested him on other actions and stayed him on execution. Thereupon the Attorney moved for the privilege of this Court, which other inferior Courts have, that a man arrested to [make him] obey an order of this Court ought not to be arrested by any other Court, for it is not [consistent] with the dignity of this Court. At first the Chief Justice denied this, because he [Fitscheuerelle] was a dangerous person and had contemptuously disobeyed all orders and executions, and if he went at large, he would not be taken again without spilling of blood. But the parties by consent referred the matter to arbitration, otherwise this seems to be the course of the Court.

HALLE *v.* FITSCHEUERELLE — Law of arrest — Arbitration

Cause of hearing between Rowlie, plaintiff, and Morgan, attorney at law, for extortion and riot.

ROWLIE *v.* MORGAN — Extortion and Riot

Morgan was one of the Deputy Stewards to the Bishop of Rochester, who held court 'from 3 weekes to 3 weekes,' sometimes at Bromlye, Gravesende or Darforde, etc.; a riot was made in a house in Rochester to which he pretended title; and for this riot, at the Court held before himself, he himself being Judge, he entered twenty-seven several plaints against the rioters, and for *habeas corpus* to remove them he took two shillings from each for his fees, and entered into the house and took an obligation from the tenant to hold possession for his [Morgan's] use.

The offence of extortion was much condemned by all, and defined to be obtaining [money] by force or fraud *colore officii*; the Attorney [said] he knew not the Latin word for this. Extortion

Morgan's Counsel did not excuse the offence in him, but [p. 115]

[1] Eight Councillors and Judges were present.

1602 June 18 confessed the same with submission to the censure of the Court as to the taking of fees; but he pleaded Not Guilty to the riot, and [Morgan] swore in his answer that he was living at London when the riot was made. But on the sentence [of the Court], four condemned him of the riot and four others acquitted him of it. Which now is the sentence? Query. For the Court had doubts as to this in Prestwood's case [1]; but Sir John Fortescue thinks that it is now resolved and agreed by all of them that [the sentence] for the Queen shall be [considered] the best. Query. Also as to the riot [*sic*, ? the extortion], five acquitted him of this and the other three condemned him and fined him £100 with imprisonment as of course. The other rioters were fined one £40, and the other £20.

Sentence

In the afternoon of this day, the Court sat to read orders, according to the course prescribed by the Lord Keeper in his time, and not before.

1602 Oct. 13

In Camera Stellata, coram Consilio ibidem, Mercurij, 13 Octobr., 1602, Michael. 44 et 45 Elizab.[2]

Perjury and Forgery

[p. 116]

In a case of perjury and forgery, a devise was produced which had been condemned by two verdicts, and was now proved good by witnesses in this Court, and by the continuance of possession according to the will. But the Court, inasmuch as this course impeached the credit of twenty-four jurors, referred the matter to Common Law to have a trial on an issue to be joined, "testament or not"; and in the meantime [the will] to be retained in Court.

Issue referred to common law

Hogge's Case

Cozenage

Another cause of hearing between Hogge and ,[3] for practice of cozenage of a curate in this manner. The defendant, knowing that the plaintiff ought to receive [some] money, pretended that he had a benefice in Gloster, and that he was to be removed to one in the County of

[1] See *ante*, p. 149.

[2] Six Councillors and Judges were present.

[3] Blank in MS.

Hereforde, and if [Hogge] would procure him money, he [the defendant] would resign, and use means with Mr Eedes, the brother of the Bishop of Hereforde, for [Hogge's] admittance and induction. And then he brought one Vivian, who took the name of Edes, and sermonized against deceite and cozenage, and prayed for the Bishop and [the defendant], whom he commended for an honest and pious man, who then sermonized also and on the same text against fraud and cozenage. And by this practice they obtained £80 from the plaintiff. But the Court was of opinion that it was fitter for the High Commissioners to determine this, and so they referred it to the Archbishop and the Bishop of London to peruse the proceedings of this Court and to finish the matter or to report to this Court, which retains it [in the meantime]. Case referred to High Commissioners

Another cause of hearing between Sallowaie, Attorney in the Exchequer, plaintiff, and Walle, defendant, for forgery of two deeds, and perjury. It lasted long, and so was adjourned to another day.[1] The Lord Keeper complained that the causes could not be heard because of the multitude of motions. The Attorney said that they did not wish to trouble them. SALLOWAIE *v.* WALLE — Forgery and Perjury — Multitude of motions

In Camera Stellata, coram Consilio ibidem, Veneris, 15 Octobr., 1602.[2] [p. 117] 1602 Oct. 15

The former cause of hearing between Sallowaie, plaintiff, and Walle, defendant, for forgery of two deeds.[3] The defendant alleged that he and his brother being tenants in common, his brother, on taking a wife, made this deed for her jointure, and gave the land to himself and his wife and to the heirs male of the husband which he should engender of the body of his wife, with remainder to the right heirs of the defendant, and at the end of the deed, *His testibus*, a thing not in use since the time of Henry VII., and there- SALLOWAIE *v.* WALLE — Forgery

[1] See below.

[2] Eight Councillors and Judges were present.

[3] See above.

1602 Oct. 15 fore a badge of forgery and fraud. First, Salloway having purchased the land, after his purchase, the defendant (to regain the land) procured one Bridgman, who had sold the land to Salloway, to make a deed which bore date after the sale to Sallowaye, and so of no force; and then he procured Bridgman to make another deed of feoffment, bearing date in December, 31 Elizabeth (whereas the deed to Salloway bore date in January, 31 Elizabeth), and this deed was first published without the indorsement of any livery [of seisin], and then the defendant procured the deed to be indorsed with the names of witnesses in January, after the date of the sale to Sallowaie, and altered the names of the witnesses. And it was agreed that the addition of the indorsement of names or of livery, or the ante-dating of a deed, if it be not to the prejudice of a third person, is not forgery; but forgery is secret, and must be proved by circumstances. This cause has continued for many years in suit in the Marches [Court] and in this Court, in the Marches [Court] at Book T., and in this Court at Book M.[1] The defendant now preferred a cross bill, but it was stayed by order until the other bill in this matter should be sentenced[2]; and it was allowed, *per gratiam specialem*, that other examinations, taken in the Marches [Court], should be read [here], notwithstanding they were examined between other parties. But the Lord Keeper gave *caveat* that it should not be used, and admonished the Council to avoid it. The Chief Justices agreed on the [following] case as to the law of feoffment: there is a deed, the deed is sealed and delivered, but no livery nor indorsement, then another purchases the land, and then the first feoffee or feoffor indorses livery on the first deed bearing date the day of the first deed, this is to the prejudice of a third person, and is forgery; but if the indorsement bears date the day that the indorsement was made, it is not forgery. The defendant was briefly sentenced by the whole Court to be a forger within the Statute,[3] for publishing the first deed, knowing

Forgery, what

[p. 118]

Depositions taken in the Marches Court

Caveat

Feoffment

Livery of seisin, indorsement of

Sentence

[1] I cannot explain these references.

[2] See *post*, p. 157.

[3] 5 Eliz., cap. 14. See Appendix X.

it to be forged, and for forging the second deed, and so to have the punishment limited by the statute for forgery.

It was ordered also by the Court, that inasmuch as it is a common thing to resist the process of this Court, and with disgrace to condemn it, and to beat him who executes it, [the punishment therefor] being only imprisonment and no more, that now if any one in time to come shall resist or condemn the process, he shall be committed to the Fleete, examined on interrogatories, and, according to the nature of his offence, he shall be fined by the Court. Order as to resisting process of this Court

[When] there are divers defendants, [and] the cause is appointed to be heard, and process *ad audiendum judicium* is served on any of them, and affidavit made thereon, this is sufficient, and the other defendants are to make appearance by their Counsel on the day of hearing of the cause at their peril: By order and course of the Court. [p. 119] Process *ad audiendum judicium*, service of

In Camera Stellata, coram Consilio ibidem, Mercurij, 20 Octobris, 1602.[1] 1602 Oct. 20

Cause of hearing between Walle, plaintiff, and the servants of Salloway, defendants, for riot.[2] There was no proof of riot, because there were but two rioters[3]; but the plaintiff, who was sentenced for forgery the day before, submitted and humbled himself to the Court, and craved favour. Whereupon the Court pitied him, and would have sentenced him and fined him £20, but forbore this in regard to his poverty. WALLE *v.* SALLOWAYE'S servants — Riot

Another cause of hearing between Arnolde, plaintiff, against Sir Thomas Lucie[4] and others, defendants, for perjury and subornation. The plaintiff, being the base ARNOLDE *v.* LUCIE and others — Perjury

[1] Seven Councillors and Judges were present.

[2] See *ante*, p. 155.

[3] Three or more persons are required to make a riot.

[4] Sir Thomas Lucy of Charlecote, eldest son of "Justice Shallow," married Dorothy, daughter of Sir Nicholas Arnold, by whom he had a son, Thomas (who died young), and a daughter Joyce, wife of Sir William Cook, knight, of Highnam, Glouc. Sir Thomas married, secondly, Constance, daughter and heir of Sir

1602 Oct. 20 son of Sir Nicolas Arnolde, claimed and enjoyed certain lands conveyed to him by a deed of feoffment to uses, made by the said Sir Nicolas, to divers persons, with power of revocation on tender of money. The said Sir Thomas Lucie, having married the sole daughter and heir of the said Sir Nicolas, and one [1] Koke, having married the daughter and heir of the said Sir Thomas, and [being] now Clerk of the Liveries in the Court of Wards and allied to the Master of the Wards,[2] sued in the Court of Wards for the land, and there pretended that the feoffment was revoked and the money paid; and the jury being present at the bar for the trial of this, one Clarke deposed that he had received the money, being one of the feoffees, and this is the supposed perjury, and that Sir Thomas Lucie p. 120] suborned it. But the jury there gave their verdict contrary to the directions given them by the Judge of the Court, being the Master of the Wards, whereupon he made decree against the verdict offered, and stayed it. And now the plaintiff relinquished that part of his bill which touched the subornation in Sir Thomas Lucie; and as to the perjury, inasmuch as it could not well appear without trial at common law, it was referred to common law; and the plaintiff moved for an indifferent jury, whereupon Surrie was agreed upon for the trial of this at the bar. The plaintiff's Counsel objected greatly to have any other place than the bar in the Court of Wards, but the Attorney said to Sergeant Healle and Phillips that they should forbear to move to cast aspersions or imputations on the Court of Wards, for the Judge there would answer them and justify what he had done. And upon the whole matter Sir Thomas moved to be dismissed and the bill to be withdrawn; but the Court wished to consider about this, and after trial at common law the cause should be sentenced here if they did not determine the matter by the trial; and then the bill shall be withdrawn if there be cause.

Richard Kingsmill of High Clere, Hants, and had by her six sons and three daughters. Burke's *Landed Gentry*, 1838, iii., 99.

[1] Blank in MS. See note 4, p. 157, *ante*.

[2] Sir Robert Cecil.

In Camera Stellata, coram Consilio ibidem, Veneris, 22 Octobris, 1602.[1] 1602 Oct. 22

Cause of hearing between Hartope, plaintiff, and Waren, defendant, in Lestershire, for riots, two bills for cutting down a tree growing in the ditch supposed to be the defendant's land, but because the defendant came in person, (having sent two persons only with a spade and an axe for the felling of the said tree), with several [people], with weapons, and used force, and maimed the plaintiff's servants, he was fined 500 marks, with imprisonment as of course, £20 to the persons maimed, to two 'surgens' 20 nobles each for their cures, and [sureties for] the good behaviour of the defendant and his servants, inasmuch as it was proved that the defendant would not have any tenants but such as would murder if they were required.

HARTOPE v. WAREN — Riot

Sentence

These bills being sentenced by the Court, another cause of hearing between Waren, plaintiff, and Hartope and others, defendants, for the same riot and another. The first was dismissed. The second was for a challenge and other riotous 'batinge' of the plaintiff Waren; and for this the defendant was fined £200, with imprisonment as of course.

WAREN v. HARTOPE and others — Riot

[p. 121]

In Camera Stellata, coram Consilio ibidem, Martis, 30 Novembris, 1602, adonque presente, Lo. Keper, l'archeuesque de Canterber., Lo. Tresorer, Lo. Admiralle, euesque de Londres, ambideux Chiefe Justices, Sr John Fortescue, diverse del Judges et Barons del exchequer, esteant le prochein iour puis le terme. 1602 Nov. 30

This was a day of orders, and casually the Lord Keeper took occasion, in as much as all the motions which were then moved were touching misdemeanours against Justices of the Peace, to deliver a brief lecture for the Justices of the Peace; firstly, that the number of them is greatly

Lord Keeper on Justices of the Peace

[1] Six Councillors and Judges were present.

1602 Nov. 30 increased, and some of them are outlawed; the Queen much dislikes this, and has given great charge to him to remove them; others are in [office] by countenance, and are idle and will not do anything, and as they do no ill, so they do no good; but others are evil and use the office to show their malice and revenge. The Judges ought to examine this, and the Lord Keeper will remove them.

1603 May 13 **In Camera Stellata,** coram Consilio ibidem, Veneris, 13° Maij, An° Do^{ni} 1603, Jacobi Regis 1°, adonque presente, Lo. Keeper, Sr Thom. Egerton, Archeuesque de Canterbery, Doct. Whitgifte, Lo. Tresorer, esteant Lo. Buckhurst, ambideux les Lords Presidents, Lo. Zouche [et] Lo. Burleighe,[1] ambideux Chiefe Justices, et Sr John Fortescue.

GRIMES *v.* CARLETON

Riot with guns in the Northern Marches

Defendant and Counsellor

Pleaded not guilty and general traverse

Cause of hearing, Grimes, plaintiff, against two Carletons, defendants, for riot and other misdemeanours. Carlton was an Utter Barrister of the Inner Temple, and steward of a court for Grimes, who removed him; he, with others, [armed] with 'gunnes, hookes, harquebusses & Coates,' assaulted Grimes in order to murder him; and in this Court is of counsel with his brother, and set his hand to his [brother's] answer wherein he pleaded the general issue, not guilty, and also a general traverse, and slandered and scandalized the plaintiff, a gentleman and esquire of two hundred years continuance; and to his own answer [p. 122] he set, as is supposed, the hand of Edwards, another Utter Barrister of the Inner Temple.

Fined 300*l*., imprisoned, disbarred, bound for good behaviour, and confession in the country

Hand borrowing to be examined by the Chief Justice and the Attorney General

Carleton was imprisoned, fined £300, disbarred, and bound for his good behaviour, and the matter was referred to the Chief Justice and the Attorney to examine Edwardes if he had set his hand to the answer, or if Carleton had counterfeited it; and the Attorney to proceed *ore tenus* against them; and the Court suspended sentence until

[1] Edward, Lord Zouch, was President of the Council of the Marches of Wales. Thomas, Lord Burghley, was President of the Council of the North.

Edwards be examined. The Court disliked that one being defendant or plaintiff, [should be] of counsel with himself in his own cause, where he is plaintiff or defendant with others, or sues or is sued in others' names. The defendant at the hearing had no counsel, and made no defence.

No party, plaintiff, or defendant, [to be] counsellor

Another cause of hearing. Rilie, plaintiff, Shellden, defendant, for riot and contempt after the command of the Queen on petition was delivered to her by the plaintiff's [Rilie's] wife, a clamorous and impudent woman, who, after two verdicts and decrees in the Exchequer and several petitions to the Queen, sued here and proved nothing against the plaintiff,[1] who was acquitted of the riot and contempt. The plaintiff [Rilie] was fined £20 for the better government of his wife, and [it was ordered] that she should be whipped and confess her fault, if the precedent of the Court would warrant this, since she is not a party to the bill. And it was moved by the Lord Keeper that no woman should be a suitor in any Court in her own person. And he and the Lord Treasurer to their great comfort have heard the King affirm that he would study to do justice to all, and there should be no prejudice [to anyone] by any private information and petition, if he be not guilty of the matter, for [the King] wishes to protect the innocent of every degree.

RILIE *v.* SHELLDEN

Riot and contempt

A clamorous woman rejected, and ordered to be whipped if there be any precedent for this

No woman to be a suitor in person

Moved, but not ordered

The King studies to do justice to all, and is the protector of the innocent

In Camera Stellata, coram Consilio ibidem, Mercurij, 18 Maij, 1603, Jacobi Regis 1°.[2]

1603 May 18

[p. 123]

The Lord Keeper sermonized that 'it is his Matie's^ pleasure to make knowne in this Cowrte that Consyderinge yt Can not be but that in gouernemente of states there will be abuses, & suche there are now founde to be as will not staye to be prouyded for by publique acte, & therefore his Matie's^ Cheifeste studye & Care beinge to prouyde for these & to execute Justice to all, hathe & intendethe by his

The King's charge, delivered by the Lord Keeper

Abuses in governments should have speedy remedy

Study and care of the King to purge abuses and to do justice

[1] Shellden, the plaintiff in the Exchequer, but the defendant here.

[2] Twelve Councillors and Judges were present.

1603
May 18

All should take notice of proclamations and observe them

Contemners or neglecters of the performance of the proclamations, severely punished

'Vulgars' shall not be judges, but shall go to the judge

Officers negligent in punishment shall make account

Contemners are pests and contemners of the royal majesty

proclamacions to redresse them, & therefore streightlye Chargethe all men to take notice of them & strictelye to obserue & perfourme them, & his Matie will seuerely punishe all Contemners or neclecters of the perfourmance of them, therefore let this be a premonition or caution to all men to take knowledge of his Matie's^ pleasure herein; & Farther yf anye offende herein, his Matie's^ pleasure & expresse Charge ys that the vulgar shall not leape into his throne & reforme any contempte herein, but shall Complaine to the maiestrate & he shall prouyde for yt, and his Matie will exacte a verye exacte accounte at his handes for neglecte of his Matie's^ pleasure herein: & whosoeuer shall Contemne his Matie's^ pleasure herein, his Matie will accounte them as pestes & Contemners of his Matie's^ roiall dignitye.'

severa levitas:
Culpabilis neclectus damnabilis contemptus.
Dignitas personae auget culpam.

ATT.-GEN. *v.* CAREWE

Recusancy

Copy of the confession shall not be delivered, nor shall the delinquent have counsel [p. 124]

Koke, King's Attorney, informed *ore tenus* against Henry Carewe, esquire, a dangerous recusant, upon examination and confession: at the time of his confession, he requested a copy of it, but by order of this Court, he could not have it, nor counsel.

'The sayd Carewe, the nexte day after her Matie was deade, comes to the parishe churche where he dwelles, & telles the parishioners that the publike seruice vsed in her Matie's^ dayes was but onelye deuysed by her Matie & in force duringe her time, & Contrarye to the rule & vse of the whole worlde, & Contrarye to that wch his Matie allowethe in his booke, & therevpon delyuers them this in wrytinge, & willes them to locke the Churche doore & giue him the keyes, vntill suche time as his Matie shall Come & determine & appointe the same, & wyshes that all people woulde so doe: & after he had Confessed this in Cowrte, he delyuers in motyues & a kinde of submission, & a noate declaringe that by the lawes of this Realme no man ys to be Condemned but vpon bille & aunsweare or originall proces serued vpon him.

'Shutts churche dores' and keeps the keys

'The Cowrte generallye Conceyues this to be a verye heynous offence (1), againste god & his seruyce: for the booke of common prayer that ys now vsed in o[r] Churche, & hathe bene 45 yeares paste, his Ma[tie] hathe hearde & bene presente at & allowed & lyked of the same; & is all the worde of god yt selfe, or warranted & grounded vpon the same, & selected & chosen oute of there popishe praiers as the gowlde, & leauinge to them the drosse & poyson as superfluous superstitions or incerteine.

Book of Common Prayer warranted as the word of God by Parliament

'(2). againste the dignitie of o[r] late soueraigne Queene, in praise of whome all spake exceedinge muche as in deede none Coulde speake inoughe: For Carewe pretended her religion temporarie & politike & by her alone establyshed, whereas all the worlde dothe knowe, that in regarde of her religion onelye god did fighte for her, & blesse her wth peace, plentie & prosperitie; & the booke of Common Prayer was establyshed by the whole state of the kingdome in parliament, & last of all assented vnto & Confirmed by her Ma[tie]: & the secretarye & Lo. Keper did affyrme that his Ma[tie] had sayde that anye scandalle or infamous defamacion or suggestion againste o[r] late soueraine Queene he woulde haue as seuerely punished, & showlde be as odious vnto him as anye offence againste his owne person.

[p. 125]

Commendation of Queen Elizabeth

The King will punish defamers of Queen Elizabeth

'(3). againste the Kinge's Ma[tie] & his booke (w[ch] M[r] Secretarie called the mirror of vertue),[1] whoe hathe allowed & Confyrmed o[r] booke of Common prayer, & no woorde againste it in his booke: for, as the Lo. Keper sayd, albeit there be a Chaunge of the gouernor, yet there ys no Chaunge neither of gouernemente nor in gouernemente.

The King's book called the mirror of virtue

The governor changes, not the government

'(4). againste the state in regarde of the time beinge seditious & stirringe the people: for in all actions the time, place & person are the most necessarye Circumstaunces to be Consydered. For the kinge's ma[tie], in his lawfull, iuste & lineall title to the Crowne of Englaunde, comes not by succession onelye, or by election, but from god onelye, (so that there is no *interregnum*, as the igno-

Time, place and person, most considerable in all actions.

[p. 126]

No *interregnum* when it is by descent

[1] It seems doubtful which book is here referred to, *Basilikon Doron*, published 1599, or *The True Law of Free Monarchies*, published 1598.

1603
May 18

Justices of the Peace are determined, constables and coroners continue

Queen Elizabeth devised the crown to King James, by parol

raunte dothe suppose, vntill the ceremonie of coronation), by reason of his lineall discente; yet Justices of peace are determyned, but Constables & Coroners, & suche pettie officers, remaine still: & the verye instaunte that the breathe was oute of her Ma$^{tie's}$ bodye, Kinge James was lawfull & rightefull kinge: & the Secretarye sayde that her late Matie in her laste sicknes did deuyse yt vnto him by parolle.' [1]

Qui pietate seditiosus est leuiter pius est vita anteacta.

Recusants are simple or dangerous

'For recusants, the Lo. Keper sayd, some are simple & lede by error; those he pittyed & was not forwarde to punishe: others daungerous, wilfull & seditious, as Carewe is one of them.

Our religion as ancient as Jesus Christ

'For o^{r} religion, it began wth *Consumatum est*, and is as auncient as Jesus Christe.'

In hoc leges seruiunt Christo quod leges fiant pro Christo.

Judgment *secundum delictum*

Relation to the King of causes and motives to mercy

[p. 127]

The King commits justice but keeps mercy

Eyes of flesh, and eyes of judgment

This Court hath warrant, of common and statute law, to proceed on confession *ore tenus*

'The secretarye sayde that there iudgemente must be accordinge to the offence, not weyghinge his estate, *saluo contenemento suo*; but it is parte of there honor to relate to his Matie the cause & occurrences to moue him to mercye: & the Lo. Keper he sayde that the Kinge Committes to them his iustice, but keepes to himselfe his mercye: & that he lookes vpon no man wth the eies of mallice or of fleshe, but wth the eies of his Judgemente: And that this Cowrte hathe aunciente warraunte & authoritie bothe by Common & statute lawe to proceede in this kinde, 10 E. 2 [?] and 12 R. 2. For the kinge's Justice is ordinarie or extraordinarie: & to proceede at the discretion of his Ma$^{tie's}$ Counselle of state is extraordinarye, & warranted by statutes.

Justice ordinary or extraordinary

Council of State warranted by statute

Fine 1,000*l*., imprisonment during pleasure, recognition of his fault in church and at the Assizes, and good behaviour

The Court differs as to the fine; the greater number is the sentence

'The greater opinion of the Cowrte was to be fined 1000^{li}, imprisonmente during the king's pleasure, recognition of his faulte in the churche & at the Assises: & to be bounde to his good behauyoure: but Sr John Fortescue, Justice Gawdy, *L'archeuesque et* Lord Keper, fine 3000^{li},' but this did not alter the sentence of the Court.

[1] See *post*, p. 177, and Appendix XI.

In Camera Stellata, coram Consilio ibidem, Veneris, 20 Maij, 1603, Jacobi Regis 1°, adonque presente, L. Keper, Lo. Tresorer, l'archeuesque, ambideux presidents,[1] ambideux Chief Justices, et S[r] John Fortescue. 1603 May 2

BAYNEHAM v. SIR THOMAS LUCAS — Writing to jurors to appear, when one is not a party to the matter, is illegal [p. 128] Defendant acquitted for default of good charge in the bill

Bayneham[2] and Sir Thomas Lucas for writing to jurors to appear, maintenance, and procuring this. It was delivered as law, that no man may write for any man to appear in any case where he himself is not interested. It was well proved that he wrote to jurors to appear, but the charge in the bill was that he procured them to give their verdict corruptly; and so, notwithstanding the offence was well proved, yet because he was not well charged in the bill, he was not sentenced: so [he was] condemned *in foro scientiae* but acquitted *in foro iudicii*, for default of a good charge in the bill.

In Camera Stellata, coram Consilio ibidem, Veneris, 27 Maij, 1603, Jacobi Regis 1°, adonque presente, Lo. Keper, l'archeuesque de Canterberie, Lo. Tresorer, Count Shrewseberie, Lo. H. Hawarde,[3] Lo. Zouche, S[r] W[m] Knowlles, Baron de Graies,[4] ambideux Chief Justices, et S[r] John Fortescue. 1603 May 27

MOYLES v. EWER — Riots — The commander is the rioter — Fine 200*l*., imprisonment as of course

Two causes of hearing between Moyles and Ewer, cross bills for several riots; where one commands his servant to enter on [certain] land and to take distress peaceably, and he enters with many others riotously, the master is a rioter. In the first cause, where Ewer was defendant, he was fined £200, and damages, the others his servants, 40 marks and 20 marks, and imprisonment.

EWER v. MOYLES — Forgery

In the second cause, where Ewer was plaintiff for

[1] See note, p. 160.

[2] Probably Sir Edmund Baynham, captain of the club of profligates known as the 'Damned Crue.' One of his exploits is recorded in this book, *ante*, p. 114. He was afterwards implicated in the Gunpowder Plot. See *Manningham's Diary*, Camden Soc. p. 142.

[3] Probably Lord Henry Howard, second son of Henry Howard, Earl of Surrey (beheaded, 1547); he was afterwards created Baron Howard of Marnhill, and Earl of Northampton.

[4] Sir William Knowles was created Baron Knowles of Greys, co. Oxford, May 13, 1603.

1603
May 27
Plaintiff fined 40*l*. for want of proof of his bill

forgery, he did not prove anything, and therefore was fined £40.

Causes retained until they are tried at common law

Other two causes of hearing were referred to be tried at common law, and retained here [in the meantime].

1603
June 1

In Camera Stellata, coram Consilio ibidem, Mercurij, 1° Junij, 1603, Jacobi Regis 1°.[1]

COUNDEN *v.* WATS and others

Counden, plaintiff, Wats and others, defendants; the defendants having a Commission of Rebellion for contempt in this Court [done] by the plaintiff, which had been pardoned, they executed it barbarously and cruelly upon him, being 'bethered,'[2] and they dragged him in his 'shirte, wast kote & stockings' only, and carried him to prison, contemptuously disobeying the letter of the Lord Keeper for the discharge of the Commission, and saying that they had authority to take him to prison, alive or dead, and that they would make 'dyce of his bones & bury him vpon a donge hill'; the plaintiff's wife and son offered £10 for his discharge, but they would not accept it. The plaintiff[3] was fined £500, pillory and imprisonment; the others £100 each and imprisonment.

[p. 129]

Fine 500*l*., pillory and imprisonment

Commissions of rebellion ought to be executed by men of good fame

It was ordered that Commissions of Rebellion should not be awarded but to men of good fame and credit, and known to the officers of this Court; for in executing of them there is great abuse.

WATERMAN *v.* VOWELL

Misdemeanours in a Justice of Peace

Another cause of hearing between Waterman, plaintiff, and Vowell, defendant, a Justice of the peace in Devonshire, for four misdemeanours in him; but it was adjourned to another day.[4]

Justices of Peace not to meddle with forgery, but Justices of Assize

It was ruled there that Justices of Peace are not to meddle with forgery, but Justices of Assize [only].

[1] Seven Councillors and Judges were present.

[2] Halliwell gives 'bedered' = bed-ridden.

[3] *Sic.* Wats is apparently meant.

[4] See *post*, p. 167.

It was also delivered as the rule and usage of the Court that if a man of Counsel with the plaintiff or defendant is served with process to be examined as a witness, he is wont in good discretion to move the Court and to have an order before he is examined. John Heall's case, of the Inner Temple.

Rule and usage for Counsellor to be examined as a witness by order and not otherwise, in good discretion

In Camera Stellata, coram Consilio ibidem, Veneris, 3 Junij, 1603, Jacobi Regis 1°.[1]

1603 June 3

WATERMAN *v.* VOWELL

Adjourned to next term

The former cause of hearing was adjourned to the first day of next term in regard that the Lord Treasurer and the Lord Knowlles, were now absent, who were present on the former day.[2]

UNDER-SHERIFF OF YORKSHIRE *v.* HOMDEN

Riot in resisting the Under-Sheriff in levying execution for the Queen

Another cause of hearing was between the Under-Sheriff of Yorkshire, plaintiff, and Homden, defendant, and others, for riot against the Under-Sheriff, for resisting him in serving execution for the Queen out of the Court of Wards.

It was adjudged a great offence, and now common and exorbitant, and in the nature of rebellion and contempt of the King. And for this [Homden] was fined £500, and the others £200 each, and 200 marks for damages, and costs as of course, and imprisonment, and bound for good behaviour, and confession at the Assizes.

[p. 130]

Sentence on behalf of an Under-Sheriff Fine 500*l.*, damages to the party 200 marks, costs and imprisonment as of course

Ut pena ad paucos, metus ad omnes, perveniat.

BURLAIE'S case

Burlaie cleared, and plaintiff fined 40*l.* for false claim Admonition to Counsel

Another cause of hearing against Burlaie for perjury and forgery, 'broughte to hearinge by the defend[te],' and the bill was slanderous and scandalous. The plaintiff was fined to the King £200. And admonition to Counsellors that they do not defame men of better credit than themselves.

[1] Seven Councillors and Judges were present.

[2] See *ante*, p. 166.

1603 June 3 PARTRIGE'S case — Petty rioters fined 10*l.* Possession under an order is not to be taken by force

Another cause of hearing against Partrige and others, for petty riot. Partrige was cleared, but the others were fined each £10. And the opinion of the Court was that it was apter for the Quarter Sessions than for this place. And it was ruled by the Court that if there be an order either in this Court, in the Chancery, or in the Marches [Court], to have possession, it is no warrant to commit a riot in taking possession, but [such a riot] is punishable here.

1604 April 19, 20, and 21

Al Cessions al Newgate, Jovis, Veneris et Saturni, 19, 20 et 21 April, 1604, Jacobi Regis 2°, Lo. Maior, Sr Thom. Bennette, ambideux Chiefe Justices, Recorder, et auters adonque presente.

SATHEFIELDE'S case

Sathefeilde, a Constable, was indicted for assault on Provost-Marshall Waldron, and for disorder in time of pestilence, his house being infected, and for resorting to the Mayor. He was fined 100 marks, and [to be] imprisoned during the Lord Mayor's pleasure, and [to be] bound for his good behaviour.

Case of THOMAS SKIDAMOR *alias* HILLE, a priest

One Thomas Skidamor alias Hille was indicted of treason for being a priest made by the power of the Pope, and being in England and dwelling there contrary to 1 Eliz.[1] and the proclamation of the now King; and therefore he was condemned as a traitor, on his own confession, being taken in the execution of his office as priest, celebrating the Mass.

p. 131] 1604 June 22

In Camera Stellata, coram Consilio ibidem, Veneris, 22 Junij, 1604, Jacobi Regis Angliae, Francie et Hiberniae secundo, et Scotiae 37.[2]

ATT.-GEN. *v.* HEALLE

Sir John Croke moved against Sergeant Healle at the suit of the Attorney-General for a better answer, and for examination on interrogatories.[3]

[1] 1 Eliz. cap. I., sec. 30, &c.
[2] Eleven Councillors and Judges were present.
[3] See *post*, p. 171, and Appendix XII.

'The Lo. Chauncellor[1] seemed to Finde greate Faulte wth the multitude of references, to the Clyente's great charge & the Judge's trouble, & therefore Coulde rather wyshe that bothe bille, aunsweare & interrogatories mighte be reade in Cowrte (especiallye in greate Causes), & by them ordered w^th^oute anye reference; wch was assented vnto by the wholle Courte, & the nexte daye appointed to heare the same; and so likewyse in the greateste Cause now of Englande betweene the Lo. Sidnie[2] & Sir Roberte Dudlye for th'earldomes of Warwike & Lester: wch the Attornie moued nexte.

SIR ROBERT DUDLEY'S case

'That whereas the Earle of Lester[3] had named Sr Roberte Dudlye in his testamente 17 times bastarde, whome he had by the Ladye Sheffeilde,[4] Sr Robert Dudlye hathe stirred vp some to Calle him bastarde, & in the Ecclesiasticall Cowrte, by the subornation of Thomas Drurye, hathe endeauoured to proue himselfe legitimate & the Ladye Sheffeilde, his mother, marryed to the Earle of Lester, to the greate dishonor of that noble and vertuouse Ladye, Lettis, now Countesse of Lester[5]; & that Sr Roberte Duddlye hathe gyven the Ragged staffe to his men that walke vpon the Thames wth the same, & Callethe himselfe Earle of Warwike & Lester, for proffe whereof an Affidauit was produced vpon the reporte of a waterman: & that this was verye dishonorable to the kinge whoe is the lyfe & fountaine of all honors & dignities, & the Countes of Lester had complayned thereof to the Kinge by petition, & the Kinge had subscrybed it & did muche dislyke the contemptuous & proude Courses & attemptes of Sr Roberte

[p. 132]

[1] Sir Thomas Egerton, Lord Ellesmere, the Lord Keeper, was made Lord Chancellor July 24, 1603. Foss.

[2] Sir Robert Sydney, brother of Sir Philip, and son of Sir Henry, by his wife Mary Dudley, daughter of John, Duke of Northumberland, and sister of Robert, Earl of Leicester. Sir Robert Sydney was created Baron Sydney of Penshurst May 13, 1603; Viscount Lisle May 4, 1605, and Earl of Leicester August 2, 1618.

[3] Robert Dudley.

[4] Douglas, daughter of William, Lord Howard of Effingham, and widow of John, Lord Sheffield.

[5] The widow of Robert Dudley, Earl of Leicester. She was the daughter of Sir Francis Knolles, and was first married to Walter Devereux, Earl of Essex.

1604 June 22 Dudlye & willed the same showlde be examyned and punished by his Counselle; the other parte of the Attornie's motion was that whereas Sr Roberte Dudlye wente to exemplifye those wytnesses that were examyned, that [he] mighte be stayed; Sr Roberte Dudlie being presente in Courte aunsweared that he neuer gaue the ragged staffe, neyther publyshed himselfe Earle of Warwike & Lester [1]: wherevpon the Lo. Chauncellor gathered that then he showlde doe well not to doe it till the Cause were determyned, but Dudlye sayde that Mr Atturnie did Caste forthe manye scandalous aspersyons and rumors to preiudghe his Cause before it Came to hearinge, & therefore desyred
[p. 133] the bille & aunsweare mighte be hearde publikelye in the Cowrte, wch was so ordered, & the nexte daye lyke wyse appointed for the same.

'This was generallye obserued to be a verye greate Cause, & manye honorable personages interested in the same eyther in bloude or righte; & for that purpose there Came wth Sr Roberte Dudlye & stoode by him w^th^in the Courte the Lo. Dudlye,[2] the Lo. Sheffeilde [3] and the Lo. of Effingham [4]: wherevpon the Atturnie tooke an occasyon to moue that whereas he serued a gracyouse Kinge, it was a strange presydente that so greate & honorable personages showlde Come so in Cowrte to Countenance & embrace any Cause Contrarye to the lawe, & therefore desyred this Cowrte woulde haue Consyderacyon of it. Wherevpon the Lorde Sheffeilde seemed to be verye muche offended & tooke it ill that Mr Atturnie showlde so indiscreatelye taxe them whoe came but to heare & to see howe the worlde

[1] I have not been able to ascertain that Dudley styled himself Earl of Warwick and Leicester before this time; he certainly did so later. See Appendix XIII.

[2] Edward Sutton, 9th Baron. He was a distant relation of Sir Robert's; John Dudley, Sir Robert's great-great-grandfather was a son of John Sutton, 4th Baron Dudley. See Burke's *Extinct Peerage*, and *Dict. of Nat. Biog.*, s.v. Edmund Dudley.

[3] Edmund Sheffield, 3rd Baron, He was the son of Douglas, Lady Sheffield, whose alleged marriage with the Earl of Leicester was the real issue of this case. He was consequently Sir Robert's half-brother.

[4] William, Lord Howard of Effingham, who was so created in the lifetime of his father Charles, Earl of Nottingham. He was nephew to Douglas (Howard), Lady Sheffield, and consequently first cousin to Sir Robert Dudley.

wente. & then the Lo. Zouche desyred to be resolued what the Course of y[e] Cowrte was, for he was allwayes of opinion that euery Baron of Englaunde mighte take place & sitte in this Cowrte. The Lord Chauncellor sayde it was no time nor place for it now, but woulde leaue it vntill the kinge's pleasure were knowne touchinge the same. For [p. 134] the matter of honor or title, this Courte vsethe not to decide, but leauethe it to the Marshall's place, & the kinge had allreadye appointed lordes for that purpose, as it was in the Earle of Kente's Cause, & Dethicke, then Garter, & M[r] Rotherham: & after the matters of honor & title are determyned then the Cause to receaue iudgemente here.' [1]

In Camera Stellata, coram Consilio ibidem, Mercurij, Veneris, Mercurij et Veneris, 10, 12, 17 et 19 diebus Octobr. 1604, ter[no] Michaelis, adonque presente, Lo. Chauncellor, Bancrofte archeuesque de Canterberie, Lo. Tresorer, Lo. Admirall, Counte Northumberland, Count Deuon, Count Northampton, Vicounte Cramborne, Secretarie Herberte, Popham Ch. Justice, Baron Sauuell, et Justice Warberton, et les 2[x] latter iours Lo. Burleigh fuit auxy presente. 1604 October 10, 12, 17, 19

ATT.-GEN. *v.* HEALLE

Four entire days were spent wholly 'in the hearinge of Sergaunte Healle's greate Cause at the suite of the kinge's Ma[tie], by the Informacion of Sir Edwarde Coke, his Ma[tie's] Attornie generall,[2] at the relation of Sir John Lucen of Kente; S[r] Edward Phillips, S[r] John Croke, the kinge's sergeaunts, & S[r] Frauncis Bacon of his Ma[tie's] Counsell, did allso speake in the Cause, & Edward Comes of the Middle Temple, sollicitor for S[r] John Lucen. The Informacyon was againste Sir John Healle, the kinge's auncyente Sergeaunte & the onelye Sergeaunte to the late Queene, William Kinge an atturnie, Dun & Bruen, the sergeaunte's men. Sergeaunte Hubberde & Sergeaunt Hutton & Randall Crue were of Counsell wth Hele, Thomas Crue for Kinge, Hide & Moore wth Bruen, for Dun was deade

[1] See *post*, pp. 186, 198, 204, 205, and Appendix XIII.
[2] See *ante*, p. 168, and Appendix XII.

1604 October 10, 12, 17, 19

[p. 135]

synce the laste terme, &, as the Atturnie informed, of an unfortunate & violente deathe, for he stabde himselfe, wch was denied by Heale, & offred to proue it by the reporte of Dun's wife, her letter, the preachers & phisicions that were presente at his deathe & now in Cowrte.

'The charge was opened by Phillippes firste by waye of inducemente to the matter, & yet not layed in the bille, nor charged to be broughte to sentence: wch was that Heale, hauing in the 42th [*sic*] yeare of the late Queene, Corruptlye to obtaine for him the M^r^shippe of the Rowlles, lente to the late Lo. Cobham,[1] attainted of treason in 1° *Jacobi Regis*, & became bounde to Sr Robt Lee, Alderman of London, & the wydowe Gurnie,[2] for the sayde Lor. Cobham, for & in the sommes of 3500^li^ of due dette, w^th^oute anie manner of intereste or loane for the same agreed vpon at the firste bargayne: but the sayde Heale in 44 Elizab., beinge oute of hope & despayringe to attaine to the M^r^ship of the Rowlles, deales wth the Lo. Cobham for his monie & sues his bondes, hauinge bondes of 10,000^li^ forfeyted vnto him; the suite Commenced w^th^oute Consente, but iudgementes had vpon all the bondes by the Consente of the Lo. Cobham: & an agreemente drawne by the Sergeaunte's man, wch he tooke to be a deffeazaunce, & ye Sergaunte himselfe penned the same & sente it to the late Lo. Cobham to peruse the same by his Counselle, whoe after twooe or three dayes, retorned the same backe againe to ye sergeaunte; & therevpon ye same was sealled and delyuered, wch was in effecte that Dayes of payemente were agreede, the due dette, at the fyrste w^th^oute any intereste agreede vpon in 42 elizab., was now Caste vp vpon a full & finalle accounte at dayes to Come to be 4660^li^ 13^s^ 4^d^, to be payde, 1475^li^ 13^s^ 4^d^ [on the] 18 Octobr. 1603, 1075^li^ [on the] 19 Januar. An° 1603,[4] 1050^li^ [on the] 22 April 1604, 1050^li^ [on the] 23

[1] Henry Brooke, Lord Cobham, attainted for participation in the alleged treason of Sir Walter Raleigh. He was not dead at this time, but is called 'late Lord Cobham' in respect to his attainder.

[2] Probably Jane, widow of Richard Gurney, of London. He was Sheriff in 1590, and was buried at S. Michael's, Crooked Lane, March 21, 1596. She died in 1612, and was buried at S. Bryde's. See *The Records of the House of Gournay*, by Daniel Gurney, F.S.A., p. 498.

[4] 1603-4.

Octobr. 1604. Tbis was done in Hillarye terme 44 elizab. *Reginae*, & by Consente a relleasse of errors. That y^e^ [p. 136] Sergeaunte did drawe & penne the agreemente subtellye & Cautelouslye, & in deede no defeazaunce, for the eye of the lawe neuer sawe any suche defeasaunce, & *Clausulae inconsuetae inducunt suspicionem*, for it was agreede by the intended defeasaunce that ye monie beinge paide at the former daies sette downe, that then after the paiementes, and a rellease of errors vpon requeste to delyuer all obligacions discharged or acknowledge satisfaction &c. so that it is no good defeasaunce, an arrowe of the Sergeaunte's quyuer made w^th^in ye Circle of his chamber cautelously & craftely done. *Primae impressiones inducunt suspicionem, res ipsa loquitur.* a blemishe of the lawe. firste to Confirme, then to Confute the Sergeaunte Contrarye to his owne agreemente, the Lo. Cobham, (15 *Julij*) and George Brooke,[1] being restrayned 13 *Julij*, to preuente the kinge of his escheate after Trinitie terme, dealethe wth Kinge, an Atturnie, the (15 *et* 16 *et*) 19th of Julye to haue Elegits retornable in June (*tres trinitat.*) then paste, but Kinge tolde him the yeare beinge paste he muste of necessitie haue a *scir. fac.*, for the law pretendes he hathe somethinge to pleade in barre, so this is to depriue the subiecte of his birtherighte; *quod contra racionem iuris introductum est, non debet trahi ad consequentiam . iudicandum est legibus non exemplis.* Hauinge done nothinge in Fyue termes before but onelye in the fyuethe [fifth] terme praye an elegit in Kente onelye, deales wth Kinge to haue the *Scir. fac.* antedated & returns them *nihil habet nec est inuentus* after the terme, when ye gates of Justice are shutt vp & retorne paste, & this [is] good by the aduyse of the Prenothorie Scotte, so as there be neither practise, fraude nor preiudice. The Sergeaunte knowinge that the 8th & 14 dayes of June the treasons were Committed, & beinge presente, & in his owne opinion thoughte them guyltye, notw^th^standinge presentes his execucion, contrarye to the truste & dutye of his place; & beinge Commanded to attende the 12th of

[1] Lord Cobham's brother.

1604 October 10, 12, 17, 19

[p. 137]

September at Woodstocke, the treasons beinge there examyned, was appointed to frame inditements againste them, & the 21th [*sic*] of September was presente at Maydenheade when they were endited, & gaue in euydence himselfe, when they were Conuycted; & farther, beinge graced wth a Judge's place, to the wronge & iniurie of that seruice & to preuente the kinge of his escheate, proceedes wth his execution vpon the landes & goods of ye Lo. Cobham & George Broke, & executes the same euen at the time of the Assises when he himselfe sate Judge in that Circuite, & sendes his man Bruen, whoe dealles wth the Lo. Cobham's men & wth the sherife & wth the Jurors to Come to the knowledge of the goods & to vndervallewe them, vsinge many perswasions to them that it woulde be ye better for the Lo. Cobham, that his Mr was his beste freinde, & the longer it woulde be before the landes showlde Come to the kinge, & the Scottes woulde not be so hastye to begge them. 29 Septembr., the daye of the assises, Jurors taken from the barre & promised to be discharged of all issues, fines & amerciamentes, & so the landes & goodes were vallewed at the tenthe parte; as a lease vallewed at 100 markes that was 177li. *per annum* & 19 yeares to Come; & so vallewes by the name of Ferme, wch is *nomen Collectiuum* & *oue les appertenaunces passe tout*: & after ye praysinge [*i.e.* appraising] the Sergeaunte geuethe one of the Jurye thanks, & promysethe one of the Lo. Cobham's men to be as good vnto him as his Lorde was; faire wordes, but foule matter: the starre chamber, the schoole of Englaunde to punishe all fraude & practises, as the Chauncery dothe all rigor & extremitie, the one a bridle, th'other a spurre: *gloriari in malitia, mala mens, malus animus*, & he is sworne dulye and trulye to minister the king's matters.' But without question the King is not entitled before attainder, 3 Hen. VI., for a petition to have relief [is] not a petition of grace but of right. 7 Hen. IV., 33 Hen. VI. fol. 51.

In 33 Hen. VIII., cap. [? 22]; Shelton, Attorney of the King's Wards.

Smithe and Younge's case.

Fatetur facinus qui fugit iudicium. [p. 138]

Qui errat ne consentit [*sic*].

'No veritie, no vnity.'

But upon the whole matter, he was condemned. And Sentence the sentence of Secretary Herberte[1] [was], that the extents were void, [Healle] to be fined £2000, imprisonment, and suspended from being King's Serjeant; and Bruen to be fined £200 and imprisonment; but Kinge to be acquitted.

Justice Warberton: to fine the Sergeant £1000, and that he should have no benefit of his execution, and imprisonment; fine Bruen £100, and imprisonment; and acquit Kinge.

Baron Sauuelle: fine the Serjeant £1000, and to be free, as [there was] no execution; fine Bruen £100, and acquit Kinge.

The Lord Chief Justice: acquit Hele and Kinge of everything, and allow the usages of antedating process, for some things the law commands and others the law tolerates, and *parua mora non est mora*; and that as to this case, this Court could not give sentence: but fine Bruen £100.

Lord Burlie: fine the Serjeant £500, and revoke the extent; acquit Kinge; and fine Bruen £100.

The Bishop of London[2]: acquit Hele and Kinge of everything, and fine Bruen £40.

Lord Cecill, Viscount Cranbourne: fine Bruen £200; acquit Kinge; and acquit Hele of fraud, corruption and practice, but fine him for the misdemeanour £1000, 'yf th'execution be not discharged'; and he protested if he had known the offence to be of such a nature, he would never have agreed to have a public hearing.

The Earl of Northampton protested the like, and was in everything of the same opinion.

The Earl of Devon of the same opinion in everything.

The Earl of Northumberland: fine the Serjeant £1000 and remove him from his place; and acquit Kinge and Bruen.

[1] Sir John Herbert, Secretary of State.

[2] Richard Bancroft, late Bishop of London, but at this time Archbishop of Canterbury. See list of Judges, *ante*, p. 171.

1604 October 10, 12, 17, 19

The Earl of Nottingham, Lord Admiral: fine £2000, the extent [to be] void, fine Bruen £100, and acquit Kinge.

The Earl of Dorset, Lord Treasurer: sentence the Serjeant guilty of all, fine £1000, the extents [to be] void, suspend [him from his office]; acquit Kinge and Bruen.

[p. 139] Lord Chancellor: find him guilty in all of corruption and ambition, craft and covetous practises; fine [him] £2000, and suspend [him]; [fine] Bruen £200; acquit Kinge.

But the greater number of the Judges acquitted the Serjeant of all note and blemish of infamy.[1]

WRIGHTE v. CONSTABLE and others

Another day in the same term; another cause between Wrighte, plaintiff, and Constable and Mathewes and others, defendants, for malicious practice in indicting Wrighte as a 'common barrettor,' for distraining his chattels to pay the entire subsidy for the whole parish, for killing his turkeys, for riotous entry, under colour of forfeiture of copyhold, to dig 'earthe, called More earthe'[2]; and it did not appear in all the depositions[3] that the plaintiff had anything against anyone but for a 'pue' or seat in the church, and that he, on behalf of the poor men of the parish, did not agree with the rich for stinting the common. Barrettor — A barrettor is *quasi Barre, traher*, 'that sues & stirres vp other men's suites, &, as appeares by the enditemente, must Sentence — be stuffed wth many other offences.' The defendants were fined each £40, with imprisonment.

FOURDE'S case

Another day in the same term, Fourde was brought up *ore tenus*. He having a cause pending in the Chancery, and foreseeing that the Lord Chancellor would grant an Injunction against him, preferred a petition to the King that he would require the Lord Chancellor to stay the granting of the Injunction, for it would undo him, his wife and his children. The King sent a messenger of the Privy

[1] This is hardly borne out by the text. As to his fine, see Appendix VII.

[2] Halliwell gives 'Moor-stone, a kind of granite found on the moors.

[3] *Liuers.*

Chamber requiring the Lord Chancellor, if it could be [consistent] with the rules of Justice and Equity, to stay the Injunction with favour to Fourde. The Chancellor, [p. 140] notwithstanding, granted the Injunction, and Fourde preferred another petition to the King informing him of this, and concluded that the question now was whether the commandment of the King or the order of the Chancellor should take effect, and such like words of injustice and shame. And so, for sowing sedition between the King and his Peers, Fourde was sentenced to have perpetual imprisonment, to Sentence lose his ears upon the pillory, having papers on his head, 'to ride wth his face to the horse taile, & to be fyned 1000^li.^.' He took the punishment grievously and impatiently. The Lord Chancellor left the Court, and the Lord Treasurer gave sentence. Lord Cecill[1] was of opinion that he should be ransomed, *salvo contenemento suo.* All the Court, being a great presence, condemned him bitterly, and commended the Lord Chancellor excellently, and condemned all petitions, especially where a Judge of the Court, a great man, or a magistrate is charged. 'Let all men hereby take heede how they complayne in wordes againste any magistrate, for they are gods; & he must haue verye good matter that will goe aboute to Conuynce them, for feare he ouerthrowe not himselfe.'

'The nexte Starrechamber daye there was no syttinge in Courte, for it was sayde the Lo. Chauncellor was wth the Kinge, vpon his knee, for Fourde's pardon, & had obtayned the same, wch was a verye honourable action in him, and added greatelye to his manye other honourable & worthye vertues.[2]

'The manner of Qu. Elizabeth's syckenes, deathe and funeralls, and the proclamacion and [p. 141]

[1] Probably Lord Burghley, Sir Thomas Cecill.

[2] Docquet, dated May 22, 1605, pardon to William Foorth of fine and corporal punishments for slanderous petitions against the Lord Chancellor. State Papers, Domestic. See also Appendix VII.

entraunce of her most lawfull successor, o^r^ most vertuous and trulye relligiouse Kinge James, by god's grace of Englaunde, Fraunce & Irelaunde the fyrste, & of Scotlaunde the sixe and thyrtythe.[1]

Queen Elizabeth's illness

'Queene Elizabethe, after she had raigned 44 yeres & fowre monethes & 7 dayes, lingringe of a melancholye syckenes, caused as some reporte for the losse of that worthye Earle of Essexe, others for the pardon obtayned for Tyrone that Irishe rebelle, others for that she sawe shee had liued longe inoughe & longed to see the ende of her dayes, for that too too [*sic*] manie abuses were Crepte in to the state, & speciallye into the gouernours of the state whoe were all so potente & rytche that lyke kinges they all ruled & raigned & no man durste speake againste what they did: it was generallye & Confydentelye reported a weeke & more before shee dyed that shee was deade, & all the better & religiouse sorte of people were muche amased & feared greatelye the dayes were now Come they wyshed neuer to liue to see; the papistes & looser kinde of people they sette there Flagges alofte & looked merrilye & feared nothinge but that yt was to good to be true: but her glasse was runne, the threede of lyfe was worne, shee wente to her Forefathers in peace, lyued, reygned & dyed in peace, & bequeathed peace to her people: For vpon Wednsedaye the 23th [*sic*] of Marche, 1602,[2] & in the 45th yere of her Raigne, aboute twooe of the Clocke in the nighte, shee dyed at Rychemonde: ymmediatelye wherevpon the Lordes of the Counselle & others of the nobilitie poasted to london; & the nexte daye, beinge Thursedaye the Foure & twentythe daye of marche, aboute eighte of the Clocke in the morninge, the Counselle & lordes, accompanied wth dyuerse Courtyars & gentlemen, entred the Cittye of London, & caused the gates of london to be shutte presentlye vpon there entraunce; & at the Crosse in Cheapeside, the

Reports of her death

Rejoicing of papists and others

Her death, March 24, 1602

The action of the Council

[p. 142]

[1] See Appendix XI.

[2] 1602–3. We should call it early in the morning of Thursday the 24th.

secretarie Cecill readinge the stile, Garter kinge at armes proclaymed o[r] kinge. (The Councell of state & nobilitie Caused at one instante the Queene's deathe & the Kinge's proclamacion of his infallible righte to be at one instante published, the proclamacion followes, fol.),[1] ☞ & the late Counselle & lordes then dyned at the sheriffes', & there sate in Councelle all that daye, & in the afternoone proclaymed him lykewyse at Tower Hille & other partes of london; & the nexte daye the Cowrte & Corpes remoued to White Halle, & there they Contynewed in the aunciente state in euerye degree, as it was in the Queene's dayes, vntill her Funeralls, (w[ch] were vpon Thursedaye, 28 Aprill, 1603, at westminster, wth greate solemnitie, as appeareth by a booke in printe, & hereafter is descrybed, fol. , buryed in the sepulchre of her grandfather).[2] & the nexte daye likewyse the proclamacion came out in printe, & so was dispersed into all the Counties of Englaunde, to the exceadinge great ioye & Comforte of al relligious & vertuous mindes: suche a good god doe wee, or showlde wee, serue, that beyonde all hope hathe turned all o[r] sorrowes into exceedinge great ioyes. god make vs all thankefull for it. Amen. (For albeit his ma[tie] did princelye acknowledge & noate the Councelle's vigilancye & well deseruinge, yet [he sayde w[th]all][3] it was no doubte a successe & euente aboue y[e] course of nature, to haue so greate a chaunge w[th] so greate a quiete; for sodaine & greate mutations, as well in state as in nature, are rarelye w[th]out vyolence or perturbacion. Bacon in his vnion of England & Scotlande.)[4] Nothinge now was talked of but the relligion, vertue, wisedome, learninge, Justice, & manye other most noble & woorthye prayses of K. James, (*lapis angularis* in y[e]

Proclamation of King James at Cheapside

☞

The like at Tower Hill and elsewhere

The Queen's funeral

Proclamation printed and dispersed

King James's approbation of the Council

Talk about the King

[1] Marginal note, with caret in the text. See *post*, p. 182. This proclamation and those mentioned hereafter are printed in a volume called *A Booke of Proclamations, publiſhed ſince the beginning of his Maieſties moſt happy Reigne ouer England, &c. Untill this preſent Moneth of Febr.* 3 *Anno Dom.* 1609. The Proclamation referred to in the text is headed, 'A Proclamation, declaring the vndoubted Right of our Soueraigne Lord King Iames, to the Crowne of the Realmes of England, France and Ireland' (p. 1).

[2] Marginal note, with caret in text. See *post*, p. 182.

[3] These words struck through.

[4] Marginal note with caret in text.

strengthe of his yeares, & ye maturitie of his experyence),[1] his bookes new printed, (Βαζιλιχον δορων [*sic*], Free monarchies, Monologie,[2] Expositions vpon the Reuelacions & the Kings, [and] the Lepanto),[1] manye bookes newe wrytten th'admiracion & prayse of him: wthin Fewe dayes after, he sente his highenes' letters to the Counselle to establyshe them, & to the Citie of London, wch is imprinted, & hereafter followethe, fol. . Not longe after he entred Barwike, & the firste woorke he did, he wente wth greate deuotion to the Churche, & herde Tobie Mathewe preache,[3] & so helde one his progresse for london, to newcastle, to Yorke, where he lykewyse visited the minster & hearde deuyne seruyce accordinge to th'use of the Churche of Englaunde, & seemed to lyke verye well thereof, & at Easter Came to Burleighe; & in all his progresse he made manye knightes, & receaued & aunsweared many petitions. He Came by diuerse lordes' & knightes' howses, to Sr Thomes Sadler's, Sr Henry Cocke's, & to Theobaulds vpon Tewsedaye, the 3rd of May, where all the lordes, the Counselle & Cowrte mette his Matie. But before his Comminge thyther he Caused all those of the late Counselle to the Q. Elizab. to be sworne of his Counselle, & more to them, the Lorde Marre & the Lo. Murrie, Lo. Tho. Hawarde, whoe was then made Lor. Chamberleine, Lo. Northumberlande, Lo. Cumberlande & Lo. Mungaie, & after the Lo. H. Hawarde: but vpon Sondaye, the 10th of Aprill, his Matie sente letters for the delyuerye of th'erle of Southampton & Sr Henry Neuell oute of the Tower, where they had lyen 2 yeare, for the late Erle of Essexes faction, Southampton was Condempned, but Sr Hen. Neuell was neuer endited: In this his Ma^{tie's} progresse, all sortes of people, bothe noble & others, of all degrees, & from all partes of the kingedomes, in infinite multitudes, did attende him wth exceedinge greate ioye & reioysinge: Vpon Satterdaye, the 7th daye of Maye, his ma^{tie} Came from Theobalds,

'The more particular receyuinge and enterteyning of his ma^{tie} you shall Finde hereafter sette downe, fol. , wch inserte above after this marke ☞'

The King comes to Berwick

Newcastle

York

Burleigh

Makes many knights [p. 143]

Theobalds

He reappoints the Council

Delivers various prisoners

'The Copie of this letter is sette downe hereafter.'

Multitudes attend him

[1] Marginal note with caret in text. 'The Lepanto' is the title of a poem, first printed in 1591.

[2] *Dæmonologie*, published 1597.

[3] He was Bishop of Durham. 'The Bishop of Durham . . . hath preacht at Berwik before the King, and said grace at his table twise or thrise.' *Manningham's Diary*, Camden Soc., p. 170.

where the sette householde was, to Charter howse, vpon horsebacke, by the marshes to [Stamford] Hille betwene Totnam Highe Cross & Newington, & so soone as he entred into Middlesexe, Martin of the middle temple made a learned speeche[1] in the behalfe of the sheriffes of london & Middlesexe, whoe there receaued him; & at the sayde Hille the Lor. Maior & his bretheren, the Aldermen, in scarlette, & 400 Citisens, in vellette Coates, & Chaynes, all one horsebacke, mette wth him, & Crooke, the Recorder, made a speache, & the Duke of Linneux[2] bare the sworde before him. Vpon Mondaye & Tewsedaye Followinge, he wente secreatelye throughe manye streates & partes of london & to Whitehalle & Westminster & St James', &c.; & at Charter Howse he made 115 knightes: & vpon Wednsedaye Followinge he wente pryuatelye to White-halle, & there tooke barge betweene twelue & one a'clocke, & wente to the Tower, & as he wafted vpon the water, a gallaunte pealle of ordynance was discharged: there he stayde vnto Fridaye Followinge, & in the morninge before he departed he made more knightes, & 4 barons; Sr Phillipe Sidnie, Baron of Penseherste; Sr Edwarde Wootton, Baron of [Maherley][3]; Sr Rob. Cecill, Baron of Essington; Sr Wm Knowles, Baron of Graies; & then he wente by water to Greenewige, & all the householde, where, vpon Sondaye, the 22th [*sic*] of Maye, his ma^{tie} delyuered a learned, relligious, wyse & Comfortable speache to the Lo. Maior & his bretheren, to the greate admiration & reioycinge of them all, & then knighted the Lo. Maior, Sr Rob. Lee, the Recorder, Sr John Crooke, and the Attornie-generall, S^{r} Ed. Coke: it is generallye reported that moste of the knightes that are made doe purchase the same, & geue to the Scotch-men, some one 100$^{li.}$, some 200$^{li.}$, some 300$^{li.}$, & that his ma^{tie} dothe not dislyke of it, but tollerate it rather then to buye or selle Juditiall places, wch is a most Commendable

Comes to the Charter-house

'A copie of this speeche followethe in this booke.'[1]

He is met by the citizens of London

[p. 144]

He makes more knights

To the Tower

He makes more knights and four barons

To Greenwich

Addresses the Lord Mayor, May 22

More knights

Purchase of knighthood

[1] It was evidently the intention of Hawarde to copy this speech, and the various proclamations, etc., already referred to, into his book, but the intention was never carried out. See next page. A copy of Martin's speech is preserved among the State Papers, Domestic, James I., vol. i. No. 71.

[2] Ludovic Stewart, 2nd Duke of Lennox. 'Lord Clanricarde, an Irishe lorde,' struck out.

[3] Blank in MS.

thinge in his ma^{tie}: & it is allso sayde that the scotche & englishe heraldes haue twentye nobles of euerye knighte that ys made to recorde his name, & that his ma^{tie} dothe expecte that euerye knighte he makethe showlde keepe three greate horse furnyshed for seruyce.

Knights to keep three horses for service

[p. 145]

Petitions to the King

'There was a petition preferred to his ma^{tie}, called the poore's petition, another called the petition of the Catholiques,[1] the Copies of them bothe are entred in this booke: His Ma$^{tie's}$ Cheifeste studye & Care showlde seeme to be for the publike good, as maye appeare by his seuerall proclamacions in printe, for the borderers,[2] for the vnitinge of the Realmes,[3] & especiallye againste protections, monopolies, saltepeter men, purueyors, lawyers, etc.[4] his charge in the starre chamber, as maye appeare before in this booke, fol. 125 [*ante*, p. 161]. Vpon Wednsedaye & Thursedaye, the 25 & 26 dayes of Maye, his ma^{tie} wente by water to Putnie, & so by Coache to Noanesuche, & to Hampton Cowrte: & then back to Greenewige.'

May 25 and 26

[The next fifteen pages are left blank, probably for the various proclamations, speeches, letters, etc. above referred to.]

[p. 161]
1604
October 29

In Camera Stellata, coram Consilio ibidem, le prochein iour puis le terme, 29 Octobr. 1604, Ter^{no} Michaelis, Jacobi Regis 2°.[5]

POUNDE'S case

Petition against judges

Mr Pounde,[6] a great and ancient recusant, was prosecuted *ore tenus* by Coke, the King's Attorney, for a petition delivered by him to the King, against Baron Sauuelle and Sir Edwarde Phillips, the King's Serjeant, Judges of the Northern Circuit, for executing one Baillie,

1 'The Papists verry lately put up a suplicacion to the King for a tolleracion; his aunswre was, Yf there were 40,000 of them in armes should present such a petition, himselfe would rather dye in the feild than condiscend to be false to God. Yet seemed he would not use extremity yf they continued in duty like subjects.' *Manningham's Diary*, Camden Soc., p. 170.

2 'A Proclamation charging all actors or partners in the incursion on the Borders, to resort to the Commissioners at a day limitted.' *Book of Proclamations*, p. 17.

3 'A Proclamation for the vniting of England and Scotland.' *Ibid.* p. 18.

4 'A Proclamation inhibiting the vse and execution of any Charter or Grant made by the late Queene *Elizabeth*, of any kinde of Monopolies, &c.' *Ibid.* p. 12.

5 No names given.

6 See Appendix XIV.

a miller, for rescuing a priest, and [also] for executing one Rauson [1] for 'receivinge & relleiuinge' a priest, and [also] for persecuting by imprisonment one Atkinson, an ancient priest in the time of Queen Marie. 'He termethe Rauson "a martir," & Atkinson, "good father Atkinson": He delyuered a petition to the Kinge, beginninge wth verses in englishe, & then wth Articles, that Baron Sauuell showlde delyuer in his Charge that whosoeuer hearde a Masse it was Felonie; wch was improbable & senceles [even] for a meane man that neuer studyed any lawe, for it is by the lawe but a pecuniarie punishemente. He scandalized Justice, the Judges whoe are sworne to do Justice & represente the kinge & haue his charge, & are to gyue to him an accounte, & for there ill Cariage are to receaue a heauye iudgemente, as [in] the Case of Justice Thorpe [2]; he sclaundered likewyse the Justices of peace & the Jurors: & yet knewe none of all this of his owne knowledge, but by hearesaye & the reporte of others. & beinge examyned, vpon his allegeaunce, whoe those others were, he refused to aunsweare; he Called them Hamans & Susanna's Judges; he taxed the lawe of Crueltye [3]; he sclaundered the time paste [past] in the late Queene's Raigne, in wch time Mr Attornie did shewe that at the beginninge of her Raigne there were no recusauntes, but all wente to Churche vntill the 9th yeare of her Raigne that Pope Pius Quintus sente his bull, & absolued them from there obedyence, & after sente there preistes & seditious bookes: he sclaundered the time presente wth Crueltie, terminge themselues Gibeonites, very fitlye, as Mr Atturnie applyed, in there olde shooes, Coates, mustie bottles, & breade, & suche like trashe: & he threatened the time to Come wth reuenge of theise men's bloode, vniustlye & Cruellye martyred, as he sayde: whereas in verye truthe there was not anie one in all Queene Elizabethe's time that suffered deathe for

Slander of Justices of the Peace and Jurors

[p. 162]

Pope Pius Quintus; his Bull

[1] Probably one of the Rawsons of Shipley near Bradford, Yorkshire, a noted family of recusants. For notes of several members of the family, see Foley's *Records of the English Province of the Society of Jesus*, vol. iii. p. 103.

[2] See *ante*, p. 136.

[3] *I.e.* charged the law with cruelty.

1604 Oct. 29

religion or Conscyence, but for treason to the person of the prince or state, or w^th^drawinge or seducinge the people from there obedience; & after Pope Pius' absolution by bull, & therevpon a generall relapse from Churche, a pecuniarie punishemente of 20^li.^ by monethe & imprisonmente yf they had not [wherewith] to paie;[1] as this man Pounde was manie yeares imprisoned, & now aged, & it seemed now decaied in his sences, for he shewed manye apparaunces of good partes, wch either yeares or troubles had now greatelye defaced in him; so that he talked muche idle talke, & impertinente, & to no purpose; yet Confessinge verye discreetelye he was to rashe & had offended in ouer forwarde blinde zealle, but yet wth extrauagante idle wordes he spoyled all againe, & was helde shorte by ye Courte; he was of ouer bolde a spirite, & full of matter, & verye plentifull in vtteringe the same. Mr Attornie tolde him the papistes woulde gyue him litle thankes for that daie's seruice, for it seemed he looked to be canonized for it; but saithe the Attornie, "god be thanked, the gospell this daye is muche more aduaunced, & error & poperie abased, & the glorie of god extolled."

Recusants to pay 20*l.* a month or go to prison

'So for theise offences he was Fyned 1000^li.^,[2] imprisonmente duringe ye kinge's pleasure in ye tower, & to stande one the pillorie here at Westminster, & in Lancashire, & to haue his eares nailled, but not cutte of; yet if he woulde produce those that informed him he showlde not haue his eares naylled, albeit those y^t^ beganne the sentence woulde haue had his eares Cutte of, but the sentence of ye Courte was otherwyse: in the begynninge of his replye to his Charge, w^ch^, as the Attornie sayde, did Caste itselfe into a tryangle, firste in three offenders, Baillie, Rauson & Atkinson; for Baillie, he was no papiste, but a protestante, & he Comminge wth 80 more to rescue a notorious preiste sendinge to the prison, he onelye was taken, & iustely Condemned for treason, & yet executed but as a Felon[3]: Rauson, for receyuinge & harboringe a preiste whoe had sayde he

[p. 163]

Sentence

Baillie's case

Rauson's case.

[1] The statute was 23 Eliz. cap. 1.

[2] See Appendix VII.

[3] That is, he was hanged, not beheaded.

Coulde raise 4000 stronge, & woulde by suche a daye surprise suche a Castle, & for Concealinge him & Conueyghinge him awaye, wch was likewyse treason, & iustly Condemned for ye same, yet executed as a Felon. For Atkinson, the olde preiste, he published at the Assises that he had authoritie vpon a man's penitencye to forgyue anye sinne, albeit it were the deposinge or killinge ye kinge, & subscrybed to this in wrytinge, for the wch he was onelye Committed, & not to Yorke Goale, by reason of ye plauge then there, but to Hull: & by suche like examples manye hundredes began to relapse & fall to error, & ye late lawe of 1° *Jacob.* did require an exacte execusion of the lawe againste recusancye: so likewise was there a tryangle of men scandalized, Judges, Justices of peace, & Jurors. & he scandalized the time paste [past], the time presente, & threatened the time to Come. He demaunded a Commission to proue ye same, wch was againste lawe, order & all Course of presidente [precedent], & so [it was] vtterlye denyed him: then he sayde there were some of note & good place that woulde iustifie the article of Charge gyuen by Baron Sauuelle that it was felonie to heare a masse, & named Sr Thom. Heskette,[1] Atturnie of ye wardes, & Mr Tilselie, & desyred to haue them produced to his face. They were sente for, & aunsweare retorned that Mr Tilselie was gone out of towne, & that the Attornie of the wardes woulde Come. Then he [Pounde] sayde he was not assured whether he [Heskette] were presente & did heare it or noe, so then it appeared plainelye he had done vnaduisedlye in all, & was rashe w^th^oute anie good grounde, wch was muche condemned in him by all ye hearers wth a plaudite & hissinge; & then [Pounde] grewe deiected & dismayed, & to wander in idle & impertinente talke, so that whereas before he was accounted before by ye wyser sorte of Catholiques an aduysed, discreete, learned & iudiciall arche man & piller amongste them, they now sayde he was distracted, he doated by reason of his age, or raued by reason of his troubles: god graunte all the

Atkinson's case

1 James I., cap. 4, against recusancy [p. 164]

[1] Hesketh.

1604 Oct. 29

enemies to him & his truthe maye proue suche, & come to lyke iudgemente, that the gospelle maye in all places be more & more aduaunced, & error & all superstitious, idolatrous poperie vtterlye abolyshed & rooted oute. Amen. Amen.'

[p. 165] 1604–5 Hilary Term

In Camera Stellata, Ter^{no} Hillarii, 1604, Jacob. Regis Britanniae 2°.[1]

SIR ROBERT DUDLEY'S case

This term the Attorney-General moved in the case between the Lord Sidnie and Sir Robert Dudlie: For 'the Lo. Admirall was to goe into Spaine to take the oathe of the kinge of Spaine for the peace, *et* Sr Roberte Dudlie, allyed vnto him, intended to goe wth him; but at the Attornie's motion he was stayed, because the nexte terme the Cause was to be hearde.[2]

1604–5 Feb. 13

In Camera Stellata, coram Consilio ibidem, Mercurij, 13 Febr. 1604, le prochein ioure puis le terme, adonque presente, Lo. Chauncellor, Lo. Tresoror, Archeuesque de Canterberye, Lo. Admirall, Count Northumberland, Count Worster, Count Deuon, Count Northampton, Vicount Cranborne, Lo. Zouche, Lo. Burleighe, Lo. Knowlles, Sr John Fortescue, euesque de Londres, touts les Judges del terre.

The Chancellor's charge

'Lo. Chauncellor, accordinge to ye accustomed manner, delyuered a charge from his Matie, accordinge to a proclamacion made the daye before in the Chauncerye for all Judges & Justices of Peace to attende this daye, as it is vsed after Hillary & trinitie terme. Firste he sayde that beinge vsuall it is had & helde a thinge of Course & in Contempte: He beganne wth the Justices of Peace, whoe generallye througheoute the wholle kingedome forgette there oathe to god, there dutye to there kinge & Cuntrye; there multitude dayllye increasethe, & they showlde be men that are of beste deserte, whoe studie to execute

Justices of the Peace

[1] No names given.

[2] See *ante*, p. 169, and *post*, pp. 198, 204, 205, 209, and Appendix XIII.

Justice & to maintaine peace, but they rather make warre: & there are too manie that doe no good, & too fewe that execute the dutye of there place, but lyue here in London the most parte of the yeare, & onelye in y[e] sommer goe downe for pleasure, & vse it for there Countenaunce, those that beginne to doe are busy bodyes so termed & troublers of the state. The kinge takes theise thinges tenderlye to the harte. [p. 166]

'And as this season speciallye requirethe to be obserued accordinge to the lawe for the eatinge of fishe & fastinge, for at this season th'increase & breedinge of yonge thinges of all kindes, beinge preserued & spared, the plentie thereof is more abundante all the yeare after, & wante & scarcitie auoyded w[ch] otherwyse woulde ensue, so that in politike & civill gouernemente it is especiallye to be looked vnto, for no kingedome vpon the earthe is more plentifullye serued wth fishe then this of Englaunde, whereby the prizes of all thinges will be abated all the yeare after, & the lande & people greatly inryched, trades increased, poore relleiued & maintayned. Season for fasting

'The multitudes of alehowses, y[e] Causes of all disorder, in w[ch] there is vsed greate prophanacion & blasphemies, riotous wastinge god's good blessinges sente for better vses: & wickednes & vice Cheryshed. Ale-houses

'The wante of mendinge highewayes, a greate & generall faulte. Justices in Eire, whoe now are the Justices of Assise, oughte to inquire of this, & of the reste, & punishe th'offenders & Fine the whole Cuntrye. Highways

'For the Judges, I knowe you all to be so learned, relligious, wyse, & graue, that you will not forgette the dutyes of yo[r] places: for you muste examine theise thinges, & make reporte to his Ma[tie], & especiallye of the Justices of peace, yf any Contemptuouslye be absente or neglygente, to be remoued wth disgrace: & yo[r] Circuites you goe not onelye to sitte upon *Nisi prius*, but you must have especiall Care of the peace of the lande & of the peace of the Churche. Some there are that Fashyon there Conscyences as they are affected, but there is no good Conscyence [p. 167] Commendation of the judges

1604–5 Feb. 13

wthoute humilitye: for they will be holye so longe as they be pleased & how they liste: suche are meinteiners & moouers of sedition: whereof there are twooe sortes of offenders in a highe degree, & deserue the greateste punishemente nexte to treason: th'one are scandalouse speakers that now saye they are depryued wthoute lawe, againste lawe, & iniustelye; wryters & lybellers that taxe kinge, state & gouernemente. Th'other are petitioners that either Come in multitudes, or presume of multitudes of subscriptions of handes, as papistes & sectaryes or puritanes: *hoc est mouere seditionem regni*, wch is treason. whoe saye that the kinge's highe Commissioners haue no warraunte by lawe to doe as they doe; whereas the kinge's Matie, as it were inheritable & descended from god, hathe absolutelye monarchichall power annexed inseperablye to his Crowne & diademe, not by Common lawe nor statute lawe, but more auncyente then eyther of them: yet in the time of superstitiouse blindenes (wch ye pope & his instrumentes specially obserued as a fundamentall pointe of pollicye to keepe ye people allwayes in blindenes and ignoraunce), & the pope then vsurpinge the kinge's supreame & absolute authorite in ecclesiasticall as well as Ciuill Causes, then the Common lawe & statute lawe, by waye of explanacion or declaracion of the aunciente lawe of ye diademe & Crowne, did plainelye shewe ye kinge's auncyente prerogatiue & iurisdiction; wch now bothe papiste & purytane doe in wordes & wth the mouthe acknowledge, but in the harte & workes denye the same.

Maintainers and movers of sedition

Petitioners

The King's Divine right

[p. 168] Religious toleration

'But especiallye he touched theise petitioners & reporters, that taxe the kinge & Counselle wth a disposition for a toleration of relligion, & that the kinge or some of the Counselle showlde Countenance & maintaine the papistes, & staye th'execucion of the lawe from them for there bodies or goods: & therevpon [the Lord Chancellor] tooke occasyon to Commende the Kinge's Matie, his manie vertues, his diuine knowledge & vnderstandinge, his zealle of Justice, & especiallye for religion; that sythence [since] Christianitie was established vpon earthe, neuer kinge that

Commendation of the King

tooke more Care or shewed lyke zealle in plantinge & settlinge true relligion :

'The Kinge's Matie hathe protested & Confydently delyuered that in this religion he was borne, bredde, schooled, broughte vp; he hathe mainteyned it wth the daunger of his life, & he will spende his lyfe & beste bloude for the same, & will dye in it: & yf he did doubte that his sonne would alter the same, & sette vp poperye, he woulde disinherite him & giue his Crowne to a straunger yf he Coulde: & as my lo. vicounte sayde, he suckte protestant's milke, he was broughte vp in the schoole of ye protestantes, & before he woulde suffer toleration of poperie, so Contrarye to truthe & true protestantes' relligion, he woulde lose his lyfe, & Crowne, & all. The King a protestant

'Theise libellers, discoursers, polititians, Censure the kinge, ye Counsell, ye Bishops, the gouernemente, & Comforte the papistes, puritanes & atheistes, wth hope of a tolleracion; whereas the kinge, ye Counsell, nor Judges, euer had worde of hope or Comforte for toleration. No toleration

'Theise reporters & scandalizers by petitions & otherwise are greate offendors, & deserue greate punishmente, *par le opinion de tout le courte.* And all the lordes Confirme thus muche of the kinge, & delyuerd it perticularlye by his ma$^{tie's}$ speciall Commaundemente.[1]

'The Lo. Tresorer [said] that there was a gentleman that had deserued well in the kinge's seruice, & made suite vnto y^{e} kinge for a recusaunte's 20$^{li.}$ by monethe [month] for not repayringe to Churche;[2] the kinge hauinge graunted it him, he, drawinge vp his pattente, had put in some wordes sauouringe of the kinge's Ma$^{tie's}$ fauourable inclinacion towardes papistes, & of a kinde of purpose to remitte the rigor of suche lawes againste them; but Comminge to inferior officers of the sealle, the Counsell & Kinge were moued in it, & therevpon the [King] reuoked his graunte, & rather oute of his grace gaue him 200$^{li.}$ *per annum* oute of his Coaffers then any suche scandale showld be offred. [p. 169]

[1] Compare this with the other charges, *ante*, pp. 19, 56, 101, 106, 159, 161, and *post*.

[2] This was the penalty enacted by 23 Eliz. cap. 1.

1604-5 Feb. 13

Prince Henry

'The Lo. Admirall he sayde that the prince[1] was a hopefull issue as euer was in the worlde, & he himselfe, hauing some Charge of him, did note this especiallye in him, that he woulde omitte & lose all sportes & pastimes whatsoeuer to intende ye sermons or his praiers.

Puritans

'The Lo. of Worster, (whoe was sayde to be wth his ma^tie^ when the puritanes delyuered the petition, & offred subscription of 2 or 3000 more of good qualitie & place), condemned it for a greate offence, & the nexte steppe to rebellion.

'The Lo. of Northumberlande to the lyke purpose.

No papist to be of the Council

'The Earle of Deuonshire verye partycularlye delyuered the kinge's Charge, & that w^th^in Few dayes he sate personallye in Counselle, & made all the Counselle delyuer there partycular religion & Faithe, protestinge that yf he thoughte any of his Counselle were popishe, or did Fauoure the papistes, or countenaunce them, or hinder the proceedinges of the lawe againste them, he woulde remoue them from his Counselle; he lykewyse delyuered his owne partycular religion wth greate & earneste zeale, that, as the kinge his Maister, so had he bene borne in ye protestantes religion, suckte protestante's milke, bene taughte in ye schoole of ye protestantes, bredde & broughte vp in the same, aduentured his bloude, & woulde spende his lyfe & dye in the same.

[p. 170]

Ambassadors not to use mass

'Th'erle of Northampton delyuered how the kinge, in his excercyse at Royston, sente to him to London, that vnderstandinge that masses were ordinarlye vsed, he showlde Charge the ymbassadors to forbeare them, & to forbydde all Companye from them, wch he did; & w^th^all did Condemne theise petitioners in multitudes as a greate offence, & deseruinge greate punishemente; & w^th^all protested that there were manye Catholickes wch otherwyse, but for there Conscyences, were men well qualifyed, & good subiectes, & loyallye disposed to the state.

A message from the Pope to the King

'The Lo. Vicounte Cranbourne spake verye muche, & moste particularlye, & declared how a scocheman, ye kinge's

[1] Prince Henry.

seruante, & one that had deserued well, Came to ye kinge wth a message from the Pope that yf ye kinge's ma^tie^ woulde permitte the prince to be broughte vp in the Catholike religion, & suffer toleracyon of religion, the pope woulde assure him of peace wth Spaine vpon what Conditions he woulde requyre; the kinge delayed him & woulde gyue him no aunsweare; but ymportuninge his Matie many times for an aunsweare, & that he durste not retorne vpon peine of the Pope's Curse w^th^oute an aunsweare, the kinge wyshed him not to retorne, but yf he woulde, then he Charged him to observe his aunsweare well & to omitte noe parte of it nor adde oughte to it, if he did, it showlde Coste him ye price of his bloude: viz. "Tell the Pope that as a temporall prince I reuerence him as I doe anye prince vpon the earthe, & as he sufferethe my subiectes in there traffickes & trauelles to be vsed Ciuillye & kindelye, I loue him for it; but before I shall either alter my religion, suffer toleration, or haue Change of this religion, I will loose my Crowne & lyffe bothe; & yf I thoughte my sonne woulde alter the religion now establyshed, esyeciallye to the rhomishe religion, so Contrarye to truthe, & so full of error, I woulde gyue my Crowne & kingedome from him, yf I Coulde, & I woulde rather die Childeles, & burye them before mee, then they showlde doe it: for in this religion I was borne, I suckte protestante's milke, I was broughte vp in ye schoole of ye protestantes, I haue aduentured my bloude for ye same, & I will dye in the same." For the puritanes, he accounted of them in another ranke then the papistes, & he woulde goe halfe waye to meete them, & he loued & reuerenced manye of them, & if they woulde leaue there opinions, there were some of them he woulde preferre to ye beste Bishoprike that were voyde: but for the papistes, he hath renewed & Confyrmed the lawe againste them.

The King's answer

[p. 171

Puritans

'*Vt pastor ad oues, sic grex*[1] *ad populum*; & no flocke free from all diseases; the kinge vnmacheable for diuine vnderstandinge & morall vertues: but wee of his Counselle & other Judges are the eies & handes y^t^ he must vse: & I

The King's learning and virtues

[1] *Sic*; a mistake for *rex*.

1604-5 Feb. 13

feare this will prooue a Criticall daye to ye disease, bothe to papistes & puritanes. (Intimidated.) [*Sic.*]

'*Diuersitas ceremoniarum non tollit consensum ecclesiae.*

'He y^t dothe not hinder y^t wch is in his power to hinder, dothe tolerate.

'An olde lawe that a sclaunderour's tounge showlde be Cutte owte.'

1605 April 19

In Camera Stellata, coram Consilio ibidem, Veneris, 19 April, 1605, Jacob. Regis Britanniae 3°.[1]

BEERELY'S case — Rout and Riot

'Cause of hearinge betwene Beerely, plaintiff, & tenne others, defendants,' for rout & riot, etc. The plaintiff is seised of the manor of D. and another lord is seised of the manor of Sale, 'betweene wch manors lyes a Common of 2000 acres; & in ye middeste [midst] of ye Common was a poole or moore wherein the tenauntes Cattelle were woonte to be myred, & in danger to be spoyled, & for feare thereof to be allwayes kepte wth a heardeman: of late the pl. improued & enclosed the same wth a diche, & set a quickeset hedge of thornes & withie stakes, & hunted of ye tenauntes' Cattelle leauinge sufficient Common besides; the tenaunts to ye number of tenne put one a 100 Cattelle, & pulled awaye ye quickesettes, & Caste downe the diche: for wch route & riote the pl. Complaines in this Cowrte.

[p. 172] Proof of service of process, required

'But firste the Courte requyred proffe by affidauit of proces to be serued *ad audiendum iudicium*: & it is ye rule & Course of the Courte yf proces be once serued vpon any one Defendaunte it sufficethe, albeit the cause be not hearde the same terme that ye proces is retornable; & so in this cause, beinge in the booke the laste terme for hearinge, was Contynewed to this terme, & affidauit was made that proces was serued vpon one of ye defendauntes to heare iudgemente the laste term, & it was sufficiente: For affidauit was requyred by the Courte, for that ye defendauntes did not any of them appeare, neyther had anye of them any Counselle, otherwyse it needed not: so then

[1] Ten Councillors and Judges were present.

there aunsweares were all reade : & it appeared by there aunsweares that time out of minde the tenauntes had vsed Common in yᵉ More, & euery tenaunte labored one daye in a yeare to clense the diches aboute yᵉ More, & put in there Cattelle onelye once in peaceable manner of purpose to trye the title & to haue an accion broughte at yᵉ Common lawe whether there [was] sufficiente Common lefte or no: & yᵉ pl. distreigninge yᵉ Cattelle, yᵉ tenauntes broughte an accion, & vpon full euydence gyuen, the yssue beinge whether sufficiente Common or not, yᵉ tenauntes were non suite, yet the Courte were of opinion that it had bene fytter to haue bene endyted in yᵉ Countrye, & so for troublinge this Courte wᵗʰ so small an offence, the tenauntes themselues beinge simple men & knowinge not but that they did as they oughte, yᵉ pl. was fyned to yᵉ kinge Xˡⁱ·; and the Tenauntes for Comminge in suche a multitude & puttinge one so many Cattelle, & for pluckinge vp the hedge, diche & settes, to the ill example of others, especiallye in those Countryes of Deuonshire, were Fyned eyther of them 20ˢ.

Sentence

Plaintiff fined

Defendants fined

'It was allso then delyuered by the Lo. Chauncellor for yᵉ rule & order of yᵉ Courte, that a suite dependinge by bill & aunsweare in this Courte, the parties, at anye time before the same be sette in the booke for hearinge, maye Compounde & ende or wᵗʰdrawe the same by the priuitie of the Courte, but yf yᵉ same be once sette downe in yᵉ booke for hearinge, the parties Can not then ende, Compounde nor wᵗʰdrawe the same, wᵗʰoute there be a Fine payde to the kinge by the pl. or defdte, or by them bothe yf there be Cause; & so was it this daye ordered in twooe particular Causes.

Rule of Court

Parties may compound a case before it is set down for hearing, but not afterwards

[p. 173]

ATT.-GEN. *v.* STOKES

Misconduct in a Deputy Purveyor

'Sʳ Edwarde Coke, th'attornie generall informed *ore tenus* againste one Stokes, a poore Carpenter, whoe, by Collor of a Commission graunted vnto his Mʳ, Sir Henry Seckforde,[1] for yᵉ prouydinge necessaryes for the kinge's

[1] 1603, Aug. 18. Grant, with survivorship, to Sir Henry Seckford and Thomas Bedinfield of the Mastership of the Tents, Hales and Pavilions. *Docquet.*
Same date. Commission for Sir

1605 April 19

toyles, tooke vpon him as a deputye Purueyor (w^{th}oute any deputacyon in wrytinge, wch by ye lawe he oughte to haue, shewinge onelye ye kinge's greate sealle, wch no deputye oughte to haue, but a deputacyon in wrytinge, & deputies oughte to be men of sufficiencye & good vallewe), tooke at Fullam in Middlesexe dyuerse timber trees, as oake & elme, growinge neere vnto men's dwellinge howses & for there defence, by Collor of this greate sealle, & prised [priced] them not, as he oughte to haue done, but agrees for a prize [price], but refuses to paye for them vnles he may haue abated j^{d} in euerye shyllinge, wch he sayde his M^{r} was to haue; whereas, by lawe, yf a tree were praysed [appraised] at 30^{s}, the kinge's price is X^{s}: he purueyed to the number of 50, solde & gaue awaye the toppes, & sayde the Chippes & knubbes were for his ladye; & this Stokes hearkened still where trees or timber were in Controuersye, & woulde be assured to take them, but paye nothinge for them by reason they were in stryfe: & tooke lykewyse Cartes to Carye them, wch he Can not doe by the lawe: so y^{t} hereby the kinge's prerogatiue is highlye abused; for it is necessarye his prerogatiue in all thinges showlde be mainteyned, & for the prouision of his howseholde it must be vsed, & it can not Contynewe w^{th}oute it; but the abusinge thereof is dishonor to ye kinge, greeuance & oppressyon to the subiecte, & the kinge woulde not in any wyse haue his prerogatiue rackte or strechte, but vsed tenderlye & wth all possible Fauoure mighte be, studyinge & desyringe nothinge more then to auoyde all manner of oppressyon, & to minister Justice to all w^{th}oute vexation or other greeuaunce; & therefore Commaunded his Atturnie generall to attende of all the Judges for there opinion in this takings of trees, whether his prerogatiue doe warrante it: for the aunciente & greate Charter of Englande, 22 times Confyrmed by ye Kinges of this realme, saythe, "*Nec nos, nec balliui nostri, nec alii, capiemus boscum alienum ad castra vel ad alia*

Claims 1*d.* in the shilling

The King's prerogative

Whether the King can take trees

'Magna Charta, fol. 4. purveyors, 1°, cap. 21.'

Henry Seckford to procure timber, iron, &c., for tents, and workmen to make them. *Docquet.*

1604, Feb. 5. Commission for Sir Henry Seckford, Master of the Toils, and others, to take up things necessary for the repair, &c., of the Toils. *Docquet.*

agenda nostra, nisi per voluntatem illius cuius boscus ille fuerit." And all the Judges of Englande, vpon delyberate aduyse, haue resolued that none of ye kinge's offycers Can take any trees growinge, for they are parcell of a man's enherytaunce & therevnto fyxed, nor take any thinge but suche as the owner hathe a purpose to sell & departe w^th^all for gaine. Purveyors cannot take trees

'So the whole Courte did muche Condemne this vsage, & did therefore sentence him to haue a fine of 20^li.^, to be sette vpon ye pillorie wth papers, to be whipped, & to haue three yeares ymprisonmente, & to be bounde to his good behauioure before he were enlarged.' [p. 174] Sentence

In Camera Stellata, coram Consilio ibidem, Mercurij, 24 April. 1605, Termino Pasche, Jacob. Regis 3°.[1] 1605 April 24

Anthonie Brakenberie and [2] Tunstall, plaintiffs, against Frauncis Brakenberie and Edwarde Coomes, Counsellor at Law of the Middle Temple, for forgery of the will of Richard Brakenberie, and 'practice in Coomes to procure it, & takinge a bribe of 200^li.^, a vellet gowne, spoones, & a Fetherbedde of Frauncis Brakenberie, for whose benefitte onely ye will was now deuysed. BRACKENBERIE *v.* BRACKENBERIE — Forgery

'This Cause allso was hearde vpon Fridaye, 26 April followinge, & not sentenced before twooe a Clocke in ye afternoone the same Fridaye.

'Richarde Brakenberie, one of the vshers of the late Qu. Chamber, beinge visited wth sickenes, was visited by Coomes, whoe, perswadinge him to sette thinges in order, gaue him verball instructions to make his will, whoe, vpon his retorne home the nexte morninge, reduced them into wrytinge, & made a formall will, & delyuered the same to his Clerke to drawe vp, & therevpon tooke the same wth him, hauinge diuerse blankes, & wente in the eueninge, 8° *Junij*, to Greewige, where Brakenberie laie sicke, & Caryed that draughte wth him; for Frauncis Brakenberie

[1] Nine Councillors and Judges were present. [2] Blank in MS.

1605 April 24 had sente to him at 9 a clocke that morninge to will him to make haste & Come awaye wth the will, or else it woulde be to late, for he woulde be voyde of vnderstandinge. After Coomes Came to him, his speache beinge allmoste gone, he spake nothinge but monosillables, "I," or "Yea," wch was his aunsweare to all questions demaunded of him, rattlinge muche in the throate, & the hearers not knowinge whether it was "I" or "Yea" that he spake, but Coomes interpreted so, & then Caused his man Holman, whoe was allso made a defendaunte, to engrosse the will in the Chamber, by the sicke, & willed him often to make haste, & when the same was ingrossinge, he [Coomes] asked him [the testator] whoe showlde be his executor, to wch he aunsweared nothinge; but Frauncis [Brackenberie], standinge behinde Coomes, biddinge aske him yf he woulde haue his vnkle Alboroughe to be executor wth Frauncis in truste to his use, to wch he aunsweared "I," or "Yea,' wch was [p. 175] his aunsweare to all questions ministred to him. So Coomes, Callinge sixe or eighte of good Credyte that were presente in ye Chamber to Come neere to the bedde to heare the wylle Reade, Reade all the will distinctlye, & to euerye partycular legacye & parte of the will, demaunded of the testator, viz. "Father, is this yor meaninge," to all wch he euer aunsweared "I," or "Yea," & no otherwyse, wch woordes Coomes interpreted to be "I," or "Yea," otherwyse the hearers doubted what he meante, & Coomes himselfe sayde that yf he did not speake, all was naughte, or nothinge worthe: yet put a penne into his hande, but he let the same Fall, & then made his man Holmas [*sic*] guyde his hande, & so subscrybed his name & sealled the same, & Holman tooke the testator's hande, & wth his fingers tooke of ye sealle. Moste of the wytnesses deposed that they iudged the testator not to be voyde of sense & vnderstandinge when the will was reade, for, yf they had, they woulde neuer haue subscrybed there names; yet they gaue Credyte to Coomes, that tolde them he had receaued instructions before, & hauinge pryuate Conference wth him now, he Confyrmed the same, & the sayde wytnesses did, notw^th^standinge, depose that the sayd testator mad no other aunsweare but "I" or "Yea," accordinge to Coomes' interpretation, & they thoughte he woulde make that aunsweare to any question whatsoeuer ministred vnto him, & Coomes very nimblye & Cunninglye fashyoned all questyons in suche a Fashyon that "I" or "Yea" was a proper aunsweare to them: Coomes, Contrarye to his instructions had inserted *de nouo* 3 or foure seuerall thinges. & so generallye by ye whole Courte Coomes was Condemned for a Cunninge & suttle practise, w^ch^, yf it had bene Complayned of by ye bill, they would haue punished him seuerelye; & I thinke it was, but he had his pardon, for it was before ye laste pardon: & they acquyted him of ye Forgerye, but all sentenced the will voyde: & it was agreede by ye Judges that yf a man giue instructions to a Clerke, by paroll, to make his will, & he puts it into wrytinge, it is a good will, but let him looke that he be able to make good prooffe of his gyuen instructions: & allso yf a man deuyse lande for lyfe, ye remainder for lyfe, the remainder in fee, ye Clerke leaues out ye remainder for lyfe, this is Forgerye; so of addition, either in will or bonde; & the Lo. Ch. Justice gaue a greate admonition to all practizers to be precise how they dealle wth men *in extremis* or *articulo mortis*.

Acquitted of forgery

Will void

'And albeit ye statute of 5 Elizab.[1] be of a wrytinge touchinge landes, yet the statute intendethe leasses for yeares, & addicion or detraction of any materiall pointe or parte of ye will is forgerye: ye Courte muche Condemned the foule practise in Coomes, thoughe verye Cunninge, wth a relligiouse preamble, & a publike shewe of greate Care & good meaninge, theise are *deuilamenta non testamenta*: for forgerie, saide Sergeaunte Hubbarde, *est malum commissum non omissum,* & it is false, subtle & secrete, & it must be not of a peece or a parte of a wrytinge, but of an entier wrytinge, wch was ouerruled by the Judges. Forgerye was punisheable at the Common lawe, before the statute, at ye discretion of the Judges to inflicte what [p. 176]

A foul practise in Coomes

[1] Cap. 14: An Act against Forgers of false Deeds and Writings. See Appendix X.

1605 April 24 punishemente they showlde thinke good: but now y[e] punishmente ys greate by 5 elizab. cap. 14.'[1]

1605 May 1 **In Camera Stellata,** coram Consilio ibidem, Mercurij, j[o] Maij, 1605, Ter[no] Pasche, Jacob. Regis 3[o], adonque presente, Lo. Chauncellor, Archeuesque de Canterberie, Lo. Tresorer, Lo. Chamberlin, Lo. Northumberlande, Lo. Deuonshire, Lo. Northampton, Lo. Vicount Cranborne, Lo. Zouche, Lo. Knoulles, euesque de Londres, Ch. Justice, Ch. Baron, Justice Yeluerton, Justice Warberton, et S[r] John Fortescue.

SIR ROBERT DUDLEY'S case

'The greate Cause betwene y[e] Lo. Sidnie & S[r] Rob. Dudlie & others, defendauntes, vpon the Attornie's informacyon[2]: shewinge that all honors, titles & dignities doe flowe from y[e] kinge, or suche as he shall appointe; & the late Queene bestowinge 2 greate earldomes w[th] diuerse landes of greate vallewe to Warwike & Lester, & the heires male of there bodies, they dyinge w[th]oute issue, the honors & landes did reuerte to y[e] Queene, & now is in y[e] kinge.

Dudley's answer

'S[r] Roberte Dudlie shewethe by aunsweare that th'erle of Lester maryed y[e] Ladye Sheffeilde, his mother, & had by her, after maryage, S[r] Roberte Dudlie, but afterwardes, growing in dislike wth y[e] Ladie Sheffeilde, he maryed the now reputed Countes of Lester: the Ladie Sheffeilde Confessethe the marriage vpon oathe, & namethe particularly [p. 177] dyuerse that were presente at y[e] maryage & wytnesses to y[e] same, as S[r] Edwarde Horsie[3] & others, & a specyall token y[t] y[e] Earle himselfe sayde that a greate personage had gyuen him a faire ringe sette wth manye table and pointed diamondes, vpon Condicion that he showlde not gyue it to anye but to suche a one whome he showlde marye, w[ch] ringe, vpon y[e] marriage, he gaue to y[e] Ladye Sheffeilde; & y[e] Duke of Norffolke beinge the onelye

[1] See Appendix XV.

[2] See *ante*, pp. 169, 186; *post*, pp. 204, 205 and 209; and Appendix XIII.

[3] Sir Edward Horsey was a friend of Leicester's; there are several letters from him to Leicester among the State Papers.

meanes of makinge this mache, the Ladye Sheffeilde woulde gladlye haue had him, & other of her honorable Freindes, presente at y[e] mariage, but Lester refused the same, alleaginge that in anye Case he woulde haue it kepte very secrete, "For yf y[e] Queene," sayde he, "showlde knowe of it, I were vndone & disgraced, & caste oute of Fauoure for euer." But, after vnderstandinge shee was wth Childe by him, he seemed to reioyce greatelye at it, & to that purpose he wrote manye letters to her by y[e] name of his wyfe; yet afterwardes growinge in some dislyke wth her, practysed by her seruauntes, & gotte theise letters awaye, & put her often in perill of her lyfe, & Caused her once to be poysened, & soone after maryed wth the Ladye Lettis, the now reputed Countes of Lester, & S[r] Frauncis Knolles' daughter; so that y[e] Ladye Sheffeilde, for her safetie, was forced to marye S[r] Edwarde Stafforde, a man very aduerse to Lester, by whom she hathe had twooe Chyldren.

'Firste Dodrige, y[e] sollicitor,[1] opened y[e] bill, & then S[r] Edwarde Phillips,[2] y[e] kinge's sergeaunte, made a large repetition thereof & added muche vnto the same, & for helpe of memorie deuyded it into Fowre partes:— The Bill opened by the Sol.-Gen.

'Firste, y[e] Consequence, or waighte of the example of y[e] Facte, lyke vnto w[ch] there hathe bene no example, nor the lyke heard of, since 9 H. 6. For it Concerne y[e] kinge's Ma[tie] in his titles & honors to twooe greate Earledomes, & in lande of greate vallewe, sixe & twentie manners, 1500[li.] rente of Assise by the yeare: & parte of the same assured to the Queene for her Joincture: & greate parte of the same solde, & 800 Families that holde parte thereof: the now Countes of Lester hathe a ioincture of parte thereof, & the Countes of Huntington & y[e] Countes of Rutlande[3] are

[1] Sir John Dodridge, appointed Solicitor-General in Oct. 1604; afterwards a Judge of the King's Bench. Foss.

[2] So appointed May 18, 1603; Speaker of the House of Commons, 1604; Master of the Rolls, 1611; died 1614. Foss.

[3] The Countess of Huntingdon was Katherine, dau. of John Dudley, Duke of Northumberland, and wife of Henry Hastings, third Earl of Huntingdon. The Countess of Rutland was Elizabeth Sydney, dau. and heir of Sir Philip Sydney, who was son and heir of Mary, another dau. of the Duke of Northumberland, and sister to Katherine, Countess of Huntingdon. Elizabeth Sydney married Roger Manners, 5th Earl of

1605 May 1 heires generall to a thirde parte thereof that showlde descende.

'The seconde parte, an introduction or inducemente for the mariage wch was 15 Elizab. [1572–3], & Sr Roberte Dudlie was borne 16 Elizab., & from 15 to 20 [Elizabeth, 1572–1578], no question at all touchinge ye Ladye Sheffeilde's mariage, when Lester maryed the now Countes
[p. 178] of Lester. There are Fyue wytnesses produced to proue ye firste mariage, all not worthe a frize Jerkin: & the minister Coulde neuer be knowne: but at ye seconde mariage, Doctor Tindall[1] was ye minister, & there were presente the Earle of Warwike,[2] The earle of Pembroke,[3] the Lo. Northe[4] & Sr Frauncis Knowlles:[5] Elizab. 22 [1579–80], the Ladye Sheffeilde maryethe wth Sr Edwarde Stafforde: in 23 Elizab., the wytnesses to ye seconde mariage, accordinge to ye vse of ye Ciuill lawe (that all Chamber, Clandestine or secrete mariages must be Confyrmed by ye oathe of ye wytnesses presente at the same), were all sworne & examyned, & Lester himselfe did solemnelye proteste before allmightie god that he was Free.

'24 Elizab. [1581–2], he Conueyghes his lande wth 15 remainders, & lymittes no estate at all to Sr Robert Dudlie.

'25 Elizab. [1582–3], he estated Sursumme lande vpon Sr Roberte Dudlie, his base sonne, 500^li.^ *per annum* of butler's lande, a fair proportion for a base sonne.

'29 Elizab. [1586–7], he makes his will and giues landes to his wife for lyfe, the remainder to his base sonne, whome he so callethe in his will 17 times.

Rutland. The two Countesses were found co-heirs to Ambrose Dudley, Earl of Warwick, on his death in 1589. They both died without issue.

[1] Humphrey Tindall, S.T.P., Master of Queen's College, Oxford, 1579; Chancellor of Lichfield, 1586; Archdeacon of Stafford, 1586; Prebendary of Halloughton, Southwell, 1588 Dean of Ely, 1591. Died 1614; buried at Ely. See his evidence, Appendix XIII.

[2] Ambrose Dudley, Leicester's brother.

[3] Henry Herbert, 2nd Earl, whose wife "Sydney's sister," was Leicester's niece.

[4] Roger North, 2nd Baron.

[5] See *Dict. of Nat. Biog.*

'After ye deathe of ye Earle of Lester,[1] th'erle of Warwike, whoe by all entendemente showlde be priuye to the firste mariage if it had bene, whoe was a trulye honorable gentleman & relligious, entred into a thirde of ye lande, for ye will was voyde for a thirde parte: & by seuerall offices [*i.e.* inquests], it was founde y^{t} Warwike was nexte heire to Lester, & ye Countes of Huntingdon & Rutlande nexte heire to Warwike. & Dudlie in his suites did not name himselfe heire, but claimed by the will. And in An^{o} 1599, in a bill in chauncerye by the Countes of Rutlande, he claimethe by ye will, & Confessethe by name the now Countes of Lester.

'And Sr James Dier,[2] Sr Edwarde Dier,[3] & Sr Wm Laighton[4] did heare Lester solempnelye vpon oathe denye the firste mariage.

'The thirde [part] is the accusation it selfe. Hillar. 45 Elizab. [1603], one Thomas Drurye, a knighte of the poste,[5] insinuate wth Sr Rob^{te} Dudlie that, yf he mighte be well rewarded, he woulde proue a mariage.

'In Auguste 1° *Jacob.*, Drurie & one Frauncis Drurye[6] goe to Sr Rob^{te} Dudlie, y^{e} 15th of Auguste, the woman denyes y^{e} mariage, Drurye instructethe her, & he is promysed to haue 200$^{li.}$, & this poore woman was but a sweeper in Warde's howse, that was the proctor at Liche- [p. 179] feilde: & then the woman, beinge instructed by Drurye, subscrybed a paper (wherein her examynacion was) before wytnesses: & yet she was a seruante wth y^{e} Ladye Sheffeilde, after the birthe of Sr Rob^{te} Dudlie.

'16 *Augusti*, an aduersarye is raysed, Buswell, that showlde Call Sr Rob^{te} Dudlie "bastarde," & ye partie is

[1] He died 4 Sep., 1588.

[2] Sir James Dyer, Chief Justice of the Common Pleas, 1559 to 1582. See *Dict. of Nat. Biog.*; Foss's *Judges*.

[3] Sir Edward Dyer, a poet and courtier, a *protégé* of Leicester's and an intimate friend of Sir Philip Sydney's. He was a favourite of Queen Elizabeth's, who made him Chancellor of the Order of the Garter. See *Dict. of Nat. Biog.*

[4] Perhaps Sir William Leighton, poet and composer (*fl.* 1603–14), as to whom see *Dict. of Nat. Biog.* There were others of the name, however, about that period. The poet's father was a William Leighton, and a Sir William Leighton was Sheriff of Warwickshire in 1591.

[5] A hired witness. Halliwell.

[6] "His wife," erased. This Francis is, of course, the woman subsequently mentioned.

1605 May 1

Cited, & appearethe, the wytnesses sworne & examyned, & sentence gyuen the same daye, & the same daye allso a Commission graunted.

'26 Aug., Drurye dies of ye plauge at ye Swanne in Southwarke; now Frauncis ys suborned & Jhones, whoe wrytethe to Sr Rob^te^ Dudlie to relleyue him in his miseries, & he sendethe him a bucke & a horse, wch were delyuered.

'The 4th is the execution of these practises of subornation & examination: Firste, ye Commission was graunted to 8 or any one of them. 7 were substantiall men to gyue countenance to ye Commission, but ye 8th was one of Sr Thom. Lee's Chapleins, (Sr Thom. Lee being Sr Rob^te^ Dudlie's wyue's Father),[1] who alone did execute the commission. & when proces was serued, they were promysed they showlde haue no dammage for Euelye, Sr Thom. Lee's man, shall beare ye Charge.

The Attorney-General's speech

'The Atturnie generall sayde this was a verye waightie Cause, & did Concerne the kinge & Common wealthe verye greatelye, & it was *Conatus sine exemplo*, & yet one presidente [precedent] Came verye neare it in 9 H. 6. Edmonde,

The Earl of Kent's case

Earle of Kente[2] had a base daughter, by Custance, late wife to Thomas, Lord Dispencer,[3] whose name was Elenor, whoe was maryed afterwarde to James, Lord of Audeley,[4] &c. *quaere le case*, for it is particularlye & largelye recyted in the statute of 9 H. 6, cap. 11, wch is a statute lykewyse restrayninge Certificates for bastardye before ye partie be Called to the same & issue ioyned, & proclamacion in the Chauncerye by 3 monethes for ye partie to appeare before ye ordinarie to make his allegations & obiections againste ye pretended *mulier*.[5]

[1] Sir Thomas Leigh of Stoneleigh, co. Warwick, created a Baronet 1611; mar. Catherine, dau. of Sir John Spencer of Wormleighton, co. Warwick. His daughter Alice mar. Sir Robert Dudley, and was afterwards created Duchess of Dudley for life. See Appendix XIII. Sir Thomas's grandson and heir was created Baron Leigh of Stoneleigh, 1643.

[2] Edmund Holland, 4th Earl of Kent. The case is set out fully in the judgment of Lord Chief Baron Fleming, *post*, p. 213.

[3] She was the daughter of Edmond of Langley, Duke of York, 5th son of Edward III.

[4] James Tuchet, 5th Lord Audley.

[5] *Mulier*, born in lawful wedlock, legitimate. The term was also used for sons.

'So then they began to reade there wytnesses, & offered some examyned in ye ecclesiasticall cowrte, but they were reiected by ye Cowrte, as ye vse there is in all cases; then they offered depositions taken by the Attornie himselfe before any bill or informacion in Cowrte. the Defendauntes' Councell obiected againste it in this kinde, that those wytnesses were examyned by Mr Atturnie in a masse before any suite, but now they are all examyned vpon particular Interrogatories in Courte, & therefore no reason why they showld be reade that were taken by Mr Atturnie himselfe. The Lo. Chauncellor seemed to be in some sorte of the same opinion, whereat Mr Atturnie was very much mooued, & Conceaued it a wronge offered to him, for it was the presidente [precedent] of ye Cowrte, & he had it allowed him in Woodde's [1] case, & Talbot's,[2] & in the Lady Gresham's case,[3] albeit they were neuer examyned in Courte; & in Cases of Treason & felonie, it is & hathe bene vsed. The Lo. Chauncellor seemed to be of another opinion; then ye Attornie desyred to be hearde, for it Concerned ye kinge & ye Common weale, & he woulde appeale to ye Che. Justice, whoe had serued in his place longe,[4] & sayde yf it mighte not be allowed him he woulde speake no more in the cause, & layde awaye his bookes, & pressed to be hearde in his appealle. The Lor. Chauncellor made aunsweare he showlde be hearde, & he [the Chancellor] woulde speake to[o], & be hearde in that place, for he woulde not be out braued; he knewe what he sayde & he had hearde & learned it before euer Mr Atturnie had: the Atturnie replyed & sayde he vsed no shiftes, but he had hearde the daye before that this cause woulde not holde, for that Mr Atturnie's examynacions taken by himselfe showlde not be hearde, but disallowed, & that Mr Budde (that is sollicitor to ye Countes of Lester) tolde him so muche: & therefore he appealled to ye Judgemente of ye Courte, & desyred he mighte haue Justice, for that belonged vnto him. The

Depositions in the Ecclesiastical Court not admitted

Nor those taken privately by the Att.-Gen.

[p. 180]

[1] See *ante*, p. 13.
[2] See *ante*, p. 16.
[3] See *ante*, pp. 22, 26, 29, 64, 94.
[4] Sir John Popham had been Attorney-General from June 1581 to June 1592.

1605 May 1 Chauncellor aunsweared there was no man here vsed any shiftes; Justice belonged to all, & he neede not doubte of it; & therefore desyred the Judges to delyuer their opinions: Wherevpon the Judges all agreede that in cases of Treason, Felonie, & criminall causes, the Atturnie generall mighte take examynacions; & if the same wytnesses were examyned for the same matter in Courte, & had made aunsweare to an Interrogatorie that there examination taken by the Attornie is true in all pointes, then the same maye be reade, otherwyse not, & not before the aunsweare to suche Interrogatorye be reade: w[ch] resolution of the Judges muche dislyked the Atturnie for that the examynacions taken before himselfe in a masse, as it were, were a speciall good inducemente to y[e] whole matter; & the Atturnie tooke not his bookes agayne, nor spake any more that wholle daye. & the Courte sate sylente a prettie space, & at y[e] laste the kinge's sergeaunte reade manye wytnesses, but nothinge to the firste or seconde of his diuisions, but to the thirde and fourthe; and spente that wholle day, yet ended not, the Courte syttinge vntill after twelue a clocke.'

[p. 181] 1605 May 3

In Camera Stellata, coram Consilio ibidem, Veneris, 3 Maij, 1605.[1]

Sir Robert Dudley's case

'The whole daye was spente in y[e] openinge of y[e] Cause betwene the Lo. Sidnie & Sir Roberte Dudlie one the pl[aintiff's] side. & y[e] Courte was of opinion that it was Fitte the Defendaunte showlde be patientelye & fauourablye hearde, & rather haue more then lesse time then the pl[t] had: & therefore Wednsedaye & Fridaye nexte was appointed for it: & the reportinge thereof I will spare vnto those times. For vpon the motion of the Lo. Cecill, the installation[2] of the Earle of Northampton was deferred that this Cause mighte be hearde.'

[1] Seventeen Councillors and Judges were present.
[2] Probably as Knight of the Garter. He was installed May 16, 1605.

In Camera Stellata, coram Consilio ibidem, Mercurij, 8 Maij, 1605, adonque presente, Lo. Chauncellor, archeuesque de Canterberie, Lo. Tresorer, Lo. Chamberlin, Lo. Northumberlande, Lo. Cumberlande, Lo. Deuonshire, Lo. Northampton, Lo. Vicounte Cranbourne ore Counte Salisberie,[1] euesque de Londres, Lo. Zouche, Lo. Knowlles, Lo. Wartton, Lo. Ch. Justice, Lo. Ch. Baron, Judge Warberton, Judge Yeluerton, Secretarie Herberte & Sr John Fortescue. 1605 May 8

The same cause was heard on the part of the defendant, '& aunsweared by Sir Henry Hubbarde, *Sergeante del leye.* Firste, in the behalfe of Sir Rob^te^ Dudlie, he renouncethe the Kinge's title, & layes all mann^r^ of title, eyther for dignitie, honor or reuenewe, at the Kinge's Feete: And for the attestation of Lester himselfe for to proue his seconde mariage, it Can not be of any force for that he is *pars rea.* SIR ROBERT DUDLEY'S case The defendant's case opened

'And touchinge the wytnesses Rouse & Reeue, they were infamous instrumentes of Drurie: & for Elizabethe Drurie, her examynacyon was taken by Mr Atturnie in wrytinge, & examynacions penned are not to be receaued, muche les when they are drawne by aduyse, & the Case the laste daye was mystaken. For then it was delyuered [p. 182] that before the bill or cause dependinge, wytnesses were examyned by Mr Atturnie before himselfe, but it now appeares that theise wytnesses were examyned before Mr Atturnie since the byll put in & this Cause Complayned of in this Courte; & there is noe presydente [precedent] to warrante it, that Mr Atturnie, informinge for ye kinge & a partie that followes it & is the Relator, maye examyne wytnesses before himselfe; & hauinge searched, wee finde no presydente in Courte againste wch any excepcyon was taken, for touchinge Boothe's Case & ye Ladye Gresham,[2] it was *ore tenus,* & he Confessed it, *et ex ore tuo te Judico,* & no man excepted againste it.

[1] Sir Robert Cecil, Viscount Cranborne, was created Earl of Salisbury May 4, 1605.

[2] See *ante,* pp. 22, 26, 29, 64, 94.

1605 May 8

'The bill was exhibited 16 *Martij*, 1° *Jacob*,' & Mr Atturnie tooke the examynacyon afterwarde.

'Touchinge Henrye Fradsome, ye defend^te's^ wytnes for the legitimacion, [he] was presente at ye marriage, & a gentleman well descended & of good worthe.

'And for Webbe, a base & poore Carpenter, Thomas Bifeilde, a runninge taylor, & his boye, & Fisher, a taylor, speake vpon the reporte of twooe bothe lyuinge & neyther of them examyned. & they are examyned vpon 13 grosse leadinge Interrogatories, from wch there aunsweares differ not 13 wordes.

The defendant's deposition not to be read

'It was desyred by them that Sr Rob^te^ Dudlie's deposition mighte be reade. It was aunsweared by the Courte that to accuse himselfe ye pl^t^ might reade him, but to excuse himselfe he mighte not be reade, vnles to ye same verye Interrogatorie y^t^ ye pl^t^ reade him; but yf there were nothinge at all proued againste him, then he mighte be reade *ad informandam conscientiam*, & so mighte the wytnesses taken by Mr Atturnie himselfe before the bill depended, and not otherwise.

[p. 183]

'Touchinge the basenes & meanenes of ye defend^te's^ wytnesses' apparelle, they followe leadinge interrogatories *verbatim*, wch was much dislyked of by the Courte, & to aunsweare generallye either affirmatiuelye or negatiuelye: & the Contrarye was proued true, that they were well apparrelled, & at there owne Charge, & noe parte at Sr Rob^te^ Dudlie's or Sr Thomas Lee's charge; so that they seeme to beate there Coates rather than there persons, & shewe manye Contradictions, improbabilities & impossibilities in ye pl^t's^ owne wytnesses.

'For Joyce Barefoote, Maudlin Salisberie & Henry Fradsom, they were w^th^oute all touche, blemishe or exception, knowne to be of Credite more than 30 yeares sythence: but Drurie fell accidentallye into this busynes, & was a man that Sr Roberte Dudlye muche dislyked, & woulde not haue anye doinges w^th^; but yet spyes in publike & pryuate states (albeit they are not allwayes the honesteste men) are necessarye to be vsed. & so did Sr Robt Dudlye vse Drurie,

& not otherwyse; but w^th^oute all kinde of subornacyon or rewarde: And for Elizabethe Drurye, Called Elizabethe Hardinge, a woman not knowne to Thomas Drurye fewe monethes before he dyed, was vsed by him as his wyfe, but I thinke neuer lawfullye marryed to him.

'And touchinge Sr Rob^te^ Dudlie's letter to the late Archebishop, that Mr Atturnie showlde therevpon saie that *Dolosus versatur in vniuersalibus*, there Can not be more particulars then there is in that letter, desyringe th'archebishop himselfe to examine his wytnes (beinge in daunger by reason of ye greate plague then in London), a wytnes of greate ymportaunce touchinge a Cause of matrimonie wherevpon all his Fortunes depended, &c.; moste vnlikelye [p. 184] to be a wytnes suborned or produced by practise, when as he woulde haue the Archb^p^ himselfe to examine him.

'For the Commission, it was dulye & accordinge to Course proceeded in, & for Sr Thomas Lee's Chapleine, wch was termed a Jewe, he is a bacheler of diuinitie, the worthieste man of his profession in ye Countrye where he lyues, a verye honeste man, & his father a germaine borne & scholemaister to Edwd the sixte; & this Commission bindes no man, & therefore Can not be vnlawfull, for it is vsuall to informe the Conscyence onelye.

'And for Buswell, it was proued that some three yeares sythence to one of Sr Roberte Dudlie's seruauntes he Callde his M^r^, "Bastarde," vpon wch Sr Rob^te's^ man woulde haue stabde him, & it is so proued; *Ideo* no aduersarye raysed, thoughe it had bene lawful so to haue done, & beinge so aduysed.

'Touchinge the Lybelle, Lichefeilde was the proper place to sue in, for the defamacion beinge w^th^in that Dyoces, the Lybelle Coulde not be else where, & the sentence showlde haue bene seuerall, for the legitimacion, & for the defamacyon; wch course had not bene to be regarded, for it can preiudice no man but Buzwell.

'And for a presidente [precedent] hereof, it is the verye booke case in 22 E. 4, Corbette's case.[1]

[1] Year Book, Trin. 22 Edw. IV., No. 47; a case of slander against the Abbat of St. Alban's.

1605 May 8 'But beinge allmoste twooe of the clocke, the Cause was adiourned to the nexte daye; & even vpon the rysinge of the Courte the Lo. of Cumberlande desyred to be hearde in a motion that touchte him very neerelye: for whereas M[rs] Chauncellor, a wytnes examyned in this Cause, delyuered Collaterallye & altogether impertinente to the question ministred vnto her, that one Dennie had tolde her, & shee affyrmed it to be true, that the Earle of Lester begotte lykewyse a bastarde of the late Countes of Darbie, the now Earle of Cumberlande his syster,[1] a ladye of as greate bloode as any subiecte in Englaunde, whoe lyued many yeares in vertue & greate honor, & hathe bene many yeares [p. 185] deade neuer spotted or blemished: And thus now to be scandalized, it touchte him neere, & stirred him very muche; & [he] desyred all the hearers to suspende there Judgementes vntill they sawe theise sclaunderous persons iustly punished for theise so greate scandalles, & desyred the Lordes to haue Consyderacyon of it, that they mighte receaue Juste punishemente.

'The Earle of Salisberie seconded him, sayinge he woulde not attribute to himselfe so highe & noble bloode, yet his sister's daughter hauinge now marryed that Ladyes sonne, the now Earle of Darbye,[2] & that Ladye beinge knowne to all the Lordes to haue lyued & dyed in greate honor & vertue, it were fitte some publike example mighte be made of so greate dishonor & scandalle to so worthie personage.

'The Lo. of Northampton immediatelye therevpon tooke occasyon to saye that this kinde of dishonerable sclaunderinge great personages & Ladies of honor was a verye greate offence & worthye of greate punishemente: for in this Case one wytnes was reade that sayde that y[e] Ladye Douglas Sheffeilde had allso another base Childe besides S[r] Rob[te] Dudlie by th'erle of Lester, "w[ch]," sayde

[1] Margaret, daughter of Henry Clifford, 2nd Earl of Cumberland, married Henry Stanley, 4th Earl of Derby.

[2] Anne, dau. of William Cecil, Lord Burleigh, and sister of Robert, 1st Earl of Salisbury, married Edward, 17th Earl of Oxford; her dau. Elizabeth married William Stanley, 6th Earl of Derby.

he, "was moste false, for that honorable Ladye," said he, "hathe protested vnto mee that it was not so": & therefore [he] desyred ye Consyderacyon allso of the Courte for the same.

'Wherevpon it was ordered by the Lo. Chauncellor that messengers showlde be forthewth sente for them all, & to be dealte wth eyther by the Kinge's learned Counselle, or by the Lordes of the priuye Counselle, to receaue suche Farther punyshemente as to there honorable wysedome shall be thoughte Fytte.

'The Cause of apparaunce, aunsweare, examinacyon, publication & sentence, all in one daye, was opened, but not stoode vpon, but adiourned to the nexte daye.'

In Camera Stellata, coram Consilio ibidem, Veneris, 10 Maij, 1605, adonque presente Lo. Chauncellor, euesque [*sic*] de Canterberie, Lo. Tresorer, Lo. Northumberland, Lo. Cumberlande, Lo. Deuon, Lo. Northampton-Lo. Salisberie, euesque de Londres, Lo. Zouche, Lo. Knolles, Lo. Ch. Justice, Lo. Ch. Baron, Justice Warberton, Justice Yeluerton, Sr John Fortescue, Secretarie Herberte. [p. 186] 1605 May 10

'The same greate Cause betwene the Lo. Sidnie & Sr Rob^{te} Dudlie helde this whole daye vntill allmoste sixe a clocke at nighte: the defend^{t's} Counselle proceeded wth there proffes, & firste they did shewe that touchinge th' examynacyon of Sir Robt Dudlie's wytnesses so secrete & speedilie as he did, they helde it no offence, but a worke of pietie and Justice to examine wytnesses either by Commission or in Courte *ad perpetuam rei memoriam*, wthout Calling any partie to the same, especiallye in time of danger. & then they reade againe Sr Rob. Dudlie's letter to the Archb^p, thereby particularlye desyringe him to examine the wytnes himselfe, & plainelye decypheringe the nature, qualitie & scope of his suite: & likewise produced presidentes [precedents] to proue it vsuall to examine wytnesses by Commission *ad perpetuam rei memoriam*, & in

SIR ROBERT DUDLEY'S case

The defendant's case continued

1605 May 10 Courte, wth that speede wch ye defend^ts had done, for now it appeared that they had done it in 2 or 3 dayes.

'Serg^te Hutton tooke an excepcion to ye bill for that it Complayned of a practise & Combinacion of 3, done since Aprill, 1° *Jacobi*, & now it appeares by proffe that the practise, yf any were, was but by one & before that time.

The Attorney-General's reply

'The Atturnie aunsweared that it was well he Came so neere the plotte as he did, for the bill he preferred in haste for feare of ye parliamente that beganne shortlye after, & so, after the bille put in, he examyned some wytnesses or parties to informe himselfe, as he mighte well doe, & after that tooke his bill or informacion oute of Courte and amended the same, & afterwardes examyninge theise wytnesses againe in Courte, & they Confirminge vpon oathe there examynacions formerlye taken before the Atturnie, & now published, the resolution of the Judges th'other daye was that they oughte to be reade & are good euydence *ad informandam conscientiam iudicis.* The Atturnie like- [p. 187] wyse delyuered that legitimacion originallye is not examynable in the ecclesiasticall Courte; generall bastardye is, but speciall bastardye is not, but at the Common lawe: but whether it be loyall [1] matrimonie or noe, that is examynable there; but yf the partie be once deade, the bishope nor the ecclesiasticall Courte Can not entermeddle wth it; for mariage *de facto* is not tryable but by the Countrye, & so the bookes are Common. 22 E. 4, 39 E. 3, 12 H. 7, fol. 22.

'For Boothe's Case,[2] he sayde it was not *ore tenus* as was th'other daye informed, but by informacyon at the relatyon of the Ladye Gresham, & in that case wytnesses so examyned by him were allowed & reade, wch yf it had not bene, the practise & Forgerye had neuer Come to lighte; & so in this case; wch benefytte, yf it showlde be taken from the Kinge's Counsell, it woulde preiudice the kinge & the subiecte bothe, manye thousaunde poundes by ye yeare.

'And for his owne parte, he made greate protestations how he dearelye affected that honorable Ladye, the Ladye Sheffeilde, & how wyllinge he woulde be to speake or doe

[1] *I.e.* lawful. [2] See *ante*, pp. 22, 26, 29, 64, 94.

any good for her, & it was an ill worke to beginne this & to rippe vp the life & deathe of so honorable a peere as Lester was in his time; theise thinges can neuer prosper wth Sr Robt Dudlie, & the liues of theise twooe honorable Ladyes, the Lady Sheffeilde beinge trayned by treason [1] & betrayed by truste: but the seruice of his greate M^r^ the kinge, his oathe & dutye to him, did in theise & suche like Cases in a kinde of ineuitable necessitie Compelle him to open some thinges wch he was sorye in harte to speake, for he must not feare the face or greatenes of any person, & therefore he hoped there Lo^ps^ wonlde beare wth him in discharginge the dutie of his place, as other there now presente had done before him.

'In Conclusion he desyred three thinges, for that this was *opus sine exemplo*.

'Firste that the testimonies taken bothe by the Commission & the ecclesiasticall Courte showlde be damned.

'Secondelye that there testimonies for euer hereafter showlde be vtterlye disabled to gyue any testimonie in this or anye other Cause.

'The thirde was that the aunsweares of the Defend^te's^ that dothe any waye Concerne ye mariage, & all other Collaterall examynacyons traducinge any honorable person, showlde be damned allso.

'And the Atturnie sayde Farther, "allthoughe, my Lordes, this be one of the greateste Causes that euer Came into this Courte, yet vpon Tusedaye nexte there will be a Farre greater, that Concerned the kinge's Matie much more." [2] [p. 188]

'1. Secretarie Herberte beganne the sentence, but the Defendaunte's Counselle first desyred to be hearde a worde touchinge the laste parte of the Atturnie's motion, & produced an order formerlye made by this Courte vpon good delyberacyon that the Defendaunte's aunsweares showlde stande: & this man was of opinion that the Former order showlde stande. Sentence

[1] This seems to refer to the execution of her grandfather, Thomas, Duke of Norfolk, in 1572.

[2] Pickeringe's case, *post*, p. 222.

1605 May 10 Secretary Herbert

'1. He [Secretary Herbert] did acquyte Sir Robt Dudlye.

'He did fine Sr Wm Laighton 300$^{li.}$ & imprisonm^{t} of course.

'Maudlin Salisberie 100$^{li.}$

'G. Gosse 40$^{li.}$

'Owen Jhones 40$^{li.}$

'Hen. Fradsam 100$^{li.}$

'All the reste of the Defendauntes he did acquyte.

Sir John Fortescue

'2. Sir John Fortescue did acquite Sr Rob^{te} Dudlie.

'Sir Wm Laighton he did fine 300$^{li.}$

'The testimonies to be suppressed, but the wytnesses not to be disabled.

Justice Yelverton

'3. Justice Yeluerton did not Conceaue the Case of suche wondermente, for the like Case is in 22 E. 4, & how greate so euer it is, greatnes must not ouerswaye truthe, but there must be one euen Course helde in all Causes: & for his owne opinion for depositions drawne or wrytten before hande maye well be suspected, but if they be not taughte or instructed they Can not be punished: & for Thom. Dennie & Joyce Bartle, that speake impertinente matter to the scandale of other noble personages, to be taken oute of Courte. & for all the Defendauntes he did acquite them all.

Justice Warberton

'4. Justice Warberton did not thinke the Case so straunge, for there are presidentes [precedents] of the like nature in o^{r} bookes; but touchinge the mariage, he woulde not speake one woorde to preiudice either parte: yet he woulde not suppresse the wytnesses, for that were to take there weapons from them; but those taken in th' ecclesiasticall courte he woulde not haue them exemplifyed, [p. 189] because they were taken behinde the backe. And so did acquite them all, & the aunsweares in Courte to Contynewe.

The Lord Chief Baron

'5. Lo. Ch. Baron.' He sayde it was the honorable Freedome of this Courte for euerye man to walke one the grounde of his owne Conscyence: but he founde he was freed from speakinge anye thinge of ye marryage, of periurye or subornacion of periurye: but onelye of the practise & of th'execucion thereof, w[ch] is notorious, vnorderlye, preiudicious and Contrarye to y[e] Course of y[e] Common lawe: for no suite oughte now to be in the ecclesiasticall Courte for bastardye, by the statute of 9 H. 6; & it will therefore be to very good purpose to reporte y[e] lawe in that pointe in this place.'

9 Hen. 6, cap. 11

The Earl of Kent's case

[1] By a supplication delivered in Parliament by the Commons, it was declared by Margaret, Duchess of Clarence,[2] 'Johne,' Duchess of Yorke,[3] (sisters and, among others, heirs of Edmund, late Earl of Kent[4]), Richard, Duke of Yorke,[5] Richard, Earl of Salisbery, and Alice his wife,[6] 'Rafe,' Earl of Westmorland,[7] John, Lord de Tiptoft and Powes, and 'Joyous' his wife, and Henry Gray,[8] the kindred and other of the heires of the said Edmonde [late Earl of Kent], (to wit, the said Duke [of York] son of Anne, daughter of 'Alinour,' another of the sisters of the said Edmund[4]; the said Alice [Countess of Salisbury], daughter to Alianour another sister of the said Edmund; the said 'Rafe' [Earl of Westmorland], son of Elizabethe, another sister of the said Edmund; the said 'Joyous' daughter of the said 'Alinour' mother of Anne; and

[1] This is taken almost *verbatim* from the preamble to the Statute, 9 Hen. VI. cap. 11.

[2] 2nd daughter of Thomas, Earl of Kent. She mar. 1st, John Beaufort, Earl of Somerset and Marquess of Dorset, and 2ndly, Thomas Plantagenet, Duke of Clarence.

[3] Joan, 3rd daughter, mar. 1st, Edward, Duke of York, 2. William, Lord Willoughby, 3. Henry, Lord Scrope of Masham, 4. Sir Henry Bromflete, afterwards Lord Vesci; she ob. s. p. 1431.

[4] Edmund Holland, 4th Earl of Kent; his elder and only brother Thomas, 3rd Earl, had predeceased him; he had 6 sisters, (1) Eleanor, (2) Margaret, (3) Joan, (4) Eleanor, (5) Elizabeth, and (6) Bridget, a nun at Barking.

[5] Eleanor, eldest daughter, mar. 1. Roger Mortimer, Earl of March, 2. Edward, Lord Cherleton of Powis. By her first husband she had a dau (and eventual co-heir) Anne, who mar. Richard Plantagenet, Earl of Cambridge, and was the mother of Richard, Duke of York.

[6] Eleanor, the 4th daughter (there were two Eleanors), mar. Thomas Montacute, 4th Earl of Salisbury; she had an only daughter, Alice, wife of Richard Neville (son of Ralph, 1st Earl of Westmoreland), who was created Earl of Salisbury *jure uxoris*.

[7] Elizabeth, 5th dau., mar. Sir John Neville (son of Ralph, 1st Earl of Westmoreland), and was the mother of Ralph, 2nd Earl of Westmoreland.

[8] Eleanor, the eldest dau., had by her 2nd husband, Edward, Lord Cherleton of Powis, two daughters and co-heirs, (1) Joan, wife of Sir John Grey, Earl of Tankerville: Henry Grey was Joan's son and heir; (2) Joyce, wife of John, Lord Tiptoft and Powis.

1605 May 10 the said Henry Gray son of Joan daughter of the said 'Alinour'), that one 'Alinour,' wife of James, Lord de Audelie,[1] pretending, calling and affirming herself to be the daughter and heir of the said Edmund, late Earl of Kent, and begotten and born in a pretended marriage had between him and 'Custance,' late the wife of Thomas, Lord Dispenser, as by the said supplication is supposed, that the said 'Alinour' wife of the said James, [Lord de Audeley,] is a bastard, and that there never was any marriage made, had or solemnized between the said Edmund and 'Custance'; but the said Edmund by the command, wish and agreement of King Henry IV., grandfather[2] of our sovereign now the King [*i.e.* Henry VI.], after great, notable and long embassy had and sent to the Duke of 'Millain'[3] for a marriage to be had between the said Edmund and 'Luce,' sister of the said Duke of 'Millain,' did take to wife, and openly and solemnly married the said 'Luce' at London;[4] the said 'Custance' then living, and being there present, did not claim the said Edmund as her husband, nor any dower after his death. The which marriage between the said Edmund and 'Luce,' so had and solemnized, continued, without any interruption by the said 'Custance' or any other, during the life of the said Edmund, as divers Lords and other credible and notable persons of the Realm have well in their remembrance: And how, after the death of the said Edmund, the said 'Luce' was endowed of his lands, as his lawful wife, continuing her estate thereof peaceably all her life. Nevertheless the said 'Alinour' wife of James [Lord de Audley] with great subtlety, imagined process, privy labour, and other means and coloured ways, to the intent that she might be certified legitimate [*mulier*] by some Ordinary in case bastardy should be alleged in her person, had brought (as it is said) in examination before certain Judges in the

[1] James Tuchet, 5th Lord de Audley.

[2] The word in the text is *ave*.

[3] Duke of Milan.

[4] The marriage took place at the Priory of S. Mary Overy, Southwark, in 8 Hen. IV. She was buried at Austin Friars, Broad Street. Dugdale's *Baronage*.

Spiritual Court, not informed nor having knowledge of the said subtlety, imagined process, privy labour and coloured ways, certain suborned proofs and persons, with her assent and covin, deposing for her that the said 'Alianour' the wife of James was begotten of a marriage had and solemnized between the said Edmund and 'Custance'; the said Duchesses, the Duke of Yorke, the Earl of Salisberie, Alice [his wife], the Earl of Westmorland, John, Lord de Tiptofte, 'Joyous' and Henry, not being warned of this, [p. 190] nor any of them, and not knowing until a long time after the said deposition was so made, of which the said suppliants do fear themselves to be grieved and impeached of their inheritance had from the said Edmund, [Earl of Kent,] by other subtlety and labour in the temporal law to be laboured and operated by the said Lord de Audelie and Alianour his wife. As if they will commence any action against any persons with their consent and covin, or otherwise will cause such person with such assent and covin to pursue an action against them (as it is supposed that they intend to do); in which action, by the covin and assent aforesaid, bastardy ought to be alleged in the person of the said Alianour wife of James, and thereupon, by the assent and covin, an issue is to be taken and a writ to be sent to some Ordinary (where it please them), not advertised of the said subtlety, assent and covin, to certify if the said Alianour wife of James is legitimate [*mulier*] or not; before which Ordinary the same Alianour wife of James will allege and prove herself legitimate [*mulier*] by the said depositions of the said suborned witnesses, and then the party reputed as adversary against the said Lord de Audlie and Alianour his wife in the said action taken or to be taken by assent and covin aforesaid, will allege no proof nor matter, nor make any defence before the said Ordinary against the said Lord de Audlie and Alianour his wife, but suffer the matter before the said Ordinary to proceed according to the meaning of the said Lord de Audelie and Alianour his wife; so that it is very likely that the same Ordinary will certify the said Alianour wife of James

1605 May 10 to be legitimate [*mulier*], which certificate so had and made, ought by the law of England to disinherit the said Duchesses, Duke of Yorke, Earl of Salisberie, Alice [his wife], Earl of Westmerland, John, Lord de Tiptoft, 'Joiouse' [his wife], and Henry [Gray], and their issue for ever, from the whole inheritance aforesaid. Whereupon the premisses tenderly considered and to eschew such 'subtell disherisons,' as well in the said case, as in other such cases like in time to come, by the advice and assent of all the Lords, spiritual and temporal, and also at the special request of the said Commons in this Parliament assembled,[1] it is ordained and established by the authority of this Parliament, that if the said Alinour wife of James be certified to be legitimate [*mulier*] by any Court before this time, that no manner of certificate heretofore made for the said Alinour wife of James, in any wise shall put to prejudice, bind, damage, nor conclude, any person or persons but him or his heirs that was party to the plea. And that from henceforth all Justices of or in the Courts, where any plea is or shall be depending, taken or moved, in which pleas, so depending, taken, or moved, bastardy is or shall be alleged against any person party to the same plea, and thereupon an issue joined which by the law ought to be certified by the Ordinary, that the Judges or one Judge of or in the Courts where the said plea is or shall be depending, taken or moved, before the time that any writ of certificate pass out of the same Court to the Ordinary to certify upon the issue so joined or to be joined, shall make remembrance under their seals or his seal, at the suit of the demandant in this plea or the defendant in the plea in which the bastardy is or shall be alleged, reciting the issue which is joined in the same plea of bastardy, and certifying to the Chancellor of the King of England for the time being, to the intent that thereupon proclamation may be made in the Chancery for three months, once in every month, that all persons pretending any interest to object against the

[1] 9 Henry VI.

party which pretendeth himself to be legitimate [*mulier*], that they sue to the Ordinary to whom the writ of certificate is or shall be directed, to make their allegations and [p. 191] objections against the party which pretendeth him to be legitimate [*mulier*], as the law of Holy Church requireth; And the said Chancellor, having notice of the said remembrance and issue joined, and being required by the said demandant in the plea, or defendant having the said remembrance, to make the said proclamation as afore is said, the same Chancellor for the time being shall cause to be made proclamation in the form aforesaid; And the proclamation so made shall certify in the Court where the said plea in which the bastardy is alleged an other time shall be depending; And that the Judges of or in the Court where the said plea is or shall be depending, taken or moved, before any proclamation so to be made in the Chancery, shall make once such proclamation openly in the same Court, and also one other time when the proclamation shall be certified by the Chancellor of England, and made in the form above rehearsed; And then the said Judge shall award the said writ of certificate to the Ordinary to certify upon the issue so joined or to be joined. And if any writ of certificate be made or granted before that all the proclamations in the form aforesaid be made and certified, that then the said writ of certificate and the certificate of the Ordinary made or to be made thereupon, shall be void in law and of none effect. And if any writ before this time be directed to any Ordinary to certify if the said Alianour wife of James be bastard or not, and up to this time not certified, if it be certified hereafter by virtue of the said writ, that the same certificate of the said Ordinary so made shall be void and of none effect.[1]

'The Cheife baron proceeded, & sayde that wytnesses were the onelye meanes of Justice & Judgemente, & are stronger en lawe then the Judges' knowledge; & therefore that famous Judge *in temps* H[enry] 4, when euydence was

[1] This is the whole of the Statute 9 Hen. VI., cap. 11. The case is wonderfully similar to Sir Robert Dudley's.

gyuen to acquite one of a murder, the kinge, being presente, demaunded of the Judge what he woulde doe, he knowinge the partie to be guyltie of the murder; he appealled to the kinge & sayde he must gyue iudgemente accordinge to his euydence, albeit the same were Contrarye to his owne knowledge: for wytnesses must *tribuere testimonium veritati ex vtraque parte*: & it is neyther necessarie nor vsuall eyther to wryte the testimonies, or to punishe them if they be wrytten: a Jury or a Judge is to haue no rewarde, onelye wytnesses are to haue there necessarye expences.

1605 May 10

'So he Fyned Sr Rob^te^ Dudlie 500^li.^; for yf wytnesses may be thus vsed there wilbe no indifferent tryall.

[p. 192]

'He fyned Doctor Babington & Warde the Proctor, eyther of them . . . . . 100 markes

'Maudlin Salisberie	100^li.^
'Rich: Gosse	40^li.^
'Georg: Gosse	40^li.^
'Sr Wm Leighton	300^li.^
'Owen Jones	40^li.^
'Henr. Framson	100^li.^

'The testimonies to be damned, the wytnesses to be suspected hereafter & helde *suspiciosi*: & the aunsweare touchinge the mariage to be remoued. All the reste he did acquite.

The Lord Chief Justice

6. 'Lo. Ch. Justice. the ecclesiasticall lawe Can not decide this cause, but for ye mariage in facte or a precontracte and after not: for albeit it appeare by there lawe to be a sinne & shall inflicte Corporall punishemente & adiudge ye mariage voyde, yet the heire shall not be disinherited *quoad peccatum solummodo*: o^r^ lawe shall take so farre notice that where a prohibicion dothe lye they haue no iurisdiction, 22 E. 4:[1] this subornacion or practise wth wytnesses is Couerte & therefore shalbe discouered by probable Circumstances: & if a man be to vse wytnesses, & doe not offer them there necessarie

[1] See *ante*, p. 207, note 1.

Charges, & they doe not Come, he is wthoute remedye againste them; & it is impossible to remoue manye inconueniencies in the Common wealthe if this be suffered. Wytnesses examyned *ad perpetuam rei memoriam*, during there lyues they shall not be published.

'Sr Rob^{te} Dudlie hathe bene misled & ill aduysed, & Sr Wm Leighton hathe bene the principall meanes. Rycharde Gosse he did acquite. For the others, he agreede wth the Lo. Ch. baron: the depositions to be damned, & the Commission damned: for the aunsweares & depositions that were impertinente, to be sealled *sub silentio* to vse when it shalbe thoughte fitte, & the wytnesses to remaine *suspiciosi*.

7. 'The Lo. Knowlles did agree wth the Lo. Ch. Justice. Lord Knowles

8. 'The Lo. Zouche did agree that there was a practise, & an execution, & he thoughte Sr Thomas Lee the principall offendor. he Cleared the reste, & agreede wth the Lo. Ch. Justice for the fines and punishementes: for the examynacions to be damned, the witnesses to be *suspiciosi*, & the aunsweares to be reserued priuate for vse.' Lord Zouche [p. 193]

9. The Bishop of London: '*nemo post mortem accusari potest.* three mariages that are voyde: 1. of those that wante discrecyon: 2. Clandestine mariage: 3. begunne wth inordinate luste. & in all thinges agreede wth the Lo. Ch. Justice. The Bishop of London

10. 'The Earle of Salisberie: that it was a Cause of greate Consequence, rare in presidente, either in his hearinge or readinge or by any reporte, & no presidente *in hoc indiuiduo*. The Earl of Salisbury

'For Sr Rob^{te} Dudlie to reuyue his legitimacion, it is naturall, it is vsuall: & he Coulde not sentence him for any fraude of harte, or of corrupcyon; but all men lyuinge are to take notice of the lawe, & he was somewhat indiscreete, & a desire of ryches & honor did misleade him. like to deceitfull marchauntes that obscure there lightes, & so are theise examynacyons.

'So he fyned Sr Rob. Dudlie for his misdemeanor . 100$^{li.}$

'Leighton . . . . 300$^{li.}$

1605 May 10 'Warde & Babington doe participate of this misdemeanor, the wytnesses to be helde suspicious: but Drurye was sometimes the Lo. Chauncellor Bacon's man, but *necessitas cogit ad turpia.* & there are no greater shufflers then the Chauncellors whoe betraie the subiectes as seruantes betraie there maisters[1]: & *in foro conscientiae* Sr Thom. Lee's Chaplein was guyltie: he muche Commended the worthe & honor of the Countes of Lester, how well she lyued wth him all his time, notw^th^standinge all his humors, how for her mariage wth him she was longe disgraced wth the Queene, beinge one of her maides of honor & discended of royall bloude; & good Ladye for her parte, he thoughte she weyghed not Sr Robt Dudlie's fine the garter vpon her legge. he agreede wth the fines & punishementes wth the [p. 194] Lo. Ch. Justice. That the proceedinges showlde be forgotten, & the wytnesses disabled. for the Ladye Sheffeilde, he dothe verelye thinke she did expecte mariage, *sed quod dubites ne feceris,* & the principall verbe is wantinge, no preist euer spoken of, & therefore they are wytnesses that are to be helde *pro suspiciosis,* & they haue bene handlede modestelye but wth dexteritie. All to be sealled vp & safe kepte; & in all other thinges Concurres wth the Cheife Justice.

The Earl of Northampton

11. 'The Earle of Northampton: he was like, he sayde, to a man vpon a narrowe bridge, either swaruinge slippinge, or must goe leasurablye; & he that hathe a weake eie, & reades a small printe wth spectacles, had not neede goe vpon this bridge.

'The La. Sheffeilde, her weakenes, error & iudgemente hathe bene traduced to the vttermoste, & made seeme most haynouse; wch if others faultes were seene they woulde appeare *in folio* that now seeme *in decimo sexto.* Hers beinge now wrytten *vngue adamantino,* wch woulde be wth a spanishe quill. For Sr Rob^te^ Dudlie's faulte, it seems he hathe proceeded earnestly, not orderlie; his mother hathe often preached & protested this mariage, &

[1] Sir Nicholas Bacon was never Lord Chancellor. He was Lord Keeper from 1558 to 1579.

he hathe but mainteyned his wytnes, *secundum qualitatem*, & relleiued him vpon his wardroabe.

'He acquyted Sr Rob^{te} Dudlye & all the reste, & the wytnesses to be damned, but not hereafter disabled in there testimonies, nor there aunsweares suppressed.

12. 'The Earle of Deuon Cleared Sr Rob^{te} Dudlie of all practise & misdemeanor, for it is naturall to euerye one to seeke his perfection; & [he] agrees for all the reste wth the Lo. Cheife Justice. that th'examinacions showlde be suppressed, *et* ye wytnesses remaine *suspiciosi*. The Earl of Devon

13. 'The Earle of Cumberlande did acquite Sr Rob^{te} Dudlie, & in all other pointes agreede wth ye Lo. Ch. Justice. The Earl of Cumberland

14. 'The Earle of Northumberlande acquites Sr Rob^{te} Dudlie & agreed wth ye Cheife Justice, & that Dudlie's guyltie Conscience & shame wth attendinge heere showlde be all the punishemente he woulde laye vpon him. The Earl of Northumberland

15. 'The Lo. Tresorer reade all his notes, & Commended as this Case was the leadinge Interrogatories [*sic*]: Sir Rob. Dudlye he fined as the Earle of Salisberie had done, & for the reste of the Fines he agreed wth the Lo. Cheife Justice. [p. 195] The Lord Treasurer

16. 'The Archebishop of Canterberie sayde that he woulde speake his Conscyence & be leade by no man's Collections; & did acquyte them all of all vndue, vnhoneste or fraudulente practise, & agreed in all thinges wth Judge Warberton & Yeluerton. The Archbishop of Canterbury

'*Quae non prosunt singula multa iuuant.*

'For it is *in tutiorem partem* to absolue & not to Condemne. wytnesses examyned *ad perpetuam rei memoriam* in l'ecclesiasticall Courte, if they are not published wthin a yeare, they are voyde.

17. 'The Lo. Chauncellor sayde th'onelye pointe to iudge vpon the bill was not periurie nor subornation, (for wthoute periurie they Can not punishe subornacion), but onelye a practise: & for that another man's Conscience was not to leade him, for if his owne sonne Come before him, god sees his Conscience, & he must doe as he will Lord Chancellor

1605 May 10 giue an accounte: but Sr Rob^te Dudlye was guyded by vnskylfull Counselle: & his faulte was wante of discretion, ignoraunce & ill aduyse, & he did acquyte him *a toto sed non a tanto*: for the righte [*sic*] of mariage, it is to be ruled by the Common lawe, & the discrecion of ye Judges will obserue rules in examinacion of wytnesses, for there is no other rule to dyrecte them: & there is no suborner wth oute periurye: *et quod iustum iuste, bonum bene, persequeris.* A wise Commissioner will heare a wytnes *viua uoce* and admitte noe wrytinge: & not sworne bindes no man. for as wordes haue seuerall soundes, so wytnesses & examynacyons haue seuerall sences: theise leadinge Interrogatories the Lo. Bacon (of whome I haue learned muche) was wonte to Call them "derogatories."[1] *forma iuramenti par le ciuill leye non sufficit per relationem.*

'He fined Dudlie . . . . . 100^li.
'Laighton . . . . 100^li.
'G. Gosse . . . . 20^li.
'H. Fradsam . . . . . . 30^li.

'Babington & Warde he did acquite, for that it was onelye ignoraunce & noe Corrupcion nor falsitie.

[p. 196] 'The wytnesses were too forwarde, yet they are to haue there charges duringe there examinacion. The examinacions to be damned, & the bille & aunsweares to be sealled vp, & the wytnesses remaine *suspitiosi.*

'And so thus was this greate Cause at 6 a clocke at nighte sentenced, but I feare not ended.'

1605 May 14

In Camera Stellata, coram Consilio ibidem, Martis, 14 Maij, 1605.[2]

ATT.-GEN. *v.* PICKERINGE

Libel against Queen Elizabeth and the Archbishop of Canterbury

'The greate Cause[3] *ore tenus* by Mr Atturnie generall againste Lewes Pickeringe, a gent. of Northamptonshire, a scholer relligiouselye disposed, & the kinge's sworne seruaunte, for a lybelle supposed to be made by him at the

[1] Sir Nicholas Bacon, Lord Keeper.

[2] Nineteen Councillors and Judges were present.

[3] This case is reported by Coke, under the title of *De Libellis Famosis* (ed. 1826, iii. 254); the facts of the case are there set out very briefly.

late Archebishop of Canterberye's deathe, & pinned vpon his herse at his Funeralls, againste him, & againste the late Queene of blessed memorie, and againste the now Archbishop, & by implication againste o^{r} Kinge that now ys.

'One Bywater, sometimes a minister but now deposed, did 11 *Martij*, 1604, delyu^{r} a booke vnto the Kinge's ma^{tie} of very treasonable & seditious Contentes, & his studye beinge searched, a lybelle was there Founde, begynninge,

'"The prelate spoke. The Cananites hope.

'"The lamentacion of Dickie for ye deathe of his brother Jockie."

'And ye burden was:

'"Jockie is deade & gone,
'"And Dum Dickie is lefte alone."[1]

'Which Copie he sayde he had from Pickeringe, & he sawe it in his studye before the Archebishop's deathe, & Pickeringe did dictate it to him & he wrote it: this he did Confesse 23 *Martij*, 1604.

'Pickeringe now aunsweared that he tooke it to be no lybelle, & that he gaue a Copie of it, & beinge of a deade man he tooke it no offence.

'This lybelle, sayde the Atturnie, Conteines 2 generall partes, 1. a defamacion of the deade & lyuinge, 2. a commaundmente wth a Comminacion proceedinge oute of popishe ambition or Cankred enuye. Coniuringe theise [p. 197]
wth ye Collyers of Croydon to sing a *Dirige* [round] aboute the Archebishop's herse

'"Masked impietie, Cunninge hipocrisie,
'"Prelates' pope, Jesuites' hope,
'"Papistes' broker, Atheistes' Cloker,
'"Latin Doctor, Deuill's Proctor,
'"Dum dog's patron, Non residentes' Champion,
'"Oure reformers' sclaunderer, True pastors' punisher,
'"Colored Conformitie, Vaine superstition,
'"Olde virgin's spectacle."

[1] *Jockie* probably refers to *John* Whitgift, the late Archbishop, and *Dickie* to *Richard* Bancroft, his successor.

1605 May 14 'But for Queene Elizabethe, she was Famous and renowned throught all the worlde for her wisedome, relligion, Constancie, & for her magnanimitie admyrable; wch is a very greate scandale to her to haue suche a spectacle, & to the kinge to be Crowned by him: but I saye to this lybeller, as it was sayde of Diogenes that hurled downe ye Chaire & Cushyons that were sette for Aristotle, that there was greater pride in him.

'*Nefas super mortuos gloriari*, it is a poison. And I will proue these three thinges to be in theise libellers, 1. Masked impietie, 2. Cunninge hipocrisie, 3. Colored Conformitie. And firste they shewe it in 2 of the beste workes, preachinge & prayer: for it was plotted by Biwater & his Complices that in there sermons & praiers they showlde stirre the people to a desyre of reformacyon, wch is not tolerable in a monarchie but in a Democracie, & theise desires haue their generacyons: & so settes downe firste his title, aduise tendinge to reformacion. secondlie, the state of Englande wealthe & strengthe (sinewes of ye warre) by sea & lande, soldiers, sailers, commaunders, Counties, hundreds, parishes, families, people. 3. Motiues to reformacion, & traduce the kinge that he woulde proue so resolute in religion as heathen kinges, as Nabuchodonozer, Cyrus, Darius: the verye title to rebellyon, [p. 198] 4 R. 2, 413, in the Chronicle. 28 H. 6, Jacke Cade, alias Mende-all. Kette's oathes of reformacion.

4. '*De iure regni et ecclesiae.*

'*Mors in olla viri dei.*

'To insinuate to the people that a generall Counselle were necessarye, & that yf the kinge will not lycence it, whether oughte not the people wthoute tumulte & sedition [to] assemble themselues, Dependinge vpon this title Clero-laicall: & so Concludinge that the kinge hathe nothinge to doe wth the Churche, nor the Churche wth the kinge, so denyethe all ecclesiasticall iurisdiction.

'5. A booke delyuered to Pickeringe wch is treason againste god, wrestinge ye scriptures & examples of the wicked kinges againste ye kinge, charginge him to bringe in poperie. a very Paschall fitte for Rome, Copied by Pickeringe.

'But againste Pickeringe onelye the libelle.

'*Infamatoria scriptura. famosus libellus quod nullus scribere vel dictare sub pena capitis.*

'19 Leuitic. 22 Exodus.

'The lawe is grounded vpon this texte 10 Ecclesi. The indignacion of the harte treason: allthoughe the libelle be true & ye person infamous, yet it is a greate offence. & by ye Course of lawe a lybelle is founde an olde sinne. for ye state & gouernmente is delyuered to ye magistrate, & therefore any priuate deliuery or wrytinge of a lybelle is a greate offence: yea, to see it, heare or reporte it.

'"Catte, ye Ratte, & Louell ye dogge," &c., coste him his life.[1] A blessed time for lawe & euen examples.

'*Summa petit venti* [?] Dauid, in there gates & drinkinge. Job impatient of a libelle: 30 Job.[2]

'For the Archbishop deade, the walles doe blesse his memorie, who hathe often spoken here grauelye & breiflye, he was slowe to anger & placable: & of greate experyence, ye loadestone of wisedome; & the belle towlinge (a Christian Ceremonie) the lybelle was made.

'*Corpore magnanimo leo et lupus et vrsus.*

'*Laudari a laudato viro vituperium est.*

'The psalmiste saythe those lips shalbe put to sylence [p. 199] y^t^ speake cruellye, disdainefullye, & despightefullye.

'3 Daniell, 6; 25 Daniell, 28; but this Courte Can not proceede wth Bywater: he drawes deeper.

[1] William Collingbourne was hanged and disembowelled in 1485 'for sondry treasons, & for a ryme which was layde to his charge, that he shulde make in derysion of the kynge and his counsayll, as folowith.

"The catte, the ratte, and Louell our dogge,
"Rulyth all Englande vnder a hogge."

The whiche was ment, that Catisby, Ratclyffe, and the lorde Louell, ruled the lande vnder the kynge, which bare the whyte bore for his conysaunce.' Fabyan's *Chronicle*, p. 672.

[2] 'Job, 30, ver. 7 & 8, *Filii stultorum et ignobilium, & in terra penitus non parentes, nunc in eorum canticum versus sum, & factus sum eis in proverbium.* And it was observed, that Job, who was the mirror of patience, as appears by his words, became *quodammodo* impatient when libels were made of him; and therefore it appears of what force they are to provoke impatience and contention.' Coke's *Reports*; *loc. cit.*

1605 May 14

'Humilitie an incidente inseparable to true religion.

Sentence

Sir John Fortescue

'1. Sr John Fortescue fined him 1000$^{li.}$, imprisonmente, to weare papers one y^{e} pillorie heere & in Cheapeside, & his eares nailled.

Justice Yelverton

'2. Yeluerton. fine 1000$^{li.}$, imprisonmente, & vnles he doe Confesse y^{e} author of y^{e} lybelle, to weare a paper at the pillorie in Westminster & Cheapeside.

Baron Saville

'3. Sauuelle. 1000$^{li.}$, imprisonment, pillorie heere, in Cheape & at Northampton, & if he doe not Confesse, his eares to be tacked.

Justice Fenner

'4. Fenner *agree al eux.*

Chief Baron

'5. Ch. Baron, fine 1000$^{li.}$, imprisonmente *duraunte le volunt le roy*, pillorye heere, in Cheape, at Northampton, & at Croydon in Surrie, & if he will not Confesse, his eares to be tacked.'

Kinloss, M.R.

6. Kinlosse, Master of the Rolls, agreed with them.

Lord Chief Justice

'7. Lo. Che. Justice. wthoute all debate a lybell is heere to be dealte wthall: & theise sorte of people woulde bringe all to disorder & confusyon, a pope in euerye parishe. For a libelle & sclaunder againste a pryuate man, he shall haue an accion of ye case; againste a noble man, *Scandalum magnatum.* a libelle is a breache of ye peace, & is not to be suffered, but punished: yf a man kill one wth a sworde or poison, there is defence & iustice for it, & this is a poison in ye Common wealthe, & no difference of ye deade or lyuinge: & th'offence to the state dyes not: & ye deade archebishop's vertues were manie, & the kinge's entraunce and gouernemente admirable. & for ye fine, imprisonmente, & tackinge vpon ye pillorie, he agreed wth the reste.

Lord Knollys

'8. Lo. Knowlles Commended ye deade Archebishop, in wisedome & learninge. Comparable to anye, & in his deathe a patterne to all; & agreethe wth the reste in all.

[p. 200]

Lord Zouch

'9. Lo. Zouche, loues breuitie, & he hathe a good grounde, & agreede in all thinges wth the reste.

Bishop of London

'10. The Bishop of London. *Episcopus signum contradictionis.* Chrisostom & Athanasius *Non scientia verborum sed scientiarum diuinarum et humanarum. rigidi puritani.*

'*Publica iniuria in omnia committitur.*

'The hate of ye Calumniator turnes ye vertues of ye deade into sinnes, & by ye Ciuill lawe it is Capitall: & in Fine & punishemente he agrees wth the reste.

'11. Salisberie. A libelle in generall & particuler, called a wrytinge defamatorie, published wth hande, worde or wrytinge, & he doe not produce an author, he is the publisher: For Pickeringe, he is a gentleman borne of noble howses, ye kinge's seruaunte, & a professor of relligion: an outwarde profession, & now shewethe his inwarde disposition: relligion dearer then life to all men of good Conscyence, & nothing hinderethe more then Calumniacion, a serpentine humor; there ende is faction, their zealle blinde Furie: & there is no presydente [precedent] to equalle the Archebishop that ys deade: & it is no vice to be an olde virgin & haue spectacles: & benefites binde mee: she was a woman by Creation, but by byrthe a Queene, by her gouernemente memorable, by her deathe happie, & the woonder of her sexe, & had all regalle partes, stoute & magnanimous, her gouernemente happie, longe, victorious, moderate, w^th^oute extraordinarye persecutions, shee did an acte of essence[1] 24 howres before her deathe, ingeniouselye & louingelye declare that shee woulde hate her selfe yf any but K. James showlde succeede her[2]: For the Archebishop, he was at his begynninge a scholler, M^r^ of a howse, a bishop, & then Metrapolitan, a Counsellor, a wryter & a preacher wrastlinge wth extremities: but vertue is ye mediocritie: to the factious, turbulente & virulente, he was ye worste; for lenitie, in theise growinge, swellinge times, drawe inconueniences vpon the state: in pointe of blood not violente: educated many; free from games; Chaste, for no woman seene in his house: he was Josyas' votarye, earlye dedycated to god's seruice: this was a barberous windinge sheete, wch faulte deserues what the Capacitie of this Courte Can laye vpon him; for it is a growinge disease, not a disipation, but a totall Corrupcyon: & for the kinge, my M^r^, a renouned, religious & iuste kinge,

Lord Salisbury

[1] Importance; 'A matter of great use and essence in studying.' Bacon, *Advancement of Learning*, II., xv., § 1. See *N. E. Dict.*

[2] See *ante*, pp. 164, 177, and Appendix XI.

1605 May 14 labouringe to auoyde scisme in Europe: For the Fine and punishemente he agrees wth the reste, but yf he make an open & honeste Confession, he freede his eares.

[p. 201] Lord Northampton ‘12. Northampton. Scipio obserued time, occacyon & place: Celebrate his memorie, redeeme his honor: & this offence was Capitall till Augustus: he hates Flatterye, & yet loues to gyue euerye man his deserued allowaunce: he woulde wrestle wth any man in skill, & endaunger any man by argumente:

‘*ad ornatum non ad essenciam.*

‘They sowe tares y[t] goe aboute *separare fratres.*

‘Demaunde a kingedome & rise againste Moses.

‘The seede of schisme & sedition springes euerye daye: Luther & Erasmus thruste & drawe: *visio pacis, lune,* Jerusalem & Jerichoe. amongste vs there are no essentiall impedimentes in doctrine, & it is not *pena sed causa* makes martyrdome. Agar had stripes & wepte.

‘He was *amator pacis, amicus reipublicae: verbo, opere, cibo.* & so for Fine & punishemente he agrees wth y[e] reste.

Lord Devon ‘13. Deuon agrees wth the reste in all.

Lord Cumberland ‘14. Cumberlande did so.

Lord Worcester ‘15. Worster did so; & Cumberlande, Worster & Zouche did all delyuer that they were at one time the dead Archebishop's pupilles in Cambridge, & that euerye nighte they Came to his Chamber, & reade a Chapter, & hearde prayers; & he laboured more to instructe them in true groundes of religion then in any other humane scyence, & wanne [1] Worster & Cumberlande from Poperie.

Lord Northumberland ‘16. Northumberlande agreede allso wth the reste.

Lord Dorset ‘17. Dorsette [2] agree in all, & added that he woulde haue him weare a Collier's sacke vpon the pillorie at Croydon.

Archbishop of Canterbury ‘18. Archebishop. *Qui expectat miraculum, ipse miraculum.*

‘*Scientia cum consensu, conscientia.*

‘For 20 yeares paste he had knowne the deade archbishop, & euerye daye 4 times he was vpon his knees at

[1] For ‘weaned.’

[2] The Lord Treasurer.

pryuate prayer, &c. & agreede in all thinges wth ye reste.

'19. Chauncellor. this lybelle is false, infamous, scandalous, lyinge & sclaunderous. Lord Chancellor

'*Qui laudatur in ore, flagellatur in corde.*

'The tonges of men Can adde nothinge to Whitgifte, nor the dyuelles take from him.

'Albeit there be a Cession, yet ye Crowne dyes not. No kinge can maintaine suche a line as ours.

'*Boni hominis facile est lacrimare.*

'*Imperio maximus: exemplo rarissimus.* & in knowledge & relligion excellente. [p. 202]

'*Mouere seditionem regni* is treason.

'The Donatistes they saye *sanctum est quando et tam diu volumus.*

'The Cause of lybellinge proceedes from an inquiete & intemperate spirite, not obeyinge gouernem^{te}; the ende is yor will, or else ouerthrowe peace of churche & Common wealthe bothe: not vniformitie, but multiformitie. *Dignitas delinquentis auget crimen.*

'Pickeringe's faulte is the Contryuinge & publishinge. A man Charged vpon his alleageaunce to aunsweare, yf he refuse it is a Contempte, & he shall haue punishemente for it.

'He agreede to the higheste punishemente: & he knowes not how to accounte to his soueraigne for this daye's worke, for that it is Capitall.

'And the lawe of the Lydians was to punishe ye lybeller *per torturam et mortem.* the Indians by drawinge bloude oute of the tonge & eares, & to be offered in sacrifice: for ye sclaunderer & hearer hathe the dyuelle.

'*Nunquam dicuntur nimis, quae non discuntur satis.*

'Kinge Edgar *et Canutus, conuitiatori lingua exciditur.*

'Gideon of Colchēster sentenced.

'*Euesque de* Chichester allso.

'Chauncellor *de* Sarum.

'Vowell *versus* Cheife Justice FitzJames. his eares Cutt of.[1]

[1] John FitzJames was Chief Justice of the King's Bench from

1605 May 14

'Chalmley recorder.

'Baker *per* Dier.

'John Snow, "no Justice in ye starre Chamber."

'Richarde Whitfeilde.

'Now it is a lybellinge time.

'His sentence was imprisonm^{te} for a yeare & then duringe the kinge's pleasure, pillorye heere, at London, Northampton & Croydon, & to weare a sacke yf it mighte stande wth the sentence of ye Courte.'[1]

[The next two pages are blank.]

[p. 205]

1604–5 March 9

Al l'Assises al Grinstede in Sussexe, Veneris et Saturni, 8 et 9 Martij, 1604 [1605], Gaudie et Daniel Judges la.

Ersefielde *v.* Bishe

Barratry

One John Bishe of Woorde, gentleman, 'was formerlie endyted at ye Quarter Cessions for a Common Barrettor.[2] And he remoued it into the kinge's benche, & there pleaded to it "not guyltie"; wherevpon yssue was ioyned, & now Sr Thomas Ersefeilde of Tilgate[3] in ye s^{d} parishe of Woorde, broughte it to a tryalle; & bothe the Judges satte to heare the same, & spente allmoste Fowre howres in it; & he was Charged wth manye Causes of mainteynaunce, & stirringe & procuringe of suites, & many other vilde practizes of desceite and mallice, of maintayninge suites, takinge monie for Compoundinge and endinge Causes, & plainelye proued againste him to the number of 26 or 28, so that all men Condemned him for a most daungerouse & turbulente person to lyue in a Cuntrye; & the people of ye Cuntrye for the moste parte stoode in awe & Feare of him, & durste scarce delyuer anye euydence againste him; but it appeared

Jan. 23, 1526, until his resignation in 1539. Foss does not mention Vowell's case, referred to in the text, but states that Sir R. Terres was condemned to pay a fine, to stand on the pillory and to lose his ears, for "a slanderous complaint" against FitzJames, "exhibited to the king in a written book." See *State Trials*, ii. 1080.

[1] He was also fined 1000*l.*; see Appendix VII. See also Appendix XVI.

[2] One who incites and encourages lawsuits and quarrels.

[3] Sir Thomas Eversfield of Tilgate near Worth, co. Sussex; he was knighted by James I. in 1603, and was High Sheriff of Sussex in 1599. His descendants are still to be found in the county.

to ye Courte y^t ye moste parte of ye offences were before 43 Elizab., that generall pardon: yet it appeared that he was nothinge bettered, for vpon Maundie Thursedaye laste, a Communion beinge appointed in ye parishe of Woorthe, where ye sayde Bishe & Sir Thomas Ersefeilde dwellethe, & the sayde Bishe, beinge requyred to be presente at itt, refused to Come to the same, hauinge indeede receaued the Communion but twyse in 25 yeares: & a litle before the begynninge of deuyne seruyce the same daye, twooe seruauntes of the said Byshe's, by his Commaundemente, did breake downe the pue or seate in the Churche (where the Ladye Ersefeilde & Bishe's wyfe vsuallye sate), & troade it into many peeces, beinge newe made of wainsekote; allso ye s^d Bishe in sommer laste, a Commission being to be sate vpon betwene 2 straungers, bishe neither partie nor wytnesse, the s^d Bishe, interceptinge ye Commissioners' warrante for the appointemente of the daye & place, alters bothe the daye & place, & Comminge into y^e Chamber where the Commissioners sate, stealethe awaye the Commission & openethe it, so seinge the Interrogatories one eyther syde; & vpon Complainte hereof in Chauncery, was ordered to aunsweare vnto Interrogatoryes; wch rather [p. 206] then he woulde doe, he gaue the pl. $4^{li.}$ to take oute a newe Commissyon: & for that Sr Thomas Ersefeilde followed this Cause, & beinge a Justice of peace, was notwth-standinge Commaunded from the Benche while the euydence was gyuen: & it seemed that he [Bishe] was accounted a Common barrettor that had stirred or maintayned 3 or more suites, for so the worde 'Common' dothe ymporte. the Jurye laye by it all nighte, & in the morninge it was sayde they woulde finde him, & Comminge to ye barre where Justice Daniell sate, & Cryinge a verdicte as the maner is, he sayde some what bitterlye to the Jurye, that none of them knewe what a Common barrettor was, yf they did they woulde not thinke theise iuste Causes of barrettrye, & bidde them be gone, for he would not take there verdicte, neyther oughte they to gyue a pryuate verdicte, so y^t now all men thoughte they woulde haue founde it, but they

1604–5 March 9 wente together agayne, & soone after before Justice Gawdie they acquyted him.'

1604–5 March 11 **Al Assises in Southwarke in Surrie,** Lune et Martis, 11° Martij, 1604 [1605], Jacob. Regis 2°, Justice Gaudye et Daniell Judges la.

MORE v. FORSTER

Slander

Sir George More, knight, brought an action on the case againste Forster senior for words, viz. in a Commission between the said Forster, &c. ' " Sr George More is a corrupte Judge, & hathe receaued bribes, & the def^te^ hathe sette him vpon horsebacke," wch were the woordes of ye declaracion; but to approoue ye mallice of ye defendaunte, they aggrauate the euydence that Sr George More was a villainouse minded man, & had taken bribes wch others refused to take. The plaintiff's Counsell doe shewe y^t^ Sr George More was a knighte of greate worshipe & Creditte, a Justice of peace, & speciallye vsed in dyuerse Commissions in ye late Queene's time, sundrye times [p. 207] Freelye Chosen knighte of ye parliamente for the shire, & a man speciallye well deseruinge manye wayes of his Cuntrye [1]; & ye defend^te^ a man of good wealthe of a 100 marks damages 100^li.^ *per annum* in landes: & so ye Jurye founde a 100 markes in dammages: wch was thoughte by ye better sorte of the Countrye to be tooe litle, Sr George More himselfe beinge accounted the vprigheste & beste disposed to the seruyce & gouernemente of ye Countrye w^th^in ye wholle Countye: & as his Counsell well mooued, the Jurye showlde wounde him more by gyuinge him small dammages then the defend^te^ hathe done by his vilde wordes.

Slander

'Another action of ye case was broughte by another againste a woman for theise wordes, viz.:—" thou arte a stronge theife, & thou wilte stealle anye thinge; thou

[1] Probably Sir George More of Losely, co. Surrey. His sister Elizabeth mar. Sir Thomas Egerton, Lord Ellesmere, the Lord Chancellor. Sir George was High Sheriff of Surrey and Sussex, 1598; he was appointed Treasurer to Henry, Prince of Wales; Chancellor of the Order of the Garter, 1610; Lieutenant of the Tower, 1615. He was M.P. for Guildford, 1584, 1586, 1588, 1592, 1603, 1623, and for the county of Surrey, 1597, 1601, 1614, 1620, 1625. See Burke's *Extinct Baronetage*.

haste stollen my Ropes." & they founde ye wordes & gaue 5^s^ dammages.

'An action of ye case vpon an assumpsit was broughte by Heathe againste Ginkes for 10^li.^ to be p^d^ w^th^in a yeare after notice of dislike of a bargayne: ye plaintiff layde ye notice in September 27, 1601: ye defend^te^ sayes he did not giue notice that daye in manner *et* forme *prout*. ye pl. takes issue that he did gyue notice that daye, & his euydence proues his notice in December 1601. yet allowed good by the Judge, for y^t^ ye time was not matter of substance but circumstance; so of ye place. HEATHE *v.* GINKES — Assumpsit

'One was saued this assises wth ye Judges spectacles: & 2 women were Condemned vpon 1° *Jacob.* for eyther of them maryinge twooe husbandes. Bigamy

'Muddles' sonne of Godstone[1] was executed for a Robberye. Robbery

'There was a tryall for ye waye oute of ye boroughe into St George's Feilde to Lambethe Mawshe & ye banke side againste ye Citie. George Knokes was a speciall wytnesse, three Aldermen were in ye Courte & ye Recorder, yet ye tryall wente againste them.' Right of way

In Camera Stellata, coram consilio ibidem, Veneris, 11° Octobr. 1605, Jacob. Regis 3°.[2] [p. 208] 1605 Oct. 11

Cause of hearing between Sir Edward Dimmok,[3] plaintiff, and the Earl of Lincolne and Bradshawe, defendants. Bradshawe in time past was servant to Sir Robert Dimmocke, father of Sir Edward, and for reward of his service [Sir Robert] gave him a lease for years binding himself in £500 to perform the covenants. The Earl, being in malice DIMMOK *v.* EARL OF LINCOLN and BRADSHAWE — Maintenance and champerty

[1] Godstone is near Tandridge, where the Hawardes lived.

[2] Twelve Councillors and Judges were present.

[3] Sir Edward Dymoke of Scrivelsby, King's Champion at the Coronation of James I. His father, Robert Dymoke, mar. Bridget, eldest dau. of Edward Lord Clinton, afterwards Earl of Lincoln, by his first wife; the defendant, Henry, Earl of Lincoln, was son of Lord Clinton by his 2nd wife. The 'malice' referred to in the text is, no doubt, connected with this relationship. Sir Edward Dymoke died 1625.

1605 Oct. 11

with Sir Edward Dimmocke, procured some part of the land by assignment by indenture, and promised to have the statute for nonperformance of the covenants, and caused Bradshawe to extend the statute, and wrote to the Sheriff and jurors to extend it, and maintained the suit, and so committed maintenance and champerty. But Bradshawe, being the defendant, was never served with process, but kept in Dimmocke's house; and therefore the cause was adjourned until Bradshawe was produced in Court to answer the interrogatories *viva voce*.[1]

THROGMORTEN *v.* STAFFORD and others — Misdemeanour

Another cause of hearing between Sir Thomas Throgmorten, plaintiff, against Sir John Stafforde, Edward Poines, and three others, defendants, for misdemeanour at the muster, principally against Edward Poines.[2] At the general muster of trained men, one Chambers being called and present, Poines said that he should not serve, being married to his sister, and drew his 'cemitere'; also his father Mathew Poines, a man weak and aged, being a Justice of the Peace and one bound for his good behaviour, Edward Poines signed[3] a *supersedeas* with the hand and seal of his aged father, and made a recognizance, and returned it in the name of his father. And for this he was [p. 209] fined by the greater part of the Court 100 marks, imprisonment and [to be] bound for his good behaviour. Sir John Stafforde, being a Justice of the Peace, and having lost two bullocks, finding them in pasture, charged two men with stealing them. They denied it. He said they should be had before a Justice of the Peace to answer it. They refused to go, and he with a 'ridinge rodde' struck one of them 'crosse the face & made him to reele.' And for this he was fined £20, for it was a great offence because he was a Justice of the Peace and ought to keep the peace, and thus [he was] a bad example. But in the opinion of the Court it was a small cause, and fitter for another place

Sentence

[1] See another case between the same parties, in which the Earl of Lincoln was plaintiff, *post*, May 6, 1607.

[2] See a cross bill between the same parties, *post*, p. 242.

[3] *Assigne* in MS.

than this Court; malice was the cause of the complaint, but although malice be the accuser, justice should be the punisher. And by some [of the Court] Sir John Stafforde would be admonished and not punished. *Dignitas delinquentis auget peccatum.* For the other three defendants, who never answered, and [there is] no charge against them, the Court would consider what should be done, for notwithstanding the course of the Court has been that if there are several defendants, and [the charge] is proved against one, the others shall not have costs, yet the opinion of the Court was that these three should have costs, otherwise this would remain as a libel against them. And it does not suffice for the plaintiff to rove for defendants, but to be well advised and instructed who are offenders, and who not, at his peril; otherwise it would be mischievous, and such defendants would not be [capable of being] witnesses.

Malice, the accuser; Justice, the punisher

In Camera Stellata, coram Consilio ibidem, Mercurij, 16 Octobr., 1605.[1]

1605 Oct. 16 [p. 210]

Dagge, plaintiff, Dunkellin and others, defendants, for forging a warrant of the Sheriff and inserting special bailiffs' names after the warrant was sealed and delivered with blanks, and also for riot in rescuing process. For the first offence [he] was fined £20, and it was ruled that such an offence had been sentenced in this Court several times. The Lord Chancellor vouched Bostocke and Lecheford's case.[2] Bostocke was removed from the Commission [of the Peace] for granting a warrant with blanks and lending his name: for it is a great offence in any, but especially in the Sheriff, if he had been made a party, because it is commonly used that the Sheriff is sworn to serve and execute process by indifferent men. But as to the riot, it was clear, and it seemed that there was a riot on the other side if it had been complained of.

DAGGE *v.* DUNKELLIN and others — Forgery

Sentence

Another cause of hearing between ,[3] plaintiff,

[1] Twelve Councillors and Judges were present.
[2] See *ante*, p. 108.
[3] Blank in MS.

1605 Oct. 16

WARREN'S case

Perjury, misdemeanour and practise

and Robert Warren the father and Robert Warren the son, defendants, for perjury and misdemeanour or practise. Robert Warren the son, having borrowed of the plaintiff £20 for one year, procured one Reache, an informer, and gave him money, and bound him by an obligation to prosecute this under the Statute of Usury, and bound himself also to the said informer by an obligation to prove this usury, and said that the plaintiff contracted for £20 lent for a year to have £22 and two days' work in the carriage of clay, which amounted to 10s. And Warren the father was privy to all this, and simply allowed it, but did not practise nor procure it. Reche, the said informer, proceeded with an information in the Exchequer Chamber, and Warren the son, by oath there, proved the usury, which is the offence now complained of. Reche was not made a defendant [in this present case]. But Warren the son, hearing that they are sued in this Court, said to Reche: "Burne yor bonde & I will burne mine, & then we will sweare there was no bondes." But this was not complained of in the bill, but proved in the depositions [*liuers*], which shows good affection in Warren the son. And the bill complains of this as an offence, before the Statute by which it is to be punished, but not without less punishment than the Act enjoins, 5 Eliz. cap. 9, which is £20 fine, six months' imprisonment and perpetual disablement as a witness. The father, for consenting to the practise, was fined £100; the son 200 marks for the practise, 100 marks for the perjury, and the punishment of the Statute. On the sentence, the Earl of Northampton delivered a noble and religious speech against usury, condemning it as abominable by God's law and man's, and accursed both in the borrower and the lender, and it is an absurd distinction between biting usury and gentle usury, for he said that by the Scripture all manner of usury is prohibited. The Lord Chancellor agreed with him, and said that it is a great 'mistakinge' [to think] that usury of £10 for £100 is allowed by our law; not so; for by 13 Eliz. cap. 8, all manner of usury is prohibited; and so by the Law of God

[p. 211]

Sentence

The Earl of Northampton on Usury

it is a sin and detestable; and the taking of more than £10 for £100 is punished, but [even this] is not allowed, nor any manner of usury; for in his opinion [*par luy*] it is 'Judaisme,' and [usurers] were called *mercatores Judaizantes*; "and for my own part it was of such force with me that I will never take use again, notwithstanding I grant my money on condition [to be fulfilled] if I be then alive, otherwise I lose as much as I shall gain if I live."

In Camera Stellata, coram Consilio ibidem, Mercurij, 23 Octobr., 1605.[1] [p. 212]

1605 Oct. 23

The Countess of Rutland's case — Arrest of a Peeress

The Attorney-General informed against one Milwarde, a goldsmith in London, Stephens, a serjeant of London, his two yeomen, and Milwarde's servant, and John Stone, the Secondary of the Counter, for arresting the Countess Dowager of Rutland:[2] and showed in his information that the King is the author of all honours and dignities, '& y^t all titles of honor & dignitie doe yssue from him, as beames of his greate dignitie & diamonds of his Crowne, & streames of that greate Ryuer,' and that by the ancient law of this realm all such honourable persons of dignity, as princes, dukes, earls and barons temporal (for he did not meddle with the 'spiritualtie,' and all persons of this realm are divided into two degrees only, the nobility and the commonality, the 'upper & lower howse'), have this privilege, that their persons cannot be attached by *capias* for debt or other personal matter, if it be not contempt; and as to this he vouched the authority of 35 E. 3, fo. , 14 H. 6, fo. 62. 48 E. 3.[3] Barons or persons of dignity shall not be of juries; and the King himself shall try honours. And he

Peers cannot be arrested

[1] Thirteen Councillors and Judges were present.

[2] Isabel, dau. of Sir Tho. Holcroft, knt., of Vale Royal, Cheshire, and widow of Edward Manners, 3rd Earl of Rutland and 15th Baron Rŏos.

1605, Oct. 24. John Chamberlain to Dudley Carleton. 'Yesterday a goldsmith in Cheapside was fined in the Star-Chamber for arresting the Countesse of Rutland vpon an execution, and yt was thoroughly argued how far noble men and women are priuiledged in theyre persons from arrests.' State Papers, Domestic, James I., Vol. 15, No. 104.

And see also Coke's *Reports*, Vol. iii. p. 360.

[3] Sir Ralph Everden's case. *Year Book*, 48 Edw. III., Mich., no. 18.

1605 Oct. 23 vouched this authority for the wives of noblemen while they keep themselves sole and do not marry ignobly; for *eodem modo constituitur, dissolvitur*, but otherwise if they be born noble.

10 H[enry] 4. Lady Spenser.

And it is a general rule that when *capias* does not lie in the original, it does not lie in the execution.

20 H[enry] 6, cap. 16. The wives of peers shall be tried by their peers also.

Contemptus nobilitatis, rebellionis praecursor. 27 H[enry] 8. For contempt process lies against the person of a countess: but the reason why it does not lie against the person of a peer or a peer's wife is not merely when he is a lord of parliament, for then their wives are not of parliament, and consequently would not have the privilege; but the principal reason is that the law intends that the King advances to dignitie such nobles as by their virtues may advance the laws and defend them and the Justice of the land, also that they are of sufficient estate to have assets to satisfy all manner of debts, so by law they are to be summoned by distress on their land and not by their bodies. And the King, if any noble has not ability, or does ignoble acts, may 'disnoble' them. All of which was the resolution of all the Judges there present. And the Attorney-General brought the law books, and showed and read the cases themselves in the books.

The reason of this

[p. 213]

The King may 'disnoble'

A peer or baron within age shall not be of parliament.

Peer or Peeress not sworn

An action of account is brought against a common person, and he craves to have an account on oath; a peer or the wife of a peer shall not do so, but only on his [or her] honour, and so [*i.e.* on his honour] he shall give his verdict. [This] was the Lady of Aburgauennie's case. But the original cause of complaint was in this way. Milwarde, a goldsmith in London, had delivered a 'border' of gold, a 'siluer howre glasse' and other commodities of the value of £90 to the Countess of Rutland, and gave a year for payment of this, and accepted her bond for it. On the day the Countess did not pay the money, and within three months afterwards, Milwarde said to a man of the Countess' that he would arrest the said Countess and drag her from her coach, notwithstanding the Lord Rosse would be there, who was her son by the marriage with her daughter, and the son and heir of the Earl of Exeter, a noble young gentleman.[1] And the said Countess, going in her coach to Charinge Crosse, the said Milwarde dealt with Stephens to arrest her, and he agreed for £10 to arrest her, the said goldsmith having an execution in the Counter [p. 214] of Woodstreete, and John Stone, the Secondary there, granted warrant thereon. And being asked if it could be served on the person of the Countess, he answered that he thought it could for anything he knew, and took only his ordinary fee for the warrant. But the serjeant said to Milwarde, "Have you not any other debt due from the Countess?" He said "Yes, £7." Then [said the serjeant], "It is good to enter an action in the Counter of the Poultrye if rescue should be made"; and thereupon he entered an action for £200. And on the return of the Countess from Charinge Crosse to Milde ende, where she lived, the said serjeant, accompanied by two yeomen, the said Milwarde and his servant, in the evening, outside Algate, came to the coach with his hat on his head, and laid his mace on the Countess' breast in the coach, and said to her, '"Madam, I doe arreste you, & you must goe wth mee." "What!" saythe shee, "doe you arreste my bodye or my goods?" "Nay, yor bodye, Madam." And very barbarouselye, vnreuerentelye & irrespectiuelye did force the Coacheman to dryue the Coache backe againe, the Sergeaunte's men turninge ye Coache wth liftinge & force, & many people gazinge into the Coache, Compelled the Coacheman to retorne his Coache & horse backe throughe the Citie to the Counter in Wooddstreate; & ye Countes Comminge to ye Counter gate grewe amazed, & desyred that ye sherife, Sr Thomas Haies, might be sente to & entreated to Come

[1] Elizabeth, daughter and heiress of Edward, 3rd Earl of Rutland and 15th Baron Roos, married William Cecil, son and heir of Thomas, Earl of Exeter; he is here called Lord "Rosse" in right of his wife.

1605 Oct. 23 to her, or to receaue her into his howse. Wherevpon the sherife Came to her to the Counter gate, & tooke her home wth him, & there entertayned very kindlye & gentleman-like. Then she asked what was the Cause of her arreste, & then they tolde her they had an execution againste her, neuer naminge the same before; whereas a Serg[te] Can not arreste any vpon an execution but he must name the same, or shewe his warrante; for w[th] his mace he Can not arreste but vpon a pleinte or action entred, but he must tell her he hathe a warrante, or that it is vpon an execution; althoughe a baillie knowne maye arreste w[th]oute shewinge a warrante but tellinge wherefore it is; but now they may be Called arrant bayllies, they are growne so skilfull. The nexte morninge the Countes prouyded the monie, payde the principall, the vse & the Costes: but shee must paye the 10[li.] to the sergaunte likewyse or else she showlde not be delyuered; w[ch] she refused to doe, & for that Cause was stayed 8 dayes longer, & then was perswaded to make a relleasse of errors, w[ch] she refused to doe lykewyse, & w[th]in twooe dayes after was delyuered, after 11 dayes ymprisonm[te].

[p. 215] 'Firste in this Case it was resolued by all y[e] Judges that the wyfe of a Duke, Earle or Baron showlde haue y[e] prIueledge that her bodye showlde not be arrested *per capias*, but in Case of Contempte, so longe as she lyued vnmaryed, or were not maryed to an ignoble man, or did no ignoble acte: & vpon y[e] reasons & aucthorities afore recyted: but for lordes of Irelande it was otherwyse, because they are distincte dignities & distincte parliamentes. Yet an Abbat here in Englande had the priuelege, 3 H[enry] 6: & for a sherife or secondarye, it was sayde that he ys bounde & sworne to execute all suche wryttes as shall Come to him. The kinge's sealle is his warrante, & he is not to examine whether it be good, or whether it will lye, or whether it be againste a person arrestable or no; he is not to dispute it, but to execute his office. W[ch] seemed reasonable, & warranted by good aucthoritie, to some of y[e] benche and barre; yet the Judges were of

Peer's wife not to be arrested except for contempt

Irish Peers

Abbats had same privilege

Legis ignorari nemini permissum est. Quod scire debes, et non vis, pro contemptu habetur.

another opinion, & delyuered that an officer oughte to be learned, & furnished wth sufficiente iudgemente & knowledge to vnderstande what he oughte to doe, & ye sherife one his perill oughte to make choyce of such a one; & therefore yf Stone, ye secondarye y^{t} made ye warrante, & Dies, the Atturnie that sued out the execucion, th'one had bene Charged in ye bill, th'other made a partie in the bill, the Courte woulde haue Censured them bothe; & for suche a faulte Complayned of in the kinge's benche of an Atturnie, he showlde haue bene hurled out of ye Courte. For the en[t]ringe of feigned actions in London & arrestinge vpon them, a Custome prescribed & vsed there, but resolued now by the Judges to be an ill Custome & againste lawe, & mischeiuous, & hathe vndone many a man; & therefore hereafter not to be vsed, for it is againste ye freedome of ye greate Charter: For ye Sergeaunte, he was muche Condemned for his Craftie & uiolent Caryage, hauinge heretofore bene allso Censured in this Courte.'

The Serjeant blamed

Sentence

And for these offences, Milwarde was fined £200, and imprisonment; the serjeant £200, imprisonment, 'stande vpon the pillorie wth papers, & disabled from euer beinge Serg^{te}. The Serg$^{te's}$ twooe men 40$^{li.}$ a peece fine, & im- [p. 216] prisonm^{te}: Milwarde's man 10$^{li.}$ fine, & imprisonm^{te}': and if the servants are not able to satisfy the fines, their masters shall pay them. The Earl of Northampton admired that the Civil Law and the Common Law agree so directly on these points of dignity; and he has another reason, that the dignity of their husbands lives in them; '& it is wth them as it is wth the eclipse of the sonne by the interposition of the terrestriall bodye, for yf she marye ignoblye, or lyue dishonorablye, her glorye is alltogether eclypsed & vanished & she losethe her priuilege.'

Semiplen probatio

20 H[enry] 6. Ladies tried by peers: but the Lord Chancellor delivered that it was a good course that great ladies and Countesses should pay their debts, so they would have no use for this privilege; and so to do is honourable.

1605
Oct. 25

In Camera Stellata, coram Consilio ibidem, Veneris, 25 Octobr., 1605.[1]

STAFFORD v. THROGMORTON and others

Maintenance, champerty, etc.

Cause of hearing between Sir John Stafforde, knight, plaintiff, and Sir Thomas Throgmorton and others, defendants, for maintenance, champerty, and other misdemeanours.[2] The case did not concern in any way Sir John Stafforde, who is the relator and informer, an evil office for so honourable a gentleman. Nevertheless malice is a good informer, but an ill judge. But now it is ready for sentence, as the Lords ought to sentence and punish it, and, the offence being proved, to raise a fine to the King. Seede the father and Seede the son are the instruments of all this suit, and reserved by Sir John Stafforde to be witnesses. First, the Court resolved that it should be heard; but if Sir John Stafforde had asked counsel of any of the Lords, they would never advise him to proceed with it: for in the former cause, Sir Thomas Throgmorton was interested as commissioner. And the Attorney said that he never allowed an informer as a witness. And another exception was objected, that the Seedes should not be witnesses since they are not only the parties solely interested in this suit and maintain part of it, but Seede the father is outlawed eight several times, and some of them after judgment, and Seede the son is outlawed five several times, and one of them after judgment also. 34 E[dward] 1. A man outlawed shall not have process. Stat. de Bigamis.[3]

Informer not to be witness

[p. 217]

It was agreed by the Court that they should not be witnesses, but if there are other witnesses to this point, they should be read also, and it would be in the election [of the Court] to give credit to them or not. For the Lord Chancellor did not think outlawed men fit persons to be in any commission or of parliament, and in his opinion [*par luy*] a relator should not be a witness.

[1] Nine Councillors and Judges were present.

[2] See a cross bill between the same parties, *ante*, p. 234.

[3] The Statute *de Bigamis* is 4 Edw. III., stat. 3; it does not appear to have any bearing on the case.

It was agreed by the Court that if a man procure a warrant in another's cause, it is maintenance A great man writes or speaks to another to appear and do his conscience or to be present at a trial: this is maintenance. But if the party speak or write to the jurors to appear, it is not maintenance, [but] otherwise to keep away [*d'estraunger*]. And a warrant for one county and served in another, is a great offence; and to keep a man in prison in his house to give evidence is an offence against the law. And a man for a personal suit may not break house, if it be not for felony or treason against the Crown. These were the offences of Sir Thomas Throckmorton, for which he was fined £200, and imprisonment. Mainten-ance, what Sentence

Dante, the bailiff, gave money; he was fined 100 marks, and imprisonment; the others £20 each, their master to pay this if they are not able.

A man may sell his land notwithstanding trespass be brought, but not if [the land itself] be in plea. And (by the Chief Justice) a man shall not arrest in another county if he has not pursued; and a special bailiff is to show his warrant, but a bailiff errant [need] not show [his warrant] but [must] show the offence. Sale *pendente lite* Bailiffs

In Camera Stellata, coram Consilio ibidem, Mercurij, 30 Octobr., 1605.[1] [p. 218] 1605 Oct. 30

Claiborne of Claiborne,[2] plaintiff, against Sir Richard Louder,[3] Gerard Louder of the Inner Temple, William Louder and Thomas Carleton, defendants, for riots, misdemeanours, and other practises to gain the land of CLAIBORNE v. LOUDER and others — Riot, etc.

[1] Eight Councillors and Judges were present.

[2] Thomas Cliburn of Cliburn, co. Westmoreland. He mar. Frances, dau. of Sir Richard Lowther, the defendant in this case. His father, Richard Cliburn, repaired or rebuilt the hall in the reign of Queen Elizabeth, and placed this inscription over the door:

RICHARD . CLEBUR . THUS . THEY . DID . ME . CAWLE .
WHO . IN . MY . TIME . BUILDED . THIS . HAULE . 1577.

[3] Sir Richard Lowther of Cumberland was knighted at Windsor, July 9, 1603; High Sheriff of Cumberland 8 and 30 Elizabeth; Lord Warden of the West Marches. One of his daughters was the plaintiff's

1605 Oct. 30

Claiborne. Which Claiborne had married the daughter of Sir Richard Louder, and Gerard Louder had married Claiborne's mother. And after the bill and answer were opened, the Lord Chancellor moved that inasmuch as this cause was between persons bound [*oblige*] in blood, it would be good to refer it to the determination and consideration of indifferent men, to establish peace and amity between them; to which the Court agreed. And thereupon it was referred to Justice Wamslowe, Baron Sauuelle and Serjeant Phillips.

Case referred to arbitration because the parties were akin

Nicholas *v.* Hichecocke and others — Forgery and riot

Another cause of hearing between Nicholas, plaintiff, relator on the Attorney's information against Robert Hichecocke, Windowe, and other defendants, for forgery and riot. The defendant Hichecocke, being bound with sureties to appear, appeared at the bar, and said that he had no Counsel and was unable to retain Counsel, and so answered for himself. The offences with which he was charged were the forgery of an injunction in the [Court of the] Marches of Wales for stay of a suit in the Court of Pipowders.[1] Hichecocke solicited a suit (not being of a House of Court or Chancery, and therefore illegal in him), and wrote to the clerk, named Crumpton, and Windowe to procure a bill and process, in the name of Lea against Weblin, and he made the process in the name of Weblin against Lea, and on the bill, without answer, procured an injunction for Weblin against Lea, and sent this to Hichecocke, who thereupon wrote to Crumpton that he had made a mistake and of necessity ought to alter the bill,
[p. 219] for he was forced to make shift. This letter Hichecocke denied, but, being compared with other letters, confessed it to be his, and by proof of witnesses it was apparent that it was his letter, written and sent by him. But it was much disliked and condemned, the granting of an injunction on a bill before any answer made. The riot

wife. He died in 1607, aged 77. Gerard and William Lowther, the other two defendants, were his sons. Gerard was appointed Chief Justice of the Common Pleas in Ireland, 1634. See *Dict. of Nat. Biog.*

[1] See *ante*, p. 88, note 3.

was in such a manner: Hichecocke, having housed corn in a barn, Nicholas, the plaintiff, with fourteen others, came with the constable to replevy, and loaded the corn on a cart, and going on the way with this, the defendant Hichecocke and others, with weapons and force, pursued the cart, turned the horses round, and stopped the corn, and wounded the plaintiff's servants, and beat the constable. And notwithstanding that replevin appertains to the Sheriff and not to the constable, the taking of the corn was illegal and riotous in them, as was complained; and the books[1] [say] and the law is that if a man be in quiet and peaceable possession of corn or other goods, he may maintain his possession with force and weapons, and if he wound another in such case it is in defence of his goods, and justifyable and lawful; for corn cannot be distrained or replevied except in cart or sacks; still when it is carried in a cart one may not fetch it again by force, for this is riotous; and so it was censured in this case. Forgery is a fruit of darkness [*obscuritie*], and "uncover" is a window that opens the proof of this. Presumptions that are vehement do not prove, but they illustrate; but if they are accompanied by preceding suspicions or by present proof, although feeble, they are good proofs. Thus, in this case, the defendant Hichecocke was formerly sentenced in this Court for forgery, and there is now great presumption and good proof against him. So he was condemned as a forger, and fined 100 marks, imprisonment, to wear papers in 'Westmester Halle' and in the Council of the Marches, and to be disabled to be a solicitor, by order of the Lord Chancellor. And the Lord Chancellor moved that he heard him graciously because he had no Counsel there. But this is *malum exemplum*, said the Attorney, and detracts from the dignity of this Court, although it was honourable in the Lord Chancellor. And at the end of the cause one Hichecocke of Counsel with him [the defendant] spoke for him and made excuse that he had not seen his client for a month past. Nicholas, the plaintiff, who informs and is the

Riot in taking corn from a barn

One in peaceable possession may maintain it by force

Sentence

[p. 220]

[1] Probably the Year Books.

1605 Oct. 30 relator, or rather *delator*, had no interest in any of the offences complained of in the bill; and the bill contains divers offences, seven or eight several forgeries of bonds, releases, etc., and charges fourteen or fifteen other defendants of good account, against whom it is only a scandalous libel, and odious to remain on the record. Nicholas had a son who was sentenced in this Court prior to this, and stirred up divers suits, because Hichecocke previously informed against him for waste in the King's wood. Now whether the bill should be withdrawn from the file or [whether] it should be entered in the Order in what manner they [the other defendants] are cleared, he[1] prayed the opinion of the Court; for in such cases [the Court] rarely assigns costs to such relators as stir and maintain suits, and [costs] by the Civil Law are not in any [such] case allowed, save *in culpa lesae maiestatis*: otherwise in all other cases by the Civil Law they [informers] are to be banished: Also he[1] prayed the opinion of the Court inasmuch as the bill complained of the forgery of an injunction for stay of a suit in the Court of Pipowders, and all the proof is for stay of a suit in the Sheriff's Court, which is very different; and now the question was, what should be their sentence. (Sentence) For the riot he was sentenced to £40 [fine], and so were three other defendants, with imprisonment of course: (Long bill) He[1] greatly misliked the length of the bill, and kept all now to the old order of the Court:—Each bill to contain but fifteen sheets of paper and not more, so it shall contain fit and necessary matter and pertinent words; and in time to come if it contain more, the Counsel shall pay the costs. And so he admonished them to take notice of this.

[p. 221] 1605 Nov. 8

In Camera Stellata, coram Consilio ibidem, Veneris, 8° Novembr., 1605.[2]

RUSWELL v. RUSWELL and others

Ruswell, plaintiff, and Ruswell and others, defendants, for riot. Hislop and others were defendants, to the number

[1] The Lord Chancellor. [2] Nine Councillors and Judges were present.

of thirteen. 'Ruswell the father, hauinge in his lyfe time aduaunced his other sonnes, the now defend^{tes}, & made a deede of guyfte to the pl^{f} of all his goods, in December 1° Jacob. dyed; & the pl. beinge in quiete possession of Cattelle & other goodes to the vallewe of 400$^{li.}$, the Defend^{tes}, to the number of 13, Come in the nighte & dryue them all awaye. & for this offence the principalles were all fyned 300$^{li.}$ apeece, & the reste a 100$^{li.}$ apeece, the pl^{f} restored to his goodes, & yet it was *in terrorem populi*, but because it was in the nighte wth suche a multitude & many that were no waye interessed in the action, all were lykewyse ymprysoned accordinge to Course: & Secretarie Herberte was of opinion to gyue the pl^{f} 200$^{li.}$ for his dammage, but it stoode not wth the sentence of the Courte, for that this Courte neuer gyues any dammage but onelye Costes.'

Taking cattle and goods by night

Sentence

Damages not given in the Star Chamber

In Camera Stellata, coram Consilio ibidem, Mercurij, 13 Novembr., 1605.[1]

1605 Nov. 13

Page, plaintiff, and Page and three other men and five women, defendants, for riot in diverting the ditch and paling [*enclosure*] of a common in the night. The proof was that the women, by the procurement of the other defendants, destroyed [*eiecte*] the ditch and the paling, and this without the privity of their husbands. And for this offence the men were fined each £40, and the women each £20. And it was agreed by the Court that it is not good to make inclosures of Commons, for this causes great offence; but it is warranted by the law. And it was ruled by the Court that if women offend in trespass, riot or otherwise, and an action is brought against them and their husbands, they [the husbands] shall pay the fines and damages, notwithstanding the trespass or the offence is committed without the privity of the husbands.

PAGE *v.* PAGE and others — Riot

Sentence

[p. 222]

[1] Seven Councillors and Judges were present.

1605 Nov. 15

In Camera Stellata, coram Consilio ibidem, Veneris, 15 Nouembr. 1605, Jacob. Regis 3°.[1]

ATT.-GEN. *v.* CLERKE and others

Sir Edward Coke, Attorney-General, informed *ore tenus* against one Clerke, 'broune baker' and purveyor to the King, and two others, deputy-purveyors, for [taking] 'Cartes.'[2] This term the Attorney also informed against one Richards, the servant of this Clerke, for taking 'pease & beanes,' and money to make provision of more, as deputy to his master. Whereas the office of purveyor is one of trust, and it is not lawful to make a deputy. And the servant was sentenced to be nailed to the pillory in two places, and to lose both his ears, and to wear papers on horseback, and was fined £40 with imprisonment. Now the master was condemned to the same punishment and £400 fine, '& to ride vpon an asse before his man,[3] & to be disabled for euer hereafter to beare any purueyor's place.

Purveyors cannot make deputies

Sentence

The law as to purveyors

'And the Attornie delyuered for lawe that noe purueyor can make any deputie: & there are certeine partycular thinges that are incidente to purueyors.

'36 E. 3, cap. 3° or 2°. 2 & 3 Phil. & Mar.

'The firste is they shall make no deputie.

'The 2d they shall be men of sufficiencie to aunsweare the kinge & the state.

'The thirde they shalbe sworne in ye Chauncerye. 23 H. 6, cap. 4; 36 E. 3; 28 H. 6.

[1] Nine Councillors and Judges were present.

[2] 1605, Nov. 14. Sir Edward Coke to Lord Salisbury: 'I had attended on yor lo. this morning, but that certen purveyors, who have egregiouslie abused themselves, & oppressed the subiect, are to be proceaded wth this morning in the Starre Chamber, the matter it selfe and the tyme requiring reformation.' State Papers, Domestic, James I., vol. 16, No. 76.

[3] The riding on an ass seems to have been suggested as an appropriate punishment in the case of another purveyor shortly before, and to have been adopted on the first opportunity.

1605, Oct. 24. John Chamberlain to Dudley Carleton: 'The weeke before there was a purveyor censured for misdemeanure in his place, to ride wth his face to the horse tayle; where in one of his iudges dissented from the rest, and wold rather have it vpon an asse, and that for two reasons, first it wold be more wonderment and gather more boyes about him, and secondly, the slowe pace of the asse wold prolong his punishment.' State Papers, Domestic, James I., vol. 15, No. 104.

'The fourthe they shall haue it vnder ye greate sealle, thereby to render an accounte.

'The 5th they shall renewe it euerye monethe, & therefore Cure's pattente for his lyfe, that was the Queene's sadler, was voyde.

'The 6th they must haue labelles annexed to there pattentes, & euery pertyculer thinge that they take must be inserted in the labelle. [p. 223]

'The 7th they must take where there is greate plentie.

'The 8th they must take in Conueniente time.

'The 9th they must take no more then needes.

'33 H. 6; 36 E. 3.

'Three score & fifeteene times the lawe prouydes againste purueyors.

'They Can not take any monie, they must purueye in kinde.

'But the twooe Carte takers were not sentenced, they excusinge themselues by the Lo. Knolles' letter, beinge Tresorer of the Householde, & the matter not fullye Confessed againste them, they were adiourned to be proceeded [against] wth all by bill & aunsweare.'

The King's prerogative

'The Atturnie & the Lo. Chauncellor did greatly aduance the Kinge's prerogatiue royall & the necessitie of purueyors, beinge both as auncyente as the Fundamentall lawes of the Kingdome: but the kinge's great Care & Clemencye to vse the same tenderlye & warilye, he beinge the originall cause of theise proceedinges, was very much Commended by all.'

1605 Nov. 20

In Camera Stellata, coram Consilio ibidem, Mercurij, 20 Nouembr. 1605, Jacob. Regis 3°.[1]

MADDOXE v. OWEN and others — Maintenance, champerty and riot

Maddoxe, plaintiff, Sir Roger Owen and others, defendants, for maintenance, champerty and riot. The Statute of 32 H[enry] 8, cap. 9, prohibits the buying of an estate [in], or title to, lands, tenements, etc., of any persons but

[1] Ten Councillors and Judges were present.

1605 Nov. 20 such whose ancestors or those whose estate they have, have been in possession, reversion, remainder, or have taken the rents or profits of the same, for one year next before, upon pain of forfeiture of the value of the land, the buyer or [p. 224] taker knowing this. And it appeared by the proofs in this case that the defendant and those whose estate he had, had the possession and took the profits, and did not know the plaintiff's title, for it was in question, and suits were pending for it. It was ruled that evidence taken in [the Court of] the Marches of Wales by the Council there in a suit to which the plaintiff was a party, should be read here; and other [evidences] were now read in suits there between others, to which the plaintiff was not a party; but the reason for this was that there was a former order for it, and upon that same order the defendant built and forbore to examine the witnesses. The plaintiff objected against this order two other orders (one taken in the Inner Star Chamber and the other at the Lord Chancellor's house), which countermanded that order. But the Lord Chancellor disallowed them, and said to the practisers that they pick their clients' purses by these house and Chamber orders; '"for," sayde he, "you are all honeste gentlemen, but I beleeue neuer a woorde you saye when you mooue mee at my howse or in the Chamber": & as it was sayde by the Attornie generall, "I finde," sayde he, "that god dothe assyste the Judge in his Judgemente seate, but not in his Chamber." The defendauntes were all acquyted, w^th^oute touche or suspition, & the Consyderacion of costes referred to the Lo. Chauncellor, & the pl^r^ helde suspected of forgerie of the late Lo. Burleighe's hande.'

Evidence in other suits, where admissible

Defendants all acquitted

1605 Nov. 22 **In Camera Stellata,** coram Consilio ibidem, Veneris, 22 Nouembr. 1605.[1]

ATT.-GEN. v. WHITHEADE

Forgery

The Attorney-General informed against one Whitheade for forginge letters of the Earl of Salisberie and Sir John

[1] Twelve Councillors and Judges were present.

Fortescue and their hands to them, to the Judges of Assize and Justices of the Peace in Essexe, commanding them to remove Sir Thomas Gardener (being a Justice of the Peace there) from the bench and from the Commission, a thing absolutely unlawful, and such as no Councillor of State in the realm could do, being Commissioners under the Great Seal of England. [p 245]

Magic and conjurations

Also he travelled in Germany for learning of the magical art, and he received instructions in conjuration, 'that he showlde baptize a dogge, & take the skinne of a Christian bodye & make him a girdle, & wth theise he showlde Commaunde all spirites & Rolles & bookes, wch suche like Coniurations were founde wth him, & now shewed in Courte; & vpon his examination he did Confesse that he Coulde turne all the rushes in a Roome into spirites & serpentes. For theise offences they were resolved they mighte by lawe impose the greateste punishemente they Coulde but deathe, & so they sentenced him to stande in 2 seuerall places vpon the pillorie & lose bothe his eares, & haue perpetuall imprisonmente; & Sir Thomas Gardener [was] delyuered wth greate Credite.'

Sentence

Al le arraignemente del Traitors por le grande treason of blowinge vp the Parliam^te^ Howse; it was in Westminster Halle.

1605–6 Jan. 27

THE GUN POWDER TREASON

'The Commissioners were the Lo. Admyrall, wch was then the Earle of Nottingham, the Erle of Suffolke Lo. Chamberlain, the Erle of worster M^r^ of the horse, the Erle of Deuonshire, th'erle of Northampton, the Earl of Salisberie principall Secretarye, the Lo. Ch. Justice Sr John Popham, the Lo. Ch. Baron Sr Thom. Flemminge, Justice Yeluerton, Justice Willyams & Baron Sauuelle, *lune* 27 *Januarij* 1605, *Jacob. Regis* 3°, *in le terme de S. Hillarie.*[1]

'There was arraigned Thomas Winter, Guye Fauxse *alias* Johnson, Roberte Caies, Roberte Winter, John Graunte,

[1] The list given in the *State Trials* omits the last three names, and adds Justice Warburton.

1605-6 Jan. 27

Ambrose Rookewoodde, Thomas Bates, all wch plede not guyltie.

[p. 226]

The King's Serjeant and

'The kinge's Sergeaunte, Sir Edwarde Phillips, did Cursorilie runne it ouer, & demonstrated it by waye of Declaracyon, Aggrauation & Approbacyon.[1]

The Att.-Gen. for the prosecution

'But the Attornie, Sir Edwarde Coke, more largelye did shewe how they had prepared 30 barrelles & 4 hogseheades of gunpowder, & had layde stones & barres & Crowes of iron vpon them: & *veritas est temporis filia*: for Fauxe's name was not knowne but w^thin fewe dayes, & they haue bene 23 dayes in examynacyon; a treason *sine nomine, exemplo, et modo*: they intended the destruction of the frame & fabrike, name & nation: ages to Come wilbe doubtfull whether it were a facte or a fiction.

'To ymagine in harte the deathe of the kinge, of the Quene or prince, is highe treason.

Treason to kill Lord Chancellor, Lord Treasurer, or a Judge while sitting

'To kille the Lo. Chauncellor, or lorde Tresorer, or a Judge syttinge *en Judgemente*, is treason: & euerye man in ye parliam^te is a Judge. *diusibile semper indiusibile.* theise men woulde haue rooted oute the tree & braunches: & in relatinge this treason I shall be forced to vse the names of some forreine princes & Councellers w^thoute any aspersyon or imputation to any of them.

'Theise treasons were plotted & wroughte 1. in Englande, 2. in Flanders, 3. in Spaine, & was begunne at Christemas was tweluemonthe before the Queene's deathe. the seconde in Marche, 1° *Jacob. Regis*. The thirde in June in Flaunders, & the 4th in Julye in Spaine.

[p. 227]

'Catesbie, *homo profundae perfidiae.*

'Thomas Winter wente wth Desmonde into Spaine: & Whalie did negotiate for an armie, promisinge the deuotion & ioyninge of the Catholiques & 2000 horse: Creswell, another preiste, was ledger[2] in Spaine for that purpose: &

[1] These were the three general heads into which Philips divided his speech, which is fully set out in the *State Trials.*

[2] A resident ambassador.

'Lord Angelo, having affairs to heaven,
Intends you for his swift ambassadour,
Where you shall be an everlasting leiger.'

Measure for Measure, iii. 1.

dealte wth Don Pedro Francisco, Duke of Lerna,[1] & so had accesse vnto the kinge, whoe sayde the Catholiques in Englaunde were as Deare vnto him as his owne Castilians: & assured them of a hundrede thousaunde Crounes: Thomas Winter retorned the Christemas before the Queene dyed: & now *mira cano* this Winter, *homo vafro et versuto ingenio*, together wth Father Baldwin the Jesuite, plottes wth Guye Fauxe that an armye showlde be landed in Milforde Hauen, broughte ouer in Spindalowe's[2] gallies. so heere is the Jesuites' treason, the preistes' treason & the pouder treason: wherein for better order 3 generall partes maye be obserued.

'1. Consideracions,

'2. Obseruacions,

'3. Comparisons of the preistes' wth Rawlie's treason.

'"Oh! but," saye the papistes, "theise traitors are no Catholikes, but the persons offendinge are men of desperate estates, of noe relligion, & of base Condition. *sine sede, sine spe, sine fide, sine re.*"

'Can this be so when as Percie the Archerebell is of the greate & honorable howse of Northumberlande; Sir William Stanlie, that greate & auntiente Traitor, of the howse of Darbie; Talbot of Grafton, guiltie in the higheste degree of misprision of Treason, of the howse of Shrewseberye? Sir Euerarde Digbie of 300 yeares Continuaunce, Winter of the beste howses, Tresham of auntiente & honorable howses.

The conspirators of good families

[p. 228]

'And that they showlde be men of noe religion, that were Straunge, when as theise preistes were the forwardeste men in them, Desmonde, Baldwin, Creswell, Hammon, Garnette, Jarrette & Westmerlande, makinge relligion there mantell of impietie, there mindes ambitiouslye bente to depose kinges & dispose of kingedomes: there religion being a religion of Distinctions; *vbi lex non distinguit, damnabilis est distinctio:* wth there distinctions they seeke

and religious men

[1] Lerma.

[2] Probably an error for 'Spinola's.' Ambrose Spinola, the celebrated general, was at this time in the service of Spain. His galleys are mentioned several times in the State Papers of the period.

1605-6
Jan. 27

to whippe kinges oute of there kingedomes wth force: & therefore it will not be amisse to obserue some of there doctrines: *omnis hereticus aut apertus aut occultus est occidendus,* & if he be kinge it is lawfull to depryue him, & if it be *morbus hereditarius,* the sonne may be depriued albeit he be a Catholique, & he that dothe it shalbe receaued *in gremium ecclesiae modo non sit ad damnum ecclesiae,* a damnable impietie: as there was an order of impietie, the templares, in one nighte were all destryde throughoute all Christendome.

Lawful to kill heretics

'Zemanchus,[1] one of there wryters, saythe that yf heretiques are excommunicate, either *facto aut iure,* it is lawfull to kille them.

[p. 229]

'*Sancta mater ecclesia nunquam gremium redeunti premit.*

'Father Creswell [2] in his *Philopater* dothe Confirme this Doctrine.

'Frauncis Tresham, whoe was one of the principall Traytors & Myners vnder the parliam[te] howse, & ys now deade in the Tower, wrote a booke *De officio principis christiani,* 5 cap., 4 lectur., approuethe this learninge.

'Sixtus quintus, after the deathe of Henry the thirde, the frenche kinge, sayde that whosoeuer drewe bloode from a Cardinall was *ipso facto* excommunicate.

Rebels absolved by Father Westmerland

'Father Westmerlande, after theise Traytors were vp in open Rebellion, and had Committed diuerse burglaries, horse steallinges, howse robbinges of armor, &c., & other outrages, did Confesse & absolue them all. Here be the instrumentes of the prince of this worlde, the pope, the Diuell, & fitte messengers for him: yet Winter & Fauxe are men of excellente good naturall partes, verye resolute & vniuersallye learned.

Winter and Fauxe resolute and learned

[1] Jacobus Simancas, successively Bishop of Ciudad Rodrigo, of Badajoz, and of Lamora.

[2] Joseph Cresswell, S.J. The work here referred to is *An Advertisement written to a Secretarie of my L. Treasurers of Ingland, . . . concerninge an other booke newly written in Latin, . . . against her Maiesties late proclamation, for searche and apprehension of seminary priestes and their receauors,* &c., 1592. It is a translation from the Latin of a work published under the pseudonym of 'Andreas Philopater,' and which is generally attributed to Father Parsons. The text rather suggests that the original work was also written by Father Cresswell. See *Dict. of Nat. Biog.*, Gillow's *Bibl. Dict. of English Catholics.*

'The kinge's lenitie towardes papistes showlde haue moued them to some better Courses, for in one whole yeare & 4 monethes he tooke no penaltie; & so his impunitie made them worse, & now they aymed at the place of Justice as well as at the persons: & Justice Fauxe showlde haue bene the gunpowder Justice. The King's lenity towards papists

'But the papistes obiecte that the Queene's lawes were bloodie, wherein they doe her greate Iniurie, for had shee bene an magnanimous kinge shee woulde haue hanged them vp all. [p. 230]

'For shee neuer medled wth any of them before Impius, and not Pius, quintus sente ouer his bulles in 13 of her raigne, whereby he did excommunicate her & absolue her subiectes from there obedience to her: then was one preiste arraigned & executed, & in 18 Elizab., father Campian, wth his treasonable bulles & bookes: & then in 23 Elizab. 20$^{li.}$ a monethe was gyuen for not Comminge to Churche: wch some seeme now to doubte whether it extende to Irelande or noe, & so manie there are reconcyled to Rome. The Pope's Bull, 13 Eliz.

'In 25 E. I. A bull of excommunication was treason by the Common lawe.

'There was a time when Rome was trulye protestante, & then there were 33 popes martirs: but now they are become temporall princes, they seeke there supremacye now vpon Earthe, & they will make there Confession in helle. & they practise to worke wth discontented persons: they all Joyne in an oathe not to disclose nor desiste: they wryte bookes of equyuocations, & corrected by father Garnette, & termed "a booke againste lyinge & Deceytefull Conueygheaunces," & suche like propositions. As if the Question be asked, "Did you see a preiste to daye," the aunsweare is, "I did not see a preiste," (wth a mentall reseruation) viz. to telle my Lo. Cheife Justice: & Mrs Vauxes butler had learned this.

'Here it is true, S.P.Q.R., *stultus populus querit Romam.* [p. 231]

'And heere he tolde a prettie tale of a fable of a Catte that killed vp all the mise & rattes in the Cuntrye, & forced them to keepe the holles, that they durste not stirre oute. The Att.-Gen. relates a fable

1605-6 Jan. 27

the Catte perceauinge this wente & shaued her Crowne, & gotte one a fryar's habite, & willed the mise to Come abroade wthoute feare, & repeated a prettie verse *non sum quod* [*fui*][1] *sed tonsum.* Oh but the mise founde that he had the same Cruell & bloodie harte still: for the inuention of pouder Came firste from a frier: & see the Juste Judgemente of god, theise men that thus intended to haue blowne vp a kingedome at one blowe, & when they were in open rebellyon & retyred to Lytleton's howse, in dryinge a li. of powder & a maide Comminge to stirre vp the fiar, a sparke set the powder one fire & blewe vp a lynnen bagge wth 12$^{li.}$ of powder in it oute at the toppe of the howse, & felle downe in a Courte adioyninge, & neuer tooke fire, & scorchte and amased them all; but god be blessed that the other pouder tooke not fier, [for] then had they bene all slaine, & this treason neuer discouered: when this had bene done, Sr Edmunde Baineham,[2] a dissolute younge gentleman, showlde haue bene the Messenger to Rome, a fitte messenger for the dyvelle, Callinge himselfe the "Captaine of the Damned Crewe": they sayde litle for themselues, but what they did was oute of there loue to there [p. 232] Freinde Catesbie & for the good of the Catholique cause: Rookebie desyred mercye, & Winter desyred that the deathe of one of them mighte suffice for both the bretheren.

The Jury find all guilty

'So the Jurie wente together & stayde not longe, but retorned againe, & founde them all guyltie; for so it appeared vpon there owne Confessyons.

Sir Everard Digby confesses

'In the meane time Sr Euerard Digbie, a goodlye gentleman, that stoode amongste the reste of ye prisoners all the daye, was arraigned, & Confessed the enditemente. & so the Lorde Cheife Justice gaue Judgemente of highe treason vpon them all: Digbie was in his tuff taffatie[3] gowne & a sute of blacke satten: & the reste were all very gallante at the kinge's Charge, they themselues desyringe to haue it so: Digbie spake muche wch did litle excuse his

Judgment of High Treason

[1] Blank in MS.

[2] See two cases of his *ante*, pp. 114, 165.

[3] A taffeta tufted, or left with a nap on it, like velvet. Halliwell.

offence, but rather aggrauate the same; what he did was for the loue of his freinde Catesbie & for the aduauncinge the Catholique Cause, but Cause of discontente he had none: he entreated mercye towardes his wyfe & children, his systers & debtors, & to haue the manner of his deathe Chaunged: the Kinge & Queene were bothe there in pryuate, & moste of all the Lordes of Englaunde, & the greater number of all the whole parliamente: but vpon the Thursedaye Followinge vpon a Scaffolde at Powle's,[1] Digbie, Grante, Robert Winter & Bates, that was Catesbie's man, were all drawne, hanged and quartered: & vpon Fridaye followinge Thomas Winter, Fauxe, Rookewoode & Kaies were in lyke sorte executed in the olde pallace at Westminster by the parliamente howse, & the lawe executed vpon them wth all seueritie, for nothinge terrified them from so horrible & bloodye a treason but this manner of deathe.

The King and Queen both there

The executions at St. Paul's

and at Westminster

'Catesbie, Percie, & some others, were slayne in there takinge in the Cuntrye, & Frauncis Tresham dyed in the tower. Catesbie's & Percie's heades were sette vpon the toppe of the parliam^te howse; & the Judges put this difference, that they beinge once in open Rebellion mighte by the lawe be so vsed, but Tresham Coulde not, for that he was not in rebellyon, neyther euer endyted; & this I haue hearde was the resolution of all the Judges.'[2]

[p. 233]

In Camera Stellata, coram Consilio ibidem, Veneris, 31 Januarij, 1605, Jacob. Regis 3°.[3]

1605–6 Jan. 31

'Doddrige, the Kinge's sollicitor, informed *ore tenus* againste Cassingherste, an Atturnie, borne at Limsefeilde in Surrie, John Dauies, fishemonger, & one Hungerforde, a citizen, that they three had taken vp monie & sealled bondes in the names of John Dauies, Haberdasher, &

SOL.-GEN. *v.* CASSINGHERST and others

Forgery

[1] S. Paul's.

[2] This account does not differ materially from that given in the *State Trials*, though the speeches vary slightly. The fact that the King and Queen were present does not appear to be recorded elsewhere.

[3] Eight Councillors and Judges were present.

1605-6
Jan. 31
Confession

Martin Freman, fishemonger.' They confessed the fact. And for this offence they were fined £10 ' apeece, to stande at the pillorie at Westminster, & at the exchange, & there to lose one eare & to be whipped, to weare papers, to be throwne ouer the barres, & to be ymprysoned vntill they finde good suerties for there good behauiour.

Sentence

[p. 234]

'This Cassingehurste was knowne to the Lorde Cheife Justice to be a verye lewde Fellowe, & the laste yeare to haue gotten a Commission vndulye out of the exchecquer for the kinge's Concealled rentes, & wente downe wth the same into Worster & Gloster shire, & had it not bene well preuented, he had done muche hurte;[1] wherevpon it was taken from him, & then he wente one in theise Courses, it beinge Conceaued in the Courte that he was the principall deuysor & actor in all theise busynesses, Dauies beinge a simple man & instructed by Cassingehurste what to saye, how to apparell himselfe in a nightecappe & a lyuerye gowne lyke vnto Martin Freman, whoe had recouered a longe sickenes & ware a nightecappe; but Hungerforde discouered it for that he Coulde not haue a share of the monie. This Cassingehurste was sometime stewarde to Mr Bostocke of his Courte at Tanridge,[2] & before him olde Richarde Fuller, a man likewyse noated of many dishoneste practyses, & a fitte instrumente to ioine in iniuste & iniuryous actions, wch in Future ages will more manifestelye appeare, (& therefore of litle Credite) to suche as hereafter shall finde iuste cause of greife & Complainte: especiallye hauinge by suche meanes endeauoured manye

Abuses at Tandridge

[1] 'The Abuse of one Cassinghurst, whoe procured A Comiss^n^ to doe the kinge service.

'This Cassingherst, his pretence was to doe the kinge service and to bring in grete somes of money. vnder the Cullo^r^ of this Comiss^n^ he gotte of one manne xl marckes, and cc^li.^ of diuers other his Ma^te's^ subiects, but the kinge gayneth nothing, but [is] only abused, and the subiect lykewise.'

State Papers, Domestic, James I., Vol. 28, No. 44.

[2] The writer, John Hawarde, lived at Tandridge, co. Surrey. Richard Bostock purchased the manor of Tandridge and other property in the neighbourhood from John Rede in 1576. He was M.P. for Blechingley 1, 27 and 31 Elizabeth. He appears to have died without issue, having settled the manor of Tandridge on his nephew Bostock Fuller, son of his sister Katherine Fuller. Manning and Bray, *Hist. of Surrey*, ii. 373. The Richard Fuller here mentioned may have been Katherine Bostock's husband.

yeares to defeate the late Queene & o^r kinge of there seigniorie in Tanridge, beinge lordes in Cheife of Tanridge, & of the waste & woodes, & doinge there seruice at his Matie's Leete, & he hauinge auncientelye a pounde there, where Edwarde's barne now standethe, but Mr Bostocke hathe of late erected a pounde in another place neere to the Churcheyarde, & hathe solde & Felled dyuerse wooddes [p. 25] vpon the waste, but Compounded secretelye wth the late Queene's officers for the same; & yf ye Rolles of the sheriffe's turne be veiwed, it will appeare there that he hathe bene Contynually presented for the same, & sometimes amerced, albeit they were neuer trulye Certifyed, as it seemethe, for that Mr Bostocke himselfe is the nexte Justice of peace & Quorum that by the lawe oughte to gyue allowaunce to there proceedinges in the sheriffe's turne, & to subscribe suche Certificate. Theise thinges & the true vnderstandinge of them will hereafter proue of no small momente to the inhabytauntes & owners in the parishe of Tanridge, to whome, if it be not speedilye preuented, greater mischeifes will insue to th'inhabitantes, & the kinge's righte loste: *Vigilantibus et non dormientibus iura subueniunt. Currat lex, viuat rex.*'

DAWES *v.* SHEREMAN — Abduction, etc.

'This daye was allso sentenced a cause wherein the kinge's Counsell informethe at the suite of one Dawes of the exchecquer againste Shereman, for Contractinge & marryinge the daughter & heire of the sayde Dawes, beinge of the age of 13 or 14 yeares, wth oute her parentes lykinge, assente, or priuitie: they informe vpon the statute of 33 H[enry] 8, cap. i, againste the Counterfaitinge of letters or priuye tokens; the scope of wch statute is, yf anye person falslye & deceitfullye gette anye monie, goodes, Cattelles, Jewelles, or other thinges, of any other person by color & meanes of any false token or counterfeit letter made in another man's name, th'offender, beinge lawfullye conuicte by witnes taken before ye Lo. Chauncellor, or by witnesses or confession in ye starre chamber, or before ye Justices of Assise or of the peace in there generall Cessions,

33 Hen. VIII., cap. i.

Obtaining goods, etc., by false tokens or counterfeit letters [p. 236]

1605-6 Jan. 31

or by action in any Courte of Recorde, shalbe punished by ymprisonm^{te}, pillorie, or other Corporall paine (excepte deathe); the Justices of Assise, or 2 Justices of peace, whereof one to be of the Quorum, shall haue power to Calle by proces or otherwise to the generall sise or Cessions, & to Committe them to warde or baile them to the nexte generall sise or Cession, there to be examyned & ordered by there discretions as abouesaide: And partelye & principallye they informed vpon 4 & 5 Ph. & Ma. cap. 8. It shall not be lawfull for anye to Conueye or cause to be Conuayde any maid or woman childe vnmaryed, wthin ye age of 16 yeares, from ye possession or custodie & againste ye will of her father, or of such person to whom ye father by his will, or by other acte in his lifetime, hathe assigned the education or gouernemente, excepte suche takinge be by or for suche person as wthout couin be ye M^{r} or mistres of suche maide, [or her] gardein in socage or chiualrie. If anie shall vnlawfully conueye any woman childe vnmaried, wthin 16 yeres age, againste ye will of ye father or mother, or from suche as by lawfull meanes haue the education, suche offender, beinge Conuicte by course of lawe (other then suche person taken awaye as holdeth landes by knighte's seruice), shalbe imprisoned 2 yeares, wthout baile or mainprise, or else paie suche fine as shalbe assessed in ye starre chamber: If anie shall take as aforesayd, & deflowre, or against ye will or vnknowing to ye father, if he lyue, or of ye mother, yf she haue ye Custodie, by secret letters, messages, or otherwise, contracte matrimonie, (excepte it be by consent of suche as hathe the wardeship), th'offender, being lawfully conuicte, shalbe imprisoned 5 yeares, wthout baile or mainprise, or be fined in the starre chamber: th'one moitie to ye kinge, th'other to the partie greiued. The starre chamber by bill or informacyon, the Justices of Assise by inquisition or indictemente, shall heare & determine. Yf suche womankinde aboue 12 & vnder 16 doe agree to any suche Contracte contrarye to this acte, the nexte of kin, to whome th'inheritaunce showlde discende or returne, shall, from ye time

Margin notes: 4 & 5 Ph. & M., cap. 8 Abduction of unmarried woman under age of 16 years — Marriage without the consent of the guardian — Punishment for this — Consent where over 12 and under 16

of suche assente, enioye all suche landes, &c., as shee had in possession, reuersion or remainder, at ye time of suche assente, duringe the life of ye person so contracted, &c.

'This Shereman had vnlawfullye, againste ye will of ye father & ye mother of ye maide, by Counterfeit letters & priuye tokens, falselye & deceitfullye Conueyghed awaye this Dawes' daughter, & not onelye contracted himselfe to her, but gotte a lycense & maryed her: but as he pretended it showlde be vpon a Condition: & so, by sentence, the Contracte was made voyde, & Shereman sentenced to paye 500^li.^, or to haue 5 yeares ymprisonmente.'

Shereman had abducted and married Dawes' daughter

Sentence

In Camera Stellata, coram Consilio ibidem, Mercurij, 5° Februarij, 1605, Jacob. Regis 3°.[1]

1605–6 Feb. 5 [p. 237]

The Attorney-general informed against Jarrette and Parsons, '2 informers whoe haue dealte for a pattente wth Sr Thom. Cornewalles, groomeporter, wch the late Queene had graunted vnto him, to allowe tablinge, Dicinge & other vnlawfull games, & to eate & dresse fleshe vpon dayes forbydden.[2] They by Collor thereof haue troubled dyuerse, & taken monie of them for a Composition, wch they Can not doe w^th^out lycence of the Courte.

ATT.-GEN. v. JARRETTE and PARSONS

Unlawful games, etc.

'For this offence they were adiudged to haue imprisonmente, weare papers, stande vpon the pillorye, & to be disabled for euer to be informers againe: in this Case there was but one or twooe partyculars proued, & many generalls, wch were allowed & reade.

Sentence

'The Attornie-generall delyuered that the Resolution of all the Judges of Englaunde was w^th^out any Contradiction that the kinge Coulde not graunte ouer the forfeiture of any penall lawe, because it was a specyall truste & auc-

Resolution of the Judges as to the granting of forfeitures

[1] Eight Councillors and Judges were present.

[2] 1604, Aug. 18. Licence to Thomas Cornwallis to nominate fit persons to keep bowling alleys, tennis courts, or other places of diversion in London and Westminster. State Papers, Docquet.

1605, Mar. 21. Grant with survivorship to Thomas Cornwallis and Thomas, his son, of the office of Groom Porter of his Majesty's house, and of the houses of the Queen and Prince, for their lives, on surrender of a former patent. State Papers, Docquet.

1605-6 Feb. 5 thoritie w[ch] the parliamentes had trusted his Ma[tie's] person w[th], but woulde not truste any other subiecte; the Lordes of his Ma[tie's] Counselle, vnderstandinge this resolution, haue Caused the same to be entred into the Councell booke, & to be locked vp in the Cheste for a monumente of greate vallewe.'

1605-6 Feb. 7 [p. 238]

In Camera Stellata, coram Consilio ibidem, Veneris, 7 Febr. [1605–6].[1]

GUIN v. VAUGHAN and JONES — Cozenage

The Attorney-general informed on the relation of Ellis Guin against Sir John Vaughan and Sir Thomas Jones. 'The pl., hauinge heretofore solde his lande to the Defd[te] S[r] John Vaughan by the practise & procuremente of S[r] Thomas Jones, pretendethe now that he was *non compos mentis*, but madde, & out of his wytte: but it is layde in the bille that beinge a simple, plaine man, & vnapte to dealle in worldlye busynes, that the defd[tes] did Circumuente him, & gotte his lande, beinge worthe a 1000[li.] or 2000 markes, they had it for 300[li.], in boxes, corne, horses, & suche lyke, of very small vallewe. the Charge of the bill beinge thus, he producethe all his proofe to shewe his madde & frantike trickes, in dyuerse kindes & of longe Contynuaunce. So the Judges did resolue that the Common lawe of Englaunde is that no man shall be receaued to disable himselfe by reason of madnes or frenzie, but the sonne maye haue a *non compos mentis*: & therevpon the Judges & all the Courte & Counsell helde it a very daungerous presydente to allowe the Charge of the Bill to tende to one ende, & the proffe to another, Contraryinge to the Contentes of the bill, for by that meanes the Defendaunte ys preiudiced greatelye in his iuste defence w[ch] he woulde produce his proofe for; & therefore by the sentence of the Courte it was dismissed.'

No man to prove himself mad

Proofs must coincide with the charge of the Bill

Dismissed

1605-6 Feb. 13 [p. 239]

In Camera Stellata, coram Consilio ibidem, Jouis, 13 Febr. 1605, adonque presente, Lo. Chauncellor, Archeuesque de Canterberie, Lo. Tresorer, Lo. Shrewsberie, Lo.

[1] Eight Councillors and Judges were present.

Northampton, euesque de Londres, Lo. Zouche, Lo. Ch. Justice, Lo. Ch. Baron & dyuerse autres Judges.

'After some Fewe motions by the kinge's Counselle & some other Fauourites, there was a motion againste one S[r] Thomas Robertes of Kente for stirringe vp of a suite, buyinge of a title, maintenaunce, riotous entries in the nighte, & suche like, beinge a Justice of the peace.

SIR THOMAS ROBERTES' case

Maintenance, etc.

'Another motion was a-made againste the excessiue lengthe of a bille Conteygninge 125 sheetes of paper Close wrytten, w[ch] S[r] Frauncis Bacon woulde haue excused wth a purpose to auoide multiplicitie of billes: but the Courte did muche Condemne it, & therevpon the aunciente order of the Courte was remembred, & now Confirmed, that no bill showlde Conteygne aboue fiueteene sheetes of paper; & for this longe bille the pl. was fyned by the whole Courte at 40[li.]. but the Lor. Chauncellor moued that he Coulde haue wished one auncyente presydente [precedent] that he hathe seene mighte now haue bene put in execution, that ys, that the Counsellor, beinge a man of infamie heretofore expelled out of the Middle Temple, showlde haue had the bille slytte wth a wholle in the middle thereof, & wore it as a heralde's Coate, & gone throughe all the Courtes in Westminster.

Motion against excessive length of a bill

Plaintiff fined £40 for it

Ancient punishment for drawing long bill

'Herevpon the Lo. Chauncellor, accordinge to the vsage at the ende of this terme & Trinitie terme to gyue a charge to the Judges & Justices of peace,[1] delyuered a partycular Charge to the Judges that they showlde diligentelye obserue all suche Justices of peace as were Carefull & diligente, & those that were troublesome & Contentyous, that they maye be remoued wth dysgrace, for there are verye manye lawes made & referred to the Justices of peace, but few executed by them; for they for the moste parte looke for precedencie, & are mainteyners of Cawses; for yf they had

The Chancellor's charge to Judges and Justices of the Peace [p. 240]

[1] Compare this with the other charges, *ante*, pp. 19, 56, 101, 106, 159, 161, 186, and *post*, p. 299, etc.

1605-6 Feb. 13

looked to there offycers & execution of the lawes againste wanderinge Rogues, theise wandringe preistes woulde haue bene mette w^th^all, & this greate treason haue bene preuented; & they woulde now endeauoure to be thankefull for this greate delyueraunce: he did exhorte the Justices to be verye carefull in the execucyon of Justice, & of the lawes againste wanderers, preistes, & Jesuites, & multitude of beggers. There ys a greate faulte in the makinge of Constables of the baser, poorer and simpler sorte of people, where as the lawe ys [that] for makinge suche kinde of officers the kinge maye seise the leete into his owne handes: that they woulde haue Care to punishe the shooters in gunnes, the libertie beinge greater albeit the lawe be streyter: he began his speache thus: "That whereas there was a brute [bruit] in London of an expectation of some greate personages heere as at this time, the kinge's Matie, oute of his gratyous wysedome, for some speciall reasons beste knowne to himselfe, thoughte it not fitte at this time": & so proceeded as is afore rehearsed. And then wente to hearinge of motions.'[1]

Laws against priests and Jesuits to be enforced

Use of fire-arms to be punished

1606 May 9 [p. 242]

In Camera Stellata, coram Consilio ibidem, Veneris, 9 Maij, 1606.[2]

KENNELLE v. GAWEN and others

Riot

A cause of hearing between Richard Kennelle, plaintiff, and Thomas Gawen and Katherine Gawen his wife,[3] Sir Edmond Ludlowe, and divers others, defendants, for riot in Wiltshire. Thomas Gawen died after the bill was

[1] Here follows 'A presydent for the grauntinge of a Stewardship of a Mannor.' This document is somewhat lengthy and of no great interest, so I have omitted it. It is a deed poll whereby Nicholas Darcie, esq., 'Lorde & Fermor of the Mannor of Kenn,' appoints William Martyn, esq., Steward of the manor; it is dated Sep. 2, 44 Eliz.

[2] Seven Councillors and Judges were present.

[3] Thomas Gawen, whose death and burial are mentioned in the text, was the son and heir of William Gawen of Norrington, co. Wilts. He married Catherine, dau. of Sir Edward Waldegrave, K.G., of Stanninghall. They had issue Thomas (died 1656) and Frances, a nun, O.S.B.; born 1576; first Abbess of Cambray, 1640. Foley, *Jesuit Records*, v. 467.

There is a pedigree of the Gawens and an account of Norrington House, with two illustrations, in Hoare's *Hist. of Wiltshire*, Chalk Hund. p. 82.

brought; but his wife, Katherine Gawen, was the principal rioter, and her sons, and one Nicholas Tooman, a tythingman, [and] Sr Edmond Ludlowe, a Justice of the peace. But before the opening of the bill, it was moved by Beere, of Counsel with the defendant, that after the examinations [were] published, the plaintiff was outlawed and *capias utlagatum* against him, [and he asked] if he now should be protected by the law [so as] to be heard as plaintiff in this Court. The Lord Chief Justice asked if he had this under seal. [Beere] answered that it was under the seal of the Common Bench. To which [the Lord Chief Justice] replied that it was of no value unless it was under the Great Seal, for then it seems it would be a good bar, and he [the plaintiff] could not be heard: Query, for it is clear, if he was outlawed before the publication of the cause, he is out of the protection of the law.

Outlawed plaintiff

Outlawry under Great Seal good bar

One Pine, of Counsel with the plaintiff, opened the bill, that Thomas Gawen being a recusant,[1] Queen Elizabeth granted his land to one Fortescue, who made a lease of it to Kennell for years; and Kennelle having servants in the kitchen and the barn, and corn growing on the land, Katherine Gawen, on the 7th of August, 1 James, with two servants, on the Sabbath day in the time of divine service, entered into the house and barred the doors. And the next day assembled more servants and friends with weapons, and kept possession by force, and took the goods, and spoilt and spent them and sent for Tooman, a tithingman, and Sr Edmond Ludlowe, the nearest Justice of the Peace. The said tithingman assembled more [people], and with his 'white rodde' (the badge of his office) encouraged

Plaintiff's case

Recusant's lands granted out

Defendant takes possession on Sunday

and keeps it by force

[p. 243]

The tithing-

[1] The Gawens were all recusants and suffered much for their faith.

'The names of such Popish Recusants as were indicted at ye Sessions holden for London and Midd., ye 15th of Februarie, 1604.

MIDD.

Robert Gowen, Thomas Gowen, Katherin Gowen.'

State Papers, Domestic, James I., vol. 1. no. 80.

List of Recusants whose fines had been granted out to various persons: Mr Gawen sonne and heyre of Thomas Gawen of Norrington, in com' Wilts.' Undated, ? 1604.

Ibid. vol. 11, no. 25.

1607, Jan. 17. Grant to John Price of the benefit of the recusancy of Catherine Gawen of Norrington, co. Wilts. *Ibid.* vol. 26, no. 13.

See also Foley, *Jesuit Records*, v. 467

1606 May 9

man encourages the rioters

the rioters, and assisted them in the King's name to keep possession; and he was received into the house, and brought others, who were also received. And Sir Edmond Ludlowe, the Justice of the Peace, came to the house, and the said Katherine Gawen at the sight of him said that he was welcome, for that he was her friend. He walked into the garden, and was immediately received into the house; and would not see but three of the rioters in the house, and no weapons, when it was proved that there were fourteen there, all with weapons. And he said to the plaintiff that there was no force nor weapons, and bound both parties to [keep] the peace; and he apprehended a servant there to send him to prison. Whereupon Mrs Gawen said, '"Let him alone, Sr Edmond Ludlowe, for he ys my man," (he indeede takinge him to haue bene one of Kennell's men), wherevpon he let him goe, & tooke one of Kennelle's men & woulde haue Committed him; & wordes increasinge, Sr Edmond Ludlowe willed Kennelle to gette suerties for the peace, or else he showlde goe to the goale, & tooke him by the Coller in greate anger, strykinge him wth his rydinge rodde crosse the face, & tolde him he woulde drawe him to the goale at his horse tayle; & thus contynued very partiall & affectionate to the Ryoters, not remouinge the force, nor takinge the weapons, nor Committinge the Rioters; but rather, together wth the tythingman, encouraginge, by reason of there offices, the riotors, & most partiallye & affectionatelye fauouringe & suffringe of them; by reason whereof muche hurte & bloude mighte haue ensued. & many dayes together there was shootinge in gunnes & bowes oute of the howse at some of the seruauntes of ye pl. And w^th^in Fewe dayes after, a Cession beinge Called to inquyre of that Riote, Sr Edmonde Ludlowe, being none of the Cession, Comes thither & challengethe one of the Jurors: And [the plaintiff's Counsel] shewes how the pl. was dampnifyed 300^li.^.

Both parties bound over to keep the peace

Plaintiff ordered to find sureties

The house besieged many days

[p. 244]

Demurrer by defendants

'The Counselle wth the Defend^tes^ offered matter for the Clearinge of Sr Edmonde Ludlowe, that hauinge put in a Demurrer & an aunsweare, for, parte beinge iointe, it was after that ordered that the bill showlde be amended in that parte for wch he did demurre, w^ch^, if it had bene so, then he showlde haue bene serued wth proces anew; but it was not so; & besydes he had repeated the substaunce of the Charge of the bille, & made a ioynte aunsweare & demurrer to the same; & so demaunded the iudgemente of the Courte; w^ch^, by the order of the Courte, he showlde haue demaunded the benefite of before publication, by reference or motion to the Courte, but now he hathe wayued it; & so ruled by the Judges: & endeauouringe to extenuate & excuse, not to Cleere or defend, the offences in all or any of the Defendauntes, they shewed that this gentlewoman conceyued by the kinge's generall pardon shee showld now haue her landes discharged; & greate waste beinge suffered & donne by ye pl. vpon the housinges & landes, shee thoughte shee mighte now enter, they beinge her ioincture: wch in Circumstaunce beinge trulye opened, did aggrauate her offence muche more; for she, beinge a recusaunte, did vpon the Kinge's Comminge reporte that the times were Chaunged for Catholikes, they showlde now haue better dayes, the blooddye Queene was deade vnder whome the Lo. Che. Justice did rule the roste, & Sr John Fortescue, & the bloud sucker, Sr Walter Rawlie; but the times were now altered, for Lo. Chei. Justice was in disgrace, & Catholikes showlde be better dealte w^th^all. But the Charge of the bille wente farther, that the Lo. Ch. Justice & Sr Walt^r^ Rawleighe showlde Conspire to kill the kinge. But some parte of them being proued it was sufficiente, & shee was sentenced for it: & the pl. bringinge an Iniunction oute of th'exchecquer for th'establishinge his possession, & the vnder sherife comminge to execute the same, wch he is to doe & not the Justices of peace, who are to aide & assiste him for the better executinge thereof; but Sr Edmonde Ludlowe, findinge the wordes of the Iniunction to be that they showlde establishe the possession of the pl. & of all suche others as then were in possession, made this partiall construction; "Why," saythe he, "Mrs Gawen ys in possessyon, ys shee not," whoe was the defendaunte that

Held to be waived, because not taken in time

Waste by plaintiff in defendant's lands

Mrs. Gawen's slanders

[p. 245]

The plaintiff gets an injunction

1606 May 9 had gotte & kepte the possession wth force: & whoe lykewyse vsed opprobrious woordes of the pl., "that a Dogge kennelle were a fytter place for him."

Sentence

'For all wch offences they were seuerallye Fyned:

'the wydowe Mrs Gawen, 500^li.^

J.P. and tithingman deprived

'Sr Edmonde Ludlowe, 300^li.^, & to be discharged of ye peace *par le* Lo. Chauncellor.

'the Tythingman, 100^li.^, & discharged, & disabled to beare office, to be bounde to his good behauyoure.

'5 other defendauntes a peece, 40^li.^

'the reste a peece, 20^li.^

'three women defendauntes a peece, 10^li.^

'& of course all to be ymprisoned; & beinge seruantes, accordinge to the ordynarie Course of the Cowrte, yf they be not able, there M^rs^ must paye for them.' [1]

[p. 246]

Slander of Queen Elizabeth, King James, and others

'The lordes insisted muche vpon the vilde woordes againste the deade Queene, againste the Kinge & the Lord Cheife Justice, & all wyshed there mighte haue bene some exemplarye punishemente vpon the woman: And the Lorde of Northampton delyuered many partyculars for approbacyon of the Kinge's Zealle & sinceritie in religion; & firste that in the late Queene's time there was a reporte broughte to some of the then Ministers of state in greate place heere that the Kinge's Matie, by a priuate messenger of noate, had sente to Rome a kinde of an assuraunce or promise for a toleration of Rhomishe religion when he showlde Come into Englaunde; wch message was very distastefull heere, & iniuryed him greatelye in his titles for Englaunde, whereof the Lo. of Northampton then Certified his Matie into Scotlaunde by letter; wherevpon his Matie retorned an aunsweare so mixte wth zealous attestations & solemne protestations of his zeale & sinceritie in that religion wherein he was baptized, & in wch he woulde dye, as gaue then full satisfaction to him & all others wch then hearde thereof: after this, vpon his Matie Comminge into Englaunde, the Lo. of Northampton mette him at Barwike,

The Earl of Northampton speaks of the King's religion

Report that the King had promised to tolerate papacy

[1] See a cross bill between the same parties, *post*, pp. 279, 281, 82.

& there, the Catholikes hauing preferred diuerse petitions to his Ma[tie], & mouinge his Lo[p] to sollicite in there behalfe, he demaunded what aunsweare the kinge gaue them; they sayde they plainelye perceaued a settled Constancie in him in the religion establyshed, but they Complayninge of the hardenes of the lawes & seuere punishementes & proceedinges againste them, & suinge for more milde vsage, his aunsweare was [that] when he Came into Englaunde he woulde examine all, & doe Justice vnto all: after his beinge in Englaunde he did so, & not onelye Confyrmed & establyshed the former lawes & gouernm[te] of that euer memorable Queene & glorious to all posterities, but so well lyked thereof, that, accordinge to the aunciente perfection of gouernemente heere vsed, added to the number of Counsellors of state & Judges of the lawe. But soone after his Comminge, being wellcommed wth a practise of a greate treason, w[ch] occasyoned a rumor to be dispersed by Watson, the preiste, that the Kinge's Ma[tie] had promised a toleracyon of Catholike religion & that he was forgettefull of his promise, the kinge, hearinge of it, & muche troubled therew[th], (hauing often protested & publikely professed his Constancie in religion to liue & dye in the same, & wyshinge often maledictions vpon his posteritye yf euer they showlde alter or Chaunge the same), sente for the sayde Earle,[1] beinge one of those Lordes that had bene ymployed in th'examynacyons of theise treasons of Rawlie, Graye & Cobham, & ymparted this vnto him wth greate passion & greife, & wylled him to repayre to Watson, whoe was now Condemned & to be forthew[th] executed, & to expostulate wth him to leaue the truthe to the worlde of this Reporte: who dealinge partycularlye wth Watson for that purpose, his aunsweare was that he was in Scotlaunde wth the kinge, & mouinge his Ma[tie] for a toleracyon, he sayde he showlde wronge his soueraigne infinitelye if he showlde saye that he made any promise for a toleracyon, for he did not, neyther did he euer reporte so, but that he founde him so strongelye settled for that religion wherein he was bap-

Petition by the Catholics

[p. 247]

[1] Northampton.

1606 May 9

tised & bredde, that there was no Cause to hope of toleracion ; & so protested vpon his soule, & so dyed.

The Lord Chancellor commends the King and the late Queen

'The Lo. Chauncellor spake muche to that purpose bothe for the kinge & deade Queene, who was so farre from bloude, that in respecte of her selfe shee woulde neuer haue had any dyed but to preuente the daunger of the state & Common wealthe & to preserue them in safetie, & that was neuer done but wth greate greiffe, & allmoste teares; & for the Lo. Cheife Justice, a most reuerende Judge, (the Queene ys now wth god, but her name & fame shall euer lyue most glorious & Comfortable to all honeste hartes), in her time, as well as sythence, most vigilante & [p. 248] diligente to punishe offendors; & by his Care to bringe offendors to iuste punishemente muche bloude hathe bene saued; & when god Calles him to himselfe, I praye god sende vs the lyke. For the Dammages to the partye, for the moste parte wee take the greateste whereof there ys any proffe, & sometimes for wante of proffe wee take the oathe of the partye himselfe; & in suche cases as theise, of vallewes of goods, entryes & Force, whoe can better proue it then the seruauntes that are & lyue aboute vs: yet in some Cases, if the wytnesses be to [much] excepted againste, or the prooffe be dubious or incertaine, we heare proffes in the negatiue, & sometimes defendaunts excusinge themselues, & geue Credyte to them as wee see Cause, for they are onelye *ad informandum Conscientiam*.'

How damages are assessed

1606 May 14

In Camera Stellata, coram Consilio ibidem, Mercurij, 14 Maij, 1606.[1]

Motion by Sir John Croke

Examinations in Chancery cannot be read here

It was moved by Sir John Crooke 'that wytnesses beinge heere examyned, they had referred themselues to there Former examynacions taken in the Chauncerye, & therefore [he] desyred the benefite of them heere. The Lo. Chauncellor aunsweared that it was *sine exemplo*, & not to be allowed, for it was th'examyners faulte to take suche an examynacyon ; & in other cases where examyna-

[1] Nine Councillors and Judges were present.

cyons haue bene taken in this Courte in seuerall causes, thoughe betwene the same parties, wee haue bene deintie to heare them, especiallye in cases of Forgerye; & therefore, it beinge before publication, it was ordered the wytnesses showld be examyned heere, but their names showlde be gyuen to the defend^{tes}.'

ASCUE v. EARL OF LINCOLN

'The Atturnie generall moued for Ascue of Lincolneshire, whoe in 35 Elizab. had a sentence againste th'erle of Lincolne, & had gyuen him[1] the vallewe, dammages & Costes; what the dammage was hathe bene referred to Justice Fenner; he hathe Certified 1700$^{li.}$ dammage, wch Ascue coulde neuer yet gette, so that *materiam superat opus*. And a doubte hathe bene now made whether the dammage [p. 249] shall include the vallewe, or whether he shall haue the vallewe ouer & aboue the dammage: the Consyderacyon whereof is referred agayne to Mr Justice Fenner.'[2]

LADY RUSSELL v. EARL OF NOTTINGHAM and others — Riot, etc.

'A Cause of hearinge was betwene the Ladye Russelle[3] pl. againste th'erle of Nottingham, Lo. Admirall,[4] Bellingem, Sugeden, Jobson, & others of his seruauntes, for 2 seuerall ryotts, & againste Thom. Dolman, A Justice of peace in Barkeshire, for a misdemeanor in the same Riote.

'Q. Elizabethe of blessed memorye graunted to the pl. the Custodie of her Castle, parke & Mannor of Dunnington,[5] & of her woodds in Barkeshire, & a fee of 2d. ob. *per diem* for her lyfe, & afterwards graunted the Fee simple of them all to the Lo. Admyrall for seruyce done[6]: & 3 Septemb.,

[1] Awarded to him.

[2] See *ante*, pp. 12, 114, 146.

[3] Elizabeth, daughter of Sir Anthony Cook, knight, mar. 1, Sir Thomas Hoby, knight; and 2, John Russell, 2nd but eldest surviving son of Francis, 2nd Earl of Bedford; she had by her 2nd husband two daughters and co-heirs, Elizabeth, who died unmarried, 1600, and was bur. in Westminster Abbey (see engraving in Dart's *Westminster Abbey*), and Anne, who mar. Henry Somerset, afterwards Earl and Marquess of Worcester, and left issue. John Russell was commonly styled Lord Russell, and it is doubtful whether he was not summoned to Parliament in his father's lifetime. On his tomb in Westminster Abbey (see Dart) he is represented in a Baron's Parliamentary Robes. *Complete Peerage*, by G. E. C.

[4] Sir Charles Howard, K.G., 2nd Baron Howard of Effingham, and 1st Earl of Nottingham; so created 1596.

[5] Donnington near Newbury, Berks.

[6] See Appendix XVII.

1606 May 14 1° *Jacob.*, dyuerse of the Lo. Admyralle's men were sente wth a loade of stuffe, & in there Carte an iron Crowe & iron barres, &c., & Came to the Castle, & tolde 2 seruantes that kepte the Castle to the pl[s] vse, that the Queene was to Come to M[r] Dolman's [1] howse, halfe a mile from the Castle, & the same not beinge able to receaue her trayne, the Lor. Admirall woulde haue lodginges prouyded for him w[th]in the Castle, & to that purpose had sente them & his stuffe; wherevpon the pl[s] seruaunts made aunsweare that they Coulde not Come thyther, neyther woulde they suffer them to enter there, beinge so dyrected by the pl., whoe was now absente w[th] her sonne in lawe, the Lo. Herberte,[2] in Worstershire: the Lo. men, vnderstandinge by the waye that they showlde be w[th]stoode, tooke a Crowe & barres of iron w[th] them, & w[th] knockinge againste the gate, broake of the locke, & put backe the bolte, & entred, & tooke the Castle, & brake into many Roomes, & tooke an Inuentorye of the pl[s] goods, and furnyshed some Roomes for there lorde, whoe sente them thyther vittaile: & vnderstandinge the Ladye was retorned, & intended to Come to the sayde
[p 250] Castle, [he] sente thyther dyuerse of his seruantes, whoe entred into the parke, & draue oute all the pl[s] Cattelle, & besette the lodge, & kepte them from vittaile & thereby made them forsake it, whereby they tooke possession. The Ladye vpon her retorne Came thyther, & findinge shee Coulde not enter into the Castle, she retorned to Newberrie, beinge w[th]in a mile, & there lodged all nighte; & the nexte daye tooke the Mayor of Newberye,[3] & diuerse Clothyers, weaponed, & in her Coache roade into the parke towardes the lodge, & beinge mette by Bellingam & other of the

[1] Mr. Thomas Dolman was an opulent clothier of Newbury, who, having purchased the manor of Shaw, near Newbury, completed in 1581 a stately brick mansion there, called Shaw Place. There he entertained James I. and his Queen in September, 1603. The royal party arrived on the 21st; how long they stayed does not appear. See Nicholl's *Progresses of James I.*, i. 266; Money's *History of Newbury*.

[2] Henry Somerset, son and heir of Edward, 4th Earl of Worcester, was summoned to Parliament as Baron Herbert of Chepstow in his father's lifetime, 1603. He succeeded to the Earldom in 1628, and was created Marquess of Worcester in 1642. His grandson was created Duke of Beaufort in 1682.

[3] The Mayor's name was Henry Cox. *History of Newbury*, by Walter Money, F.S.A.

lorde's seruaunts, was tolde in verye respectiue fashyon that shee Coulde not enter into the lodge nor the Castle, & her seruauntes offringe to passe, a sworde was drawne, & no more hurte done; & before this time, a Cession being holden for the former riots, & enditementes preferred, & Councelle hearde one bothe sides, & founde against the Ryotors; but because it seemed doubtefull by reason of the title, & the Quarter cessions being wthin Fewe dayes, they referred it to a full benche, & woulde not then Fine the riotors, nor graunte restitucion: the Lo[rd's] men keepinge the possessyon, & the Ladye beinge there, as aforesayde, & walkinge & spendinge the daye there, shee sente for Mr Thom. Dolman, the nexte Justice of p., & willed him to restore her possession, to Committe ye ryotors, & to binde the reste to the p[eace]; but he, seinge no force nor ill beseeming woorde or vsage, did neyther committe nor binde to the peace any of them, & for restitution, he thoughte he Coulde not doe it, beinge but one, & beinge a case of some doubte in lawe whether the possession of my Lo. in parte were the possession of all or no; he desyred it mighte be respited till the Quarter Cessions that they did all meete, & perswaded the pl. to Contente her selfe, & haue patience, & betake her to her Lodginge, eyther at Newbery, at his owne howse, or wthin the Castle. For Bellingem did offer her, yf [p. 251] she woulde acknowledge to holde it of my lorde, or passe her honorable woorde to departe peaceablye & to yealde the possession thereof the nexte morninge, she showlde enter wth her gentlewoman, & suche other necessarye attendauntes as she woulde haue, & they woulde geue her the beste wellcome they Coulde eyther in the Castle or lodge; but she aunsweared shee woulde not, for shee scorned to be keeper to anye subiecte whatsoeuer, & so of willfullnes meerelye shee kepte wthoute by the Castle walle all nighte: wthin Fewe dayes after, the kinge's Matie Came to Mr. Dolman's, & the pl. vpon his Comminge made her Complainte to his Matie by petition, wherevnto the kinge made aunsweare [that] the Castle, parke or Mannor were none of his, but the Lo. Admyralle's by the graunte of the late Q. Elizabethe, ("& I

The plaintiff petitions the King

1606 May 14 woulde they were better for his sake"),[1] but wyshed her to referre it to some honorable personages, or to the Judges, to make some good ende betwene them, but she desyred Justice that the lawe mighte ende it; wherevnto the Kinge replyed, "Madame, is there none wthin the kingedome that you dare or will truste?" "I beseeche yor Matie," quothe shee, "let mee haue Justice, & I will truste the lawe." & shortelye after broughte an Assise in the kinge's benche for the Custodye of the Castle & parke, wch the Lo. Admirall supposed she had forfeyted in fellinge of wooddes & killinge of the game; but shee recouered in the Assise, & then proceeded wth this suite, in wch shee woulde not be stayed in any kinde, albeit my Lo., when he wente aboute to gette the graunte of this Reuersion from the Late Queene, acquainted the pl. therewth, & for her good will gaue her [p. 252] 1000$^{li.}$ in regarde of some Costes shee had bestowed there:

Defence

'The Counselle wth the Lo. Admirall & the other Defendauntes made defence firste by the Lo[rd's] aunsweare & th'other defendaunts' [answers], & by wytnesses, & some of those produced & examyned by the pl., in effecte thus, that the Castle & parke beinge my Lord's, & the pl. hauinge but the Custodye thereof, the Lorde's owne seruauntes entringe but into his owne howse could not be riotors; & for suche a kinde of entraunce into his owne wth his owne people, a greate & an honorable Earle, Lorde highe Admirall of Englaunde, to be thus produced as a delinquente heere, they did humbly leaue it to the Consyderacion of the Courte how fittinge they showlde iudge it to be; and for the lorde's men, that they did was but lawfull, & in peaceable manner, wthout blowes or any ill be-seeminge woorde; for Dolman, the Justice of peace, whoe saw nothinge but signes of peace & good vsage, & vnderstandinge the questions & doubtfullnes of the Case, had good warraunte to doe as he did; for in the Commission of the peace there is a prouisoe, that for anye matter of difficultie or doubte they showlde respite it, & referre the decision thereof to some of the Judges or Justices of Assise:

Plaintiff had custody only

[1] Margin.

'The Counselle for the pl. vrged what they Coulde againste the defendauntes, &, as they sayde, by Commaundemente, beinge as it seemed not willinge to be of Counselle wth the pl., or against the defend[te], vnles they had bene Commaunded: but the daye beinge now spente, & the Lordes beinge to attende the kinge there M[r] after dinner, for his Ma[tie's] aunsweare to some greeuaunces delyuered him by the lower howse of parliamente,[1] whoe now sate euerye daye, expectinge an ende. Reply

'The Lo. Chauncellor moued that forasmuche as it seemed doubtefull what was graunted the pl. by her pattente, w[ch] was materiall to be rightelye vnderstoode before this Courte showlde be able to sentence this Cause, that it were necessarye it [the patent] showlde be veiwed; wherevpon it was reade in Courte, & appearinge thereby that shee had but the Custodie of the Castle and parke granted her, & not the lodge, in w[ch] [*i.e.* the lodge] there was onlye some proffe or lykelyhoode of a Ryote, the Judges, doubtfull thereof, began to mooue the Courte; but the Ladye, interruptinge them, desyre'd to be hearde, & after many denyalls by the Courte, vyolentelye & wth greate audacitie beganne a large discourse, & woulde not by any meanes be stayed nor interrupted, but wente one for the space of halfe an howre or more; & in her beginninge of her speache excepted against my Lo. of Nottingham for that he had not aunsweared vpon his oathe, but vpon his honor: To w[ch] the Lo. Chauncellor replyed that it was her Atturnie's faulte that he moued not for it, for so longe as he sate in that place, the greateste peere in the kingedome showlde aunsweare vpon oathe, & so was the Course of this Courte, & so had he verye latelye vsed in the Earle of Shrewseberye [2] & the Earle of Cumberlande's Case.

[p. 253] The plaintiff's patent to be read

The plaintiff insists on addressing the Court

Peers to answer on oath

'Then shee did wth bitternes obiecte that my Lo. Admirall in the begynninge of his aunsweare had denyed her to be Ladye Dowager to the Lo. Russelle, & that he knewe none suche: for shee sayde shee had bene Lady

[1] See Appendix XVIII. [2] See *ante*, p. 16.

1606 May 14 Dowager before Nottingham was,[1] & that if the Lorde Russelle had lyued, bothe for worthe, honor & iudgemente, he had farre excelled the Lo. of Nottingham ; & that he [p. 254] had dealte verye dishonorablye wth her in gettinge the Castle & parke from her, for shee her selfe had a promyse of the late Q. Elizab. to haue the same, & for the same purpose had gyuen her 1500^li.^, & when shee ynformed the Queene that ye Lo. Admyrall woulde be a suitor for the same, her Matie's^ aunsweare to her was, "God's deathe! my Castle of Dunnington! I thinke he will haue my Crowne and all." And yet after this shee graunted the same to him, & the pl. neuer had her 1500^li.^ againe.'

The Lords try to stop her

But in vain

'The Lordes seuarallye herevpon woulde haue stayde her, & muche distasted theise fonde speeches, but shee still wente one, & all the Courte & presence murmuringe & makinge greate noyse, gyuinge no eare to any thinge shee sayde, her owne Counselle goinge from the barre allso; yet shee wente one w^th^oute any chaunge, or any waye abashed at all, in a verye boulde & stoute manner, w^th^oute any shewe of any distemparature, or any loude speakinge, but shewinge a very greate spirite & an vndaunted Courage, or rather will, more then womanlike, whose reuenge by her tounge semed to be the summe of her desyre; in a meaner personage it is vsuallye termed 'mallice' & 'enuye,' but in her, beinge honorable, learned, & indued wth many excellente guyftes, wee grace it w^th^ 'a great spirite,' wch I feare the worlde conceauethe to be more then blemyshed, if not vtterlye extinguyshed, wth extreame pryde.

The Lord Chancellor interrupts

'Herevpon the Lo. Chauncell. tolde her, "Madame, you must geue vs leaue; we haue suffered you to wronge yor-selfe, this Courte, & o^r^ M^r^ his seruice:" & the Lo. of Northampton Coulde not forbeare, but stayed her, & tolde her she had endeauoured to wronge a righte noble Earle, "& firste, out of the place I holde, as one to whome [p. 255] the office of Earle Marshall is commytted, that by the lawe of armes you are no Ladye Dowager, nor [there are] none

The Earl of Northampton on dowagers

[1] John, Lord Russell, died in 1584; the Earl of Nottingham was so created in 1596.

vnder the degree of an Earle's wyfe:" & vpon that shee plucked him by the cloake, & tolde him the lawe was otherwyse before he was borne: he, muche mislyking of that vsage, tolde her in manner of a reproffe that it was neuer offered to the Courte before, suche violente interruption of any Judge in delyueringe his sentence when they had bene formerlye hearde, & bidde her forbeare, & heare him, "for," sayde hee, "the Lo. Russelle, yo[r] husbande, was a noble gentleman, but ill beseeminge you wth so many vnfittinge detractions to compare him to the Earle of Nottingham; & he dyed in his father's lyfetime, so you Coulde not be Lady Dowager, for yo[r] husbande was never Earle." [1]

'The Lo. Tresorer then stayed her, (for shee was begynninge againe), & tolde her shee greatelye wronged the deade Queene, his M[rs]. Shee was so farre from breache of anye promyse, especiallye a Consyderacion beinge gyuen, "w[ch] you shall geue mee leaue to beleeue that there was neuer any suche thinge, nor you coulde neuer speke more dishonorablye of her:" The Lord Treasurer stays her

'Then the Lo. Chauncellor, & bothe the reste of the Lordes, muche condemned the Ladye for those wordes of [concerning] the Lo. Admyrall, of whome they spake very muche good, & that of there owne knowledge the late Queene helde him as loyall a harted man as any w[th]in the kingedome, & euerye waye very honorably accounted, & of exceedinge good merite: then the Lo. Chauncellor perceauinge the Judges to doubte whether the pl. had barelye the Custodye of the parke and not of the lodge, w[ch] was a matter laye lykewyse in proffe, & now noe wytnesses examyned, how this Courte coulde now judge of it he did not see. And the Judges seemed to be of that opinion allso, wherefore the consyderacyon of this & the reste was referred to the Judges: & they all wyshed it had bene ended, & neuer broughte to this, all condemninge greatelye the pryde & wyllfullnes of The Court censures the plaintiff [p. 256] Questions of evidence

[1] This supports the view that John Russell was never summoned to Parliament. If he had been it must have been well known, and would certainly have been mentioned here. See *ante*, p. 271, n. 3.

1606 May 14

the pl. See *puis*, fol. 289, the case sentenced. & all the defend^{tes} acquited wth Costes againste the pl.'[1]

1606 May 16

In Camera Stellata, coram Consilio ibidem, Veneris, 16 Maij, 1606.[2]

ATT.-GEN. *v.* GRAVES, and others

Unlawful felling of timber

The Attorney general 'informes againste 5 purueyours *ore tenus*; Graues & Brennan, the 2 M^{rs} [masters], & the other 3 there seruauntes, had a Commission to take timber boordes & poules [poles] for the Kinge's toyles, & that they did in Aprill now laste paste take & felle in Mr Backehouse' grounde in Barkeshire, vpon the sabaothe daye in the morninge, 360 saplinges of oake & ashe for poules, & gaue for them 12^{d} the hundrede, & had sixe score to the hundrede, & 4^{d} a loade for cariage. Whereas the Attornie delyuered that by Magna charta they can not take any subiecte's woodde or timber growinge, nor boordes in his howse, because they are annexte to the enherytaunce, wthoute he doe agree wth the partie; wch lawe hathe bene now 34 or 35 times contynewed & establyshed, & a proclamacyon latelye publyshed to that effecte. Theise offences were confessed by the partyes, but not so fullye as by twooe affidauits wch were taken before the Lo. Chauncellor, & now reade in Courte, but, as the Lo. Chauncellor well opẽned, for the aggrauation of the offences, but not to leade them in their iudgemente.

Magna Charta cited

Sentence

'They were sentenced, the 2 maisters fyned 20$^{li.}$ a peece, imprisonm^{te}, & to be bounde to there good behauyoure: the 3 seruauntes to stande vpon the pillorye wth papers, & imprisonm^{te}, to signifye especiallye there dishonoringe god in breache of the sabaothe daye, an offence muche increasinge th'offenders punishm^{te} in the sentence of this Courte. The Lo. Chauncellor did likewyse delyuer that before Magna charta was, the prerogatiue was; for Magna Charta is but a declaracyon or manyfestacyon thereof; & if a t[enant] for yeares suffer suche trees to be cutte

[p. 257]

King's prerogative older than Magna Charta

[1] See *post*, p. 309, and Appendix XVII. See also Moore's *Reports*, 786.
[2] Nine Councillors and Judges were present.

downe by the kinge's takers, the lessor shall in an action of waste recouer *locum uastatum*, & treble dammages. For as w^th^oute the prerogatiue the kinge's crowne & dignitie can not be mainteyned, so he can not be more dishonered then, vnder shadow of his prerogatiue, his subiectes to be oppressed and burdened; for his greateste care in the worlde, nexte to the seruice of allmightye god, is the welfare & prosperous libertie of his subiectes, and no greater greife vnto him then to haue them oppressed & burdened.'

'Another cawse of hearinge was opened betwene the wydowe Gawen & Kennelle but deferred to Fridaye nexte, that it mighte then be a full Courte.' [1] GAWEN *v.* KENNELLE

In Camera Stellata, coram consilio ibidem, Mercurij, 21 Maij, 1606.[2] 1606 May 21

Tenaunte and others, plaintiffs, against Sir Stephen Proctor and others, defendants, for a practice and a misdemeanour in the examination of witnesses in the Chancery *ad perpetuam rei memoriam*, and for default of good proof it was returned into the Chancery to be ordered there. TENAUNTE *v.* PROCTOR and others — Practice

In Camera Stellata, coram consilio ibidem, Veneris, 23 Maij, 1606.[2] 1606 May 23

Cause of hearing between Wildegoose, plaintiff, and Parrie '& others, defendauntes, for riote in reapinge of Corne, & Comminge wth a dromme, gunnes, bowes & arrowes, & welche hookes, & misdemeanor againste a Justice of peace, Thom. Johnes of Grayes Inne, Counsellor at the lawe,[3] whoe came thither, & tooke the weapons from somme of the Ryotors, & Committed them. WILDEGOOSE *v.* PARRIE and others — Riot

'For this greate Ryote all the Defendauntes were fyned [p. 258]

[1] See a cross bill between the same parties, *ante*, p. 264; and see *post*, pp. 281, 282.

[2] Eight Councillors and Judges were present.

[3] Admitted to Gray's Inn, Aug. 9, 1599; then of Staple Inn, gent.

1606 May 23 Sentence

eache a 100li., & imprisonmte for a yeare, as 2 H[enry] 5, cap. 8, dothe enioyne for greate Ryottes. & a man's beste dyscrecyon, as the Lo. Chauncellor well sayde, ys *discernere iustum iuste secundum leges*.'

Parrie v. Wildegoose and others

Maintenance, misdemeanour, and riot

'Then there was a Crosse bille broughte by some of theise defendauntes againste the pl. & the sayde Thomas Jones, for mainteynaunce in Jhones, misdemeanor as a Justice of peace, & a ryote; & this bille was put in before the other & a *subpoena ad audiendum Judicium* taken oute before th'other, & therefore the Counselle desyred it mighte firste be hearde, albeit in th'other they had gotte the starte of them in the paper; but it woulde not be graunted: the case was thus, that Jhones, beinge a Counsellor at the lawe & a Justice of peace, was requested by Sr John Wildgoose & Thom. Wildegoose,[1] his brothers in lawe, to retaine an Atturnie, & to doe the beste he coulde for there & his sister; wch he did, & gaue an Atturnye 3s 4d, & gaue his owne Counsell gratis, & this by all was adiudged no mainteynaunce: this Johnes consultinge the nighte before how this Corne showlde be reaped, for John Parrie hauinge marryed olde Wildegoose' daughter, & growinge vnthriftie & wastefull, & sellinge some lande, they endeauoured to gette a Joyncture, or some prouision, for there syster & her Childe, & procured to the 2 Wildegooses a lease for 99 yeares to the vse of the wife yf shee lyued so longe, & of her childe: the wyfe sowed the lande: & the sayde Jhones, deuysinge how this Corne showlde be reaped, fearinge Parrie's & his seruauntes' resystaunce, procured a *capias vtlagatum* from the vndersherife (beinge Jhones' kinseman), & arrested & ymprysoned Parrie, albeit the vtlarye was

[1] This Thomas Wildgoose, or some one else of the same name, invented a new method of propelling boats. Writing to Viscount Cranborne [letter undated; attributed to 1604], he says that his 'first woorke shall be a boate of pleasure for his matie & his fayre queene to sporte vp & downe the rivr of Thames, in as stately and as stronge as his matie will, to run as sweeft or as slow as they list themselues, & no man perceave how it goeth: but as if swannes swimminge or flyeinge, or horses of the race of Pegasus beatinge their winges in the ayre, or stagges, vnycornes, or lyons, trampling on the waves, should draw it forward.' State Papers, Domestic, James I., vol. 11, no. 1.

longe before satisfyed, & the dette dyscharged, & allso vpon Latytats made speciall baillies of his owne seruauntes & other of his freindes, to the number of 9 or 10, for the arrestinge of Parrie's seruauntes: by Collor whereof they came thyther wth swoordes, billes, wealche hookes, & other weapons, & did arreste Parrie's men: & Mr Jhones himselfe, hauinge grounde adioyninge to the hedge where the Corne did growe, came thither earlye in the morninge, wth his rapyer by his side & a shorte truncheon in his hande, & there stayd all daye, & Commaunded them to keepe the [p. 259] peace; & seinge one wth his hatte one his heade, strouke him one the heade, & tolde him there were better men in place then himselfe, & bidde him be vncouered; wherevnto he made aunsweare that there was more Cause to keepe one his hatte to keepe his heade. wch strykinge by a Justice of p[eace] was muche myslyked of by the Courte, for that he was to geue all good example for the preseruatyon of the the peace; his carte was there, & helped to howse the Corne.

Assault by Justice of Peace

'For theise offences they were all acquyted by the Lo. Tresorer, Lo. Zouche, *euesque de Londres*, Justice Yeluerton & Sr John Herberte, but clerelye sentenced & Fyned for the Ryote by the Lo. Chauncellor, th'erle of Exeter and the Lo. Cheife Baron, but there sentence coulde not alter the former opinions, because of the moste voyces; but Jhones was muche Condemned for the Cunninge & suttle Conueyaunce hereof, & Condemned very bitterlye *in foro conscientiae et in foro Judicij*.

Acquitted by the majority

Jones censured

In Camera Stellata, coram Consilio ibidem, Mercurij, 28 Maij, 1606.[1]

1606 May 28

The Cause of hearinge between Mrs Gowen, plaintiff, and Kennelle, defendant; 'one side onelye was hearde & so adiourned to the nexte daye.'[2]

GAWEN *v.* KENNELLE

[1] Eight Councillors and Judges were present.
[2] See *ante*, pp. 264, 279; and next page.

1606 May 30

In Camera Stellata, coram consilio ibidem, Veneris, 30 Maij, 1606.[1]

Gawen v. Kennelle

Riot and misdemeanour

The said cause of hearing between M[rs] Gawen, plaintiff, against Kennelle, Willoughbie and Tines, ministers, the Constable and Tithingman, two Coroners of the County of Wilts, and one Richard Coomes, defendants, for two riots, 'misdemeanor, in takinge vp & buryinge the bodye of Thomas Gawen, the pl[aintiff]'s husbande, now Contynewed in hearinge twooe whole dayes, & layde seuerallye for distincte offences, but in one bill.

[p. 260]

Gawen a recusant

'The offences were layde thus, that M[rs] Gawen's husbande beinge a stiffe & a roughe recusante, his lande, as it appeares before, was leased to one Fortescue, & so to Kennelle, for the life of M[r] Gawen: in Auguste, the firste yeare of Kinge James, M[r] Gawen died, as it was supposed vpon a sondaye at nighte or vpon mondaye morninge, & beinge a fatte & Corpulente man, his wyfe made haste the nexte daye to burye him: & at one parishe M[r] willoughbye denyed them buryall, for that he sayde M[r] Gawen was excommunicate, & therefore was not to be buryed in churche or Churcheyarde; therevnto they replyed that yt was pardoned, & shewed his Ma[tie's] generall pardon vnder the greate sealle. But M[r] Willoughbie saide he woulde repayre to his ordinarie, & be aduysed by him; whoe, searchinge wth the officer for that purpose, was Certifyed it was so, & therevpon were of opinion that he oughte not to be buryed in Consecrated grounde: they, goinge to another parishe, where Tynes was mynister, in the nighte time, w[th] dyuerse to the number of tenne or twelue, gotte into the Churche, & buryed him in the Chauncelle of the same Churche, w[th]oute eyther Mynister, Clerke or sexton, & locked the Churche doore to them, & the nexte daye range [the bells] all daye in twooe seuerall parishes; & in this they range so disorderlye that the Constable, Tythingman, the minister, & dyuerse of the parishe, were raysed, to the number of 30 or 40, doubtinge some fyer or other disordred assemblinge,

His death

Burial refused

Buried at night in another church

[1] Ten Councillors and Judges were present.

& repayred to the Churche, but Coulde not be permitted to enter, but gotte in at a lytle pryuie doore, & examyninge that assemblye, what they made there, or why they range in suche a Fashyon, they began to be muche offended, & tolde them they woulde Contynewe there in so doinge, & woulde haue thruste them oute of the Churche; the Constable & Tythingman Commaundinge them to be gone, & forcinge them oute of the Chauncelle, the woman spatte in the tythingman's face. Herevpon the Constable had [p. 261] her to the stockes, & put all the reste out of the Churche. After this there was a brute [*i.e.* bruit] that Mr Gawen was not deade, but fledde beyonde sea, or hydde him; for the daye before he was supposed to dye, he was seene rydinge throughe Blamforde. Now Kennelle, havinge an estate for Gawen's lyfe, grewe suspicious of his deathe, & in the nighte time wth his man wente to the Churche, & dygged vp one ende of his graue, & founde his Coffen, & so lefte, & did no more, but lefte the graue open, & filled not the earthe in againe, & wente his waye. And w^th^in Fewe dayes after repayred to Sr James Maruin, a lyuetenaunte & a Justice of peace,[1] & suggested vnto him that it was bruted & muche suspected that eyther Gawen was not deade, or that he Came to some violente or vntimelye deathe, that he was strangled, or his wife had hastened his ende, & desyred that the Crowners mighte viewe the bodye; therevpon he wrote to the Crowners theise partyculer suggestyons, & wyshed them to sommon a Jurye to haue *visum corporis*; the 2 Crowners soone after sommoned a Jurye, & appeared at the place at the daye, and the foreman of the Jurye suggestinge that it was very suspicious (by reason of the Infectyon of the plauge in those partes & his sodaine deathe)

Gawen reported not dead

Kennelle digs up the body

He writes to the Coroners

Inquest

Fear of the plague

[1] Sir James Mervyn of Fonthill Gifford, co. Wilts, knight; aged 37 at the death of his father in 1566; will dated 1610, proved 1611. He left an only daughter, Lucy, who married George Tuchet, Lord Audley, created Earl of Castlehaven 1617. Their son, Mervyn Tuchet, was beheaded in 1631, when the manor of Fonthill Gifford was forfeited to the Crown. [See *State Trials.*] About 1750 the property was sold to Alderman Beckford, whose son rebuilt the house on a magnificent scale, and called it Fonthill Abbey. The present owners of the estate are Sir Michael Shaw-Stewart, Bart., of Fonthill Abbey, and Alfred Morrison, Esq., of Fonthill House. See Hoare's *Wiltshire*, iv. 12.

1606 May 30 that it was muche to be feared that he might dye of the plague, & therefore desyred that he mighte lye in the grounde some longer time for feare of infectyon; wch the Inquest adjourned Crowners yealded vnto, & adiourned the Jurye for 14 dayes; at wch daye they all appearinge, the Crowner Commaunded the tythingman to digge vp the graue & take out the bodye, wch he vtterlye refused to doe, & then Kennelle hyred one [p. 262] to do it. Whoe was enforced by reason of the waighte of the Corps to dragge him at the lighteste ende, whereby, his Feete being vpwarde, the whole waighte of his Corps swayed to his heade & necke (wch Kennelle himselfe was Charged to doe & to dregge him into a meadowe farre of); whereas the Jurye desyred, that the body hauing longe lyen in the earthe, & of very stronge sauoure, the Churcheyarde small, & the assemblye of people greate, allmoste a 100, that he mighte be broughte into a meadowe close adioyninge, where there woulde be more & better ayre, wch was done accordinglye; but none of the Jurye but one durste for the stronge sauoure of the Corps come nere him, but Kennelle Caused one to reape the shrowde, & gaue euydence himselfe to the Jurye that there was a suspicious Circle aboute his necke that he showlde be strangled; but Verdict of natural death the Jurye did acquite him, & founde he dyed of a naturall deathe & a naturall disease, (& as it was generallye suspected, an impostume in the stomacke). So they all departed; the Crowner gaue charge to the parishe & officers Parish officers refuse to bury the body to burye the Corps, wch they refused to doe. Kennelle Caused it to be drawne into the Churche poarche, & hidde awaye the keye of the Churche doore, & there let him lye dyuerse dayes; whereby all the parishe were so annoyed that they durste not Come to the Churche. & w^th^in Fewe Kennelle does so dayes after, Mr Kennelle gaue dyrections that he showlde be buryed in the Churcheyarde, but whereas all for the most parte are vsuallye buryed easte & weste, he Caused Grave made north and south his graue to be made northe & southe, & some findinge faulte wth it, he sayde, "as he was an ouerthwarte neighboure Overthwart while he lyued, so he shalbe buryed ouerthwartelye, & if you mislike it, I will haue him dregde at a horse taile, & layde vpon the downes.'

'Theise were the offences wherew^th^ the defendauntes were charged. At the firste openinge they did sounde most barbarouselye & inhumanelye, but in the ende they were well qualifyed, albeit Kennelle, in the opinion of the Courte, was muche Condemned to haue begonne & proceeded in this busynesse wth greate malyce againste Gawen, lyuinge & deade, his goods & reputation: for Willoughbye & Tines they were acquyted, & muche Commended to haue dealte well & discreatelye, & the Bishop allso; for yf the excommunication be pronounced, the pardon dothe not discharge it; otherwise if it be but graunted & not denounced; & before 16° Elizab. *Reginae*, vtlaries were excepted in the pardons, & not pardoned. but to saye the Kinge Can not pardon ecclesyasticall causes ys very iniurious, for he ys supreame heade of the churche, & before Q. Eliz. was borne mighte haue pardoned outlaries: so were lykewise the Constable & Tythingman acquyted & Commended for that they did well & as they oughte to have done, for vpon any suche outrage they oughte *ex officio* to Commytte the parties: [p. 263] The Ministers acquitted King can pardon ecclesiastical offences Constable and Tythingman acquitted

'For the Coroners, there office ys that vpon complainte that any person ys come to an vntimelye, vnnaturall, or violente deathe, they are to haue *visum corporis*; for the Kinge is so interessed in euerye subiecte that he hathe, that there must an accounte be made vnto him how he came to his deathe, whereof the lawe dothe presume the Coroner Can not haue notice but *super visum corporis*: & the inhabytantes oughte to giue notice to the Coroner of any person suspected to Come to suche a deathe. And it is not the Coroner's office to take vp the bodye, or to burye the bodye, but the Inhabitantes of the parish oughte to doe bothe, & yf they doe not they are to be fyned: for Kennelle, he was muche Condemned in that of himselfe, w^th^out any dyrection by aucthoritye, [he] tooke vpon him to breake vp hallowed grounde, & to leaue it vnreuerentlye not closed up againe. but for the Coroners to take vp the bodye, albeit yt haue lyne longe, they maye doe it by lawe, & so is the booke case of 21 E[dward] 4, adiudged in 2 R[ichard] Duties of Coroners [p. 264] Parish must take up and re-bury the body

1606 May 30 Coroners acquitted Kennelle much condemned

3 by all the Judges of Englaunde after Complainte made to the Kinge.[1] The [coroners were] acquyted by the Courte: but Kennelle was muche Condemned by all the Courte, & thoughte in truthe to be the firste inuentor of all theise rumors, but it was not proued in the bookes,[2] yf it had they woulde haue Fyned him more heauilye. The charge in the Informacyon was that he & his seruauntes, &c., wch the Judges thoughte noe sufficiente charge, albeit the prooffes did artyculate some of them: but the principall offence againste Kennelle wherevpon the Cowrte grounded there sentence was his inhumane vsage in the buryall of the Corps ouerthwarte, his malicious woordes of him, for *de mortuis nil nisi bonum*; & o^r^ vsuall manner of buryinge ys very auntiente, as Basill notethe, & vsed by the Apostles in the primatiue churche: & so we praye to the Easte.

Overthwart burial

Sentence

'For this he was fyned by some 200^li.^, but by the sentence of the Cowrte a 100^li.^, & imprisonmente:

Coome's offence

'Coome's offence was that this vsage beinge complayned of to the Lordes of the Councelle, & soundinge muche worse then it now appearethe to be by the proffes (a practise of the popishe sorte to caste a scandale vpon o^r^ religion),[3] whereas wee all deteste & abhorre all suche Cruell & barbarous vsage, & Condemne it as heathenishe & inhumane, & rather leaue it to them to glorye in then wee o^r^ selues [p. 265] woulde be once blemyshed wth it, but vpon this complainte the lordes graunted oute there warrante, & Coomes beinge tolde thereof, he made aunsweare he Cared not for the same the leaste heare [hair] of his bearde: for wch his Contempte to aucthoritie, he was fined 40^li.^ in regarde of his pouertie, otherwyse it had bene greater, & adiudged to stande vpon the pillorie wth papers.

Contempt of the Council

Sentence

The Lord Chancellor moves that defendants, when acquitted, shall have their costs

'In the Conclusyon, the Lo. Chauncellor moued the Judges to this purpose, that forasmuche here ys but one defendaunte or 2 sentenced, the reste acquyted, & no Cause of Complainte against them, albeit the bill or informacion be ioynte againste them all, yet it Chargethe them seuerallye,

[1] *Year Books*, Mich. 21 Edw. IV., no. 55; Mich. 2 Ric. III., no. 5.
[2] The depositions.
[3] The Gawens were papists.

& wth seuerall offences, & of sundrye natures, whether the reste that are acquyted shall haue there costes; he Cyted a presydente where in the lyke Case Costes was awarded; & so the Judges & Courte were now of opinion that those defendauntes that were now acquyted in this cause showlde haue allso there Costes. *quod nota bene.* The Archebishoppe delyuered a secrete practise of the papistes, that of late dayes they vse to wrappe there deade bodyes in 2 sheepes,[1] & in the one of them they strawe earthe that they themselves haue hallowed, & so burye them they Care not where, for they saye they are thus buryed in Consecrated earthe.' The Archbishop on burial of Papists

In Camera Stellata, coram consilio ibidem, Martis, 3 Junij, [1606], le prochein iour puis le terme, adonque presente Lo. Chauncellor, Archeuesque de Canterberie, Lo. Tresorer, Lo. Admirall, Lo. Chamberlin, Lo. Shrewsbery, Lo. worster, Lo. Northampton, Lo. Salisberie, Lo. exeter, Euesque de Londres, Lo. Zouche, Lo. Knowlles, Ch. Just., Ch. Baron, Justice wanslowe, Justice williams, S[r] John Fortescue & S[r] John Herberte. 1606 June 3 [p. 266]

On motion it was ordered that if the parties, without licence, agree in compounding a cause, pending in this Court, they shall pay the Costs. Compromise without leave

The Attorney-general informed *ore tenus* against the two Lords in the Tower for the powder treason. 'Lo. Sturton[2] & Henrye, Lo. Mordante,[3] standinge w[th]in a barre made of purpose for them: He firste shewed them there examynacion, & they reade them, & acknowledged them to be true: then he began to shewe that when the kinge had peace *infra et extra quatuor maria* then he was in most daunger: *vbi* THE KING *v.* LORDS STOURTON and MORDAUNT — Contempt

[1] Query sheets, or sheep skins?

[2] Edward, 9th Baron Stourton, succeeded his brother John in 1588; *ob.* 1632. He mar. Frances, dau. of Sir Thomas Tresham of Rushton, co. Northampton; her brother, Sir Francis, was involved in the Gunpowder Plot, and attainted of High Treason; her sister, Elizabeth, mar. William, Lord Monteagle, to whom the celebrated letter was written. Burke, *Extinct Baronetage, s.v.* Tresham. See also Bell, *Ruins of Liveden.*

[3] Henry, 4th Baron Mordaunt, succeeded his father, Lewis, in 1601; *ob. cir.* 1608.

1606 June 3 *maxima securitas, ibi maximum periculum,* & when all showlde haue bene destroyed *uno flatu, uno ictu,* then these 2 lordes showlde haue bene saued. Whose offences he deuyded into fowre partes :—

1. the qualitie of th'offence.
2. the Circumstaunces.
3. the excuses.
4. presidentes or examples ; *nam periculosum existimo quod non bonorum virorum iudicio approbatur.*

Misprision is a greate offence, & punishable in another kinde, yet the kinge hathe pardoned it, & ys pleased to haue yt punished as a Contempte onelye : and so to disobeye the royall Commaundemente of the kinge. *Causa legationis, epistolae regis habent vim legis.* heere in this cause is disobeyinge the greate sealle, & for the greateste cause : & therefore let vs examyne the wrytte. the partes of the wrytte Conteine 2 causes of assemblinge the parliamente, the firste of Commaundemente to appeare for counselle, *de aduisamento consilii de arduis et vrgentibus concernentibus nos, statum*
[p. 267] *ecclesiae christianae, et regni nostri.* The seconde ys *iniungendo mandamus cessante omni et quacunque excusatione sicut nos, honorem nostram* [sic], *saluationem et defensionem, nullatenus omittatis.* In the feweste woordes the most matter ys conteygned that maye be. *et dignitas personae auget culpam.* Elie's faulte hindred the sacrifice & seruice of god. the philosopher saithe *corruptio optimorum pessima.* yf a litle corrupte bloode come to the harte, yt is either deadlye or daungerous ; & this offence is farre greater in theise greate lordes, for it is an offence againste there creation ; & therefore he ys called *nobilis ad consulendum et ad defendendum* ; & twooe honorable Ceremonies are vsed in there creation, for they are not fallen noble from heauen, but a gowne & a swoorde ys gyuen them, & they deryue all there nobilitie & honor from the brighte beames of the kingelye dignitie ; & this there offence ys *eclipsus nobilitatis,* for *eclipsus est defectus lune cum sol opponitur,* &c.

Excuses '3, there excuses : & yf we obserue there affections, they are infected, & there houses peruerted, Jesuited. *mors in olla*, & by the lawe it is felonie to harbor preistes. *et societas habet in se quoddam attractitium* [sic], &c. In the Lo. Mordant's howse a prouisoe ys agreede vpon by the powder traytors that theise twooe elected lordes shalbe preserued. *Judicis officium, vt res, ita tempora rerum* [*querere*]. Theise damnable & detestable preistes are serpentes, vipers. & saithe Senica, *serpentes paruulae fallunt.* An olde preiste maye easilye be founde oute, but theise younge preistes, in fethers & fashions, they doe infecte & affecte too, & ouerthrowe all wth whome they conuerse.

'A greate prince is resembled to an elephante. *et elephantem propter iustas causas serpente percusso terra non patitur. ille tibi semper insidiari potest,* but you can not allwayes finde him. [p. 268]

Lord Stourton's excuses

'The Lorde Sturton's excuses doe rather accuse him: he hadd no monie, & he was in dette, his wyfe delyuered but twooe monethes before, & her father deade, Sr Thomas Tresham,[1] the plauge increased in London. all theise were hinderaunces [so that] he Coulde not come vpon Tusedaye, yet they were no hinderaunces vpon Fridaye, for then he came.

Lord Mordaunt's excuse

'The Lorde Mordante's excuse that beinge in London wth Catesbie in October he wente downe to looke vp his euydence for asserte landes; he had all the sommer before to doe it; & kepte Contynuall Companie wth all the greate Traytors.

Precedents

'4. presidentes. *erubescere sine lege loqui.* noe gouernemente w^th^oute lawe. *quod non lego non credo,* a greate Lorde heretofore sayde it.

In temps E[dward] 1, *roye presente al benefice en Yorke Dioces, archeuesque de Yorke refuse,* for that the pope had presented to the same benefice. '14 E[dward] 3. *Quare non admisit*; *plac.* 3°. He refused the kinge's chaplein, & made aunsweare *nec ausus fuit nec potuit.* For this Contempte he forfeited all his goods and temporalties.

'19 E[dward] 2 *et* 3 Phip. & Mar. in my lorde Dier &

[1] See *ante*, p 287, n. 2.

1606 June 3 Trivit, 19 Edward 2 in l'exchequer; William, Earle of Richemonde, goes w[th]out leaue ouer in to Brittanie, & a priuie sealle ys sente to him for to retorne, & he, not Comminge, forfeited his goods & landes.[1]

'Bartie in Queene Marie's time maryed the Duches of Suffolke, had leaue to goe ouer into Flanders to gette in dettes, & for not retorninge, beinge sente for, he forfeited [p. 269] his landes & goods.[2]

'4 H[enry] 3 in the Tower; Earle Henrye de Cornewall departed from y[e] parliamente w[th]oute leaue, he forfeyted all his landes & goodes.[3]

'3 E[dward] 3, fo. 18, 19;[4] Vmbran', 11; John *euesque de* Winchester, one of the parliamente, was arraigned, for that he was sommoned & Came not, & greeuouselye fyned.

'When the kinge or his lyuetenaunte goethe to the warres, the nobles and Commons, that are the strengthe of the lande, oughte to attende vpon sommons, & to departe w[th]oute leaue ys felonie; for then allso ys the Counselle of y[e] lande assembled.

'6 H[enry] 8, cap. 16. a Burges can not departe w[th]oute leaue.

'Blessed be god, those are preserued that showlde have bene destroied, & all those that showlde haue bene preserued (but that the kinge extendes greate mercye) showlde haue

[1] Dyer's *Reports*, ed. 1794, fo. 128 b. The reference to Trivet suggests the *Annales* of Nicholas Trivet, but I cannot find any reference to the Earl of Richmond's case there. No *William*, Earl of Richmond, is mentioned by Courthope, *Historic Peerage*, or Burke, *Extinct Peerage*; John de Dreux, 4th Earl of Richmond and Duke of Brittany, succeeded his father in 1305, and died 1334. He is probably the nobleman referred to in the text.

[2] Katherine, Baroness Willoughby d'Eresby, dau. and heir of William, Lord Willoughby d'Eresby, mar. 1st, Charles Brandon, Duke of Suffolk. He died 1545, and his widow mar. Richard Bertie, of Bersted, co. Sussex, in 1553. Being both zealous Protestants, they retired to the continent during Mary's reign, and did not return till her death. See Burke's *Extinct Peerage; Dict. of Nat. Biog.; Five Generations of a Loyal House*, by Lady Georgina Bertie; Dyer's *Reports*, 176 a.

[3] Henry (or Richard) Fitz Count, Earl of Cornwall, natural son of Reginald de Dunstanville, Earl of Cornwall, natural son of Henry I. See Dugdale's *Baronage* and Burke's *Extinct Peerage*.

[4] *Year Book*. The case is not quite correctly cited in the text; the Bishop came, but departed without leave.

bene destroyed. He is a blessed man therefore whome a traitor dothe not affecte: thoughe they Curse, wee will blesse.

'Then he reade the Confessions of Roberte Winter, Guie Faux, Thomas Winter, Euerard Digbie, [Robert] Caies, Henry Garnette, superior of ye Jesuits. *non libens loquor, res ipsa loquitur.*

'For theise offences by the sentence of ye Courte they were fyned, the Lo. Mordante tenne thousaunde markes [1] & the Lorde Sturton syxe thousaunde markes,[2] & ymprisonmente in the tower from whence they Came duringe the kinge's pleasure. Sentence

'Justice williams delyuered that yf a man departe out of the Realme w^th^oute leaue, he shall forfeite his goods. Justice Williams on departure from the Realm

'20 E[dward] 1. the kinge presentes to ye archedeakonrye of Norwige, & the partie for that cause ys excommunicate, the bishop was fyned 2000^li.^

'25 E[dward] 3. Sr Frauncis Englefeilde wente beyonde seae, & was serued wth a priuye sealle to retorne. *quaere le case.*

'5 R[ichard] 2, cap. 4. to be absente from the parliamente ys a greate Contempte, & was fined & imprisoned.[3] [p. 270]

'The Lo. Ch. Justice. a Contempte ys greatlye aggrauated or minished by ye Circumstaunces. the absence in progres, in warre, or embasie, ys a greate Contempte. The Lord Chief Justice

'The erle of Salisberye spake some thinge againste the questionistes of this age, & called them the Antagonistes. The Earl of Salisbury

'*conuersatio consiliorum concio.*

'This Damnable plotte had broughte desperate Calamitie, & a masse of confusyon.

'The greater the offences are, the more hydden they lye: but the kinge of his grace hathe bowed the Cedar so lowe as to stoope to the iudgemente of this Courte.

[1] £6,666 13*s*. 4*d*.
[2] £4,000.
[3] Stat. 2. 'Every one to whom it belongeth, shall upon summons come to the Parliament.'

1606 June 3 | The Earl of Northampton

'Northampton. *cedant priuata publicis.*

3 remedies in phisique to cure diseases { Diete, medecine, bloud lettinge } Diacatholicon

'*Excusatio infructuosa, aliquando inutilis, aliquando nulla.* Assuerus' iudgmente for the Queene's Contempte in not Comminge to the Feaste. Ciceroe did obserue Catiline's Companie. *Quorum est commune simbolum, eorum facilis est transitus, non in fulmen, sed in sonitum. Estote in speculis ne dignitate vestra priuemini.*

The Archbishop of Canterbury

'The Archebishop. *in re manifesta non eget probatione*: he woulde be shorte, for that all that had gone before him had marched vnder the Atturnie's inuention.

Lord Chancellor

'The Lo. Chauncellor sayde that theise exorbitante offences are not subiecte to an ordinarye Course of lawe.

'*Qui non corrigit peccatum, assentit.*

'*Nobiles, quia noscibiles,* for there religion & virtues. *nobilitas gentis ignobililatem mentis,* &c. *quod scire debes et non vis, non pro ignorantia, sed pro contemptu, habetur.* Saint Barnarde.'

He agreed with the fines and imprisonment.[1]

1606 June 27 [p. 271]

In Camera Stellata, coram Consilio ibidem, Veneris, 27 Junij, 1606, adonque presente, 1. Lo. Chauncellor, 2. archeuesque de Canterbery, 3. Lo. Tresorer, 4. Lo. Admirall, 5. Lo. Chamberlin, 6. Lo. Shrewseberie, 7. Lo. worster, 8. Lo. Northampton, 9. Lo. Salisberie, 10. Lo. Exeter, 11. Lo. Zouche, 12. Lo. Knolles, 13. Lo. wootton, 14. Lo. Stanhoppe, 15. euesque de Londres, 16. Lo. Cheife Justice, 17. Lo. Cheife Baron, 18. Sr John Fortescue, 19. Sr John Herberte.

THE KING *v.* EARL OF NORTHUMBERLAND — Contempt

A greate scaffold was erected for the courtiers and other men of great account, and the side bar with a seat for the prisoners.

The Attorney-general, Sir Edward Coke, informed *ore*

[1] See Appendix XIX.

tenus against the Earle of Northumberland[1] (brought from the Tower of London by Sir William Wade, Lieutenant of the Tower, and Sir William Lane), for the powder treason, '& begins wth very greate respecte, beinge of highe & emynente place, & the greateste person & Cause that euer was broughte into that Courte.

'He deuided the Cause into 4 partes: the firste for the honor & order of the kinge's Ma$^{tie's}$ proceedinge againste him, his highe & greate offence beinge now drawne downe to a small Contempte:

'2. the offences that he ys now charged wthall.

'3. the Circumstaunces, that doe aggrauate the offence wherewth he ys charged.

'4. his greate & many misfortunes.

'In all wch he woulde deale succinctlye & sincerelye, wth protestacion of respecte of honor, & that truthe showlde be his Center & temperaunce his Circumference: Tullye in all his oratyons tooke pleasure in defences, but neuer in inuectiues: the Atturnie Can not defende any offendor *contra coronam et dignitatem regis*, but dothe defende the honor, ye dignitie, ye Justice, & ye mercye of the kinge. *Nunquam oppugnaui quod non salua conscientia impugnaui:* In all the examynacyons there hathe not bene one Interrogatorie againste him or of him, but was allwayes [p. 272] examyned by his peeres, & herein maye Momus & Momis be satisfied. *Summa petit liuor.*

[1] Henry Percy, K.G., 9th Earl of Northumberland; born 1564, died 1632. The question of his complicity in the Gunpowder Plot is gone into very fully by Mr. E. B. de Fonblanque in his *Annals of the House of Percy*, 1887, vol. ii., chap. 12, where many letters and documents on the subject are printed. An account of the proceedings in the Star Chamber is preserved in Cotton MS., Vesp. C. XIV. 451, and a copy of the Decree, apparently Coke's rough draft, in Harleian MS. 589 (15), fo. 111. The balance of the fine of 30,000*l*. was remitted after 11,000*l*. had been paid, Nov. 8, 11 James I, 1613; but the Earl was kept a prisoner in the Tower until July 18, 1621. See also Collin's *History of the Ancient and Illustrious Family of the Percys*, p. 106.

1606, June 25.—John Chamberlain to Dudley Carleton. 'The Lordes sat much in counsaile about yor Lorde [Northumberland] and on Monday morning were wth him in the towre, but what passed I cannot learne, only the common voyce goes the K[ing] wold haue him to the Star-chamber.' State Papers, Domestic, James I, vol. 22, no. 20.

1606 June 27

Presumptions

'There are three kinde of presumptions. the first *leues aut temerariae.*

'2. *probabiles, aut veresimiles.*

'3. *violentae, aut necessariae, aut vehementes.*

'*Neruus sapientiae non temere credere.*

'The leaste of all theise presumptions drawethe restrainte.

'11° E[dward] 4. Common fame sufficethe to examyne & restrayne not to a howse but of fauoure and not of righte.

'*semiprobaciones ac solae presumptiones concludunt et condemnant in causa lesae maiestatis.*

'*mors in olla.*

'Yet his ma^tie^ out of his greate grace hathe fashioned them but as Contempts & misprisions.

'*misericors et iustus est deus, poet condonare sine meritis, quia misericors, non condemnare sine malis operibus, quia iustus.*

'This greate Earle the ninthe Earle in discente: no man makes auntiente nobilitie but god: yet [for] damnable offence the kinge hathe proportioned a punishemente *ad instructionem, non ad destructionem.*

'But there are some that make *Cornutum argumentum*, a boollheaded argumente, *vt haec ficta, non facta, videantur* to posterities.

The Jesuits

'*Patienter audire, causam discernere, et recte iudicare, sapientis est iudicis.*

'Theise Jesuites or Jebusites are the cause of all theise. they may be lykened to the harpies, *virgineas volucres, excecando, coinquinando* by equiuocation, & *praeripiendo.* euery heretike *ipso facto est* excommunicate, & any man maye kille him, & it is a disabilitie to him & to his posteritie.

'*Qui adheret hereticis amittit regnum et gentem.*

'*Quos hostis ad malum inuenit, deus ad bonum disposuit.* Laddes of ye Northe shall stande for this defence: & now substaunces are made but Circumstaunces, & bodies but shadowes.

'Garnet was the prouinciall or superior of ye Jesuites. *Father Garnet*

'Thomas Winter was the messenger; the Catholikes offer assystaunce, & prepare horses for inuasyon, & to lande them in Milforde Hauen. But the Atturnye protested he woulde delyuer nothinge to preiudicate the partye nor preiudge ye Courte. [p. 273]

'In ye beginninge of the kinge's Raigne, & at the ende of ye Queene's Raigne, ye Lo. of Northumberlande became the heade of ye Catholikes, & a freinde to ye Catholique Cause, & he desyred the Catholikes mighte depende vpon him. *exteriora et extrinseca demonstrant interiora.* the Spaniardes showlde lande in Milforde hauen, & in the righte of his wyfe he had Carewe Castle neere vnto it[1]: & at that time he increasethe his stable, so that he tolde ye kinge his hole reuenue woulde scarcelye mainteyne it. *Northumberland the head of the Catholics*

'There were 2 damnable & detestable bulles againste the kinge, &c. *Quandocunque contigerit miseram feminam illam Elizabetham ex hac vita excedere, excludantur omnes successores quantumcunque propinquitate sanguinis, &c., nisi catholicam religionem non solum tolerare sed eam omni opere et studio promouere, et iureiurando,* &c. *Two Bulls against the King*

'After the Earle of Northumberlande knew of theise 2 bulles, he sente Percie into Scotlande for a toleration, wth 2 letters & a message pretendinge the more easye entraunce yf he woulde geue hopes of toleration : wch were intollerable & not to be indured, for that an englisheman's harte greues to see another kinde of woorshippe: vpon Percie's retorne out of Scotlaunde, the Erle of Northumberland tolde the Catholykes that the kinge's Commaundemente was that they showlde be assured of ease of there persecutions : *The proposed toleration*

[1] His wife was Dorothy, dau. of Walter Devereux, Earl of Essex, and widow of Sir Thomas Perrott, knight. Carew Castle was forfeited to the Crown on the attainder of Rhys ap Griffith, son of Sir Rhys ap Thomas, K.G., for high treason. He was beheaded Dec. 4, 1531. The Castle and Lordship of Carew were leased to a Mr. Parrott or Perrott, who is called Sir John by Fenton (*A Historical Tour through Pembrokeshire*, p. 250), and Sir Andrew by Lewis (*Topographical Dict. of Wales*). This lease probably descended to Sir Thomas Perrott, the first husband of the Countess of Northumberland, and formed part of the dower, or jointure, assigned to his widow.

1606 June 27 wch the kinge himselfe *in verbo regio* saythe he neuer did promise or Commaunde.

'The Lo. windsor broughte the Catholiques' petition to the Erle of northumberlande, & he presented it to the kinge. Beinge interrogated of the Catholique parte, he aunswearethe he remembrethe not. *vt res ita tempora rerum.*

'Percie he sayde, "Well, I must kill the kinge." But p. 274] Catesbie aunsweared, "No, Tom; yf thou wylte be a traytor, thou shallte doe it to some purpose. I am thinkinge," &c. "Well," sayes Percie, "wee are allwayes talkinge, but wee doe nothinge." After this they plotted this pouder treason, & were all sworne & tooke the sacramente to effecte it, & to Concealle yt: & soone after this he [Thomas Percy] was made a pentioner, a fitte man to put an axe into his hande to carrye it ouer the kinge's heade.

'*veniam leso numine casus habet.*

'A man maye Justifie ye killinge of a traytor Comminge to kille the kinge.

'9 *Julij*, he was made a pencioner, & neuer tooke anye oathe: Staplie, clerke of ye Checke, showlde haue ministred it:

'*Omne falsum dolum in se continet.*

The Catholic Lords to be saved

'Theise Traitors, assembled together, Consulte for sauinge the Catholique Lordes: Northumberlande, Mounteagle, a blessed name to the worlde's ende, vicounte Mountague, Sturton, Mordante. Alas! I thinke they neuer meante to make any of theise protectors.

'At eleuen of clocke, Percie sendes muche to Fauxe after he came from Northumberlande: & after the acte done, then there showlde be viceroyes & mariages. wrighte's sister nursed the Ladye Marye. Percie sayde, wthin 24 howres before the time, that yf the proiecte by powder tooke no effecte, Northumberlande woulde curse him.

'Monie flewe abroade, & the englishe regimente showlde come ouer, & Catesbie showlde haue Sir Charles Percye's place.

'*vbi non possum discernere, non teneor diuinare.*

'A Counsellor restrayned oughte not to wryte to any

w[th]out leaue, but Northumberlande wrote that his treasure showlde be in safetie, w[ch] was but a wache worde to Persie that the plotte was discouered, but noe worde to apprehende Percie.

'*Coalescunt et crescunt presumptiones.*

'Sion (a heape of benefittes) was gyuen to Northumberlande, & leaue to selle. Sion House

'*Qui reddit malum pro bono, non recedet malum a domo eius.* [p. 275]

'Dissimulation in religion had neuer goode ende; a fearfull thinge.

'Simeon and Leuy meante fraude in there hartes. Dauid was a states man, & yet it is sayde he Can not gouerne that can not dissemble. Northumberlande had neyther discontente, wante, nor disgrace: but he must Calclate [*sic*] the kinge's natiuitie by S[r] Roberte Carre.[1] & causethe him to wryte to Topperine & to Herriotte:[2] *par le Canon ley* suche persons are excommunicate. 21 Isaiah; 19 Job. "all ye that loue the lorde seeke the thinge that ys good."

'but for matter of religion he cares not muche.

'The Confessyon of a delinquente ys in the nature of verdicte.

'Henry Garnette broughte 2 bulles *sub anulo piscatoris*: they neuer bellowed. The bulls that bellowed not

'*Tutius est ledere temporalem quam eternam maiestatem.*'

The king himself ought to appoint all pensioners. *Et quae non prosunt singula multa iuuant.*

'Calculatinge *occupatissima vanitas et indocta doctrina.*

'Herriott is a funerall beaste. 13 Elizab.

'Inwarde essences are beste knowne by outwarde properties, as greate ryuers by litle springes, trees by there rootes or braunches.

'3. Circumstaunces w[ch] my lorde vsed: to geue hopes to Catholiques by Commaundemente to be eased of there Northumberland encouraged the Catholics

[1] Apparently not Sir Robert Carr, or Ker, who was afterwards created Viscount Rochester and Earl of Somerset, as he was not knighted until Dec. 23, 1607. See *Dict. of Nat. Biog.*

[2] Probably George Heriot, the King's Jeweller, the founder of Heriot's Hospital, Edinburgh. See *Dict. of Nat. Biog.*

1606 June 27

persecutions, & to holde them in hopes. 2 daungerous knowne Jesuyted recusauntes offered to kill the kinge, sworne and taken the sacramente to doe it: & an axe put into his hande to Carye ouer the kinge's heade, & yet not sworne.

'*Scilicet in superis fortuna luenda est.*

'*vbi dolor, ibi digitus.*

'An accusation of a delinquente ys stronger then anye wytnes: it is an olde tricke of a traitor to rayle vpon his accuser.

[p. 276] '*Fictae excusationes iustam accusationem inducunt.*'

Sentence: Herbert

'For this his offence, Secretar. Herberte fined him 10,000li.,[1] the losse of his Counsellor's place & Captaine of the pentioners: & imprisonmte duringe the kinge's pleasure.'

Fortescue

Fortescue agreed.

Chief Baron and Chief Justice

By the Chief Baron and the Chief Justice: every pensioner oughte to be sworn, '& the Captaine of the pentioners oughte to be presente when he is sworne; it is a truste reposed in him; & by them bothe helde a greate offence to wryte when he was restrayned. they agree to the fine & imprisonmte & losse of offices.

Lords Stanhope, Wootton, and Knollys

'Stanhope, wootton & Knoulles agree allso.

Lord Zouche

'Zouche: 2 religions Can not stande together; for Percie either had no feelinge of religion, or was a knowne papiste, before he was a pentioner. & agreed wth the reste in sentence.

Bishop of London

'*Euesque de Londres: non minuit delictum dignitas personae.* & agrees to the reste.

Lord Exeter

'Exeter agreed allso. *Amicus usque ad aras.*

Lord Salisbury

'Salisberie. "I haue taken paines," sayde hee, "in my nowne harte to cleare my lorde's offences, wch now haue leade mee from the Contemplation of his virtues; for I knowe him vertuous, wyse, valiaunte, & of vse & ornamente to the state. The more perylous wyse men's actions be, there the more industrye they vse to gouerne them. Actions doe conteigne *euidenciam operum.* The Cause of this Com-

[1] This is a mistake of Hawarde's; the fine was 30,000*l.* See *ante*, p. 293, n. 1.

bustion [was] the papistes seekinge to restore there religion. *Non libens dico sed res ipsa loquitur.*" '

He agreed as to the fine with the Chief Justice, and imprisonment for life during the King's pleasure.

'Northampton : *solem e mundo non cum mundo.* a kinge most gracyous, clemente, sweete & worthye prince that euer was. many greate princes haue suffered for lesse faultes. Buckingham for a wenne in his forheade. warwicke. Perkin warbecke. mountsurroy. verona *et* placentia in Italie. He agreede wth Salisberie. Lord Northampton [p. 277]

'worster, Shrewsberie, Suffolke, Admirall, & Tresorer, agree. *et l'archeuesque auxy.* Others agree

'Chauncellor. *vt audio sic iudico, non sic vt amo aut odio.* rather blushe then bleede at so heynous a plotte, *occulta et latens, demonis inspiratio.* Theise figure flingers : a daungerous thinge to raise a pryuate man's name aboue or neere the kinge's name. my Lo[rd's] letter to the kinge gyue hopes to the Catholikes, & winde & worke himselfe in. *ignorantia affectata* ys naughte; they woulde not vnderstande because they woulde haue more lybertie to sinne : & so agrees wth the reste, delyueringe that perpetuall imprisonm[te] & ymprisonmente duringe lyfe was all one.'[1] Lord Chancellor

In Camera Stellata, coram consilio ibidem, Jouis, 10 Julij, 1606, adonque presente, Lo. Chauncellor, Lo. Tresorer, les Ch. Justices,[2] dyuerse Judges et auters. 1606 July 10

'The Chauncellor delyuered a charge to the Justices of peace that they showlde conserue the peace & punishe peace breakers. The Lord Chancellor's charge

'1 E[dward] 3. they are Called Conseruators of the peace.

'18 E[dward] 3, 24 E[dward] 3, 34 E[dward] 3, 14 R[ichard] 2, by theise there aucthoritie is increased, & they showlde be men learned. they showlde regarde there oathes & their Commissyon.

[1] See Appendix XIX.

[2] Sir Edward Coke, Attorney-General, was appointed Chief Justice of the Common Pleas, June 30, 1606.

1606 July 10

'And especiallye he Commended to there Care & truste, the findinge out of preistes & suche perylous persons: to the poore & to all beggars: the Judges of Assise are the visitors of the Realme, showlde fauoure none, but cherishe the good & rewarde them, & remoue the euell.

[p. 278]

'That they showlde wth all diligence looke to the gouernem^te of there Alehowses.

'The pretensed greeuaunces in parliamente to the kinge, he takes it to harte, & more Carefull he ys to satisfie them, and hathe Commaunded his Counselle & Judges to Consyder of them: & of all suche as abuse there pattentes. for he Can not holde his Crowne yf he showlde loose his prerogatiue. but he woulde haue it vsed tenderlye, & to the greateste ease to his people that mighte be.'[1]

1606 Oct. 31

In Camera Stellata, coram Consilio ibidem, Veneris, 31 Octobr., 1606.[2]

ATT.-GEN. *v.* MILES

Perjury, maintenance, etc.

'The Attornie generall, now Sr Henrie Hubbarde,[3] *informe* against one Miles, a Common informer, for periurie, mainteynaunce & other misdemeanors. 1. periurie vpon an indictemente, for wch the Judges did forbeare to Censure him because of the Inconuenience thereof, for that all men are so slowe to gyue euydence for the kinge, & this woulde hynder them muche more: 2. for mainteynaunce in buy-

Maintenance

inge & suinge many bondes & dettes of other men's, wch the Judges resolued no man Coulde doe, excepte it were for a true & a due dette *bona fide* assigned; wch dothe ouerthrowe the vsuall & Common Course of making letters of atturnie to sue for another man, wch is Commonlye helde a good warraunte in lawe: 3. his misdemeanors were, in that he was sometimes a Clothier in Suffolke, & not thryuinge

Misdemeanours

in that trade, & enuyinge the prosperitie & thryfte of other Clothyers there, he turned Common ynformer, & informed againste more then threescore seuerall times, but neuer

[p. 279]

broughte any of them to any tryall, but merelye for

[1] Compare this with the other Charges, *ante*, pp. 19, 56, 101, 106, 159, 161, 186, 263 and *post*. As to the grievances, see Appendix XVIII.

[2] Nine Councillors and Judges were present.

[3] Sir Henry Hobart, appointed July 4, 1606.

vexatyon; & in the examynacyons of this Cause yt appeared by one deposition that he had vsed greate blasphemye, (viz:—yf god showlde Come downe from heauen & tell him he woulde teare him into 4 quarters, he woulde not yet leaue his suites); a fearefull & most prophane sayinge, & for wch the Courte did most speciallye and sharpelye Censure him, not as a thinge Complaynable or examynable properlye in this Courte, but now appearinge vnto them in Judgemente, they Coulde not let so greate prophanation & blasphemie go w^th^oute exemplarye punishemente: & therefore for all these offences they founde him guyltie, but for the periurye they woulde not sentence, but for the reste they adiudged him to a fine of a 100^li.^, three yeares ymprisonmente, to stande vpon the pillorie at westminster & in Suffolke at the Assises, & to weare papers declaringe his mainteynaunce, misdemeanor & blasphemie, & to make his submission by humble confessyon, & neuer after to be admytted an ynformer. Mr Richardson, a Counsellor at the barre, of Counsell wth Miles, moued to the Jurisdiction of the Courte, yf they Coulde determine periurie not declared by 6 E. 6;[1] to wch Koke, Ch. Justice *del Commonplace*, replyed bitterlye, marueylinge to heare suche grosse ignoraunce, fruites of abridgemente men that neuer reade the bookes at large: for it was resolued by all the Courte, that this Courte maye determyne all periuries at the Common lawe, & that it was an aunciente Courte longe before H[enry] 7,[2] & determyned Causes, & R[ichard] 3 sate iudiciallye in this Courte:[3] & the Lo. Chauncellor sayde

Sentence

'The lorde Ch. Just. Popham delyuered muche of his owne knowlage extenuatinge th' offences, wch made the sentence more milde.'

Coke, C. J., on Abridgments

The Star Chamber an ancient court, and can try all perjuries

[1] This appears to be a mistake for 5 Eliz. cap. ix.; An Act for punishment of such as shall procure or commit any wilful Perjury.

[2] This refers to the statute 3 Hen. VII. cap. i., which has been considered by many as first creating the Court of Star Chamber. It certainly did not do so, and Coke is perfectly correct in what he says about the ancient jurisdiction of the Court. See *Introduction.*

[3] The authority for this statement seems to be the *Year Books.* Case 4, Michaelmas Term, 2 Ric. II, commences, *Coram Rege & Consilio in Camera Stellarum*; but this does not necessarily imply that the King himself was actually present. Case 22 of the same Term commences, *Dominus Rex interiori Camera stellata appellavit coram se omnes Justiciarios suos*; but this was to get from the Judges a declaration on certain points of law, and was not a judicial proceeding. Still it is quite possible that Coke's statement is true.

1606 Oct. 31

that in Chauncellor Bromlie's time,[1] Serg^te Louelace & Ployden had set there handes to a demurrer for suche a bille of periurye, & were Conuented & bitterlye reprehended in this Courte, to wch Louelace made his excuse that he was a younge man, & when he sawe St Austine goe before he thoughte he mighte safelie followe.

[p. 280]

Coram Rege

'There [are] but 3 *Coram Domino rege.*

'1. *Coram Domino Rege in Cancellaria.*

'2. *Coram Domino Rege in Camera stellata coram consilio ibidem.*

'3. *Coram Domino Rege in Banco vbicunque fuerit.*'

'*Ebrietas dissipat sensum, confundit intellectum, et destruit vitam.*'

1606 [? Nov. 5]

In Camera Stellata, coram consilio ibidem, Mercurij, 1606, [*sic*, ? 5 November], Jacob. Regis Britanniae 4°.[2]

BRIDGEMAN *v.* GLOVER and others — Pre-emption of Tin

The Attorney-general informed on the patent of the Stanneries of emption and pre-emption, made by Queen Elizabeth to Bridgeman and another named Wenne,[3] of London, against one [Richard] Glouer, and others[4] of the Pewterers' Company, for practises and misdemeanours to defraud and deceive the King in his prerogative in the pre-emption of tin, and conveying this without custom, and calling court at their Hall without the Master, in deposing the Master (not warranted by their charter), and in assembling tumultuously and riotously at their Hall, and entering with violence on the treasure without keys, and other like acts. 'Fuller, of Counselle wth the Defendauntes, did confydentelye alleage that pre-emption was newe starte vp, & neuer hearde of before the latter ende of the late Queene's Raigne; but the Lo. Chauncellor did reprehende him bitterlye for it, & wished him to learne better wordes, & seeke to knowe more; for the kinge's Counselle did ap-

[1] 1579 to 1587.

[2] Eight Councillors and Judges were present.

[3] Thomas Brigham and Humphrey Wemmes.

[4] The others were Roger Glover, John Hethe, and Habbakuk Curtes.

proue by many presydentes [precedents] that the kinge & all his predecessors & the princes, Dukes of Cornewall, haue allwayes had bothe emption & pre-emption of all the tinne mines in Deuonshire & Cornewell in whose groundes soeuer they were, as a flower of the Crowne of Englaunde.'

4 *Johannis regis Angliae*; the king grants to the Bishop of Exeter the tithes of the pre-emption of tin in Deuonshire & Cornewell. [p. 281] Precedents as to the pre-emption of tin, etc.

1 Henry III.; a grant to 'Jhone,' the King's mother, of all the Stannaries.

10 Henry III.; the king grants to his brother Richard the Stannary by the name of *stagnarium*.

15 Henry III.; prohibition for merchants not to intermeddle if it be not signed.

33 Edward I.; report in the Commentaries. Quere. For it was read and commended for an excellent precedent.

'12 E[dward] III.; a Commission *par graunte* to take tinne, & Carriage for the same, & all w^th^standers to be rebelles; & there bothe pre-emption & sole emption are graunted.'

31 Edward III.; a grant of the coinage of the stannary [*cunagium stannariae*] by the Prince for three years, and the emption of all the tin, for 3000 marks fine and 500 marks rent.

7 Edward VI.; lease for 21 years for 3000 marks yearly rent, emption of all the white tin.

18 June, 43 Elizabeth; Patent to Bridgeman and another, named Wenne.[1]

And upon the opening of this part only it was adjourned to the Wednesday next following.

On which day, &c., all the evidence was heard for the plaintiff, and Fuller replied to the first part as to the right of the King. As to the precedents, he affirmed that it was never used in [time of] peace, but in time of trouble it was used to raise money to maintain wars; *et necessitas est lex temporis*; and the King shall [then] have pre-emption [of tin] as he shall have pre-emption in victualls and other 1606 [Nov. 12 (?)]

[1] Otherwise called Brigham and Wemes or Wemmes.

1606 [? Nov. 12] provisions by his prerogative, viz:—'he shall buye before euerye man, & no man shall buye before the kinge be [p. 282] furnyshed.' But all the Court reprehended Mr Fuller sharply for such a construction. And the King's Solicitor, Dodrige, proved that all the Kings of this realm at all times had this, and it is the custom also in foreign countries: in France: and the Dukes in Germanie have it.

The Judges' opinions

And the Court moved that the 'Judges showlde geue there resolution in this pointe: wherevpon firste the Lo.

Coke, C. J.

Ch. Justice Koke sayde that Mr Fuller woulde yealde the kinge no more in one kinde than the Maior of London, the Duke of Cornewall, & the Archebishop of Yorke had for the buyinge of vittailles: & in the other kinde he yealdes to more then euer the kinges of Englaunde had or euer he hoped any kinge of Englaunde woulde desyre to haue, by his rule of *necessitas lex temporis*; for in the time of troubles or warres, god forbidde it showlde be lawfull that the kinge mighte take any man's goods, albeit euery man showlde be wyllinge to Contribute reasonablye to suche times: but for the matter it selfe bothe the Judges did cleerelye resolue that all the stannaries & tinne w^th^in Cornewall & Deuonshire did 1700 yeres sythence belonge to the kinges of this lande, wch he proued out of Diodorus Siculus, & that now in whose groundes soeuer they are, they belonge to the kinge, not in pointe of prerogatiue, but in pointe of intereste, or otherwyse the kinge Coulde not graunte them ouer: & proued farther that all those presidentes were soughte by petition to be Confyrmed as, 4 E. 1, 1 E. 3, 12 E. 3, 8 R. 2, 1 E. 4, 3 H. 7, 11 H. 7, cap. 4, 23 H. 7. *Bene docet qui prudenter interrogat.*'

And so it was adjourned to the next [Court] day.

1606 Nov. 14

At which day being Friday, November 14th, 1606, the Counsel for the defendants was heard and all their witnesses.

[p. 283] The defendant's case

'And the wytnesses that were produced one the Defendauntes' behalfe did sweare lyberallye that the wardens, & the reste of the assystauntes & Companie, did preferre a petition to the Lordes of ye Counselle, whereas the petition yt selfe was that one warden & some fewe of the Companie did preferre the petition; but the 2 Glouers did seeke to gette handes to the petition, & were the principall actors in this busynes; & the scope of all was to ouerthrowe the pattente & breake the backes of the pattentees; & the Lo. Cheife Justices did bothe delyuer that it was lawfull for any man to sue to the kinge by petition, but in a iuste & euen course, not by gatheringe of handes, for that ys a greate offence, & of late hathe Caused muche trouble, & bene punished in this Courte: & for th'offence layde to the defendauntes' Charge in transportinge goods w^th^oute Custome, it is an offence not inquirable nor to be punished in this Courte, neyther ys the refusinge to enter into bonde, but yf any of them be accompanyed wth an vndue practise thereby to deceaue the kinge, to hinder his righte or pattente, it ys punisheable heere: yf any twooe will Conspire together to enhaunce the prices of any Commodity w^th^in the kingedome, it is punisheable heere, for it is the worste kinde of engrossinge: & this beinge an inheritaunce annexed to the Crowne of Englaunde, the subiecte allso hathe an inherytaunce in it, & may haue a *scire facias*, & if it be a prerogatiue, he maye haue a *Quo warranto*.

Petitions to the King are lawful, but signatures must not be 'gathered'

Affectus iste malus licet non sequatur effectus

'Euerye Companie by there Charter maye electe a M^r^, &c., but it is *pro bono regimine societatis*.

'20 Ass. and 43 Ass. *plac.* 38.[1] twooe Conspire together to abate the prises, or rase the prises, of woolle, the greateste Commoditie of the kingedome, & nexte vnto it ys Tinne, *par* Kneuette, then Cheife Justice & Chauncellor, they were put to there fine & ransome: for Ingrossers of any Commoditie were punisheable by the Common lawe before any statute was euer made: & it is allwayes beste for the Common wealthe when the home Commodities are Cheape, & forreine deere, & that ys the reason that the greate Custome ys for out-Cariage[2] of home Commodities,

[p. 284] Conspiracy to raise or lower prices

[1] *Le Liver des Assises & plees del Corone*, 1580. The first of these references seems to be incorrect; the second will be found on fo. 276.

[2] Exportation.

1606 Nov. 14 & the litle Custome for forrein Commodities that are broughte [in], thereby to incourage Forreiners to bringe there trade into o[r] Cuntrie.

'*eger animus semper errat.*

'And the not punishinge of offences is the Cause at this daye of the Contempte of honor & order in all places.

'For the displacinge of the M[r] of the Companie, or the disfraunchisinge of men or officers, ys not properlie to be examyned in this Courte, vnles it be accompanyed wth a ryote, a misdemeanor & a practise, as it was in this Cause.

Popham, C.J. 'By the Lo. Cheife Justice Popham: the Commoditie of tinne had bene vtterlye ouerthrowne yf the pattente in 43 elizab. had not bene graunted, & occasioned principallye by some particular Merchauntes that woulde at some times forbeare to buye any tinne of a longe time vntill they mighte make there owne prise, leauinge in the Tinners' handes threescore thousande poundes of tinne; whereas, synce the pattente, it is ordered that the Tinners shall allwayes haue tenne thousande poundes in monie [p. 285] beforehande. And the Condicion of a bonde deuysed by the lordes of the Counselle, & by them ordered, was to haue & take Tinne as the kinge payde for it, so as they wroughte & vttered the same to the subiectes w[th]in the lande, & yf they woulde transporte it, then they payde a greater rate for it. w[ch] to yealde vnto, the 2 Glouers not onelye refused them selues, but disswaded others, terminge it slauerye to be so bounde, & therevpon remoued the M[r] & chose another: whereas, by the opinion of the Lo. Cheife Justice Popham, no Companie or fraternatie Can by there Charter remoue any officer w[th]oute iuste Cause; yf they doe, he hathe his remedye in Chauncerye or kinge's benche, where he shall haue a wrytte to settle him in his office againe.

Lord Chancellor and Coke, C.J. City of London commended 'And by the Lo. Chauncellor & Lo. Ch. Justice Koke, the gouernemente of the Citie of London was muche Commended, as it was *epitome totius regni*, & by the good gouernem[te] thereof the whole kingedome receaued muche good, & as it was allwayes true & neuer false to the Crowne of Englaunde, so at this time there are as grave and wyse a Counselle & senate in the same as euer was, whoe haue gyuen an excellente testimonie to all the worlde of there religious & peaceable gouernemente in these greate times of alteration & of infection longe lingringe amongste them. & it was the rather spoken at this time bothe to encourage [p. 286] them in there well doinge, & allso to Commende them in that they endeauoured to order & dispose of theise thinges peaceablye amongste themselues, & to staye any Farther proceedinge in them, vpon a petition delyuered vnto them by theise defendauntes; w^{ch}, for that it did Conteigne in it some false matter wherein they were abused, it was ordered by the sentence of the Cowrte that the Defendauntes showlde, at a publike Cowrte at the Guylde halle, make recognition & acknowledgemente of there faultes & fauxitie to the Lo. Maior & his bretheren: for it was noted by the Lo. Chauncellor, that in the hearinge of this Cause there hathe bene now spente three whole dayes, & neither at the firste nor seconde did any of the Defendauntes submitte themselues, but defended all they Coulde eyther by witte or arte of there Counselle, & opposed againste the pattente & kinge's righte all they Coulde deuise, euen after the opinion of the Judges, & therefore vnworthye of any fauoure, for the iudgemente belongethe to the Courte, & mercye to the kinge.

Petition by the defendants

'But for the opinions of the Courte in sentence, they were somethinge differente. Herberte, Koke, *euesque de Londres*, & Exeter, fined the twooe Glouers onelye 200$^{li.}$ a peece: but the opinion of the reste, wch seemethe was the sentence of the Courte, viz:—Popham, Zouche, Northampton, Tresorer, *Archeuesque*, & the Chauncellor, were all of opinion that the twooe Glouers showlde be Fyned a thousaunde markes[1] a peece; Curtes & Dunninge, three hundrede poundes a peece; Hethe 200$^{li.}$; & that the twooe Glouers showlde paye 200$^{li.}$ Dammage to the 4 plaintifes; & the other 4 defendauntes showlde be fyned 100$^{li.}$ a peece; to make recognition of there Faultes as

Sentence

[p. 287]

[1] £666 13*s.* 4*d.*

1606 Nov. 14

before to the Lo. Maior & Courte of Aldermen ; to haue all ymprisonm[te] accordinge to the Course of the Courte duringe the kinge's pleasure.

The Lord Chancellor moves that Coke's antiquarian information be put in the Order

'And the Lo. Chauncellor moued that forasmuche as the Lo. Cheife Justice of the Common place had taken greate paines & delyuered manye excellente thinges touchinge the kinge's intereste in matters of tinne, & those of greate antiquitie, whereof the worlde neuer tooke knowledge before, that one of the kinge's Counselle showlde attende his beste leysure for the settinge them Downe, to the ende they may be inserted in the Order; w[ch] the whole Cowrte lyked verye well of.

'*Par* Lo. Northampton. *nummus non gignit nummum, neque metallus metallum. Par* Lo. Chauncellor. *pater* [*sic*] *familias vendacem non emacem esse oportet*; otherwyse let him looke well to his stocke, for it will soone decaye.'[1]

[p. 288]

FARWELL *v.* FARWELL

'The same daye vpon motion made of a reference of a bille wherein Farrwelle, an Atturnie at the lawe, was pl. againste John Farrwelle, his sonne, of the Inner Temple, outer barrister.[2] The Lo. Ch. Justice Popham had certified that the Defendaunte had firste in the begynninge of his aunsweare pleaded not guyltie, & afterwardes layes downe much impertinente matter, very scandalouse to his Father, & in no sorte materiall to the Causes Complayned of in the bille, & to this aunsweare he had sette to his owne hande: & for this, by order of Courte, he was to be imprisoned, & not to be delyuered vntill he were bounde to his good behauyoure, & had payde suche Fyne as the Cowrte showlde ympose vpon him. And by waye of aduyse, the Lor. Chauncellor did admonishe all men to beware how there practise began vpon themselues, & that it is not fytte in good dyscretyon to be of Counselle wth himselfe & in his owne Cause; men of iudgemente & discretion haue allwayes refrayned so to doe, for a man Can not looke into himselfe wth indifferente eies. Euerye man naturallye

Counsel punished for a scandalous Answer

The Lord Chancellor advises counsel not to act for themselves

[1] See Appendix XX.

[2] John Farwell of Holbrook, Somerset. Admitted Nov. 1594; called to the Bar 1603; Bencher 1620.

ys a louer of himselfe, & partiall in the iudgemente of himselfe.'

In Camera Stellata, Coram Consilio ibidem, Veneris, 7 Nouembr. 1606, adonque presente, Ellsemere, Lo. Chauncellor; Bankrupt,[1] archeuesque de Canterberie; Dorset, Lo. Tresorer; H. Hawarde, Lo. Northampton; Burleighe, Lo. Exeter; Zouche, Lo. Zouche; Vaughan, euesque de Londres; Popham, Ch. Justice; Koke, Ch. Justice; et Flemminge, Ch. Baron. [p. 289] 1606 Nov. 7

LADY RUSSELL *v.* EARL OF NOTTINGHAM and others — Riot, etc.

'The Former Cause betwene the Ladie Russelle, pl., & the Earle of nottingham, formerlye referred to the Judges, was now this daye hearde one bothe sides againe.'[2]

'And the Judges did all wth Consente delyuer there opinions vpon the reference in there sentence, & woulde not before.

'The Lord Cheife Baron Cleered the Lo. Admirall from procuringe any Riote, for his Commaundemente was lawfull, & therefore he was Cleere, albeit the riote was subsequente. Sugden was onelye presente at the firste, & this vsage was no ryote, for the Lorde Admyrall had th'enheritaunce of the Castle, & the Ladie had onelye the Custodie to the vse of the Lo. Admirall, & her possessyon was my Lorde's possessyon; & therefore yf a seruaunte that keepes a howse will keepe his M[r] out of possession, the M[r] maye breake the howse, for he dothe not eiecte another out of possession. But the 2[d] riote ys of greater difficultie, for the ladye hathe the Custodie of the parke, & yf the lodge were an auntiente lodge at the time of the pattente made, then it dothe apperteigne to the keper, as proper to the keper to haue a lodge. yf it apperteigne to the keper in pointe of intereste, then the 2[d] was a ryote; but as the Case stoode, no restitution Coulde be graunted. And the Justice of peace[3] did very discreatelye, for there was no [p. 290] (Fleming, C. B.)

[1] A curious misspelling of Bancroft. [2] See *ante*, p. 271.

[3] Thomas Dolman.

1606 Nov. 7 breache of the peace, therefore no Cause to binde any to the peace. He acquytted the Lo. Admirall, & that he had done honorablye & discreatelye. & he acquytted all the reste for the firste ryote, but he Coulde not acquite nor condemne them for the seconde ryote, because it coulde not appeare vnto them in iudgemente whether it were an auncyente lodge or no, nothinge beinge mencyoned wthin the bookes [depositions], (wherevpon they must onelye iudge), Concerninge the same.

Coke, C. J. 'The Lo. Ch. Justice Koke agreede that the Lo. Admirall was not to be touchte wth any procuremente, nor any other, for the firste ryot: for the Lo. Admirall gaue a lawfull Commaundmente, & yf his seruaunte execute vnlawfullie, that shall not Charge him: but otherwyse it is of an vnlawfull Commaundemente, as I Commaunde my seruaunte to beate one, & he beatethe him vntill he kill him, this ys my faulte. The Ladye Russelle ys the Lo. Admirall's seruaunte, & keper of his howse; yf he or his seruauntes breake the lockes or doores, it is noe wronge, for she hathe but the bare Custodie, for him & not againste him; & she hathe noe intereste, yf there be not an auntiente kepershippe & lodginge appurteigninge to that; for a Freeholde maye appurteigne to an office, as to the Fleete: but she hathe her salarie for her keepinge, 2^{d} ob. [2½*d.*] *per diem*, & shee ys *servus servi.*' A man grants the keepership of a house or park, and the grantor destroys the house, or destroys the park, or disparks it, where is the keepership? *Erubescimus sine lege loqui.* 7 Edward VI., in Dier.[1]

'He Commended Dolman, the Justice of peace, & he did very discreatelye, for he had done iniustice yf he had graunted restitucyon. A Justice of peace ys not bounde to gyue restitucion, but he maye yf he will: & so he freede him wth Commendacion *a poena et culpa.*

[p. 291] 'For the 2^{d} ryote. for there number, there were 17; for there weapons, they had swordes & other weapons of offence; they vsed ill wordes, "kill them & hocke them";

[1] Apparently the case of Lord Willoughby *v.* Foster is referred to, Hil., 6 & 7 Edw. VI.; Dyer's *Reports*, i. fo. 80 b.

for the time, they kepte there three dayes & three nightes, & the time onelye may make a ryote greate. yf a man haue had a possession for three yeares, he maye keepe it wth force, but he Can not enter vpon his possession, *nec manu forti nec multitudine gentium.*' 22 Henry VI., 14 Henry VII. a disseisee may not enter on the disseisor by force, notwithstanding he had 60 years possession. *Nihil vi faciendum,* for the law abhors force; *nihil magis contrarium legi quam vis.* 'But he Coulde neyther acquit nor Condemne them by Judgemente, for a Judge showlde not, neyther Can he, iudge accordinge to his owne pryuate knowledge, *mes secundum allegata et probata.* And the dryuinge of the Cattelle ys lawfull, for the keeper shall haue but the surplusage onelye, & it dothe not appeare that there was anye; & for this laste, he referred to the Common lawe to receyue a tryall there.

'Cheife Justice Popham agreede that the firste was no riote, neyther the seconde, that he Coulde Judge of: for a man may resiste wth force beinge in possession, but not enter wth force.' The keeper who has no grant of herbage and pannage shall have only the surplusage, and if he take agistment [*gisemente*] or destroy the wood, it is a forfeiture. Popham, C. J.

Without inquiry, a Justice of the Peace cannot grant restitution, if he did not see the force; and the Sheriff ought to restore to possession.

Zouche and London agreed with the two Chief Justices. Lord Zouch, Bishop of London

Exeter censured the second as a riot, and fined [them] £40 *pro exemplo.* Lord Exeter [p. 292]

'Northampton. the kinge by his prerogatiue maye take vp any howse in his progres. By the Ciuill lawe the wyues are fauoured in Cases of treason, *propter imbecillitatem sexus.* Lord Northampton

'Lo. Tresorer acquites them all, & referres them to the lawe; for in iudgemente *quod dubites refeceris.*' Lord Treasurer

The Archbishop acquits them all. Archbishop

'Lo. Chauncellor acquites the Lo. Admirall, & that he hathe Carryed himselfe honorable, & greate temper, & good respectes. But for the 2^d^ ryote, he woulde sentence it yf Lord Chancellor

1606 Nov. 7 the wytnesses did agree w[th]in the bookes [depositions]. *Ideo liberavi animam meam.* euerye man ys to delyuer his Conscyence: "I Cannot Cleere nor Commende Dolman, the Justice of peace, for yf he had done [well], vpon the sighte of suche an assemblye, suche weapons, suche an occasyon, suche woordes, yf he had done well he showlde haue bounde them all to the peace for most safetie." '

1606 Nov. 19, 21 **In Camera Stellata,** coram Consilio ibidem, Mercurij, 19 Nouembr., et Veneris, 21 Nouembr., 1606.[1]

MORGAN *v.* MORGAN and others

170 defendants

20 to be chosen

'A greate Cause of hearinge betwene Edwarde Morgan, pl., againste S[r] William Morgan,[2] & 170 other Defendauntes, a welche Cause: there ys a Crosse bille dependinge allso, that is to be hearde the nexte daye, againste as many defendauntes; & therefore it was formerlye ordered by the Courte that one bothe sydes they showlde eyther make Choyce of 20 defendauntes a peece, & they showlde onelye proceede againste them, to auoyde the drawinge vp so many dwellers so farre of from this towne.

[p. 293] 'The Charge in the bille was that Sir W[m] Morgan, beinge a Justice of peace & a greate man in his Cuntrye, vpon former malice & quarrelle wth Edwarde Morgan, had Caused a Challenge to be sente to the pl. & his sonnes, & againste a quarter Cessyons at Chrystemas, had sente & spoken to dyuerse of his Freindes & kinsemen to Come stronge to meete him at the Cessions; & therevpon he himselfe Came accompanyed wth 40 men, some wth swordes, rapyers & daggers, steele Cappes, priuie Coates, Jauelins, & swordes & buckelers, & billes, & longe staues, in so muche as the towne was full of weapons, & there Came 140 to assyste Sir Wylliam Morgan: The Defendaunte he alleaged that he, hearinge how the plaintifes meante to dysgrace him, Came thus prepared to defende himselfe, & that there was nothinge done, not a blowe gyuen: & that the pl.,

[1] Eight Councillors and Judges were present.

[2] Sir William Morgan was knighted by James I. at Whitehall, July 23, 1603.

beinge a recusaunte,[1] did the nexte Sondaye after the Queene's Deathe, take the Cuntrye armoure, from the place where yt did vsuallye lye, home to his owne howse; wch the Defend^te^, muche mislykinge, did labor to w^th^stande; wch was the Cause of the fyrste mallice: so vpon the whole matter, 2 entier dayes beinge spente in the hearinge of the Cause, the Courte seemed to be doubtefull what sentence to gyue, & differed in there sentence the one from the other. The 2 Ch. Justices, ye Lo. Zouche, the twooe bishops & the Lo. of Northampton, iudginge but a small faulte, rather an error onelye, & wante of a litle good discretion; for his Comminge to ye Cessyons he was bounde by his oathe, & for ye wearinge of weapons by 4 H[enry] 7 & 24 H[enry] 8, they are all forfeyted to the Kinge, beinge w^th^in Wales, w^ch^, as they thoughte, was punishemente inoughe; & the Defendaunte a gentleman that had done good seruice in the Cuntrye, & the pl. a recusaunte, but otherwyse a man of honeste & Ciuill Conuersatyon; yet the sturringe of armor at suche a time was very ill, & mighte haue proued very daungerous, & the defend^te^ did well in seekinge to staye it as he did; yet because suche are the dispositions of the people in those partes that to gyue waye to theise thinges were very daungerous, & for example sake therefore, they fined the Defend^te^ 40^li.^, & many of the reste 20^li.^ & 10^li.^ a peece, & imprisonmente of course.[2] Sentence

'But the Lo. Chauncellor, the Lo. Tresorer & Secretarie Herberte were of an other opinion, & blamed the defend^te^ very muche, for that he was sworne to preserue & keepe the peace, & this sekinge to be greate & beare a side, in those Cuntryes especiallye, ys very daungerous; & for his offence they fyned him 300^li.^ markes [*sic*] & the reste of the defendauntes 20^li.^ & 40^li.^ apeece.'[3] [p. 294]

[1] 1605? Undated. Grant to Robert Hales of the recusancy of Edward Morgan of Swinnerton, co. Stafford. State Papers, Domestic, James I., vol. 17, No. 82.

1607, March 19. Licence to Edward Morgan to exercise his religion, paying £20 a month to the King. *Grant Book*, p. 25.

1610, March 4. Grant to John Carse, Page of the Bedchamber, of £300, debts due to Edward Morgan, recusant, which ought to come to the King. Docquet.

[2] This, being the sentence of the majority, would be the sentence of the Court.

[3] See a cross bill between the same parties, *post*, p. 314.

1606 Nov. 26

In Camera Stellata, coram Consilio ibidem, Mercurij, 26 Nouembr., 1606.[1]

MORGAN v. MORGAN — Riot, etc.

Seizing the county armour

'Cause of hearinge betwene Sr Wm Morgan, pl., againste Edwarde Morgan, his twooe sonnes, & dyuerse other Defendauntes, vpon a Crosse bille for the Former Cause: but the bille did allso Conteigne the riotous takinge awaye the armoure wth multitudes, wch, upon a reference to the Judges, was thoughte, for some pryuate reasons, not fytte to be opened nor dealte wthall; but vpon the latter parte of the bille, for that Wm Morgan & George Morgan, the Defendauntes 2 sonnes, & dyuerse other defendauntes, Came wth multitudes to the sayd Quarter Cessions at Vske, (hauinge no occasyon of busynes there), some armed wth priuie Coates, quylted Cappes, swordes & bucklers, holbertes, iauelinge & pike staues, & troupte vp & downe the towne wth there weapons after proclamacyon made by the sheriffe for keepinge of the peace, & one George Morgan, a defendaunte, strake one of Sr Wm Morgan's kinsemen a greate blowe in the face standinge neere to the Courte, for wch he was endyted & Fyned 10s; whereas by the opinion of the Courte yf any man kille the Lo. Chauncellor, or any Judge syttinge in iudgemente, it is treason; & yf any stryke in the Face of the Courte, he shall loose his hande for yt, and be put to Fyne & Raunsome, & imprysoned duringe his lyfe. [p. 295] & by the Judges, this small Fine imposed by the Justices of the peace ys a greate faulte, the offence beinge so greate, & theise lighte punishementes of offences wch, when they are Complayned of heere, are fined at 200li. or 300li. or 500li. fine, are the Causes of many more offences & Complaintes thereof heere; for *vt res, ita tempora rerum*, & therefore wyshed them to haue Care to redresse the same: & for theise defendauntes, the Father was acquyted,

Sentence

for that he was not presente at that Ryote, nor he was not Charged in the bille as a procurer (in that parte of the bille that Came now to hearinge); but his twooe sonnes were Fyned 200li. a peece, & he that stroke the blowe was

[1] Nine Councillors and Judges were present.

fyned 200 markes, those 4 that ware priuye Coates $40^{li.}$ a peece, the reste $20^{li.}$ a peece.'[1]

In Camera Stellata, coram Consilio ibidem, Saturni, 29 Nouembr. 1606, le prochein iour puis le fine del terme, adonque presente, Lo. Chauncellor, euesque de Canterberie, Lo. Tresorer, euesque de Londres, ambideux Cheife Justices, Baron Sauelle, Justice Yeluerton et Justice williams. 1606 Nov. 29

ATT.-GEN. v. WELBY and others — Riot, etc.

'After dyuerse motions made, the Atturnie generall informes *ore tenus*, vpon the Confessyon of the parties, againste 5 younge gentlemen, 1. welbye of graies Inne,[2] 2. Vauxe of the middle temple, a Citizen's sonne, & lefte $50^{li.}$ lande by the yeare, beinge a younger brother, 3. Gosnall, the sonne of a Counsellor at the lawe of the Middle temple, 4. Fitche of Clifforde's Inne, & a Clerke, 5. Losse, a Clerke. There offences were that they, wth 3 others that were escaped, beinge at supper together the 7th of this nouember in Holborne, did resolue to doe somethinge that they maye be spoken of when they were deade. And therevpon late in the nighte after supper tooke a boate [p. 296] & wente ouer to Lambethe Marshe to the Swanne, where one Dauis dwelte, a lewde Fellowe & a very lewde howse, & there Called for drinke & a wenche, & beinge denyed, brake the windowes of the howse & of tenne or twelue howses more there, in somuche as the Constable wth the wache sette vpon them & tooke them, but beate some downe to the grounde before they Coulde take them, & the nexte morninge Caryed them to the Lo. Ch. Justice, whoe vpon examynacyon Commytted them to the kinge's benche prison, where they haue lyen euer sythence: & all this they Confessed vpon there examynacyons, & it was Confyrmed allso by the examynacion of the Constable & the other wachemen.

[1] See a cross bill between the same parties, *ante*, p. 312.

[2] Probably William Welby of Gedney, co. Lincoln, gent., admitted Nov. 16, 1604.

1606 Nov. 29 'It was generallye Condemned for a greate & a base offence, ill beseeminge gentlemen, as the moste of them were reputed to be, bothe in name & bloude: & they are now to punishe it, not so muche an offence in them, as to prouyde that by the example of this punishem^{te} others maye be kepte from offendinge in the like kinde; yet wee see they haue Confessed it, there ys Confession, Contrition, & some parte of satisfaction, in that they gaue the nexte daye 16^{s} recompence to the parties whose windowes they brake: *et come le Lo. Cooke dit, Cum sponte confitente mitius est agendum, ad reformacionem, non ad ruinam, ad emendationem, non ad destructionem. iter iuuentutis lubricum.* "this dronkennes," sayd the Lorde Chauncellor, "ys *voluntarius Demon*, it Caries a legion wth him." Welbie,

Sentence

Vauxe & Gosnall were fyned 50$^{li.}$ a peece; Fitche & Losse 20$^{li.}$ a peece; & imprisonm^{te}.'

[p. 297] 1606-7 Jan. 28

In Camera Stellata, coram Consilio ibidem, Mercurij, 28 Januarij, 1606, Termino Hillarij.[1]

KINGE *v.* LUDLOWE

Riot, and misdemeanour

'A Cause of hearinge betwene Kinge, a minister, & Joel Kinge his sonne, pl., againste Henry Ludlowe, esq^{r}, the sonne & heire apparaunte of Sir Edwarde Ludlowe,[2] John Younge, a minister, Lancaster, Hockenet, & others, the seruauntes of Sr Edwarde & Henrye Ludlowe, defend^{tes}, for 2 ryots & a barbarouse misdemeanor. This Joel Kinge, the pl., heretofore seruaunte to Sr Edwarde Ludlowe, very lewdlye & wickedlye betrayed his M^{r}, & stoale awaye his daughter & maryed her, he beinge a very meane & base fellowe; for this base indignitie the defendauntes maliced him, & manye times attempted his ouerthrowe; & in December in the 45th yeare of the late Queene,

Assault

the sayde Joel Kinge in rydinge to Readinge was assaulted in Bishops roade, & there taken from his horse, & wth the raines of his horse bridle he was hanged vp in a tree vntill he was allmoste deade, & then lette downe, & his handes & legges bounde very harde together behinde him, & they

[1] Nine Councillors and Judges were present. [2] Knighted 1601.

tooke one of his girtes & strangled him harde wth the same, & wth a sticke thruste downe dyuerse pinnes into his throate, & so lefte him, this beinge done in the morninge very earelye: he laye there vntill the eueninge, & then was founde, his handes [and] his other limmes were growne very blacke & muche swollen, his tounge hanginge oute of his mouthe as blacke as a shooe, & to all men's thinkinge deade, & wthoute sense, & so disfigured that none knewe him but by a marke in his hande. And then Caryinge [p. 298] him to a howse, & rubbinge him wth warme Cloathes, & powringe *aquavite* into his eares & mouthe, they perceaued he had lyfe, but laye in greate paine & extremitie, & three dayes speecheles; & despayringe of his recouerye, they broughte him penne and inke, & he wrote the description of John younge, his apparelle, the horse that he roade vpon, wch was Henrye Ludlowe's, & descrybed three other of Mr Ludlowe's men, & all there names, w^{ch}, vpon other prooffes & there owne Confessyons, were prooued to be all there the same morninge & verye neere to the place where Joel laye bounde; but [they] pleaded not guyltie to the Facte: Joel laye in greate extremitie for dyuerse dayes, & wthin 8 or 10 dayes, after takinge honie, butter & oyle, & vsinge a wyer made Crooked, & a feather put downe into his throate, after greate strayninge by vomitinge, he Caste vp dyuerse pinnes, & some water & flegme therewth: & then had one of H. Ludlowe's men sworne the peace againste Joel, & gotte a warraunte from a J. of peace for him, & H. Ludlowe sayde, "yf yor Conscience will sweare safelye, you may take the peace of him;" & Sr Edwarde Ludlowe sayde, "yf he Can not Come, you maye bringe him vpon a horse or in a Carte;" & sente 2 of his men wth them for the bringinge of him, a very Scithian & barbarous practise, & more Cruell then either Lion or beare, whoe will not destroye there owne kinde: & moste of all Condemned in the parson, & as the Lo. Kooke sayde, "*Clericus in oppido, piscis in arido.*" & they all wyshed Sr Edwarde Ludlowe had bene made a partie, they would haue sentenced him; they vpon the presumptions & Circumstaunces con- Sentence

1606-7 Jan. 28 demned Henry Ludlowe in 500$^{li.}$, John younge the parson in a 1000$^{li.}$,[1] the other 2 in 100$^{li.}$ a peece, & the other thirde in 50$^{li.}$, to be bounde to there good behauyoure, & im-
[p. 299] prisonm^{te}; & referred [Younge] to the Lo. Archebishop for his remoouinge oute of the ministrye.

'*Condemnare innocentem et iustificare nocentem, vterque abominabilis apud deum.*

Slander in the King's Bench

'Henry Ludlowe broughte an Action of the Case againste Joel Kinge for woordes, whereby he Charged him wth this facte, & recouered againste him a 100$^{li.}$ for dam-

Indictment

mages; but Joel preferred an inditemente vpon this facte & it Coulde not be founde, so that it seemes Mr Ludlowe's strengthe ys greate in the Cuntrye; & therefore the Courte gaue him a 100$^{li.}$ dammages. & the Lo. Ch. Justice of

Written evidence, when good

Englaunde sayde that yf a man be robbed or wounded, & he wrytes downe a perfecte description of the men, wherebye they are knowne, & so dyes, this wilbe good euydence to Conuycte them: the Defendaunte in this Cause had examyned no one wytnes, but had firste preferred a Crosse bille againste the plaintiffs, pretendinge that this was a practise & a iuglinge tricke, & in that bille, as they suggested, they had examyned many wytnesses, whereof they prayde to haue now the benefitte to reade them in this Cause, & the rather for that it was broughte firste into the Cowrte; but it was resolued by the Cowrte it was againste the Course of the Cowrte, & was not allowed not one to be reade *ad informandam conscientiam. Quod nota.*

'*Judicandum est de manifestis, non de occultis.*'

1606-7 Feb. 13

In Camera Stellata, 13 Febr., 1606.[2]

Savage, Nethersie, Martin, Gennings, and Johnson

John Sauage, £100, John Nethersie, 100 marks, Thomas Martin, £100, George Genninges, £30, and William Johnson, £30, were sentenced for building contrary to the proclamation of [3] Elizabeth and 4 James,[4] causing by this

[1] See Appendix VII.

[2] No names given.

[3] Blank in MS.

[4] The *Booke of Proclamations* before referred to, *ante*, p. 179, *n.* 1, does not include any proclamation as

death, dearth, depopulation, disorder and waste of timber. The tenements to be pulled down. fined for building contrary to the proclamations

There are 6,000,000 [*sic*], six hundred souls in the suburbs. London beinge *Camera regni* by the residence of the King. 'the Maior, y[e] Recorder, & those that haue bene Maiors are [the] onelye Justices of p. in London.'[1]

In Camera Stellata, coram consilio ibidem, Veneris, 24 April. 1607, termino Pasche.[2] [p. 301] 1607 April 24

Cause of hearing against Gallette and others for riot and other practises and misdemeanours in receiving a blank warrant of the Under-Sheriff and putting a name in it, a usual fault and common with Sheriffs. And for this offence only as for a misdemeanour they fined Gallette £20, with imprisonment, and they acquitted him of the other offences, also the other defendants. 'And wished that the sherife had bene made a partie, vpon whome they woulde haue layed a heauyer Fyne for example sake.' GALLETTE'S case — Practice and misdemeanour — Sentence

In Camera Stellata, 29 April. 1607.[3] 1607 April 29

Cause of hearing between Robinson, plaintiff, against Nethersall, formerly Mayor of Canterberrye, 'for forgerie and periurie, & againste twooe others; & did shewe forthe that Nethersall, Comminge to olde Leuette, a Clerke in Canterberye, & findinge him full of greife & sorrowinge for the deathe of his sonne, he shewed him a bonde of his sonne's of 200[li.] to be paid to y[e] father yf the sonne dyed vnmaryed, & Nethersall Copyed oute this in parchemente: ROBINSON v. NETHERSALL and others — Forgery and perjury

to buildings in the fourth year of James. On p. 101, however, is printed *A Proclamation for Buildings in and about London*, which is probably the one referred to in the text, dated at Thetford, March 1, 2 James, 1604. No timber trees were to be used for charcoal or firewood; after Michaelmas then next 'no person shall build or erect any new house, or the forefront of any house in any new building, where any former building was, within the same Citie of London, or the Suburbs thereof, or within one mile of the sayd Suburbs, except all the vtter wals and windowes thereof, and the forefront of the same be wholly made of Bricke, or Bricke and stone,' etc.

[1] Page 300 is blank.

[2] Five Councillors and Judges were present.

[3] Seven Councillors and Judges were present.

1607 April 29 p. 302] & afterwardes nethersall, vpon a triall for the sayde dette vpon the sayde bonde, deposethe that he did see a true bonde out of w[ch] he made that Copie; but it Coulde not appeare by any mann[r] of proofe that euer there was any true bonde; and this bonde was therefore sentenced in this Cowrte to be a Forged bonde, but no Forger then found; yet now it was proued that nicholas Leuette, one of the defendauntes, did sealle & delyuer this bonde in his brother's name after his brother was deade; & so was the sentence of the whole Courte that he was the Forger, & had his sen- 5 Eliz. cap. 14 tence for his punishemente vpon the statute of 5 Eliz., cap. 14.[1] Nethersall & the other defendaunte, Henry Sentence Leuette, were condempned of periurye & forgerye by bothe the cheife Justices, the Lo. Knolles & Lo. of Northampton, & were acquyted by the Lo. Tresorer, lo. Archebishop & the Lo. Chauncellor as a case *non liquet*. 4 againste three: but I Qv, if Lord Chancellor has a casting vote haue hearde y[e] Lo. Chancellor hathe a Castinge voyce yf there be 4 againste 4 or three againste three, but what this Judgemente will prooue to be *Quere*; for it was well sayde by them that it were better to acquite 20 that are guyltie then Condempne one Innocente.'

1607 May 1

In Camera Stellata, coram Consilio ibidem, Veneris, 1° Maij, 1607.[2]

MARGERY *v.* DRUE

Forgery

[p. 303]

Cause of hearing between Margerie, plaintiff, and Henry Drue, brewer and Mayor of Boston,[3] defendant, for the forgery of the will of Richard Margerie, deceased. 'The defend[te], as he Confessed by his aunsweare, Comminge to Richarde Margerie when he was sycke, he gaue him instructions by worde onelye to make his will; w[ch] the defend[te] did not then wryte any thinge; & the sayde Rych[d] Margerie, w[th]in 2 howers after suche instructions Forgery of a will gyuen, dyed, & the defendaunte, w[th]in 14 dayes after, wrote downe a formall wille as any Lawyer Coulde make, & sette

[1] For the punishment see Appendix X.

[2] Eight Councillors and Judges were present.

[3] He was Mayor of Boston in 1595.

downe the perfecte disposition of all his landes & goodes, wth many legacyes, so speciallye & so artificiallye, as it was altogether impossible for any man to doe, no, not any lawyer whatsoeuer; neither coulde the memorye of man Carye awaye so muche; wth a Clause of reuocation of all former willes, & a solemne witnessinge by the partie himselfe, as thoughe it had bene done in his lyfe time, & not as a declaracion of the intente & meaninge of his laste will; wch had bene good for goods yf aftewardes prooued as the declaracion of his intente by parolle onelye: & so bothe the cheife Justices delyuered there opinions:

'In this will the Defend^{te} had for better Collor to the same deuysed parte of the sayde Rich^{de} Margerie's estate to ye Maior & Aldermen of Boston for the vse of ye poore, & other parte of it to ye Churche, to one Doct^{r} wright, but ye pl. beinge a simple, weake, younge Fellowe, & an apprentice, he woulde haue boughte his yeares; & as soone as he Came to full age he [the defendant], pretendinge to prooue a Father vnto him & to protecte him, gotte a Feffemente of his lande, vpon truste as he supposed, but then he tolde him there was a will wch tooke ye lande from him, & yet allwayes after that, & now allso, denyed that there was any will; & yet, not longe before this suite began, he gotte a relleasse from him, so deuysed & penned as the lyke hathe bene seldome seene, *et clausulae inconsuetae inducunt suspitionem.* & in that was all questions, suites and controuersies touchinge ye will relleased; whereas there was then no question or suite concerninge ye same.

The defendant's cunning

and fraud

[p. 304]

'For this offence he had a very sharpe sentence by ye generall Consente of all ye Courte, accordinge to ye statute of 5 Eliz., cap. 14:—He shall paye doble Costes & dammages to ye partie greiued, shalbe sette one the pillorie & haue bothe his eares cutt of, his nosthrilles to be slitte & cutte & seared wth a hotte iron, & shall forfeite to the kinge ye proffittes of all his landes duringe his lyfe, & haue perpetuall imprisonm^{te} duringe life.'[1]

Sentence

5 Eliz. cap. 14

[1] This is the punishment imposed by the statute.

1607 May 6

In Camera Stellata, coram Consilio ibidem, Mercurij, 6 Maij, 1607.[1]

Earl of Lincoln *v.* Dimmock — Riot, etc.

'Cause of hearinge *enter* Th'erle of Lincolne, pl., againste Sr Edwarde Dimmocke, & other, his seruauntes, Defendauntes,[2] for 2 ryottes & a practise or misdemeanor in ioyninge together to delyuer a petition to ye kinge againste the pl. the firste riot was in breakinge a pounde & takinge forceablye Cattelle from thence, (wch are sayde to be *in Custodia legis*, & therefore to be repleuid); th'other riote was in breakinge downe 20 rodde of sawed pale in ye nighte time, digginge vp the postes, & Carryinge them into ye defendaunte's yarde. Sr Edwarde Dimmocke denieth all vpon his oathe. the wytnesses proue that th'other defendauntes did saye that they did it by ye Commaundem^{te} or procuremente of Sr Edwarde Dimmocke, or else they thinke they durste not haue bene so bolde:

Breaking a pound

Breaking down a pale at night

[p. 305]

Sentence

'For the practise, one Dethicke, one of the Defendauntes, was sentenced for y^{e} author of it & y^{e} agente in it, & he & th'other defendauntes were fyned 40$^{li.}$, some 50$^{li.}$, some 60$^{li.}$, & imprisonm^{te}: but Sr Edwarde Dimmocke it seemethe was acquyted by most voyces, albeit Condempned by some.'

1607 June 10

In Camera Sellata, coram Consilio ibidem, Mercurij, 10 Junij, 1607.[3]

Death of Sir John Popham, Lord Chief Justice of the King's Bench

While the Courte was sitting, 'Newes was broughte that Sr John Popham,[4] the Lo. Cheife Justice of Englaunde,

[1] Nine Councillors and Judges were present.

[2] See a cross bill between the same parties, *ante*, p. 233.

[3] Eight Councillors and Judges were present.

[4] Sir John Popham was born about 1531; educated at Baliol Coll., Oxford; called to the Bar at the Middle Temple; Autumn Reader, 1568; Serjeant at Law, 1578; Solicitor-gen., 1579; Attorney-gen. and Treasurer of his Inn, 1581; Speaker of the House of Commons, 1581; Lord Chief Justice of the King's Bench, 1592; he died June 10, 1607 (aged 76), as stated in the text, and was buried at Wellington, co. Somerset, where he had built himself a house, and where he founded a hospital for the maintenance of 12 poor men and women and the education of two poor children. See Foss's *Judges*, Chalmers' *Biog. Dict.*, Collinson's *Hist. of Somerset*, ii. 483; etc.

was deade, some sayde of an vlcer in his bladder, others that he had taken pilles & the phisique neuer wroughte vpon him, others that he dyed of greife for sharpe wordes from the kinge's Matie; but howsoeuer, he was a moste worthye man, & the state & Common wealthe receaued the greateste losse of him that euer felle since Queene Elizabethe's deathe; he was a Father of the Common wealthe, a maine piller of the gospelle and true religion, a seuere & an vprighte Justicer, & the onelye supporter of the Common lawes of Englaunde; an infinite losse the lawe & professors thereof haue of him, the gouernemente & gouernors will haue a greate misse of him, the lewder & looser sorte of people will reioyce, the godlye and vertuous doe lamente and mourne, & not w^th^oute iuste Cause.'

'Cause of hearinge by wydowe, pl., and Longe & others, defendauntes, for a ryotous entrye into a howse, & lockinge vp the pl., a wydowe of 80 yeares of age, & keepinge her lockte vp for 3 weekes, destroyinge her goodes, & eatinge her prouision, a very barbarous & Cruell matter: & for wch offence the principall defendaunte was Fyned 100^li.^, the reste 20^li.^ a peece, beinge seruauntes, & ymprisonmente of Course, & the pl. had 50^li.^ for her dammages, & was restored to her possessyon: but vpon this difference by the Lo. Chauncellor, for that he woulde not haue it Conceaued that this [Court] medlethe wth takinge or gyuinge possession by Iniunction or otherwyse, but yf vpon hearinge & sentence it appearethe a possessyon was gayned or taken by force, forgerye or Fraude, or the lyke, then by sentence this Cowrte will settle the pl. or defendaunte for the possessyon, as he was at the time of the forgerye, Fraude or Force.' [p. 306] LONGE'S case — Riotous entry, etc. — Sentence

'Another Cause of hearinge betweene wydowe Rape & ,[1] plaintiffs, & Girlin & others, defendauntes, for a ryote, lykewyse in seruinge of proces & arrestinge a woman: the baillyes of the libertye of Blythinge[2] in Suffolke laye all nighte at Girlin's howse, & the nexte RAPE v. GIRLIN and others — Riot

[1] Blank in MS. [2] Blything is one of the Hundreds of Suffolk.

1607 June 10 morninge, an howre before daye, wth swordes & staues & lightes, wente, wth some of Girlin's seruauntes wth them, to the wydowe's howse, whoe kepte very secrete & hydde herselfe, & beinge let in at the firste doore by a mayde seruaunte of the howse, Came to the doore of the roome where the pl. laye, & entreated her to open the Doore, for they were to arreste her vpon an execucion as one sayde; & she refusinge, they broke open the Doore & wyshte her [p. 307] to make her readye to goe wth them, & so tooke her & Caryed her to pryson, where shee laye 30 weekes.

'But by the defendauntes shewinge, the truthe of the Case appeares to be that Girlin, the defendaunte, (by whose procurem^te all this ys intended to be done), was bounde wth the wydowe Rape, & for her dette payde 60^li. vpon an execucyon vpon that bonde, & the wydowe hydinge her selfe, & refusinge to discharge him, he sued oute a *latitat* oute of the kinge's benche, & had a warraunte from the highe sherife to a knowne baillye, whoe wente earlye in the morninge accompanyed wth twooe other his inferior bayllies, & one seruaunte of the Defendauntes, & beinge let in at the firste doore by a mayde seruaunte, they wente to the doore of the Chamber where the pl. laye, & desyred her to open the Doore for they had a warraunte to arreste her at suche a man's suite, naminge Girlin, but shee refused. And therevpon they peaceably & w^thoute any other force or terror thruste open the Doore, & beinge entred into the Chamber, they wyshed her to make her readye, & eyther procure them sufficiente baylle, or else she must goe to pryson, wch she refusinge to doe, they Carryed her to the defendaunte's Girlin's howse, & from thence to the prison.

Riot or not? 'And whether vpon all this matter the Defendauntes showlde be Condemned or no, the Cowrte muche doubted, & in sentence was dyuyded, & by the greateste number (wch I [1] take to be the sentence of the Cowrte) they were acquyted, & dismissed to the Common lawe to trye it there.

[p. 308] Sentence 'The Lo. Cheife Baron, the Lo. Ch. Justice, the Lo. Zouche, the bishop of London & the Lo. of Northampton

[1] John Hawarde.

did acquyte them, but the Lo. Chauncellor, the Archebishop & Secretarye Herberte did Condemne them, & fine them $20^{li.}$ & $30^{li.}$ a peece.

'And by occasyon of the sentence, the Lo. Ch. Justice delyuered good & necessary matter of learninge for seruinge & executinge of proces, whether the sheriffe or baylife mighte breake & enter a howse, or no, to serue proces. One booke saythe he maye, another saythe he maye not, so it seemethe *vexata questio* & that the bookes showlde differ: but of late vpon resolution it is adiudged & published in Lo. Coke's reportes p. [V], fol. [91], Seman's Case,[1] that where the kinge is partie either in originall or iudiciall proces, he maye breake & enter a howse, & so in a *Capias vtlagatum*, for there the kinge hath an intereste: but in an originall or *Latitat* where the subiecte ys onelye partie, there he Can not enter & breake the howse, for it is euerye man's Castle; but, yf the doore be shutte or lachte, he maye lifte the lache & open it & goe in, but not vnlocke or vnbolte it; but yf he doe breake open the doore, as in this case, the arreste notw^th^standinge ys lawfull, but the partie shall haue an action of trespass for breakinge the doore, but th'arreste ys lawfull notw^th^standinge: & so the bookes vpon this difference doe not contrarye one th'other as hathe bene conceaued, for this iudgemente & difference reconcylethe them. *quod nota.* And touchinge th'arreste by nighte, he helde it no offence by lawe, for otherwyse Fewe dettes woulde be payde; but a man can not distreine for a rente seruice by nighte, & the reason ys for that the lawe intendethe that the tenaunte woulde paye it yf it were by daye, or repleue [replevy] the distres.

Lord Chief Justice on the serving of process

Seman's case

Arrest at night is lawful, but not distraint

'But the Lo. Chauncellor seemed to dislyke muche theise arrestes by nighte, & helde opinion there was no aucthoritie to proue them, for where the bookes are that a man maye distreigne in the nighte for dammage fesante, the reason ys because otherwyse the Cattelle maye destroye the Corne or pasture before the morninge, & when they are in the pounde they are *in gremio legis*. Theise new writtes,

[p. 309]

Lord Chancellor on arrests at night

[1] Semayne's case; Peter Semayne *v.* Richard Gresham, Mich. 2 Jac. I.

1607 June 10 atitats theise *latitats*, of late muche in vse, but in auntiente time neuer knowne nor hearde of, haue done muche hurte and tle good; but the originall wrytte is the true, auntiente & beste course, & safeste for euerye man to vse: but yet he experyence in London approouethe that it were very daungerous & mischeiuous to haue noe wryttes or proces serued in ye nighte, for then woulde Fewe dettes be payde & manye deceites vsed.'

The Lord Chancellor's charge to the Judges and Justices of the Peace

'The Lorde Chauncellor, the daye after th'endinge of this terme, in his speache delyuered to the Judges & Jusices of peace,[1] did shewe how the kinge had an incessante Care for the good of his people & quyetnes of the Cuntrye: & that he hathe gyuen Commaundmente that all persons showlde departe into there Cuntryes,[2] not for there idle pleasures, but to haue speciall care to the peace of the Cuntrye at this time: for the same is disturbed either by popishe or sectaries: theise vsurpacions & anarchies are daungerous; & the magistrates must haue Care that the people be not idle nor stirre vp discontente by prophecyes or pamphelets, & there be order in ecclesiasticall gouernors, & that there be not a pope in euerye parishe: it is the parte of a J. of peace to foresee & prouide againste theise thinges, & not to vse the laste parte, wch ys the worste and the hangman's parte, punishemente, but to wth stande the beginninges: as now in theise late depopulations, a greate & wicked offence, a faulte in J. *de* peace & Sheriffes, that p. 310] showlde haue preuented & foreseene theise thinges. You must therefore looke carefullye to all seminaries & there Followers, & to there Conuenticles, to all vagrauntes stronge to labor, yet idle & like gentlemen in apparrelle & diete, yet wth out meanes, lybellers & deuysers of plottes.

'*Iniquum est iusticiam inire per gradus.*

'This *nescientia*, grosse ignoraunce, in some was a greate faulte. *erudimini iudices terrae.*

'17 R[ichard] 2, cap. 8, Riot.

[1] Compare this with the other charges, *ante*, pp. 19, 56, 101, 106, 159, 161, 186, 263, 299, and *post.*

[2] Counties.

'13 H[enry] 4, cap. 7.

'Looke to the Justices of peace that are turbulent or neglecte there dutyes: for you that are Judges of Assise, the kinge hathe made Choyse of you for men of learninge & integritie, & hathe made you the visitors of his kingedome principallye & speciallye for the preseruation of the peace of the lande. & to punishe depopulators wth all seueritie: to looke Carefullye to sherifes and vndersheriffes & there officers, whoe buye & selle the people, & retorne base & simple iurors: & yo[r] Constables for the moste parte are the simpleste & meaneste of the people, a greate Faulte.'

In Camera Stellata, coram Consilio ibidem, Mercurij, 14 Octobr. 1607, adonque presente, Ellsmere, Lo. Chauncellor; Dorsette, Lo. Tresorer; Northampton; euesque de Londres, Rains; Lo. Zouche; Flemminge, Ch. Justice[1]; Coke, Ch. Justice del Common place; S[r] Julius Cesar, Chauncellor del exchequer, le primer temps que il seie en ceo Courte.[2] 1607 Oct. 14

SNEGGE v. SHERSTON and others — Riot

Cause of hearing between Baron Snegge,[3] plaintiff, Sherston,[4] Mayor of Bath and Justice of the Peace, and others, defendants, in the matter of a riot. Sherston, being a lessee for years, and having paid his rent for fifteen years to Baron Snegge, at the end of his term, when the Baron was in the King's service on the Northern Circuit,

[1] Sir John Popham, Chief Justice of the King's Bench, died on June 10th, 1607; Sir Thomas Fleming, Chief Baron of the Exchequer, was appointed Chief Justice on June 25th following.

[2] See *post*, p. 336, n. 3.

[3] Sir George Snigge was born at Bristol *cir.* 1545; admitted to the Middle Temple, 1567; called to the Bar, 1575; Treasurer, 1602; Recorder of Bristol, 1592 to 1604; appointed Baron of the Exchequer, 14 Oct. 1604; *ob.* 11 Nov. 1617; buried in S. Stephen's church, Bristol. See Evans, *Hist. of Bristol*, ii. 181; Barrett, *Hist. and Ant. of Bristol*, 514.

[4] William Sherstone was the first Mayor of Bath under the Charter granted by Queen Elizabeth in 1590. The rent mentioned in the text was in respect of Berton farm in the parish of Waldcot, which had been purchased by Sir George Snigge from Edmund Colthurste. The citizens claimed certain rights of common in this property, which led to a further dispute with William Snigge after the Baron's death. The matter was eventually settled by arbitration in 1619. See Warner's *Hist. of Bath*, 186.

1607 Oct. 14

kept possession by force, and he had in the house a 'drumme, caliuer, crossbowe, powder & shotte, 2 holberds, 6 prongs & diuerse staues,' but he did nothing but keep possession for five months. And he practised, by the advice of Chambers, another defendant, to 'stirre auncient title.'

Sentence

[p. 311]

And for these offences he was fined £100 and Chambers £200, for *plus peccat autor* [sic] *quam actor*. The other defendants, being servants of Sherston's, were fined £20 apiece, the Master to pay this by the course of the Court. And imprisonment [for them all] as of course.

1607 Oct. 16

In Camera Stellata, coram Consilio ibidem, Veneris, 16 Octobr. 1607.[1]

SOL.-GEN. *v.* LOUCHE and HOLLAND — Building contrary to proclamation

Sir Francis Bacon, now the King's Solicitor,[2] informed *ore tenus* against one Louche, 'a kooke, & Roberte Hollande, a scryuener at temple barre,' on their confession, for erecting new buildings contrary to two several proclamations and in contempt of them; the one 22 Elizabeth, the other 4 James, and another published this day. (Coke, Chief Justice: *Vbi non est lex ibi non est transgressio.*) 'theise buyldinges are againste the common lawe & the kinge's prerogatiue. *Quaere* the proclamation before in this book, where the particular mischiefs are set down.'[3] 'We had neede of a lawe againste Inmates in London & outmates in the Cuntrye; for depopulations haue destroyed & decayed all other good townes, & seruauntes for husbandrye are not now to be gotten.

'In buyldinge 3 thinges considerable, 1. *necessitas*, 2. *salubritas*, 3. *ornatus*.

'*Frequens et generalis contemptus est rebellionis prodromus.* In o[r] punishemente therefore wee must not looke backewarde. Lameche's punishem[te] was tenne times to Cain's. *Interest reipublicae ne quis re sua male vtatur*; & as it is the kinge's prerogatiue, so it is the auntient lawe

[1] Eight Councillors and Judges were present.

[2] He was appointed Solicitor-General June 25th, 1607.

[3] This seems to refer to the case of Savage and others, *ante*, p. 318; in the MS. there is a blank page left, apparently for the Proclamation.

that no noble man or subiecte whatsoeuer maye buylde any forte or howse wth battlem^{tes}: 5 E. 2; Britton & Bracton; *quaere*.

'*Nihil est illicitum quod est necessarium. Necessitas lex temporis*; but the Lo. Chauncellor said he had learned a rule that the prerogatiue meddles not wth *meum et tuum*; the kinge Can not take my lande or goods & giue it to another, but where the Common state or wealthe of the people or kingedome require it, the kinge's proclamacion bindes as a lawe, & neede not staye a parliam^{te}; & as a father saythe, when lawes are in making euery man may speake, but being made *iudicandum est secundum leges*.

[p. 312] Sentence

'Louche was fined 200$^{li.}$,[1] imprisonm^{te}, & his howse to be plucked downe, & for contemptuous wordes againste a J. of p., Sr John Granger, he was to be bounde to his good behauioure.

'Hollande, in respecte of his milde & modeste caryage, wch was much Commended by the Courte, he was fyned 100$^{li.}$, imprisonm^{te}, & the forefronte of his howse to be newe buylte wth bricke before whitsontide nexte, or else to be plucked downe.'

Sir Henry Mountague,[2] Recorder of London, and now the King's Counsel at large, the place that Sir Francis Bacon had, informed, that these Causes being infinite, this Court two years ago appointed a Commission, and by it they found three hundred faulty in this, and in four large houses they found now 8,000 inhabitants, & the last great plague 800 out of one of them died of the pest; and if it be not reformed the people cannot have food, nor can they be governed.

[1] See Appendix VII.

[2] Third son of Edward, eldest son of Sir Edward Montagu, Chief Justice of the King's Bench and Common Pleas in the reigns of Henry VIII. and Edward VI. Elected Recorder of London, 1603; M.P. for the City of London, 1604; King's Serjeant, 1611; Chief Justice of the King's Bench, 1616; Lord Treasurer, 1620, when he was created Baron Montagu of Kimbolton and Viscount Mandevil; Lord President of the Council, 1621; created Earl of Manchester, 1626; Lord Privy Seal, 1628; *ob.* 7 Nov. 1642. See Foss's *Judges*; *Complete Peerage* by G.E.C.

1607 Oct. 16 *Ore tenus* on confession only

Cooke [Coke] said that on *ore tenus* they ought only to proceed on confession, and not otherwise, notwithstanding it appear plainly to be true.

This last vacation John Rennols, Utter Barrister of the Inner Temple,[1] Johnson, a Bencher of the Middle Temple, Atkinson of Lincoln's Inne,[2] and Ellis of Graie's Inne,[3] died.

1607 Oct. 21

In Camera Stellata, coram Consilio ibidem, Mercurij, 21° Octobr. 1607.[4]

STANDISHE *v.* WOOLNER — Riot

'Woolner, knighte, a Justice of peace, defend^{te}, & Standishe,[5] plaintiff, for a riot. Standishe had a lease for yeares from the late Queene, & Woolner gotte a leasse in reuersion, bothe wth a Clause of re-entrie for non paiemente of rente, Standishe makes defalte of paiem^{te}, & Woolner not knowinge thereof, he makes no tender neyther; so bothe leasses were forfeited: & Standishe he takes a newe leasse in possession, & woolner, supposinge that Standishes [p. 313] first lease was in beinge, & that vpon the determinacion thereof his leasse in reuercion showlde Commence, sendes at seuerall times seuerall persons, & but 2 at any one time together, to enter & take the possession, & to dryue off Standishe's Cattelle; & woolner's men wente & draue of the Cattelle, & beinge put in agayne by Standishe, they resyste them, beate & wounde them, & kille some of the Cattelle. & for this woolner was fyned 1000$^{li.}$, his men, some 30$^{li.}$, some 40$^{li.}$ a peece, imprisonm^{te}, woolner to be thruste oute of the Commission, & he & all his people to be bounde to there good behauyoure.'

Sentence

[1] John Reynolds of Chesterford, co. Essex; admitted, Nov. 1586; called to the Bar, 1595.

[2] No one of this name appears in the books of the Inn for this period; there were several 'Atkins.'

[3] There were several Ellises of Gray's Inn at this time.

[4] Eight Councillors and Judges were present.

[5] The Standishes are a well-known Lancashire family, whose principal seat is at Duxbury. In the absence of any Christian name it seems impossible to identify the plaintiff in this case. I cannot identify the defendant either.

In Camera Stellata, coram Consilio ibidem, Veneris, 23 Octobr. 1607.[1] 1607 Oct. 23

'Sr John Stafforde,[2] relator *versus* Parmeter, an Atturnie of the Common place, for mainteynaunce & buyinge of a bonde; but the Defendaunte was acquyted by the Cowrte, yet blamed for that he woulde intermeddle in sollicitinge or followinge any Cause in any Cowrte but where he ys an attornie, for no man Can be a generall sollicitor, & the lawe takes knowledge of none to intermeddle wth lawe busynesses but *homo consiliarius et in lege peritus, et Attornatus siue procurator*; & they must doe it for there Fees; neyther can they disburse monie for Fees or Copies, but in there owne Cawses: & therefore that Atturnie sayd well, wch was olde Crowe, when his Clyentes woulde haue him paye Fees & disburse monie for them, "I doe not loue," quothe he, "that any man showlde goe to lawe wth my monie." Which was Commended for a good & an honeste aunsweare, & the man ys yet lyuinge, & hathe 500li. lande by the yeare. Yet yf a man wryte vnto an attornie to instructe or reteyne counselle, or take out proces for him, it is so Common & necessary for the poore of ye Cuntrye that, albeit yt be an offence againste the lawe, yet this Cowrte will not sentence yt:

STAFFORD v. PARMETER — Maintenance — Acquittal — No man can be a general solicitor — [p. 314]

'For a man to buye a dette or a bonde, it is againste a rule in lawe, that noe man Can graunte a thinge in action, excepte it be for the satisfaction of a trewe dette, *bona fide, sine fraude et dolo*, as it is 24 H. 6, 5 H. 7, 5 E. 4, & so did this defendte; but he was blamed allso for Compoundinge a Cause wthout lycense of the Cowrte, for no man oughte to doe it.

Buying debts or bonds

'Sr John Stafforde was greatelye blamed by the Cowrte that beinge so worthye a gentleman, so honorablye discended, & otherwyse so well deseruinge in himselfe, that he woulde stoope to so base an office as to be an ynformer, whoe

Sir John Stafford blamed for becoming an informer

[1] Nine Councillors and Judges were present.

[2] Knighted by he Lord Admiral and the Earl of Essex at Calais, 1596. Metcalfe, *A Book of Knights*, 137.

1607 Oct. 23

albeit they be necessarye in euerye well gouerned state, yet for the moste parte they are of the meaner & worste kinde of people; but for feare of danger & discourage to others to doe the lyke, they spared to fyne him *pro falso clamore*, & the Lo. Chauncellor he sayd he would be sparinge in his bille of Costes: for it is not mayntenaunce for any man to ynforme in this Cowrte or in an inditemente, for all is for the kinge, & 1 R. 2, cap. 4, & 4 H. 4,[1] doe not extende to this kinde of Relators; but the Cowrte founde greateste faulte for that, vnder Collor of relation, he vsed the parties greeued for wytnesses, whose testimonie was disallowed by the Cowrte, & ordered now that none showlde vse it hereafter: & that a man vtlawed Can not be a wytnesse nor receaued to wage his lawe. It was allso muche mislyked by the Cowrte that Commissioners vse to take depositions *affirmatiue aut negatiue*, a greate trouble to the Cowrte & not to be receaued, neyther any discreete Commissioner to vse it or admitte of them.'

Not maintenance to inform in the Star Chamber

[p. 315]

Outlaw cannot be witness

ROGERS *v.* MACHIN

'Another Cawse of hearinge betwene Rogers & Machin, for 5^s. fine for a Copieholde, was dismissed as vnworthie of the Cowrte.'

1607 Oct. 28

In Camera Stellata, coram Consilio ibidem, Mercurij, 28 Octobr. 1607.[2]

GOSSE *v.* BADCOCK and others

Riot

'Cause of hearinge, Gosse, plaintiff, Badcocke, defend^te^, for a riot in entringe to a howse forciblye & keepinge the possession; but the ryote was suche that they thoughte it vnfytte to trouble the Cowrte therew^th^; yet beinge now posseste wth the same, they sentenced yt, & fyned the defend^te^ 50^li.^ & his 2 seruauntes 10^li.^ a peece, & imprisonm^te^ of course. The Lo. Kooke sayde he remembred a prettie storie in Plutarche: an ill painter had painted a Cocke, &

Sentence

Coke quotes Plutarch

[1] 1 Ric. II., cap. 4. 'The several Penalties of several Persons that do maintain Quarrels.' I cannot identify the statute of 4 Hen. IV., if indeed the reference is to a statute.

[2] Eight Councillors and Judges were present.

one asked what yt was, & he sayde, "a Cocke;" then quothe he, "yt is a very Bad cocke, you are beste wryte ouer his heade 'this ys a Cocke,' or else they will saye it is a goose." The Lo. Northampton [said] that the propertie of a good Cocke ys to be *vocalis* to Calle men to there woorke, viz. to there lawfull vocation, but heere was a Badcocke indeede that Called them to this vnlawfull woorke.' Lord Northampton's joke

'Another Cause of hearinge, Russe, plaintiff, and Fraunklin, defend^{te}, for Forgerye of a deede of Feoffem^{te}; but yt was proued by 5 wytnesses that the partye did sealle & delyuer the Deede, & that the same was reade vnto him, so yt Coulde be noe Forgerye, albeit the Clerke had inserted other matter in the Deede then the partye gaue him instructions for, he seallinge & delyueringe the same as his Deede. & so he was acquyted & dysmissed.' RUSSE *v.* FRANKLIN — Forgery [p. 316] Acquittal

In Camera Stellata, coram Consilio ibidem, Veneris, 30 Octobr. 1607.[1] 1607 Oct. 30

'Cause of hearinge betwene Rowlie, plaintiff, & Penkethe, defend^{te}, for matter of Riote vpon the sabaothe daye in the time of diuine seruice, comminge wth a Carte wth vittaile & other prouision, wth men & women, & entringe into a barne, & holdinge possession againste Irelande, a Justice of peace. but the proces was not dulye serued vpon the principall defendaunte, but vpon one of the Defendauntes onely, wch albeit it be sufficiente for an apparaunce or to make aunsweare, yet *ad audiendum iudicium* it is not sufficiente; & therefore althoughe they were guyltie yet the Courte woulde not sentence them: & the Lo. Ch. Justice Coke sayde that albeit the Common lawe did not punishe the breache of the Sabbaothe daye, yet for his parte he woulde binde them to there good behauyoure that vsed prophanation of that Daye, & he had good warraunte so to doe.' ROWLIE *v.* PENKETHE — Riot

[1] Seven Councillors and Judges were present.

1607 Oct. 30 MOORE v. JACKSON and others

'Another Cause of hearinge *enter* Moore, widow, plaintiff, & Jackson & others, defend[tes], but no affidauit was made that any proces was serued, & the Defend[tes] did not appeare: & so it was dysmissed.'

STEPNEY v. WARREN — Misdemeanours

'Another Cause of hearinge, Steptney, plaintiff, againste Warren, defend[te], a Justice of peace in Breaknokshire, for many vilde misdemeanors: & referred to the nexte daye to be sentenced.'

[p. 317] 1607 Nov. 4

In Camera Stellata, coram Consilio ibidem, Mercurij, 4° Nouembr. 1607.[1]

STEPNEY v. WARREN — Misdemeanour

'The same Cause of hearinge betwene Stepnie, plaintiff, againste Warren, defend[te], a Justice of peace in wales, who had Committed many vilde, lewde & odious misdemeanors, & hauing no Counselle nor any matter of excuse or defence, pleaded in generall wordes the generall pardon, w[ch] by th'opinion of the Judges was nothinge, for that he oughte to haue pleaded it speciallye, wth all the exceptions: his offences were either suche as Concerned his priuate person, as multiplicitie of causeles suites againste dyuerse in moste Cowrtes, stirred oute of malice, & causeles, for vexatyon & reuenge, & to raise & drawe matter of benefytte to himselfe, keepinge twooe of his owne seruauntes to be Common ynformers, & takinge very baselye of some 10[s] & 20[d] for composition; or his publike offices that he bare, either as a Justice of peace takinge a Cople of oxen & other bribes, Countenauncinge offendors, baillinge & suffringe to escape Felons, persons suspected of murder, & suche lyke offendors, goinge to the goale, takinge of irons from malefactors & others in vpon executions for dettes, gettinge possession of Cattelle by collor of a repleuin, (a thinge heretofore vsed & by th'opinion of the Lo. Coke adiudged felonie, & they dyed for it), rescuinge himselfe being arrested vpon a *Capias*, &c.: or, as he was a Commissioner for the subsidie, admittinge of some Cessors that payde nothinge, takinge monie of

[1] Eleven Councillors and Judges were present.

others to discharge them; or, as he was tresorer for the poore, hauinge Collected & gotten into his handes 46$^{li.}$, & disbursed noe parte of it for the vse of the poore: or, [as] he was an eschetor, thereby defraudinge the kinge of his rightes. For any one of theise offences seuerallye by it [p. 318] selfe the Cowrte was of clere opinion that it was worthye of sharpe & seuere punishemente, & in iudgem^{te} or punishmente the person of any man ys not to be respected, but th'offence, *pena delicto non delinquenti*; & the punishm^{te} or offence of one Justice of the peace ys no disgrace to all the reste that are vertuous, honeste, painefull, & an honorable & necessarye callinge or office, wthout whome the fabrike of the gouernemente Can not Contynewe: but th'offence is the greateste when Justice is made th'instrumente, Collor, shadowe, or stalkinge horse to offende, forgettfull of his othe as a J. of peace, of his othe as a leige man taken at 12 yeares of age, a necessary law & fitte to be still obserued; yf theise periuries had bene pertycularlye Compleyned of, the Cowrte woulde haue sentenced him in that kinde. He made a *supersedeas* for felonie, a thinge neuer hearde of before: For his offence as a Commissioner of the subsidie, it was verye greate, & albeit he be not ymmediatlye sworne, yet by his oathe as a Justice of peace he is sworne to execute the same trulye, & all men haue assented to the same in parliam^{te}, & it is the kinge's dette euen as tythes are due to ye Churche, so let the kinge at the leaste haue the tenthe, for it is a miserable thinge that the state & kingedome showlde be so riche & the kinge's treasurie so poore. Sythence the Queene's deceasse many necessarye & needefull Charges haue bene imposed vpon the kinge, suche as the lyke were neuer hearde of in this kingedome, as the Queene's buriall, in wch the kinge Commaunded very honorablye that noe Coste showlde be spared for her whose memorye will be euer blessed & honorable, yet she wanted one greate blessinge, wch to o^{r} exceedinge greate Comforte we are now more happie, the yssues of his [p. 319] Matie: his Comminge in the Queene's, the prince & all the posteritie [*sic*]. The Lo. Treasorer, as proper to his place,

1607 Nov. 4

spake very muche to this purpose: & the Lo. Coke helde it a greate offence, the defraudinge of the poore, a good & a Charitable lawe, & *panis pauperum vita pauperum, qui defraudat eos vir sanguinis est*: & by all it was Conceaued a masse of offences; for all wch he was Fyned 2000 markes, ympri-sonm^te^ of course, to weare papers aboute Westminster halle, at the Assises & at the Commission for the subsidye, to be bounde to his good behauyoure, to be disabled from bearinge any ministeriall or iudiciall office, to repaye the 46^li.^ to the vse of the poore, & 5^li.^ a peece to all those that he hathe wrongefullye sued, & good Costes: & there was one other defend^te^ againste whome they did not proceede, he was dismissed wth Costes.'

Sentence

1607 Nov. 6

In Camera Stellata, coram Consilio ibidem, Veneris, 6 Nouembr. 1607.[1]

EARLNE *v.* WATKINS

'Earlne, plaintiff, Watkins, defendant; *mes* Sr Nicholas Hide [2] was the man that Followed it againste one Chase for a bargaine of his timber; after 2 trialls & the bargaine proued, he sued the wytnesses & some of ye Jurye heere for periurye, a very tryflinge Cause; & the defend^te^ was dismissed wth Costes, & the pl. fyned 40^li.^, & 20^li.^ dammages to the defend^te^.'

Acquittal

Plaintiff fined

DUDGEON *v.* BURINGTON and others — Riot

'Another Cause of hearinge, Dudgeon, pl., & Burington & others, defend^tes^, for matter of riote in beatinge, woundinge & mayminge the pl., in the Churcheyarde in Herefordeshire: three of the defend^tes^ were fyned 200^li.^ a peece, commytted, & before there delyueraunce to be bounde wth good suerties to there good behauyoure, & the pl. to haue good Costes, & 60^li.^ dammages in regarde of his woundes & innocente bloude that he shedde.

Sentence

[p. 320] 'But Secretarie Herberte and Sr Julius Cesar [3] gaue

[1] Eleven Councillors and Judges were present.

[2] Probably Sir Nicholas Hide of Albury, co. Herts, Sheriff 17 James I.; created a Baronet 8 Nov. 1621. Burke, *Extinct Baronetage.*

[3] Sir Julius Cæsar was the 3rd son of Cæsar Adelmare, physician to Queens Mary and Elizabeth. At this time he was Master of the Court of Requests. He was afterwards appointed Master of the Rolls. Died 1636. Foss, *Judges.*

there sentence accordinge to ye statute of 5 E[dward] 6, cap 4,' which is, if any one shall by words quarrel or brawl in a church or churchyard and the offence is proved by two witnesses, the offender, if a layman, shall be suspended by the Ordinary *ab ingressu ecclesiae*, and if a clerk, from his office. If any one smite or lay violent hands on another in church or churchyard, *ipso facto* he shall be deemed excommunicate. If any strike another with a weapon, or draw a weapon with intent to strike another, and be convicted of this by the verdict of 12, on his own confession, or by two lawful witnesses, before the Justices of Assize, the Justices of *oyer et terminer*, or the Justices of the Peace at their Sessions, he shall be sentenced by the Justices before whom he is so convicted to have one of his ears cut off, and if he have no ears, he shall be burned on the cheek with the letter 'F' for 'fraymaker' or 'fighter,' and he shall be *ipso facto* excommunicate.

Herberte and Cæsar differ

5 Edw. VI., cap. 4

'But the Judges differed from them as before, firste for that the bill was not framed vpon this statute nor any other speciall statute, but generallye, & allso this statute lymitethe pertycularlye the Judges of th'offenders againste that lawe.

'Yet the Lo. Chauncellor was of opinion that this Cowrte mighte giue that sentence, or any other Corporall punishem[te] but lyfe: yet the Lo. Coke sayd that *maxima pecuniaria pena maior est quam minima corporalis.* & in that respecte the sentence was the greater, for Churcheyardes are consecrated to pious vses, the places where the temples of the holye ghoste lye, the bodyes of the sayntes, men are to be in peace to doe there deuotion; a growing euell, men gyuen to prophanenes, the nexte waye to Atheisme, whereas heretofore they were sanctuaryes & places of refuge; & by the aunciente lawe noe preiste either goinge or comminge from the Churche Can be arrested in his person: & so they all wyshed that there mighte Care be had to punishe those that vsed either prophanation one the Sabaothe daye, or in Churche or churcheyarde, and that the people mighte resorte & Contynewe at y[e] Churche wth deuotion all the time of diuine seruice.'

Churchyards

[p. 321]
1607 Nov. 12

In Banke le Roy, Jovis, 12 Novembr. Termino Michaelis, 1607, Jacob. Regis Britanniae 5°.

HOLLIDAY v. KENRICKE — Ejectment

A Jury was adjourned to this day between Sir Leonard Hollidaie, Mayor of London,[1] plaintiff, and Roberte Kenricke[2] of Northamptonshire, defendante, *in eiectione firme*. The names of the Jurors:—

Wm Clerke; Wm Lie;

Challenge of Juror

Thomas Lete;—(He was challenged, because the plaintiff claims a lease for 2000 years in a Manor which the defendant had purchased from the Earl of Darby, and the said Juror is a tenant [?] of this manor for freehold and copyhold. It was allowed as a good challenge.)

Thomas Watts; John Berrowe;
Thomas Judgate: Edwarde Ashbie;
Edwarde Arnoll; Henrye Leake;
Thomas Muscotte; Henrye Hickeman;
Roberte Gennowaye.

Adjourned

It was adjourned to Easter Term for default of appearance of the Jurors.

1607 Nov. 12

In Curia Wardorum, Jovis, 12 Novembr. 1607, Jacob. 5°; adonque presente, Sr Roberte Cecill, Mr del Gardes, Principall Secretarie al roye, Vicounte Cranborne, Counte de Sarum, et del priuie Counselle; Flemminge, Ch. Justice de Banco; Coke, Ch. Justice de Banco Communi; Tanfeilde, Ch. Baron; Pepper, Attornie del Gardes; Sr Roger Wilbrom, Surueyor del Gardes, and Mr del Requests et Chauncellor al Roigne.

The great cause between the executors of Lord Mount-

[1] Sir Leonard Halliday, Merchant Taylor; knighted at Whitehall, July 26, 1603; Lord Mayor, 1605. Son of William H. of Rodborough, co. Glouc. See *Remembrancia*, 495. There is a pedigree of the Hallidays of Rodborough in Burke's *Commoners*, ii. 131.

[2] Robert Kendrick or Kenwrick purchased the manor of King's Sutton, co. Northampton, from William, 6th Earl of Derby in 1598. He died 1 Mar. 1616-7, and was bur. at Sutton. See Baker's *Northamptonshire*, i. 694; Bridges, i, 178.

ioye, Earl of Deuonshire,[1] viz.:—Lord Danuers,[2] [3] Earthe & Wakeman, executors, and Sir Henry Baker[4] and Sir Richard Champernowne, claiming to be the heirs of the said Earl of Deuonshire, now dead without issue, and the question now was which of them is the heir to the Earl. A Jury was now returned to find the office and the heir. Serjeant Forster, Hide, Thomas Crewe, Richard Martin and Sir Henry Mountague, the Recorder, were of Counsel with the executors; Serjeant Nicholls and Whitlocke with Sir Richard Champernowne; George Crooke and Richardson with Sir Henry Baker. The Counsel for the executors moved that the first thing according to the writ is to inquire what lands descend, for if no lands descend, the heir shall not sue out livery, but by previous consent they may proceed, and also they may examine their witnesses.

THE EARL OF DEVONSHIRE'S case

'The pedegree produced for Sr Rich^de^ Champernoun was that Charles, [8th] Lord Mountioye, was sonne to James, [6th] Lord Mountioye, who was sonne to Charles, [5th] Lord Mountioye, who was sonne to William, [4th] Lord Mountioye. Charles, the laste Lord Mountioye, Earle of Deuonshire, dyed w^th^oute yssue, so there the dyrecte lyne ended; & now theise challenge in the Collaterall lyne. Constance was syster to W^m^ [4th Baron], &

[p. 322] Sir Richard Champernoun's case

[1] Charles Blount, 8th and last Baron Mountjoy, succeeded his brother, William, in 1594; he was elected a Knight of the Garter in 1597; General of the Army in Ireland and Viceroy (with the title of 'Lord Deputy') 1600 to 1603, and as 'Lord Lieutenant' from 1603, having during that period subjugated the great Irish rebellion under the Earl of Tyrone. He was, in reward, created Earl of Devonshire, 21 July, 1603. He went through the ceremony of marriage, 26 Dec. 1605, with Penelope, Lady Rich [see *ante*, p. 172, and Appendix IV.], dau. of Walter Devereux, Earl of Essex; she had obtained an ecclesiastical divorce *a mensa et thoro*, 15 Nov. 1605, from Robert, Lord Rich, her husband. The Earl died without legitimate issue 3 April, 1606. *Complete Peerage*, by G. E. C.

[2] Sir Henry Danvers, 2nd son of Sir John Danvers of Dantsey, co. Wilts, and of Danby, co. York, was created Baron Danvers of Dantsey, 21 July, 1603, and Earl of Danby, 5 Feb. 1625-6. His elder brother, Sir Charles Danvers, was attainted for participation in Essex's rebellion in 1602. See *Complete Peerage* by G. E. C. See also the case of Danvers *v.* Long, *ante*, pp. 49, 61, and Appendix III..

[3] Blank in MS.

[4] Sir Richard Baker of Sisinghurst, co. Kent, knight, mar. Catherine dau. and heir of John Tirell, youngest son of Sir Thomas Tirell, knight; he was succeeded by his eldest son, John, whose eldest son was Henry Baker, the claimant in the text. See Burke's *Extinct Baronetage*.

1607 Nov. 12

daughter to John [3rd Baron], & marryed to Thomas Terrelle, by whome shee had yssue John Terrell.[1]

'William [4th Baron Mountjoy] had 3 wyues, by whome he had yssue. The firste Elizabeth was maryed to the Marques of Exeter,[2] who died wthoute yssue, & John Baker was her Collaterall heyre. The seconde was Alice Keble, the wydowe of Keble,[3] an alderman of London, & the daughter of Browne, an alderman of London, by whome he had issue Charles, Lord Mountioye, & Katherine whoe was marryed to John Champernoune,[4] by whome he had issue Henry Champernoune, who had yssue Richarde Champernoune.

'This pedegree they prove by 5 wytnesses & by a booke. 1. Charles Browne, grandchilde to Sr Wm Browne; 2. Thomas Parrie; 3. Lady Dorothy Parrie; 4. Margaret Pagette; 5. Michaell Blunte, knighte.[5]

Sir Henry Baker's case

'Sr Henrye Baker discended from Constance.

'Dorothye was the 4th wyfe of Wylliam & by her he had a sonne & three daughters, by one of wch daughters

[1] Sir Thomas Tirell of Heron, co. Essex, knight, mar. Constance Blount. Their eldest son, Sir Thomas, mar. Anne, dau. of Sir William Browne, Lord Mayor of London, and had a son John, whose only dau., Catherine, mar. Sir Richard Baker. Burke's *Extinct Baronetage*.

[2] This is not correct. Lord Mountjoy's first wife was Elizabeth, dau. and co-heir of Sir William Saye of Essendon, co. Herts. She died in 1506, leaving two daughters and co-heirs, Gertrude and Mary. Gertrude mar. Henry Courtney, Earl of Devon and Marquess of Exeter, and had two sons, who both died *s.p.* Mary mar. Henry Bourchier, Earl of Essex, and had issue a dau. Anne, who *ob. s. p. legit.*

[3] Alice Keble was the third wife according to *The Complete Peerage*, where she is called dau. of Henry Keble, and widow of Sir William Browne, Lord Mayor 1513.

The issue of this marriage is correctly stated. Catherine Champernowne mar. 2ndly, Sir Maurice Berkeley of Bruton.

Sir Thomas Tirrell, father of Catherine Baker, Sir Henry's grandmother, mar. Anne, dau. of Sir William Browne.

Lord Mountjoy's fourth wife was Dorothy, dau. of Thomas Grey, Marquess of Dorset, and relict of Robert, Lord Willoughby de Broke. By her he had issue, John *ob. s. p.*; Dorothy mar. Roger Blewet; and Mary mar. Sir Robert Dennys. See *Complete Peerage* by G. E. C.; Burke's *Extinct Peerage*.

[4] Eldest son of Sir Philip Champernowne of Modbury, co. Devon; Sir Richard Champernowne, the claimant in this case, mar. Elizabeth, dau. of Lord Chief Justice Popham, but *ob. s.p.* Burke's *Commoners*, ii. 272.

[5] Sir Michael Blount of Maple Durham, co. Oxford. He was descended from Sir Thomas, brother of Sir Walter, 1st Lord Mountjoy. On the death of the Earl of Devonshire in 1606, he claimed the Barony of Mountjoy, but without success. Burke's *Commoners*, iii. 163.

S[r] Rich[de] Champernoun comes, sayde the Counselle of S[r] Henrye Baker: & that they proue by a visitacion by Commission by the heraldes, & by th'accounte & estimation of th'erle of Deuonshire.

'But the daye beinge spente it was deferred to Satterdaye Followinge, to be then hearde agayne. And then to the seconde satterdaye in the nexte hillarye terme.'[1] Adjourned

In Camera Stellata, coram Consilio ibidem, Veneris, 13°, et Mercurij, 18° Nouembr. [1607]. adonque presente, Lo. Chauncellor, archeuesque de Canterberye, Lo. Tresorer, Count Northampton, Count Exeter, euesque de Londres, Lo. Zouche, ambideux Cheife Justices, S[r] John Herberte et S[r] Julius Cesar. [p. 323] 1607 Nov. 13, 18

'Pemlie, a minister in Kente, vpon an *ore tenus*, his owne Confessyon, for a libelle againste Bishops & the gouernemente of the Churche, set vp vpon a poaste of an In gate in a markette towne in Kente, was Fyned 2000[li.], to stande vpon the pillorye at westminster wth papers & there to lose one eare, & vpon the pillorye at Cheapeside & there to lose another eare, to be whipped at bothe places vnles he Confesse his faulte, & to be perpetuallye ymprysoned, but fyrste of all to be degraded from the ministrye before he receaue any Corporall punishemente; w[ch] he was the nexte thursedaye Followinge at Lambethe.'[2] PEMLIE'S case — Libel — Sentence

In Camera Stellata, coram Consilio ibidem, Veneris, 20 Nouembr. 1607.[3] 1607 Nov. 20

'Cause of hearinge betwene Warren, plaintiff, *et* Steptney, defend[te], being highe sheriffe in wales, & for sellinge his hundredes or bailliwikes, & for holdinge his hundrede euerye twooe weekes contrarye to the lawe, for it oughte to be kepte from three weekes to three weekes; but of theise WARREN *v.* STEPNEY — Misdemeanour as Sheriff

[1] This case is not reported further in the MS. See Appendix XXI.

[2] See *post*, p. 343.

[3] Eleven Councillors and Judges were present.

1607 Nov. 20

Adjourned

twooe the Judges woulde aduyse before they woulde delyuer there resolution, for it was a generall case & vsed by moste of the sheriffes of Englaunde; & so the cause was referred to another daye.' [1]

[p. 324]

LEWES v. LANY and others

Taking bribes, and riot

Lord Coke speaks in favour of the defendants

Judges must not take fees

except in some special cases

Commissioners may take rewards for their trouble and travelling expenses, if not done corruptly

Acquittal

'Another Cause of hearinge, Lewes, pl., & Lany [2] & Goldsmithe of Graie's Inne, 2 Counsellors at the lawe, Fisher, an attornie at the Lawe, & others, defendauntes, for that they beinge Commissioners vpon the statute of Bankrupts had corruptelye taken rewardes & caryed themselues vndulye in th'executinge of the Commission: vpon there aunsweares yt appeared that they had trauayled & bestowed many dayes & tooke greate paines to execute the Commission, & after all was ended Lany had $5^{li.}$, Goldsmithe $5^{li.}$, & Fisher $12^{li.}$, to beare there rydinge Charges, & for there paines: & before any proffe was reade, the Lo. Coke spake very muche in the Commendacion of Lany & Goldsmithe, & it were harde to nippe them thus in the budde; he neuer hearde nor knewe but they were honeste men, hopefull & lykelye to proue good members to there Cuntryes; & for generall Judges of the lande, they can take nothinge, eyther before or after, for they haue there Fee of the kinge; yet in speciall cases some Fees are allowed them by the parties, as in a specyall assise, or in errors in london; but Commissioners, put in truste & not sworne, yf they Contracte not or bargaine Corruptlye before hande for some greate rewarde or Fee, & so that be an occasyon to demeasne themselues partiallye or corruptelye or affectionatelye in execution of that truste, he was of opinion that by lawe they may well take rewarde for there trauelle & paines, & it was no offence; (yet he was sorrye they had taken anythinge). But all the Cowrte was Cleare of opinion that yt was no offence, but iustifiable by the

[1] See a cross bill between the same parties, *ante*, p. 335.

[2] John Lany, eld. son of John Lany, Lent Reader of Gray's Inn, was adm. there 1590–1; John L. the father was adm. 1567. The son is probably the one mentioned in the text, as Coke speaks of Lany and Goldsmith as though they were young men. There were several Goldsmiths of Gray's Inn about this time, and it is impossible to identify the one here referred to.

Common & ciuill lawe; & the Lo. Chauncellor sayde he was sorrye they tooke no more, (for wth a Lawyer *Cessans lucrum damnum est*), & yf Commissioners showlde not haue rewarde for there trauell & Charges, no Commissions woulde be executed. So they were acquyted by the sentence of all the Cowrte, wth very greate Commendation, especiallye of Lanie, vpon knowledge of many of ye lordes.

'But some other defendauntes, for a riot in goinge wth gunnes & other weapons vpon the sabaothe daye in the time of deuine seruice (wch none can doe) to execute a warraunte of the Commissioners for the takinge the bodye of the Bankroupte, Lewes, for this riote they were Fyned, th'one a 100^li.^, th'other 100 markes, the thirde 100 nobles, & imprisonm^te^ as of Course. The Lo. Chauncellor woulde haue yt entred in the order wth some touche of delyueringe theise [Lany and Goldsmith] wth Credyte & note of greate Commendacion by so manye honorable personages, & that they showlde haue good Costes, & the pl. to acknowledge his Faulte vnto them.'

[p. 325]
The Riot
Sentence

In Camera Stellata, coram Consilio ibidem, Veneris, 27 Nouembr. 1607.[1]

1607 Nov. 27

PEMLIE'S case

'This daye Pemlye (beinge degraded by the archebishop) was accordinge to the former sentence, 18 Nouembr., put to his punishemente, firste he had 25 ierkes,[2] & then stoode in the pillorye, & had papers, & one of his eares Cutte cloase from his heade, & after that he had 25 ierkes more.'[3]

EDWARDES v. WOOTTON and others — Libel

'This daye allso a Cause was hearde betwene Thomas Edwardes, a phisitian of Exeter, pl., & Doctor Wootton, a phisitian, Norris' wyfe, an apothecarye, one other phisitian, & an apothecarye, defend^tes^. Th'offence was a lybelle made by Doctor wootton, & by him & the reste published in the manner ensewinge. Edwardes & Doctor Wootton fallinge oute & vsinge bitter tearmes, Doctor

[1] Ten Councillors and Judges were present.

[2] Apparently lashes; his sentence was that he was to be whipped. Jerk, to beat: Halliwell.

[3] See *ante*, p. 341.

1607 Nov. 27 wootton wrytes a letter & begins "Mr Docturdo & fartado," &c., more then 2 sides of paper full of vilde matter, [p. 326] ribaldrie & defamacyon, & enclosethe yt as a letter, & subscrybes it, & sendes yt to Mr Edwardes, & keepes a Copie thereof, & afterwards publyshethe the same, & delyuers Copies to dyuerse whoe lykewyse reade & publishe the same to dyuerse, & saye that Doctor Edwardes will forweare them & beare them out in yt, howsoeuer or whatsoeuer yt coste him. This was greatelye to the defaming & damnifyinge of the pl., Edwardes, being broughte vp as an Apothecarie & allowed a phisitian by the College of Phisitions in london vpon examynation had, & otherwyse reputed a very honeste & discreete man: The Defendaunte Doctor wooton pretended that the pl. himselfe had firste published this lybelle, but made no proffe of it, & had mynistred 80 Interrogatories, 4 yardes of parchemente by the measure of the Lo. Chauncellor, againste the pl., thereby examyninge all the principall men of those Countryes touchinge the honestye, Credite, reputation & Caryage of the pl. (a very daungerous presydente & not to be suffred, for the pl. Can haue no knowledge thereof before publication); yet they all did generally wth one Consente aprooue the sufficiencye, honestye & good Course & Caryage of the sayd Compl., & no one wytnesse accused or touched him wth any blemishe in any kinde.

Interrogatories 4 yards long

Libel or not

'The question was whether this was a lybelle or no, & resolued by the Judges & all the Courte that yt was a lybelle: for yf a man will wryte a pryuate letter defamatorye & not otherwyse publishe yt eyther before or after the wrytinge, he shall not haue an action of the case; but forasmuche as the same dothe prouoke malice & breache of the peace & reuenge, yt shalbe punished in this Cowrte & nippe it *dum seges in herba*; for being a letter onelye kepte cloase yt gyuethe no cause of accion because he hathe [p. 327] no dammages. & this beinge an offence that dothe prouoke reuenge, bringe daunger to the state & common weale, *et interest reipublicae*, & therefore an offence in this Cowrte to be seuerelye punished.

'Therefore the Lo. Coke beganne a sharpe sentence, & the greateste number agreed therevnto: the Defendaunte Doctor Wootton in regarde of his degree he woulde spare for corporall punishemente, but he fyned him 500$^{li.}$, & th'other three defendauntes 40$^{li.}$ a peece, & 200$^{li.}$ dammages to the pl., th'other three defendauntes to paye 10$^{li.}$ a peece & the Doctor the reste: he had learned that there were *duae partes medicinae, remouens et promouens*; so woulde he remoue his monie from him by his Fine, & he would promote him to, for this was *crimen lese dignitatis, et lese maiestatis; et dignitas personae auget culpam*; & Mercurye was now exalted in the howse of Scorpion. & this libeller hathe a faulte that no other sinne hathe (for naturallye all other sinnes desyre to hide themselues & to be concealed), but the libeller seekes to reueale himselfe wthout penitencie. Here's Craft by a letter & palleated mallice: & by 10 H[enry] 7, Bagnall's case,[1] Scott & others were hanged for lybellinge. This is a Common faulte, & it is vsuall: the publishinge of seditious bookes, wch is treason if any man doe receaue wth assente any suche bookes, or y^{t} dothe aduaunce the authoritie of Rome, or ye Rhomishe religion, it is a *premunire*. 11 Elizab. Dier.[2] *piccides continent venenum*, they be apotecaries' boxes full of poyson; & to be an apothecarye & then a phisition is no disparagemente, but a meane to proue the better phisition, as an [p. 328] Atturnie or a Clerke maye afterwards proue the better Judge: so was Catiline[3] & Browne[4] 2 attornies, & Dier[5] a

Coke gives sentence

[1] This case is referred to *post*, p. 372, where it is assigned to the year 5 Henry VII. I have not been able to find it.

[2] This was a resolution of the Judges made at Serjeants Inn, Fleet Street, 9 Feb., 11 Eliz., 1569. Dyer's *Reports*, 282 a.

[3] Robert Catlin; Judge of the Common Pleas, 1558; Chief Justice of the Queen's Bench, 1559; *ob.* 1574. See Foss, *Judges*, and *Dict. of Nat. Biog.* It is not elsewhere stated that Catlin had been an attorney.

[4] It is doubtful whether Anthony or Humphrey Browne is here referred to. The former was Chief Justice of the Common Pleas, 1558, but was afterwards reduced to a puisne Judge in the same Court. Humphrey Browne was appointed a Judge of the Common Pleas in 1558. It is not recorded that either of these Judges had been an attorney. See *Dict. of Nat. Biog.* and Foss, *Judges*.

[5] James Dyer, Judge of the Common Pleas, 1558; Chief Justice of the same Court, 1559; the compiler of the *Reports* so often cited in this MS. Foss does not mention that he had been a prothonotary's clerk. See also *Dict. of Nat. Biog.*

1607 Nov. 27

prenotarie's clerke. So maye a schoolemaister proue a good bishop, as one of the learnedste this daye in Englaunde ys Bilson, bishop of winchester.[1] It is a faulte in aunsweares, & it is noe good aduise, to aunsweare vpon oathe to any matter of forme or of lawfull or vnlawfull, & the Clyente ys endaungered in his oathe, for he oughte but to aunsweare matter of Facte.

Wootton to sit in a public place with the interrogatories round his neck

'And the Doctor at a publike markette at the nexte generall Assises at Exeter showld be sette in some eminente place, & were aboute his necke for a typpette the Fowre yardes of Interrogatoryes, & Confesse his Faulte, & then the Interrogatories to be retorned to the Cowrte, & to be defaced & Cancelled; the Doctor to be ymprysoned and bounde to his good behauyoure.

The Lord Chancellor on slanderers

'By the Lo. Chauncellor yt did appeare that there was an auntyente lawe that the sclaunderer showlde be lette bloude in the tounge, & he y[t] woulde heare lybelles showlde be lette bloude in the eares. He vouchte Pickeringe's Case,[2] vicar Bruerton's letter, & agreed in his sentence wth the Lo. Coke.' [3]

1607-8 Jan. 27

In Camera Stellata, coram Consilio ibidem, Mercurij, 27 Januarij, [1608].[4]

Maynarde v. Moone and others — Riot

Cause of hearing between 'Richarde Maynarde, plaintiff, and Thomas Moone, [5] Jarrette, & others, defend[tes], for ryot: the pl. hauinge a Coppis woodd adioyninge to a waste, & in wh[ch] Coppis woode the tenauntes vsed to haue Common, as they pretended, & the pl. vpon the fellinge thereof enclosinge the same wth postes & rayles, the sayde postes & rayles were plucked vp twice or thrice in the nighte time, & placed there agayne by the pl., & at the laste digged vp & burnte vp in the nighte time by the defend[tes],

[1] Thomas Bilson, Bishop of Worcester, 1596, and Winchester, 1597. He was appointed Warden of Winchester College in 1576; Anthony à Wood (*Athenae*) says that he is stated by some to have been a schoolmaster. See *Dict. of Nat. Biog*

[2] See *ante*, p. 222.

[3] This case is reported very briefly in Coke's *Reports*, xii. 35.

[4] Eight Councillors and Judges were present.

[5] Blank in MS.

& by them a Coaleharthe sett one fire in the nighte, of the plaintiff's.

'The Judges especiallye & all the reste of the Cowrte [p. 329] did muche lamente & Complaine of the waste & destruction of woods, & it is the Common error of Englaunde that, where by the statute diuerse steddles or standers are to be lefte vpon euerye acre, those are vsuallye Felled at 16 or 18 yeares growthe, whereas by the lawe they oughte to Contynewe untill they were tymber, a greate mischeife in the Common wealthe, and necessarye to be looked vnto in time; for this being an ylande, the strengthe thereof consystethe principallye in his woodden walles, & it is ympossible that Dwellinges & habitations showld Contynewe yf woods be not maynteyned: yt is allso as daungerous to geue waye to the popular sorte to take the sworde of Justice into there handes, they must not be there owne Judges; & especiallye the offence ys greate to execute busynesses in the nighte, albeit thinges lawfull, & theise small begynninges woulde be nypped in the budde, w^{ch}, yf they were well looked into by the Justices of the peace, in time they woulde be stayed, or else they will growe in litle time to the popular rebellyons of Northamptonshire; & the number of the Justices of the peace ys to greate, they trust so muche one to another that they doe nothinge, they lurke in the towne all the winter, & goe downe to take the pleasure of the Cuntrye & to receaue presentes of there Freindes & neighbours: For preseruation of woodds there was vouched 13 H[enry] 3 & 8 E[dward] 3, that where parsons woulde fell the woods of there Churche, vnles yt were for reparacyons of there Churches, prohibicyons did lye at the Common lawe.

Law as to timber

Too many Justices of the Peace

'The Defend^{ts} Wm Moone & Thomas Jarrette were Condemned in the pryuate opinions of dyuerse of the lordes: but Thomas Moone was fyned 50$^{li.}$, to stande vpon the pillorye in the nexte markette, imprisonm^{te}, & bounde to his good behauyoure.'

Sentence

1607-8 Jan. 27

LORD MORLEY v. COLTE and others

'The Lo. Morlye[1] in another Cause was plaintiff & Sr Henry Colte[2] & his brother & twooe men were Defendauntes: the case was thus, that the Lo. Morlye wth his twooe men, rydinge in Hatfeilde Chase partlye for his pleasure & partlye to look to his game of Deere there, mette wth the defend^te^ Sr Henry Colte, his brother, there 2 men & there syster, & a greyhounde wth them, they [p. 330] trauaylinge in the highe waye from there Father's howse in Suffolke to there Father's howse in Suffolke [*sic*][3]; & the Lo. Morlye demaundinge of Sr Henry Colte what he was, he, not then knowinge him to be the Lo. Morlye, made aunsweare for oughte he knewe he mighte be as good a man as he; & after many ill wordes of passyon and prouocation, the Lo. Morlye bidde him "god buye, goodman Colte," & Sr Henrye Colte in greate passyon replied, "god buye, goodman Morlye." But exceptyon was taken

Uncertainty in the Bill

to the bill for that the same was incerteinlye layd, sayinge in the Charge thereof "this instante September," & layinge no yeare, so it mighte be before the pardon; & albeit the defend^tes^ had by there aunsweares & examynacyons reduced it to a Certeintye, yet the Charge in the bill was

Bill dismissed

that the Cowrte must iudge of; & so for this Cause yt was dismyssed by the opinion of the Judges.'

HUETT'S case

'In a motyon made by Serg^te^ Phillips in Sr Wm Huett's case sentenced in the Ecclesiasticall Cowrte, & therefore

[1] Edward Parker, 12th Baron Morley, succeeded his father, Henry, 1577; he was one of the Judges at the trial of Mary, Queen of Scots, in 1586; he mar. Elizabeth, dau. and heir of William Stanley, 3rd Baron Monteagle, and in her own right Baroness Monteagle; she died *cir.* 1603, leaving a son, William, who succeeded to both Baronies. *Complete Peerage*, by G.E.C. See *ante*, p. 287, note 2.

[2] Sir Henry Colt, son of George Colt, of Colts Hall, Cavendish, co. Suffolk, and Clay Hall, near Barking, and Nether Hall, Roydon, co. Essex. His eld. son, George, was a zealous royalist and 'was almost cut to pieces at Worcester fight, and after that battle fled abroad with several of his children, and lived in Holland and Flanders; he was drowned at sea, 20 Jan. 1658, sailing for Ireland; an Earl's warrant is said to have been found on him when picked up.' Foster's *Baronetage*. Mary, dau. of John Colt, great-grandfather of Sir Henry, mar. Sir Thomas More. See Morant's *Essex*, ii. 491, etc.

Hatfield Chace would lie between Colts Hall and Nether Hall. A view of the ruins of the latter house is given in Wright's *Essex*, ii. 299. See Appendix XXII.

[3] A mistake for 'Essex.' See *ante*, note 2.

demurred heere, ruled by the Cowrte th at in a Demurrer the matter ys all Confessed, & albeit the Cause be examyned & finallye sentenced in the Ecclesiasticall Cowrte, yet this Courte shall deale wth the periurye.'

'**In the Checquer Chamber,** *Martis*, 31 *Maij*, 1608, there presente Sr Thomas Egerton, Lo. Chauncellor; Sr Rob. Cecill, Lo. Tresorer; Lo. Northampton, Lo. priuy seale; Lo. worster; Lo. Knowlles; & *auters* honorable auditors; Ch. Justice Flemminge; Ch. Justice Coke; Ch. Baron Tanfeilde; Justices *del banke*, Fenner, Yeluerton, Williams & Croke; Justices *del common banke*, wamslowe, warberton, Daniel & Forster; Barons *del exchecquer*, Snegge, Herne & Altham,' in the great cause of *postnati* in Scotland.[1] [p. 331] 1608 May 31

'In ye kinges benche an assyse was broughte by Robert Caluin againste Richard Smithe & Nicholas Smithe for a howse in Shordiche: the tenauntes pleade that the demaundaunte was in Nouembr. 3° *Jacobi* borne at Edenboroughe in Scotlaunde, *infra ligeanciam* of Scotlaunde & *extra ligeanciam* of Englaunde, & that time oute of minde they haue bene twooe auntiente, distincte & seuerall kingedomes, & therefore the tenauntes oughte to haue iudgemente againste the demaundaunte. CALVIN'S case

'And this Daye Justice walmslowe argued, & after some shorte preamble that the matter was waightye & of greate Consequence, yet he was sworne to doe Justice, & [if] he were his brother he must delyuer his opinion out of his iudgemente & vnderstandinge accordinge to his small knowledge. he was of opinion that iudgemente oughte to Judgment of Walmsley, J

[1] This case will be found reported at great length in Coke's *Reports*, vii. 1, *State Trials*, ii. 559, Moore's *Reports*, 790, etc. Coke does not record the presence of any of the lords mentioned in the text, except the Lord Chancellor. Hawarde's report of this case is in many parts little more than a collection of disconnected quotations and references, which it would be almost impossible to verify. And as there are several excellent reports of the case already in print (see above), I have cut down Hawarde's slightly. Justice Walmsley's judgment I have left nearly intact, as he was one of the two Judges who considered that the *Post-nati* were aliens, and moreover his speech does not appear to be reported elsewhere. See Appendix XXIII.

1608 May 31

be gyuen againste the Demaundaunte. & his difference was vpon the worde *ligeanciam*, vpon the pleadinge of *extra* & *infra*: albeit wee are all vnder one kinge, yet *ligeancia* ys not bounde to the naturall person, but Conteygned in a litle roome.

Bracton *de officiis* cited

'Bracton, in his booke *de officijs*, shewethe what *ligeancia* betwene the lorde & tenaunte ys. *Cum ante tam ex parte matris quam patris*: the solemnitie of doinge [p. 332] homage likewyse by the tenaunte to the Lorde. The statutes of Scotlaunde & the booke at th'ende of them *De verborum constructione* [1] dothe sette downe what *ligeancia* ys, from the kinge's leiges or from the leiges of the realme: & thereby the kinge and subiecte are bothe bounde: then he shewed that the Courte leete was before the Conqueste, in Edwarde the Confessor's time, called the liege Courte of Englaunde, where the oathe of allegeaunce ys gyuen to all: & they are Called "Deceners," or by tens, or "the ten man's Daye": & when W^m^ the Conqueror came in he did assemble 12 of euerye Countye, whoe did sette downe the Customes, & doe yet remaine in a booke of parchemente: wch was in deede *quedam maxima securitas*: Edwarde the Confessor before had deuysed it so: so is Bracton.

The Court Leet

The Statute for View of Frank pledge

'& 18 E[dward] 2, the statute dothe appointe that in a leete yt showlde be inquyred of the Capitall pledges & Dezeners, yf any at twelue years of age be wantinge, the towneship shalbe amerced: & whoe hathe receaued any of them the tenthe man ys to yealde an accounte: & by that oathe he is *infra legem* vnles he be after outlawed & so *extra legem positus*.

'The statute of 18 E[dward] 2 is false printed, for it oughte to be "all of twelue yeares of age" & not [" all the dozens "].[2]

'The statute of Marlbridge 12 H[enry] 3 dothe exempte

[1] *De Verborum significatione: The Exposition of the Termes and Difficill Wordes, ... Collected and exponed be M. John Skene, Clerke of our Soveraine Lordis Register, Councell and Rolles.* Edinburgh, 1597.

[2] Blank in MS. The reference is to the English edition of the Statutes printed by Henry Wykes in 1564. In the edition of 1556, the words are *toutes de douze ans*.

bishops & greate lordes from there apparaunce at the leete,[1] but before that statute by the Common lawe all oughte to appeare there, or else oughte to be distreyned for there resyauncye for an amercem^{te}. 2 H[enry] 4. by the common lawe euerye one wthin the leete oughte to make his oathe of ligeauncye, particularlye sette downe in Britton: *d'estre loial & foial*, viz.:—to obeye ye lawes[2]: but Scotlaunde comes not to o^{r} leete: & there ys no greater assurance then his oathe. in Scotlaunde the fealtie ys to the kinge himselfe. in the booke *De verborum significatione*[3] yt dothe appeare: the lawes of the kingedomes doe differ, & the kinge ys sworne to defende his subiectes by the lawes; That ys, his subiectes of Scotlaunde by the lawes [p. 333] of Scotlaunde, & his subiectes of Englaunde by the lawes of Englaunde.

'Fitsherbert, in his *Natura breuium*, in his wrytte *de Idiota*, dothe explane this.

'& so it dothe appeare in the iudgemente in *premunire*, he ys put out of the protection of the lawes of the kinge, that ys of the lawes of Englaunde. so that hereby yt may appeare the subiectes of the twooe kingedomes haue seuerall ligeaunce, seuerall lawes, & seuerall oathes: & this appeares in a pardon of K. James the thirde. The case ys that he is an alien borne at Edenboroughe *extra ligeanciam*. for euerye subiecte ys either *natus aut partus*; if he be borne, it is his birtherighte, & betwene Englaunde & Scotlaunde there was allwayes a partition walle, & thoughe it be in an open Feilde, a man saythe *quare clausum suum* &c. Juryes here in Englaunde can not enquyre of tresons, felonies or other offences committed in Scotlaunde & *sic econtra*.

'32 H[enry] 6. here can be no triall of one borne in Scotlaunde.[4] but I woulde doe as the good huswyfe dothe when she hathe made a good threede & woulde vtter the same, shee seemethe to drawe it oute to Cutte yt, but yet

[1] The Statute of Marlbridge is 52 Hen. III. Cap. x. is the part referred to.

[2] See Coke's *Reports*, vii. 6 b.

[3] See *ante*, p. 350, n. 1.

[4] *Year Book*, Hil. 32 Hen. VI. fol. 23.

1608 May 31 Cuttethe [not]; neither woulde I cutte threede in Englaunde or Scotlaunde.

'The kinge hath 2 persons, Scotland & England, politike and naturall, *separalia iura*, & can not be Confounded. *quod subintelligitur non deest*: otherwyse yt it is when the kingedome dothe discende vpon a subiecte, as in the case of the Duke of lancaster: & Scotland ys an auncyente kingedome, there haue bene 108 kinges: & the kinge by his greate seale of Englaunde or his letters pattentes Can geue nothinge in Scotlaunde: neither by Consente in parliamente, for they are twooe bodyes & as twooe Corporatyons: There are 2 abbottes, & lande ys gyuen to them twooe, they haue seuerall rightes & are tenauntes in Common: so one kingedome dothe not drowne [p. 334] an other. Abbot & parson haue deuyded rightes; 14 E[dward] 3,[1] & so the kinge of Englaunde & Fraunce. 22 H[enry] 6, one borne in scotlaunde is an alien.'[2]

25 E[dward] 3, 21 E[dward] 3[3]; *infra ligeanciam* of England and of the King of England is all one: 'one heade to haue twooe bodyes were monstrous: & to confounde the kingedomes. the grande Jurye ys Called the bodye of ye Countye.

'To come ouer the wale to plucke an apple ys holden no greate offence, but to take orcharde, apples, appletrees & all, were not tollerable: yf this Demaundaunte beginne to purchase at twooe yeares of age, what he will doe by that time he shall be 70 yeares olde; and I knowe not whether all his nation be of that minde, so it will be sans number: the kinge maye make as many denizens as he pleasethe, but a kingedome is but as a great family into wch no more are to be receaued then the M^r^ will & knoweth of: yf a waye into a hauen be stopped by tempeste, another

[1] This refers apparently to 14 Edw. III., Stat. 5: 'The Realm and People of England shall not be subject to the King or Kingdom of France.'

[2] ? a mistake for 32 Hen. VI.; see above.

[3] 25 Edw. III., Stat. 2. This was the Act for declaring the rights of children born out of the realm of parents in 'the faith and ligeance of the King of England.' The Statute referred especially to the King's children. The second reference should be 42 Edw. III. fol. 2, according to Coke's *Reports*, vii. 12. See *Year Books*, Hil. 42 Edw. III., no. 9.

Can not be made before a write *de Ad quod damnum* be broughte. Solomon saythe that the multitude of people ys the kinge's honor, that ys yf he Feede & breede them, otherwyse not. so shall there be *post nati in saecula saeculorum*, wch were no good manners in them.

'The statute of 25 E[dward] 3 [1] did naturalize the kinge's Children that were borne in Gascoigne out of the Realme, & but three of them. King's children

'The kinge ys Called *pater patriae*, & he will haue Care that all his subiectes maye lyue, & allthoughe he may denizen all, yet it is hoped he will doe no more then reason will moue. yt hathe allwayes bene the pollicie of Englaunde to keepe straungers out, as the pope & his beneficed men, & so to vse straungers as not to hurte his owne Children.

'The kinge maye saye *hoc possumus facere quod per legem possumus facere*; & the kinge Can not graunte that an alien maye sue an englisheman. [p. 335]

'The kinge ys bounde by his oathe at his coronacion to obserue the lawes, & specially the lawes of Edwarde the Confessor: & all innouations are daungerous, & in all good gouernementes much Condemned. The King's coronation oath

'When H[enry] the 7th Came to the Crowne the outlawes that were wth him receaued no Comforte, the subiectes helde there liberties: & one greate libertie ys that an englisheman shall not be impleaded by an alien, & that [liberty] the subiecte Can not lose: *sua sorte sit quisque contentus*: Englaunde's lotte ys fallen into a faire grounde, let him be Contente therewth.

'For the Case of Normandie, it became parcell of the kingedome, being gained by Conqueste, as Irelande is. 19 E[dward] 4.[2] Normandy and Ireland

'But to saye that ligeaunce followes the kinge is absurde & improper. I am to Come when the kinge sendes for mee: no more then Corne followes him that buyes it, or the Deere him to whome yt is gyuen: & so an alien to the

[1] See *ante*, p. 352, n. 3.

[2] Apparently a mistake for 17 Edw. II. cap. 12, a statute declaring the King's rights in Normandy.

1608 May 31

kinge is a straunge speeche; there maye be a villein to the kinge. 7 E[dward] 4.

'And so he Concluded: he sayde he Coulde not be longe, he had an oulde memorie,[1] & yf he showlde looke muche vpon his paper he showlde be oute; he coulde tell them no newes, but some olde thinges wch he had rede; & so ended that Judgemente was to be entred for the tenaunts againste the Demaundaunte: he argued Confydentelye and boldlye; he was well lyked and muche Commended; & so agreed wth Justice Forster.[2]

Judgment for defendants

[p. 336]

Tanfield, Chief Baron

'The same Daye the Lo. Cheife Baron, Sr Lawrence Tanfeilde, argued allso; & firste he put the Case as before: & then he proued yt a vsuall thinge to referre Causes of greate waighte or difficultie to this place, & that yt hathe bene called *Camera Consilij*. the statute of 31 E[dward] 3 [cap. 12] dothe enable yt to reuerse iudgementes, & 13 H[enry] 4 for Causes retorned hither out of ye Chauncerye.

'He was of opinion that the *post nati* were no aliens, & for the plea, he woulde Confesse & auoyde it.

'And for *ligeancia*, yt is neither to the Crowne, nor to the lawe, nor to the kingedome, but to the person of the kinge; and the particion walle is not broken as to the lawes: the generall allegeaunce ys to the person of the kinge & to all the powers of his person, & it is the power and workinge of god.'

The King's person cannot be divided, as if he had a natural and a political body.

'Euerye man had his allegeaunce by his byrthe, & after[-wards] yt is Confyrmed in a leete.

'*Cor regis in manu domini*, & the kinge's person is an adamaunte that drawethe allegeaunce vnto yt. & to deuyde the allegeaunce from the kinge's person to the Crowne, kingedome or lawes, was Spencer's opinion, a case censured & Condemned in parliamente, & it is an opinion that dothe hatche and protecte treason.[3]

Spencer's case

[1] He was born about 1537.

[2] They were the only two Judges who held that the *post-nati* were aliens.

[3] This refers to the trial of Hugh le Despencer, father and son, in 1320. See Coke's *Reports*, vii. 11.

'An alien ys he that ys borne oute of the kinge's allegeaunce, & there ys an alyen enemye or an alyen Freinde. *mes parliamentum omnia potest.* & there are 4 markes: 1. *extra ligeantiam et potestatem*; 2. *poier del roy*; 3. *in fide alterius regis*; 4. an enemye to the kinge: & yt is a rule that whome the kinge can not disable, the subiecte Can not disable: & from whome the kinge Can not take lande, the subiecte Can not take lande. [p. 337] An alien, what

'& the lawe dothe operate nothinge idle, yf it gyue the thinge, yt gyues the meane allso. & so in this Case he Concluded that iudgemente oughte to be gyuen for the Demaundaunte, but his argumente was farre shorte of expectatyon: Walmseloe & he argued bothe in a daye, but the satterdaye followinge, beinge 4 *die Junij*, the Lo. Coke had a whole daye by himselfe.' Judgment for the plaintiff

'Sabbati, 4 Die Junij, 1608.' 1608 June 4

'Lo. Coke, Cheife Justice *del common banke*. Fyrste he Cyted Columella that there are 4 nounes, *nomina operatiua*, leaders to the vnderstandinge of the Case: 1. is *alienigena*, firste in place, laste in operation of the allegeaunce; 2. *regnum*; 3. *leges*; 4. *iura*.[1] theise doe shewe more lyfe & dexteritye, & oute of these he woulde drawe 7 seuerall & materyall argumentes, but woulde be shorte & perspicuous: 1. *extra natus est alien, mes Caluin est extra natus, Ideo est alien.* 2. *natus infra scotiam est alien al corone d'angliterre.* 3. *duo iura, duo regna, equum est si in diuersis personis, cum concurrunt in vna persona.* Coke, C. J. C. P.

'4th. where th'allegeaunce ys due to ye person hauing twooe distincte Capacityes. but Caluin ys borne vnder the allegeaunce of Scotlaunde. *Ideo* he is an alien. [p. 338]

'5. where the kinge hathe twooe seuerall kingedomes, by twooe seuerall tytles & discentes, there Can be no vnyon of allegeaunce.

'6. where there are twooe seuerall lawes, any one borne

[1] Coke's Report gives *Ligeantia*, *Regnum*, *Leges* and *Alienigena*.

1608 June 4 out of th'extentes & reache of the lawe of Englaunde is an alien.

'7. he that at the time & place of his byrthe ys not partaker nor inherytable to the lawes of Englaunde, can not haue the benefytte of the lawes: & hee that ys borne out of the iurisdictyon of the lawes of Englaunde, Can not be tryed by the lawes of Englaunde.[1]

'For the etimologie of the worde allegeaunce (*aut ligeancia ex vi termini*) *hoc est aliene gentis.* this is *paruum in magno, et magnum in paruo*; litle in sillables, but greate in substaunce; the greateste Case that euer was in westminster halle: & protested he woulde delyuer his Conscyence & oute of his harte, & woulde followe the Counsell of him that Coulde beste gyue yt. 8 Job. *hesterni sumus et ignoramus.*

'*neminem oportet esse sapientiorem lege*: he woulde not be bedazeled wth any popularitie, frighted wth no terror; & protested that no one of them all did knowe before they argued what was another's opinion, nor neuer had message in one kinde or other; tenne had allreadye argued one waye & 2 th'other: & Companye is a greate Comforte to a man in his iournye, but he woulde not go wth the greater number for Companye, but that they had Chalked oute the righte waye before him.

'He was of opinion that Caluin was no alyen.

[p. 339] 'obedyence & subiectyon are bretheren by byrthe & make a naturall subiecte: & this is better explaned & Confyrmed in the leete. & there ys a recyprocall bonde betwene ye kinge & the subiecte: *ligeancia mutua debet esse connexio membrorum: et regis est regere et protegere.*

'*ligeancia* ys fourefolde, 1. naturall, 2. *facta et acquisita*, 3. *legalis*, 4. *localis.*

'Denisation ys eyther by pattente, parliamente or conqueste.

[p. 340] 'a man ys made *legalis* by the leete, & it is indefinite to all.

[1] These were the arguments advanced on behalf of the defendants. See Coke's *Reports*, *loc. cit.*

'& this opinion of seueringe the allegeaunce from the kinge's person can haue no defence from Spencer's treason.

'A more happie Coniunction of the twooe lyons then there was of the twooe roses; for it seemes the heauens reioyce & Conspyre in this vnion, for at this time the sunne ys in *gemini*, twooe twyns; & as Paul's signe was Castor & Pollux, so now the Constellation is in *Corona*, & goes out w^th^in 7 dayes. The two lions and the two roses

¶ 'this he delyuered in his Conclusion of all his argumente, but spake much more; & so this was wrytten out of his proper place by mistakinge my noates in seuerall wryting tables.¶

'& so was of opinion that obedyence was not locall nor Confyned to any place, but the oathe in the leete ys vniuersall, & so spacyous ys his oathe of allegeaunce as is the kinge's gouernemente. Obedience not local

'we that are Judges are men of state, but not states men, neyther must we argue so: theise are qualities of the soule not prescrybed to any place.

'I finde a straunger in the case, but not an alyen. [p. 341]

'11 H[enry] 4; Irelande; for allegeaunce dothe extende as farre as the kinge hathe any territoryes.[1] *nullis claustris coercetur: nullis metis refrenatur: nullis finibus restringitur.* Ireland

'there is a questyon *Cui?* A secrete euill to restraine allegeaunce to the kingedome, to the person, or to the politike capacitie. for the kinge hathe 2 distincte Capacities: his naturall person ys accompanyed wth his politike Capacitie. & there are 3 Causes of policye, *maiestatis, vtilitatis et necessitatis.*

'H[enry] 7th was attainted of treason, purged by being kinge. the kinge was heire to the Earle of Marche, beinge but of the halfe bloode, & yet did inheryte.

'The prince purchasethe & afterwardes ys made kinge, he shalbe now seised *in iure corone*, as in his politike Capacitye: & he hathe a soule, wch man can not Create.

'*probationes debent esse per notiora.*'

The law of England consists of the laws of 1. nature, [p. 342]

[1] *Year Books*, Mich. 11 Hen. IV. no. 17.

1608 June 4 the gift of God, which cannot be changed, 2. customs, 3. statutes.

Nature writes the law of government in the heart [1] of man for his preservation, by government and in obedience.

'wheresoeuer the kinge hathe gouernement there allegeaunce ys ioyned to it.

[p. 343] Gascony

'a man borne in Gascoigne was a naturall subiecte to the kinge of Englaunde.'

1 Henry IV. fo. 1. A man banished out of England *religatus fuit Gascogniae*, when it was exile, an 'alienatinge from his Cuntrye, lawes, & preseruation, & a change of the soyle.' [2]

10 Edward III. fo. 41. A man in England exchanged land with a Gascon.[3]

'theise thinges are adiudged good in a petition, viz., that a man borne in Gascoigne shall inheryte in Englaunde.

'Stamforde hathe the Cases, & saythe that it "appears" and not that it "seems" [*appeare nemy que semble*],[4] & that those borne in Gascoigne shall inheryte in Englaunde.

Normandy

'Normandye was had by discente, not by Conqueste.'

17 Edward II. lands in England descend to Normans.[5]

'Gernsye was parte of Normandye.

Isle of Man

'The Ile of man was an absolute kingedome, & Came not into Englaunde w^th^out leaue, the little Kinge of Man.' [6]

Calais

Calis and Guies [Guînes] in Fraunce; men born there [were] natural subjects to the King of England.[7]

Berwick [p. 344]

27 Edward III., *secundum legem regni Scotiae.* in Barwike & Rosse in Scotlaunde.[8]

42 Edward III. a man born there, natural.[9]

Ireland

Ireland is not part of England: treason there tried in the King's Bench. Oruck's case. and so Sir John Parrette

[1] '*In ceux de home*'; the letter *r* is written above the *x* of '*ceux.*'

[2] *Year Books*, Mich. 1 Hen. IV. no. 2.

[3] *Year Books*, Trin. 10 Edw. III. no. 44.

[4] Sir William Staundford, Stanford or Stamford, *Les Plees del Corone*, 1583; *ut patet* are the actual words he uses, fo. 59 c, ed. 1607.

[5] 17 Edw. II. Stat. I. cap. 12.

[6] 'The little, but yet ancient and absolute kingdom of the Isle of Man.' Coke, vii. 21.

[7] Calais, see Coke, vii. 22; Guînes, *ibid.*

[8] 11 Edw. III. Coke; *Ex Rotulis Scotiae anno* 11 Ed. III.

[9] See Coke, vii. 23 b.

was tried there.[1] Diar, 20 Elizabeth, and still are distinct kingdoms.[2]

Attribuat lex regi quod rex attribuat regi [*sic*]. A Conqueror may change the law where he had it by conquest and the inhabitants are 'infydelles,' but otherwise where they are Christians.

Errors in Ireland are corrected by the parliament in England.

14 Henry III., *leges figendae et refigende perniciosa.* A noble man and his wife [are] carried in time of conquest to France and have issue there, [the issue] is liege and natural. 'There is no alien in the Case, but this kinde of pleadinge is a stranger neuer seen before. *alienigena* (*per* Litleton) *est qui natus est extra ligeanciam in tali patria que nemy in legeaunce del roye.* [p. 345]

alienigena est duplex { *amicus aut inimicus* { *perpetuus.* *infidelis.* / *temporalis.* / *permissus.*

'He maye haue tresure & goods.

'*Subditus est datus, aut natus.*'

It is the destruction of the realm for an alien to purchase [land] and by this means build castles, if strangers 'showlde purchace in peace.' and also they are not returned on Juries.

It is a rule that no one can be an alien by birth who cannot be an enemy by accident.

Magna Charta, 3°.

19 Edward IV. fol. 7.

ante nati may be enemies by accident.

Where there cannot be war, there cannot be an alien.

19 Edward IV., if the king does not make war, it is a tumult.

Where the protection of the subjects by the king is equal, in general the obedience is equal.

One born in natural allegiance is no alien.

'What is due by Constitutyon of a man may not be altered, *mes* naturall obedyence ys due by Constitutyon,

[1] See Appendix XIX. [2] Dyer's *Reports*, Mich. 19 & 20 Eliz., 360 b.

1603 June 4 therefore yt can not be altered or taken awaye: yf the parliamente doe enacte that the kinge shall not be obayde, it is voyde.

[p. 346] 'He that at the time of his birthe can not be an alien to the kinge of Englaunde, can not be an alien to the subiecte of Englaunde.'

[If] an alien purchase land held of a subject, the king shall have it, and yet the subject shall plead this for the king's benefit.

An alien may be made liege by the king.

If the king make war, the liege subject is bound to assist him.

'yt is obiected it will cause confusyon. To that he aunswearethe that there wilbe a vnyon in 4 thinges: 1. person, 2. allegeaunce, 3. protection, 4. alliaunce.

'A separation in 4 thinges: 1. kingedomes, 2. lawes, 3 parliamentes, 4. nobilitie.

'a kinge is a kinge, & a poore knighte is a knighte, in all the worlde; so are no other degrees.

'20 E[dward] 4. *vt valeat status iunxerat ante rosas. consociasse rosas. Cor vnum et via vna.*

'yf the allegeaunce showlde be locall many inconvenyences woulde ensue: for yf there showlde be stirre in Scotlaunde, what woulde ensue yf those in Englaunde were not bound to assyste: *utlage: premunire. hors de lour witte* if they be out of there allegeaunce. & therefore this Can haue no defence out of Spencer's treason; but he thankte god none of his bretheren were of that opinion: & no one Judge had Conference wth another, nor receaued any message: at this daye there is a Concurrence of iudgementes: but H[enry ?] 2 rose wth a syde winde: & at this daye no opinion of any learned man to the Contrarye: &

[p. 347] at this the heauens reioyce. "for at this time the signe is in *Gemini*, that are twins, & the Constellation ys *de Corona* & goes out w^th^in seauen dayes: & as Paul askinge it was in Castur & Pollux, so I doubte not but yt will proue a happie Coniunction: & I will not giue litle Caluin so muche as the apple, excepte he Can gette monie to purchase it, then in the name of god let him haue bothe apple & tree & orcharde & all; for I haue founde by some experyence that monie & tresure [are] as the synewe of purchacinge. & thoughe he be but litle, the flye ys as perfecte a creature as the eagle or the Elephaunte."

'& so ended his argumente wth greate admyration of the better & wyser sorte, infinite commendacyon of all, & good satisfactyon of very manye; he Contynued to the ende with strong voyce, excellente memorye, rare delyuerye, & with small or no perturbacyon or alteracyon.'

'Tusedaye Followinge. Martis 7 Junij, 1608, Sr Thomas Flemminge, the Lo. Chiefe Justice of Englaunde, & Sr Thomas Egerton, Baron Ellesmere, Lo. Chauncellor of Englaunde, argued bothe in one daye.' 1608 June 7

'The Lo. Cheife Justice first put the Case accordinge to Course. Fleming, C. J.

'yf they abyde in Scotlaunde yt dothe not Concerne them, otherwyse yf they Come into Englande. [All persons] borne out of the realme shalbe naturalls yf they be not borne vnder another kinge: agreede by all that he is no alien that ys not borne out of the king's seignioryes, as Ireland, Normandie, Man, Gascoigne, Guyan.'

Colt's case adjudged in the Exchequer [2 James I.]; the wife was delivered in Flanders, when she had left Calais where her father and mother were born; and he was adjudged natural, and by the office his lands were given unto him.[1] [p. 348]

'The onelye rule to make a naturall is to be borne wthin the kinge's allegeaunce. *est vltimus terminus. extra et infra*' extended to Ireland as well as to Scotland.

'The deriuatyon of *ligeancia* is from *liga*, a bonde, *obligatus et ligeus*, allegiaunce. *fedus, confederatio inter principes*.

'This is a Conuentiall bonde, & not naturall. th'other ys begonne by byrthe & ended by deathe. as betwene the

[1] See Dyer's *Reports*, fo. 224 b, note.

1608 June 7 father & ye sonne. this oathe ys onelye to the kinge & to no other naturall leige lorde: o^r naturall leige people, & they are subiectes onelye that haue taken this oathe. & this oathe ys recyprocall as well on the kinge's as on the subiecte's behalfe. & this allegeaunce begyns wth euerye man's byrthe, & ys by the lawe of nature: & the oathe at the leete dothe Confyrme it & remembrethe him of his dutye, & ys to instructe them in the lawes & of there dutye to the kinge & the subiectes.

'An alien may be sworne in a leete, & yet this makes him no denizen, 4 H[enry] 4.

'None can take an aduauntage of an alyen where the kinge Can not take aduauntage: the bonde of allegeaunce is not a bonde of seruitude but of Freedome: *come liber homo.*'

An alien shall not have a real action against the subject; but if a subject sell lands or goods to an alien, the king shall have them and the subject shall never have any advantage of it.

An alien may depart the realm when he wishes; therefore this is one reason why he cannot purchase. But the King may command him to stay for the defence of the realm under pain of his protection.

[p. 349] Allegiance cannot be bound to the kingdom: 'they are twooe kingedomes *non quoad intellectum, sed quoad oculum.* They will make fearefull conclusyons yf they laye th'allegeaunce vpon the kingedome, vpon the crowne, or vpon the lawes, this is to make to muche of this Conceite: as yf the scottes conspire in Scotlaunde or adhere to an inuasyon.

'*Duo iura in vna persona ac si vn person.*

'Queene Elizabethe dothe yet lyue in the person of the kinge, & the kinge hathe no more then the Queene lefte him, & in her time this had bene a good plea. this ys entended of her bodye politique, for her naturall bodye ys deade. he is a subiecte borne in respecte of the lawe of god, & not of the municipall lawes of this kingedome of Englaunde. *leges sunt mutae et mortuae, rex est autor* [*sic*] *et vita legis.* Bracton. he is aboue the lawes, but not to abrogate them, w[ch] he Can not doe. his absolute power hathe no lawe to dyrecte him: he is absolute in warre & peace, & maye Commaunde the subiecte to goe whither he pleasethe; & so Concluded that iudgmente oughte to be entred for the plaintife or demaundaunte in the Assise.

Judgment for plaintiff

The Lord Chancellor

'The Lorde Chauncellor [1] argued the same daye. And began to excuse himselfe that he had longe sythence bene Called from theise legall exercyses, & so bereaued of all meanes to argue this case after so many learned & graue Judges: but beinge adiourned out of Chaunceryе vpon a demurrer there into this Cowrte, not for any difficultye that he Conceaued in the Case, but for the weightynes of the Cause, for a person excommunicate or an alien is disabled to sue *en* chauncerye.

[p. 350]

'There was one did petition againste the Lo. Keper Bacon [2] for that he had made a decree againste the lawe: he made aunsweare that he had done accordinge to equitye, & that yt was out of there learninge, he had done his Conscience, & the Chauncellor was not to make accounte to anye but to the kinge's Ma[tie] himselfe.

'He sayde he Coulde tell them no newes, nor prophecye of so weightye thinges, neither vse exordium or preface, but order woulde he showlde put y[e] Case, w[ch], for y[e] gayninge of time, he spared.

'The generall Case is *magnum in magno*, & the partycular case is *paruum in paruo*: by the passages & proceedinges in the generall & partycular case, he was of opinion he was no alien, thoughe he were borne in Scotlaunde.

Commissioners to treat of the Union, 1603

'He spake much of 1° *Jacob.*, for the Commissioners that showlde treate of the vnion: [3] there ys one royall person, therefore there can not be twooe allegeaunces. 20

[1] The Lord Chancellor's speech was printed for the 'Societie of Stationers,' 1609; pp. 118.

[2] Sir Nicholas Bacon, Lord Keeper 1558 to 1579.

[3] The Commissioners consisted of 2 Privy Councillors, 2 Ambassadors, 4 common lawyers, 2 civilians, 4 merchants and 16 country gentlemen. The list is printed in the *Journal of the House of Commons*, May 12, 1604. See Moore's *Reports*, 790.

1608 June 7 Octobr. 2 *Jacob.* a proclamatyon for greate britaine.[1] & the same daye the Commissioners mette, & then non did openlye gainsaye it, the Judges did delyuer there opinions in the vpper howse, & after conference betwene bothe howses, the Judges Confyrmed there former opinyons in bothe howses: one of the lower howse did then saye that a proclamacyon was not binding;[2] but he [the Lord Chancellor] did admonyshe them by waye of Cautyon not to contemne or set lightlye by proclamacions.

'Judges are sworne, & speake vpon there oathe in parlyamente, & so it is consented, & this is the higheste Cowrte of all others, & the Judges are Called thyther by wrytte vpon there oathe; & for Assises, *nisi prius, oier & termyner,* beinge once sworne yt suffycethe: & there estimacyon is suche that they haue no cause to feare, flatter or fauoure.

[p. 351] 'Of all the 12 apostles onelye Thomas doubted the resurrectyon of o^{r} Sauyoure, wch was a Cause that the same was better Confyrmed to the whole Churche. so they haue bene Thomases onelye that haue doubted in this Case, & there Doubtinges haue bene the greateste Causes of the reasons of this iudgemente in this place.[3]

'I will not vse any sillogisticall argumente; the case is rare & difficulte & neuer before adiudged; noe transcendente case, but to be adiudged by the Common lawe, that rulethe & ouerrulethe it.

'The Common lawe is *ius scriptum et non scriptum*: & this I fyrste learned of him whose name will be euer blessed & the memorye thereof happye, The Lo. Tresorer Burleighe,[4] that at the firste yt was not wrytten, but [was] reduced into wrytinge: but this is an age of questyons,

[1] 'A Proclamation concerning the King's Maiesties Stile, of King of Great Britaine, France and Ireland.' *Proclamation Book*, 82.

[2] 'It was discreetely and modestly saied by a learned Gentleman of the lower House.' Ellesmere, *loc. cit.*

[3] Here the printed speech goes on: 'The two woorthy and learned Judges that haue doubted in this Case, as they beare his Name, so I doubt not but their doubting hath giuen occasion to cleare the doubt in others,' p. 29. The two Judges were *Thomas* Walmsley and *Thomas* Foster.

[4] Ellesmere's *Post-nati*, 33.

all is in *Quomodo et Quare*: & therefore some haue not spared to saye that the lawe ys weake & incerteine: & so they obiecte againe, yf it be not wrytten how Can it be knowne.

'1. Firste, the common lawe ys the Common & generall Custome of the whole realme. [p. 352] Common law, what

'2. it dothe consyste of Certeyne auntyente princyples & Customes: as, there is no tenaunte in dower nor tenaunte by the Curtesye of the Crowne of Englaunde.

'*vbi non est directa lex, standum est arbitrio Judicis.* yet the Ciuill lawes are too generall, but he reuerencethe the professors. but spaine & Fraunce doe not receave the Ciuill lawe, but for a dyrectyon, not to be governed by it; neyther dothe Rome, to be bounde by it.

'There is 3 kindes of presumption:—*presumptio*, 1. *temeraria*, 2. *probabilis*, 3. *violenta*.' Presumptions

There are four kinds of interpretations of laws:—1. *historica*, 2. *etimologica*, 3. *analogica*, 4. *practica*.

'*Historica* ys darke & daungerouse.

'The kinge dyscended from bothe monarches of theise 2 kingedomes, Fergus[1] & Enas.[2]'

Ligeancia, ligum or *liga*, an Italian word, signifies *totalem subiectionem*.

'Analogicall. [p. 353]

'Irelande & Fraunce by discente, & so turne the Case, & it will be cleare allso. Ireland and France

'Normandye & Aquytaine were absolute princes & had auncyente soveraigne power: one kinge hathe had one seale, & another kinge hathe had another seale. Maude the Empresse had no seale. the kinge of Englaunde by his seale of Englande maye Commaunde all his subiectes in any parte of the worlde. Normandy and Acquitaine

[1] Fergus, son of Ferchard, the first King of Scotland according to the fictitious chronology of Boece and Buchanan; said to have come to Scotland from Ireland about 330 B.C. See *Dict. of Nat. Biog.*

[2] The marginal note in the *Post-nati*, p. 59, says 'Inas.' Perhaps Ina, King of the West Saxons, who died 726. See *Dict. of Nat. Biog.*, *s.v.* Ine. Can it possibly refer to Æneas, who is said by Geoffrey of Monmouth to have been the grandfather of Brutus, the first King of Britain?

1608 June 7 Cheshire

'Chester was a Countye palatine before the Conqueste & had a speciall seale. 33 E[dward] 2.'

The 'Irishe & the Aquitaines' are the subjects of the king, and yet not sworn in England.

'reason & knowledge ys infinite: yet no man can borowe his neighbor's braine.

'Ottelius,[1] *de vera Juris prudentia.* Interpreters of the lawe oughte to be *etate graues, eruditione docti, vsu rerum prudentes, autoritate induti. vitium est si rationem non inuenias.* yet there remayne seuerall crownes, severall *leyes* [laws] & seuerall legeaunces.

[p. 354] '*veritas docendo suadet et non coercet. rex solus iudicat vbi ius non iudicat.* 1 *Cod. fo.* 13. & so Concluded that *magna est veritas & preualet,* & god is the author of all truthe: and so decreede for the pl. that Judgemente showlde be entred for him.

Judgment for the plaintiff

'He argued very profoundelye & was exceedinge longe, but reade muche in his booke, & had taken infinite paines, for he had wrote a greate volume, & was allmoste 4 howres in his argumente. So this was the ende of this greate Cause, the greateste Cause, I[2] thinke, that euer was adiudged in this Cowrte; & euerye Daye there was an honorable presence of many of the priuye Counselle & other noble lordes, knightes, & gentlemen, but especiallye as this Daye, & I thinke for the most parte they were all well satisfyed: god graunte it proue a blessed vnion for the kinge & all his posteritie, & for all his kingedomes & people. Amen. Amen. Amen.'

[p. 355] 1608 June 16

In Camera Stellata, coram Consilio ibidem, Jouis, 16 Junij, 1608, le prochein iour puis trinitie terme, adonque presente Lo. Chauncellor, baron de Ellesmere, Lo. Northampton, adonque Lo. priuie seale, euesque de Londres, et touts les Judges d'angliterre.

WALTHAM FOREST

'There was a Cause of hearinge appointed this daye for the huntinge in waltham Forreste, pretendinge it to be

[1] Ellesmere's *Post-nati*, p. 85, says 'Hopperus'; Joachimus Hopperus, *De Juris Arte*; 1555.
[2] Hawarde.

purleiwe,[1] formerlye hearde in parte in this terme, but adiourned to this daye for wante of a recorde wch the defend^tes^ stoode muche then vpon, but coulde not then shewe. & now they Confessed that they were mystaken in that recorde, & did now therefore confesse that the vsage had misledde them, & that the same was part of the Forreste, & therefore in all humblenes submytted themselues to his Matie for there offences paste & for there vsage of the same as parte of the Forreste or purleiwe; & so ordered *ex confesso*, & referred to the nexte terme.' Purlieu Adjourned

'After the kinge's Councell had moued, the Lo. Chauncellor delyuered a Charge from the kinge's owne mouthe to the Judges & Justices of peace that speciall Care showlde be had for the due executyon of the kinge's proclamacion,[2] the printed articles & the Lorde's letters for Corne busynes;[3] "for we force the dearthe o^r^ selues w^th^out cause; that ye kinge hathe speciall care to preuente all causes whatsoeuer, hathe requyred ye Lo. Maior of London to make prouisions from forren partes, hathe restrayned all transportatyon, & hathe forgyuen all Custome of importation: that Corne Maisters, ingrossers & forstallers of graine, be looked vnto, that ye poore be prouyded for w^th^in there paryshes, for now more wanderers then ever were; & it is Justices' of peace faulte, The Chancellor's Charge to the Judges and Justices of the Peace

[1] The purlieu of a forest is the land near to it, added thereto by Henry II., Richard I. and John, and afterwards disaforested by the *Charta de Foresta*. Jacob's *Law Dict.*

An owner of lands in the purlieu had certain rights of hunting there. He must have free land within the purlieu to the yearly value of 40*s.*; he might hunt with dogs, but was not allowed to use guns, bows and arrows, or other weapons of the chase; he must not 'forestall' the deer (that is, get between it and the Forest); he might hunt only with his own servants, and only three times a week; he might not hunt on Sundays, nor at night, nor within the fence-month, nor within 40 days before or after the King's hunting there. See W. R. Fisher, *The Forest of Essex*, 166.

[2] 'A Proclamation for the preuenting and remedying of the dearth of Graine, and other Victuals;' 2 June, 1608. *Booke of Proclamations*, 174.

[3] 1608, Sept. 25.—Earl of Southampton to Earl of Salisbury. 'The skarsity of corne is so greate in this contry that mayny are driuen to supply themselues wth seede for this sowing time out of other partes, it beeinge not heere to be had. . . . There hath been payed att Hampton w^th^in these six weekes last past out of the contry the summe of 14 thousand pound in redy mony vnto strangers for corne brought thether by them, as I am enformed from the Mayor.'

State Papers, Domestic, James I. vol. 36, no. 34.

1608 June 16 whoe showlde Correcte Constables for not executing there offices, & gyue them Charge to be more Carefull; neuer more Justices & lesse done; he puts in few into Commission but vpon Commendacyon from the lordes or Judges, whoe [p. 356] showlde Certifye vpon knowledge, & not informacyon; for in all partes the numbers are so increased that those that are the doers & beare the burden of the busynes can haue no place at the benche, nor hardelye gette into the Cowrte but as they are Called, for the number of newe & younge knightes, that Come in there braueryes & stande there lyke an Idoll to be gazed vpon, & doe nothinge, ys so greate & pressinge for place, Countenaunce & estimacyon: but they must knowe they are not Justices for there Countenaunce onelye; let them remember there oathes & dutyes, that they are for the Justice, peace & gouernemente of the Cuntrye, & not to be quarter Justices, as many of them are, that lye aboute this towne 3 partes of the yeare, & goe downe onelye for there pleasure in hawkinge & huntinge; but the Lo. Maior of london must now make accounte what they are that lurke aboute the towne, & the Judges retorne to his Matie the names of them that abyde not in there Cuntrye dwellinges & keepe hospitalitye, wch now his Matie by his proclamacyon[1] inioynethe them all to doe, & that the sommes Collected for the poore be ymployed accordingelye: & what they are that attende there quarter Cessions, to veiwe the Clerke of the peace's booke for it, whoe retorne recognizaunces, whoe are Contentyous; that the good maye be Comforted & aduaunced, & the badde remoued & punyshed.

'" The Judges, the visitors for tooe times in the yeare, not for Justice alone, but for the peaceable gouernem^{te} of the Cuntrye, put in greate truste by his Matie, & to make an accounte to him wch he will expecte from them, that they, the J. of peace, sheriffes, & all other officers, looke diligentlye to preuente in the begynninge all assemblyes in riotous manner, as this laste yeare the Leuellers in Northampton & other shires, that Coste many lyues, & some were executed, & when they are in Companyes they proue

[1] See *ante*, p. 367, n. 2.

Rebellions; w^th^stande there begynninges, or else yt wilbe yor faultes: for yor disorders in alehowses, looke now Carefullye to them, & let them be seauearelye [severely] punyshed; & there, as well as in yor owne howses, keepe order for dayes forbydden, wch is a greate Cause of muche waste & greate expence.

' "& let vs now vse the good Creatures of god soberlye, for I Can not saye what ys the Cause of this dearthe, whether the vnseasonablenes of the weather, the greedye mindes of Cornemaisters, Ingrossers or Forstallers, that loue to Feede vpon there owne bretheren, or o^r^ owne synnes that hasten god's iuste iudgementes vpon vs: & then obserue well what the Prophete Ezekiell saythe. Ezekiel, 16 cap., vers 49, "This was the iniquitye of thy syster Sodom. Pride, fulnes of breade, & abundaunce of idlenes was in her & her daughters, neither did she strengthen the hand of ye poore & needye. vers 50. but they were hautye, & Commytted abhominatyon before mee: therefore I tooke them awaye as pleased mee": for o^r^ pride yt is to muche seene, & the greate waste in tauernes, alehowses & ordinaryes prouethe o^r^ Fulnes of breade; let vs beware of the reste, for as wee haue a gracyouse & a good kinge, whome god hathe bleste, so let vs not hasten god's iudgementes wth o^r^ synnes." And so Concluded.'[1] [p. 357]

In Camera Stellata, coram Consilio ibidem, Mercurij, 12° Octobr. 1608, termino Mich'is.[2] 1608 Oct. 12

This day Mr Edward Jones, after the death of Mr Mill, took the place of his deputation of the Clerk of the Council's place in this Court, as Deputy to Sr Francis Bacon, who has the grant of the reverson of it after the death of the said Mr William Mynne [Mylle]. Jones, Deputy Clerk of the Star Chamber

The same day a cause of hearing, Copping, plaintiff, against Palmer and others, defendants, for two riots in [p. 358] COPPING v. PALMER — Riot

[1] Compare this with the other charges, *ante*, pp. 19, 56, 101, 106, 159, 161, 185, 263, 300, 326, and *post*.

[2] Nine Councillors and Judges were present.

1603 Oct. 12

carrying *fene* or 'haie' in the night time with a multitude of seven or eight, [armed] with pike staves and other weapons, and in beating the plaintiff and his wife, and the second riot in arresting and striking the plaintiff in the Church and churchyard on the 'Sabaothe' day in the time of divine service. It seems that as to the title, it was not greatly material, for the defendants, by their Counsel, Randall Crewe & John Walter, showed that the plaintiff has no title, and that the defendant Palmer has a title from the Committee of the Ward, and that there was a decree and an injunction out of the Court of Wards against the plaintiff, the which he contemptuously disobeyed, and that the defendant had trial with a verdict and judgment for £8 damages against the plaintiff for the same assault and battery, tried before the Lord Chief Justice Popham, and all those then gave evidence, and that the plaintiff was a 'lewd & contentious fellowe'; and to prove this they showed a certificate of divers Justices of the Peace and other gentlemen testifying this; which the Lord Chancellor greatly disliked, and he said that 'he neuer saw theise testimonyalles speede well.' Also on behalf of the defendant they took exception as to the second riot that the bill is indorsed on the 'backside' "R^d^ the same 23 Nouembr. 22 Elizab." a thing of new use, '& the bill complaines of the 2nd riote done the 21th [*sic*] of June nexte before,' and the proof is for a riot made in June, 23 Elizabeth. For which the Lord Chancellor found great fault with the 'Counsellors,' and advised them to insert the particular day and time without any manner of reference or relation.

Arrest in church yard on Sunday

Sentence

As for the sentence of the Court, the defendants were acquitted by Cesar, Coke, and Zouche, and by Parrie [1] were condemned only in 40 marks for the second riot. But by Lord Chief Justice Flemminge, the Bishop of London, the Lord Privy Seal, the Archbishop of Canterbury and the Lord Chancellor, the defendants were condemned by three of them in 100 marks apiece, and by the Archbishop and the Lord Chancellor in £100 apiece, and imprisonment. And

[p. 359]

[1] Thomas Parry, Chancellor of the Duchy of Lancaster.

it was ruled by the Lord Chancellor that, notwithstanding the Court differed in their sentence, yet the defendants are fined, for £100 includes 100 marks, and such is the course of the Court. And it was also ruled as the course of the Court that if divers defendants are named in the bill and process is prayed against all of them, all those who are not served with process may still be examined as witnesses. But Lord Cooke condemned the acting in the night, which is a time of rest, and lawful things cannot be done in the night, as for instance, a man cannot distrain for his rent in the night, and if a man travel at night and be robbed, the country shall not be charged. And as to the profanation of the Sabbath day (for both the riots were made on the Sabbath day), and in the church and cemitary, which are sanctuaries and the places for prayers and places of rest for the bodies, which were and will be temples of the Holy Spirit, the law forbids 'chidinge, quarrelling, strykinge, buying & selling in Churche or Churcheyarde, 5 E[dward] 6, cap. 4;[1] brawling in Churcheyarde' is a great offence, and excommunicates *ipso facto*; if he lay violent hands 'to strike, or drawe any weapon, in churche or churcheyarde to lose one eare; if he haue none eares then to be marked in the Cheeke wth a letter F.' *Die dominico cessat vox pretoris*: & in some cases words or the holding up of the hand make an assault; *qui primo percutit, aut ictum dat, incipit rixam.*

vultus, visus, gestus, instruunt iudicem.

And the Lord Chancellor said that in all courts, when he meets with one who serves process in a church or churchyard, 'he layes him by the heeles.'

A special bailiff ought to show his warrant for arresting a man, but otherwise in the case of a bailiff known, as appears by Lord Cooke's Reports. Lord Cooke said that he did not wish to be both Judge and witness, but he knew the plaintiff to be a lewd fellow. And the Lord Chancellor said that he would not now be muzzled by any former verdict, but his tongue should speak freely what his heart

Bailiffs

[p. 360]

[1] See *ante*, p. 337.

1608 Oct. 12

and conscience thought; and in some cases time is material, and the defendant ought to take advantage of this in pleading, but in this case it was not material *modo constat de facto*: the riots were proved by the confessions of the defendants themselves. And so sentence [was passed] upon them as above.

1608

In Camera Stellata, coram Consilio ibidem, adonque present, Lo. Chauncellor, archeuesque de Canterberye, Lo. Priuie seale, euesque de londres, Lo. Zouche, ambideux Cheife Justices, Justice Yeluerton & Sr Julius Cesar.[1]

Case of the three ALDERMEN OF GLOUCESTER

Libel

Cause of hearing, three Aldermen of the City of Gloster,[2] plaintiffs, and Machin and Bruster, sons of two Aldermen of Gloster, and seven others, defendants, for publishing and dispersing an infamous libel against the plaintiffs and their wives, persons of honest reputation, good fame and credit, and great value. They proceeded to hearing on the defendants' own confession, but did not sentence any of them for making, contriving or devising the said libel, for it was ruled by the Judges that if a defendant, in his examination, excuse himself and accuse another defendant, it is not good proof to convict the other defendant, but that if he accuse himself and the other defendant, it is a good conviction of the other defendant also. Libelling generally was condemned as a great and heinous offence, and a breach of two great commandments of the Omnipotent, viz.:—of stealth, and of taking away the good fame of a neighbour; and by the laws of [some] nations punished with death, for instance, by the Romans, by the Cretans; and by some laws with banishment and loss of lands and goods. By the ancient law of this kingdom *Conuitiatori lingua exciditur*, for the first offence *premunire*; libelling the King or the State is treason, *mouere seditionem regni*. 5 Henry VII., Bagnall's Case:[3] if against private persons, 'pillorye,

Bagnall's case

[1] No date is given; it is presumably after Oct. 12, and before v. 9.

[2] Taylor and others; see Appendix VII.

[3] See *ante*, p. 345, n. 1.

whippinge, losse of eares, nailing, weare papers, confessyon in publike places, &c.'

'Publishinge or receauing sclaunderous bookes, extolling [p. 361] Publishing slanderous books
y[e] pope or his religion, power or gouernem[te], or aduauncinge or allowinge of them, is for the firste offence *premunire*, the 2[d] treason.

'The 2 firste defendauntes, for that they were gentlemen Sentence
ingeniouselye borne and bredde, very younge, & Machin of the Middle temple, a studente of good towardnes & likely to proue a good member in y[e] Common wealthe, were spared for there Corporall punishemente, but fyned 200[li.] a peece, & to acknowledge there faultes at the Assises, Cessions, & in a publike place before the Maior and aldermen, to be bounde to there good behauioure, & ymprisoned: twooe of them that were the Cheife publishers & delyuerers of Copies of the sayde lybell were sentenced to be whipte & stande vpon the pillorye, & they & all the reste to acknowledge there Faultes as before, to be fyned fiftie poundes a peece, bounde to there good behauyoure, & ymprisoned. yt appeared by the opinion of the Cowrte, it seemethe to be a perylouse thinge to keepe a lybelle, especiallye yf it touche the state, or if it be a magistrate or a publike offycer to whome the same is delyuered, he oughte to examyne the matter & (if it be in his power) to punishe the same; otherwyse w[th] all possible speede to acquaynte the lordes of the kinge's Councell w[th]all, and not to conceale the same, or to doe nothinge aboute the same.'

In Camera Stellata, coram Consilio ibidem, Mercurij, 9° Nouembr. 1608.[1] [p. 362] 1608 Nov. 9

'A Cause of hearinge, S[r] Will[m] Haule,[2] pl., againste John Ellis, Defend[te], for lybellinge onelye by letter, John Ellis hauing sente 3 letters to the pl., subscrybinge his name to them, being very obscene & wanton, & full of very vilde knauerye; & it was resolued by the Judges that theise HAULE *v.* ELLIS — Libel

[1] Eight Councillors and Judges were present.

[2] Sir William Hall of Kent was knighted at Greenwich, July 3, 1604.

1608 Nov. 9 were lybelles Conteygninge matter of disturbaunce of the peace & gyuinge occasyon of breache of the same: & for
Sentence this he was Fyned 500li. & imprysonmte.'

1608 Nov. 11 **In Camera Stellata,** coram Consilio ibidem, Veneris, 11° Novembr. 1608.[1]

HAWARDE *v.* WHITBROKE

Practise and misdemeanour

'Captaine John Hawarde,[2] pl., *versus* Sr John Whitbroke,[3] for practise and misdemeanor in seekinge vndulye to gette the pls lande: firste, by a mortgage for 40li. he hathe an absolute bargaine & sale of 40li. lande *per annum*, wth a Couenante onelye on his parte to reassure the lande againe, vpon the repayemente of the monie, to Captaine Hawarde himselfe, so he showlde haue thereby but an estate for lyfe, & a prouiso in the same Deede that yf the bailies, seruauntes, or receauors of Sr John Whitbrooke were molested or incumbred, all showlde be voyde; & a bonde for performaunce of Couenauntes of the same Deede. & longe before the Daye of payemente, the Defendte arrestethe
[p. 363] the pl. vpon the bonde, & layes [him] in the Common goale, & practisethe wth the Goaler that he showlde haue xli. to vse the pl. in that manner that he mighte be forced to sell his lande; the gailer vsethe him wth all hardenes, placethe him in the toppe of the goale in December in a very colde roome buylte of stone, & sufferethe him not to haue eyther Fire, candle, bedde, or strawe to lye vpon, nor for 5 dayes either meate or drinke, no, not the kinge's allowaunce of 1d *per diem* to eache prysoner; in so muche as he had Famyshed, but by the deuyse of a Corde he had some small thinges Conueyghed to him by a poore wydowe, & was forced to drinke his owne vryne: & so kepte him in pryson for the space of twooe yeare and a halfe; & when the monye was to be tendered, he sendes a Cople wth a letter of

[1] Eight Councillors and Judges were present.

[2] Sir John Hayward of Salop was knighted at Windsor, July 23, 1609.

[3] Sir John Whitbrooke of Salop was knighted at Greenwich, June 12, 1604.

1610, Mar. 19.—Grant to Clement Corbet of the benefit of the recusancy of Sir John Whitbrook of Bridgnorth, co. Salop. State Papers, Domestic, James I., vol. 53, no. 21.

Attornye to receaue the same, but gyues them no auctoritie to reassure the lande. Sentence

'For theise offences he was Fyne a 1000$^{li.}$ & 250 $^{li.}$ dammage to the partie, & he to haue his lande againe, the Defend^{te} to be bounde to his good behauyoure, & ymprysoned; & the Lo. Chauncellor gaue a good charge to all Counsellors at the lawe to haue Care of there Clyentes' Causes, for they must yealde there accounte to god at the laste Daye, & to beware how they be of Counsell wth suche manner of Conueyghaunces.

'The Lo. priuye seale woulde gladlye haue excused the defend^{te}, being his seruaunte and one, as he sayde, that deserued well and had many good partes, but he was now to iudge *secundum allegata et probata, et non secundum optata.*' [1]

In Camera Stellata, Martis, 14 Febr. 1608, ter^{no} Hillarij, le prochein iour puis le terme, adonque presente Lo. Chauncellor, Lo. Tresorer, archeuesque de Canterbery, Lo. Zouche, Herberte, Cesar, touts les Judges. 1608-9 Feb. 14 [p. 364]

The Lord Chancellor's charge to the Judges

'The Lo. Chauncellor onelye made a speache to the Judges that yt was his Ma$^{tie's}$ expresse charge that the Judges showlde haue greate Care in there Circuites to mainteine the kinge's peace & to punishe all malefactors, to looke Carefullye to the Justices of peace that they be diligente & circumspecte in there places, for there are some that are not sworne, & most of them neuer studye there oathes.' [2]

[1] See Coke's *Reports*, vi. 481. It does not appear that John Hawarde, the plaintiff in this case, was any relation to John Hawarde, the writer of the MS.

[2] Compare this with the other charges, *ante*, pp. 19, 56, 101, 106, 159, 161, 186, 263, 299, 326, and 367.

APPENDICES

APPENDIX I

The Navigation of the River Lea

PAGE 10

'BEFORE Sr John Popham, knight, L. chieff Justice of England, and Sr Edmound Anderson, knight, L. Chief Justice of the Common Plees, sitting to here prooffes for the right of the passage wth barges vppon the Ryver of Ley from Ware to the Tames, and of the convenience and inconvenyence wth the vsage thereof for most parte of xx^{tie} yeres last.

Apud Serjaunt Inne in Fleete-streate *die Lune vj^{to} die Maij A^{o} xxxvj^{to} Regine Eliz.*

It hath benn well proved by the Plt^{s} and confessed by the Defft^{s} that the Ryver of Ley runninge from Ware to the Thames is an auncyent navigable Ryver and one of the great navigable Ryvers of the Realme, and that there hath benn common and contynuall passage vppon the said Ryver wth Barges by the space of xvj^{ne} or xvij^{ne} yeres wthin xx^{tie} yeres nowe last past through Sr Edward Dennye's newe Locke, and that the Bargemen have had libertie to pull vpp and passe throughe the olde locke if they coulde not passe through the newe.

The Ryver proved and confessed to be navigab'e and so vsed for xvj^{ne} or xvij^{ne} yeres wthin xx^{tie} yeres last

But it is obiected by the defft^{s} that the great streame or Ryver runninge along close to the towne of Waltham Abbey should not be the auncyent Ryver of Lea, but that the little streame wch runneth to Chesthunt myll and so downe to Smalley bridge alias Smalling bridge should be yt.

A question

And by waye of argument to maynetaine there said allegacion, the said defft^{es} saie, wthout shewing any proof for it, that the auncyent navigable Ryver of Ley should devyde the Sheres of Essex and Hertford, and that the streame that runneth to Chesthunt myll and Smalling bridge is the streame wch devydeth the said Sheires and therefore is the auncyent Ryver of Ley, and that Smalling bridge is in Waltham and is the bridge wch is called by the Pl^{tes} the highe bridge in Waltham Hollycrosse.

The defft^{es}' prooffes

The pl^{tes} saie that the towne of Waltham Hollycrosse is the inhabited towne of that name wthin the parishe of Waltham in

The Pl^{te}'s prooffes

the Countie of Essex, soe called to distinguishe it from Waltham Crucis otherwise called Waltham Crosse w[th]in the parishe of Chesthunt in the Countie of Hertford.

And to prove that the navigable Ryver of Ley runneth and aunciently hath run to the said towne of Waltham Sancte Crucis, they prove that there was a Commission xxix[o] *Edwardi tercij* to enquire of the annoyzaunces in that navigable Ryver by theis wordes *In aqua vocata la Ley que currit a villa de Ware vsque* Waltham Sancte Crucis.

And by an Inquisicion taken by a presentm[t] of a Jury of Essex made by vertue of the said Commission it appeareth that the said streame that runneth to Chesthunt Mill, where the Defftes woulde lay out the said navigable Ryver, was then but a Ditche running out of the Ryver of Ley to the Myll of Chesthunt conteyninge xvj[tene] foote of bradthe *ad magnam diminutionem dicte aque*, wherby it appeareth plaine that that Ryver w[ch] the Deff[tes] woulde nowe have to be the navigable Ryver of Ley was not then taken to be the navigable Ryver of Ley, but was presented to be a hurte to the Ryver of Ley for taking to muche water awaye.

Item, it appeareth by the same Inquisicion that the navigable Ryver of Ley did then run downe beneathe the said Chesthunt Myll ditche by Hallifeilde in the parishe of Waltham Sancte Crucis and by Netherlock w[ch] is the locke in questyon and soe to Waltham towne and to the highe bridge of Waltham by theis wordes *inter alia*; *Johannes de Gulford habet in Hallifield in parochia de Waltham vnum fossatum currens extra transitum dicte aque de la Ley; in villa de Waltham iuxta le Netherlock sunt duo montes de arena in medio aque de la Ley et impediunt transitum navium ibidem; Thomas Spalding habet vnum gradum a domo sua in la Ley que potest impedire transitum navium. Item Ricardus Collworth fecit purpresturam in dicta aqua de la Ley iuxta altum pontem de Waltham ad magnum impedimentum transitus navium.* By this presentment that Spalding had made stares from his howse into the Ley to the hinderaunce of passage, it is very manefest that passage of vessells was in the Ryver of Ley that runneth by Waltham Sancte Crucis and under the highe bridge there, for that at or nere Smalling-bridge ther neither is nor was ever any howse.

By an other Inquisicion taken by vertue of the said commission at Waltham Crosse by a Jurye of the Countie of Herts, it was presented as followeth by theis wordes, *inter alia: Item le damme mowthe molendini de la Chesthunt mylle est maioris latitudinis quam antiquius esse solebat, de latitudine xvj pedum per quod,* &c. By this it appeareth plainely that the streame that runneth to Chesthunt mylle is but Chesthunt mylle dam and not the navigable Ryver of Ley, and it seemeth that the navigable Ryver of Ley in that place devydeth the Sheeres, because the Jurors of both Sheeres did present the fault of Chesthunt myllstreame.

It is also presented by the said Jury of Herts in theis wordes: *Item est in predicta aqua contra solum dicti Abbatis apud le Netherlock vna insula magna per quod,* &c. By this it appeareth that the Ryver of Ley is found by the Jury of Herts, like as it was by the Jury of Essex, that the navigable Ryver of Ley did run by the Nether locke nere to the towne of Waltham Sancte Crucis, wch is the Locke in questyon, and it seemeth by the presentment of bothe the Juryes that the Ryver in that place devideth the Sheres.

By the same Inquisicion it is also presented thus: *Item est in piscaria Abbatis ad caput ville de Waltham vna fractio in aqua per quod cursus aque de la Ley maxime impeditur.* By this it appeareth plainely that the very inhabited towne of Waltham Sancte Crucis is ment and not the large parishe of Waltham.

By an Inquisicion taken xxij^{do} *Edwardi quarti* it is presented by a Jury in the Countie of Hertford that the heade at the entry of the Abbott of Waltham's Myll, where water goethe out of the king's streame, is of xvj foote broade wher it should be but fower foote, by the wch the king's streame is sore hurte. Also the said Abbott hath a locke wch is but xv^{ne} foote broade where it should be xviij^{ne} foote, for which cause it must be broken vpp, for it is great Jeopardy to all manner of Barges and boates that goe vppon the water there; by this presentmente it is also very manifest that the navigable Ryver of Ley did run the same waye that the Pl^{tes} affirme, viz: to the locke in questyone and to the highe bridge of Waltham Sancte Crucis wch was riotously throwen downe by the said Deff^{tes}, and that the same Ryver or some parte of it at the same locke was taken to be wthin the Countie of Herts, for that the Jury did there present it.

It is also presented by the said Inquisicion that there is a bridge in Waltham called the Highe Bridge wthin the liberties of Chesthunt wch must be made newe, for there maye noe bardge passe except that the bridge be made in height that the barges maye goe there wthout any letting, or ells that there be a man reddy to drawe the same bridg att all times wthout any charge of the Passengers or commons, for the streame oweth to be free wthout any Custome or dutie taken at any place in the said water, and there the Passengers be compelled to paie a Dutie for drawing of the said Bridg by the wch there shall growe a dutye and a charge to the passengers and the Country, wheras ther oweth noe such to be. Also beneath the said bridge in the Ryver there benn certaine stakes, hyees,[1] &c., wch noyeth the kinge's streame sore, wch must be pared, rydd and scowred by theis persons following every man during his grownd (that is to saie) Conesby of London the holder of the next tenem^{t}, &c. By this it appeareth plainelie that the high bridge in Waltham presented by this Jury is the same highe bridge that standeth over the navigable Ryver of Ley, and was late layed lowe by the deff^{tes}. And wheras the Deff^{tes} doe obiect against this presentm^{t}, that Smalling bridge that standeth vppon Chesthunt Myll streame is higher then the bridge in Waltham towne and is also wthin the parishe of Waltham and standeth vppon the Ryver that devideth the Sheeres, therefore this is Waltham highe bridge presented by the Jury. This obiection is allreadye aunswered fully by that wch goeth before, and is further aunswered thus, viz. that Smalling bridge was ever called by the name of Smalleybridge alias Smallingbridge and is knowe by that name onely and not by the name of Highebridge and is wholy wthin the Countie of Hertf. as by a Collection made wthin late yeres for the repaying therof wthin the Countie of Hertf. by order taken amongst the Justices of that Shere, and as was testifyed before yor Ll^{s} by the viccar of Chesthunt, and it is further manifested that the Jury might well present the Highe bridge in Waltham towne to be wthin the Liberties of Chesthunt for that the parishoners of Chesthunt haue of longe time and still doe pretend that theire liberties doth extend to that Bridge and that they have gonne thether wth there presession of late yeres, but there is noe meaninge nor necessarye to take knowledge of theire controuersye, because it is not materiall to the proof of the navigable Ryver of Ley; But to make the matter plaine that th'other is the navigable streame and not this small streame that runneth to Chesthunt mylle, it hath bene sufficientlie proved by the presentm^{t} aboue mencioned and many others that vessells haue passed vppon the Ryver of Ley from Ware to the Thames, but none coulde passe through Chesthunt Myll streame by reason it is but a shallowe narrowe ditche and by reason that the Myll dam of Chesthunt Mylle standeth crosse the streame, soe that noe vessell be it never so little coulde ever passe

[1] Qy. hays, hedges.

that waye, and therfore the passage was vnder Waltham highe bridge, and throughe the olde locke otherwise called Netherlocke of Waltham, as is before alledged.

The Comission of Sewers directed to the L. Treasurer and others *Anno xvij^{o} d^{ne} Regine nunc Eliz.* for the scowringe of the Ryver did declare the Ryver to runne from Ware to Waltham, from Waltham to Templebridge, from Templebridge to Bullyfant, and from thence to Clobbes Hill, and from thence to the olde Forde and soe to Bowebridge and to the Locke, and soe to Leymouth to the Ryver of Thames, wch Comission was made by former Presidentes and sufficient proves [proofs], and it is to be gathered thervppon that the course of the auncyent Ryver of Ley was lymitted to runne by places of name standing vppon it, and not by parishes, in wch sence Waltham is to be taken for the very village or towne through wch the Ryver runneth, and not for the whole parishe of Waltham, and in none of the olde or newe Inquisicions the Ryver of Ley is declared to run through any parishe but is called the water of Ley in the Counties of Hertford, Essex and Middelsex. *Quequidem aqua se ducit a ponte ville de Ware vsque ad aquam Thamisie.* The Jurors of the Counties of Essex and Hertford that were charged to inquire according to this last Commission have presented the Ryver of Ley that was navigable to goe through Waltham locke and Waltham high bridge according as other Jurors had donn before and as it is nowe alledged by the pl^{tes}.

Commissio iiij^{ti} H. quinti

The owner of the Manno^{r} of Theobaldes paied xxvj^{s} viij^{d} *per annum* to the L. of the Manno^{r} of Perryers for the course of the water goinge throughe his grounde from Ley to Chesthunt Mille vntill both the Manno^{rs} came to my L. Treasurer.

It is alledged in the bill of Compl^{t} in the Starr chamber that the locke and bridge wher the Ryottes were commytted doe stand vppon the Ryver of Ley, and the deff^{tes} doe not denye the same, and some of them, namely, Henry Cokarelle, Myller of Chesthunt Mylle, and Ralph Curle of Chesthunt, beinge examyned vppon the Ryott doe confesse that they thinke the said Mylle and highbridg doth stand vppon the said Ryver of Ley, and Thomas Robynson of Waltham Hollicrosse, one other of the Deff^{tes}, confesst vppon his oathe that he knoweth the Ryver of Ley, wch is her Ma$^{te's}$ Ryver, and saiethe that the highe bridg in Waltham doth stande over the mayne streame of the said Ryver, and Rob^{te} Browne of Waltham Hollicrosse, one other of the Deff^{tes}, age lxv yeres, saieth vppon his oathe that he knoweth the Ryver of Ley, wch he taketh to be one of the greatest Ryvers of the land, and that the highebridge in Waltham dothe stand over or vppon the Mayne streame of the said Ryver, and that the olde locke wch is aboute three q^r^ters of a Myle beyonde Waltham, wch of late hath benn stopped, did stand vppon the Mayne streame of the Ryver of Ley.

By an Inquisicion taken *apud Waltham sancte Crucis in Com' Essex anno quarto Henrici viij^vi^ coram Henrico Frowicke, Escaetore*, &c., *virtute officii sui*, remayning in the Exchequer, it is presented *inter alia* thus: *Quod Abbas exempti Manerii Sancte Crucis de Waltham et eiusdem loci conventus sunt seisiti de Manerio siue dominio de Waltham sancte Crucis in Com' predicto*, &c., *Et dicunt vlterius iidem Juratores quod predictum Manerium siue dominium de Waltham Sancte Crucis extendit se per metas et bundas, viz: a quodam ponte vocato Smalleigh-bridge que est in confinio Com' Essex' et Hertford' per parvam riperiam ibidem vocatam le Smalleighe quequidam riperia est de parte occidentali in extrema parte Communis Marisci de Waltham predict'*, &c., *Quiquidem mariscus iacet de parte orientali dicte parve Riperie et sic predictum Manerium siue dominium se extendit in longitudine per parvam Riperiam predictam vocatam Smalleigh et vsque ad pratum vocatum Frithey*, &c.,

* * * * *

and it is plaine that vessells called 'Cimbe' then passed vppon Highe Leigh, wherevppon it may be necessarilye concluded that they passed through the olde locke and the highebridge at Waltham Hollycrosse where the passage hath benn lately stopped by force, for other waye they coulde not passe. This Inquisicion beinge taken for the benefitt of the Abbott of Waltham and noe doubte by his privitye and good lyking, ioyned to the other proofes maye suffice to satisfye Sr Edward Dennye, knighte, who hath the Manno^r^ of Waltham wth like liberties as the Abbott had, and may move him to desist from theis wronges and yelde to right.

Towchinge the burthen of Shutes and barges; obiections and aunsweres

Wher it was alledged that certaine vessells called Shoutes, wch were proved of auncient time to have passed downe the Ryver, were of very small burthen, it was proved by Recordes that in kinge Edward the thirdes time ther passed three Shoutes downe carryinge xij loades of tymber, wch is fower tonne to a peece, and in kinge Henry the fowerthes his tyme a Shoute carryed xij tonne of tymber atte one time downe the Ryver, and the barges lately passinge that waye be some of sixe or seaven tonne burthen, and some of lesse burthen and yet doe passe wth a shallowe water.

It was alledged by the Defftes that allbeyt the Ryver was navigable, yet it was not lawfull for the Bargemen to goe a lande to towe there barges. To this aunswere was made that the Ryver being one of the great Ryvers of the Realme hath such liberties and priviledges as other great Ryvers haue, and that Bargemen and keelemen have allwayes vsed and do goe a longe by the bankesside to drawe there vesselles by the Ryver of Thames, Severne, Trent, and the Ryver betweene Wisbich and Cambridge, and all other great Ryvers, and in some places they vse the helpe of horses to towe vpp ther vesselles and that the like libertie is allowed to all the navigable Ryvers in Holland and Zeland and all forren partes. The aucthoritie of Bracton that the vse of the banckes of Ryvers is publique *de Jure gentium* like as of the Ryvers themselves, and also the aucthoritie of the booke case in the time of kinge Edward the fowerth that alloweth Fishermen to goe a lande vppon any man's grownde to drye ther nettes because it is good for the Common welthe, were alledged. It appeareth by the said Inquisicion taken in kinge Edward the fowerthes time that the owners of the ground one either side of the Ryver should take awaye all the trees, busshes and hedges growing vppon the banke of the said Ryver wch could serve to noe other ende but that the Bargemen might goe vppon the banckes to towe there barges. It appeareth also that the Lord Treasurer and others late Commissyoners of Sewers attending vppon him, following that example, caused all the trees, willowes and busshes, and other ympedymts vppon the Ryver banckes to be taken awaye, and bridges to be made over the mouthe of Millstreames for the Bargemen to goe along the banckes and towe there barges. And it is alledged that for asmuch as it is vnpossible to carry vpp barges or boates against the streame wth owers [oars] onely that be of any convenyent burthen, nor allmost any other wth any convenyent nomber or in any convenyent tyme, and for that vessells wth good burthen haue allwayes heretofore passed vpp and downe the Ryver as is afore proved, therefore it cannott be but that they were towed. And lastlie it is said and cannott be denyed that the Bargemen going one land one the bancke side to towe ther barges and keeping one pathe can doe but little or noe hurte to the land. Towching towing of Barges; obiections and aunsweres

The Defftes counsell said that they would saie nothing towching the conveniencye or inconveniency of the passage but leave the consideracion thereof to the Lls [Lords] the Judges.' The convenyencie and inconveniency

State Papers, Domestic, Elizabeth, vol. 248, no. 97.

APPENDIX II

Gresham v. Markham

PAGES 22, 26, 29, 64, 94

1595 Dec. 5 'RIGHT HONORABLE, my dewtie in all humillitie remembred, when in the cawse of the Lady Gresham, consernenge the Annuyties graunted by Sr Thomas Gresham, I am depely chardged, and was drawen into the same by the means of Sr Thomas Reade and his mother for the vse of the said lady Gresham, and by reason thereof haue disbursed and laide oute to the vallew of Fiften hunderyth poundes, And now bothe my self and others towched in credytt by the informacion of moste lewde and slender witnes; The cawse beinge weightie my meaneinge ys, right honorable, that yt might be couered and ended wth pacience, wherein all parties maye have their desyer, and myself eased and releeved, as to yor honorable consideracion in Justice and charetie shalbe thowght convenient, to whose Judgement in all respectes I will submytt myself, beinge sory that I did not acquaynte yor hono^{r} soner herewyth, then yt had never come to this extremetie; Therefore, yf yt maye please yor hono^{r}, or who you shall appoynte, to looke into this cawse, I do verely thincke that bothe my lady gresham, and all hers, and my self, my poore children and frendes to the nomber of Forty persons who are lyke to peryshe and be distroyed by reason hereof, shall haue more then cawse not onely to pray for yor hono^{r}, but be bounden in all dewtie to the same duringe o^{r} lyves. Cravinge pardon for my boldenes herein, do beseche almightie god to prosper yor hono^{r} in all yor procedinges, this vth of december, 1595

Yo^{r} hono$^{r's}$ moste humble
to commaunde
Ro: BOUTHE.

To the right honorable
Sr Robert Cicill, knight,
one of her ma$^{te's}$ moste
honorable prevy counselle.'

State Papers, Domestic, Elizabeth, vol. 255, no. 4.

'The Humble Peticion of John Markeham th'elder. 1596 ?

The cause or grounde.

Sr Thomas Gresham, knight, did make a marryage betwene the sayde Markham and Anne Hurst, his servantes, and in consideracion thereof did giue and graunte vnto them cxxx$^{l.}$ for 99 yeares and a bonde of M$^{t\ li.}$ to paye vc$^{l.}$ the First of February, 1596; and in the first graunte was mencioned to the childe she then went with, were it mon or woman.

That Sr Thomas Gresham bounde Markham by obligacion in a greate penalty to marry her by a daye, wch was performed.

The childe was a boye, called John Markham the Yonger.

To whome Sr Thomas Gresham did giue and graunt when the boye was almost thre yeares of age, Two seuerall Annuityes at sondry tymes for vjc$^{l.}$ per annum for 99 yeares from the decease of him and Dame Anne his wyfe.

With a prouiso or lymitacion, That yf the sayde Sr Thomas Gresham at the tyme of his decease sholde haue issue male or female of his body lawfully begotten, That then all the annuityes and bonde to be voyde.

That Sr Thomas was beneficiall to them duringe his lyfe.

That Sr Thomas frequented at tymes the company of the sayde Anne Hurst vnto his decease,[1] wch was almost thre yeares after her marryage.

That Sr Thomas deliuered those deedes, acknowledged the 5 July a^{o} 21 E. [1579], to the handes of the sayde Anne Hurst the same daye after he had acknowledged the same before Doctor Mowse.

The practys for the overthrowe of the sayde deedes by a supposed forgery.

Thomas Crosse, prest, Richard Bilbroughe, vintner, two common cosoners, and men of very lewde behauio^{r}.

The sayde Crosse and Bilbroughe aboute two yeares past, beinge acquainted wth the sayde Markham th'elder, came to the sight of some of the sayde deedes.

They searched two dayes in the notarye's booke that made the deedes.

They caused a falce entry to be made in another scryveno$^{r's}$ booke of the bonde of vc$^{l.}$.

They caused a falce informacion to be drawne in the lady

[1] He died Nov. 21, 1579.

Gresham's name, and yett did not knowe her name, neyther was she acquainted therewth.

That Markham can neyther wryt nor reade.

That they w$^{th\cdot}$ Sr Thomas Reade, knight, deceased, vsed all meanes and devices to bringe Markham wthin the compas of the late robbery of the Lady Gresham.

That Sr Thomas Reade graunted his warrant vnder his hande to apprehend the body of Markham vpon state and treason.

That Markham by virtue of the sayde warrant was taken oute of his bedde at midnight and brought to Sr Thomas Reade, who kept him two dayes close prysoner, examyning him onely touchinge the sayde deedes, supposinge by this practys to gett them.

That Sr Thomas Reade comytted the poore man close prysoner in Newgate wthoute baile.

Crosse caused a seale to be made in Aprill, 1594, wth a greshopper.[1]

Crosse was the first setter of this practys who brought Bilbroughe into the action.

That Bilbroughe hath confessed forgery and that he forged the deedes.

The one was appoynted to confesse forgery, and the other to witnes.

What rewardes, bondes and promyses were giuen and promysed by Sr Thomas Reade and his mother and others for the effectinge of this practys, lett the witnesses declare.

What rewardes and promyses were giuen and promysed by Sr Thomas Reade and his mother to one Richard Charles aboute this practys, beinge one of the witnesses, is very shamefull.

Also what imprysonment and other devices were vsed to take awaye the testimony of one Thomas Manson, beinge a witnes, wilbe proved.

The proceedinges of the cause
in this honorable Courte.

First, the sayde Markham th'elder in the beginninge of Easter terme last ehibited [*sic*] his bill in to the Starr chamber against Sr Thomas Reade, Crosse, Bilbroughe, and their consortes.

Within few dayes after yt pleased her Ma$^{te's}$ attorney to send for Markham and examyned him and commytted him and his soliciter close prysoners.

Also, vpon a mocion made by Mr Attorney, the bill of Markham stayed and no proceedinges.

Then yt pleased Mr Attorney, aboute x or xij dayes after he had commytted Markham and his soliciter close prysoners, to

[1] The Gresham crest.

cause a crosse bill in the Lady Gresham's name to be exhibited in to this honorable courte against the sayde Markham and all his witnesses to the sayde deedes, and made them and diuers his freindes all defendantes.

In wch crosse bill the sayde Bilbroughe was made a defendant, who before had promysed to confesse forgery, and was a defendant in the first bill exhibited.

That Bilbroughe saieth that he forged the deedes sythence the xxxvj^th^ yeare of her ma^te's^ reigne [1593–4].

And yett the Lady Gresham and Mr Reade w^th^in v or vj yeares past sent diuers to Markham for the buyinge and takinge in of the sayde deedes.

That Markham, his wyfe and children, haue lyved theis v or vj yeares only vpon such monyes as they haue borrowed vpon the credytt of the sayde deedes.

That theis deedes graunted by Sr Thomas Gresham haue byn seene and rede many yeares past.

That Bouthe was appoynted to buy some of the deedes by the assignement of the Lady Gresham, Sr Thomas Reade and his mother, aboute three yeares past.

That Mr Reade offered in the Lady Gresham's name MM^li.^ for the sayde deedes.

That Roger Bouthe beinge sent for to Mr Attorney did giue him the true dates and witnesses of all the deedes, otherwise no bill colde haue byn drawne against Markham.

That the sayde Bouthe was commytted to the Fleete, vpon a contempt ignorantly commytted, lxx dayes, whereof he remayned close prysoner xiiij daies.

That Markham remayned close prysoner aboute xix weekes.

Of wch tyme the sayde Markham remayned in a howse of office aboute xv dayes, hauinge but a hole to take and receyve a peece of bred and a cupp of beere.

That Markham and Bouthe were close prysoners those xiiij dayes that were appoynted for the examynacion of the witnesses.

That Markham cold neyther speake wth counsell nor freindes all the tyme of his imprysonment.

And nowe this cause proceedinge to hearinge, he hath not as yett examyned any witnesses to testify the deedes nor for the layinge out of this wicked practys.

The lyfe and behauio^r^ of
Thomas Crosse, prest.

That he was the first setter of this supposed forgery.

That he is excomunicated and outelawed.

That he is put from the ministry for his bad and lewde conversacion.

A lewd man of his body.

That he sayeth and affirmeth that he maye take an oathe to benefytt himselfe or his friende.

That he is a comon cosoner and hath liued many yeares by deceyvinge and cosoninge her ma^te's^ subiectes.

The lyfe and behauio^r^ of
Richard Bilbroughe.

That by forgery he hath cosoned diuers of her ma^te's^ subiectes before this practys, and [it] hath byn the best part of his maintenance longe tyme.

Item, in sellinge of a howse lefte him to thre or foure persons.

Item, in forginge and counterfeytinge a will.

Item, in forginge the clarke's hande and seale of the company of mercers in London.

Item, that he maye be diuers wayes charged for misdemeano^r^ of Filchinge wch by the lawe is supposed to be fellony, as by a siluer cupp or boole oute of a tavorne, and other thinges elles where that he maye be charged w^th^.

Wherefore the sayde Markham humbly prayeth to haue compassion and consideracion of his cause and that such witnesses as he hath to produce (hauinge yett examyned none) maye be examyned for the tryall hereof, and for the layinge oute of the practys, Or elles referred to suche as the honorable lordes shall appoynte, whereby their Lo: maye be certifyed of the trothe herein.' [Undated; ? 1596]

State Papers, Domestic, Elizabeth, vol. 261, no. 46.

1607 Oct. 6 Grant to Edward Kendall, Deputy Clerk of the Hanaper, of the goods, etc., of John and Charles Markham, outlaws, indebted to him.

State Papers, Docquet.

See also Reade *v.* Booth, Coke's *Reports*, vi. 438.

Sir Thomas Gresham, the founder of the Royal Exchange, m. in 1544 Anne dau. of William Femely of West Creting, Suffolk, and widow of William Reade, citizen and mercer of London. She died at Osterly House, Nov. 23, 1596, and was buried in S. Helen's, Bishopsgate. See *Dict. Nat. Biog.* and the authorities there cited.

APPENDIX III

Danvers v. Long

PAGE 49

'A TRUE DECLARACION of the ground of the conceaued mislike of Sr Walter Longe, knighte, & Henry Longe, gent., his Brother, againste Sr John Danvers, knighte, his Sonnes & Followers. 1595 ?

Firste, For y^{t} the said Henry Longe & one Nich^{as} Reade, Sr Walter Longe's Servaunte, having committed a Robberie, vppon Complainte made, weare discouered by the Industrie of the said Sr John Danvers.

Secondlie, For y^{t} a second Robberie was discouered by the said Sr John Danvers to be committed by one Mathewes, A Seruaunte in Sr Walter Longe's howsse.

Thirdlie, For y^{t} the said Sr Walter Longe was by the Justice of Assizes sharpelie reprehended for vndue proceeding in matter concearning the said Robberie, vppon Examinacion taken by the said Sr John Danvers.

Fourthelie, For y^{t} the said Sr Walter Longe was by the order of the Ho. Ll^{s} committed to the Fleete, for his vndue Course againste the said Sr John Danvers, for his due proceeding in Hir Ma^{ts} service.

Fiftelie, For y^{t} the said Sr John Danvers as A Justice of the Peace, comytted iiij^{or} of the Seruauntes of the said Sr Walter Longe, for A murther by them latelie comitted.

The Abuses offered by Sr Walter Longe & his Brethren ageinste Sr John Danvers, his Sonnes & Seruauntes, in regard of the premisses.

Firste, the said Sr Walter Longe, his Brothers & Followers, by manie Insolent behaviours & termes provoked & moued quarrell ageinste the said Sr John Danvers.

Secondlie, the same not sorting to theire desired effecte, A Servaunte of the said Sr John Danvers was murthered by Servauntes of the said Sr Walter Longe's, and one other Servaunte verie daungerouslie wounded.

Thirdlie, no occasion of brall being thereby taken, the said Sr Walter Longe's Brother, to give further occasion of quarrell, being gardyd wth many of Sr Walter Longe's Servauntes, in verie disordered manner entred the howse of A Tenaunte of the said Sr John Danvers, and in Insolent manner (wthout anie culler of occasion) A glasse of Beere was throwne in the face of the principall officer of the said Sr John Danvers: Saying in derision They had nowe doubbed him a knight also.

Fourthlie, Sr Charles Danvers (finding theis Insolent behaviours offered) by gentlemanlike Letters (wthout [anie cause ?] of offence) desired to be satisfied by Sr Walter Longe, whether the same weare done by his privitie, whereof, vppon mutual Letters passing betweene them, he remayned satisfied.

Which being to the said Henry Longe knowen, and finding the same sorted not to suche publique offence as he desired, and purposing to moue quarrell, by what meanes soeuer he cared not, thereby to effecte his mallice conceaued (wthout any shaddowe of Cawse) wrote his Letters of defyaunce to the said Sr Charles Danvers, giving therein (besides manie rude termes) manie times the Lye in the throate, for no matter concearning himself, and sondrie times sending him word That wheresoeuer he mett him he would vntye his pointes, & whippe his &c. wth A Rodd; calling him Asse, Puppie, Foole & Boye.

The manner of the Affraye and deathe of the said Henry Longe.

The said Sr Charles Danvers being moued by the Continuall Extremitie & Insolencie of the said Cawses, determyning wth some small disgrace to requite so many & greate disgraces as before offered, repaired to the place of the said Henry Longe's aboade being an Ordinary, where giving the said Longe ijo blowes wth A Cudgell (wthoutoffring any other weapon or violence) and being therewth satisfied, offered to departe the Chamber, but the doore being fastened by one of Longe's Companie, & himself pursued by the said Longe, and by him daungerouslie wounded in vij several places, and therewth faynting, Sr Henrie Danvers, his Brother, then (& not before) comming into the said Chamber, & finding his Brother bleeding & faynting, to prevent his deathe, dischardged his Pistoll, wthout wch the said Sr Charles had byn then slaine.

The Indirect proceeding of the said Sr Walter Longe, since the deathe of the said Henry Longe.

Firste, to prevent all due & indifferent Course of proceeding for th'examinacion of the premisses, he by himself, his vncle, & Brothers in lawe (w^th^out anie others) hathe taken vppon them (being in nature parties to the Cawse) to examyne & sett downe the testymonie of divers verie parciall & vndue wittnesses.

Secondlie, he hathe by one Thomas Tromplin, & Edmond Powell, his Instrumentes, practised to corrupt wittnesses to accuse your humble Peticioner wth matters of felony, tending to the endaungering of hir [1] liffe & estate, by rewardes given & promised.

Thirdlie, he hathe incyted divers Riotous persons (in moste Contemptuous & owtragious manner) to pretend tytle, & to pull downe divers Inclosures, many yeeres Contynued in & vppon the ground of the said Sr John Danvers (himself pretending no tytle therein).' [The remainder has been cut off.]

With this document is a letter from Sir Charles Danvers to Sir Robert Cecil begging his favour and countenance in the matter of the suit. It is not dated, but is indorsed "Apr. 1595," and sealed with a seal bearing a chevron between three spur-rowels of six points.

State Papers, Domestic, Elizabeth, vol. 251, no. 123.

See also *Some Old Wiltshire Homes*, by S. J. Elyard, 1894, p. 72.

[1] Dame Danvers, the plaintiff.

APPENDIX IV

Lady Penelope Rich

PAGE 172

LADY PENELOPE RICH was daughter of Walter Devereux 1st Earl of Essex, and sister of Robert Devereux 2nd Earl of Essex, who was beheaded Feb. 25, 1601. The letter referred to in the text is probably the one printed in Birch's Elizabeth, vol. ii. pp. 441, 442, and also in Cal. State Papers, Domestic, Elizabeth, Addenda 1580–1625, p. 398, where the date is given as '1600, Nov. ?.' The letter is mentioned frequently in the State Papers. 1600, Feb. 8; Dudley Carleton to Sir Edward Norris. 'My L^{d} of Essex came not to the Starrchamber on Wednesday, as was expected, nor any extraordinary matter happened, saue onely that the Bishop of London satt there as I aduertised y^{r} L^{p} he should. The La: Rich hath written againe to her Matie, but in other kind of language.' State Papers, Domestic, Eliz., vol. 274, no. 37. 1600, Feb. 22; John Chamberlain to Dudley Carleton. 'The Lady Rich hath ben called *coram* again about her letter, but she excused herself by sickness and (as the Scottish man says) did not compeere.' [*Ibid.*, no. 48.] 1600, March 29; Carleton to Chamberlain. 'The La: Rich, who hath beene once more summoned to appeare abowt her letter, excused herself by sickness, and is now stollen into the cuntrie to be further owt of harmes way.' [*Ibid.*, no. 86.]

1600, May 28; Chamberlain to Carleton. 'There is a meaning to call the Earle of Essex before the counsaile and other noblemen assistants on Satterday next, at the L. Keper's; where according to his aunswers to such matter as shalbe obiected by the Q [ueen's] learned counsaile, there is hope he may haue further inlargement. His apologie was lately printed wth the Lady Riche's letter in the end, and some few of them sold, but they were presently suppressed, and, vpon search, found not to be don so much vpon frendship or faction, as vpon hope of gaine: the poore Lady is like to haue the worst of yt, being sent for and come vp to aunswer and interpret her riddles.' [*Ibid.*, no. 150.] 1601, Feb. 10?; Lady Rich is a prisoner at Mr Sackford's. [*Ibid.*, vol. 278, no. 39.]

See *Lives and Letters of the Devereux, Earls of Essex*, by the Hon. W. B. Devereux, ii. 152.

APPENDIX V

Daniel's Case

PAGE 119

1596 May 2 'KNOW all men by theise presentes that I, Ladie Fraunces, Countesse of Essex, haue remised, released, and quite claymed for mee, mine executo^rs and Administrato^rs, to my seruaunte Jane Daniell, as well the summe of eight thowsand and odd powndes conteyned in her bookes of accomptes, as also all and all manner of Actions, Debtes, Duties, and Demaundes whatsoeuer from the beeginninge of the World vntil this present daie. In Wittnes whereof I haue sett to my hand and seale. Dated the seconde of May 1596. In the xxxviij^th yeare of her Ma^ts Raigne.'

FRA: ESSEX.

State Papers, Domestic, Elizabeth, Addenda, vol. 33, no. 60.

1600 April 7 'Be it knowne vnto all men &c. That we Robert Devoreux, Erle of Essex, Erle Marshall of England, and the Lady Fraunces his wief, For and in Consideracion of the true and faithfull services of John Daniell of Deresbury in the County of Chester, Esquire, and Jane his wief. . . . Have remysed released, discharged and quite claymed . . . vnto the said John Daniell and Jane his wief . . . all and almanner of accions, suits, receipts, . . . and acompts . . . whatsoeuer which against the said John Daniell and Jane . . . we nowe haue or euer haue hadd or . . . at any tyme hereafter may haue.' Dated, April 7, 42 Eliz. 1600.

This document has never been executed.

State Papers, Domestic, Elizabeth, vol. 274, no. 96.

1601 June ? Statement by G. Lisle of the facts in Daniel's case; it agrees exactly with the text, *ante*, p. 119.

Ibid., vol. 279, no. 124.

A long account of the proceedings in the Star Chamber, with marginal notes and comments in Daniel's hand. These notes and comments are printed in italics and inclosed in square brackets. The remainder of the document agrees mainly with the text. It is too long to print in full. 1601 June

Twelve months since when the late Earl of Essex was confined at the Lord Keeper's house, his Countess [*for feare her house shuld haue ben searched and the l'res found, therfore she delyuered them to my wyffe*] gave a casket of letters [*conteynyng matters of dysloyaltie & contempt agaynst her ma^tie's person*] to Jane, wife of the prisoner, Daniell: he, finding the casket under his bed, secretly opened it [*thys excuseth my wyffe*], and took out some of the letters, intending to make gain thereof; [*no such purposse, But labored to dyscov^r matter of state in the l'res wth entent to have revealed the same & soe haue performed his dutie: whereof hee prevented bie the means of those that escaped vnpunished & yeat procured me to detract my lawfull course*] and took them to Peter Bales, a scrivener, to counterfeit them [*wch he dyd the better to reade all the l'res, wch were xxx^tie & only vj brought to Bales*] pretending he had been sent by the Countess; he dictated some of the letters for Bales to copy [*wch was fyrst done by hys greate paynes & help to reade them bie Bales' meanes & not of hys owne knowledge, &c.*], and found fault with him for not imitating the Earl's hand better, and corrupted the copies by adding thereto and forging matter in his reading, [*these wordes, 'the Queene's Comandm^t,' &c. were then shoed to be Reesolved whether they were matter of State*]. Subsequently the Countess sent for the casket, and missing many of the letters, she went to Daniell's house [*a moneth before Bales knew of the l'res*] and being perplexed lest the Earl might conceive some dislike against her for suffering his love letters to be divulged [*the l'res of secresie were kept most secretly, wch was my overthrow*], she questioned Daniell and his wife about them; they denied having them [*the l'res were not denyed, but deteynyd for matter of estate*], and Daniell used very discourteous speeches [*no such matter nor speaches spoken on neyther part*], and pretended to be offended with his wife for keeping the casket without his privity; but being told by the Countess that the letters were neither of importance nor dangerous to the state nor to any particular person, [*both wch was then vnknowen, & therfore he dysyred to be truly resoulued*], but that the loss thereof troubled her, Daniell pretended that he would use his utmost efforts to find them, and shortly afterwards he wrote a letter to the Countess [*she first wrote to my wyffe ; hee wrote to her after she had wrytten & sent dyuers messages*], confessing that he had them, and that as they might greatly concern her lord, it behoved her to be careful to regain them, but that he had become very much impoverished and decayed of late, and had only about 3000*l.* during his service with the Earl, he would restore the letters upon some honourable consideration of his necessity [*a 1000^{li} offred before any such l're or demaund of 3000$^{li.}$ by mee wrote*]. The Countess sent one of her servants [*Sr Edward Dyer & Mr Lylle*] to have the letters returned, but Daniell demanded 3000*l.* The Countess herself then treated with him, but he would not part with them unless she paid him 1720*l.* [*Sr Edward Dyer made this Contracte at the Countesse request and offred me* 1720$^{li.}$], he alleging that if he carried them to Lord Cobham and Sir Walter Raighley, they would give him 3000*l.* for them [*no such words*]. Not having so much money as 3000*l.* the Countess was glad to Compound, [*Sr Edward Dyer dyd Compounde & brought the money*], but to raise the money she was forced to sell her jewells [*sould before ; Borowed of Lyngley & Crompton & Sr Edward Dyer, as he tould mee, & Peter Vandalore*], and having made up the 1720*l.*, she paid it to Daniell and received her letters ; but Daniell, thinking his evil practises might come to light, demanded a general release from the Earl and Countess [*a Release was offred before any money payd*], so as to prevent any danger that might ensue. All this plainly appeared to the Court, both by the prisoner's writing [*not one worde of my hand wrytinge tuching the Release*] and his confession [*nor no word confessed But I could have dysproved by good matter, yf I had been duly dealt wth all*], and he was unable to defend or extenuate his offences [*because yt lay in matter to bee prooved, wch could not be obtayned, for I was both denyed Counsell & prouffe*]. The Court asked if there was any truth in his speeches against Lord Cobham and Sir Walter Rawlieghe, and he admitted his report [*never reported nor spoken by me*] to be most false and slanderous, for they never offered him any money. It also appeared that Daniell had lately written a letter to the Countess impeaching her of some supposed unkindness towards the late Earl [*she knowes this matter to be most true*]. The Attorney-General remarked on Daniell's treachery, being a servant to the late Earl [*noe servante of two yeares before but retyred vpon just cause of dyscontent & vnconstant dealing both bie th'erle and hys Countesse*]. The late Earl, at the time of his arraignment, pretended that the aforesaid letters had been forged and counterfeited [*th'erle's letters were truely wrytten & not counterfeyted; but ymytated for the Queene's servyce, from wch he was w^th^drawen bie the Countesse & her friends*] by his adversaries, whereas it now appears to have been done by his servant, Daniell, and therefore the imputation which the Earl endeavoured to lay upon others was most unjust [*he had no better pretext to color his treasons, wch at his death hee confessed to bee false ymputacions, as appeareth by Mr Barlowe's sermone, wch proueth that Danyell was made an instrumen^t^ to excuse others*], and ought to have been imposed upon the prisoner, on whom the Attorney-General prayed for some extraordinary and exemplary punishment [*my vniust desartes in seekyng to discou^r^ the truth, & meanyng to reveale the same to her ma^tie^ as afforesayd*]. The Court, considering the heinousness and falsity [*made falsetie in pollicie*] of his offences, sentenced Daniell to a fine of 3000*l.* and imprisonment in the Fleet Prison for life, [*wch I thinke to bee an vndeserued censure*]; and pitying the wrong and injury which the Countess had sustained, [*greater wronge done by her to mee*], cleared her from all suspicion of any ill intention towards the Earl [*the effecte of her actyons haue proued contrarie*]; and stated that they could testify of their own knowledge as to her true and honourable regard for him, [*but after hys death she dyd sho some unkyndnesses agaynst the Earle's chyldren*].'

[Indorsed] 'Cossyne Danyell, yf you can Contryue this Censure 1603–4 Jan. 26
bryflie, heare you shall fynd the Cause therof at large, But how the same may be aunswered sauflie I know not, and therefore I leave yt to yor good Consyderacion, For I neu^r^ Complayned of the Centence agaynst mee, yeat haue I Complayned aboue 100 tymes of such wronges and oppressyons as haue be Comytted agaynst me & myne synce I was Condempned, wch are as heavie to mee as treble the fyne, And soe referring the same to yor good endeavour, doe salute yow kyndlie. From my lodging neare Charing Crosse, thys xxvj^th^ of Januarie, 1603.

Yo^rs^ to hys vttermost,

JOHN DANYELL.'

Ibid., vol. 279, no. 126.

Examination at the Fleet Prison of Jane, wife of John 1601 Sept. 7
Daniell, esquire, of Hackney, aged 36 years, and of Mary Harper servant of John Daniell. These documents relate chiefly to the seizure and sale of the goods in the house at Hackney, and contain many interesting particulars. They are unfortunately too long to print here. Jane Daniell mentions among other things,

'the Countisse of Essex picture, one Stone Ringe for the spleene, an Eagle stone, and the picture of the depon$^{t's}$ brother in lawe ;' all these were valued at 3*l*.

Ibid., vol. 281, no. 77.

1600 July 31

1601 Oct. 3

'Be it knowen to all men by theis presentes That I, Peter Bales, of London, gent., have received divers letters from Mr John Daniell (when he was Prisoner in y^{e} Gate house) by the handes of his servant John Lewys : In some of wch letters he charged me as a Christian to manifest my dealing wth him in the late Earle of Essex letters : Therefore I will trulie discharge my conscience, as followeth ; First, Mr Daniell repaired to me about this busynes in the begyning of Lent 1599 : And after at severall other tymes he brought me 5 or 6 letters, directed from the said Earle to his Ladie : for reading & writing of wch letters, he came to me divers tymes within the space of three weekes : And because I coulde not reade those letters perfectlie, I endevoured first to conceive them myself : And after I taught Mr Daniell to reade those letters so well, that he dictated some of them as they were copied forth : wch copies I did not imitate so neare as I could, though he gave me xij *d.* for everie copie. For I ment rather to have charged a Constable wth hym, if I had found matter of treason in any letters : wch I something suspected, because there was conteyned in one of the letters, theis wordes, or the like in effect : *The Queen's commaundem^{t} may breake my neck, but my enemies at home shall neuer breake my harte.* W^{ch} letter was directed from the said Earle in Ireland to his Ladie in England : and dated in August before his coming thence. Then followed that I at Mr Daniell's request wrote that letter divers tymes ouer : By reason whereof, those wordes were sundrie tymes inserted into divers Copies : For it did conteyne some matter more then the rest of the letters he brought to me ; and was as hard to reade as any other : So that out of that letter, and the other letters, I wrote above a doozen Copies at seuerall tymes when he came to me : Nevertheles I did insert no words into any of my said Copies that could be preiudiciall to the Earle or his Countesse, other then such wordes as I found in his hono$^{r's}$ letters : Albeit the wordes before remembred, & some other matt^{r} in that letter, made me thinke there might be greater matter discovered : But fynding no wordes of importance in any [of] the other letters wch came to my handes, I desired Mr Daniell to shew why he caused me to write one letter so often over : To wch he aunswered at his last being wth me, that the Countesse of Essex had commaunded him to take that course, to the end he might the better gull somebodye: W^{ch} saying greatelye troubled me; for I could neither finde out the reason of those wordes, & his dealing with me as afore, nor yet the cause why he did not retourne to me afterward: So that being in this perplexitie, I was the rath^{r} persuaded by one Peter Feryman of London, gent., to repaire to the Countesse of Essex three severall tymes before shee would be satisfied touching these matters: And in the end, at her La: request, I yeelded to conteyne such thinges in a declaracion as was then required by ye Countisse & thought fitt for her purpose: W^{ch} Declaracion being agreed vpon by me, Mr Feryman & Mr Lyle, her La: Secretarie, wee all subscribed our names therevnto, in the begynning of Aprill, 1600: And when wee had perfected the same, they willed me to deliver that declaracion to ye Countesse of Essex: Who vpon the sight thereof promised me good recompence for that service, when her Lord was received into the Queene's favo^{r}: whereupon I delivered ye same Declaracion to her La: Hoping the said Earle would recouer his creditt, and then obteyne an office for me, touching her Ma^{ts} billes to be signed: wch was before promised & vndertaken by his servant, Mr Wiseman, to be performed by his hono^{rs} meanes: Yet notwthstanding I fayled thereof and of all oth^{r} recompence for my service, contrarie to my expectacion: So to conclude this my dealing in the premisses (for a testymonie of ye truthe) I have setto my Seale and subscribed my name: Besides I will be readie to iustifie all these thinges by oath if neede shall require: Dated the last day of Julye, 1600.

PETER BALES.'

Postscript:

'Calling bett^{r} to my remembrance; the said letter before recited began as followeth: *Franke, I send vnto you Cuffe, my man, whome you may belieue in what he saith:* And further in the end of the same letter, I remember his Lo: writt these wordes: viz: When yor bellye shalbe layd, I will prouide for yor being here, &c.'

Ibid., vol. 281, no. 34.

There is another copy of this letter, with some slight alterations, dated Oct. 3, 1601; This sentence in addition:— 1601 Oct. 3

'And lastly touching Mr Feryman, I must confesse that he laboured me from the begynning till the said Declaracion was finished, otherwise I had never entred into this matter wth the said Countesse, being fullie determined to haue revealed the

1601 Oct. 3 same to some of the privie Counsell: But I was perswaded by Mr Feryman to geve the Countesse satisfaccion as afore.'

Ibid., vol. 282, no. 3.

1601 Oct. 5 Inventory of the goods of John Daniel, in Hackney parsonage. Total value, including 400*l.* for the term of years and next presentation to Hackney parsonage, 510*l.* 12*s.* 2*d.*

Note that this inquisition was taken by an Exchequer commission, to seize the same to the Queen for a fine of 3000*l.*

Note that the said goods, &c., were sold to Ferdinando Richardson, Groom of the Privy Chamber, for 530*l.* 12*s.* 2*d.*, of which he paid 232*l.* 12*s.* 2*d.* at Michaelmas, 1601, and 98*l.* at Michaelmas, 1602, and 200*l.* is still due.

Some of the articles mentioned in the inventory are noteworthy:—

[In the Parlour] Itm one greate Booke Called a French Herballe, iij*s.* iiij*d.*; Itm one mappe of Ireland and an old Brushe, x*d.*; Itm a Chest bord with the men, xij*d.*; Itm one other little French booke called the contentmt of the spiritt, vj*d.*; Itm one Psalter and a Dutch booke, j*d.*; Itm one thrummed Cushion, xvj*d.*; [In the Mylke howse] Itm one vennice glasse, iiij*d.*; Itm one saltseller, a Mawdlyn Cuppe and a wyne Cup of pewter, xij*d.*; Itm 2 narrow mowthed glasses, ij*d.*; [In the Hall] Itm one Chaire covered wth Silke called Cavendish stuffe, and a highe stoole covered wth needleworke, xv*s.*; [In the Buttrye] one old standerd, v*s.*; three staues, vj*s.*; a lyttle old spinning wheele, vj*d.*; [In the groundes] 6 Chaldron or thraboutes of Coales called Seacoles, iiij*l.*; [In one Square White box] in goulde, vj*l.* 10*s.*; in silver, xj*s.* xj*d.*; one Carcanett wth xven buttons of gould and pearle, xxxvij*s.* vj*d.*; [In a blacke chest bound wth Iron] one Childes mantle of Crimson taffata garded wth velvett, and a gould and silke fringe, xl*s.*; [In a trunke in the Chambr called Mr Daniell's chamber] one nightcap wrought wth black silke and gould, and a purse imbrodered wth goulde, vj*s.* viij*d.*; one ould riding hood, xij*d.*; one shirte, iiij*s.*; one vellett Cappe, xij*d.*; one peice of Cloath rounded of a Cloake, ij*s.*; 5 fallinge bands, viij*s.*; one girdle, a paire of hangers of greene silke and gould, and a string of gould to hang his dagger on, xx*s.*; one Ruffe with purled lace, v*s.*; one Flannell wascote wrought wth red Cruell, ij*s.* vj*d.*; one dammaske Cloake wth Sleeves garded wth vellett, l*s.*; one paire of Fuger sattyn hose payned wth vellett, xxvj*s.* viij*d.*; one peice of blewe cloth, vj*s.* viij*d.*; twoe peices of Tawnye vellett, old, iijs. iiijd.; one greene quilted Cappe, xxd.; [In the same Chamber] 4 pictures, xs.; [In the studye] one hatt and one Munmouth Cappe, vs.; 2 Rapiers, xvjs. viijd.; one little Turkye Carpett, ls.; [In M[ris] Daniell's chamber] 2 Bibles, iiijs.; [In one other Chamber] twoe Muskettes and one Flaske, [*inter alia*]. The terme of yeares and next advowson [*sic*] of the parte of the parsonage of Hackney, w[ch] M[r] Danyelle hath in graunte from M[r] Georg Smithes, Citizen and gouldsmith of London, valued at iiij c *li.* *Ibid.*, vol. 282, no. 4.

Petition of Jane Daniell to the Council. The fine of 3000*l.* imposed upon my husband in the Star Chamber was agreed to be paid 1200*l.* the first year, and then 200*l.* yearly, whereupon the Lord Treasurer ordered our goods to be in safe guard, and divers evidences relating to Deresbury manor and Hackney and Minshull parsonages, and bonds for about 2000*l.* were to be delivered to the Attorney-General to frame a book thereon; but while this was preparing, the Sheriff and other officers have made prey of my husband's goods, valuing Hackney parsonage and the goods, worth 2000*l.*, at 700*l.*, to our loss of 1300*l.*, which would have satisfied both her Majesty and the Countess of Essex. On Dec. 10, the Attorney-General told my husband that the Queen had bestowed 2000*l.* of our fine on the Countess of Essex, who was content to accept 1000*l.* for the same, which her secretary and solicitor confirmed, and offered to procure my husband's pardon and release from prison. He in return offered her the yearly rent of all he has left, viz., Deresbury manor and Minshull parsonage, but she wants the 1000*l.* within the year, which we cannot pay. He then offered her 2000*l.* in debts, deducting 300*l.* to make the 1000*l.* for the Queen, and 200*l.* to redeem him from prison, and to store his domain with cattle; she accepted this, if the debtors would be transferred into her name; as there are more than 200 persons concerned in different places, there will be difficulty in it, yet it was offered to be done if her ladyship would bear the charge, but this she refused. I fear she will now urge my husband's corporal punishment, and procure a lease of Deresbury and Minshull to herself, whereby the whole family would be extinguished, and her Majesty hindered in her payments. I beg that we may be restored to our former ability, the Sheriff and his officers punished in the Star Chamber, and Deresbury and Minshull extended for the Queen. We will then perform the first agreement to the uttermost of our power. 1601 Dec. 13

Ibid., vol. 283, no. 20.

1601 Dec. 13 Jane Daniell to the Queen. Similar in effect to the preceding. 'All my husband's lands were extended, and all his goods for the most part sould for little or nothing; both contrary to the said L'res [of the Lord Treasurer] and agrement; whereby my husband is altogether disabled to performe the said agrement. And yet he is threatned to have his punishment, except he will paie as much nowe they have ymbeselled his goods, as when he had the goods in his owne handes; which is altogether vnreasonable and vnpossible, as may plainly appeare by their severall extents. Wherefore, and for that I am the daughter of one Ryhova, Governor of the Cittie of Gaunt, who most resisted the Spanish tyrannie in Flanders my native contrey, from whence I am exiled for that Faith which your Highnes defends: and nowe am vnder the wings of your highnes blessed harbor, where I cannot live nor contynue without your Ma^ts^ Protection. And forasmuch as I am dailie afflicted by the Countesse of Essex, whome I have served most faithfullie (as my Saviour is my witnesse), and yet because we are not able to paie her La^p^ 2000^li.^ of your Ma^ts^ said fine so speedelie as she would, therefore by her frends she hath not onely overthrowne the said agrement, to your Ma^ts^ great hyndraunce, and my vtter vndoing; but also found meanes to cause my poore Children to be turned out of the Personage of Hackney, and procured others to take the same over their heads, and so to leave them in danger of beggerie; vnlesse your Matie of your accustomed goodnes wilbe pleased in some sorte to raise vs vpp againe, by granting me and my foure small children (before a stranger) the said Personage and lands, with the rest of my goods, as they are valued and extended, together with my husband's free pardon. And he wilbe readie to doe your Highnes such good service as may be greatlie for your Ma^ts^ benefitt. And according to our bounden dueties, we shall dailie praie to God for your Ma^ts^ long and prosperous Raigne over vs.

Your Maiestie's most
distressed Subiect,
JANE DANYELL.'

Ibid., vol. 283, no. 21.

1602 Jan. Petition of Jane Daniell to the Queen. Although you promised an order about my husband's lands and parsonages, the Sheriffs and officers have embezzled and undervalued them and our goods. The corrupt prosecutors intend to ruin us, and to enjoy all our living for 40 years, whereas my husband would have paid the debt in 10. I entreat a grant of Deresbury and Minshull, and present relief for myself, husband and children.

Ibid., vol. 283 A, no. 22.

Lord Treasurer Buckhurst to Mr. Fanshawe. I have directed John Daniell, prisoner in the Fleet, to receive from the Attorney-General bonds value 200*l.*, for relief of himself and family; but without aid from the Court of Exchequer in attaching the persons indebted, the money cannot be recovered in time for his present wants. You are therefore to accept the bonds, and issue process thereon, that Daniell may be the sooner relieved, and that the Queen may recover something towards her fine due from him. [etc.] 1602 Aug. 20

Ibid., vol. 284, no. 104.

Petition of Jane Daniell to the Queen. In Trinity term, 43 Elizabeth, my husband was fined 3000*l.* in the Star Chamber, for which commissions were sent into Cheshire and Middlesex to seize his lands and goods. The Lord Treasurer then made an agreement with my husband as to the fine, and in accordance therewith I delivered to the Attorney-General bonds, etc., to the amount of 2000*l.* The manor of Deresbury and the parsonage of Minshull, my husband's inheritance, and the lease of the parsonage of Hackney, were also charged with the payment of the fine, which would have been paid in 3 years, or 10 years at the most. But now, though we have been deprived of all our property, the fine will not be paid for 36 years. Thomas Aston, esq., then Sheriff of Cheshire, seized my husband's goods, to the value of 414*l.*, and divided them between himself and his friends, and only put them down as worth 114*l.* The same thing was done with the said manor and parsonage; the goods at Hackney, worth 330*l.*, were only valued at 110*l.*, and the lease, worth 1000*l.*, was valued at 420*l.* The Lord Treasurer refuses to interfere. The Countess of Essex has all my husband's inheritance, and 'Mr. Ferdinadon Ritchastson' has the parsonage of Hackney far under value. My husband is thus disabled to perform the said agreement. I pray for your Majesty's aid and my husband's liberty. 1602 Sept.

Ibid., vol. 285, no. 22.

Petition of Jane, wife of John Daniell, to the King, for restoration of her children's lands, unjustly detained for payment of 2500*l.* the unpaid balance of a fine of 3000*l.* due from her 1604 Feb. 22

1604 Feb. 22 husband to the Crown. She prays that the fine may be pardoned, and that a commission may be directed to the Lord Chief Baron, Mr Justice Gawdie, Mr Baron Savile, Mr Justice Walmesley, Mr Justice Kingsmill and Mr Justice Warberton, or any two of them, to inquire into the whole matter. An order is indorsed referring the cause to the Court of Exchequer, which is thoroughly acquainted with it, 'for speedie Justice according to the merites of the cause;' the suppliant to be admitted to sue *in forma pauperis*.

State Papers, Domestic, James I., vol. 6, no. 76.

1604 Petition of Jane Daniell to the King. Her husband was persecuted in the Star Chamber by great persons, and imprisoned for non-payment of his fine. He obtained his liberty at the general pardon on the King's accession, but no allowance for support, though others received pardon for debts, as well as freedom. Their lands are detained for the fine, although they would have paid it, if allowed to retain them. She begs discharge from the fine, and restoration of their estates.

Ibid., vol. 11, no. 43.

1604 'A true declaratyon of the mysfortunes of Jane Danyell, wyffe of John Danyell of Derysburie in the Countie of Chester, Esquyre, and the onlie daughter of Francys Rethulle, Lord of Ryhove, who was Gouernour and High balyffe of the Cytties of Gaunte and Dendermond in Flanders, Coronell of 25 Companyes of footemen, and Captayne of 200 horse.'

A very lengthy and verbose document of 29 sheets of paper written on both sides, with a dedication to the Queen. The agreement already mentioned made by Daniell as to the payment of the fine, dated Aug. 7, 1601, is set out on p. 11. It is stated that the agreement was written by the Lord Treasurer in his great chamber at Salysburie Court, and signed by him and by Daniell in the presence of Sir John Fortescue and about 20 others. Signed 'Jane Danyell.'

Attached is a draft letter to Lord Cobham and Sir Walter Rawleigh, signed 'John Danyell,' but in the same handwriting as the preceding, charging them to declare the truth of the allegations made by the Countess of Essex respecting the dealings between them and Danyell as to the letters.

Ibid., vol 11, no, 44.

Grant to Richard, Earl of Clanricarde, and Lady Frances, his wife, of the remainder of a fine of 3000*l.* imposed on John Danyell of Dorsbury, co. Chester, for cozening the said Lady Frances, then Countess of Essex; and also of the benefit of an extent made on his lands. 1607 Sept. 25

State Papers, Docquet.

Petition of John Daniel to Lord Chief Baron Tanfield. The petitioner, having been censured in the Star Chamber and fined 3000*l.* and had all his estates (worth 500 marks a year) taken, was allowed by the King's favour to sue for his debts *in forma pauperis*. He sued Hamnett Grigge accordingly on a bond for 40*l.*, but he resisted payment, and obtained an injunction in the Court of Exchequer staying the proceedings in the Court of Common Pleas. The petitioner begs that the Commission to examine witnesses may be executed at Hackney or Westminster and not in Cheshire, as he is very weak and not able to travel. His wife, Jane, made affidavit, June 20, 1608, that her husband 'is at this present soe weake and sicklie that he is not able to travell into Chesshire w[th]out greate daunger of his liefe.' The petition was granted by order dated June 22. 1608 June

Ibid., Addenda, vol. 39, no. 56.

Statement by Peter Bales that he had been urged by John Danyell to tell the truth about the Earl of Essex's letters, which was that in 1599 Danyell brought him some letters from the Earl to the Countess, which they read together, and of which several copies were made. Bales thought there was some mystery in the letters, and determined to reveal them to the Council, but was persuaded to give them up to the Countess of Essex. 1608 Aug. 16

Ibid., vol. 36, no. 18.

Petition of John Danyell to Lord Salisbury. Has been turned out of his estates in spite of his willingness to pay his fine; the fine is given by the King to the Earl of Clanricarde; and certain bonds due to the petitioner are detained in the Exchequer; solicits the return of the whole or some part of them, for the relief of his family. 1608 Sept. ?

[Note by Salisbury.]

'Let the petitioner be ready with his counsell to move this matter in full Court the first day of the Terme; for I will alter no orders in my chamber.'

Ibid., vol. 36, no. 19.

1608 Sept. ? Petition of Robert Thickpenny, servant of the Earl of Clanricarde, to Lord Salisbury. Asks for a confirmation of the order that the bonds given into the Exchequer by Danyell shall be kept in Court until the fine is discharged.

Ibid., vol. 36, no. 20.

1610 Jan. 28 Petition of John Danyell to Sir Lawrence Tanfield, Chief Baron of the Exchequer. For permission to enter a suit in the Exchequer against the Earl and Countess of Clanricarde, for wrong done him in the matter of the Star Chamber fine; or else to continue the suit he has already commenced there, to which they endeavour to put a stop.

[Note by the Chief Baron.]

'28 Jan. 1609 [10], Lett the Court be moved & this petyconer shall haue Justice.'

Ibid., vol. 52, no. 30.

1610 Jan. ? Petition of John Danyell to the King. Appeals to His Majesty as standing in the place of God upon earth, to protect him from the oppressions described by himself and his wife, in some discourses which he begs permission to publish. Complains of the unjust proceedings of certain great persons against himself and his wife, through which he was fined 3000*l.* in the Star Chamber, and deprived of all he had in the world, on pretence of levying the fine.

Ibid., vol. 52, no. 31.

1610 Jan. ? License to John and Jane Danyell to print and publish the works entitled, *Danyell's Disasters*, *The Varyable accidents in a pryvatt man's lyffe*, and *A Declaracion of the fatall Accydents of Jane Danyell.*

Ibid., vol. 52, no. 33.

1610 Jan. ? *Danyell's Disasters*, being an account of the proceedings in Chancery in reference to the payment of his fine, etc. 8 pages.

Ibid., vol. 52, no. 34.

1610 Jan. ? *The varyable accedents of a pryuat man's lyffe*, being an account of 'The vnexpected Calamytys dyscouered in the tyme of my meserable trobles, Hapnyng in the lyffe of me John Danyell of Deresbury in the Countie of Chester, Esquyre.' 32 pages; incomplete.

Ibid., no. 35.

Copy of a Bill in the Court of Exchequer by John Danyell 1610 Feb. 8
'Tuttlestrete,' Westminster, *in forma pauperis*, against the Earl and Countess of Clanricarde. He sets out all the facts of the case at great length; his wife he calls 'Jane Ryhova;' he mentions his wife's 'laboure and skill in making of Tyres and other necessarie ornamentes and thinges as her Hono^{r} [the Countess of Essex] did vsually weare vpon her heade and other partes of her bodie, and wch were then esteemed by very honorable and greate Ladies of England to be verie rare invencions, and wch deserved a very good reward, for by her like ymployment since that tyme, the said Jane hathe gotten, by the like laboure of her handes, aboue a hundred poundes yearelie;' he says that the Earl and Countess of Essex persuaded him to marry Jane by promises of reward and advancement in Queen Elizabeth's service, 'althoughe he might then haue had farr greater and more valuable mariages in diuerse places'; he defends his action as to the letters on the grounds of fear for his own safety and zeal for the Queen; he took the letters to Bales because they were written 'in suche a ragged Romane hande as yor orator coulde not reade'; he complains that certain officers of the Earl of Clanricarde have 'spreade abrode diuerse vntrewe rumors' to the effect 'that yor orato^{r} sholde haue betraied the said Earle of Essex, and that yor orato^{r} was an arrante Thefe, and one that brake a slaunder of the said Earle, and stole a Baskett of the said Countesse wth Jewelles of greate worthe,' 'and coosoned the said Countesse of her letters, and deliuered her counterfett letters insteede of her trewe letters, and thereby wrought the said Earle's confusion'; he says that he was 'soe farre from hurtinge the said Earle, as that he neuer procured his little Fynger to ake'; he prays for a *subpoena* to Richard, Earl of Clanricarde, and Frances, his wife. The result does not appear.

Ibid., no. 56.

Peter Bales was at one time tutor to Prince Henry. In 1590 he published *The Writing Schoolemaster*, for teaching 'Swift writing, true writing, faire writing'; the volume was dedicated to his 'singular good lord and master,' Sir Christopher Hatton. He was alive in 1610, but the date of his death is not known. See *Dict. of Nat. Biog.*

See also Camden's *Annales*, ii. 640; *The Egerton Papers*, Camden Soc., 321, 357, 358.

APPENDIX VI

Robert Pye

PAGE 129

THE statement that Pye's father was a butcher seems to be a mistake. According to the printed list, *Students admitted to the Inner Temple*, 1547–1660; he was the second son of William Pye of Meend [or Mynde] Park, co. Hereford. He entered at the Inner Temple, 1584; was called to the Bar, 1595; Auditor of the Exchequer under James I. and Charles I. Knighted at Theobalds, July 13, 1622. Purchased Faringdon House, co. Berks, 1622, which he defended for the King against the Parliamentary forces, 1645–6. See Lyson's *Magna Britannia*, I, 277.

He was M.P. for Bath, 1620–1 and 1623–4; Ludgershall, co. Wilts, 1625; Westminster, 1625–6; Grampound, co. Cornwall, 1627–8; Woodstock, 1640; Berkshire, 1654 and 1658–9. He died in 1662.

Sir Robert is said in C. J. Robinson's *The Mansions of Herefordshire*, 1872, p. 86, to have been a son of Roger Pye, and to have been baptised in 1584.

'Contemporary gossip called him [Sir Walter Pye, Sir Robert's son] the grandson of a Southwark butcher, but there is no foundation for the story.' *The Castles of Herefordshire*, C. J. Robinson, 1869.

APPENDIX VII

PAGES 143, 168, 176, 182, 222, 316, 328, 373

FINES, TAXAT' IN CUR' CAMER' STELLAT' TERMINIS SEQUEN', VIZ^{t},

Termino Trin' Anno 44 Eliz. R^{ne}

Attorn' R' plt^{e} for falselie sclaunderinge the Ll^{s} of the Counsell	Anthonye Atkinson	XM m'kes	C^{li}
	Michaell Cawlye	XM m'kes	C^{li}
	William Elson	XM m'kes	C^{li}
	Gilberte Wilkinson	XM m'kes	C^{li}

Termino Mich'is Anno 2do Jacobi Regis

Attorn' R' plt^{e} contempt & misdemean^{rs}	Joh'es Hele miles seruiens ad legem . .	M^{li}	
Attorn' R' plt^{e} Sclaunder against his ma^{tie} magistrates & Justice	Willm^{s} Forthe gen'	M^{li}	C^{li}
Attorn' R' plt^{e} Sclaunderinge the Justices of assize	Thomas Pounde gen'	M^{li}	C^{li}

	Termino Pasche Anno sexto Ja. R'		
Attorn' R' pl^{te} for most infamous libellinge	Lewis Pickeringe, gen'	M^{li}	
	Termino Hillar' Anno 4 Ja. R'		
Attorn' R' pl^{te} for the barberous vsage of Joell Kyne	John Younge, Clarke	M^{li}	C^{li}
	Termino Mich'is Anno 5 Ja. R'		
Attorn' R' pl^{te} for contemptuous buildinge	Richarde Louche	CC^{li}	X^{li}
	Termino Pasch' Anno sexto Ja. R'		
Gage pl^{te} for riottous breakinge into an Inclosure	Michael Pickeringe, gen'	VC^{li}	XXX^{li}
	Henrie Selbye	VC m'kes	XX^{li}
	Richarde Perrott	C m'kes	V^{li} a peece
	Silvester Malbie	C m'kes	
	Thomas Brokesbie	C m'kes	
	John Eykins	C m'kes	
	Rob^{te} Eykins	C m'kes	
	Richarde Selbie	C m'kes	
	Henrye Clarke	C m'kes	

Termino Mich'is Anno sexto Ja. R'

Taylor & al. pl^{tes} for publishinge a libell in Gloucester	Edwarde Machynn, gen.	VC^{li}	Respectuantur
	Laurence Brewster, gen.	VC^{li}	
	James Cowarne	L^{li}	
	Morrice Atwoode	L^{li}	
	Pauncefoot Pell	L^{li}	
	John Tullye	L^{li}	
	Thomas Shewringe	L^{li}	
	Henrye Boll	L^{li}	
	Willm Chamberlyn	L^{li}	
For not bringinge in the boddye of one Hellier	The Sheriffe of Cornewall	X^{li}	

Termino Hillar' Anno 6 Ja. R'

pro falso clam'	John Charmon	XX^{li}	
Giib^{te} Wakeringe, k^{t}, pl^{te} Riottes & misdemeano^{rs}	Willm Clare	L^{li}	XXX^{li}
	Richard Hawkes	XX^{li}	X^{li} a peece
	Thomas Tayllor	XX^{li}	
	Frauncis Taylor	XX^{li}	
	John Chorme	XX^{li}	
	Thomas Chorme	XX^{li}	
	John Hamson	XX^{li}	

Littleton, kt, & al', pltes Riott & mainteyn'nce	Sr Gilbte Wakeringe, kt	Cli & VC m'kes	CC m'kes
	John Wakeringe senr, gen.	C m'kes	Xli
	Willm Ager	Lli	Vli
	Willm Smithe	XXli	XLs apeece
	John Walker	XXli	
	James Wilkenson	XXli	
	Richard Hayes	XXli	
	Richard Stone	XXli	
	Raphe Harrison	XXli	
Attorn' R' plte Riott and other misdemeanors	Sr Edward Littleton, kt	CCCli	Cli
	Sr Walter Leveson, kt	M m'kes	CCli
	Roger Fowke, esqr	M m'kes	VC m'kes
	Willm Comberford, esqr	CCCli	Cli
	Willm Smithe	Cli	
	Richarde Drakeford	XLli	XX m'kes apeece
	John Barnesley	XLli	
	John Wossall	XLli	
	John Firchilde	XLli	Vli

State Papers, Domestic, James I. vol. 43, no. 33 d.

The sums in the first column are the amounts of the fines as fixed by the Court; those in the second column the amounts at which the fines were taxed or ultimately adjusted.

APPENDIX VIII

Plymouth Water Works

Page 144

'Right hono^{bl}' : our duetyes humbly remembred. As we haue allwayes heertofore founde yor honorable fauour in any our affayres, so we now humbly craue the contynuance of the same in this our present occasyons : we procured from her ma^{ty} by acte of parliamente, in the 27th yeere of her happie raigne, some parte of the Riuer of Meuy to be brought to our towne, which cost vs and Sr Frauncis Drake, (who vpon Composicion with vs vndertooke the bringeinge home of the same), a greate some of money ; we haue compounded, and p^{r}chased of the owners the lande ouer which the same runneth. And so haue held & enioyde the same euer since, vntill now of late that Willyam Gryms, esquier, and some of his Complices, seekeing our disherison, and the keepeinge away of the same water from vs, hath lately erected certaine classe milles and Tann pittes, where were neuer any before, And hath and doth rioutously and vnlawfully diuerte and torne out a greate parte of our said Riuer to his said milles and Tanpitts, for which we haue suets dependinge in the starre chamber before yor hono^{r} and the rest of her ma^{ts} most hono^{bl} privy counsell ; where the said Grymes founde such fauo^{r} the last terme vpon his motion, as the same matter was referred by their hono^{rs} to the three cheefe Justices and the two Justices of Assises of this Circuit ; and conceavinge his doeinge and proceedinge were against law and Justice, And findeinge the said Justices inclyninge to certify so much vnto that hono^{bl} Courte, He procured Sr John Gilberte, knighte, Tristram Georges and Henry Coplestone, esquires, to sett downe an order vnder their hands, that the said Mr Grymes and his heires shall diuerte and haue some parte of our said ryuer to serue his said milles, payeinge vs. xijd. by the yeere, which will tende to o^{r} vtter disinherisoun, and the ouerthrow of our wholl towne ; For if the said Crymes [*sic*] be permitted to tourne out and take any parte

1601 Sept. 14

of our said water, Others ouer whose lande the same ryuer is convaide will do the like, and so we shall haue none to come to our Towne, as by a particular of our greevances (wherewith this bearer will acquaynt yo[r] hono[r]) may appeare, wherein we most humbly crave yo[r] hono[bl] favour; And so, with our humble duetyes, and harty prayers for your hono[r]s longe preseruacion, humbly take our Leaue.

Plymouthe, the xiiij[th] of this instant September, 1601.

Yo[r] hono[r]s at
Commandemente,

Thomas Payne, mayor,
and his bretheren.'

[addressed] 'To the Right Hono[bl] S[r] Robert Cycill, knight, principall Secretary of our Soueraign Lady the Queene.'

State Papers, Domestic, Elizabeth, vol. 281, no. 84.

APPENDIX IX

Serjeant Yelverton's case

PAGE 150

'MATTERS wherein the L. Presydent of her Ma[tie's] Counsell in the Northe findeth himselfe grieued with M[r] Sergeant Yeluerton, one of the Justyces of the Assise in those North partes to the dyscountenance of him & the Authority of that Counsell established by her Ma[tie]. 1602 Feb. ?

First, Whereas the L. President and that Counsell haue a Commyssion of Oyer and Termyner contynewally to be executed, as occasion serueth, wherein the Justices of Assyze are & by w[ch] they haue vsed to sitt at the Assize tyme at Yorke, And therefore when the Charge is to begynne, being commonly vppon Wednesday in the Forenoone that Weeke, The Lo: President (or in his absence, the Vicepresident) and Counsell attendant do alwaies resorte to the Castle, & sitt with the Judges, duringe the tyme the charge is giuen, And that they sitt vppon the Gaole, where and in all other Assemblyes the L. President's place is the Cheife, & at the Assizes to sitt betwixt the two Judges, And the Vicepresident by her Ma[tie's] Instruccions is in his absence to haue, and hath alwaies had, the reuerence & place dewe to the L. President: Yet in Sommer Assyzes last was Twelumoneth, the L. Eure then Vicepresident beinge sett next vnto Baron Sauylle, M[r] Sergeant Yeluerton Comminge from the Nisi-prius at the other end of the Hall, thrust aboue him, & satt next vnto Baron Sauylle, and so put downe the Vicepresident, w[ch] was much noted by the countrey, the rather because the Moonday before at the Mynster Sermon, he tooke the vpper place also of the Vice-president.

Item, in farther disgrace of the L. President, Whereas he and the Counsell haue vsed to sitt with the Judges vppon the Gaole by the generall commyssions aforesaid: In Sommer Assyzes last, the L. President sittinge in his vsuall place with them at the charge, M[r] Sergeant Yeluerton cawsed there spetial Commyssion of Goale Delivery to be read, Wherein Watkinson, Somerskales,

& certaine other meane clerkes are ioyned and not the L. President and Counsell, And afterwards before they did ryse Cawsed the Statute of 20 R. 2, ca. 3, to be read likewyse publickly, whereby all Barons and others are forbidden to sitt with the Justyces in their Assyze, wch was taken to be a disgrace to the L. President beinge there, &c. Who came not to sitt but only at the tyme of the Charge and Gaole in hande, and was the more noted to be done for the L. President's disgrace, because he read it not in any other place in his Cyrcuyte, but in that place only.

The L. President therefore desireth, That it may be ordered that the Justyces of Assyze, L. Presydent and Counsell, may sitt by the vsuall Commyssion of Oyer and Terminer, as hath bene heretofore accustomed, whereby the Authority beinge conioyned may be stronger, and not by their disioyninge themselves from vs, the Authority of the L. Presydent & Counsell to be disgraced, wch is established to gouerne the countrey all the yeare after.

Item, Whereas the vsuall tyme of the Assyzes in Lent at Yorke hath heretofore bene the first Monday in the third Weeke of Lent, Mr Sergeant Yeluerton in respect of his priuate gayne in the Cyrcuyte, wherein he goeth as a Practyser, hath twyse synce he serued there, put of the Assyzes vntill the last Weeke of Lent, so as they haue ended eyther on Good Frydaie or Easter Eve, to the great trouble of the Justyces of Peace & Countrey, and the evill example and scandall thereof; so as they haue bene forced to travell to their home vppon Easter daye.'

[Indorsed] 'L. Presidente of Yorke's Articles agaynst Seriant Yelverton.'

State Papers, Domestic, Elizabeth, vol. 283 A, no. 42.

In February, 1602, the Council commissioned the Archbishop of York, with the assistance of Sir Thomas Fairfax, Sir Edward Stanhope, and Thomas Hesketh, Attorney of the [Court of] Wards, or any two of them, to inquire into the matter, and to report 'what place the vicepresidents haue held in former tymes'; 'Her Ma^ts^ pleasure is that there shalbe a lookinge backe for xxv or xxx^ty^ yeares into the Carryadge of that matter, And as you shall perceaue that most of the vicepresidents in this processe of tyme haue vsed it, so to advertise vs, to the intent that vppon such certificate all Partyes may be dyrected to conforme themselfes.'

Ibid. no. 43.

'Proofe, that as the Lo: Presid^{t} hath, so likewise the Vicepresid^{t} when there is any, in ye assize weeke is to haue the precedencie of ye Judge and to haue the cheefe place likewise when they sitt vpon the gaole deliuerye, & that he & her Ma^{ts} Counsell do sitt wth them as Commissioners for ye same gaole deliuerye. 1602 April 22

* * * *

'That the Lo: Presidente hath had that precedencie at ye assizes himself allwaies when he hath bene at ye assizes, appereth by the recordes of ye assizes so many as be extante now in ye Clarke of ye assizes handes, from 4° Eliz. Regine till this daie, namely in ye precedentships of the Earle of Rutlande, Archbishop Yonge, Earle of Sussex, Earle of Huntingdon, & my Lo: Burgheley.

* * * *

'How ye vsage hath bene aswel for precedencie as ye seruice at the gaole deliuerye for thes 30 yere, being the time limitted by there Lo^{ps}' l'res to be enquired of.

'It was never in question but y^{t} the Lo: Presid^{t} allwaies had ye place of ye Judges in all places when he was presente at ye assizes.'

* * * *

[Indorsed] '22 April, 1602. Concerninge the precedencie of ye Vicepresid^{t} at Yorke & ye vsage of ye Commission of gaole-deliuerye.'

Ibid., vol. 283 A, no. 82.

APPENDIX X

The Punishment for Forgery

PAGE 156

THE punishment for forgery under the Statute 5 Eliz., cap 14, was as follows:—

He 'shall pay unto the Party grieved his double Costs and Damages . . . and also shall be set upon the Pillory in some open Market Town . . . and there to have both his Ears cut off, and also his Nostrils to be slit and cut, and seared with a hot Iron, so as they may remain for a perpetual Note or Mark of his Falshood, and shall forfeit to the Queen our Sovereign Lady, her Heirs and Successors, the whole Issues and Profits of his Lands and Tenements during his Life, and also shall suffer and have perpetual Imprisonment during his Life.' Section II.

APPENDIX XI

Queen Elizabeth's death, etc.

PAGES 164, 177

John Chamberlain to Dudley Carleton. 1603

'I make no question but you haue heard of our great losse March 30
before this come at you; and no doubt but you shall heare her ma$^{tie's}$ sicknes and manner of death diversly related: for euen here the papists do tell strange stories, as vtterly voyde of truth, as of all ciuill honestie or humanitie. I had goode meanes to vnderstande how the world went, and find her disease to be nothing but a settled and vnremouable melancholie, insomuch that she could not be won or perswaded neither by the counsaile, Diuines, phisitians, nor the women about her, once to tast or touch any phisicke: though ten or twelve phisitians that were continually about her did assure here wth all manner of asseuerations of perfect and easie recouerie yf she wold follow theyre aduise. So that yt cannot be saide of her as yt was of the Emperor Adrian that *turba medicorum occidit regem*, for they say she died only for lacke of phisicke. here was some whispering that her braine was somewhat distempered, but there was no such matter, only she held an obstinate silence for the most part, and because she had a perswasion that yf she once lay downe she shold neuer rise, could not be gotten to bed in a whole weeke till three dayes before her death; so that after three weekes languishing she departed the 24 of this present being our Ladie's eue between two and three in the morning, as she was borne on our Ladie's eue in September:[1] and as one Lee was Maior of London when she came to her crowne, so is there one Lee Maior now that she left yt. the archbishop of Caunterburie, the bishop of London, the Almoner, and other her Chaplaines and Diuines, had accesse to her in her sicknes diuers times, to whom she gaue goode testimonie of her faith by word, but specially towards her end by signes when she was speachles, and

[1] The Nativity, Sep. 8.

wold not suffer the archbishop to depart as long as she had sence, but held him twise or thrise when he was going and could no longer indure both by reason of his owne weakenes and compassion of hers. She made no will nor gaue any thinge away, so that they wch come after shall finde a well stored iewell house and a rich wardrobe of more then 2,000 gownes wth al thinges els aunswerable . . . . Surely the counsaile haue dealt very prouidently and beyond that was to be expected or hoped for in so sodain an accident: and no doubt but God did direct them, seing all things past so quietly and in good order. during the Quenes sicknes some principall papists were made sure, and some daungerous companions clapt vp, among whom Sr Edmund Bainham was committed to the marshalsea for some desperat speaches (they say) against the Kinge: but yt shold seeme there was no great matter, for I heare he is now at libertie again . . . . the counsaile went on Satterday to Richmond and that night late brought the corps wth an honourable attendaunce to whitehall, where the houshold remaines: the body was not opened, but wrapt vp in seare-clothes and other preseruatiues . . . .'

State Papers, Domestic, James I., vol. 1, no. 6.

1603 April 12

John Chamberlain to Dudley Carleton.

'The Quene's funerall is appointed the 28th of this present, wth as much solemnitie as hath ben vsed to any former prince, and that by the king's owne direction: yt shalbe kept at Westminister, and the Lady Arbella is to be cheife mourner, accompanied wth 2 marquisses, 16 countesses and 30 barronesses, wth all theyre traine; besides the greatest part of the nobilitie, all the counsaile and officers of houshold.'

Ibid., vol. 1, no. 21.

'The Death of Queene Elizabeth
wth her declaracion of her successor.

'About the Friday sevenight after Christemas last being about the 14 [of January] in the 45 yeare of her Raigne, the late Queene about 2 dayes before [sickened of a cold] (being euer forwarned by m^r^ Doctor Dee to beware of whitehall) and the [said 14th day] remoued to Richemonde. But a litle before her going, euen the same morn[ing the] Earle of Nottingham, High Admyrall of England, Coming to her partly to sp[eek with] her as Concerning her

Removall, and partlie touching other matters wherein her pleasure and direction was to be knowne, they fell in to some speeche of the Successyon, and then she told him that her seate had ben euer the throne of kinges, and non but her next heire of bloud and dissent should succeede her: after falling into other matters they left that speeche, and she departed to Richemonde, where she was well amended of the Cold: But on Monday the 28 of February she begane to sicken againe, and so Continved tyll monday the 7th of march, at wch tyme notice was given to the Lordes of the Counsell that she was sicke of a Cold, and so she Continved sicke till Tusday the 15th of marche folowing, after wch day she begane somwhat to amende, but the 18 of marche following being friday shee begane to be very ill, wherevpon the lordes of the Counsell were sent for to Richemonde and there contynued till wednesday the 24th of March about 3 of Clocke in the morning (being our lady Even) at wch tyme shee died, but on the Tusday before her Death, being the 23 of March, the Lord Admirall being on the Right side of her bed, the Lord keeper at the left and Mr Secretary Cecill (after Earle of Salesbury) at the bedes feete, all standing, the Lord Admyrall put her in Minde of her speech concerning the succession had at whithall, and that they in the Name of all the Rest of her Counsell Came vnto her to know her pleasure who should succeed: wherevnto she thus replied, "I tould you my seat had bene the seate of kynges and I will have Noe Rascalle to succeed me: And who should succeed me but a king." The lordes not vnderstanding this darke speech, and looking the one on the other, at length mr Secretary bouldly asked her what she ment by these wordes, "that No Rascall should succeed her"; wherevnto she Replyed, that her Meaning was that a kinge should succeed her, "and who," quoth she, "should that be but our Cosen of Scotland;" They asked her whether that were her absolut resolucion: wherevnto she answered, "I pray you trouble mee no more, Ile have none but him:" wth wch answer they departed. Nothwthstanding after againe about 4 a Clocke in the after noone the next day being wednesday (after he Archbishope of Canterbury and other Devines had bene wth her, and left her in a Manner speechelese) The 3 lordes aforesd repaired vnto her againe asking her if she remained in her former Resolucion, and who should succeed her; but shee, not being able to speake, was asked by Mr Secretary in this soarte, "wee beseeche yor matie, if you remayne in yor formore resolucion, and that you would have the king of Scottes to succeed you in yor kingedome, shew some signe vnto vs": whereat soddenly heaving her selfe vpwardes in her bed and pulling her Armes out of bed she held bothe her handes ioyntlie toguether ouer her head in Manner of a Crowne: whereby as they guessed she signefyed that she did not only wishe him the kingdom but desired the Conynuance of his estat: After w[ch] they departed: And the next morning (as is aforesayd) she Dyed: Imediately after her Death all the lordes, aswell of the Counsell as other Noblemen that were at the Courte, came from Richemond to Whithall by 6 a Clocke in the Morninge, wher other Noblemen that were in London mett them. But as they begane to sitt in Counsell in the privie Chamber at Whithall the Lord keeper (S[r] Thomas Egerton), and the Reste of the Counsell that were no Barones, offered to sitt at the Lower ende of the Counsell table, and not aboue any of the meanest nobillitie, but the noblemen in respecte of theire formor Authoritie called them to the hier ende of the table and wished them to keepe their places, wherevnto the Lord keeper made answer (viz) "if it be yo[r] Lordshippes' pleasures we will doe so, but that is more of yo[r] Curtezie then wee can demaund of Dutie," and soe they sate Doune everie Man according to his Degree, in Counsell touchinge the Successyon, where after some speeche had of Divers Competitores and matters of state, at length the Lord Admyrall Rehersed all the afforesaid premyzes w[ch] the late Queene had spoken to him, and to the Lord Keeper & M[r] Secretary, wth the manner thereof, w[ch] they being asked did afferme to be true vpon theire Honors.'

Ibid., vol. 86, no. 150.

This account is printed in Lord Somers' *Tracts*, i. 246. It may be compared with that given by Sir Robert Carey in his *Memoirs*.

1603 April 12 John Chamberlain to Dudley Carleton.

'We haue no certaintie where the kinge is, they that come last say he appointed to be at Berwick the seuenth of this moneth, and thincke he is now on the way to York, where he will make no long stay, but comes to worsop, a house of the Earle of Shrewsburie's, so to Beuer Castle, thence to Burghly, then to Oliuer Cromwell's by Huntington, to S[r] Thomas Sadler's in Hartfordshire, to Hartford Castle, to Tiballs, to the Charterhouse or Howard house, and so to the towre till his coronation.'

Ibid., vol. 1, no. 21.

APPENDIX XII

Serjeant Hele's Case

PAGE 168

Serjeant Hele to Secretary Cecil. 1603 Oct. 13

'My L. Cobham owes me 4,666$^{li.}$ 13^{s} 4^{d} or thereaboute as hit shall appeare to yor Lo^{p} vnder his hand and seale the 17th of Maye laste. yor ho: hath hard howe this moneye was drawne from me, and what wronge I have receaved. god forgive hym, he is not able to right me . . . . . It is true that I have caused muche of my Lo. Cobham's land in course of Justice and somme of his goodes in Kent att my verye greate chardge to be extended and deliuered to me, the riche and beste thinges being before conveyed awaye. This that I have done was in myne absence by this bearer my Servaunte according to the lawe and wthout anye indirect course or meanes. I humblie beseeche yor Ho: (the case standing as yt dothe) that I maye have yor Ho: favo^{r} and proteccion. I thinke all men woulde have taken the same Course that I have donne, to take the helpe of the lawe, rather then to expect favo^{r} by secondarye meanes.'

State Papers, Domestic, James I., vol. 4, no. 16.

A document headed 'Seriant Hele's extent in the countie of Kent,' showing that he had valued the lands of Lord Cobham and George Brooke at £683 16*s.* 4*d.* *per annum* which were worth £2314 12*s.* 0*d.* *per annum*; the goods at Cobham hall, the leases and coppices, he had valued at £790, which were worth £3926 0*s.* 8*d.* Among the goods were 'tapistrie hanginges' valued at £165, but worth £633 4*s.* 8*d.*

Ibid., vol. 10, no. 85.

'Lo. Cobham's debts payd by the King.

To Sr John Heale, Knighte, for money due to him vpon Judgmentes & extents vpon the Lands of the Late Lo. Cobham, 3,500$^{li.}$'

Ibid., vol. 12, no. 77.

APPENDIX XIII

Sir Robert Dudley's case

PAGES 169, 186, 198, 204, 205, 209

1580-1 March 13 IN his palace or house, commonly called Leicester Howse, near Temple Barre, in the presence of me, Edward Barker, notary public, and of the witnesses named below, there personally appeared Robert Dudlei, Earl of Leicester, and Lady Leticia, Countess of Essex, and said they, fearing (as they asserted) on the one hand that by the untimely public discovery of the truth, they might be subjected to the royal indignation and other inconveniences, and on the other hand, that by the superstitious suppression of [the evidence] they might go under the suspicion of cohabitation, and their children, if by the blessing of God they should haue any, might by succeeding heirs be questioned as to their status and legitimacy, desired that the marriage formerly solemnised between them should be made known to the world; and they swore on the Holy Gospels that they, being then free from any matrimonial contract, were on September 21, 1578, married according to the rites of the English Church by Humfrey Tindall, Clerk in Holy Orders; and in proof of the same, they requested me, as a notary public, to take the depositions of Ambrose Dudley, Earl of Warwick, Roger Northe, Baron of Kirtlinge and Francis Knowelles, knight, and also the said Humfrey Tindall and others: in order to perpetuate their testimony as the marriage was clandestine.

'Ambrose Dudley, Earl of Warwick, aged 48, saith :—

'That he, beinge Brother to the Erle of Leicester and very familier wth him and his affaires, was by him made acquainted wth the good Loue and likeinge grounded betweene him and the Countesse of Essex, and lastlie how he was resolved to make her his wief, whervppon this Deponent for the dispatch therof at the Request of his said Brother vppon a Satterdaie (as he now remembreth) Came to Wansted Howse (her Ma^{ty} then lyinge, so far as he likewise remembreth, at one Stoner's in Waltham Forrest, in wch howse (as he sayth) and in a litle Gallery therof, the next Morninge followinge (beinge, as he nowe remembreth, the xxjth daie of September in Anno Dni 1578) his said brother and the said Countesse of Essex were Marryed together, after the order of the booke of Comon prayers, by one Mr Tindall, a servaunt and chaplein to his brother Leicester, in such like Manner and forme as other folkes are accustomed to be Marryed, Att wch tyme he well remembreth Sr Frauncis Knowlles, Father vnto the Countesse, did giue her for wief vnto the aforenamed Erle of Leicester, in the sight and presence of this Deponent, The Erle of Pembrooke, The Lord North, Sr Frauncis Knolles, Mr Tindall and Mr Richard Knowlles, all wch were prsent and saw the said mariage solemized as he hath Deposed.'

Roger North, Baron of Kertlinge, and the other witnesses deposed to the same effect.

State Papers, Domestic, Elizabeth, vol. 148, no. 24.

Sir Robert Dudley to the Earl of Northampton. 1607 April 29

'The Ambassadors to his Ma. at Venice sent hether to mee a privye Seale, wch beinge a writinge of Record and the Labell of Superscription derogating from my due pretences and right wch I clayme, being lawfull sonne and heire to my father, I durst not open as consenting to, so to receave the same privie Seale, least in so doing it might bee preiudiciall to my right and tytle to the premisses . . . . What are the Treasones manifested against mee . . . . That abroad I take vppon me the Tytles of my pretences. To wch I aunswere I maye better doe it abroad, being my undowbted right thoughe questioned by his Ma :, then the Lord of Westmerland, the Lord Beauchampe, and the Lord Mounteagle did before he hadd the graunt from the King, and did it and doe it at home daylie not only by the examples of this tyme but all other. But I may saye I have more reasone to doe it here in all Catholique partes then they, bycause I have not only made my full proofe thereof in England, and past the assaye of the Starchamber, and have the same examinacions as Evidence to defend my right, as no other nobleman hath more but these to defend them; But also publique storries doe give sufficient testymonie to all the Catholique partes of the world by these lawes to account mee lawfull sonne and heire to my father, and so consequently Earle of Warwicke and Leicester. Yf I hadd made no other proofe but that, it were sufficient, and no more excepted at here then that my Lord of Arrundelle's younger sonne is called Count Arrundell over Germanie . . . . Ligornia [Leghorn], April 29, 1607.

WARWICK & L:'

State Papers, Domestic, James I., vol. 27, no. 12.

1614 July 15 Writing from Florence, Sir Robert says that he has no wish to return to England, as he has received too many discourtesies from his friends and kindred.

Ibid., vol. 77, no. 65.

See also Nicholas' *Barony of Lisle*, Dugdale's *Baronage*, Burke's *Extinct Peerage*, *Dict. of Nat. Biog.*

The two following examples of Sir Robert Dudley's signature as Earl of Warwick and Leicester are from the State Papers (Domestic, James I., vol. 71, no. 35, and vol. 77, no. 65), and are dated 1612 and 1614 respectively.

APPENDIX XIV

Thomas Pounde's case

PAGE 182

THOMAS POUNDE of Belmont near Winchester. See a long and interesting account of him in *Records of the English Province of the Society of Jesus*, by Henry Foley, S. J., vol. iii., p. 567. Speaking of the trial reported in the text, it is stated that it lasted for eight hours, and that the Attorney-General's speech lasted an hour. The account there given is wrong as to the date of the trial, said to have been Nov. 29. 160¾, and in a few other details. The sentence is said to have been a fine of 4,000 scudi [quoting Bartoli's *Ecclesiastical History of England*], and 'because, continued the Lord Chancellor, a man of the age of 65 would not, perhaps, be able to survive the pain [of having his ears cut off], let him, instead of this, be nailed by one of his ears to the public pillar of justice at Westminster; after a certain number of hours let him be unfastened, and taken to Lancaster, and there let him be nailed by the other ear to the public pillar of Justice.'

Foley, *op. cit.*, pp. 603, 604.

What the 'public pillar of justice' is, is not stated; probably the pillory is meant.

In the same vol., p. 614, is printed a narrative of his sufferings, written by himself; the original is among the State Papers, Domestic, James I., vol. 21, no. 48. Also another State Paper, endorsed 'Proceedings at the Assizes at York and Lancaster.' As this document cannot now be found, I transcribe it here from Mr. Foley's work.

'In Yorkshire.—First, Mr Pounde by Order of the Starre Chamber, being there to make acknowledgment of his faulte, refuseth the same, otherwise than that if he had offended, then was he sorry for it . . . .

'The Proceedings at Lancaster.—First, Mr Pounde being there resolved both by the attorney of the Wardes[1] and Mr Fildesley,[2] to whom he appealed in the Starre Chamber for testimonie, and by all other Justices of the Peace at the former and these Assizes p'sent, of the untruth of his information to his Ma^tye^, he thereupon confessed his faulte and with humilitie submitted himself.'

The reference to this document *was*, State Papers, Domestic, James I., vol. 13, no. 52 B.

See also *The Rambler*, vol. ii., 1857.

1605 May 18 'A like pardon graunted to Tho. Clifton, Henrie Clifton, Rich. Carter, Rich. Hardman, & James Smyth, for the traiterous rescueing of James Gardner, a Seminary preist, in the County of Lancaster, for wch offence one Lawrence Bayly was executed, & the parties aforesaid have sithence conformed themselves. Subscribed by Baron Savile and Sergeant Phelipps, & procured by Sr Roger Wilbraham.'

State Papers, *Docquet*.

[1] Sir Thomas Hesketh, mentioned in the text *ante*, p. 185.

[2] Called 'Tilselie' in the text, *loc. cit.*

APPENDIX XV

Brackenbury v. Brackenbury

PAGE 198

HUDSON, in his *Treatise on the Star Chamber* (*Col. Jurid.* ii. 69), relates an anecdote which seems appropriate to this case, and may well have been told on this occasion.

Lord Egerton (he says) would 'merrily tell a tale: That a friar coming to visit a great man in his sickness, and finding him past memory, took opportunity (according to the custom of those times) to make provision for the monastery whereof he was; and finding that the sick man could only speak some one syllable, which was for the most part "Yea" or "Nay," as an imperfect voice, forthwith took upon him to make his will; and demanding of him, "Will you give such a piece of land to our House to pray for your soul?" the dying man sounded "Yea." Then he asked him, "Will you give such land to the maintenance of lights to our Lady?" The sound was again "Yea." Whereupon he boldly asked him many such questions. The son and heir standing by, and hearing his land going away so fast by his father's word "Yea," thought fit to ask one question as well as the friar; which was, "Shall I take a cudgel and beat this friar out of the chamber?" The sick man's answer was again "Yea"; which the son quickly performed, and saved unto himself his father's lands.'

APPENDIX XVI

Pickering's Case

PAGE 230

LEWIS PICKERING was the son of John Pickering of Tichmarsh, co. Northampton, by his second wife, Ursula, dau. of Thomas Oxenbridge of Itchingham, co. Sussex. His half-sister, Margaret Pickering, mar. Robert Keyes, one of the Gunpowder Plot conspirators. See Burke's *Commoners*, ii. 195.

1605 March 5 Henry, Earl of Northampton, to Sir Thomas Lake.

'It was very strange in D. Mountagew to tell Bywater that his M^{ty} entendid to release him had not letters from the councell thwarted his intention of clemency. For we haue founde him worthy of a sharpe censure, and the libell written was impartid to another befor euer it came to our Master's handes.'

State Papers, Domestic, James I., vol. 13, no. 13.

1605 March 6 Viscount Cranborne to Sir Thomas Lake.

'Bywater hath ben examined and will not tell who advised ye Courss wch is contained in a writing, wher of I sent my L. of Worster a Copy yester night . . . and therfore we meane to be a little rownde wth him.'

Ibid., vol. 13, no. 15.

1605 March 12 Sir William Ryder to Sir Thomas Lake.

'Ther was dyvers of the Lordes about one Bywater, a minister, one of those whott curse, I thinke about a book y^{t} was d^{d} to his Matie at Ware as he went downeward.'

Ibid., vol. 13, no. 24.

1605 March 24 The Council commissioned Sir Julius Cæsar and others to examine 'Thomas Bywater, a minister, and some others that are charged to haue bin partakers and of Counsaile wth the said Bywater in some seditious matter verie offensive vnto his ma^{tie}.'

Ibid., vol. 13, no. 33.

'My Ho^{d} good Lord,

'I was an humble sutor vnto y^{r} Ho^{r} y^{t} I might have ye liberty of ye prison, otherwise my close imprisonment will bee 1605 March? a meanes to shorten my life. Since by yor Lo. favour my servant hath accesse vnto me, for ye wch I humbly thanke y^{r} Lo. desiring y^{t} y^{r} Lo. wold bee pleased so much to respect my health, y^{t} I may have ye same liberty wch other prisoners have. I protest vpon my salvation y^{t} I never heard or read of any thing in Bywater's booke concerninge his ma^{tie} before I sawe it in ye kinge's hande, neither was I of his counsell in ye delivering of it. When he shewed it me at Royston, I warned him not to give a coppy of it to any bodye, & when he told me y^{t} he was to appeare before ye LL. of ye Counsell, I desisted from taking any notes out of it, wherof I never gave coppy to any, but shewed them to Mrs Russell, a kinswoman of ye Lady Bedford's, on whom she attendeth, & one who, I am assured, prayeth dayly for y^{e} good of y^{e} kinge, my fact being so much y^{e} more excusable in y^{t} she is one whom I purposed to make my wife, if his ma^{tie} wold bee pleased (as he promised) to repaire my meane estate, weakned in his ma$^{tie's}$ service, of whom *I never receaved the worth of one pennye.* S^{r}, I am bolde to remember y^{r} Lo. of those words deliuered vnto me at Basinge when y^{r} Lo. protested vpon y^{r} honor & reputation to bee my frend, & when y^{w} meant to bee otherwise to tell me soe. Except I heare to y^{e} contrarye, I will expect a forable [*sic*] answer from y^{r} Lo., for whom I will dayly praye y^{t} ye God of heaven wold encline y^{r} Lo. heart to pitty ye poore Countrymen of Northamptonshire & ye rest of those parts wher the ministers are silenced, then the wch noe one thing in ye world can winn y^{r} Lo. more honor wth God nor love wth men.
From ye Gate howse.

Y^{r} Lo^{pp}'s perplexed prisoner

LEWES PYKERINGE.'

Ibid., vol. 13, no. 37.

APPENDIX XVII

Lady Russell v. The Earl of Nottingham

Pages 271, 309

Donnington Castle and manor and other property were granted by Queen Elizabeth on May 15, 1600, to Nicholas Zouche and Thomas Hare, and their heirs, as nominees of the Earl of Nottingham; 'forasmuch that he did render very great services to us and our kingdom, with our ships and our royal fleet; and did with our armament in the year of our Lord 1588, and of our reign the 30th, conquer in an open naval battle the Spanish fleet, prepared to invade our kingdom.' (Money's *Donnington Castle*, 7. See Patent Roll, 42 Eliz., part 19.) The following year the property was settled on the Earl and Catherine his wife for their lives, with remainder to William Howard, son and heir apparent of the Earl, and his heirs male, and with divers remainders over. On Sep. 11, 1603, Sir Thomas Edmonds writing to the Earl of Shrewsbury, says, 'His Lordship [my Lord Admyrall] in his passage hither by the waie of Neweberrye, hath recovered the possession of Donnington Castle from the Ladye Russell, she being absent in Wales wth her daughter the Lady Harbet' (*The First and Second Battles of Newbury*, Walter Money, F. S. A., p. 268). On Sep. 24, 1603, the Earl of Worcester writes to the Earl of Shrewsbury, 'Yf I had paper spare I would haue wryten of my Lord Admirall's taking possession of Dunington vppon my Lady Russell, and kepethe the Castell and her lady[-ship] owt of dores; who complayned to the King, but found littell redress, and so is turned to the Lawe' (Nicholl's *Progresses of James I.*, i. 274).

The grant to Lady Russell, referred to in the text is as follows:

1590 March 17 Elizabeth, etc. Whereas by our letters patent dated Nov. 14, 13 Eliz. 1571, we granted to Richard Beeke, one of the Equerries [*quirreis*] of our Stable, the offices of Keeper [*custos*] of our Castle of Donington, in co. Berks, and Keeper and Paler [*palaciator*] of the Park of Donington, and Bailiff of our Honour, Lordship and Manor of Donington, and of all other Manors, etc., in co. Berks, which were late of Charles, Duke of Suffolk, and Keeper of the woods of the said Honour, Lordship and Manor, and of the other Manors, and Master of the drift of wild animals [*deductus ferarum*] of Donington Park, also Keeper, Warden or Paymaster of the Almshouses in Donington, and taking the fees, wages and emoluments of the said offices, all of which Thomas Cawarden, knight, late deceased, held, To hold and enjoy the said offices, together with the herbage and pannage of Donington Park, for the term of the life of the said Richard Beeke; Know that we have given and granted to our well beloved Elizabeth, Lady Russell, widow of John, Lord Russell, deceased, all the above mentioned offices, to hold to the said Elizabeth, Lady Russell, for the term of her life, to be enjoyed immediately on the vacation of the offices by the death, resignation, or forfeiture of the said Richard Beeke, taking the herbage and pannage of the said Park without rendering any account thereof, and taking the following wages, namely; as Keeper of the Castle 2½*d.* a day, as Keeper of the Park 3*d.* a day, as Paler [*palaciator*] of the Park 1*d.* a day, as Bailiff of Donington Manor and the other Manors as above 2*d.* a day, as Keeper of the wood as above 1*d.* a day. Dated at Greenwich, March 17, 32 Elizabeth.

Privy Seals, March.

APPENDIX XVIII

The Grievances of the Commons

PAGE 275

THE grievances here referred to, though mentioned repeatedly in the Journal of the House of Commons about this date, are not there set out at length. The following list is taken from a document preserved among the State Papers.

'The Judgment of the Lords of the Privie Councelle wth what answeres were fitt to be gyven, and what Course to be holden Concernynge the seueralle grievances presented to his Matie by the Common House of Parlyament, in order as they are Conceyved in the Instrument Conteyninge the same.

'1. Concerninge the pattent graunted to my Lord Davers and Sr John Gilberte of three partes in foure to be devyded of the yearlie overplus of twoe thousand and eight hundred pownds arysynge of Issues, fynes, amercyam^ts^, forfeytures of Recognizances, and the lyke, throughe the Realme.

'2. Concernynge a pattend graunted to Sr Roger Ashton of all fynes, amercyaments and other penalties and forfeytures knowen vnder the name of greene Waxe, growinge from the tenauntes of the Duchie of Lancaster.

'3. Touchinge a pattent made to Sr Henry Bronker of the Issues of Jurors not appearinge throughout England.

'4. Concernynge my Lord Admyralle his Lycence to sell wynes by Retaile at a greater price then the Lawes nowe in force allowe.

'5. Concernynge a pattent wch permitteth the vse of a stuffe for dyinge, made of a mixture of Lockwood or Blockwood with other things, which, in that manner vsed, is alleaged to be good and proffitable for dying.

'6. Concernynge the Raysing of his Matie's^ Customes.

'7. Touchinge the Imposycion vpon Currantes.

'8. Concernynge the Imposycion vpon Tobaccho.

'9. Touchinge a pattent graunted to the Duke of Lynoxe for the searchinge and sealinge of dyverse stuffes by the name of the Newe Draperies.

'10. The great Chardges that Shereffes of Counties are putt to by the Clarkes and offycers in the Escheaquer vpon their accountes wch are made meerlie for the kynge's service.

'11. Concernynge Muster Masters.

'12. Concernynge pre-empcion of Tynne.

'13. Concernynge the pattent of Makinge of Smalte or blue starche.

'14. Concernynge purveyances.

'15. Concernynge lycencynge of transportacion of Iron Ordynance and Bulletts.

'16. Concernynge the abuses Committed by the Salt Petermen.'

State Papers, Domestic, James I., vol. 23, no. 66.

APPENDIX XIX

The King v. The Earl of Northumberland, Lord Mordaunt, and Lord Stourton

PAGES 287, 292

1606 Marc Lord Salisbury to Sir Henry Bruncard, President of Munster.

'For any thing wch you may expect of the Lords, that wch I can say is this, that Mordant, Sturton and Montagu are lyke to come to the Star Chamber, such being his $Ma^{ty's}$ gracious disposition, as notwithstanding the circumstances to proove their warning to be absent might imply (yt it were strayned and racked) some dangerous consequence, that they were privy to the fact, adding thereunto their Religion, their neere allyance with the principall Traytors, and the particuler confession of my lord Mordant to haue had most of them continually in his house all this sommer; yet his Ma^{ty} rather construeth their absence to grow vpon some generall advises in respect of vncertaine troubles, then to putt them to answer for their lyfes, where it would goe hard with them: for the other great man [the Earl of Northumberland], you know the King's noble disposition, to be alwaies such as although he may not, in such a case as this, forgett the providence and foresight necessary in cases publiq, and therefore was constrained . . . to restraine liberty where he had cause of jealousy, yet considering the greatnes of his howse, and the improbability that he should be acquainted with such a barbarous plott, being a man of honor and valour, his Ma^{ty} is rather induced to beleeue, that whatsoeuer any of the Traytours haue spoken of him hath ben rather their vants then vpon any other good ground; so as I think his liberty will the next terme be granted vpon honorable and gracious termes; wch for myn owne part, though ther hath neuer ben any extraordinary deerenes between vs, I wish, because this state is very barren of men of great blood and great sufficiency together.'

State Papers, Ireland, vol. 218, no. 21.

Carew Castle and the Perrotts

PAGES 295, 358

Margaret, dau. of Sir Thomas Perrot of Haroldston, co. Pembroke, was the 2nd wife of Gruffyd ap Nicholas of Newton, the grandfather of the celebrated Sir Rhys ap Thomas (of whom Lord Dynevor is the lineal descendant). Sir Rhys was the 3rd son of Thomas, eldest son of Sir Gruffyd by his first wife, and succeeded to the family estates on the death of his elder brothers without issue. Thomas Perrot (*ob.* 1474), son and heir of the above mentioned Sir Thomas, had issue Sir William (*ob.* 1503), who had issue Sir Owen (*ob.* 1513), who had issue Sir Thomas. This Sir Thomas married Mary, dau. of James, 2nd son of Maurice, Lord Berkley, and was nominally the father of Sir John Perrot, who is said to have been really the son of Henry VIII. Sir John obtained a grant of Carew Castle from Queen Mary, the exact date of which seems to be unknown. He was appointed Lord President of Munster, 1572. He was found guilty of high treason, 1592, but not executed. He, however, died in the Tower shortly afterwards. The family estates were speedily restored to his son and heir, another Sir Thomas, who married Dorothy, daughter of Walter Devereux, Earl of Essex, and sister of Robert, the unfortunate favorite of Queen Elizabeth. Sir Thomas is stated to have died shortly after his father (1592), when his widow married Henry, Earl of Northumberland. *Perrot Notes*, by E. L. Barnwell; printed for the Cambrian Archæological Society, 1867.

See also Lord Somer's *Tracts*, vol. i. p. 268.

APPENDIX XX

The Pre-emption of Tin

PAGE 308

1603 June 7 — Allegations against the patent granted to Thomas Brigham and Humphrey Wemmes by the late Queen for pre-emption of tin.

State Papers, Domestic, James I., vol. 2, no. 4.

1603 June 7 — Proceedings in Council upon the revocation of the above patent on complaint of the Pewterers of London. With a draft of a proposed proclamation.

Ibid., no. 5.

1603 June 16 — Proclamation revoking the patent for pre-emption of tin.

Proclamation Book, p. 22.

1604 Feb. ? — Statement by the tinners, of the injuries caused to them and to the patentees for pre-emption of tin, by the suspension of the patent at the suggestions of the two Glovers and of the Pewterers' Company; and request for relief, by a loan to themselves, and a prohibition to export tin, till the patentees have sold the quantity remaining on their hands.

State Papers, Domestic, James I., vol. 6, no. 79.

1604 July ? — The tinners of Devon to Lord Cecil, complaining of the proposed renewal of the suspended Patent for the pre-emption of tin.

Ibid., vol. 8, no. 136.

1604 July ? — Tender of contract for tin for 21 years, as the last farmers had it, paying £10,000 yearly for the pre-emption.

Ibid., no. 137.

Treatise relating to tin and the stannary customs, being "The Substance of Gayer's booke touching the Tynn causes"; with replies thereon. The King is advised to favour the pre-emption of tin. 1604 July ?

Ibid., no. 138.

Warrant to Sir Richard Smith, Receiver General of Cornwall, to deliver tin at a certain rate to such persons as now lend money, in repayment thereof; and to re-deliver to Thomas Brigham and Humphrey Wemes the tin sold by them to the Company of Pewterers. 1604 Sept. 25

State Papers, *Docquet.*

Reply of Thomas Brigham and Humphrey Wemes to an annexed petition to the King from the Master, etc., of the Pewterers' Company, against the monopoly granted to them of the pre-emption of tin. 1604 Oct. 14

State Papers, Domestic, James I., vol. 9, no. 75.

The King to Sir Richard Smith. For relief of the tinners, and for the benefit of the realm in upholding the price of tin to foreign nations, we keep the pre-emption of tin in our own hands, and have written to our Lord Treasurer to deliver you £17,000, which we require you to carry, with a sufficient guard, to the coinage towns of Devonshire and Cornwall, and there buy to our use all the tin coined in Helston, Truro, and Lostwithiel, by the end of the present month; and in Devonshire and Liskeard in Cornwall, by the end of the midsummer coinage, giving £28 the thousand weight for the good, with abatement for what is defective. Also for the tin of Devonshire according to our former directions. All which tin, and that already in your custody, we require you to see safely conveyed to London and to places assigned, to be there vented to our use. We also require you to send to our Treasurer a perfect account of your proceedings, and for your pains, charges and losses, we have given him warrant to make you full allowance. 1605 Feb. 20

Ibid., Addenda, vol. 37, no. 20.

The Earl of Dorset to the Earl of Salisbury, concerning Irish accounts, and money received from Sir Richard Smith for sale and pre-emption of tin. 1606 Sept. 24

State Papers, Domestic, James I., vol. 23, no. 23.

1606 Nov. ? Notes by Lord Treasurer Dorset on the principal points to be considered in the question of the King's right to the pre-emption and exportation of tin, questioned by Richard Glover and the Pewterers' Company.

Ibid., no. 56.

16 6 Nov. 14 Decree of the Court of Star Chamber against Richard Glover and others, Pewterers of London, for endeavouring to frustrate a patent granted to Brigham and Wemes for the pre-emption of tin in Cornwall and Devon.

Ibid., no. 57.

1608 May 31 The Earl of Salisbury to the Officers of the Customs, ordering them not to permit any tin to be shipped for exportation within their jurisdiction, but such as has been licensed by Sir Thomas Bludder and Company, merchants of London, patentees for the pre-emption and exportation of tin.

Domestic Correspondence, July 29.

1608 July 10 Release to Richard Glover of 150*l.* part of a Star Chamber fine of 500*l.* on payment of the remainder.

State Papers, *Docquet.*

1608 Dec. 21 Warrant to pay certain sums to John Eldred and Martin Freeman, of London, Farmers of the pre-emption of tin, on resignation of a late patent to them and others for the same.

Warrant Book, II, p. 77.

1609 Oct. 3 Edward, Lord Wotton, to Salisbury, requesting an order to be given to the patentees for tin, to deliver 16,000 lbs. weight of tin yearly to the King's pewterer.

State Papers, Domestic, James I., vol. 48, no. 80.

1610 May 7 Thomas Jones to Salisbury. He was employed by the late Lord Treasurer to prosecute those pewterers who had fraudulently induced the King to relinquish the pre-emption of tin. By his means they were fined, and the pre-emption was re-established; craves a reward for his services.

Ibid., vol. 54, no. 25.

Statement of the origin and progress of the pre-emption of tin from the first grant thereof, shewing the mischief that would ensue by the surrender of the present patentees, on account of a proviso in their patent that no other shall sell tin for a year afterwards, if they have a stock in hand. 1614 Oct. 1

Ibid., vol. 78, no. 1.

See also *The Egerton Papers*, Camden Soc., 283; Coke's *Reports*, vi. 202.

APPENDIX XXI

The Earl of Devonshire's case

PAGE 338

Dudley Carleton to John Chamberlain.

1606 April 17 'My L^{d} of Deuonsheire's funerals will be performed in Westminster abowt three weekes hence. There is much dispute amongst the Heralds whether his Ladie's armes shall be empalde wth his, wch brings in question the lawfulnes of the mariage, and that is sayde to depend vppon the maner of the diuorce, wch though it run in these termes that she was to be separated from her late husband a thoro et mensa propter varia et diuersa adulteria, confessata et commissa tam in suburbiis quam intra muros civitatis London, yet are they tied in the conclusion not to marry any other.'

State Papers, Domestic, James I., vol. 20, no. 36.

Same to same.

1606 May 2 'My L^{d} of Deuonsheire's funerals will be performed on Wednesday next: in wch my L^{d} of Southampton is cheife morner . . . . It is determined (not to have my La. Riche's armes empalled wth his)[1] his armes shall be sett vp wthout his wife's.

Ibid., vol. 21, no. 4.

[1] These words struck out.

APPENDIX XXII

Morley v. Colte

PAGE 348

'Whilst the Abbots and Monks of *Waltham* were vexed and perplexed with the Men of *Cheshunt* they found more Favour from some loving and beautiful Women of that Parish, I mean, from the Holy Sisters of *Cheshunt Nunnery*; though they sufficiently suffered Disgrace, for the kind Entertainment they had often received from those dear and loving Sisters.

'I shall entertain my Readers with the Story, namely,

'One Sir *Henry Colt* of *Nether Hall*, in *Essex*, much in Favour with King *Henry* the Eighth for his merry Conceits, suddenly took his Leave of him late at Night, promising to wait on his Grace early the next Morning; hence he hasted to *Waltham-Abbey*, being informed by his Confederates or Spies, that the Monks thereof would return in the Night from *Cheshunt* Nunnery, where they had privately been regaling themselves, and had secretly quartered themselves there. Sir *Henry* pitched a Buckstall (wherewith he used to take Deer in the Forest) in the narrowest Place of the Marsh, where they were to pass over, leaving some of his Confederates to manage the same. The Monks with some of the obliging Nuns, being come out of the Nunnery, hearing a great Noise behind them, and suspecting to be discovered, put out the light they had with them, whose Feet without Eyes could find the Way home in so frequented a Path, they had been us'd to. But making more Haste than good Speed, they ran themselves all into the Net. The next Morning Sir *Henry Colt* brought and presented them to King *Henry*; who laughed at the Trick, and said he had often seen Sweeter, but never more beautiful or fatter Venison.'

The History of the ancient Town, and once Famous Abbey, of Waltham, by J. Farmer, of Waltham Abbey, Gent.; London, 1735; p. 76.

This Sir Henry Colt is not mentioned either by Morant or Wright in their *Histories of Essex*, nor does his name appear in the State Papers of the period. Perhaps Farmer has confused him with the later Sir Henry Colt, the defendant in the case reported in the text. The heads of the family during the reign of Henry VIII. were John Colt, who died in 1521, and George, his son and heir, who succeeded him. George's name occurs frequently in the State Papers, but he is not described as a knight.

APPENDIX XXIII

Calvin's case

PAGE 366

Opinions of the Law Officers of the Crown on questions 1604
relative to the naturalization of Scottish subjects, born after the Nov. 16
accession of King James to England.

State Papers, Domestic, James I., vol. 10, no. 15.

Speech by Sir Francis Bacon in the House of Commons, 1607
concerning the article of naturalization of the Scottish nation. Feb. 17
Printed; 4to; London, 1641.

Ibid., vol. 26, no. 53.

Note of Lord Chief Justice Coke's speech at the conference 1607
between the two Houses, on the naturalization of Scotchmen. Feb. 25

Ibid., no. 64.

See also, *Ibid.*, nos. 65, 66, 69, 70, 72, 73, 74, 77, 78, 79, 80, 81, 85, 86, 87, 88, 90, vol. 27, no. 9.

Speech of Justice Yelverton in Calvin's case relative to a 1608
messuage in Shoreditch. May 7

Ibid., vol. 32, no. 40.

Speeches of the Judges, etc., in the Exchequer Chamber, on 1608
the question of the *ante nati* and *post nati*, in reference to the June 7
naturalization of Scotchmen [in Calvin's case].

Ibid., vol. 34, no. 10.

Licence for ten years to Sir William Woodhouse to print 1608
report, etc., of Calvin's case. Aug. 1

Grant Book, p. 37.

1608 Dec. 9 John Chamberlain to Dudley Carleton.

The King is anxious for Parliament to meet, that the House of Lords may confirm the Judges' sentence as to the *post nati.*

State Papers, Domestic, James I., vol. 38, no. 17.

'The Conference held the 25th of February, *Anno* 1606, betwene the Lords Committees and the Commons, touching the Naturalizinge of the Scots,' etc.

Lord Somer's Tracts, ii. 132.

APPENDIX XXIV

Henry Hawarde

PAGE xiii

Edward Somerforde of London, 'inholder,' the administrator of the estate of William Buckley of London, deceased, complained whereas Buckley had agreed with Henry Heywarde of Tandridge, gentleman, as to a lease to be made by Heywarde to Buckley of a messuage in 'Temes' Street, London, 'commonlie called the Signe of the Shipp,' and had paid him £40 for the same; the lease was not made in Buckley's life, and since his death the plaintiff, as his administrator, had requested Heywarde either to return the £40 or else to grant the lease, which he had refused to do; The agreement between Buckley and Heywarde was a verbal one, so that the plaintiff has no remedy at common law; but he prays for a writ of subpœna, as he 'hopeth that the said Henry Heyward is a man of conscience, and feareth God, and will not vntruelie sweare and forsweare vppon his answere.' Dated May 5, 1587.

The answer states that Heywarde, about December last, was possessed of a messuage in Thames Street, 'nere vnto Billingesgate,' known by the sign of The Galley, for a term of years; and he agreed to sell the lease to Buckley for £350; Buckley paid £40 on account, which sum was to be forfeited if the remainder was not paid by a certain day. Heywarde says that he had 'diuerse greate somes of monye then to paye,' and that, not receiving the balance due from Buckley, he 'was thereby driven to make present sale of the said premisses to paye suche sommes of monye as he then stode bounde to paye, to his greate losse and hinderaunce by reason of the sodayne sale thereof.'

Chancery Proceedings, Elizabeth, Bundle S. 26, no. 43.

APPENDIX XXV

John Hawarde

PAGE xix

To the Quene's most excellent Ma^{tye}.

Humblye complayninge sheweth vnto yor most excellentt Matie yor Highnes' true, Faithffull and obedient Subiect, John Hayward, of Clyffordes Inne, wthin the parishe of Saynt Dunstones on the West, gentelman, That whereas yor Highnes Subiect by Reason of some nessary [*sic*] and vrgent busynes vupon the First daye of January now last past Repared to the Towne of Maydestone in your Highnes' County of Kent, Beinge Newyeres Daye, youer subiect passinge throwe the Towne one Fonteone leading his gelding by hym, and tow gentelmen Talking wth hym, Determyned not to staye in the Towne drawing towardes Eaveninge, and to Followe one his Determynatt affayres and Bussynes, and as he was passinge Forth of the Towne in quiett and peceable manner, There happened one Gabrell Warcope suddenly to Come vnto hym, They and as yett vnknowne to yor subiectt, To Come into yor subiecte's Company, who entered into many vayne and Friuelosse discourses wth yor subiect, and in manner enfforsed yor subiect to answere to many very ydle and Folishe questyons and demaundes, To th'ende as hytt should seme to drawe yor subiect into some such Convenyent place For his purposse as he expected, and passinge one in this manner wth many Crosse and overthwart speaches to the end to move yor Highnes' subiect to some ympatience distemperature of mynde, But yor Highnes' subiect, perceavinge the dryfte and determynatt purposse of the sayd Gabrill Warcopp to be to quarrell, still suppressed his Coller and contynewed hyme selff wth in the Boundes of patience ; And in th'ende when the sayde Warcopp had brought yor Highnes' subiect to his desyered place, and had provided hym selff of such Company as he thought Featt For his purpose, So hytt is, pleseth yor most Excelent

Matie that the sayd Gabrill Warcopp, assocyating to hym selff Richard Reve, Thomas Reve, Katheryn Reve, Thomas Fylcott, Anne Fylcott, Fraunces Bourne and John Bourne, and Dyuerse others lyke Ryotours, Routors, and evell disposed persones To the number of Twenty or thereaboutes, the Resydewe beinge as yett to yor Highnes' subiect vnknowe, and being armed wth swordes, dages, longe picle-staues, Forrest Bylles, wth such warlick and vnlawffull weapons, aswell invasiue as defensyve, one the sayd First daye of January nowe last past, att and in the sayd Towne of Maydstone, did assembell them selues together, and not haueing the Feare of god beffore their Eyes, ner [neither] dewe Regard of yor Highnes' good and Comendable Lawes, Statutes and Ordynaunces mayd and provyded against Ryottes, Routes, vnlawfull assembles and such lyke misdemenures, nor the punishment dewe For the same, yor Highnes' subiect then and there being in gode's peace and yor highnes', they, the sayd Gabrill Warcopp, [and the others], In and vppon yor highnes' subiect did make an assault and hym did beate, hurt, wounde and evell entreate, and hym did put in greate perill of his lyffe, and yor highnes' subiect haueing a long whined Hauke of Great vallewe vppon his Fist, They the sayd Gabrill Warcopp wth the Resydewe of the sayd maleffactors in most Bucherly, and Ryetous mannor the sayd Hauke, being one yor sayd subiect Fist, dyd kyll, spoyle and Teare asunder, one lyme From another, And the sayd Richard Reve, Thomas Reve, Thomas Fillcott, Anne Fylcott, Fraunces Bourne and John Bourne, Crying maynely out, "Downe wth hym, kyll hym & kyll hym." Wth wch wordes of Incoredgment, the sayd Ryotors so Fiersly Followed yor subiect, as he grevesly beaten, wounded and leaft for dead, to the greatt losse, hinderaunce and indempnity of yor subiectes, and Contrary to dyuerse yor highnes' good and Comendable Lawes and statutes in thatt behalfe mayd and provyded; In Tender Consideration whereof and For somuch as Ryottes, Routes and vnlawffull assembles, and such lyke misdemenures, so donne and Comytted by the sayd Gabrill Warcopp, Richard Reve and other the maleffactors and Ryotors afforesayd, are hateffull to god and hurtffull to the Comen-wealth and nearely Repugnant to dyuersse yor Highnes' good and wholesome Lawes, statutes and ordynaunces mayd and provyded in thatt behalffe, The Presydent and example whereof ys such and so perillowes, as yf spedy Remedy and Refformation be not therein had, and seveare punishment mynistred to the offendors accordingly, maye tende to the decaye of Justis, to the subbernation and overthrowe of diuerse yor Hignes' good and Comendable lawes and statutes, & to th' encoraging and ymbolding of such lyke Riotous, wicked, & evell disposed personis to attempt practice & put in vre the lyke, Hyt maye thereffore plesse yor most excelent Matie, the premyses Considered, to graunt vnto yor Highnes' subiect yor gratious wryttes of Subpenas to be dyrected vnto the sayd Gabrill Warcopp [and the others] & dyuerse others, To Commaund them and every of them Thereby att a Certen daye and vnder a Certen payne therein to be lymyted, personably to be and appeare Beffore yor most excelent Matie in yor Highnes' Court of Star-chamber, then and there to answere to the premyses and to stande to and abide such further order & direction therein as to yor Highnes' and yor Ma$^{te's}$ most ho: privie Counsell shalbe thought meete. And yor said Subiect accordinge to his bounden duetie shall daielye praie to god for the preservacion of yor most excelent Matie longe to Rule & Rayne over vs.

HARRIS.

Indorsed: Martis, primo Februarii, Anno xxxix^{o} Elizabeth Regine [1597]; Will'm Mill.

Warcopp, Richard Rive and Thomas Rive put in a joint defence; each of them 'saith that he is not guilty of the rioutes, Routes & speeches mencioned in the said Bill, nor of anie of them, nor of anie othe^{r} the Misdemeanoures mencioned in the same, determinable in this most honorable co^{r}te, in suche sorte, mann^{r} & forme as in ye said Bill of Compl^{t} is most vntrewely surmised.'

Star Chamber, Elizabeth, Bundle H. 70, no. 13.

APPENDIX XXVI

The Star Chamber

PAGE xlv

WORKS at Westminster, 21 & 22 Edw. III, Peter de Bruges, Clerk of the Works.

October 15, a° 21, 1347.

Wages of 22 masons working for 6 days on the works of the Chapel and upon the making of the wall of the new house near the Receipt [*supra facturam muri nove domus iuxta Receptam*] at 5½ a day, 60*s*. 6*d*.

October 22, 1347.

23 carpenters working upon the vaulting [*vosura*] of the Chapel, and upon the new house near the Receipt, 6 days at 6*d*. a day, 69*s*.

Wages of William Herland, carpenter, working on the Chapel, and on the said new house, and on the Queen's bridge, and on other works, at 3*s*. 6*d*. a week, 7*l*. 11*s*. 0*d*.

November 19, 1347.

2,000 laths bought at Kingston, and used for the walls of the said new house and for the walls and roofs of divers chambers, 6*s*. 8*d*.

William Odyn, for 37 'plaunch bords' for the works of the said new house & other chambers, 16*s*. 1*d*.

500 'Estrich bords' bought of John Wesenham for the Chapel and the said new house, at 13*s*. 4*d*. the 100, 66*s*. 8*d*.

100 'Rygolbords' bought of the same for the same works, 30*s*.

November 26, 1347.

15 carpenters working on the Chapel and on the new house near the Receipt for 5 days at 5*d*., 31*s*. 3*d*.

2 plumbers working on the said works at 9*s*. 4*d*. a week.

2 sawyers sawing timber for the works of the same Chamber for the same time, at 4*d*. a day, 3*s*. 4*d*.

December 3, 1347.

William Deynes for 1000 nails for the said new house, 2*s*. 6*d*.

To the same for 500 nails for the same, 20*d*.

6000 'travers' nails for the walls of the same, 2*s*. 6*d*.

6000 sprigs for the same house, 2*s*.

2000 'bord nails' for the same house, 3*s*. 4*d*.

2000 laths for the walls of the house, bought at Kingston, 6*s*. 8*d*.

Boatage of the same from Kingston to Westminster, 6*d*.

Katherine Smith for divers 'crampons' and other ironwork for the same house, weighing 38lbs, 3*s*. 2*d*.

The same for 120 great nails for fixing the said ironwork, at 5*d*. the 100, 6*d*.

To William Cornwaill and his fellow, two lathers, lathing the walls of the said new house, 4 days at 3½*d*. each, 2*s*. 4*d*.

December 10, 1347.

William Deynes for 4000 'traversnails' for the walls of the said new house near the Receipt, 20*d*.

To the same for 1000 'lednails' for the works of the said house, 20*d*.

To the same for 2000 nails for the said house, 3*s*. 4*d*.

To the same for 1000 nails for the said house, 12½*d*.

Hugh de Tyngrith for 6 'mouncells' of plaster for the walls of the said house, at 6*s*. 6*d*. the 'moncell,' 39*s*.

Carriage of the same from S. Paul's Churchyard to Westminster by land, 23*d*.

Katherine Smith for certain ironwork for a window in the said house, weighing 9 score lbs., 15*s*.

The same for half a hundred great nails for the works of the said house, 2½*d*.

For 800 'Talsthid' for the office of the plumbers for the same, at 2*s*. 10*d*. the 100, 22*s*. 8*d*.

Boatage of the same from Hamilton to Westminster, 13*s*. 4*d*.

Two lathers lathing the walls of the said new house, for 6 days, at 3½*d*. a day each, 3*s*. 6*d*.

December 17, 1347.

William Deynes for staples and hasps for the door of the said new house, 9*d.*

The same for 8000 'travers nails,' 3*s.* 4*d.*

The same for 4000 sprigs for lathing the walls of the said house, 16*d.*

The same for 1500 nails for the windows of the said house, 2*s.* 6*d.*

The same for 500 nails for the works of the said house, 6¼*d.*

The same for 500 nails for fixing the 'planch-bords' 15*d.*

Three locks [*serura*] for the doors of the said house, 18*d.*

Divers hinges and hooks for the windows of the said house, 15*d.*

Two plasterers for burning plaster for the walls of the said house, for 5 days, at 13*d.* a day, 5*s.* 5*d.*

Two lathers lathing the walls of the said new house for 4 days, at 3½*d.* a day each, 2*s.* 4*d.*

December 31, 1347.

William Deynes for 8000 'travers nails' for the walls of the said new house, 2*s.* 11*d.*

The same for 500 nails for the works of the said house, 6¼*d.*

The same for 3000 nails for fixing divers 'plaunch-bords' on the floor of the said house, 7*s.* 6*d.*

500 nails for the scaffolding of the said house, 10*d.*

Agnes Dishe for 100 logs of alder for the said scaffolding, 16*s.*

The same for 50 hurdles [*cratr'*] for the same, 8*s.*

500 withes [*scortic'*] for the same, 3*s.*

The carriage of the logs, hurdles, and withes from London to Westminster, 8*d.*

The same Agnes for 12 standards of alder for the works of the said house for the scaffolding, 3*s.*

300 tiles for the walls of the said house and the roofs of other houses, 13*s.* 8*d.*

The carriage of the same from Southwark to Westminster, 12*d.*

1000 laths for the walls of the said house, 3*s.* 6*d.*

16 carpenters working on the Chapel and on the said new house near the Receipt for 6 days, at 5*d.* a day each, 40*s.*

Walter Dachet, plumber, working on the casting and laying [*fundatione et jactatione*] of lead for the roof of the said new house, for a week, 4*s*. 8*d*.

William Dachet, his servant, for 5 days at 2½*d*. a day, 12½*d*.

4 plasterers burning and mixing plaster for the walls of the said house, for 5 days at 3*d*. a day each, 5*s*.

2 lathers lathing the walls of the said house for 1½ days, at 3½*d*. a day each, 10½*d*.

William Suthwerk and his mate and John Sawier and his mate, sawing planks and boards for the said chamber near the Receipt, for 5 days at 4*d*. a day each, 6*s*. 8*d*.

January 7, 1348.

William Deynes for 1500 nails for the works of the said new house, at 2*d*. the 100, 2*s*. 6*d*.

The same for 2000 nails for the said house, at 3*d*. the 100, 5*s*.

The same for 8000 'travers-nails' for the works of the said new house, 3*s*. 4*d*.

The same for 250 nails for works of the said house, 2½*d*.

2000 tiles for the repair of the walls of the said house and for other necessaries, 9*s*.

Carriage of the same from Southwark to Westminster, 4*d*.

Agnes Dishe for 25 logs, 12 hurdles [*crat'*] and 100 withes [*scortic'*] for scaffolds for the repair of the walls of the said house, 6*s*. 4*d*.

Carriage from London to Westminster, 2*d*.

Nicholas de Rameseye for 3 'mouncells' of plaster of Paris for the repair of the walls of the said new house, at 6*s*. 6*d*. the 'mouncell,' 19*s*. 6*d*.

Carriage from S. Paul's Churchyard to Westminster, 12*d*.

John Leycester and his mate, plasterers, for making the walls of the said new house, 6 days at 7*d*. a day each, 7*s*.

6 other plasterers helping them for the same time, at 3*d*. a day each, 9*s*.

January 14, 1348.

William Deynes for 800 'lednails' for the works of the said new house, 16*d*.

The same for 1000 nails for fixing 'plaunch-bords' in divers floors of the said chamber, 3*s*. 4*d*.

2000 tiles for the repair of the walls of the said house, 9*s*.

Carriage from Smithfield to Westminster, 8*d.*

1000 laths for the walls of the said house, 4*s.* 2*d.*

300 'withes' for the scaffolds of the said house, 12*d.*

Tallow [*in sepe*] for the plumber, 2*d.*

13 large nails for the works of the said house, 3*d.*

19 carpenters working on the Chapel, and the said new house, and other works within the Palace, for 6 days at 5*d.* a day each, 47*s.* 6*d.*

4 carpenters working there for 4 days, at 4*d.* a day each, 5*s.* 4*d.*

John Leycester and William Plastrer, plasterers, working on the repair of the walls of the said new house, for 6 days at 7*d.* a day each, 7*s.*

5 other plasterers burning plaster and helping them on the works of the said new house, for the same time, at 3*d.* a day each, 7*s.* 6*d.*

Walter Dachet making the roof of the said new house, for a week, 4*s.* 8*d.*

3 labourers helping him for the same time, at 2½*d.* a day each, 2*s.* 6*d.*

2 sawyers sawing planks for the works of the said new house, for 3 days, at 4*d.* a day each, 2*s.*

The lather lathing the walls of the same for 2½ days, at 4*d.* a day, 10*d.*

John Werkman and Robert Squadder, two daubers, repairing the walls of the said chamber with clay, for 6 days at 2½*d.* a day each, 2*s.* 6*d.*

January 21, 1348.

William Deynes for 1100 nails for the said new house, at 1½*d.* the 100, 16½*d.*

The same for 4000 nails for the works of the said new house, 3*s.* 2¼*d.*

Walter Dachet, plumber, working on the roof of the said new house for a week, 4*s.* 8*d.*

3 labourers helping him for 5 days, at 2½*d.* a day each, 3*s.* 1½*d.*

John Leycester, plasterer, working on the repair of the walls of the said new house, for 6 days, at 7*d.* a day, 3*s.* 6*d.*

3 plasterers helping him for the same time, at 3*d.* a day each, 4*s.* 6*d.*

2 sawyers sawing timber and boards for the works of the said new house, for 4 days, at 4*d.* a day each, 2*s.* 8*d.*

January 28, 1348.

William Deynes for 1000 nails for the said house, 2*s.* 6*d.*

The same for 500 nails for the works of the said new house, 6¼*d.*

The same for 6000 'travers-nails' for the walls of the said house, at 5*d.* the 1000, 2*s.* 6*d.*

The same for 2000 sprigs for the same, 8*d.*

The same for 500 'led-nails' for repair of the roof of the said house, 10*d,*

The same for 1000 nails for the same, 15*d.*

2 lbs of pig's tallow for the plumbers, 2½*d.*

2 ells of canvas for the plasterers, 6*d.*

500 laths for the walls of the said house, 2*s.* 6*d.*

1500 tiles for the walls of the said house, 6*s.* 9*d.*

Boatage from London, 10*d.*

Walter de Merdon for 2 cartloads, 2 waggonloads, and 7 [*clav'*] of new lead for the roof of the said new house, 6*l.* 2*s.* 4*d.*

Cartage and boatage of the lead from London to Westminster, 12*d.*

William Dachet, plumber, working at the repair of the roof of the said new house, for a week, 4*s.* 8*d.*

3 labourers helping him, 5 days at 2½ a day each, 3*s.* 1½*d.*

The plasterer working at the repair of the walls of the said new house, 5 days at 7*d.* a day, 2*s.* 11*d.*

3 plasterers helping him, 5 days at 3*d.* a day each, 3*s.* 9*d.*

The lather working there, 5 days at 4*d.* a day, 20*d.*

February 4, 1348.

Walter Mordon for 100 'estrich-bords' for the rafters [?; *sper'*; spars, rafters], windows and battlements [*in parte bataill'*] of the said new house, 15*s.*

Carriage from London to Westminster, 4*d.*

William Deynes for 8000 'travers-nails' for the works of the said house, 3*s.* 4*d.*

The plumber working at the repair of the roof of the said new house, for a week, 4*s.* 8*d.*

3 labourers helping him at 3*d.* a day each, 4*s.* 6*d.*

The plasterer working at the repair of the walls of the said house, for 6 days at 8*d.* a day, 4*s.*

3 plasterers helping him for the same time, at 4*d.* a day each, 6*s.*

2 labourers working 3 days at the repair of the walls of the said house, at 4½*d.* a day each, 2*s.* 3*d.*

February 11, 1348.

William Deynes for 1000 nails for the works of the said new house, 22½*d.*

Nicholas Tyngrel for one 'moncell' of plaster for the repair of the walls of the said house, 6*s.* 6*d.*

103 lbs of tin bought at London for soldering the leaden tiles [*in soldacione tel' plumbi*] on the top of the said house, 13*s.* 9*d.*

Tallow for the same, 3*d.*

13 carpenters working 6 days on the Chapel and the said new house, at 6*d.* a day, 39*s.*

2 sawyers sawing timber and boards for the said house for 6 days, at 5*d.* a day, 5*s.*

February 18, 1348.

William Deynes for 800 'lednails' for the battlements [*bataill'*] of the said new house, 12*d.*

Walter Dachet, plumber, and his three men, working 6 days at repairing the roof of the said new house, 9*s.* 2*d.*

John Leycester, plasterer, and 3 others, for working 6 days at the repair of the walls of the said new house, 10*s.*

2 sawyers sawing timber and boards for the works there for 5 days, 4*s.* 2*d.*

2 lathers working 5 days on the repair of the walls of the said new house, 3*s.* 9*d.*

February 24, 1348.

Hugh de Tyngrith for one 'mouncell' of plaster for the walls of the said house, 6*s.* 6*d.*

Carriage from London to Westminster, 4*d.*

Walter de Mordon for 11 waggonloads and 8 [*clav'*] of lead for the roof of the said new house, 52*s.* 9*d.*

Walter Dachet, plumber, working 5 days on the repair of the roof of the said house, 4*s.* 8*d.*

John Leycester, plasterer, working 5 days on the repair of the walls of the said new house, 3*s.* 4*d.*

3 plasterers helping him and preparing plaster for the said walls, for 5 days, 5*s.*

March 3, 1348.

500 tiles for the repair of divers walls in the new house, 2*s.* 3*d.*

John Leycester, plasterer, working for 6 days on the repairs of the walls of the new house, 4*s*.

3 plasterers helping him, 6*s*.

March 10, 1348.

500 tiles for the repair of the walls of the said new house, 2*s*. 3*d*.

28 masons working for 6 days on the works of the Chapel, and the repair of the walls of the said new house, and on the conduit,[1] at $5\frac{1}{2}$*d*. a day, 77*s*.

John Leycester, plasterer, working 6 days at the new house, 4*s*.

March 17, 1348.

400 nails with tin heads for the door of the said new house, 21*d*.

John Kent, William Hunt, and 11 other carpenters, working 6 days on the Chapel, the house, and other works in repair of the King's Chamber, 39*s*.

John Leycester, plasterer, working 6 days on the repair of the said house and other defects within the Palace, 4*s*.

March 24, 1348.

4 carpenters working 5 days on the repair of the [*stanum* or *scanum*] within the said new house, at 5*d*. a day each, 8*s*. 4*d*.

March 31, 1348.

17 carpenters working for 6 days on the Chapel and the new house, at 6*d*. a day, 54*s*.

April 7, 1348.

John Lokier, for 6 locks and keys for the doors of the said new house, 5*s*.

William Deynes for divers 'rynges' for the same, 15*d*.

One lock and 2 keys for 'le Wyket' in the door of the new Receipt, 9*d*.

April 28, 1348.

Katherine Smith for an iron bolt for the door of the new Receipt.

[1] This stood in the middle of Palace Yard; it is shown in the small map on page xlii.

May 26, 1348.

4 'mouncells' of plaster of Paris for the new house of the Receipt.

July 14, 1348.

Richard de Nottele for 28 cartloads of sand for mortar and for raising a certain place between the new house of the Receipt and the kitchen of John Bray, 3*s.* 6*d.*

Queen's Remembrancer's Ancient Miscellanea, $\frac{871}{6}$.

ACCOUNTS from 21 June, 25 Edw. III., to 25 August, 28 Edw. III.

February 22, 1352.

Thomas Elyot for a ship-load of Portland stone for repairing the foundations of the Palace wall near the water, £11.

Thomas Draper for 2 ship-loads of Ragg [stone] containing 75 cartloads, for the repair of the said wall, 42*s.*

Carriage and boatage from London to Westminster, 7½*d.*

February 27, 1352.

Thomas Draper for a ship-load of 'Ragg' stone for the foundations of divers houses in the Palace, containing 50 cartloads, 28*s.*

6 carpenters working on the dressing [*stapulacione*] of timber for a certain new house newly made, 6 days at 6*d.* a day, 18*s.*

March 26, 1352.

5 masons working on the dressing of stone [*stapul' petr'*] for the repair and emending [*pro reparacione et emendacione*] of the Palace wall on both sides [*ex vtraque parte*] of the Watergate, 6 days at 5*d.* a day, 12*s.* 6*d.*

April 2, 1352.

10 masons working on the dressing of stone for the said Palace wall, 6 days at 5*d.*, 25*s.*

April 16, 1352.

6 masons working on the dressing of stone for the wall near the Queen's bridge, 6 days at 5*d.*, 15*s.*

April 23, 1352.

Ditto.

May 13, 1352.

Robert Lokyere for a ' cliket ' and 6 keys for the door of ' Hell ' in the Exchequer, and for a lock for the door of the Council House in the Exchequer, and for a plate for the door of the chamber of the Clerk of the Kitchen, 3*s.* 6*d.*

July 2, 1352.

John Coventrie, glazier, working on [*cylect'*] of the windows of the new chamber of the Receipt for a week, 3*s.*

Queen's Remembrancer's Ancient Miscellanea, $\frac{872}{10}$.

ACCOUNTS for 21 & 22 Edw. III.; 25 Jan. 1347, to 24 Jan. 1349.

4 tilers working on the roof [*tecturam*] of the House of the ' Chaundelerye ' and on the covering [*coopertura*m] of divers houses within the privy Palace, stripped by strong winds [*per validos ventus*], for 26 days at 6*d.*, 73*s.*

3 tilers working on the laying of the tiles of the ' Hale ' made within the Palace, against the last sitting of Parliament [*contra Parliamentum ultimo tentum*], 24 days at 6*d.*, 36*s.*

6 tilers working on the repair of the roof [*tecturam*] of the house called ' Sterred Chambre ' within the Palace, 18 days at 6*d.*, 54*s.*[1]

16 tilers working on the same works, 6 days at 6*d.*, 48*s.*

8 tilers working on the same works, 12 days at 5½*d.*, 44*s.*

2 shinglers working on the roof of the house of the King's Exchequer and of a window called ' Gapier ' upon the said Exchequer, 4 days at 5*d.*, 3*s.* 8*d.*

Queen's Remembrancer's Ancient Miscellanea, $\frac{873}{22}$.

ACCOUNTS of Peter de Bruges, Clerk of the Works at Westminster Palace; from Oct. 15, 1347 to Aug. 10, 1348.

For divers pieces of timber, boards, ' talwood,' and laths, bought for the works of the Chapel and the new chamber near the Receipt, and for other houses and chambers within the Palace; 204*l.* 9*s.* 8½*d.*

For 15 ' mouncells ' of plaster of Paris bought for the walls of the new house near the Receipt and for the chimneys of othe chambers there; 4*l.* 13*s.* 4*d.*

Pipe Roll, 29 Edw. III.

---

[1] The date of this seems to be in January or February, 1348; see *ante*, pp. 458, 459.

Accounts of William de Weston, Clerk of the Works at Westminster Palace and the Tower of London.

For divers pieces of timber and boards bought for and used in the making of a certain chamber annexed to the Receipt of the Exchequer and on the repairing and mending [*super reparacione et emendacione*] of other houses and chambers in the Palace; and 'talwood'[1] for the glaziers and for melting lead; and logs and hurdles for the scaffolds; between Michaelmas, 25 Edw. III commencing [1350] to June 19 following; 44*l.* 9*s.* 2¾*d.*

Pipe Roll, 25 Edw. III.

Accounts of Walter de Weston, deceased, late Clerk of the Works, etc., presented by his executors.

For divers pieces of timber, boards, laths, 'talwood,' logs, and hurdles for the scaffolding, bought for a certain chamber near the Receipt, and for the repair of the Steward's Chamber, and for other works within the Palace of Westminster, by the King's verbal order, from January 19, 23 Edw. III [1350] to Michaelmas following; 12*l.* 0*s.* 4½*d.*

Pipe Roll, 26 Edw. III.

'But many of these rooms appear to have been rebuilt; those on the south about the time of Henry VIII, those on the East in that of Queen Elizabeth, and accordingly this last mentioned range bears over one of its doors the date 1602, the figures of which are, however, divided for the admission of the device of two roses, which, in allusion to her descent from the houses of York and Lancaster, was one of her cognizances. It is here also placed on a star, the reason for which last circumstance has not appeared, unless it was in allusion to the name of the room to which it led, though perhaps it might be one of the multitude of devices she is known to have used. The door over which this date occurs, may be seen in the view of the entrance to the Speaker's Court Yard, already given, and the room to which it leads was once the famous Star Chamber. The ceiling of this room, which is extremely beautiful, and of oak, and was formerly gilt, is constructed on squares, 9 in breadth and 15 in length. It is apparently not older than the time of Queen Elizabeth, as the roses and date on the outside seem to have been carved by

[1] Fine wood, cut into billets. Crabb, *Tech. Dict.*

the same hand. . . . In this ceiling are also the devices of two roses, one placed on the other, portcullises, pomegranates, and fleur-de-lys. This Star-Chamber is said by Strype, book vi, p. 51, to have been the ancient council chamber within the King's Palace of Westminster. In the reign of Edward III, the East side of New Palace Yard consisted of the Star Chamber, and under that a chamber belonging to the Clerk of the Kitchen, both of which have since been rebuilt.'

Antiquities of Westminster, J. T. Smith, 1807, pp. 29, 65.

INDEX I

Cases

H H

INDEX II

Matters

INDEX III

Persons and Places